Behavior in
Organizations

McGRAW-HILL SERIES IN PSYCHOLOGY
Consulting Editors

Norman Garmezy   Lyle V. Jones

Adams   Human Memory
Berkowitz   Aggression: A Social Psychological Analysis
Berlyne   Conflict, Arousal, and Curiosity
Blum   Psychoanalytic Theories of Personality
Brown   The Motivation of Behavior
Brown and Ghiselli   Scientific Method in Psychology
Butcher   MMPI: Research Developments and Clinical Applications
Campbell, Dunnette, Lawler, and Weick   Managerial Behavior, Performance, and Effectiveness
Cofer   Verbal Learning and Verbal Behavior
Crafts, Schneirla, Robinson, and Gilbert   Recent Experiments in Psychology
Crites   Vocational Psychology
D'Amato   Experimental Psychology: Methodology, Psychophysics, and Learning
Deese and Hulse   The Psychology of Learning
Dollard and Miller   Personality and Psychotherapy
Edgington   Statistical Inference: The Distribution-free Approach
Ellis   Handbook of Mental Deficiency
Ferguson   Statistical Analysis in Psychology and Education
Fodor, Bever, and Garrett   The Psychology of Language: An Introduction to Psycholinguistics and Generative Grammar
Forgus   Perception: The Basic Process in Cognitive Development
Franks   Behavior Therapy: Appraisal and Status
Ghiselli   Theory of Psychological Measurement
Ghiselli and Brown   Personnel and Industrial Psychology
Gilmer   Industrial and Organizational Psychology
Gray   Psychology Applied to Human Affairs
Guilford   Psychometric Methods
Guilford   The Nature of Human Intelligence
Guilford and Fruchter   Fundamental Statistics in Psychology and Education
Guilford and Hoepfner   The Analysis of Intelligence
Guion   Personnel Testing
Haire   Psychology in Management
Hirsch   Behavior-Genetic Analysis
Hirsh   The Measurement of Hearing
Horowitz   Elements of Statistics for Psychology and Education
Hurlock   Adolescent Development
Hurlock   Child Development
Hurlock   Developmental Psychology
Jackson and Messick   Problems in Human Assessment
Krech, Crutchfield, and Ballachey   Individual in Society

McGRAW-HILL SERIES IN MANAGEMENT
Keith Davis, *Consulting Editor*

Behavior in Organizations

Lyman W. Porter
University of California
Irvine

Edward E. Lawler III
University of Michigan

J. Richard Hackman
Yale University

McGRAW-HILL BOOK COMPANY

New York St. Louis San Francisco Düsseldorf Johannesburg
Kuala Lumpur London Mexico Montreal New Delhi Panama
Paris São Paulo Singapore Sydney Tokyo Toronto

Library of Congress Cataloging in Publication Data

Porter, Lyman W
  Behavior in organizations.

  (McGraw-Hill series in psychology) (McGraw-Hill series in management)
  1. Organization. 2. Management. 3. Psychology,
Industrial. I. Lawler, Edward E., joint author. II. Hackman, J. Richard,
joint author. III. Title.
HD31.P645   658.4   74-8027
ISBN 0-07-050527-6

Behavior in Organizations

  10 11 12 13 FGFG 8 9 10 5 4 3 2 1

This book was set in Times Roman by Black Dot, Inc. The editors were
Richard R. Wright and David Dunham; the designer was Joseph Gillians; the
production supervisor was Thomas J. LoPinto. The drawings were done by
J & R Services, Inc.

Contents

ix

Preface

This book is an introduction to the study of behavior in organizations. It focuses on both the *individual* and the *organization*—and, especially, on their interaction. Throughout, our objective is to provide the reader with ways of "looking at" and "thinking about" behavior in organizations. Rather than presenting a mere compendium of undigested facts and theory, we have tried to use research findings and behavioral science concepts to advance the reader's understanding of the subject. Considerable emphasis is thus placed on analysis and on implications to be drawn from the material.

This book centers on the behavior of people *in work situations*. The overall approach is one in which major topical areas in organizational behavior are dealt with in an integrated fashion. We begin with a consideration of the nature of individuals and organizations and of the basic forms of their interaction. Then we discuss the emergence and growth of individual-organization relationships—how each party chooses the other, adapts to the other, and develops continuing relationships. The third section of the book delineates the nature and impact of structural factors—both organizational and job-related—on individuals' behavior. The fourth section analyzes the influences of various organizational practices and social processes on employees' experiences and feelings and on their performance. The final section reviews and critically assesses the methods and goals of changing and developing organizations, and concludes with some rather personal thoughts of the authors concerning where organizations *should* be going in the future.

We have written this book for students—particularly those enrolled in junior-senior and beginning graduate-level courses in organizational behavior, organizational psychology, and management. No extensive background in the behavioral or social sciences is assumed. We also believe the book can prove useful for the practicing manager who wants an analytic, noncookbook approach to the subject.

The mechanics of writing a book such as this by three widely separated authors (from California, Michigan, and Connecticut) have presented some interesting organizational problems in their own right. At one time or another, we have held meetings or discussions in such distinctive—and diverse—locations as: an Italian restaurant in Chicago; the hotel at Detroit Metropolitan Airport; Newport Beach, California; a conference room at Newark Airport; New Haven, Connecticut; and hotels in Washington, D.C., and Montreal, Canada. By the time we had finished with all our meetings, correspondence, and phone calls and had interchanged comments on various drafts of portions of the manuscript, no chapter could be considered the exclusive property of any one of us. The book represents a true amalgam of our individual and joint ideas.

A large number of people have assisted us on this project. We would like to thank our graduate students and professional colleagues—and especially Eugene Stone, John Campbell, Thomas Atchison, Keith Davis, Lloyd Suttle, William Crampon, and Gerrit Wolf—for their many helpful suggestions on earlier drafts. Portions of the manuscript were typed by a corps of faithful secretaries, including Betty Ann Reinecke, Eve Mount, Gini Nordyke, Jane Doberstyn, Maryellen Holford, Esther Lucibello, and Margaret Steinmetz. The final version of the manuscript was expertly typed by Susi Lavasseur.

Finally, we want to gratefully acknowledge the patience and support of the members of our families: Meredith, Anne, Bill, Judy, Beth, Laura, Leslie, Cindy, and Eve.

Lyman W. Porter
Edward E. Lawler III
J. Richard Hackman

Part One

Individuals, Organizations, and Their Interaction

Chapter 1

Introduction

Consider the Plight of Eric

Eric is a new manager of product information for a national firm which wholesales electrical components. He's proud because he was assigned a "tough" office right out of management training. He's challenged because he can see as clearly as everyone else in the office that the work is not getting done on time—and that mistakes are far above the 2 percent target. And he's scared because he finds himself utterly incapable of figuring out what he ought to do to make things better.

The office is a new, one-story building in a wooded suburban location—complete with carpeting on the floor and Muzak in the walls. The people are thirty-five female employees, ranging from recent high school graduates in their first job to experienced middle-aged housewives. And the job is to provide salesmen in the field with current information about price, availability, and delivery times of an exceptionally large inventory of electrical equipment and supplies.

Eric spent his first day on the job—some three months ago now—just watching and listening. While in management training, he had thought a lot about how he would handle that first day. He knew that everyone in the office would be as eager to find out what he was like as he was to learn about them and their jobs. And he wanted to make a good impression.

But Eric finally decided not to put on any false faces. The fact was that he knew virtually nothing about the people he would be managing, or the kind of work they did. So why, he asked himself, act otherwise? Besides, if the people saw that he was genuinely interested in listening to them and learning from them, perhaps that would help establish good mutual rapport between him and his people. So he would just watch, and listen, and try to learn in his first few days on the job.

The first day was fun. Soon after arriving and being introduced to the four first-level supervisors, he asked to be "plugged in" to one of the complicated-looking operating consoles at which the women received calls from the field. A green light would blink on the console, and the information clerk would be connected to the salesman in the field—all taken care of by an out-of-sight computer, which assigned calls sequentially to the waiting clerks. The salesman would ask for information about the availability of a certain piece of equipment. The clerk would then look up the stock number of that item in a large catalog at her side and punch the number into a keyboard on the console. Immediately, the computer would present full information about stocks and delivery times of that item on an electronic display panel on the console, and the clerk would relay the appropriate information to the salesman. When the call ended, the green light would extinguish itself, and the clerk would then wait for the light to flash again, signaling the arrival of a new call.

Eric was fascinated by both the efficiency of the operation and the pleasantness of the surroundings. His biggest worry at that point was that everything was so efficiently designed that he, as manager, would not have anything to do with his time.

He soon learned how wrong he was. When, on his second day at the office, he began to attack a pile of paper work on his desk, he found messages from nearly a dozen field salesmen, all wanting him to return their calls. Each of these salesmen, it turned out, had a significant complaint about the product information service—and some were obviously quite angry. Eric managed to maintain a calm, responsive stance toward the complaining salesmen, but he also felt his stomach tightening as he heard what they had to say. By the day's end, he had made a list of three general problems which seemed both frequent enough and serious enough to warrant his immediate attention and action:

    1   Salesmen often were unable to get through quickly to information clerks. Since salesmen's calls usually were made from customer offices, this meant that they were left holding the telephone of a client for up to ten or fifteen minutes waiting for a clerk—while both the salesman and the customer became increasingly impatient.

    2   Errors were excessive. Salesman after salesman reported that, on the basis of information provided by the clerks, they would promise delivery of materials on a specific date at a specific price—only to hear later from an irate customer that the materials had not been delivered or that the price was different from that quoted or (all too often) both.

    3   The clerks were often abrupt and unfriendly to the salesmen when they called. According to more than one salesman, the clerks acted as if they were being imposed upon, rather than providing the salesmen with help in carrying out the company's business.

In the next week, as Eric attempted to track down the reasons for these difficulties, other problems came to light. First, absenteeism and turnover were extremely high. Part of the reason, it appeared, for the excessive delays was that 15 to 20 percent of the clerks were unlikely to show up for work on any given day—especially Monday and Friday—and that up to an hour's tardiness was not uncommon. This created call "backups" on the computer. The computer, of course, calmly held the calls for as long as necessary, oblivious as only a machine can be to the rise in tempers in the customer's office.

When absenteeism was particularly high on any given day, part-time employees would be called to fill in. Many of these individuals were not entirely familiar with the job and often did not remember some of the procedures to be used in looking up equipment numbers in the catalog—resulting in wrong catalog numbers and erroneous information being given to the customers. Worse, even experienced clerks had a high error rate. Eric's hope that the error problem was in the computerized information displayed on the clerks' consoles rather than a fault of the clerks themselves was clearly misplaced. And since reports of errors arrived weeks after the information had been provided (when orders failed to arrive on the customer's premises, or arrived with unexpected prices), it usually was impossible to determine who had made the mistake or why.

Finally, quite contrary to the impression he had received his first day, Eric learned that loafing on the job not only was widely practiced among the clerks, but it had indeed been developed into a rather elegant art form. It turned out that the clerks had devised ingenious ways to "busy out" their consoles (i.e., to manipulate the console in order to provide the computer with a "busy" indication when in fact the console was free). All a clerk needed to do, then, when she wanted a break from work, was to busy out her console and, if a supervisor happened to be nearby, act as if she were listening intently to a salesman on her headset.

Worse, there appeared to be a highly efficient system of informal communication among the clerks, which alerted everyone when a supervisor was about to appear on the scene (or was monitoring calls surreptitiously from the private listening room). This informal network also was heavily used for creative coordination of "personals" (i.e., brief relief from work to use the rest room) and for making sure that none of the clerks were violating the generally accepted norms about how hard one should work on a given day.

Given his own observations and impressions, Eric was not surprised when, a few weeks after he had taken over management of the office, he was visited by the regional vice-president of the company. The vice-president informed him that sales were falling companywide, and that at least part of the problem had to do with the quality of the information with which salesmen were being provided. Eric's operation was one of the most critical points of coordination in the entire company, he said, and it was important to everyone in the company that Eric reduce both the error rate and the number of delays salesmen currently were experiencing. The vice-president said he had enormous confidence in Eric's managerial ability, that he was sure the problems would be remedied quickly, and that he viewed Eric's future in the company with great optimism.

Eric panicked.

Within two days he had instituted a crash program to increase efficiency, reduce call-in delays, and slash the error rate. He held a half-day meeting with his four first-level supervisors, impressing upon them the urgency of the situation and the need for them to work with their people, individually if necessary, to improve service. He held an evening meeting with all staff members (with everyone receiving both refreshments and overtime pay), at which he announced a set of officewide performance goals, and encouraged each employee to do her best to help achieve the new goals. He even had one of the supervisors construct four large signs reading Increase Efficiency (each with a line drawing of a smiling face under the words), which were placed on the four walls of the operating area.

Beginning the day after the kick-off meeting, all supervisory personnel (himself included) were to spend at least three hours a day on the floor, helping the employees improve their efficiency, making spot checks for errors, and generally doing anything possible to smooth the flow of work.

The first two days under the new program seemed to go reasonably well: the average waiting time for incoming calls dropped slightly, spot checks of errors showed performance to be close to an acceptable level, and everyone seemed to be working hard and intently. No longer, for example, did the employees take time to look up from their work and smile or exchange a few words when Eric entered the room. That bothered him a bit because he always had enjoyed chatting with the clerks, but he accepted the loss of the smiles as a small price to pay for the increases in efficiency he hoped for.

On the third day disaster struck. Eric did not notice until midmorning that someone had carefully lettered IN before Efficiency on each of the four posters—and the smiles on the line-drawing faces had been extended into full-fledged, if subtly sarcastic, grins. Worse, everyone seemed to be studiously ignoring both the posters and him. Even the first-level supervisors said nothing to him about the posters—although Eric noticed that the supervisors, like the clerks, collected in pairs and threes for animated conversation when they were not aware of his presence. When he walked out into the operating area to start his three-hour stint, all eyes looked away and stayed there. He had never felt so completely alone.

That evening Eric stayed after everyone else had left; he removed the posters and pondered what to do next. With possibly one or two exceptions, he was sure that the people who worked for him were decent human beings. And he knew that he himself was only trying to do his job, to get performance back up to standard. As he had told the employees at the kick-off meeting, this was in the best interest of everybody: the customers, the salesmen, the clerks, himself. So why the hostility toward him and his program?

Gradually he began to suspect that the problems he had confronted— high errors and delays, excessive absenteeism and turnover—were merely outcroppings of some more basic difficulty. Perhaps, he thought, he had attacked the symptom rather than the disease.

But what was the disease? He considered each of the possibilities. He knew that there was a lot of complaining about the pay and the inflexibility of the hours. But the pay was actually very good, higher than for almost any other nonskilled job available to females in the suburban area—and every year there was a raise for everyone, which almost always was greater than the increase in the cost of living.

The hours were a problem, he knew. But even those employees who complained the most knew that he had tried mightily to convince the regional office to let him introduce a flexible scheduling plan that would allow the employees to better coordinate their personal and work lives. He had been told that company policy dictated an 8:30 to 5:00 workday and that hours (just like all other personnel policies) were centrally controlled in the interest of companywide efficiency and regularity. Eric didn't like the decision (he felt he needed to be given much more personal authority to be able to run his own operation effectively). He did, however, understand that there was some need for central coordination of policy, and he thought that the employees also should be able to see the necessity for it. The hours, he decided, could not conceivably be the root of all the difficulties.

He considered briefly the possibility that the employees were simply not capable of doing the work at satisfactory levels of speed and accuracy. But he knew that could not be the case: all had passed a company-administered ability test before they were hired and all had gone through a rigorous training program which covered every contingency a person conceivably could face as an information clerk. Besides, the job was not all that difficult; he personally suspected that even the requirement of a high school diploma was superfluous, that anybody who could read and write could handle the job without significant difficulty. No, lack of ability was not the core of the problem.

Indeed, as Eric reflected further, it seemed that the reverse could be true: that perhaps the job was so simple and routine that the clerks were bored—and therefore chose to be absent a lot and to loaf whenever they could on the job. But surely the high pay and the pleasantness of the work setting should more than compensate for any such feelings of boredom. Also, holding errors below 2 percent could provide a real challenge. And besides, loafing on the job would itself probably be more boring than working.

Supervision? It seemed most unlikely that this was the root of the difficulty. Each of the four supervisors had been information clerks themselves (although in the old days, when there was no computer and you had to look everything up in a set of reference manuals), and they knew the job inside out. Moreover, he knew from talking with the supervisors that they were genuinely committed to spending as much time as needed to help each clerk do as good a job as possible. Eric had observed each of them working on the floor many times, and there was no question in his mind about how much time and energy they spent in assisting and developing individual clerks.

Then what? Maybe, he finally concluded, the key was Kipsy. Kipsy had been a thorn in his side (the supervisors agreed) ever since Eric started the job. Although she herself had been working as a clerk for less than a year, she already had emerged as one of the informal leaders of the work force. Eric found himself agreeing with one of his supervisors who had suggested over coffee one morning that Kipsy alone created as many problems as any other dozen clerks taken together. He was 99 percent confident, for example, that it was she who had mutilated his signs. And he recently had been hearing rumblings that Kipsy was informally talking up the possibility of the clerks unionizing, probably even affiliating with some national outfit that had no understanding of the local situation.

He had tried to talk with her once. She had showed up unannounced at his office one day, with a long list of complaints about him and the work. His approach had been to listen and hear her out, to see what was troubling her, and then to do something about it—for her own sake, as well as for her supervisor and the company. Thinking back now, however, the main thing he remembered about the conversation (if you could call it a conversation) was her incredible anger. He was perplexed that he could not remember specifically what it was that she had been so mad about. Eric did recall telling her, as the conversation ended, that if she worked hard and effectively on her job for a year or two she would become eligible for enrollment in a company-run training course for a higher paying job. But again, he could not recall whether or not that had interested her.

In any case, it was clear that Kipsy was the link pin in the informal network among the clerks—and if they were turning against him and the company, you could be pretty sure that she was right in the middle of it. The question, though, was what to do about it. Fire her? In a very important sense, that would be admitting defeat—and publicly. Talk to her again? That probably would result in nothing more than his getting another load of hostility dumped in his lap, and that he didn't need.

Eric was in trouble, and he knew it. He realized it first when he could not think of a good way to repair the damage that his new motivational program apparently had created. But he knew it for sure when he found that he was no longer thinking about work except when he was actually at his desk in the office and had to do so. When he started this job he had expected to become totally immersed in it; indeed, he had wanted to be. But now he was psychologically fleeing from his job as much as the clerks seemed to be fleeing from theirs.

Consider the Plight of Kipsy

Kipsy has been an information clerk in Eric's office for almost a year. In that year she has become increasingly frustrated and unhappy in her work— and she doesn't know quite what to do about it. Things certainly have not worked out as she had expected them to. She had applied for the job because a friend told her that the company was a great place to work, that the pay was excellent, and that the people she would be working with were friendly and stimulating. Moreover, it was well known that the company was growing and expanding at a fast clip. That, Kipsy concluded, meant that there was a good chance for advancement for anyone who showed some initiative and performed well on the job.

Advancement was important. Throughout her high school years, Kipsy had always been seen as a leader by her classmates, and she had enjoyed that role much more than she had let on at the time. Her grades had been good, mostly A's and B's, and she knew if she had pushed a bit harder she could have gotten almost all A's. But she had decided that participation in school activities, doing after-school volunteer work, and (importantly) having friends and learning from them was just as important as grades. So she had deliberately let the grades slip a little.

The man who interviewed Kipsy for the job was extremely nice—and what he said about the job confirmed her high hopes for it. He even took her into the room filled with the complicated-looking consoles and let her watch some of the people at work. It seemed like it would be great fun—though perhaps a little scary—working with all that computerized equipment. She didn't know anything at all about computers.

When they returned to the hiring area from their visit to the console room, Kipsy's employment tests had been scored. The interviewer told her that she had scored in the top 10 percent of all applicants for the job, that all signs pointed to a great future for her in the company, and that she could start training the next day if she wanted. Kipsy accepted the job on the spot.

Training for the job was just as exciting as she had expected it to be. The console seemed awfully complicated, and there was no end to the special requests and problems she had to learn how to deal with. The other people working on the job also were very nice, and Kipsy soon had made many new friends.

But after a few weeks the fun wore off. The kinds of difficult problems she had been trained to solve on the console seemed never to occur. Instead, the calls began to fall into what Kipsy experienced as an endless routine: the green light flashes, the salesman gives the name of a piece of equipment, you look it up in the book and punch the number on the keyboard, you recite the information displayed by the computer back to the salesman, and the green light goes off. Then you wait, maybe only a second, maybe five minutes, for the light to go on again. And you never know how long you are going to wait, so you can never think or read or even carry on an uninterrupted conversation with the girl next to you. It was, Kipsy decided, pretty awful.

Worse, many of her new friends were quitting. The rumor was that nearly 80 percent of the people on the job quit every year, and Kipsy was beginning to understand why. Neither she nor any of her friends knew of anybody who had been promoted to management or to a better job from the ranks of the console operators, at least not in the last couple of years. And Kipsy was smart enough to realize that in time the whole operation would be automated—with salesmen punching in their requests for information directly from the field—at which time, she surmised, she and everyone else who had stuck out the job in hopes of something better would be laid off.

The only good thing about the job, she concluded, was that she was becoming the informal leader of the work group—and that had its moments. Like the time one of the girls had her planned vacation postponed on short notice, supposedly because absenteeism was so high that everyone had to be available for work merely to keep up with the flow of incoming calls. The girl (and two of her friends) had come to Kipsy and asked what she could do about it. Kipsy had marched straight away into the manager's office with the girl, asked for an explanation, and got him to agree to let her take the vacation as planned. That felt awfully good.

But such moments were too infrequent to keep her interested and involved—so she found herself making up interesting things to do, just to keep from going crazy. She developed a humorous list, Rules for Handling Salesmen, which she surreptitiously passed around the office, partly in fun but also partly to help the new girls (there always were a lot of new girls) learn the tricks necessary to keep from getting put down by the always-impatient, sometimes-crude salesmen. She also found that girls having difficulties on the job (again, usually the new workers) often came to her rather than to the supervisors for help—which she gladly gave, despite the obvious disapproval of the supervisors. She even found herself assuming the role of monitor for the group, prodding girls who were not doing their share of the work, and showing new girls who were working too hard the various tricks that could be done to keep the pace of work at a reasonable level (such as "busying out" the machine, when you just couldn't take any more and needed a break).

That was all fun, but as she reflected on it, it just didn't compensate for the basic monotony of the work or for the picky, almost schoolmarmish attitude of the supervisors. So she was buoyed up when she heard that a new manager was coming, fresh out of school. The rumor mill had it that he was one of the top young managers in the company, and she decided he surely would shake things up a bit as soon as he found out how miserable it was for people who worked in the office.

Eric's first few days on the job confirmed her high hopes for him: he seemed genuinely interested in learning about the job and in hearing what changes people had to suggest. And he talked directly to the people doing the work, rather than keeping safely out of sight and listening only to what the schoolmarms said people thought and felt. All to the good.

Her opinion about Eric's managerial abilities dropped sharply a few weeks later, however, by what came to be known around the office as the "flexible hours fiasco." Kipsy and two other girls had come up with a proposal for prescheduling work hours so that there would be substantially more flexibility in the hours each person would work. The plan was designed so that management would know at least two days ahead of time who would be coming in when. The only cost to the company would be some additional clerical time spent on actually doing the scheduling, and Kipsy had gotten agreement from almost everyone in the office to share in the clerical tasks, on their own time.

Eric had seemed receptive to the plan when Kipsy first presented it to him, and said only that he would have to check it out with higher-ups before instituting it. Nothing more was heard about the plan for about two weeks. Finally Eric called Kipsy into his office and (after a good deal of talking around the issue) reported that "the people upstairs won't let us do it."

Kipsy's respect for Eric plummeted. Rather than give a flat no, he had wiggled around for two weeks, and then lamely blamed the decision on "the people upstairs." She knew very well that the manager of an office could run his office however he pleased, so long as the work got done. And here was Eric, the bright new manager on the way up: he wouldn't go along with an employee-initiated proposal for making their life at work more bearable; he refused to take personal responsibility for that decision; and he even had the gall to ask Kipsy to help "explain to the girls" how hard he had tried to get the plan approved, and how sad he was that it had been turned down. Kipsy's response was a forced smile, an elaborately sympathetic "Of course I'll help," and a quick escape from his office.

She took the Monday of the next week off, to think about whether or not she should quit and try to find a better job. At the end of the day, she made up a list of what she wanted from her work, what she was getting, and whether or not things would improve if she stuck with the job:

My wants	Am I getting them?	Hope for improvement
1. Good pay	OK, not great	Little, till my hair turns gray
2. Interesting people	Fine	No change, except friends keep leaving
3. Interesting work	Dismal	Zero
4. Chance to show initiative and personal responsibility	None	No hope
5. Chance to contribute to an organization I believe in	Low	Ha!

The next day, Tuesday, she took her list and went to see Eric. After listening to a fatherly lecture on the importance of not missing work, especially on Mondays when the work load was heaviest, she began to tell him how upset she was. She told him that the only thing she got from working hard on the job was a backache every evening. She told him she had been misled about the chances for promotion on the job. And she asked him, as politely as she knew how, what he would suggest she do.

Eric's response blew her mind. There was a new program, he said, in which people who did well on entry-level jobs for a few years could apply for advanced training in a technical specialty. This training would be done at company expense and on company time, and would qualify her for a promotional-type transfer whenever openings in her chosen specialty developed. If she worked hard and was rated high on the quarterly supervisory assessments, Eric said, he would be prepared to nominate her for the advanced training. But it was important, he emphasized, that she behave herself—no unnecessary absences, high work productivity, good ratings by her supervisors. Otherwise, she certainly would not be selected by "the people upstairs" for the new program.

Something snapped. What kind of a fool did he think she was? How long did he expect she would be willing to wait for a "chance to be nominated" for some foggy "technical training program"? She started telling him, no holds barred now, no false politeness, exactly what she thought of the job, of the supervisors, even of the way he was running the office. And the more she talked, the madder she got—until finally she got up, almost in tears, and ran out leaving behind only the reverberations of a well-slammed door.

She was ashamed later, of course. She knew she would be, and she was. But she also was too embarrassed to go up to Eric and apologize. Which was too bad, because she suspected that behind it all Eric was probably a decent man, and maybe even somebody she could learn to like and respect—if only he would let himself be human once in a while. But she knew there was nothing she could do to change the way Eric did his job; the first move clearly had to be his. It could be a long wait, Kipsy decided. In the meantime she would come to work, try to minimize her backaches and upsets, and continue to think about finding another job. Of one thing she was sure: no more "bright ideas" for improving things at the office would come from her; that got you nothing but grief. And no longer was she going to worry so much if she happened to misremember a catalog number or accidentally disconnect a salesman. If all they wanted was a machine, that was all they were going to get.

Kipsy found herself much less able to be cavalier about her work than she had thought she could be. As hard as she tried not to care when she made errors, the distressing fact was that mistakes still *did* bother her. And she still felt like an unreconstituted sinner when she was a few minutes late for work.

It took the "increase efficiency" program to finally break her completely. It was not to be believed: an evening meeting, complete with supposedly inspirational messages from all the bosses about how we all had to pitch in and help the company make more money; grade school posters on all the walls imploring people to work harder; and, to top it all off, all the bosses, even Eric, standing around hours at a time looking over everybody's shoulders, day after day.

Did Eric really believe that treating people like children would make them work harder? She could have told him straight out beforehand that the program would make things worse rather than better. But of course he didn't ask.

Kipsy went on the offensive. She knew it was wrong, but she also knew she had to do *something* to preserve her sanity. Her first target was the signs; she and another girl stayed late in the rest room and, when everybody else had left, carefully changed the lettering of the signs to read "Increase INEfficiency," and turned the smiling face on each sign into an obviously sarcastic grin. Kipsy also began discussing with the other girls the possibility of forming a club, which would be partly social but which could possibly develop into a vehicle for doing some hard-nosed bargaining with Eric.

It didn't work. Changing the signs, after the initial thrill, only made her feel more guilty. And even though virtually everyone in the office shared her dismay about the monotony of the work and was as upset as she about Eric and his "increase efficiency" program, nobody was very excited about forming a club. Some thought it wouldn't have any impact and would be a waste of time; others thought it sounded like the first step toward unionization, which they didn't want. So the club idea died.

Kipsy was depressed. What should she do? Quit? Her preliminary explorations had not yet turned up any jobs which were much better—and most paid less than this one. Besides, to quit would be to admit publicly her inability to change anything in the office. She was supposed to be the leader of the girls in the office; she shouldn't become just one more tally toward the 80 percent a year who left.

Talk to Eric again? She seriously doubted that he would listen to one word she said. And she doubted equally seriously that she could keep herself from blowing up again at him—which would accomplish nothing and help no one.

Shut up and stick it out? That was what she had been trying for the last three months. Without noticeable success.

What, then?

Consider the Plight of the Student of Organizational Behavior

If he is sophisticated in his understanding of behavior in organizations, the student of organizational behavior should be able to draw from his kit the tools needed to understand and analyze organizational problems such as the one described above—and thereby assist in the solution of such problems. But this is no easy task: if there is a single obvious solution to the problem shared by Eric and Kipsy, it has escaped the authors of this book.

Indeed, one of the features of organizational behavior that makes the field simultaneously intriguing and frustrating is the general absence of "right answers" which neatly solve the problems of organizational life. Understanding organizations is much like understanding the weather: it is usually fairly easy to generate convincing explanations of what has already happened, and general future trends can be predicted fairly reliably if one knows the basic laws governing the various elements. But often it is impossible to say for sure exactly what is going to happen tomorrow or next week. The phenomena are simply too complex and affected simultaneously by too many factors for simple predictions or explanations to be correct.

How, then, is one to approach the study of organizations in order to generate the capability to analyze, understand, and change what happens within them? Despite the youth of the field of organizational behavior (or perhaps because of it), there is a diversity of approaches—each with some merit, and none without its own difficulties. As will be seen, how one would go about addressing a specific organizational problem (such as that of Eric and Kipsy) depends substantially on the particular approach to the study of organizational behavior one favors.

One way to think about these approaches is to identify some of the major "themes" or issues which characterize the field of organizational behavior. In the next section we try to do this, in the hope that the reader will be provided with a general sense of the terrain of the field. Then, in the following section, we set forth several basic premises which have guided the writing of this book, and which reflect the authors' particular perspective on the field.

SOME RECURRING THEMES IN ORGANIZATIONAL BEHAVIOR

The themes discussed below can be viewed as bipolar dimensions which describe the central analytic issues of organizational behavior. They apply to the consideration of virtually every problem in the field, whether it is the design of work, the socialization of new employees, the effects of different reward systems, or the impact of work groups on individuals. Since they are so pervasive, it is important for the reader to consider them at the beginning of his study of the field—so that they can serve as a context for thinking about particular topics that will be discussed later in the book.

Theoretical–Empirical

Any field of scientific inquiry requires both sound theory and well-conducted empirical investigations. The field of organizational behavior has historically been more oriented toward empirical than theoretical issues— although in recent years the two types of contributions have been moving toward a better balance.

Part of the reason for the empirical emphasis in the field is the roots of organizational behavior in the field known as industrial psychology. Early industrial psychology focused heavily on the use of tests to develop and standardize instruments that could be used for the selection and placement of employees in organizations. In recent years, industrial psychologists have broadened the scope of their investigations to include problems of training, job satisfaction, supervision, the effects of various motivational plans (such as wage incentives), and so on. But the orientation of that field has continued to be strongly empirical.

Only in recent years has a trend developed which emphasizes the importance of conceptual formulations of behavior in organizations. Within the past decade or so, we have seen the emergence of several different theories of employee motivation, of leadership behavior and effectiveness, and of organizational change and development. Many of these conceptual developments have been accompanied by supportive empirical findings, and some potentially exciting knowledge and understanding of organizational phenomena are now emerging. Nevertheless, there are still many areas—for example, communication in organizations—where there remains a great need for better theory and for theory-based empirical research.

The importance of having both theory and empirical research for the development of understanding about behavior in organizations can be seen by reflecting back on the organizational situation shared by Kipsy and Eric. An enormous number of factors could be important in determining what happened in that organization: the personal characteristics of Eric, of the first-level supervisors, or of Kipsy and the other information clerks; the structure of the organization itself; the design of the jobs held by organization members; the nature of the reward system; the selection and training procedures; and so on. There are, in fact, so many potential influences on the behavior of the people in that organization that it would be literally impossible to measure all variables and look at all the empirical relationships among those variables as a strategy for understanding the organizational situation.

Usually in such cases the researcher selects some subset of variables for measurement, and attention is restricted to those factors which have been selected for empirical analysis. It is important to realize that at precisely the point when some variables are selected for study and others are rejected as "not so relevant," a theoretical statement has been made. It may be merely a vague statement, and it may reside in the observer's head and nowhere else, but it is a theoretical statement nevertheless—because it specifies what is and what is not important to the understanding of a particular problem in a particular set of organizational circumstances. Therefore when a researcher claims that he sticks close to the data and does not deal with issues of theory when he collects and analyzes data about behavior in organizations, in most cases a better statement would be simply that the individual is not using theory deliberately, but that he is using theory nonetheless.

A more typical use of the term "theory" involves the specification of a set of internally consistent propositions about what variables are related to what other variables, complete with specification of the means by which the variables considered are to be measured. The collection of empirical data is critical in assessing the validity of such theorizing. The theory specifies what is expected to hold—what variables in the organizational situation should be found to relate to what other variables—and the empirical data show the degree to which such predictions are borne out in reality. Indeed, some of the most important learnings about organizations have emerged when a set of theory-based predictions has *failed* to stand the test of empirical data; such failures of prediction often have led to the identification of previously overlooked factors, which have turned out to be crucial to a complete understanding of the phenomena under investigation.

Empirical relationships collected and stored away without the benefit of theoretical or conceptual organization often turn out to be little more than a jumble of hard-to-understand facts; and it is also true that theorizing in the abstract, without the tie to reality provided by empirical data, often represents little more than vacuous speculation. Clearly data and theory need each other and grow from each other. As the reader proceeds through this book and considers the various topics covered, he should keep in mind questions prompted by both sides of the theoretical-empirical issue: Is there theory available to explain the research findings presented, and is there research evidence available to support the theoretical viewpoints proposed?

Descriptive–Prescriptive

This theme addresses the distinction between what *is* and what *ought to be.* In a field such as organizational behavior, which has such obvious overtones of applications, there is a strong temptation to move beyond the level of description and to prescribe what is "best" for organizations and the people who work in them. Reflection on our organizational case, for example, prompts almost automatically some highly prescriptive statements about how much "better" it would be for everyone if Kipsy and Eric's organization were different in certain ways: The organization *should* provide Eric more autonomy, Eric *should not* initiate programs without more thought in advance, Kipsy *should not* get angry so easily, the jobs *should* be redesigned, and so forth.

While it often is relatively easy to obtain consensus from like-minded friends and colleagues about what "ought to be" in organizations (and, indeed, precisely because it *is* so easy to obtain such agreement among people similar to ourselves), we must be on guard against making premature prescriptions about organizations and behavior within them. In many cases, our descriptive understanding of organizational behavior is so meager and superficial that the consequences of attempting to achieve various prescriptive goals for organizations are not known to us. This, obviously, means that prescriptive recommendation in the absence of solid descriptive understanding is a risky and sometimes dangerous process.

It is true that every manager in every organization must, as a necessary part of organizational life, make decisions and take actions with incomplete or inadequate knowledge. This does not imply, however, that individuals who have gained special expertise in the field of organizational behavior should also make the leap from the data and findings which now exist to general prescriptive conclusions which have the trappings of scientific proof. For the state of the field is such that, in general, the proof is not yet available. While we strongly believe that the findings from research on problems of organizational behavior have some clear-cut and important implications for practice, we also believe that prescriptions based on these findings should be made with considerable caution—and with full acknowledgment of the tentativeness of much of what we know about behavior in organizations.

In point of fact, in a field such as organizational behavior there can be an effective symbiotic relationship between description and prescription. Those who would prescribe need the insights and data from descriptive-type studies and examinations of topics. Description thus forms the basis for much that is prescribed. On the other hand, and not so frequently recognized, is the fact that even premature prescriptions can have their place in the development of an applied-type field. This is because such prescriptions (or, more likely, an integrated set of them), when stated forcefully, often have the effect of stimulating a great deal of research. While the motivation for such research sometimes may be to prove the incorrectness of the prescriptions, it still often results in advances in knowledge.

Our own emphasis throughout this book (with the exception of the final chapter) will lie somewhere between pure description, on the one hand, and the advocacy of a set of prescriptions on the other. We will focus on the *analysis* of problems with the aim of attempting to increase the understanding of them. For this purpose, we will make use of both descriptive material and some of the major prescriptions that have been put forth. (Chapter 16, "Goals for Organizational Change and Development," for example, is a place where we will make rather extensive use of social scientists' prescriptions.) We believe both approaches are helpful to a sound analysis of life in organizations.

Macro–Micro

When analyzing topics in organizational behavior, it is possible to take either a *macro* "big picture" perspective, or a *micro* "small details" view. Basically, it is a question of which unit is going to be emphasized: the organization or the individuals who make up the organization. The macro approach places the organization in the foreground and the individuals and groups that make it up in the background. It emphasizes the totality of the organization as a unit and concentrates on its relation to the larger social-economic-political environment. Such a perspective might be particularly utilized by those interested in a sociological analysis of organizations.

As should be clear from the way in which we chose to describe the case of Eric and Kipsy, we lean more toward a micro orientation in our approach to behavior in organizational settings—focusing on the immediate or proximal causes of behavior in organizations and emphasizing the psychological aspects of that behavior. Individuals and groups tend to be the "figure" in our discussions, and the organization is the "ground" or context.

Actually, of course, both the macro and the micro perspectives are necessary for understanding the complex human processes which take place in organizations. One of the most significant events in determining what happened in Eric's office, for example, was the disapproval of the flexible-hours proposal (on grounds of maintaining organizational "regularity"). While it had clear and substantial effects on the attitudes and behavior of individuals in the office, the disapproval clearly was a manifestation of a characteristic of the organization as a whole. Thus, throughout the book, we will need to examine both macro and micro approaches to understanding organizational behavior and we will attempt to keep salient the legitimacy of approaching the study of organizations from either end of the continuum: that is, from the macro view, moving inward toward an analysis of smaller units; and from the micro view, moving outward toward the total organization.*

Structure–Function

Another theme that pervades the literature on organizations and organizational behavior is the twin emphasis on both structure and function. This is analogous to medicine's concern with, and distinction between, anatomy and physiology. Medical diagnosis requires a knowledge of both, and the same is true in the area of organizational psychology: to understand the behavior of people in organizations, it is necessary to study both the structure of organizations and their functions.

Structure involves the particular arrangements among parts, their relatively enduring patterns of relationships. Since formal organizations can be considered as contrived social systems, it is clear that their structures are man-made and not inherently determined by a particular set of circumstances. This is what makes the structures of organizations interesting to the student of organizational behavior: structures are a matter of choice, and hence they can be altered. An emphasis on structure, then, involves a study of how these parts are put together to form a coherent whole and how the resulting structure affects the types of actions and behaviors that take place. In the organizational arena, the effects of structure sometimes tend to get overlooked because of the seemingly more obvious—and perhaps more glamorous—impact of functions. What is neglected, often, are the ways in which particular structures can help determine the nature of events that take place in an organization.

An emphasis on the functions that are carried out within organizations focuses attention on ongoing processes and activities. Many books on management, for example, are written from a functional standpoint, basing their analysis on a listing of management functions: planning, organizing, directing, staffing, etc. Such an approach can be useful, but it also can be limiting if sufficient attention is not paid to the interaction between these functions and the structural aspects of organizations.

It is difficult to imagine any topic in organizational behavior that does not demand a combined structural-functional approach. What developed in Eric and Kipsy's office, for example, was obviously partly rooted in structure (e.g., the way the work was designed; the size of the work group; the authority structure in the office) and partly in function (e.g., the way

---

*For a further discussion of the question of levels of analysis, see Chapter 3.

management related to the employees; the informal social processes which evolved among the information clerks). Clearly both sets of factors must be taken into account if one wishes to try to predict the behavior of an individual in that organization.

Similar breakouts of structural and functional properties are useful in examining other topics in organizational behavior (e.g., motivation, communication, leadership, and so on), as will be seen throughout this book. While it may be useful, for analytic purposes, to emphasize structure more than function (or vice versa) in a given instance, in general a combined structural-functional approach provides the greatest leverage in understanding behavior in organizations.

Formal–Informal

Complex organizations in which people work are, as we noted previously, constructed social systems. Indeed, they often are called "formal organizations" because they involve certain prescribed or specified relationships and functions. Such specifications come from those who founded the organization and/or those who currently control its resources. However, as the reader knows, there are untold numbers of nonprescribed and nonspecified relationships and activities that take place within a so-called formal organization. Because of this, the notion of the "informal organization" has developed. Thus, the formal organization in Eric's office specified a pattern of relationships extending from Eric to the first-line supervisors to the information clerks—with the clerks being generally undifferentiated, except that each clerk had a reporting relationship to a specific supervisor. The informal organization of the office, however, was quite different. Clearly, Kipsy occupied a strong position of leadership in the informal organization, probably having as much or more legitimacy to influence individual clerks as did the formal supervisors. Moreover, Kipsy also had developed a direct informal link with Eric, which was sometimes used to bypass the first-level supervisors (who, in the formal organization, stood between her and Eric).

Historically, analysts of organizations (particularly early management theorists) tended to focus only on the formal, prescribed aspects of organizations. They were particularly concerned with how greater rationality and efficiency could be built into the design of organizations. Any organizational problems that developed—especially in relation to "recalcitrant workers"—were ascribed to inadequate designs of the formal structure. Even early industrial psychologists devoted their attention rather single-mindedly to formal procedures, such as the operation of employee selection systems.

Concentration on the formal aspects of organizations began to weaken in the 1930s, as it became increasingly apparent that attention to the formal organization by itself was insufficient either to understand behavior in organizations or to change it. Playing a central role in this change of orientation was the now-famous research project known as the Hawthorne studies (Roethlisberger & Dickson, 1939).

This extraordinarily broad interdisciplinary project was carried out over a number of years (primarily 1927–1932), although the major results were not published until several years after the last data were collected. The initial aim of the studies was to obtain data on factors affecting variations in employee performance. The overwhelming significance of the studies, however, lies in their demonstration of the existence and influence of the informal social structures which pervade organizations. From the time of the publication of the results of the Hawthorne studies onward, no one interested in the behavior of employees could consider them as isolated individuals. Rather, such factors and concepts as group influences, social status, informal communication, roles, norms, and the like were drawn upon to explain and interpret the voluminous data from these studies and other field investigations that followed them. In effect, the Hawthorne researches were the first to emphasize the social complexities of organizations and the necessity of what we now would call a "systems" approach for explaining various behavioral phenomena.

In the years since the Hawthorne studies, the informal aspects of organizations have come in for considerable attention by both researchers and practitioners. Indeed, one might argue that in recent years there has been almost too much concern with the informal, to the exclusion of attention to the more formal characteristics of organizations. The expression "the informal organization" is too-often bandied about when, in fact, there is no single informal organization. Rather, there are various different patterns of nonprescribed relationships that take place within the formally structured contexts of organizations. What might constitute an informal communication structure would not necessarily correspond to an informal structure of friends or to an informal work-flow structure. At the very least, we should recognize that we are not dealing with a dichotomy between a formal organization and *an* informal organization. Rather, in organizational behavior we are confronted with a great diversity of structures, relationships, and actions that are to varying degrees prescribed and specified.

Objective–Subjective

In any area of scientific endeavor one of the major goals is to obtain objective, factual information about phenomena. The field of organizational behavior is no exception. Researchers and scholars in this field are making continuing efforts to obtain more reliable and valid data, data which can be objectively verified by others using similar methods of observation and investigation.

The fact that a goal of science in this area is to be as objective as possible should not, however, mislead us into ignoring or downgrading the very real importance of subjective phenomena. That is, if we are interested in the behavior of people in organizations, we must be concerned with their subjective interpretation of events; that is, their perceptions. The reason we must be concerned with perceptions is simply that behavior is based on them. It is not the "real" properties of events or situations that determine the actions and attitudes of people, but rather what people think—subjectively—the real properties are. Of course, in many instances, an individual who is motivated to do so can determine fairly quickly and easily whether his perceptions are confirmed by other indices of reality. However, when a person is dealing with social events and social interactions, as he is in organizational work settings, it is much more difficult for him to check his interpretations. He is forced to rely on his subjective impressions.

It would not be an easy task, for example, to construct a reliable picture of objective reality in the office managed by Eric from either Eric's or Kipsy's perceptions. Both individuals had access to only a partial view of reality, because of their occupancy of different positions in the social structure, and both did a good deal of interpreting and assumption making—some of which was clearly inconsistent with objective reality. The series of events surrounding the flexible-hours proposal is a good case in point. Kipsy wrongly interpreted the rejection of the proposal to be Eric's personal decision, and made a number of wrong inferences about Eric because of that; and Eric wrongly interpreted Kipsy's forced smile and statement, "Of course I'll help explain" as indicating that she understood and would help the other clerks understand how hard Eric had tried to get the proposal accepted.

Throughout this book, we will continually emphasize how individuals utilize objective information (i.e., sensory input) to form their perceptions, which in turn become the basis for their actions and reactions. For example, in Chapter 10 we will discuss the question of how the designs of jobs affect the behavior of employees, and we will particularly stress that it is not the objective job that is being reacted to but rather the "redefined job"—the job as the employee comprehends it. This redefined job may or may not coincide with the way the designers of the job conceived it when they put a set of tasks together to form the job. Because of this possible discrepancy, organizations are often surprised to find that employees' behaviors are far different from those which were intended and expected. And, the more the "objective" features of the job are emphasized, the more difficult may be the communication between the organization and the employee on that job. That is to say, the failure to take into account the subjective experiences of individuals at work can result in quite misleading conclusions if one wants to arrive at an objective analysis of a situation.

The crux of the matter is that we must be careful to avoid any invidious comparisons between something labeled "objective" and something labeled "subjective," when we are dealing with phenomena pertaining to behavior in organizations. Objectivity, as a characteristic of observer-scientists, is to be valued; but subjectivity, as an aspect of individuals' behavior, is also to be valued—and studied.

Cognitive–Affective

Our last theme addresses the distinction between two modes of behavior: cognitive and affective. The former refers to the thought processes of individuals, and emphasizes rationality, logic, and the use of the mind. The latter refers to the feelings of individuals, and emphasizes the emotions and (one might say) the use of the glands. When Kipsy made up her list of what she was getting from her work and what she expected to get in the future if she stayed on the job, she was operating in a dominantly cognitive mode; when she found herself unable to contain her anger in trying to discuss that list with Eric, the affective side had become dominant. The way in which the affective and cognitive sides of a person can affect each other is well illustrated by Eric's subsequent inability to remember (a clearly cognitive act) the content of what Kipsy had been saying to him. His own affective reaction to the exchange was, in effect, protecting him from the need to take rational action regarding a personally distressing and anxiety-arousing matter.

While both modes of behavior constantly are exhibited in organizational settings, the balance between them can be markedly different depending upon the nature of the immediate situation. Where there are few direct consequences to the individual because of what is happening, or where there are no time pressures to make decisions or come up with reactions or responses, an individual will tend to behave in a cognitively dominated manner. However, when events or people produce tension or anxiety, when the pace is fast, or when the individual will be directly impacted by the events, the affective mode tends to predominate.

For many years there was an overemphasis by both social scientists and managers on the cognitive-rational components of behavior to the exclusion of a concern with the affective-emotional components. Countless examples of employee behavior, however, seemed inexplicable when looked at only from the perspective of the employees' supposed logical reactions. Questions such as the following seemed nearly unanswerable: Why is the new office building disliked more than the old one with the dingy walls? Why is the carefully designed incentive pay plan resulting in no greater production than when there was no such plan in existence? Why should group A be concerned about how group B is doing? And so forth. It is only fairly recently that we have come to realize what perhaps should have been obvious before: that any explanations of behavioral events in work settings that ignore the emotional or affective aspects of behavior are bound to be inadequate. Even more important is the notion that such aspects of behavior are to be regarded as normal and natural. Individuals at work, like individuals everywhere, are both thinking *and* feeling creatures. Human phenomena in organizations cannot be understood without this perspective, and hence it will be one that prevails in our analyses in this book.

SOME PREMISES ABOUT LIFE IN ORGANIZATIONS

Just as no organization member can experience what happens in his organization with true objectivity, neither can textbook writers fully achieve the oft-espoused goal of letting the data speak for themselves. We have tried to write a book which illuminates and interprets current knowledge about behavior in organizations without imposing our own normative biases on the theories and findings we discuss. But since we know that our own views must necessarily color our interpretations—not to mention our decisions about what to include and what to leave out of the book—we have set forth in the next few pages several of our own basic premises about life in organizations. Our hope, whether the reader agrees or disagrees with these premises, is that they will provide him with a richer context and perspective for reading and understanding the material to follow.

1 The quality of the interaction between individuals and the organizations for which they work can be improved to the benefit of both parties. Throughout this book, we stress that it is the *interaction* of individuals and organizations that is the key object of our concern and of the field of organizational behavior. On the basis of all the evidence we have available, from strictly scientific studies as well as from perceptive observations from other sources, we believe that considerable potential exists for improving the quality of this interaction. Furthermore, we think that such improvements will aid not just employees or not just organizations themselves, but rather will redound to the benefit of both.

Considerable evidence exists, ranging from the highly quantified to the anecdotal, that points toward a fairly widespread degree of dissatisfaction of many citizens with their jobs. (See, for example, the 1972 study sponsored by the U.S. Department of Health, Education, and Welfare, *Work in America*.) This is not to say, by any means, that all employees or even a heavy majority are highly dissatisfied with their work. Rather, it is to say that a significant percentage of employees are less satisfied than they could be with their job and organizational circumstances. Looking at the situation from the organization's perspective, the performance of a portion of employees is often regarded as barely adequate (if not substandard) and well below what individuals are capable of demonstrating. "If only Joe (or Sally) would work up to his (her) capacity" is a not infrequent complaint.

Still additional evidence of the problem of individual–organization interactions in many work environments is the relatively high rate of turnover among employees, particularly in the early months after a person joins an organization. While it is unreasonable to expect that every employee–organization match will work out so well that neither side will want to discontinue the relationship, the rates of turnover in many work situations are clearly (it seems to us) higher than they need to be.

Our first premise, therefore, is the firm belief that more potential exists for improving the quality of individual–organization interactions than is commonly utilized or even, perhaps, recognized.

2 The responsibility for improving the quality of individual–organization interactions rests with both the individual employee and the organization. It is all too easy in the world of work to attach blame. "Management is autocratic . . . ," "Employers are unfair . . . ," "Workers are lazy . . . ," "Unions are power hungry. . . ." On and on goes the list of complaints that members of one segment of the work situation have about some other part of the system. It seems clear, though, from all that has been learned over the years, that the responsibility for the state of affairs that exists in any given organization is widely shared. Therefore, the responsibility for improving individual–organization relationships is also jointly shared.

If progress is to be achieved in making work and organizational life more satisfying for the employee, and the employee a more satisfactory performer, *mutual* efforts will be required. Organizations (i.e., the influential people in them), for their part, cannot safely or complacently assume that they have already done everything that is possible to bring about a quality working environment. They have not, or at least not often enough, done so. For example: Only a relatively small fraction of organizations have systematically examined their whole range of jobs to determine which ones might usefully be enlarged or enriched to the benefit of the jobholder and at no cost, or little cost, to the organization. Only a small portion of employing enterprises have *really* stopped to evaluate the quality of their supervisors' relationships with subordinates. Many have given supervisors some sort of training but then have proceeded to assume that once a supervisor has been trained there is no need to keep monitoring constantly the effectiveness of his relationships as seen from the vantage point of the subordinate. Only a limited number of organizations have thoroughly investigated their reward practices to determine if they are helping to generate the types of employee actions that are simultaneously beneficial to both the employer and the individuals themselves.

For their part, organization members would seem to have an obligation to help better the enterprise of which they are a part as well as themselves. It is organizations, after all, that provide the circumstances that permit most of us to realize many needs and aspirations. Individual performance that is clearly substandard or individual behavior that contributes only to self-enhancement at the sacrifice of a more common good invites organizational responses that lead away from, rather than toward, an improved quality of organizational life. So-called self-actualization carried to an extreme in organizational settings may perhaps provide increased gratification for one individual, but it is unlikely to result in a better organizational situation for his work colleagues. Thus, while individuals in organizations have every right to expect that the collectivity owes them something beyond a mere fair day's pay for a fair day's work—namely, a high-quality working environment—they in turn must help the process along.

3 A systems perspective toward organizations is inevitable: the phenomena of organizational life are not isolated segments or incidents. We believe that it simply is not possible to look at particular aspects or topics of organizational behavior without adopting a systems perspective. One must always assume, it seems to us, that most things that go on in organizations are in some way related to a number of other things that are occurring or will occur; and, further, that any given action by the organization (e.g., a new training program, the creation of an organizational unit, the recombination of several job duties) or by an employee (e.g., changing his production speed, being late for work, coming up with a new problem-solving idea) *will* have ramifications and implications beyond the immediate situation. While this seems patently obvious, it is remarkable how many individuals in organizations—both managers and rank-and-file employees alike—ignore this simple proposition. Often, it will be to their detriment, as things later turn out.

On a broader scale, the major topic areas covered in this book in separate chapters clearly interrelate to each other in a meaningful way. The manner in which a new employee is recruited and the reasons why he chooses Company A over Company B will affect his response to various organizational actions during the early adaptation period. These events in turn help determine the kind of reactions he will have to his job and the ways in which he relates to supervisors and others in the organization. All of these provide a context as to whether various efforts to change or develop the organization will be successful, and so on. The message on this point is clear: If one starts with the assumption that aspects of organizational behavior have systemic and meaningful relationships to, and impacts on, other areas, then he is much less likely to be surprised by organizational events than he would be if he made a different assumption. It is possible, of course, to assume stronger connections than actually exist, but the errors in this direction seem much less than if the assumption of systems-type relationships is not made in the first place.

4 Organizations and individuals need to become more cognizant of the fact that work in organizations is typically carried out in a social situation—and use that fact to their mutual advantage. The essentially social character of work in organizations is emphasized at a number of places throughout this book. Regardless of any views of an organization about whether such social interaction in the job situation is good or bad, it occurs. And it occurs with consequences that are sometimes positive and sometimes negative both for the organization and for its members. Employees often "fire up" each other by communicating their own enthusiasms within a group; in other circumstances, the opposite occurs with social influence being exerted decidedly in the direction of holding down production or getting back at the boss. The norms that are developed can go in a variety of directions with regard to absenteeism, production, cooperation, and the like. Social situations also can serve to increase or decrease the satisfaction level of employees: an argument with a fellow worker leads to angry feelings; a compliment from the boss or a word of encouragement from the "old pro" makes one feel a little—or a lot—better about how things are going at work.

The key, it seems to us, is for organizations and individuals to take advantage of the fact that work *is* social and turn this feature to the benefit of both. This means, of course, both members and the enterprise working together to try to create social climates that are conducive to positive outcomes. This is not to deny the reality, or, in certain circumstances, the desirability of conflict. It does mean helping the conflict to be channeled into constructive rather than destructive outcomes. Social climates can be a very rewarding part of work situations, but positive climates do not come about without a great deal of care and feeding by those who populate *all* the parts of the organization.

5 There exists a commonality of organizational phenomena across all types of organizations and in a wide variety of cultural settings. Anyone who has ever worked in an organization has encountered the statement: "But *our* organization is different. . . ." True, but only in a very narrow and specialized sense, just as no two individuals are identical. We contend that the kinds of events and human behaviors that take place in organizational settings have a commonality that far transcends the boundaries of particular enterprises. If an employee has been curtly dealt with by a supervisor, this is likely to bring a resentful response whether the location is Central Hospital, Midland University, or the Lane Shoe Company. If an employee receives a tangible form of recognition immediately upon the completion of a significant task, this is likely to strengthen performance-reward beliefs whether it is the tax department of a state government or a professional baseball team. Elaborate systems of informal communication networks form in Army regiments as well as in the State Department.

The point to be made and kept to the forefront is that although much of the research that has been carried out to date on organizations has been done in business and industrial enterprises, the phenomena are just as likely to be found in any other setting where people come together to work. Just because a company turns out steel products for profit does *not* make it unique with respect to the existence of organizational socialization attempts and reactions, the formation of informal groups and the existence of group norms, the desire of many employees for more meaningful work, the need to select the best possible employees, or the resistance to organizational change.

Organizational behavior phenomena are essentially universal. Period.

6 The development of both individuals and organizations will continue to be both a necessity and an objective. Neither individuals nor organizations are ever "finished" products. Both have potentials that are capable of responding to concerted development efforts. With respect to individuals, we take it as a premise that people want to develop and be assisted in this development. Put simply, most of us would like to be better than we are at whatever we see ourselves capable of doing. The problem lies, therefore, primarily in knowing how to do this rather than in the latent motivation to do it.

We believe that organizations should see themselves as potentially one of society's most powerful instruments for assisting individuals in improving and developing their skills—intellectual, manual, and psychological. While it is obviously true that a number of opportunities exist for individuals to engage in self-development activities—taking correspondence courses, for example—in practice such opportunities are somewhat limited. The employing organization—the place where the individual spends thirty-five to forty waking hours per week attempting to exercise some of the skills he considers most important—offers a prime set of resources for aiding individual development. This implies that the organization's role in development of employees must be seen in a broader context than merely one in which an individual is trained for his entry-level job or for a job to which he is transferred or promoted. Rather, organizational efforts to help employees develop themselves should permeate all the activities the organization carries out that have relevance for the use of its human resources. However else the organization's climate is characterized, it should at least be viewed as *developmental.*

Further, organizations must be constantly alert to opportunities to develop themselves. The history of employing organizations for the past 100 years or so seems fairly clear in pointing to the conclusion that those that remain static and do not attempt continuously the tasks of renewal and development are likely to decline and atrophy if not go out of existence entirely. The problem for many years was that while the leaders of organizations were often aware of the need for development, they were unable to bring to bear appropriate methods and techniques. The reason for this, at least insofar as the human side of organizations was concerned, was primarily that such methods and techniques did not exist. They could not be applied because they had not yet been developed. In the past decade or so, however, behavioral science has begun to provide techniques—however imperfectly they may be developed in their present state—which offer, we think, significant possibilities for organizational development. Therefore, there appears to be little excuse for employing enterprises not to undertake vigorous attempts at improving and developing themselves. Employees and, indeed, society, increasingly will expect it.

7 Behavioral science research has much to offer in improving both the quality of the work experience for individuals and the productivity of work organizations. This is a research-oriented book. We have little sympathy for theories or management prescriptions which are not supported by data; and we have little use for anecdotes or specific research findings which have no accompanying interpretative context. We believe, and strongly, that behavioral science research and theory—when linked together—are among the most useful means for developing both the knowledge and the practical methods which are required for life in organizations to be improved.

We admit the legitimacy and usefulness of a wide diversity of research strategies and techniques for gaining understanding of behavior in organizations. Studies reported and discussed in this book include those done in both laboratory and field settings, and using both correlational and experimental research strategies. We reject the proposition that laboratory studies, because of the artificiality of the setting, cannot yield findings of use in ongoing organizations; we also reject the notion that studies done in real organizations necessarily have relevance or importance merely because they were conducted in the "real world."

For us, the criteria for the usefulness of organizational research have to do with (1) the degree to which *real* psychological or social processes have been created (whether by experimental manipulation in the laboratory or by occurrences in an ongoing organization), (2) the degree to which these processes and their consequences are measured reliably and in such a way as to minimally distort their meaning as experienced by the research participants, and (3) the degree to which the interpretations of the data are congruent with the actual measures which were obtained and, importantly, do not extend beyond the constraints of the setting in which the data were collected.

Actual experiments (in which variables are manipulated and controlled by the researcher or his agent) offer the most logically "tight" assessment of what is *causing* what. We realize, however, that for many organizational problems (especially when the research is conducted in the field), it is impossible to have the level of experimental control that usually character- izes research done in cognitive or social psychology. We are, therefore, sympathetic to attempts to use correlational techniques (in which the degree of association between two variables or sets of variables is measured, without the necessity of experimentally controlling any of the variables). Our interpretations of correlational findings, however, tend to be cau- tious—since it is not logically possible to know merely from a high correlation between two variables which one is causing which. There has long been controversy in organizational behavior, for example, about whether or not "satisfaction causes increases in productivity." Study after study has correlated measures of employee satisfaction and measures of productivity—and the results of these studies have been anything but consistent. Recent research and theory have suggested that one reason for such inconsistencies is that, in some situations, a person's productivity level may be substantially more the cause of his satisfaction rather than vice versa. There is no way that this could have been known from those studies which simply correlated one with another, and attempted *post hoc* to interpret the size of the correlation obtained.

In sum, we are strongly inclined toward a research-oriented approach to the study of organizations and organizational change, and we favor the use of a wide diversity of research tools and techniques in doing research on organizational phenomena. We urge the reader to share with us, however, a friendly skepticism about the research studies we report in this book—and to consider on his own the degree to which they validly and meaningfully reflect and extend our understanding of behavioral processes in ongoing organizations.

Chapter 2

The Nature of Individuals

All attempts to understand why people behave as they do in organizations necessarily involve some basic assumptions about the nature of human beings. Assumptions are typically made about what people seek and what they avoid; how people make choices about what they will do; what they are capable and incapable of accomplishing, and so on. Sometimes these assumptions are not made explicit but they are always present. This chapter reviews some of the major assumptions about the characteristics of man which have been influential in the discussion of his behavior at work, and it makes explicit the ones which will guide our discussion in the chapters to follow.

VIEWS AND MODELS OF MAN

There is no dearth of "ready-made" models of man in the literature of psychology and philosophy. Indeed, a good deal of scholarly effort has been expended over the years to develop an understanding of man which is general enough to allow prediction of human behavior in a variety of situations. Such models have varied on a number of dimensions that are discussed in the following paragraphs.

Rational versus Emotional Some writers have viewed man as a highly rational organism, which operates much as a computer would if it were alive. Thus, man is seen as systematically collecting information relevant to whatever task is at hand, analyzing that information carefully and logically, weighing and evaluating alternative courses of action with precision, and eventually charting and embarking upon an entirely rational course of action. Some psychologists have carried out very informative lines of research (especially on human problem solving and decision making) based upon a rational "information-processing" model of man (e.g., Edwards, 1954).

At the opposite conceptual pole is the "emotional" model of man. Human beings are seen by scholars of this persuasion as being controlled heavily by their emotions—many of which are not under voluntary control, and indeed may not even be accessible to the consciousness of the individual. Those of the Freudian persuasion, for example, work from the assumption that many of the most important determinants of one's adult behavior are unconscious, and often are based upon unresolved conflicts and crises faced in childhood. From this perspective, in order to understand phenomena such as leader-subordinate relationships in organizations, it is necessary to unearth and deal with early and perhaps repressed issues such as the person's father-child relationships.

Behavioristic versus Phenomenological Some scholars maintain that man can be adequately described in terms of his behavior alone; that no concept of "consciousness" or theories of consciously controlled behavior are necessary to understand human behavior even in the most complicated social settings. The behavioristic school usually is attributed to John B. Watson (1930, p. 104), who strikingly illustrated his view of man in the following well-known quote:

> Give me a dozen healthy infants, well-formed, and my own special world to bring them up in and I'll guarantee to take any one at random and train him to become any type of specialist I might select—doctor, lawyer, artist, merchant-chief and, yes, even beggar-man and thief, regardless of his talents, penchants, tendencies, abilities, vocations and the race of his ancestors.

Thus, in its radical form, behaviorism holds that all behavior is environmentally controlled. In contemporary psychology, the behavioristic tradition is carried on by B. F. Skinner, who has shown how everything from human language to the behavior of patients on a mental ward can, at least in principle, be analyzed and understood completely in behavioral terms. Moreover, Skinner's thinking has recently been applied by some to behavioral change attempts in organizations *(Psychology Today, 1972)*.

The phenomenological view of man is directly opposed to that of the behaviorists. As described by one scholar (Hitt, 1969, p. 657), it maintains that:

> Man can be described meaningfully in terms of his consciousness; he is unpredictable; he is an information generator; he lives in a subjective world; he is arational; he is unique alongside millions of other unique personalities; he can be described in relative [rather than absolute] terms; he must be studied in a holistic manner; he is a potentiality; and he is more than we can ever know about him.

Thus, from a phenomenological view, to understand the behavior of a person in a social setting we must somehow get "inside" the head of the person because that is where the determinants of his behavior reside (Buhler, 1969). Those with this perspective argue that man is so complicated and his true potentialities are so thinly revealed in his day-to-day activities that a scientific understanding of him and what determines his behavior cannot be obtained from behavioral observation.

Economic versus Self-actualizing Man   Many early writers on organizational theory and management practice conceptualized man in strictly economic terms. As described by them, economic man:

> . . . is a rational creature who uses his reason primarily to calculate exactly how much satisfaction he may obtain from the smallest amount of effort, or when necessary, how much discomfort he can avoid. "Satisfaction" does not mean pride in one's job, the feeling of having accomplished something, or even the regard of others; it *refers only to money.* Similarly, "discomfort" refers not to failing in one's task or losing the respect of one's comrades, but solely to the fear of starvation. Economic man is naturally competitive, basically self-interested, and in the battle of life strives hard to outwit every other man; so far from helping the weak or the underdog, his sole concern is with his very own survival (Brown, 1954, p. 16).

The economic model of man had considerable influence on the management of organizations early in this century and was central to the development of the "scientific management" school of thought (Taylor, 1911). According to scientific management, people are expected to perform most effectively when work functions are highly specialized and standardized. It goes on to state that people will work effectively if they are sufficiently well paid. The twin design principles of specialization and standardization lead to the creation of jobs which are simplified and repetitive, and which can be performed by almost anyone after a short period of training. The highly paid assembly-line job is a classic illustration of a job designed according to the dictates of scientific management. If people cared only about economic issues, they would be expected to find these jobs quite satisfying. Unfortunately, people who work on such routine, specialized and simplified jobs usually are *not* well satisfied (Blauner, 1964; Shepard and Herrick, 1972; Upjohn Institute, 1973), which casts considerable doubt on the general usefulness of a strict economic model of man in organizational settings. (A more complete discussion of the issues relevant to work design and people's reactions to various job designs is provided in Chapter 10).

The self-actualizing view of man is, in many important ways, directly opposed to the concept of economic man. Psychologists such as White, McClelland, and Maslow note that many people seem to be motivated by the opportunity to increase their competence and to grow and develop as individuals. Therefore, they conclude, man cannot be adequately described solely in terms of economic or physiological considerations. Instead, they posit, man ultimately strives toward loftier ideals, such as self-fulfillment and self-actualization. Maslow, (1943, p. 382), for example, describes self-actualization as follows:

> Even if all these [lower-level] needs are satisfied, we still may often (if not always) expect that a new discontent and restlessness will soon develop, unless the individual is doing what he is fitted for. A musician must make music, an artist must paint, a poet must write, if he is to be ultimately happy. What a man *can* be, he *must* be. This need we may call self-actualization. . . . [Self-actualization] refers to the desire for self-fulfillment, namely, to the tendency for one to become actualized in what one is potentially. This tendency might be phrased as the desire to become more and more what one is, to become everything that one is capable of becoming.

Maslow and other humanistic theorists argue that while baser considerations may divert a person's orientation from the ideals of growth and fulfillment, the nature of man is such that he will strive toward those ideals when he is given a realistic opportunity to do so. The problem in designing social systems (including organizations), then, from this point of view, is to create conditions under which this natural tendency of man can be supported and encouraged—for the betterment of both the individual and the social system.

Theory X versus Theory Y   Two opposing sets of assumptions about man, which summarize several of the views reflected in the models of man described above, have been described by McGregor (1960). The special usefulness of the McGregor formulation is that the *way one would treat an individual in an organization* (and indeed, the way the organization itself would be designed) follows rather directly from whether one holds "Theory X" or "Theory Y" assumptions about people.

The Theory X assumptions are the following:

1   *The average human being has an inherent dislike of work and will avoid it if he can.*
This assumption has deep roots. The punishment of Adam and Eve for eating the fruit of the tree of knowledge was to be banished from Eden into a world where they had to work for a living. The sometimes undue stress placed on productivity, on the concept of "a fair day's work," on the evils of featherbedding and restriction of output, and on explicit rewards for performance reflects an underlying belief that an organization's management must counteract an inherent human tendency to avoid work. The evidence for the correctness of this assumption would seem to many managers to be incontrovertible.

2   *Because of the human characteristic of dislike of work, most people must be coerced, controlled, directed, threatened with punishment to get them to put forth adequate effort toward the achievement of organizational objectives.*
This Theory X assumption maintains that the dislike of work is so strong that even the promise of rewards is not generally enough to overcome it. People will accept the rewards and demand continually higher ones, but these alone will not produce the necessary effort. Only the threat of punishment will do the trick.

3   *The average human being prefers to be directed, wishes to avoid responsibility, has relatively little ambition, wants security above all.*
This assumption of the "mediocrity of the masses" is rarely expressed so bluntly. Many supervisors and managers will give private support to this assumption, and it is easy to see it reflected in overt practice.

The Theory Y assumptions are the following:

1   *The expenditure of physical and mental effort in work is as natural as play or rest.*
This Theory Y assumption asserts that the average human being does not inherently dislike work. Depending upon controllable conditions, work may be a source of reward (and will be voluntarily performed) or a source of punishment (and will be avoided if possible).

2   *External control and the threat of punishment are not the only means for bringing about effort toward organizational objectives. Man will exercise*

self-direction and self-control in the service of objectives to which he is committed.

   3   *Commitment to objectives is a function of the rewards associated with their achievement.*
The most significant of such rewards (e.g., the satisfaction of ego and self-actualization needs) can under the right conditions be the direct products of effort directed toward organizational objectives.

   4   *The average human being learns, under proper conditions, not only to accept but to seek responsibility.*
Avoidance of responsibility, lack of ambition, and emphasis on security are generally consequences of experience, not inherent human characteristics, according to this view.

   5   *The capacity to exercise a relatively high degree of imagination, ingenuity, and creativity in the solution of organizational problems is widely, not narrowly, distributed in the population.*

   It clearly makes a large difference in understanding individual behavior in organizations which view of man is accepted. Under the first view, Theory X, the assembly-line worker who occasionally puts the letters *FORD* on a car in the wrong sequence so they make some other combination of letters is seen as irresponsible and in need of tighter controls. Under the second view, he might be seen as bored and seeking some legitimate increase in the variety and self-expression he experiences at work.

Toward a Realistic View of Man in Organizations

Which view of man is valid: Theory X or Theory Y? Probably both of them have some validity. There certainly are some people who probably can best be characterized in terms of the assumptions of Theory X, just as there are others who can best be viewed in terms of Theory Y. It is equally impossible to characterize man unequivocally on either end of the other dimensions discussed: economic versus self-actualizing, behavioristic versus phenomenological, or rational versus emotional. All have some elements of truth to them; but *no* single model of man is in itself capable of explaining the full diversity and richness of behavior which is observed in organizations, because none of them adequately recognizes the large and significant differences that exist among people. Not only do different people behave in diverse ways when faced with the same situation (the "individual differences" problem that has been the focus of attention of many industrial psychologists for years), but also the same person behaves differently at various times and in various organizational environments. Behavior in organizations is simply too complex and diverse for any model that assumes, for example, that all people are motivated by economic or self-actualization needs.

   How, then, are we to develop a realistic view of man in organizations that will help analyze, understand, and predict his behavior—but still allow for the important individual and situational differences which exist? There is no thoroughly satisfactory answer to this question, but our intention is to deal with it by stating several general propositions about man, and then discuss how individual differences modify these general propositions. The focus, of course, will be on those propositions and individual difference characteristics which are necessary to understand the nature of the interaction between individuals and the organizations in which they work.

MAN IS PROACTIVE

The behavior of people at work often is discussd in terms of the way individuals *react* to organizational policies and practices. Thus, individuals are seen as resisting the institution of a new pay plan; or as increasing in work motivation because of the leadership strategies used by a supervisor; or as becoming more skilled in their work because of an organizational training program; and so on.

It is quite true, of course, that individuals react and respond to the things that happen to them—at work, and in their lives outside the organization. These events often influence their goals and change the methods they use to obtain their goals. The impact of such events, however, should not obscure the great deal of personal initiative—proactive behavior—that individuals demonstrate in seeking means to satisfy their personal needs and pursue their goals and aspirations. Moreover, such personal initiatives are taken in virtually all settings in which individuals find themselves. Thus, like most behavior, work behavior is often goal oriented. Although individuals cannot always report accurately on what their goals are, there is evidence which shows they frequently can and that these reports often are predictive of their future behavior (Locke, 1968; Steers & Porter, 1974). Thus, as will become apparent when we discuss topics such as job design and pay systems, examination of employees' mental states can help us predict how they will react to certain organizational policies and practices. An important theme of this book, then, is that behavior in organizations is *jointly* determined by organizational practices and by the proactive, goal-oriented behavior of individual organization members.

MAN IS SOCIAL

Membership in organizations is a central and highly important part of the lives of most people. Part of the reason for this is that people spend such a large proportion of their waking time in organizational settings of one kind or another. But more than this, some involvement with other people in groups or organizations seems to be necessary for most people to maintain their identity as people and their psychological well-being (Freeman & Giovanni, 1969; Scheidlinger, 1952).

The need of individuals for "belonging" often is heightened under conditions of psychological or physical stress. For example, soldiers in World War II were found to increase their group identifications under combat conditions (Janis, 1963); similarly, a number of studies have shown that people have strong desires to be with other people when they are in a state of experimentally induced anxiety (e.g., Schachter, 1959).

There clearly are significant individual differences in how important social involvement is to people. One reason for this seems to be that a person who becomes excessively involved in, and identified with, a set of other people can risk losing his identity (Bion, 1959). Thus, the individual faces conflict in determining just how involved to become in a group or organization. The consequence of this conflict between social dependence and independence is frequently a pattern of vacillation on the part of individuals between group (or organizationally) centered activities and individual-centered behavior (Ziller, 1964).

Individuals often use their relationships with other people to obtain valuable information about themselves and the environment in which they operate. The data supplied by others constitute a "social reality" for the individual and the group. Individuals often use social reality to test and compare their own abilities, ideas, and views in order to increase their self-understanding. Indeed, a number of writers have shown that a person's social relationships, probably more than any other single factor, determine the nature of his self-concept. Thus, the notion of Cooley (1922) of the "looking glass self" specifies that an individual comes to gain self-understanding and a self-concept by inferring what he "must be like" given the way others behave toward him in social settings.

It should be noted that socially controlled information—whether it be about external reality, about the self, or about specific behaviors and skills—can be sought by the individual for either (or both) of two reasons. First, individuals may derive *intrinsic* satisfaction merely from learning about and coming to "know" the proximal world. Festinger, for example, posited a drive for people to know about the accuracy of their beliefs and opinions about the world in his theory of "social communication" (1950); and he suggested an analogous drive to know about oneself in his theory of "social comparison" (1954). Thus, individuals would be expected, for intrinsic reasons alone, to seek information from others.

In addition to the intrinsic reasons for seeking information from others, there often are some very good *instrumental* reasons for doing so. If an individual wishes to behave so as to achieve rewards which exist in the organizational environment, he must have a good understanding both of that environment (e.g., what behaviors lead to what outcomes there) and of himself (e.g., his own skill level relative to job requirements). Thus, the need for information in organizational environments is substantial; the degree to which a person can obtain it on his own is severely limited by his restricted time-and-place perspective. A reliance on other organization members for assistance in obtaining needed information is inevitable and is one of the reasons social relations are so important to individuals.

MAN HAS MANY DIFFERENT NEEDS

Ever since philosophers began trying to understand why people behave the way they do, there has been controversy about what it is that motivates a person to action. The earliest theories were "one-factor"—i.e., they attempted to postulate a single explanatory concept which would make it possible to analyze in simple terms the complexities of human behavior. One such principle, which still has some credence today, is "hedonism": it states that man's primary orientation is toward avoiding pain and seeking pleasure, and that all man's behavior ultimately can be understood if one only determines what a person experiences as pleasurable or painful. Unfortunately, what was considered pleasurable or painful was usually determined by observing what a person chose to seek out or avoid, thereby resulting in a circular analysis which did not allow for the *prediction* of behavior.

Gradually one-factor theories of human motivation were replaced by attempts to identify and document lists of basic human instincts, drives, and needs. Such lists, unfortunately, began to grow endlessly long; every time a new pattern of behavior was observed for which there was no available explanation, it became necessary to add yet another instinct, or drive, or need. And as the lists expanded in length and diversity, they became less and less useful for understanding and predicting human behavior. One list, for example, included over 14,000 instincts, one of which was the need "to eat apples from one's own orchard." Much of the criticism of this approach that has been made by behaviorists such as Skinner has focused on the long and often useless lists of needs that have been drawn up.

It has become increasingly clear that human beings are motivated toward a great diversity of ends, and that what particular factor motivates a person today may or may not be potent in determining his behavior tomorrow. Moreover, there are large differences among people in what they need and value—making the task of developing any complete and internally consistent list of factors virtually impossible. This, however, does not mean that the concept of need is not a useful explanatory concept in dealing with

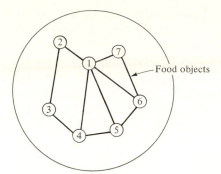

Figure 2–1 Need for food.

human behavior in organizations. It can serve to help explain a considerable amount of the goal-oriented behavior that occurs in organizations. As McGregor's statement of Theory Y illustrates, different assumptions about the nature of human needs lead to quite different explanations of behavior and quite different principles of organization design.

How Many Needs Must Be Considered to Understand Behavior in Organizations?

Originally, needs (and drives) were said to exist only when a physiological basis could be established for the attractiveness of the objects sought by a person (e.g., food, water, sex). This restricted usage is no longer in vogue, however, and the term "need" now is used to refer to *clusters* of goals or outcomes that a person seeks. Consider, for example, food as an outcome which is sought by people. Food objects cluster together, in the sense that when a person desires one food object he often desires some others as well; and when he gets enough of one, he may lose interest in the others. Thus, we say people have a need for food rather than saying that people have a need for roast beef or milk. By doing this we move to a more general level and begin to group outcomes more conveniently. The question that then arises, however, is where to stop? That is, at what level of abstraction or generality should we stop grouping outcomes and start calling them needs?

In general, those theorists who have developed longer lists of needs (e.g., Murray, 1938) have settled for a lower level of abstraction than those who have formulated shorter lists (e.g., Alderfer, 1971). As an example, consider again a particular food object. This particular object is one of a number of objects sought by a person who has been without food. This can be represented diagrammatically as shown in Figure 2-1. The figure shows a cluster of outcomes linked together because the outcomes are all food objects and when one is desired, the others are desired. It would be possible

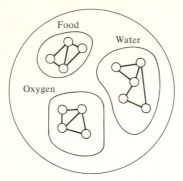

Figure 2-2   An "existence" need.

to stop at this level and simply say that people have a need for food. However, it also is possible to go to a higher level of abstraction and combine food outcomes with water and oxygen and call this cluster an "existence need." This need (which is illustrated in Figure 2-2) includes all outcomes which people need to sustain life. The criteria for grouping of the food objects in Figure 2-1 specified that when one outcome is sought the others will be sought, and when one is obtained a person's level of desire for the others is affected. The basis for grouping objects in Figure 2-2 is different: in this case, all objects have as a common property their necessity to human existence. Thus, one would say that people desire food objects because of their existence need, while at the other level of analysis one would say people desire these objects because of a need for food or nutriment.

Both approaches are in one sense correct. Ultimately the level that one chooses should be dictated by the degree to which the level permits one to predict and understand behavior in organizations. Unfortunately, there presently is not enough research evidence available to allow one to draw any final conclusion about which level of analysis leads to the greatest predictability. Conceptually, the best approach would seem to be to group only those outcomes whose attractiveness is found to have an empirical relationship to each other. This means that a group of outcomes can be called a need only if when one of the outcomes is obtained the attractiveness of the others changes, and if as more of one is obtained a person's satisfaction with the whole cluster of outcomes is affected. Using this criterion in an organizational context suggests the following needs (similar to the listing by Maslow, 1954):

1   A number of existence needs, including sex, hunger, thirst, and oxygen

2 A security need
3 A social need
4 A need for esteem and reputation
5 A need for autonomy and independence
6 A need for competence, achievement, and self-actualization

Is There a Hierarchy of Needs?

Although several theorists have proposed theories which have needs arranged in a hierarchy, Maslow's (1943, 1954) work has been the most influential. He views man as moving successively up a need hierarchy such that as his lower-order and most essential needs are satisfied, his higher-order needs become more important. According to his view, a person will be concerned with self-actualization only if his existence needs, his security needs, his social needs, and so on, are well satisfied. Maslow implies that needs are arranged like a ladder that must be climbed one rung at a time. In general, this means that at any particular stage of a person's development one need will be most important for the individual. If, however, the satisfaction of a lower-order need is threatened, that need will again become prepotent and the person will reduce his efforts to satisfy all higher-order needs. For example, when a person's sense of security is endangered, he will ignore esteem, self-actualization, and other higher-order needs.

Maslow also points out that a satisfied need is not motivating. Thus, once a person has obtained a satisfying amount of food, the need will become unimportant and he will not be motivated by the opportunity to obtain more of the outcomes which satisfy it. It would be expected, therefore, that the kinds of things which will motivate a person may change as his career in an organization progresses and as he moves up the need hierarchy ladder.

The issue of whether needs are arranged in a hierarchy is an important one since it directly affects how behavior in organizations can be analyzed. If a need hierarchy exists, for example, definite predictions can be made about what the impact will be of giving people a high level of security or of paying people high wages. What, then, does the evidence show?

There is strong evidence to support the view that unless the existence needs are satisfied none of the higher-order needs will come into play. There is also some evidence that unless security needs are satisfied, people will not be concerned with higher-order needs (Cofer & Appley, 1964; Alderfer, 1972). There is, however, little evidence to support the view that a hierarchy exists once one moves above the security level (Lawler & Suttle, 1972). Thus, it probably is *not* safe to assume more than a two-step hierarchy, with existence and security needs at the lower level and all the higher-order needs

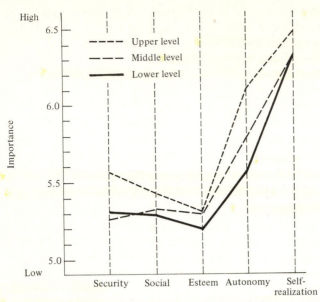

Figure 2–3 Importance attached to five needs by managers at three organizational levels.

at the next level. It is safe to assume that unless the lower-order needs are satisfied the others will not come into play in any major way. However, which higher-order need or needs will become salient after the lower ones are satisfied (and the order in which they will develop) cannot be stated. In fact, it is probable that many people are simultaneously motivated by several higher-order needs. While a person might be motivated by either a set of higher-order needs or a set of several lower-order needs, it is less likely that a person will be motivated simultaneously by both sets. Thus, one person might be motivated by social needs and by autonomy needs, while another is motivated by hunger and by security; it is doubtful, however, that a person would be simultaneously motivated by, say, security and autonomy.

Can Needs Be Satisfied?

There is a substantial amount of research showing that as needs are satisfied they become less important and that other needs emerge. Figure 2-3 shows the stated importance of certain needs to a group of over 1,900 managers, and Figure 2-4 shows their satisfaction with these needs (Porter, 1964). Note that the least satisfied needs are also the most important. This has been a general finding in the research on need satisfaction. Typically, need satisfaction leads to reduced need strength. Thus, it appears that most needs are in fact capable of being satisfied and that once this occurs people stop seeking—at least temporarily—outcomes which satisfy that need.

The one exception to the above conclusion is the need for self-actualization or growth. This need seems to be relatively insatiable in the sense that the more it is satisfied the more important it becomes. This need, unlike others, appears to stay important (Alderfer, 1972). The only thing that makes self-actualization or self-fulfillment lose its importance is a threat to the satisfaction of the person's lower-level needs. Thus, once self-actualization appears, it generally should continue to be a strong motivator.

Can Both Intrinsic and Extrinsic Outcomes Satisfy Needs?

One of the things which seems to distinguish most needs from those at the highest level of Maslow's hierarchy is that they can only be satisfied by outcomes which are external to the person and which have a concrete reality (e.g., food, money, praise from another person). The need for self-actualization and competence, on the other hand, seems to be capable of being satisfied only by outcomes which are internal to the person and which are essentially given by the person to himself (e.g., feelings of accomplishment and growth). It is true that certain environmental conditions need to be

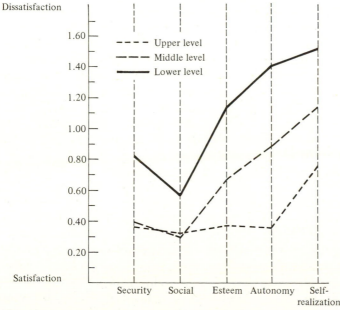

Figure 2–4   Dissatisfaction attached to five needs by managers at three organizational levels.

present before the internal outcomes can be obtained, but the outcomes themselves are not observable by others and they are controlled by the recipient. Thus, outcomes which satisfy needs can be both intrinsic and extrinsic.

Can Outcomes Satisfy More Than One Need?

A number of research studies indicate that some types of outcomes (i.e., certain events, objects, behaviors) are useful in satisfying several different needs. A classic example is pay. Pay appears to be able to satisfy not only existence needs but security and esteem needs as well (Lawler & Porter, 1963; Lawler, 1971) because it can be used to buy articles such as food which satisfy existence needs; it provides a measure of personal security; and it confers on the person receiving high pay a certain amount of esteem and respect in many segments of our society. Thus, if a person is trying to satisfy any one of these three needs (i.e., existence, security, esteem), pay will be important to him.

Engaging in a behavior considered "socially useful" also potentially can satisfy a variety of needs. Thus, while a person probably would not join the Peace Corps out of a concern for existence-need satisfaction, joining often does reflect a desire to satisfy a number of different higher-order needs. In particular, membership in the Peace Corps could lead to opportunities to gain satisfaction of social, esteem, autonomy, and even self-actualization needs. Thus, even though there undoubtedly are large individual differences in needs which membership in the Peace Corps will satisfy, it, like pay, can satisfy many different personal needs simultaneously.

How Important Are Different Needs?

The data shown in Figure 2-4 provide some indication of the importance of various needs. In particular, the data suggest that for the 1,900 managers sampled, higher-order needs clearly are more important than are needs lower in the hierarchy.

There are some data which suggest that pay and certain lower-level needs are rated as more important by workers than by managers (Porter & Lawler, 1965). Moreover, Dubin (1956) argues that the work place is *not* a central part of the life of most industrial workers and that it is unwise to expect them to be strongly concerned with fulfillment of higher-order needs on the job. There is also evidence to suggest that higher-order needs are important to people at *all* organizational levels today but that they are more important at the higher than at the lower levels of organizations. However, it is dangerous to place too much faith in data of this sort. People have difficulty reporting accurately on how important different needs are to them. Different approaches to asking people which needs are most important to them frequently produces quite different results. Therefore, any conclusion about the relative importance of different needs must be tentatively stated.

Has the Importance of Needs Changed?

A number of writers have speculated that the strength of various needs in the population in general has been changing over the past several decades. They argue that only recently has a significant proportion of the population been concerned with higher-order needs, such as self-fulfillment and autonomy. Only in the last few years have psychologists themselves conducted research on self-actualization needs; an emphasis on the concept of self-actualizing man is clearly a development of the 1960s, even though Maslow and others identified it much earlier.

Two reasons have been proposed to explain the recent emergence of higher-order needs. First, there is the rising education level in contemporary society. Second, the standard of living has increased in the United States so that relatively fewer people are concerned about satisfying their existence needs. In effect, this frees them to focus on the satisfaction of higher-order needs.

Unfortunately, there is very little evidence to either support or refute the view that need strength is changing throughout society. To test this view adequately, it would be necessary to have need-strength data collected many years ago on a random sample of the population and to have comparable data collected recently. Such direct data do not exist. There is, though, some data that can be used to support the view that higher-order needs have become more important. It has been shown, for example, that younger managers place greater importance on self-actualization needs than do older managers (Porter, 1963). This could, of course, simply be a function of age, but it could also be due to the higher education level of these managers and the fact that many of them have never experienced a threat to their existence needs. The latter interpretation is supported by research which shows that higher-educated people are more concerned with self-actualization than people who are less well educated. In addition, it is significant that the *idea* of self-actualization has only recently gained fairly wide attention in the society. It now seems "in" to talk about self-actualization, which may reflect an increased level of desire for the satisfaction of higher-order needs. All the above is, of course, only indirect evidence. But it does point rather consistently toward the view that concern with self-actualization has increased recently.

Individual Differences in Need Strength

In our discussion thus far we have focused on general statements about the nature of man's needs. We have not emphasized the differences in the strength of needs that exist from one person to another. Large differences are clearly evident and must be considered when viewing the individual in the organization. These differences lead to individuals seeing different things when they perceive the same job and to their performing their jobs differently. Because of these differences, a job which is satisfying and motivating to one person will often be seen as boring by another. Similarly, a pay system that will motivate one person is often seen as irrelevant by others simply because the rewards provided by the pay system are differently valued by different people.

Many individual differences in need strength are related to other characteristics of people. For example, urban workers tend to have different values than do people who come from rural settings (Hulin & Blood, 1968). In particular, urban workers seem to be more alienated from their work and less desirous of obtaining higher-order need satisfactions on the job (Hackman & Lawler, 1971). There also are the already mentioned differences among people who have different education levels.

By comparing the personal characteristics of people who have strong versus weak desires for various need satisfactions, it is possible to construct profiles which illustrate the personal characteristics which typify a person oriented toward certain needs. An example of such a profile, for people who are strongly oriented toward money, is provided from research data:

> The employee is a male, young (probably in his twenties); his personality is characterized by low self-assurance and high neuroticism; he comes from a small town or a farm background; he belongs to few clubs and social groups, and he owns his own home and probably is a Republican and a Protestant. (Lawler, 1971)

MAN PERCEIVES AND EVALUATES

What an individual experiences in an organizational setting can be substantially different from what another individual experiences in the same situation or from what an outside observer would describe as "objective" reality. How one experiences his environment is a quite *active* process: a person selectively notices different aspects of the environment; he then appraises what he sees in terms of his own past experiences; and he evaluates what he is experiencing in terms of his own needs and values. Since people's needs and past experiences often differ markedly, it should not be surprising to learn that their perceptions of the environment do likewise. In the paragraphs to follow, we examine some of the implications of these processes for understanding the behavior of individuals in organizations.

Perceiving the Organizational Environment

To make sense of his environment, an organization member faces two perceptual tasks: first, he must decide what to attend to and what to ignore, and secondly, he must interpret and make sense out of those items he does attend to in the context of his experience. The processes people use in perceiving their environments are discussed below.

Selective Noticing   Organizations provide their members with many more stimuli than any individual is cognitively able to handle. Therefore, in perceiving the organization at any given time the individual must decide not to notice many potentially relevant aspects of his environment. What aspects of the environment *are* noticed depend partly on the nature of the stimuli themselves and partly on the previous experience of the individual.

Stimuli which are highly distinctive within the usual organizational context are more likely to be noticed than are stimuli which do not "stick out" in some unusual way. Thus, the written memo from the central office may not serve as a very distinctive input to organization members in an organization which generates dozens of such memos every week, but a videotaped message from the company president (which occurs rarely) will have high distinctiveness and will very likely be attended to by almost all employees who watch the televised message.

In addition to stimulus distinctiveness, the previous learning of organization members plays an important part in determining what is noticed. Organization members quickly become able to discriminate between those sources of stimulation that one needs to pay attention to—and those which may be safely overlooked. For example, the college student may find that it is generally unnecessary to read the longish memos which emerge with regularity from the office of the associate dean for student activities, but that he had better read carefully any material which comes from the academic dean of the college.

In summary, then, we assume that organization members are not able to attend to all organizationally initiated stimuli which they encounter and that they therefore must be selective in what stimuli they do attend to. It is proposed that what *is* noticed will be a joint function of the distinctiveness of the stimuli in the organizational context and the previous experience of the organization member about what kinds of messages have important personal consequences for him and what kinds do not.

Appraisal Even when a stimulus is noticed or attended to by an organization member, there is no guarantee that it will be perceived accurately. The meaning which any given "objective" stimulus has for an individual member is inextricably bound up in the needs and values of the member, and individuals often distort stimuli so that events are more congruent with the needs and values of the person than they actually are (Jones & Gerard, 1967, Ch. 7). It is difficult to predict for any given individual the specific nature of his distortion of a particular event which occurs; there are simply too many idiosyncratic factors involved, both in the nature of the event and in the psychological makeup of the individual, for much specificity in prediction to be achieved.

It is possible, however, to predict the *amount* of distortion which is likely to occur rather than the particular *kind* of distortion which will take place. In particular, distortion will be especially likely (with a resultant lowering of the degree of congruence between the "objective" organizational event and the way it is experienced by the member) *when the member has a high emotional investment in the event that takes place.* Such investment comes about when the stimuli in the situation engage important needs of the member, for example, by threatening or challenging his self-esteem or by signaling opportunities for the achievement of important personal goals. When, for example, the supervisor in an organization announces a new policy about company promotions, the possibility of distortion and misunderstanding of that message would be expected to be high for those individuals who aspire to "make it big" in the organization. In such cases, the organization might well consider undertaking steps to ensure that the message was heard as it was sent, perhaps by structuring small group discussions in which each member could ask questions and restate the new policy until all agreed that it was understood.

In essence, then, it has been suggested that (1) it is very difficult to predict the specific nature of perceptual distortions of stimuli in an organizational environment for specific organization members but (2) it often is possible and useful to try to identify those situations in which such distortion is likely to reach such high levels that special steps to improve perceptual accuracy are warranted.

Redefinition There are many events which take place in organizations which individual members simply take note of and store away for future reference. Examples include an impression that "the boss is irritable today," that "a coworker left work fifteen minutes early and got away with it," that "every time I push a bit to get ahead with my work they bring me more to do," etc. These kinds of messages are subject to being overlooked or distorted, as discussed above. But once they have been heard and understood, whether with or without distortion, then they are simply retained as part of the member's accumulated wisdom about the organization which may be of help at some future time, and no more active processing of the stimuli takes place.

There is, however, one class of stimuli which does require additional processing after perception. These stimuli are those which reflect, either explicitly or implicitly, a request or demand regarding the behavior of the perceiver. When the individual perceives that the stimulus he is receiving implies that he should do something, then he must assess the acceptability to himself of that message. That is, before a person accepts a communicated request and begins to act on it, he thinks about the various costs and rewards of engaging in the behavior. The outcome of this exploration can range from acting on the request or demand, to rejecting it in its entirety, to modifying or redefining it in some way to render it more acceptable. The last alternative, of course, introduces an additional level of distortion into the message as it was originally communicated, but this distortion is more deliberate and conscious than that associated with the process of perceiving the message (discussed earlier).

Assume, for example, that an organization member's supervisor suggests that he undertake some relatively onerous task, such as cleaning up the debris around a very noisy machine. The costs and rewards that the member considers in such a case might have to do with the degree to which doing the task will please the supervisor (a potentially positive factor) compared with the degree that doing it will be intrinsically unpleasant and get his clothes dirty (negative factors). If the expected positive and negative payoffs of accepting the request are roughly equal, it is reasonably likely that the individual will *redefine* the request in such a way that he will be likely to retain the rewards of accepting the request but, at the same time, will not have to incur all the costs. In the present example, the member might redefine the request to read "Get the debris cleaned up" as opposed to the original form, "*You* clean the debris up." Such redefinition opens up many new alternatives for meeting the request, including persuading someone else to do it for him.

Expectancies   The result of the process of perceiving, appraising, and redefining stimuli from the environment is a set of beliefs held by the individual about various aspects of the organization. Such beliefs specify "the way things are" in the organization as viewed by the individual, and may include everything from the color of the paint on the walls to whether or not hard work really pays off in the organization.

One very important class of beliefs is called "expectancies." Expectancies are simply the beliefs individuals hold about what leads to what in the environment. Thus, a belief that "hard work leads to quick promotions" is an expectancy, as is "buttering up the boss increases the chances of getting time off for personal business now and then" and "a person working on my job feels good inside when he does a particularly high-quality piece of work." Expectancies, therefore, can serve as a "map" for the individual in planning how he will go about fulfilling his needs and achieving his goals in the organization since they are predictions about the likely future consequences of a course of action.

Behaviorists such as Skinner argue that it is not necessary to focus on expectancies. Their view is that future behavior can best be predicted by observing past behavior. It is true that past behavior is often a good predictor of future behavior in similar situations, but our view is that the prediction and understanding of human behavior can be improved by considering expectancies. The behavior of employees in organizations, for example, is clearly influenced by what the employees are told about situations and what they see happening to others. Thus, their behavior in a situation is influenced by more than merely what has happened to them in the past when they have been in similar situations. Further, employees often find themselves in new situations and it is difficult to know what past behavior of the person should be looked at as a guide to future behavior. One way to understand employees' behavior in new situations and to understand how observation and reports of others influence behavior is to study expectancies.

To summarize, people develop beliefs about their organizational environment as a natural and necessary part of their experiences in the organization. There are, however, several factors which militate against accurate perception of stimuli present in the organizational environment. Among these are (1) factors which determine which stimuli are noticed and which ones are ignored; (2) perceptual distortions, based on the particular needs and values of the individual; and (3) active redefinition of the expectations (or demands) sent from others, based on the expected rewards and costs of accepting those demands as they originally were understood. Expectancies were defined as a special (and very important) class of beliefs which specify the relationships between what a person does and what outcomes he obtains in the organizational environment. How expectancies influence the voluntary behavior of individuals in organizations is discussed in greater detail later in this chapter.

Evaluating What Is Perceived

The above discussion focused on how people develop perceptions and beliefs as a part of their experiences in organizations. In addition to such "cognitive" reactions, however, people have strong "affective" reactions to what they perceive in the organization and what happens to them there. Affective reactions include a person's likes and dislikes, good feelings and bad feelings, satisfactions and dissatisfactions, and various states of emotional arousal.

Three general types of affective reactions are of special importance in understanding individual behavior in organizations and are discussed separately below: (1) an individual's satisfaction with various aspects of his job and with his overall job, (2) the level of psychological "arousal" an individual experiences in the organization, and (3) the "valence" an individual attaches to various outcomes which he potentially can obtain from the organization.

Feelings of Satisfaction   People are rarely neutral about things they perceive or experience. Instead, they tend to evaluate most things in terms of whether they like or dislike them. Moreover, as suggested by Osgood et al. (1957), this evaluative response (or "gut reaction") is one of the most important factors in establishing the *meaningfulness* of something to people. For many years psychologists have been concerned with measuring and understanding the feelings people have about their work, and literally hundreds of studies have been done on the satisfaction of organization members.

Part of the reason for the early interest in job satisfaction was the widely held belief that people who are satisfied should perform better in organizations. The failure of researchers to find such a relationship between satisfaction and performance has, in general, decreased this belief. This has by no means signaled the end of interest in studying job satisfaction, however. Psychologists still are concerned with it, but it now is seen more as a *reaction* to one's work and one's organizational membership than as a determinant of one's performance. Viewed in this way, satisfaction has become an important topic of study in its own right. Moreover, satisfaction has turned out to be a reasonably good predictor of absenteeism and turnover; the more satisfied an employee, the less likely he is to be absent or to resign from the organization (Porter & Steers, 1973).

Unfortunately, no real theory of job satisfaction has yet been developed, although some attempts have been made (see Locke, 1969, for a review). In general, it appears that satisfaction is determined by the difference between the amount of some valued outcome that a person receives and the amount of that outcome he feels he *should* receive. The larger the discrepancy, the greater the dissatisfaction. Moreover, the amount a person feels he *should* receive has been found to be strongly influenced by what he perceives others like himself are receiving (cf. Lawler, 1971). People seem to balance what they are putting into a work situation against what they feel they are getting out of it and then compare their own balance with that of other people. If this comparison reveals that their outcomes are inequitable in comparison with those of others, then dissatisfaction results.

Much of the research on job satisfaction has focused on its determinants. Sufficient research has now been done so that it is possible to specify in general how people react to various managerial and work practices which they experience in organizations. It is also possible to point out how individual differences influence the effects of practices on satisfaction. In the chapters to follow, the effects of organizational policies and practices on employee satisfaction will be discussed in detail.

Arousal   A different type of affective reaction people have to their life in organizations is the level of psychological and physiological arousal or activation which they experience. Among the stimulus characteristics which have been suggested as potent in raising an individual's level of arousal are the intensity, variation or novelty, complexity, uncertainty, and meaningfulness of stimuli which impinge on him. It should be noted, however, that what is intense or novel for one person will not necessarily be so for another.

It usually is assumed that there is an inverted "U" relationship between the level of arousal and general performance effectiveness. When the level of activation is very low, individuals tend not to be alert, to have trouble with motor activities requiring muscular coordination, and to be relatively insensitive to changes in sensory input. At moderate levels of arousal, performance approaches optimal levels. When arousal is too high, individuals have difficulty with muscular coordination and experience a general state of muscular and mental hypertension which can greatly handicap performance effectiveness.

It has been suggested that there is some level of activation which is characteristic of each individual at each stage in his sleep-wakefulness cycle, and that changes toward the characteristic level are experienced as affectively positive (as when an individual becomes "less bored" or "less tense and excited"), whereas changes away from the characteristic level are experienced as affectively negative (Scott, 1969; Fiske & Maddi, 1961). Perhaps a somewhat more sophisticated conception of the relationship between arousal level and affect has been proposed by Hunt (1963). He cites the considerable literature which indicates that individuals find slight incongruities from the usual or characteristic state of affairs affectively positive, and that they will exert energy to achieve such incongruity. However, movement away from the optimal level of incongruity tends to be experienced as negative [either as "boring" (when stimulation drops below the optimal level of incongruity) or as "panicky" (when it goes above the optimum)]. In an analogous fashion, movement toward the optimal level of incongruity is experienced as positive (either as an increase from a boring state or as a decrease from a hyperactivated state).

Valence of Outcomes   The third general type of affective response to be considered is the "valence" an individual has for various outcomes he might obtain as a consequence of his activities in the organization. Valence refers simply to the degree to which the individual desires the outcomes in question. Thus, valence may be either positive or negative, depending upon whether the outcome is one which is sought or avoided by the person.

An outcome can become valent for an individual in two ways:

1   It can be directly satisfying of one or more of the person's needs. For a very hungry person, food would be an outcome which would directly satisfy his existence needs. Similarly, being allowed to interact informally with his coworkers would be a positively valent outcome for someone with strong social needs.

2   An outcome can be valent because it leads to *other* outcomes which satisfy an individual's needs. Thus, money by itself is not directly need-satisfying to a hungry man; but money will be highly valent for that man because it can be used to purchase food which will satisfy his needs. The valence of a particular outcome, then, can be seen as determined by the valence of other outcomes for which the first one is instrumental (i.e., effective in acquiring the outcomes). Many outcomes in organizations (e.g., "performing well") are highly valent to individuals because they are instrumental in leading to other valued outcomes (e.g., higher pay, quicker promotion, esteem from one's supervisor, and so on).

The way in which the concepts of valence and expectancy can be combined to yield predictions of the voluntary behavior of individuals in organizations is discussed in the section to follow.

MAN THINKS AND CHOOSES

Because man is a purposive, proactive, cognitively active being, his behavior can be analyzed in terms of the behavioral plans he develops and executes (or, alternatively, the choices he makes) about how to deal with stimuli he encounters and how to achieve his personal goals. Two very important questions arise if man is viewed in this way:

1 How are behavioral plans selected (or choices made) from the large set of possibilities available to the individual?

2 How does the individual tell how he is doing in executing his behavioral plan, and how does he know when to stop?

These two questions are examined below.

How Plans Are Selected and Choices Made: The Expectancy Model

The general "expectancy-theory" model of human motivation provides one way of analyzing and predicting which courses of action an individual will follow when he has the opportunity to make personal choices about his behavior. This theory, which was originally formulated by Tolman and Lewin in the 1930's, recently has been usefully applied to behavior in organizational settings (e.g., Vroom, 1964; Porter & Lawler, 1968).

In essence, the model posits that the motivational "force" to engage in a behavior is a multiplicative function of (1) the expectancies the person holds about what outcomes are likely to result from that behavior and (2) the valence of these outcomes. Or, in symbols:

$$MF = E \times V$$
where MF = motivational force
E = expectancy
V = valence

Since there are likely to be a number of different outcomes expected for any given behavior, the terms in the equation are summed across those outcomes to arrive at a single figure reflecting the attractiveness of the behavior being contemplated.

Thus, if the behavior being considered is "working hard on the job," one needs to do the following to predict the effort exerted by the individual on his job:

1 Identify the outcomes the individual expects as a consequence of working hard. These might be "Being tired at the end of the day," "Feeling that I'm really getting something done at work," "Getting promoted out of the job sooner," "Receiving negative reactions from my coworkers," and so on. Most people consider fewer than six or seven salient outcomes for any contemplated behavior, so such lists are usually not long.

2 Determine the degree to which the individual is sure that each outcome will result from engaging in the behavior. Estimates of *confidence* can be made on a probability scale from zero (totally unsure whether or not the outcome will result) to one (completely sure that the outcome will occur).

3 Determine the valence of each of the outcomes for the individual. Valence can be assessed on any scale which is symmetrical around zero: for example, −3 to +3, −1 to +1, and so on. The only requirement is that it be possible to determine whether the individual finds each outcome attractive, unattractive, or neutral (zero). It will be recalled from the discussion of outcomes that the valence associated with a given outcome is determined jointly by (1) the degree to which the outcome is directly need-satisfying itself and (2) the degree to which it leads to other outcomes which have valence.

4 Multiply the expectancy and the valence for each outcome, and then proceed to sum up the resulting products. The figure which results will indicate whether the individual has a basic tendency to engage in the behavior (positive numbers), to avoid engaging in the behavior (negative numbers), or is neutral about whether or not to engage in the behavior (number near zero). To make actual predictions of behavior, however, it usually is necessary to know how the motivational forces toward engaging in various *alternative* possible behaviors compare. It might be, for example, that the only choices open to an individual are low in attractiveness. If one looked only at any one of the alternative behaviors, the value obtained might lead to the conclusion that the individual would *not* select that behavior. If, however, all the other behavioral alternatives led to less positive estimates of force, that conclusion would be erroneous.

Most researchers who have applied expectancy theory to work organizations have asked employees to report on their expectancies and valences. Strict behaviorists would reject this approach and predict behavior by a careful analysis of the situation and the past behavior of the people involved. Studies have shown, however, that people's reports of their expectancies and valences *can* predict later behavior, although not all studies have found that valence measures are useful. The reason that valence measures have not aided prediction is not clear at this point (see Lawler & Suttle, 1973). Thus, while there are some technical difficulties associated with exact formulations of expectancy theory, there seems to be widespread research support for the utility of a general expectancy-theory approach to understanding the behavior of people in organizations.

Application to Work Performance in Organizations It should be emphasized that the expectancy-theory model applies *only to behaviors which are, in fact, under the voluntary control of the individual.* Unless the individual is actually free to make a choice regarding his behavior, the model is not applicable. In considering work performance in organizations, there are two general types of choices over which the individual has voluntary control:

1 The amount of effort and energy he puts into his work activities
2 The performance strategies or approaches he uses in going about his work

The distinction between effort and strategy is a simple one: effort refers to the *intensity* of a person's work activities, and strategy refers to the *direction* of those activities. For example, a person's decision about whether to work hard or take it easy on the job is a decision about effort; his decision about whether to try to do high-quality work or to produce large quantities of work instead is a decision about strategy. Performance effectiveness on most lower-level jobs in contemporary organizations tends to be more strongly determined by how hard one works than by how one goes about his work. Strategy considerations, on the other hand, are more important in many complicated, higher-level jobs.

It should be emphasized in conclusion that the expectancy model is just that: a model and no more. People rarely actually sit down and list their expected outcomes for a contemplated behavior, estimate expectancies and valences, multiply, and add up the total unless, of course, they are asked to do so by a researcher. Yet people *do* consider the likely outcomes of their actions, do weigh and evaluate the attractiveness of various alternatives, and do use these estimates in coming to a decision about what they will do. The expectancy model provides an analytic tool for mirroring that process and for predicting its outcome, but it does not purport to reflect the actual decision-making steps taken by an individual.

How is Progress Monitored during the Execution of a Behavioral Plan?

In the above section we focused on factors which determine what plan of action will be adopted by an individual; here we turn to the question of how an individual knows how he is doing as he implements his behavioral choices, and how he knows when to stop.

A model of how behavioral plans are executed has been proposed by three psychologists (Miller, Galanter & Pribram, 1960). It suggests that the basic unit for analyzing human action is a "TOTE" sequence. TOTE is an

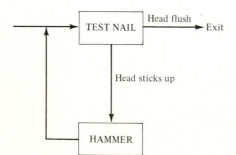

Figure 2–5 Hammering as a TOTE unit. *(From Miller, Galanter, & Pribram, 1960, p.34.)*

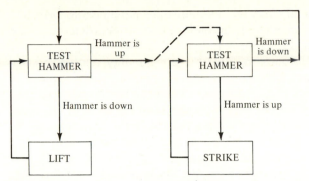

Figure 2-6 Assembly of two TOTE únits into one larger unit. *(From Miller, Galanter, & Pribram, 1960, p. 35.)*

acronym for "Test-Operate-Test-Exit." The sequence is illustrated in Figure 2-5 for the plan "hammering a nail." The performer tests whether the nail is sticking up; if it is, he hammers again; he then tests again; and so on until the head of the nail is flush and he "exits" from the performance sequence.

Very complicated patterns of behavior can be assembled from basic TOTE units in very much the same way that large computer programs are made up of numerous subprograms, each of which is called at the appropriate time by the main program and each of which can have subprograms of its own. The way in which TOTE units are assembled is illustrated in Figure 2-6; the figure breaks down the "hammering" unit shown in Figure 2-5 into two subunits: lifting the hammer and striking the nail.

The same general paradigm can be used to describe and analyze the work activities of individuals in organizations. Individuals select (and organizations provide) indicators of the degree to which various personal and work goals are being reached by their activities. Based on how the present state of affairs compares with the standard (the "test"), the individual knows whether to continue his activities ("operate") or to stop ("exit"). Moreover, if the individual finds that the more he engages in the activities, the *further* he is getting from the goal, he presumably would be prompted to stop the entire performance sequence and reconsider his choice of performance strategy.

Rationality and Work Behavior in Organizations

Both the expectancy model of choice making and the TOTE model described above implicitly suggest a high level of rational analysis and effective decision making on the part of the individual. It is tempting to assume in the expectancy-theory paradigm that an individual will select the behavioral alternative that actually will maximize his payoffs. Similarly, it is implicit in the TOTE paradigm that an individual will continue his work activities until the performance goal is fully met.

Such assumptions imply a good deal more rationality than is actually characteristic of the behavior of individuals in organizations. People do not have (and do not attempt to obtain) complete knowledge of the outcomes of their behaviors; nor do they proceed rationally and methodically toward their objectives, even when these objectives are ones they personally endorse. If man truly attempted to optimize his behavior, he probably would be so heavily involved in search and evaluation activities and in constant "operating" activities aimed at meeting the test for optimal performance that he would never do anything. Simon (1957) has argued that, in general, man's behavior is directed more toward "satisficing" than toward "optimizing." By this he means that a person will look for a course of behavior that is satisfactory or "good enough" and when he finds it he will act. Or, for ongoing performance activities, he will persist until he feels his performance has reached some level of personal acceptability, even though that level of performance may be less than optimal.

Does this mean that man's behavior in organizations is irrational and unpredictable? Not necessarily. Behavior generally *is* predictable if we know how the person perceives the situation, but it often does not appear to be rational or optimal to those who observe it. While man's behavior may not appear to be rational to an outside observer, there is reason to believe that it is usually *intended* to be rational by the actor and that it is seen as rational by him. Behavior often is seen as nonrational by an observer simply because the observer does not have access to the same information or hold the same expectancies the actor does and because the observer may value outcomes quite differently than the observer. This can lead to observations such as "I'd never do it that way; what's wrong with him anyway?" at the same time that the actor is feeling that he knows exactly where he is going, why, and what good things are going to happen to him when he gets there.

Sometimes people tend to view their behavior as rational when, in fact, it is not. For example, when one outcome of a contemplated course of action has an emotionally potent payoff that the individual is unwilling to acknowledge, he may find himself rationalizing his behavior in terms of other outcomes which are not, in fact, as objectively important to him as he is attempting to make them. The employee who transfers to a new job where he can be near someone for whom he has romantic feelings, for example, may never admit to himself that those feelings were crucial in reaching the decision to transfer. Instead, he is likely to exaggerate the importance of various other outcomes he expects as a consequence of the transfer in order to justify his decision, to himself as well as to others. This tendency toward maintaining the appearance of an internally consistent and rational stance is very pervasive and powerful. People have been shown to engage in considerable attitude and belief change merely to achieve a state of experienced consistency (Festinger, 1957; Bem, 1970). Thus, while people tend to have strong desires to *appear* rational, the machinations they go through to achieve that appearance often are quite the opposite.

MAN HAS LIMITED RESPONSE CAPABILITIES

Thus far our discussion has focused on factors that influence man's disposition or motivation to behave in a certain manner. An important additional determinant of man's behavior is his *capacity* to perform as he intends. Psychologists interested in individual differences traditionally have focused on this issue and have found that people vary considerably in their ability to behave in certain ways. To state the issue simply: People are not capable of behaving in all ways; in fact they are decidedly limited in their response capabilities.

People's response capabilities are a function of both innate aptitude and learning. Stated as a formula this becomes:

Response capability = (aptitude × learning)

Traditionally, psychologists have classified behaviors into those that are innate (and therefore not subject to improvement by training) and those that can be altered and learned. This way of thinking about human behavior seems to be outmoded. It now appears that even measures like IQ (which was once thought to be innately determined and fixed) can be influenced to an extent by training and experience. Thus, it now seems reasonable to think of human response capacities in terms of a continuum. At one end of the continuum are those responses that are relatively uninfluenceable as a result of training and experience, and at the other end are those responses that are relatively open to change and not significantly constrained by genetic or physiological factors.

Figure 2-7 presents an illustration of the kind of continuum that can be constructed. It shows that some capabilities (e.g., reaction time) are relatively fixed, while others are relatively malleable and can be improved by training. Unfortunately, there is relatively little data available on just where certain kinds of responses should be placed on the continuum. The arrangement shown here represents a rough approximation of the actual position of the responses included. The significance of this issue for understanding behavior in organizations is substantial since it directly questions what type of training and development programs organizations should run. If, for example, managerial style is relatively fixed, it hardly

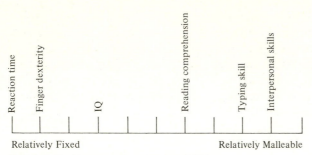

Figure 2–7 Human response capabilities.

makes sense to spend money training managers. It would seem far better to attempt to *select* managers who have the desired response capabilities. Fortunately, as will be seen in Chapter 7, there is some evidence to indicate that management style (as well as some other response capabilities of high importance to organizations) is open to influence and development through training programs.

Measuring and Classifying Individual Differences

A number of social scientists (primarily psychologists) have worked on the development of valid measures of people's response capabilities. A large number of tests have been constructed, and research has shown that some of them can reasonably accurately predict some types of future behavior in organizations. Tests have been developed to measure response capabilities which are relatively fixed and also those which are more susceptible to change as a result of experience and training. The latter tests are usually called skill tests, while the former are called aptitude tests. Both kinds of tests often play an important role in organizations since, as will be discussed in Chapter 5, they often are a key element in the selection process of organizations.

In addition to tests which are designed to measure people's response capabilities (often called tests of maximum performance because they are designed to measure how well a person can perform a given task) tests of people's typical behavior have been developed. These tests—usually referred to as personality or interest tests—are designed to measure how a person typically behaves in a situation; and they, like aptitude and skill tests, show large individual differences. Overall, personality and interest tests have not proved as useful in predicting behavior in organizations. This is unfortunate, since valid tests of typical performance are needed to aid our understanding of behavior in organizations.

Attempts to classify abilities have encountered problems similar to those involved in efforts to develop definitive lists of human needs. While there obviously are a number of different kinds of abilities, it is difficult to group them in any internally coherent framework. In general, researchers have attempted to cluster abilities according to how strongly performance in one specific area relates to performance in another. Even this procedure, however, has resulted in a diversity of classification schemes. There is enough agreement among these approaches, however, for us to conclude that it is important to distinguish among mental, physical, and interpersonal response capabilities.

Mental Capabilities

Clearly one of the most important areas of an individual's response capacities concerns mental abilities. Most of the research which has attempted to relate such abilities to job performance can be examined in terms of a relatively simple two-way classification scheme (Ghiselli, 1966). One dimension of the system is quantitative or numerical ability, and the other is verbal ability. The distinction turns out to be important since quantitative and verbal abilities do differentially predict success in various jobs. For some jobs (e.g., certain sales jobs) verbal ability scores seem to be the best predictor, while for others (e.g., engineering jobs) quantitative ability scores predict better. This is not surprising, given the different demands which jobs make on people. Thus, for understanding individual behavior in organizations it probably is important to maintain this distinction. It is not clear, however, that it is necessary to break down mental abilities into more than two categories because of what has been called the "g" or general factor in intelligence. The "g" factor reflects the fact that almost all kinds of mental ability are highly related to each other. It suggests that one's level of general intelligence may influence *all* kinds of mental performance. Thus, while it probably makes some sense to distinguish between verbal and quantitative mental abilities, further classification seems unnecessary for our purposes.

Manual and Physical Response Capabilities

In addition to varying in mental ability, people also differ in manual response capabilities. These differences have obvious implications for organizations. Many organizations have jobs that require people with specific manual response capabilities that often are not generally available in the population (e.g., baseball teams). In filling these jobs, then, the emphasis must be upon measuring people's manual skills and selecting only those people who have the manual capabilities necessary to do the job successfully.

Just as there are problems in developing an adequate classification system for human mental abilities, there also are difficulties in developing a classification system for human physical abilities. About all that can be concluded at this point is that a truly adequate classification system for human physical abilities presently does not exist.

Interpersonal Skills and Personality

A person's interpersonal style (how he deals with others) and his personality frequently are thought of in terms of response predispositions, i.e., as reflecting largely how a person *wants* to respond or behave. But interpersonal behavior is influenced not only by response disposition but also by response capability (Wallace, 1966). This view leads to an abilities conception of personality, which considers the response capabilities of people to be a key determinant of their personality and interpersonal behavior.

Much of the research on the interpersonal behavior of executives would strongly support the idea that the abilities concept does have relevance for the study of personality and interpersonal relations in organizations. For example, a number of cases show how personality and interpersonal style actually do influence organizational effectiveness and how interpersonal competence can be thought of as a skill that can be learned and that is a particularly vital skill for upper-level managers to have (Argyris, 1962). Interpersonal competence, then, can be likened to calculus, in that many people can be taught it but few people can discover it for themselves.

Analysis of interpersonal behavior strongly points to the conclusion that how a person comes across in situations demanding such skills is a function of *both* his response capabilities and his behavioral dispositions. It is quite clear that at any given point in time, people are limited in the interpersonal behaviors of which they are capable. Some people cannot, for example, easily express emotions in groups or develop high degrees of trust in others. These behaviors often are difficult for some people not because of dispositional tendencies but simply because they *do not know how.* They have never learned to express emotions openly; instead, they have learned only how to cover them up or, at most, express them indirectly. It is also clear, however, that people's interpersonal behavior is strongly influenced by their dispositional tendencies. Sometimes people do not *want* to express emotions even though they may have the capability of doing so.

In summary, then, the argument is that interpersonal behavior is strongly influenced by both "can do" and "want to" issues. This conclusion has some important implications for the kind of training that should be done on interpersonal behavior. Time needs to be spent working not only on dispositional issues but also on capability issues. People need to be taught and to practice different styles of interpersonal behavior so that they will have available a variety or repertoire of response capacities. This is particularly true if people do not know what is effective interpersonal behavior because the only styles they have experienced are dysfunctional ones (Argyris, 1971).

The classification and measurement problems that were discussed above for mental and physical response capacities are again relevant here and, if anything, are even more severe in the interpersonal behavior area. There are few, if any, well-validated scales presently available for measuring interpersonal capabilities, nor are there any well-developed and widely accepted classification systems for these capabilities.

CONCLUSION

This chapter has focused on general processes and characteristics of individuals which are central to understanding the behavior of people in organizations. While we have attempted throughout to emphasize processes and characteristics which are true of all people, it has been constantly necessary to qualify our conclusions by statements about the importance of individual differences for understanding and implementing the principles discussed.

This tension between general processes and individual differences will be characteristic of our discussions throughout the book. As will be seen again and again, effective organizational management (or, as far as that goes, effective research on organizations) depends upon the development of a way of conceiving behavior in organizations which allows one to consider simultaneously the general psychological laws which govern all people and the idiosyncrasies of particular organization members—idiosyncrasies which, if not present, would make management an easy job, organizational behavior beautifully predictable, and life in organizations rather boring.

REVIEW AND DISCUSSION QUESTIONS

1 What similarities and differences would be found in organizations whose managers hold Theory X and Theory Y assumptions?
2 What is the basic problem associated with viewing all individuals from either a Theory X or a Theory Y perspective?
3 Is it possible to have the same reward satisfy, simultaneously, needs at several levels in the Maslow need hierarchy?
4 Management's use of behavioristic (Skinnerian) principles might be infeasible in some work organizations. Why?
5 How does hedonism relate to the various motivational models presented in this chapter? (For example, expectancy theory, behaviorism, etc.)

6   If Maslow's need hierarchy is valid, what are its implications for the design of reward systems in organizations?

7   What is meant by the statement, "A satisfied need is not a motivator"?

8   What is the relationship between need satisfaction and need importance? Is it the same for all needs?

9   Why did psychologists originally study job satisfaction? Why do they continue to study it?

10   List some organizational events that are particularly likely to be misperceived by organization members and explain why.

11   What implications does Simon's theory (i.e., limited search for alternatives and limited knowledge of consequences of acts) have for the Motivational Force = Expectancies $\times$ Valences formulation?

12   Although a manager may find that he is able to substantially increase the motivation of his subordinates (MF in the MF = E $\times$ V model), productivity or some other index of performance may not rise. Why?

13   What is an expectancy? How does it influence voluntary behavior?

Chapter 3

The Nature of
Organizations

In the previous chapter we examined some views about the nature of individuals. If we are to understand the behavior of people at work, it will be necessary next to look at the other major variable involved: organizations. They will be the focus of the present chapter, where we will review some of the major conceptual and theoretical ideas that social scientists have put forth as ways of thinking about them.

DIVERSITY OF VIEWPOINTS

The basic nature and features of organizations, as will become evident, have been the object of intense scrutiny and debate during the past two decades. They have been dissected from virtually every conceivable perspective. One sometimes gets the feeling that organizations must mean all things to all people because often what one author chooses to emphasize in an analysis is virtually ignored by someone else. The situation has been likened by Haire (1959) to the proverbial story of the blind men describing an elephant—each believes he is describing a different animal. Apropos of this, one scholar

(Waldo, 1961, p. 216) has commented: ". . . one must conclude that if they [organization theorists] all concern the same elephant it is a *very* large elephant with a generalized elephantitis."

Despite the fact that there is considerable variability in how scholars choose to analyze organizations, there is also a certain amount of commonality among the viewpoints. As we shall note later, when we abstract some of the more prominent definitions of organizations, there are certain aspects of them that seem to be emphasized with some degree of regularity. The fact that there is by no means perfect agreement merely serves to emphasize that complex organizations are, indeed, complex. The important point for the reader to keep in mind is that there is no ultimate "right" or "wrong" way to look at organizations. There are, however, some conceptualizations that may be more helpful than others in understanding them, depending in large part upon the uses which one wishes to make of such viewpoints.

The fact that there are a variety of viewpoints available concerning the basic nature of organizations indicates that the study of organizations is not the exclusive province of any single academic discipline. This point has been stressed by a number of writers (e.g., Waldo, 1961; Haire, 1959; Pugh, 1966). Each disciplinary orientation tends to focus on a particular aspect or set of features of organizations. For example, economists tend to deal with how organizations allocate resources and how decisions are made under conditions of uncertainty. Industrial engineers focus on the technological underpinning of organizational activities. Sociologists have been concerned largely with the structure of organizations and the ways in which organizations in toto cope with their external social environments. Political scientists are concerned with such issues as the exercise of power and authority in organizational settings. Psychologists, by and large, have concentrated their study on the behavior of individuals and groups within organizations.

None of these disciplinary perspectives has a fundamental advantage over the others. Indeed, it is often found that an organization researcher from one discipline tends to utilize concepts that have been more frequently associated with some other discipline. Thus, for example, one can find psychologists who study types of power, sociologists who put particular emphasis on technology, and political scientists who address themselves to role relationships. In essence, the analysis of organizations is a fertile meeting ground for a number of disciplines and has the distinct character of a truly interdisciplinary field.

ORGANIZATIONS DEFINED

As with other key terms in the behavioral sciences (e.g., leadership, role, power, motivation), what we mean precisely by the word "organization" is not easy to define. In fact, there are some who would doubt the utility of attempting to do so. March and Simon (1958), for example, in a widely referenced book entitled *Organizations,* choose not to define this word but instead state that "it is easier, and probably more useful, to give examples of formal organizations than to define the term" (p.1). With tongue in cheek, another organizational analyst notes that "[he] who has not tried his hand at framing a one-sentence (or even one-paragraph) definition of organization has denied himself an educational experience of high value" (Waldo, 1961, p. 218). Nevertheless, our position is that there is value to be obtained by examining some representative definitions provided by a variety of social and behavioral scientists. Such a sampling of definitions will serve to focus attention on the presumed essential features of organizations. This, in turn, will permit us later in the book to identify some of the major issues dealt with by organizational theorists as these issues relate to the question of how people at work interact with organizations.

A summary of fundamental characteristics of organizations, as abstracted from a representative sample of some of the more widely cited definitions, is shown in Figure 3-1. This summary set contains five major features that can be conceived of in the terms of a typical lead paragraph of a news story:

Organizations are:
1 Who: composed of individuals and groups
2 Why: in order to achieve certain goals and objectives
3 & 4 How: by means of differentiated functions that are intended to be rationally coordinated and directed
5 When: through time on a continuous basis

For each of these basic features, Figure 3-1 permits us to see the range of definitional attributes. Thus, for the question of composition of organizations, Barnard talks about a size as small as two or more persons, while Strother speaks of groups of two or more people and Scott uses the term "collectivities." The common element here, however, is that organizations are, first and foremost, *social* entities in which people take part and to which they react. The second fundamental feature stresses the purposeful, goal-oriented characteristic of organizations. This focuses our attention on the instrumental nature of organizations; that is, they are social instruments set up to *do* something. The third and fourth features concern the means by which organizations go about the process of trying to accomplish objectives. As indicated in Figure 3-1, there are two major types of methods that are seen as essential for this: the differentiation of functions and positions, and the deliberate, conscious, intendedly rational, planful attempts to coordinate and direct the activities thus produced within the organization. Finally, some

1 *Composition: individuals/groups*
   . . . "two or more persons" (Barnard)
   . . . "a number of people" (Schein)
   . . . "a group or cooperative system" (Gross)
   . . . "groups of two or more people" (Strother)
   . . . "at least several primary groups" (Simon)
   . . . "social units" (Litterer)
   . . . "social units" (Etzioni)
   . . . "collectivities" (Scott)

2 *Orientation: toward goals*
   . . . "devoted primarily to attainment of specific goals" (Etzioni)
   . . . "achievement of some common explicit purpose or goal" (Schein)
   . . . "obtaining a set of objectives or goals" (Litterer)
   . . . "some kind of collective goal(s) or output(s)" (Strother)
   . . . "pursuit of relatively specific objectives" (Scott)
   . . . "an accepted pattern of purposes" (Gross)
   . . . "toward ends that are objects of common knowledge" (Simon)

3 and 4   *Methods:*
   3 *Differentiated functions*
     . . . "differentiation of function" (Gross)
     . . . "some kind of differentiation of function" (Strother)
     . . . "[differentiation in] terms of authority, status, and role" (Presthus)
     . . . "division of labor and function" (Schein)
   4 *Intended rational coordination*
     . . . "rational coordination of activities" (Schein)
     . . . "high degree of rational direction of behavior" (Simon)
     . . . "conscious integration" (Gross)
     . . . "consciously coordinated activities" (Barnard)
     . . . "subject to criteria of rationality" (Thompson)
     . . . "structured interpersonal relations" (Presthus)

5 *Continuity: through time*
   . . . "more or less continuous basis" (Scott)
   . . . "continuity of interaction" (Gross)

Note: Sources for these definitional characteristics, along with the general disciplinary orientation of the authors, are the following:
Barnard, 1938, p. 75 (Sociology/management)
Etzioni, 1964, p. xi (Sociology)
Scott, 1964, p. 488 (Sociology)
Thompson, 1967, p. 10 (Sociology)
Gross, 1968, p. 52 (Political science)
Presthus, 1958, p. 50 (Political science)
Simon, 1952, p. 1130 (Political science)
Schein, 1970, p. 9 (Psychology)
Litterer, 1965, p. 5 (Management)
Strother, 1963, p. 23 (Management)

Figure 3-1 Fundamental characteristics of organizations (as abstracted from representative definitions given by behavioral and social scientists).

(but not all) commentators point to a fifth basic feature: the continuity through time of the activities and relationships within organizations. This latter aspect implies that when we are talking about organizations we are not dealing with one-time-only actions or relationships, but rather ones that have some prospect of becoming regularized and of lasting for some indefinite amount of time.

These five features, taken together, supply something of an anatomical look at organizations. They are, if you will, skeletal definitions that delineate the minimal outlines of what organizations are and do. They serve to help us distinguish the types of entities we refer to as "formal organizations" (especially those in which people work) from other social groupings such as families, social classes, ethnic groups, and random gatherings of individuals. The five features, by themselves, do not provide a flesh and blood picture of the nature of actual, ongoing organizations. To say that organizations are composed of individuals and groups per se says nothing about where people come from, how many there are, and what capabilities they have. To say that organizations are goal oriented tells others nothing about what kinds of goals, whose goals, changing goals, overlapping goals, or conflicting goals. And so forth. It is obviously necessary to examine each of these five features in considerably more detail to learn something of their implications for furthering our understanding of individual behavior in the organized work setting. This is the task for the remaining sections of this chapter.

THE COMPOSITION OF ORGANIZATIONS

Question of Units

In analyzing the composition of organizations, one is immediately faced with the problem of specifying the "units" that compose organizations. At the same time, it is possible to think of organizations as units themselves, and ask how they relate to some more encompassing entity. That is, organizations can be considered as "parts" of a larger total system.

One way to look at the units question is to adopt a classification or "levels of analysis" system that has been proposed by a number of organization theorists (e.g., Simon, 1952; Indik, 1968). This classification scheme is shown in Figure 3-2.

It can be seen in Figure 3-2 that this approach considers individuals as the smallest units of analysis, and society at large as the most encompassing. In between are groups, organizations, and institutions. This kind of conceptual scheme has been referred to as a "nest of Chinese blocks" similar to such sequences as elementary particle → atom → molecule in physics, and gene → chromosome → nucleus → cell → tissue → organ → organism in biology (Simon, 1952).

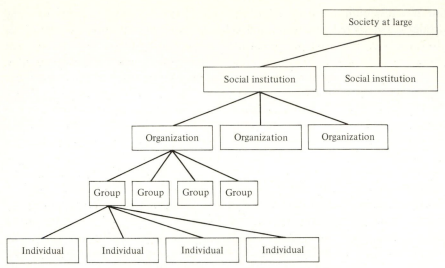

Figure 3-2   A classification system of units relating to organizations.

It should be noted that the individual → group → organization → institution → society sequence does not specify *how many* of each type of smaller units there are in the next larger unit. As the summarized samples of definitions given in Figure 3-1 imply, the minimum number in each case is assumed to be two (i.e., two or more people form groups, two or more groups form organizations, two or more organizations compose institutions, and so on). The maximum number of units is not specified and is assumed to vary widely for different types of groups, different types of organizations, and the like.

Perhaps the most important implication of the approach shown in Figure 3-2 is the idea that each larger unit operates as a major aspect of the *environment* of the preceding unit. Thus, typically, people do not relate to organizations as isolated individuals. Normally, though not always, they are parts of groups and their interaction with the organization is as a part of some type of group. The group or groups of which they are a part often are the most crucial feature of their surroundings. Hence, John Jones's view of the XYZ organization strongly reflects his attitudes toward, say, his immediate work group. For him, the XYZ organization *is* virtually the same as his immediate group. Similarly, at one step up the sequence, the key influencing environment for the group is the organization of which it is a part. A group that is part of a relatively unsuccessful organization, for example, may not pay much attention to the fact that the institution (e.g., the banking industry) of which the organization is in turn a part is relatively successful within society. What really matters are the opportunities and problems presented by the immediate environment—the organization. This is not to say, of course, that units one step or more removed are not influential. Clearly, they are in many instances. John Jones may find that what the organization does to him or for him has more impact on him than the activities or interactions occurring in his group. The point is that each level of unit above a given unit constitutes a part of its environment, and the more immediate the level the greater is the assumed influence on the particular unit.

Individuals in Organizations

As we have mentioned earlier, a fundamental aspect of the definitions of organizations relating to their composition is the fact that they are *social* entities. When we study the behavior of individuals in the organizational situation we must take account of the fact that they work with other people around them—either directly, as on a factory production line or a hospital floor, or indirectly, as in a managerial job where others may not be physically present all the time but where their influence is strongly felt. The inevitable knowledge that the individual has about this fact—that he is not working alone—is presumed to have considerable impact on his behavior and his thinking (as discussed in detail in Chapters 13 and 14). In this sense, then, the organization can be considered a *social home* for each individual employee that takes part in it.

In viewing individuals as units that form organizations—whether as parts of distinct groups or not—it is necessary to keep in mind what they *bring* to organizations. What is often overlooked is that individuals bring both more and less than might be ideal for the organization. Certainly, as has been pointed out in Chapter 2, a man at work has made available to the organization certain physical attributes, certain aptitudes and abilities. In addition, he also brings along a whole set of attitudes, personality disposi- tions, feelings, emotions, and the like, that might—from the organization's point of view—impede his usefulness to the organization. The organization employs more than just a nervous system or a pair of hands.

At the same time, however, no employing organization ever obtains the total person from a psychological point of view. The concept of *partial inclusion* has been utilized to describe this "segmental involvement of people in social groups" (Allport, 1962; Katz & Kahn, 1966). Since each individual is a member simultaneously of many groups or organizations (a family, a church, clubs, etc.), no one of them is able to command his total commitment to the complete exclusion of all the others. He is partially included in each and totally included in none. Even people occupying positions at the very top of organizations, those who have the most to gain or lose in relation to the organization's fate, have ties to other social entities that they cannot shut out entirely even if they desired to do so. In essence, organizations would prefer to have particular psychological parts of individuals, but they are consistently obtaining more or less than those specified parts.

Groups in Organizations

Groups are the other key element in the social composition of organizations. As ordinarily defined, groups consist of a limited number of individuals who have common interactions and some degree of shared values and norms (standards of behavior). In organizations, such groups are of two major types: (1) those specified and created by the organization and (2) those that occur naturally in the process of individuals having the opportunity to interact with each other. The first type is typically referred to as "formal groups," and the latter as "informal" or "social groups."

Formal Groups   Some groups are specifically designated by the organization and are set up to further the attainment of its goals. These can be considered "formal groups." Their creation represents an attempt by the organization to structure itself in the most efficient manner possible. The fact that such groups, for example, those composed of a number of subordinates reporting to a given superior, can be created by the organization also means that they can be dissolved by it. Hence, there is no necessary time span for the life of a given formal group. Some continue in operation for very long periods of time, during which individuals enter and leave the group, but the structure and functions of the group remain relatively constant. Such relatively stable groups tend to be particularly characteristic of the lower levels of organizations. Other formal groups may be in existence for relatively short periods of time. These groups, more likely to be found at middle and higher echelons, are referred to by some as "temporary systems" (Bennis, 1966). Examples would be task forces and project teams set up by the organization for limited tasks of rather specific duration. Individuals would be likely to remain members of such groups for their duration (since they are often in existence for quite short periods of time), and hence the composition would remain fairly constant.

It should be noted that any given employee can be simultaneously a member of two or more formal groups. The fact that such groups are specified by the organization in no way precludes multiple membership—and, thus, multiple influences on the individual's behavior. Indeed, almost every individual above the lowest level of the enterprise is the member of at least two such groups. First, he is a member of the group over which he is the supervisor or boss, and second, he is a member of a group of which he is one of the subordinates. This kind of multiple formal-group-membership role has been termed by Likert (1961) as "linking pin." The implication of the linking-pin concept is that any supervisor or manager who fails to take into account this type of dual group membership will inevitably find that he has created difficulties for both himself and the formal organization. Multiple formal-group membership is not confined to just the superior-subordinate relationship, however. Frequently, a person will find himself in a situation where he has at least two superiors to report to and thus he is a member of two different subordinate groups. A common example would be the personnel manager of a branch operation (whether it be a decentralized industrial firm or a multicampus university) who is responsible both to the head of that branch and also to the head of personnel services in the headquarters of the organization. Other multiple formal-group-membership situations would occur, for example, when the individual is a member of one or more project groups.

Organizations attempt to summarize the pattern of relationships among formal groups by constructing organization charts. (An example of such a chart is shown in Figure 3-3.) These charts try to map both the distance of the groups from each other as well as the network of linkages among them. In this way, any individual in the organization can locate where he is in relation to the *formal* structure of the organization. Closeness to the top or the bottom, or distance from the center (main functions), as pictured on the chart, is often an important source of information for the individual in terms of developing his own plans and behavior in the day-to-day work situation and over a period of time.

Nonspecified (Informal) Groups   While an organization chart may be of some help in representing the set of relationships among specified formal groups, it almost never reveals usable information about the *social* group composition of organizations. One major reason for this is that there is no single set of nonspecified or *informal groups*. The kind of chart one might attempt to draw of informal groups would depend upon what *type* of such group is under consideration. Even a relatively limited part of an organization, such as an office with twenty or thirty employees, may contain several quite different informal groups. Examples (and others could be listed) would be:

Informal task groups: a set of individuals that work together on formal tasks of the organization, but who develop patterns of interaction in carrying out the tasks that are left undesignated by the organization.

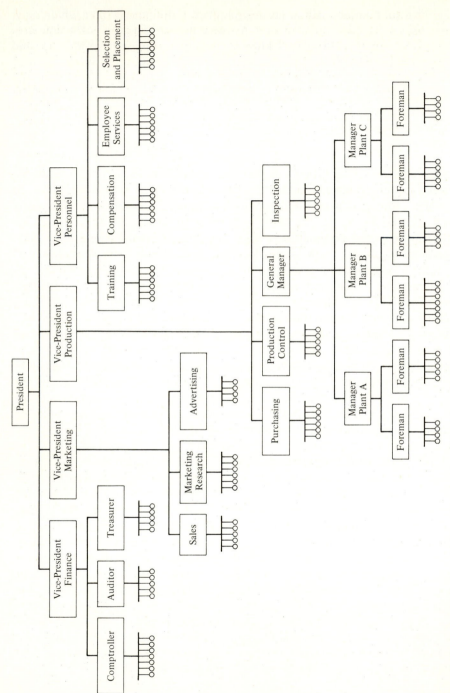

Figure 3-3   An example of an organization chart (for a business company).

Informal communication groups: a set of individuals who may or may not be close friends, but who have voluntarily developed certain types of interactions for the purpose of passing various types of information from one person to another.

Informal friendship groups: a set of individuals who may have no formally designated interactions with each other, but who decide voluntarily to interact either during the work situation—whether or not such interactions are relevant to carrying out "work"—or during nonwork periods such as coffee breaks or lunch hours.

Again, as with formal groups, an individual may, and usually does, simultaneously belong to several such informal social groups.

The number of informal social groups within an organization tends to be rather large relative to the total number of individuals employed by it. Furthermore, their boundaries, in terms of who is or is not a member are often blurred. Some such groups make it quite clear who is considered a member and who is not. Other groups, however, function with a number of individuals on the periphery in the sense that these people sometimes interact with the group's members and at other times do not. This fact, coupled with overlapping membership across groups, makes it exceedingly difficult to summarize explicitly, in a given organization, the informal social composition of the organization. While certain questionnaire-type techniques are sometimes helpful in specifying members of a given group, they are usually inadequate for the purpose of giving an overall view of the social group composition of the total organization. The fact that such a picture cannot be easily drawn so that it is analogous to the organization chart for the formal organization in no way implies, however, that the social composition does not exist or that it is not important.

The chief aspect of nonformal groupings that we need to consider here is their tremendous influence on the behavior of the individual member of the organization. This has been well documented in research for fifty years from the influential Hawthorne studies of the late 1920s onward. The impact has been in all areas of behavior, from producing, to communicating, to deciding to stay with or leave the organization. As will be discussed in greater detail later in this book (Chapter 13), individuals join or become members of social groups for a variety of reasons, some of which they may be very conscious of—such as the desire to gain friendships—and others of which they may be relatively unaware—such as to gain emotional support. Once an individual is attracted to a group and becomes a part of it, he or she is affected by it—its values and standards of behavior. Deviation from these accepted patterns of behavior is often at the expense of leaving the group or at least not receiving all the benefits of membership in it.

THE ORIENTATION OF ORGANIZATIONS:
TOWARD GOALS

Organizations are considered to be oriented toward goals and objectives. This is the clear message one gets by looking at the definitions of organizations that are summarized in Figure 3-1. This feature, in fact, is taken by many theorists (e.g., Etzioni, 1964; Parsons, 1960; Schein, 1970) to be the *sine qua non* of organizations. Parsons puts this most forcibly when he says that it is "primacy of orientation to the attainment of a specific goal [that is the] defining characteristic of an organization which distinguishes it from other types of social systems" (1960, p. 17). Presumably, according to this view, the more specific and explicit the goals of a social collectivity are, the more it should be regarded as an organization (rather than, say, an informal group, a crowd, etc.).

Goals, as organization theorists tend to use the term, are defined as *desired future states of affairs* (Vroom, 1960; Etzioni, 1964). While in some cases they may never be realizable, the organization is viewed as intending to reach them. Here, also, we should keep in mind that there is no necessary requirement that an organization have only a single goal. In fact, most organizations that we will be considering throughout this book, (that is, organizations that employ people) will very likely have multiple goals.

Importance of Organizational Goals

Viewed in broad perspective, the presumption that organizations are purposeful in nature can be potentially quite important for affecting the behavior of individuals in relation to organizations. People tend to react to organizations *as if* they were going somewhere. To the extent that a given individual believes this with respect to a particular organization, it may influence his desire to join and stay with it. If he comes to believe that the organization is lacking in purpose, this also can have an impact on his desire to perform even if it does not drive him away from the organization. For these types of reasons, organizations that are concerned about employee participation and performance often go to great lengths to ensure that "ends are objects of common knowledge" (Simon, 1952). It is obvious, of course, that some organizations succeed in doing this much better than other ones. Those that are able to make their goals sufficiently prominent so that the objectives are, indeed, *common* knowledge throughout the organization, are presumed to have a competitive advantage in mobilizing collective human effort.

In more specific ways, organizational goals serve several important functions (Etzioni, 1964; Zald, 1963; Steers, 1971):

1 *Focus attention:* To the extent that goals are emphasized and made known to organization members, they can serve as one kind of guideline to

focus the efforts and activities of individuals and groups. They thus can be thought of as one type of prescription of what "should be" done.

2 *Provide a source of legitimacy:* Not only can goals have the function of indicating to an organization member what he should be doing, they also help legitimize or justify his actions or decisions. In this way they can be a type of defense for any member if his activities are criticized or questioned.

3 *Serve as a standard:* Goals, in conjunction with various measurement procedures (e.g., profit-loss calculations, determination of number of clients served) can help organization members determine how well they are performing their work or carrying out certain actions.

4 *Affect the structure of the organization:* Organizational goals and the structure (relatively stable patterns of relationships among members and positions) of organizations interact. Each can affect the other. What the organization is attempting to do can influence how it will be set up to do it, and how it is set up can also affect what it will try to do.

5 *Provide clues about the organization:* The goals of an organization can be an important source of information about and insight into the character and nature of it, both for members and nonmembers. Goals are a part, sometimes a key part, of the picture: What is this organization really like?

Although so far we have been stressing the purposeful nature of organizations and thus the importance of goals, we should not lose sight of the fact that there is much that goes on in organizations that is not highly purposeful in character. We are referring here to the many normal routines that exist in all organizations and the many habitual types of activities that each member carries out day in and day out. Therefore, while we can say that organizations are goal oriented and that this orientation can have significant impact on the behavior of individuals, such influence is not all-pervasive. Members spend a fair portion of their time in organizations acting and reacting without engaging in overtly conscious, purposeful behavior.

Formulation of Goals

To state that organizations have goals places us in danger of reifying the concept of organization and talking about it as if it were a concrete "thing," rather than some sort of abstraction denoting a system of interacting people (Simon, 1964). On the other hand, we cannot talk about organizational goals as being simply the sum of the personal objectives of all the individuals in the organization. Barnard (1938, p. 85) makes this point by stating:

> We have clearly to distinguish between organization purpose and individual motive. It is frequently assumed in reasoning about organizations that common purpose and individual motive are or should be identical. With the exception noted below, this is never the case; and under modern conditions it rarely even

appears to be the case. Individual motive is necessarily an internal, personal, subjective thing; common purpose is necessarily an external, impersonal, objective thing even though the individual interpretation of it is subjective. The one exception to this general rule, an important one, is that the accomplishment of an organization purpose becomes itself a source of personal satisfaction and a motive for many individuals in many organizations. It is rare, however, if ever, and then I think only in connection with family, patriotic, and religious organizations under special conditions, that organization purpose becomes or can become the *only* or even the major individual motive.

If we accept the above viewpoint, we are left with something like the following way of looking at the question "Whose goals?" when we use the term "organizational goals": Organizational goals are established *by* individuals, usually in some collective fashion (that is, by some number of individuals cooperating together), and usually *for* the intended benefit of the total entity *as these individuals see it*—which, of course, in some instances, may in actuality mean for the primary benefit of the particular individuals who formulate the goals. When the organization is originally created, such goal formulation will be by the founders; thereafter, however, it will tend to be by those individuals who "have sufficient control of organizational resources to commit them in certain directions and to withhold them from others" (Thompson, 1967, p. 128). While these individuals will ordinarily be those holding the highest formal positions in an organization, this will not be necessarily so if there are others lower down who have "sufficient control of organizational resources." An example of the latter situation is where a technical expert has extremely specialized knowledge available to no one else in the organization. He might not hold a particularly high position in the chain of command, but he controls a scarce but vital organizational resource (technical expertise) and thus may be able to influence organizational goal formation.

We have previously defined an organizational goal as a desired future state of affairs. There is a somewhat different (but not opposite) way to look at goals that may be helpful in understanding aspects of the "Whose goals?" question. This alternate way of viewing goals is from the vantage point of decision theorists (Cyert & March, 1963; Simon, 1964). To illuminate this position we shall present in some detail the ideas of one of the major developers of this theory, Herbert Simon.

Simon (1964) regards goals as, in reality, *sets of constraints* that limit the scope of actions. Thus, he states that

> in the decision-making situations of real life, a course of action, to be acceptable, must satisfy a whole set of requirements, or constraints. Sometimes one of these requirements is singled out and referred to as the goal of the action. But the choice of one of the constraints, from many, is to a large extent

arbitrary. For many purposes it is more meaningful to refer to the whole set of requirements as the (complex) goal of the action. This conclusion applies both to individual and organizational decision making. (1964, p. 7)

This analysis of what constitutes a goal can be summarized by an epigram that Simon quotes: "If you allow me to determine the constraints, I don't care who selects the optimization criterion."

With this way of looking at goals, we may ask whether every individual in the organization must be guided at all times by the primary goal(s) of the organization. Simon answers "no," and provides an interesting example with respect to the often-cited goal of "profit" in a business organization:

"Profit" may not enter directly into the decision making of most members of a business organization. Again, this does not mean that it is improper or meaningless to regard profit as a principal goal of the business. It simply means that the decision-making mechanism is a loosely coupled system in which the profit constraint is only one among a number of constraints and enters into most subsystems only in indirect ways. It would be both legitimate and realistic to describe most business firms as directed toward profit making—subject to a number of side constraints—operating through a network of decision-making processes that introduces many gross approximations into the search for profitable courses of action. Further, the goal ascription does not imply that any employee is motivated by the firm's profit goal, although some may be. (1964, pp. 21–22)

In effect, the point is being made that the overall goal (constraint) of profit is sufficiently diffuse to permit members of lower echelons in organizations to be guided in their day-to-day actions by more immediate goals (constraints) that are not directly related to profit but which also do not ultimately violate that overall organizational goal. Again, it is necessary to stress that although lower-level individuals in the organization may not have been in on the setting of the overall organizational goal(s), and may not be affected very directly by them in their daily behavior, they nevertheless are affected by the *assumption* that such goals have been set and that those leading the organization know what they are. This does not, also, preclude the possibility in some organizations that lower-level employees will want to participate in the goal-formulation process to the same extent as those who (at the higher levels) control more of the organization's resources.

Official, Operative, and Operational Goals

The preceding discussion leads directly into an additional type of consideration with respect to organizational goals. This is the relationship among "official," "operative," and "operational" goals.

Official Goals   "Official goals" are the publicly stated goals of an organization, as annunciated in its charter, its official documents, the policy statements of its officers, and the like. Typically, the broadest official goals are ones that society expects of a given type of organization—e.g., "to provide such and such a service at a profit" for a business organization, "to provide higher education and to disseminate knowledge" for a university, and so forth. More specific official goals would be ones consistent with these broad goals for a category of organizations, but they would differ from one organization to another (e.g., for one business company it might be "to achieve sales of X million dollars by 1980;" for another it might be "to achieve a 10 percent annual increase in net operating revenues"). A key question surrounding official goals, however, is whether or not they are "operative"—that is, whether they are in fact the objectives that are actually being pursued by elements of the organization at any given point in time.

Operative Goals   Clearly, in some organizations most of the time, and in most organizations some of the time, there will be a close correspondence between official and operative goals. In such cases we can infer that operative goals are largely determined by the official goals. In other instances, however, there may be relatively wide discrepancies between the two, such that some of the official goals can be considered "nonoperative." (An example of a nonoperative official goal would be where a company states that one of its objectives is to be a "good corporate citizen," yet seldom does anything directly to help the community in which it is located.) It is clear that if operative goals are different from the official ones, the situation can be due to a variety of reasons. These would include sources or factors both inside and outside the organization. The official goals may be too difficult to meet, they may not be ones that certain influential people in the organization want to pursue, they may be outdated by recent but unacknowledged changes in the environment (e.g., a change in the competitive situation for a business organization, a change in interests of college-age youth for universities, etc.), and so forth. In any event, we make the assumption that it is the operative goals rather than the official goals that have the greater impact on the behavior of individuals in the work situation.

Operational Goals   Somewhat akin to the concept of operative goals, but not identical with it, is the notion of "operational goals" or "goal operationality." Goals are said to be operational when there are "agreed-upon criteria for determining the extent to which particular activities or programs of activity contribute to these goals" (March & Simon, 1958, p. 194). Operative goals, therefore, will be more or less operational to the extent that there is agreement on how their attainment will be measured.

Promoting "exemplary research" or providing "sound training" in hospitals may be much less operation*al* (though still opera*tive*) than increasing bed capacity by 10 percent, for example.

Means-End Analyses   The concept of operational goals raises the issue of how goals relate to the means used to accomplish them. This is, in effect, the question of how relatively broad nonoperational goals are broken down into more specific and concrete operational goals and subgoals.

We can start with the assumption that goals that are nonoperational are soon converted into a set of subgoals because most organization members will want and need some basis for carrying out their own individual actions. Thus, because individuals are presumed to have a need for organizing their world around them, they will proceed to develop such subgoals. This being the case, it indicates that throughout the organization as a whole a series of larger and smaller (in terms of scope) goals will be developed, each having a particular (and, usually, predictable) relationship to the others. Except for the broadest, most encompassing objective, each goal that develops in an organization can be considered to be both a goal in itself and a *means* of reaching some other goal.

An illustration of such means-goal chains (or, as they are usually called, "means-end chains") is given in Figure 3-4 for a hypothetical organization. This organization has an official goal of "providing travel services to the general public." Such a goal, as stated, is not operational because no criteria are provided for determining whether or not any given action that might take place in the organization will lead toward its attainment. (It is necessary, at this point, to keep in mind that whether a goal is operational or nonoperational cannot be answered in a simple yes or no manner. There are, as March and Simon (1958) note, "all degrees of 'operationality.'") However, this nonoperational state of affairs does not prevent the creation of various means or mechanisms that people *think* will lead to such an overall goal. Thus, in our illustration, the organization can decide that there are at least two ways (and, ordinarily many more) it could provide useful travel services to the general public: one would be to set up a service that would transport people from one city to another; a second means might be to set up a service to provide hotel accommodations. The organization could decide to pursue either or both of these means (level B in our diagram) toward its overall goal (level A). (Levels in the means-end chain do not necessarily correspond to formal levels in the organization. It is entirely possible for several means-end levels to be in existence within any given hierarchical level of the organization.) For purposes of illustration we will assume the organization decides to do at least the former. This particular means can then be considered as a subgoal to be pursued in some fashion or other. At level C in

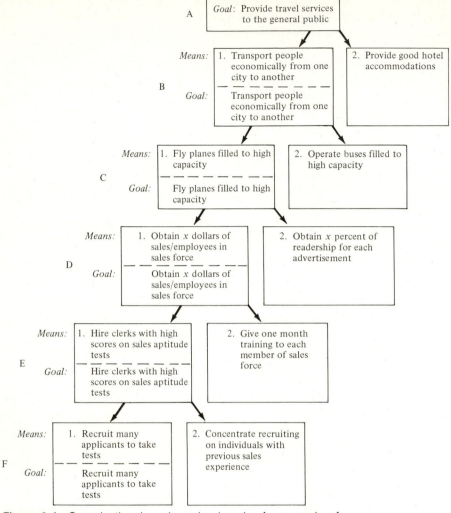

Figure 3-4 Organizational goals and subgoals: An example of means-end chains.

the diagram we see that again there are at least two (not incompatible) ways to meet the level B goal: fly planes at high capacity and operate buses at high capacity. If flying planes at high capacity is selected as at least one of the ways of meeting the level B goal, it now becomes a goal in itself and in turn can be pursued by several different means such as obtaining a large volume of sales per member of the sales force and obtaining a high readership of advertisements. The means-end chain can, in turn, be carried on down to more and more specific goals, each being a means to some larger goal. (The recent emphasis in many organizations on "management by objectives" is, in effect, a concrete illustration of a formal elaboration of means-end chains.)

How far one wishes to carry out this means-end analysis depends upon the uses to which it is to be put. It can be continued until it reaches a level of specificity where an existing set of known (i.e., familiar) means can be put into action (March & Simon, 1958). The more innovative or novel the goals, the greater the necessity for carrying the analysis to greater lengths. The major point to be kept in mind is simply that a means-end analysis is a convenient way of thinking about the question of goals and subgoals in an organization. It helps the observer—whether in or out of the organization— to understand why certain goals appear in certain parts of the organization, and what their relationships may be to each other. It also helps to demonstrate how nonoperational goals become translated into operational goals that directly affect the behavior of individuals in the organization.

Goal Changes

It is essential to realize that goals for the organization as a whole or for primary units rarely remain completely unchanged over long periods of time. Two factors account for this: first, since organizations are composed of people, and since the particular composition changes through time—that is, people are constantly entering and leaving the organization—it should not be expected that goals set by past members will automatically stay fixed as the goals the present members hold for the organization. Second, and perhaps more importantly, the environment in which the organization operates is in a constant state of flux. Goals appropriate to a previous environmental state may become irrelevant or outmoded in such a way that if the organization is to survive, it must change its goals as well as the means for attaining them.

Goal Displacement   Sociologists tend to distinguish two different types of major goal changes: "displacement" and "succession" (Blau & Scott, 1962; Etzioni, 1964; Sills, 1957). The former type of change in goals—"displacement"—is considered to occur when new (operative) goals are developed that entirely subvert or go counter to the official or sanctioned goals. Frequently, this occurs where behavior or actions that were considered to be means to some more inclusive goal become in themselves an ultimate goal for the individual or the unit—in other words, this is a situation involving a *means-end inversion.* This kind of process can occur, for example, in governmental agencies where overzealous and rigid enforcement of rules becomes the desired state of affairs rather than being regarded as one way of achieving some larger goal such as service to the public (Merton, 1940). On a more total organizational level of analysis, organizations will often carry out activities that serve to preserve their own existence even though such behavior tends to violate their stated goals of contributing in some way to society at large. Usually, when we refer to goal displacement, we are talking about covert goal changes that are not explicitly made public—because, if they were, their contradiction with the stated goals would become obvious and the apparent discrepancy would cause individual and/or organizational embarrassment and difficulty.

Goal Succession The second fundamental type of goal change—succession—refers to situations where new or modified goals are incorporated into, or substituted for, existing ones in such a way that the latter are not violated in spirit. That is, the new goals are ones that individuals or organizations are willing to state explicitly and openly. They are presumed to be, by members or others connected with the organization, more worthy or more relevant than the previous ones. It is also usually presumed that goal succession will facilitate the organization's continued or improved adaptation to changing environmental circumstances. [Of course, it can turn out that this presumption eventually is incorrect in a given situation—the new goal(s) may prove to be in actual practice a mistake for the organization to have adopted.]

An example of relatively successful implementation of goal succession is cited by Sills in his book (1957) describing the process that took place in the National Foundation for Infantile Paralysis in the 1950s. This organization faced a particular problem in that its previously stated goal—eliminating polio—was becoming completely achieved (in large part, of course, through the efforts of the foundation itself). If it were to continue to maintain its present resources (e.g., the commitment of its employees) and to continue gathering additional ones (e.g., money) from the environment, it needed to find a new goal or goals to succeed the previous one. This it did, as Sills describes, by changing its goal to the reduction and treatment of birth defects and arthritis. Had not the organization come up with this goal which appealed to enough people within the organization and to the larger societal environment, it might well have gone out of existence as an organization.

Even though environmental changes may be drastic in terms of their effect or potential effect on particular organizations, necessary goal succession may not take place. The reasons for this will vary with the particular circumstances, but we can hypothesize that at the time changes in goals would need to be made, those controlling organizational resources would be unwilling or unable to bring about such modifications. Example of organizations cited by Sills that did not carry out goal succession, and thus went into decline, include the Woman's Christian Temperance Union (W.C.T.U.) and the Townsend Organization, established in the 1930s to help individuals deal with the effects of the Depression. One could, of course, add numerous examples of goal-succession failures from the world of business—e.g., the turn-of-the-century buggy-whip company that persisted in the aim of turning out a better product in the face of a complete decline in the need for that product. In short, it is clear that almost all organizations need continually to exercise some degree of the goal-succession process, but not all of them will do this fast enough or in a way that will ensure continued viability of the organization.

THE METHODS OF ORGANIZATIONS: DIFFERENTIATED FUNCTIONS

If organizations are indeed oriented to some desired future state of affairs, that is, if they are goal oriented, then they must possess some methods for attaining their goals. While goal achievement can occur occasionally by chance or serendipity, it would be unlikely to happen frequently enough for organizational survival to take place. Hence, organizations must contain in their very nature some more systematic means to facilitate the attempt to reach goals. One of these inherent features involves the "differentiation of functions," and referring back to Figure 3-1 we can see that it is the third basic defining characteristic of organizations.

By differentiated functions, organization theorists simply mean that everyone in the organization does not do the same thing. This feature helps distinguish organizations from some other types of social collectivities such as crowds or audiences. In the latter case, for example, a group of individuals attending a musical performance are all essentially carrying out the same set of activities: watching the musicians and listening to the sounds. The audience is not purposely divided in any *systematic way* into those who primarily watch and those who primarily listen (though by chance certain individuals may be only watching and not actively listening, and others are listening without watching). This does not come about because the situation does not require it and because there is no collective goal orientation of the audience—they are not trying to achieve something together. In an organization, especially a work organization, on the other hand, the environmental situation and the goal orientation more or less require that *some degree* of differentiation take place. Without it, the organization is assumed to become some other type of social grouping or to cease existence entirely.

Reasons for Differentiated Functions

The overriding reason why differentiated functions are an inherent feature of organizations is the one we have already mentioned; namely, they are a means for goal achievement. However, it is possible to divide this general reason into two subsidiary ones: the nature of tasks and the nature of people.

The Nature of Tasks For the types of organizations that we are considering in this book, organizations that employ people, the kinds of tasks that must be performed—as part of the means-end chains referred to in the previous section—are such that they are of too many types and of too much complexity for any single individual to be able to perform them adequately, let alone master them. In other words, task requirements enforce a necessity for functions to be subdivided in some way and allocated to different individuals. (It must be stressed, of course, that the general necessity in no way determines how the differentiation is to occur or to what degree). The chief reason for this is that almost any work organization utilizes some kind of technology, and the technology dictates that one person or one group cannot possibly perform all the needed functions at the right time and in the right place.

The Nature of People Even in those organization situations where tasks or sequences of tasks are relatively simple and straightforward, the limitations of individuals will still require differentiation of functions. As has been discussed in Chapter 2, members of an organization are not equal in either the total amount or the pattern of their skills and capabilities. Thus, each individual can carry out some tasks better than others, and any two people differ in how well they can carry out a given task. This means that in any organization that is attempting to achieve goals, efforts will be made to assign tasks differentially to individuals in such a way that this type of resource is utilized more effectively than would be the case with random assignment. This does not imply, however, that each person will necessarily carry out only those tasks he performs best or on which he is the best performer. Many other constraints will operate in the situation that will frequently prevent this, including individuals' preferences and values for different kinds of work.

Types of Differentiated Functions

While it is possible to think of many diverse ways in which the total work to be performed in an organization can be subdivided, for analytical purposes it is most useful to think of two major varieties of differentiated functions:

those differing along the "horizontal" dimension of the organization, and those differing along the "vertical" dimension. In fact, it is a basic characteristic of organizations in comparison with other social groupings that functions will indeed be differentiated along both dimensions. Since, in an organization of any size, there are at least several horizontal levels within it as well as several vertical lines (of authority, responsibility, etc.) leading from bottom to top, this means that in effect we have a matrix of differentiated functions. In general, the larger the organization the more complex the matrix becomes, especially in terms of the ability of any individual working in the organization to understand and comprehend the matrix.

Horizontal Differentiation Differentiation of functions along the "horizontal" dimension of the organization refers to the division of activities among individuals and groups all of whom occupy the same (or roughly the same) authority and responsibility level. Frequently, this kind of differentiation is labeled "division of labor." Unfortunately, this phrase carries connotations of applying only to industrial or manufacturing types of organizations and only to their lowest level—i.e., the rank-and-file worker level. In point of fact, division of labor occurs in *all types* of organizations—governmental and educational as well as industrial—and at *all levels* within the organizations. Thus, it is a universal phenomenon throughout organizations.

At the lower levels of many kinds of organizations, especially industrial ones, the particular way in which functions are differentiated is strongly affected by the technological requirements that prevail. In other kinds of organizations (e.g., schools), and at the higher levels of almost all types of organizations, technology fades into the background somewhat and other factors, such as the type of problems to be solved or the clientele to be dealt with, become more prominent. It must be noted, however, that the farther the division of labor is removed from technological imperatives, the greater the possibility that nonrational aspects will enter into the ways in which functions are differentiated. As has been pointed out, what we frequently witness are "clear-cut instances of the intrusion of the organization as a social system on the organization as a rational tool" (Scott, 1964, p. 496). What is meant here is that such factors as the personal motivations of the most influential top personnel in the organization, or the status differences among various categories of employees, may enter into the decision-making process with respect to allocating functions among organization members.

The general concept of division of labor leads to various ways in which employees may be grouped together in an organization. Though it is not our purpose here to go into detail on the questions of organization structure (since this topic will be dealt with in detail in Chapters 8 and 9), it may be helpful to mention briefly several bases for grouping by means of division of labor within horizontal levels of organizations. Perhaps the most useful set of categories was provided some years ago by Gulick (1937), a well-known management theorist. He stated that every employee in an organization could be classified by four categories: the *purpose* he is fulfilling, the *process* he is using, the *persons or things* on which he is acting, and the *place* in which he is carrying out his work.

If we were to generalize across organizations, we would probably find that some combination of purpose and process (since often these two categories are not independent of each other) was the most frequently used basis for allocating differential functions. Indeed, elaborate prescriptive theories have been constructed to tell organizations how they should best group their employees along these dimensions in order to obtain maximal goal attainment. The problem with these prescriptions is that while they may be quite helpful for relatively small and simple organizations they tend to be much less effective for large and complex organizations operating in dynamic and fast changing environments. Thus, prescriptions for the division of labor that have any degree of generality are not very much in evidence. Regardless of what is supposed to work out best, our concern in this book is much more with what actually happens in terms of impacts upon the individual employee when particular divisions of labor are adopted. The key thing to keep in mind here is that most employees have a sense of how the work is presently divided and they have a perception of which dimension (purpose, process, etc.) is most important to them. This in turn is likely to affect their behavior in the work situation.

Vertical Differentiation Turning to the "vertical" differentiation of functions, we are dealing with differences along such dimensions as the amount of authority or power an individual has to influence organizational actions, the degree of responsibility he has for these actions, and the number of individuals he supervises or manages. In other words, vertical differentiation occurs with respect to the breadth of domain of a job, with higher positions involving greater breadth. The primary reason for vertical differentiation within organizations, of course, is to provide for specialized types of coordinative activities. The division of labor on the horizontal level creates the need for this type of separate function.

Generally speaking, in relatively large organizations vertical differentiation results in four major types of groupings of activities:

Top management positions:	concerned with overall goal formation and policy decisions regarding allocation of resources

Middle management positions:	concerned with subgoal formation and plans for implementing decisions from above and coordinating activities from below
Lower management positions:	concerned with implementing decisions made at higher levels, and coordinating and directing the work of employees at the lowest level of the organization
Rank-and-file positions:	concerned with carrying out specific task activities

In smaller organizations, of course, the four groupings get compressed into only three or perhaps even only two groupings (i.e., a manager and his rank-and-file employees).

There are two things to note about the vertical differentiation of functions. The first is its relation to means-end chains that we discussed in the preceding section. A vertical distinction among position in organizations results in each individual having a particular role with respect to means-end chains. Those people who are in the top positions will be primarily oriented to goal formation while those at the very bottom will be primarily functioning to carry out goals. Individuals in the middle of the vertical hierarchy will be oriented both to goals—for their segment of the organization— and to means for achieving more comprehensive goals that exist for larger segments of the organization than their own. Thus, individuals in these positions, i.e., middle and lower management, will more than any others in the organization need to be alert simultaneously to both ends and the methods for accomplishing them.

This brings us to our second point concerning vertical differentiation. This is the fact that different psychological and role requirements are made upon individuals occupying positions at various levels of the enterprise (Porter & Ghiselli, 1957; Katz & Kahn, 1966). This in turn implies that an individual who is an effective performer at one level may not necessarily be well adapted to the requirements at other levels. In the somewhat sardonic terms of a popular book (Peter & Hull, 1969), "individuals rise to a level of their incompetency." However, the important psychological point to emphasize here is that the extent to which this happens is affected both by the nature of the individuals working for an organization, in terms of their abilities and capacities, and by the ways in which the organization chooses to divide work along the vertical dimension. There is absolutely no *necessary* reason, however, for a given individual in a given organization to reach eventually an organizational level at which he is incompetent. Again, as with horizontal division of labor, there tend to be few if any universal guidelines for the "best" way to differentiate functions vertically.

Consequences of Differentiated Functions

Differentiated functions are a necessary part of any organization. Without this feature, people who are members would not be able to achieve anything beyond what would result if they all worked as isolated individuals. Without differentiated functions it is unlikely the organization would be able to survive—as an organization—for very long. Hence, the benefits of this feature are fairly obvious. However, there are also other consequences that occur which may or may not be so beneficial to the health of the organization. We will briefly look at two of these more important consequences below; they and others will, of course, be discussed at much greater length in succeeding chapters of the book.

Impact on Individuals' Interactions   The first impact of differentiated functions is the effect their existence has on the interactions that occur among members in an organization. The ways in which functions are divided and parceled out among different members, particularly with respect to the horizontal division of labor, strongly determine who will be able to interact with whom. While the division of labor in no way completely determines these interactions, it does place certain kinds of limitations on those that can occur. In essence, differentiation increases the likelihood that certain types of interactions will occur—e.g., sales manager X talks frequently with salesman Y—and on the other hand will decrease the likelihood that other interactions will take place—e.g., sales manager X seldom talks with production manager Z. Thus, even the most rational or logical differentiation of functions within an organization will have interactional consequences that cannot be entirely predicted in advance. The particular interactions that are encouraged or discouraged may or may not contribute to organizational goal attainment. Similarly, they may or may not contribute to individual satisfaction. In any event, the longer the period of time over which particular patterns of interactions occur, the more stabilized they become. This in turn leads to the development of the actual (as opposed to the official) *structure* of the organization. In this sense, structure and differentiated functions with their resulting interaction patterns cannot be considered as two separate entities.

Impact on Individuals' Attitudes   The second major type of consequence of differentiated functions is the effect on attitudes of individuals in different positions within the organization. When a person can or must concentrate on a particular or limited aspect of the total work of a group or section or organization, this will result in his developing certain viewpoints about these specialized activities since they are so much a part of his immediate experiences (e.g., Dearborn & Simon, 1958; Dalton, 1959; Herman & Hulin, 1972; Schneider, 1972; Porter & Stone, 1973). The viewpoints or attitudes that are developed about these activities will in turn affect the individual's relations with other people and such things as his motivation to perform effectively and his degree of commitment to the organization. While the nature of the differentiation of functions within a particular organization is not by any means the only influence on an individual's attitudes toward his job, peers, and organization, it is certainly one of the more crucial factors. We shall see this demonstrated at various points throughout other chapters in this book.

THE METHODS OF ORGANIZATION: INTENDED RATIONAL COORDINATION

If differentiated functions constitute one of the integral methods of organizations, their inevitable twin, so to speak, is "intended rational coordination." The former creates the need for the latter, which is the fourth defining characteristic of organizations (refer back to Figure 3-1).

"Rational coordination" refers to the putting together of the activities or effort of individuals in such a way that it makes sense—seems logical—to members of the organization, particularly to those who are most influential in the allocation of its resources. Although it is people who perform the activities, the coordination is centered on only certain things a person does, not all of his behavior. (See the earlier discussion of "partial inclusion" on p. 73.) Even in the most totalitarian organizations, only certain activities of individuals are coordinated, not the entire behavior of the person.

The other point to stress in the definition of rational coordination is the emphasis on its *conscious* nature (Barnard, 1938). In any organization at any time, coordination may fall apart due to unexpected events in the environment or poor planning or other factors, yet what is *attempted* in organizations is a conscious effort to put together activities in a meaningful way. In this sense, the coordination is "intendedly rational" whether or not it is successful in any ultimate sense. It is nonrandom even though it is surrounded by many events that are random.

We have referred to rational coordination as the twin of differentiated functions. This is because of the fact that the two must exist together if we are to have an organization. One is inextricably linked to the other in the following manner (Figure 3-5): The goal orientation of organizations leads, as we have discussed, to the existence of goals, and this fact in turn creates the necessity for differentiated functions; the combination of goals and differentiated functions leads to a situation where the functions become dependent upon each other, thus creating the need for rational coordination

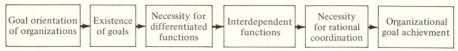

Figure 3–5 Sequence of relationships among certain organizational characteristics.

if organization goals are to be achieved or approached. Without rational coordination, differentiated functions lead, if not to chaos, at least to end results that are less than what could be achieved by individuals acting alone. Without differentiated functions, there is no necessity for rational coordination. The linkage between differentiated functions and rational coordination might well be summed up by a sort of reverse paraphrase of a well-known biblical quotation: "What, therefore, has been put asunder, the organization must put together."

Mechanisms for Achieving Rational Coordination

To achieve coordination, the organization relies on a variety of types of mechanisms or devices. Some of them will be elaborated on in greater detail in later chapters of this book, but it is useful to enumerate a few of the more important ones at this point in our discussion of coordination.

Subgoal Specification   The more tangible and specific subgoals of the organization can be made, and the greater the acceptance of them that can be obtained, the more likely it is that individual organization members will be able and willing to coordinate their activities with each other. Uncertainty on the part of members as to specific objectives is likely to interfere with any attempts to bring about an orchestration of individual effort toward common ends.

Hierarchical Authority Structure   We have already talked about the vertical differentiation of functions involving the creation of functions that differ in terms, among others, of the amount of authority involved. In organizations, such vertically differentiated functions are *arranged* in such a way that individuals occupying certain positions have *authority* over the activities of others and hence can attempt to achieve the rational coordination of such activities. By authority is meant a situation where "[a subordinate] permits his behavior to be guided by the decision of a superior, without independently examining the merits of that decision" (Simon, 1957, p. 11). That is, when authority is exercised the individual is voluntarily obeying a decision of someone else. In an organization, authority is said to exist in a *hierarchy* because some individuals are given more authority than others and each individual stands in some kind of authority relationship to every other individual. This provides one way for differentiated functions to take place in an integrated fashion.

Roles As a means of bringing about coordination, organizations attempt to develop stabilized expectations of behavior, particularly in relation to organizational positions (or sets of specialized functions). We speak of such sets of expectations that are attached to organizational positions as "roles." The existence of roles provides a coordinative device both for the members who occupy the positions to which the roles are attached and for other members of the organization who come into contact with them. For the occupants, the role helps define the limits of the activities to be performed by providing a basis for deciding what should be done, what is permissible to do, and what should not be done. If others who come into contact with the occupant are aware of the occupant's role—and hence of the activities expected, permitted, and prohibited—they in turn can adjust their own efforts to mesh with the occupant's.

Communication Organizations depend upon communication—the transmission of information from source to recipient—to facilitate the coordination of activities of members. Particularly where unanticipated environmental circumstances are encountered, communication is an essential device for achieving rational coordination. The pervasiveness of complaints about "communication problems" that exists throughout all types of enterprises attests to the important place that communication has in the life of organizations. If activities did not need to be coordinated, communication would be relegated to a much more peripheral position in the operation of organizations.

Individual Self-control A final type of mechanism that organizations depend on to achieve coordination is one that is not often made explicit in discussions of coordination, namely, individual self-control. If organizations had to rely entirely on external means—e.g., a hierarchy of authority—of establishing coordination it is unlikely that society would witness very much concerted activity. Individuals bring to the organization certain values, needs, and expectations (see Chapter 2) that serve to aid the coordination process. Many of these belief systems and motives that a person brings to the organization will contribute to coordination almost as a matter of course without the individual having to pay attention specifically to the problem. Others will contribute to deliberate coordination attempts by the individual. And, still others may, of course, hinder or impede the process of coordination. Despite the latter possibility, the fact remains that organizations, whether they know it or not, whether they like the idea or not, are dependent to a rather large degree on individual self-control to achieve coordination. That is why, in many organizations, attempts are made to increase the individual's identification with, and commitment to, the organization. The presumption is that where identification and commitment are obtained, it is easier to achieve coordination of individuals' effort and hence there are greater possibilities for organizational goal attainment.

Consequences of Rational Coordination

Rational coordination of activities produces consequences both for the organization and for the individual. From the organization's point of view, when disparate functions and activities can be brought under successful rational coordination, the organization achieves some measure of control over, or impact on, its environment. It is enabled, thereby, to cope with a dynamic set of conditions that surrounds it. Instead of being overwhelmed by the environment and falling prey to forces that would tend to dissolve or destroy it, it is enabled to maintain a continuity through time (which is the subject of the next section). Thus, both the necessity for, and the advantages of, rational coordination are obvious for the organization.

For the individual member, however, rational coordination may be more of a mixed blessing. On the one hand, it certainly contributes in a positive way to the individual's ability to achieve something beyond that which he could obtain by acting alone. Thus, it permits him to gain all the advantages that are attainable by associating himself with his fellows in an organization. Not only are organizational objectives facilitated by rational coordination but so are many individual goals. On the other hand, the requirements for rational coordination and the mechanisms the organization employs to bring it about serve to limit the freedom of the individual. If he is to coordinate his actions with others he must restrict his own actions or allow them to be restricted by others. This may lead to various types of individual-individual or individual-organization conflicts. Such conflicts, while sometimes ultimately quite beneficial to both parties, may prove harmful to the individual. Though a person in effect has no choice concerning participating in some types of coordinated activities if he is to join or remain with an organization, the extent to which this characteristic will be disadvantageous for him will depend on his own needs and beliefs as well as on the way in which the organization itself handles the requirement for rational coordination.

CONTINUITY OF ORGANIZATIONS

The fifth and final defining characteristic of organizations is their "continuity through time." (Refer back to Figure 3-1.) Presumably because it is a feature that tends to be so obvious, it is not as frequently mentioned in the various definitions of organizations as are the other four previously discussed characteristics—social composition, goal orientation, differentiated functions, and intended rational coordination. Nevertheless, it is a key defining element of organizations that serves to distinguish them from at least certain other social groupings such as casual parties, crowds, audiences, etc.

By "continuity through time" we do not mean an existence through any necessarily long or infinite amount of time. The phrase simply refers to an extension of relationships and interrelated activities longer than momentarily and on more than a one-time-only basis. The prospect of continuity is influential at the founding of an organization and continues to have an impact throughout its life. Nevertheless, organizations can and do go out of existence by design or even in spite of the best efforts of their members. So, the fact that an organization is operated by its members in such a way as to try to attain its perpetuity does not in any way guarantee that it will be able to survive over a given period of time.

What Is Continuous?

One may well ask, "*What* is continuous in an organization?" One theorist (Scott, 1964) would say: "The pursuit of . . . objectives" is what is continuous. Another (Gross, 1968) would say "interactions." We would say it is the totality of the goal-oriented pattern of both interactions and activities that tend to recur on a more or less regular basis through time that constitutes the continuity of an organization. This in no way implies a series of exact recurrences, since this would be impossible. Organizations and their environments are much too dynamic and complex to permit duplication from one point in time to the next. What is central here is the *regularity* in actions and relationships that seems to form some sensible thread from one time point to the next. Organizations definitely have this thread, while many other social groupings do not.

One element of organizations that ordinarily does not have continuity is the specific set of members. In fact, most organizations are purposely designed in such a way as to anticipate and take into account the fact that membership will be changing so that the continued existence of the organization will not depend on the continuity of membership of a particular individual or set of individuals. The organization thus attempts to preserve its own continuity by fostering the *substitutability* of its members. In actual practice, of course, organizations are often able to achieve only partial or limited substitutability. Hence, the organization's continuity is made much more dependent upon the continuity of membership of a particular individual than might be desired from the point of view of the organization. This is especially so to the extent that particular members contribute unique and highly needed personal resources (ideas, experience, abilities, etc.).

Impact of Continuity

The most important aspect of the continuity characteristic of organizations for our purposes in this book, however, is the influence it has on individuals' behavior. That is, individuals *assume* an organization will have continuity (except under unusual circumstances where there is reason to believe the organization will not survive), just as they assume that it is oriented toward some kind of goal or goals. This assumption by members—that the organization has a future—pervades all aspects of an individual's actions and his interactions with others. (In laboratory situations with artificially created groups it is the lack of such a belief in a group's future that makes it so difficult to replicate real-life organizational behavior.) Such assumptions are, of course, frequently more implicit than explicit. Nevertheless, even the fact that the individual takes for granted that there will be continuity is likely to influence his attitudes toward his job (e.g., "it will get better"), his organization (e.g., "this company has a good retirement plan"), his relations with others (e.g., "that ought to show him that next time I mean business"), and the way in which he performs his activities (e.g., "if I work too fast, the boss may give me more work"). If individuals did not hold the assumption that organizations have a degree of continuity, it is unlikely that organizations would ever be able to last for very long in the first place. It is, therefore, a rather critical feature.

ORGANIZATIONS AS SOCIAL SYSTEMS

For analytical purposes, up to now in this chapter we have focused successively on the fundamental defining characteristics of organizations. We have treated them separately, when in fact they are necessarily and intimately related to each other. Here in this final section we will stress these relationships among the characteristics.

In recent years, it has become increasingly common among organization theorists to treat organizations as "systems" (see, for example, Etzioni, 1964; Thompson, 1967; Berrien, 1968; Katz & Kahn, 1966). As typically defined, a "system" is thought of as "a set of components surrounded by a boundary which accepts inputs from some other system and discharges outputs into another system" (Berrien, 1968, p. 111). Thus, "system theory is basically concerned with problems of relationships, of structure, and of interdependence rather than the constant attributes of objects" (Katz & Kahn, 1966, p. 18). In other words, when we are talking about organizations as systems we are attending to the *combination* of parts and elements that form some sort of a unique whole. The focus is not on a part as it stands by itself, but rather on how the part interacts with and is related to other parts.

Most, if not all, organization theorists who take an explicit systems approach go one step further in their analysis and designate organizations as "open" systems. By the word "open" in this context is meant the fact that the parts of a system (organization) do not completely determine the system's outcomes by themselves, but rather interact with an outside environment that represents situational uncertainty. Thus the parts of the organization system are subject to influence by environmental stimuli not directly contained within the system.

For our purposes here, and throughout the remainder of this book, the two major aspects of an open systems approach to organizations that will be most important are (1) the fact that different characteristics or attributes of organizations do have a mutual interdependence with other attributes and cannot be regarded as completely separate and independent features and (2) the fact that organizations are in a constant exchange interaction with— receiving input from, and discharging output into—an uncertain environment. Let us examine each of these points in greater detail.

By abstracting from definitions of organizations, we have earlier identified five key characteristics of organizations:

1   Social composition
2   Goal orientation
3   Differentiated functions
4   Intended rational coordination
5   Continuity through time

If we now look at them together as a group, we can see how each one cannot stand alone but must be considered as interdependent with the others. Each one influences the others and in turn is influenced by them.

If we pick the social composition of organizations as a starting point for examining the interrelatedness of these five characteristics, we can think of the following: the kinds of individuals—in terms of abilities, needs, interests—who form the social composition of (or, input into) organizations will have a decided impact on which particular organization goals are pursued, how the different functions will be divided up among the membership, what kinds of coordinative processes will be most effective, and whether the organization is likely to be able to survive through a given period of time. A change in the nature of the social composition, such as a different recruitment strategy (for example, in universities the possible change from restrictive admission policies based on high school performance and test scores, to an open-enrollment policy), can drastically affect what happens to each of the other characteristics in a given organization. A failure, for example, to recruit employees with a certain level of abilities, may result in the organization having to modify the kinds of goals it is aiming for, allocate functions on a different basis, restructure the authority hierarchy, and so forth.

Now, let us pick a different characteristic, say, intended rational coordination, to again illustrate the interconnectedness of the five character-istics. If, in a given organization, certain kinds of information are communi-cated from one source to a set of recipients, this can impact the social groupings that occur, the nature of the goals adopted, the assignment of tasks to individuals, and the degree to which continuity is assured. This of course does not mean that each and every communication will have widespread repercussions. It simply indicates one cannot understand com-munications in organizations without taking into account their relationship to other organization characteristics.

The other essential systems point to emphasize is the embedment of the organization in an uncertain and changing environment. The in-terdependence of characteristics we have discussed above takes place not in a static situation but in a dynamic one. The organization, and its members, cannot control all, or even most, of the parts of the environment that have a potential for impact on it. This implies that "the central problem for complex organizations is coping with uncertainty" (Thompson, 1967). System the-orists would say that for organizations to survive they must reach some sort of equilibrium—or steady state—with the environment. They must be able to tolerate and adapt to the changing forces in the environment. In practice, of course, some organizations are not able to do this successfully and their survival is jeopardized. The important point is that even organizations that have been successful in the past in achieving such an equilibrium with the environment cannot in any way be guaranteed continued survival without making constant changes. If the environment were static, the organization's characteristics could remain fixed and what worked in the past would preserve the organization. The environment, unfortunately for organiza-tions, is not static. Therefore, nothing is, or can be, ever really "set" in an organization—a system composed of people.

REVIEW AND DISCUSSION QUESTIONS

1 Does the fact that there is considerable variability among organizations preclude one from studying them? How does this variability affect the precision with which organizations can be described?
2 Organizations are seen differently by scholars from different academic dis-ciplines. How does the student of administration benefit from being able to "dissect" organizations in several ways? Would the study of organizations be facilitated if attention were limited to only *one* perspective (that of the sociologist, that of the psychologist, etc.)?

3 Consider the "five fundamental characteristics" of organizations. How can various social and physical collectivities be contrasted with organizations? For instance, how would organizations be contrasted with mobs? How would an organization be contrasted with a physical system (e.g., a computer)?

4 Does the fact that individuals are generally only partially "included" in making objectives hamper the ability of organizations to reach objectives (i.e., accomplish goals of the organizations)?

5 Contrast various organizations on the degree to which their members are "included" in making objectives. Consider such organizations as business firms, universities, correctional institutions, hospitals, etc.

6 Compare and contrast formal and informal groups in terms of how they originate and what effects they have.

7 Organizational members are generally part of not only the formal organization but also several informal sets of employees associated with the larger formal organization. How does such overlapping membership influence the operations of the formal organization?

8 What functions are served by organizational goals?

9 Compare and contrast official, operative, and operational goals.

10 Explain the importance of "means-end chains" in organizations.

11 Are there any functional features of "means-end inversions?" That is, does the fact that in some instances means become the end indicate some form of "pathological" behavior on the part of the organization and its members?

12 How can horizontal differentiation and vertical differentiation be contrasted? Is it possible to simultaneously differentiate along both the horizontal and vertical dimensions?

13 How has your own behavior in an organization been affected by the knowledge that the organization would continue (at least for a while)? Cite an example.

Chapter 4

Behavior in Organizational Settings: The Interaction of Individuals and Organizations

When human behavior in complex social situations is discussed in the research literature, mention frequently is made of the classic formulation of Kurt Lewin that $B = f(P,E)$—that is, that behavior is some interactive function of both the person and his environment. This formulation is surely correct in principle. It is, however, sometimes subtly seductive, in that it can lead one to think that he knows much more about what causes people to act the way they do than is actually the case.

Consider, for example, an organizational setting in which two workers are observed on the same job, under the same supervision. One worker is producing large amounts of output of apparently high quality. He is singing to himself as he works, and seems to be prospering in his job. The other individual is turning out neither very much nor very high quality work, and is observed frequently muttering to himself as he works and finding excuse after excuse to take breaks from his work activities. The Lewinian formulation can help keep us from falling into an interpretative trap that has caught many a manager—namely, that one individual is a "good" employee and that the other is a "bad" one. Instead, we are prompted by Lewin's equation to explore the possibility that the observed behavioral differences may be a function of some *interaction* between the characteristics of the organization-al environment and the characteristics of the individual worker. The performance of Kipsy on the information clerk job described in Chapter 1 is another example of how both the characteristics of the individual and the nature of the work environment must be considered if we are to understand behavior at work.

Critical to such an analysis, then, is the goodness of the fit between the specific work situation and the specific individuals under consideration. This approach raises—and forces consideration of—the rather optimistic possibil-ity that there is another type of job or work situation in which the apparent-ly "bad" worker described above might prosper and perform quite effectively.

The problem with analyzing behavior in terms of individual-environment interactions—and this is the point at which the Lewinian notion can become seductive—is that it is all too easy to conclude that the observed differences in performance come about simply because one person fits better with his environment than does another. Such an explanation in fact explains nothing at all, and provides no clues about how things might be changed (e.g., by selection or placement, by redesigning work, by reorienting supervision) to achieve a better person-environment fit.

To achieve an understanding of individual-environment interaction which will provide a basis for predicting and for changing human behavior in complex situations, we will require considerable elaboration of the terms in the basic Lewinian equation. In particular, we must be able to specify in some detail (1) those attributes of the individual which are relevant to the behaviors of interest, (2) analogous attributes of the environment—or, in the present case, of the organizational environment—and, importantly, (3) the way or ways in which these two sets of attributes interact.

In Chapters 2 and 3 of this book we examined, at a fairly general level of analysis, the characteristics of individuals and of organizational environ-ments which we believe may be especially relevant to understanding behavior in organizations. In this chapter we will attempt to set forth some ideas about how individual-level factors and organizational-level factors *jointly* determine individual behavior in organizations. Our intent is to provide a general framework within which it will be possible to discuss many of the organizational problems and processes which are the focus of chapters later in the book.

A VIEW OF INDIVIDUAL-ORGANIZATION INTERACTION

One important way that organizations contribute to the individual-organization interaction is by providing the *stimuli* to which individuals in the organization are exposed. These stimuli differ, of course, in nature, pattern, and sequencing depending upon the particular organization of interest and the position of a specific individual within that organization. Since many individuals in an organization will be exposed to the same or to similar organizationally supplied stimuli (e.g., the same physical building, the same supervisor, the same technology, etc.), it obviously can be useful to examine the patterns of stimuli which impinge on the members of a given organization.

But different individuals, of course, do not react the same way, even to identical stimuli. So such an analysis also would have to include those individual-difference factors which affect the way in which stimuli are perceived, processed, and acted upon. Just as different organizations provide different sets of stimuli to their members so do different members respond differently to those stimuli. Both sources of variation must surely be included in any adequate analysis of individual-organization interaction.

While it would be possible to discuss individual-organization interaction in detail using general terms (such as "stimuli"), it probably makes more sense for present purposes to conceive of the contributions of both organizations and individuals to the interaction in somewhat more substantive terms. In the paragraphs to follow we will suggest one way of putting some "flesh" on the bare-boned analysis of individual-organization interaction outlined above—which, hopefully, will enhance our ability to make predictions about the behavioral outcomes of given interactions. In particular, it will be suggested that both organizations and individuals bring identifiable demands to the interaction, and that each contributes its particular kind of resource as well. The dynamics of individual-organization interaction, then, have to do with the ways that these demands and resources are combined and exchanged.

What the Organization Contributes to the Interaction

The stimuli that the organization supplies to individuals within it may be partitioned into two classes. One class of stimuli is manifested in the *expectations* that are communicated by the organization to its members, and the other can be conceived of as *resources* that are available in the organizational environment for use by members of the organization.

Expectations   An organization communicates expectations to individuals within it as a consequence of their membership and their specific position within the organization. Indeed, by their very nature, organizations *must* communicate expectations to their members—and enforce compliance with those expectations to some extent. To do otherwise would be to allow the inherent tendency of social systems toward *dis*order (i.e., the law of entropy) to prevail, ultimately resulting in the dissolution of the organization itself.

This point can be illustrated in terms of the defining attributes of organizations discussed at length in Chapter 3. It was proposed there that (among other things) organizations are characterized by (1) orientation toward goals or objectives, (2) differentiated functions within the organization, and (3) rational coordination of the various subsystems of the organization. All three of these attributes require that there be limits on the amount of discretion each organization member has to choose what he shall do, when, and with whom.

In other words, organizations must, to some extent, develop and use systems of *control* which ensure (1) that the activities of organization members are, in fact, oriented toward the goals of the organization; (2) that organization members who are assigned responsibility for carrying out specific functional activities in the interest of organizational objectives actually perform those functions—and *not* other functions which are the assigned responsibility of others in the organization; and (3) that explicit means of coordinating among individuals and subunits of the organization be developed and followed—so that the activities of organization members are in fact *organized*, and organized in such a way that the various "pieces" of the organization combine effectively toward achievement of organizational goals.

To ensure that the demands or expectations that organizations place on individuals are experienced and responded to by them, various formal mechanisms are used. Examples of these mechanisms (which will be discussed in detail in subsequent chapters in this book) include (1) selection systems, which are intended to ensure that only individuals who *can* meet the expectations that the organization will place on them are permitted membership, (2) socialization and training procedures, to help members increase their understanding of organizational expectations and their capability to fulfill them, (3) evaluation and reward systems, which provide explicit contingencies between whether or not an individual meets the expectations of the organization and his receipt of rewards from the organization, (4) measurement and control systems, which monitor the degree to which the objectives of the organization are being met, and provide the means for remedial action, and (5) supervisory practices, which can be designed in order to help the individual effectively meet organizational expectations—as well as to check on the degree to which he actually is doing so. In effect, the needs of the organization are translated down through the means-end chain described in Chapter 3, and the ultimate result is that individual organization members experience a set of expectations or demands relevant to their own personal behavior.

From the point of view of the individual, the organizational expectations of him may seem to come from a variety of different sources. They may be communicated by the individual's supervisor (e.g., "John, we encourage employees here to get to work right at 8:30"), by his peers and subordinates acting to perpetuate and enforce traditional ways of doing things in the organization—or at times even from people who themselves are not members of the organization (e.g., a client of the organization).

Further, expectations may be either an *explicit* part of the individual's regular terms of employment with the organization, or they may be *implicit* in the activities he does at work—e.g., when an assembly-line employee confronts a very fast-paced line and decides that he is expected to produce large quantities of work, but that he need not try to do especially high-quality work. The fact that expectations are not always explicit deserves emphasis: Many of the most potent and pervasive demands of an organization on its members can be very subtly or implicitly communicated to them—as, for example, when no one tells the junior faculty member that he does not go to the faculty meeting of a prestigious Ivy League university in a sport shirt, but he quickly finds out what the expectation is when he attends his first faculty meeting in informal attire.

Resources   The second kind of contribution organizations make to the individual-organization interaction is the provision of a diversity of resources for use by organization members. While a "resource" can be anything which an organization member potentially can find useful, money is of course one of the important resources organizations offer their employees. Sometimes resources are deliberately and explicitly supplied as an inducement to organizational membership (e.g., "our plant has an excellent gym and pool for you to use during lunch hours and after work") but more often they are made available nonintentionally as a by-product of something which is done more directly in pursuit of organizational goals. Thus, organizations may provide as potential resources for employees items as diverse as interesting work activities; friendly colleagues; a pleasant, comfortable work place; a good technical library; etc. Organizational expectations, of course, in themselves can sometimes serve as resources, depending upon the attributes of the organization members. An example is the expectation that a salesman will spend a good portion of his time on the road. For an employee who likes to travel, the chance to do so is a resource for personal fulfillment which is available to him because he holds that particular job in that particular organization. We will have more to say about some of the implications and motivational advantages of achieving a congruence of organizational expectations and resources for organization members shortly.

What the Individual Contributes to the Interaction

The contributions of the individual to the interaction also may be partitioned into two classes: *needs and goals* and *skills and energies.*

Needs and Goals First, the individual brings to the organization his own more or less unique pattern of needs and goals. He has a strong *personal* stake in his organizational membership, and the nature of this personal stake can and does powerfully affect the nature of his behavior in the organization and his response to organizational demands. As was suggested in Chapter 2 it is incomplete (and incorrect) to view the individual solely as a reactive entity who responds only to organizational initiatives. Indeed, researchers have shown that individuals actively seek out opportunities to satisfy their own personal needs and to achieve their own goals within the organizational context. The personal needs and goals of organization members, of course, vary widely from individual to individual. One person may be oriented toward achievement and growth in his career; another may care most strongly about achieving important social satisfaction; a third may consider his career in the organization exclusively in terms of maintaining his job security.

It should be noted that one philosophy of management maintains that "irrelevant" individual differences (such as needs and goals) should be stamped out as far as possible in the organization through the standardized design of jobs, the development of potent and uniform incentive systems, the institution of close supervisory practices, etc. The intent of these practices is to ensure uniform behavior of all employees working in particular positions in the organization (cf. the example of Eric's firm in Chapter 1). Our view, as will become apparent at many points throughout this book, is that this philosophy underestimates both (1) the degree to which it is *possible* to "stamp out" such individual differences and (2) the negative organizational consequences of doing so. Some of the reasons for this view should become apparent in the pages that follow.

Skills and Energies Second, the individual provides skills and energies which may be applied to organizationally relevant activities.* Both skill and energy may be considered as resources provided by organization members (analogous to the resources made available by organizations). Considering skills and energies as resources assumes, of course, that the

*By skills we mean those attributes of the individual which determine his competence to perform activities—be they motor activities, cognitive activities, or interpersonal activities (see Chap. 2 for a more detailed discussion of human skills and abilities). "Skill," as used here, is more specific than "ability" which is seen as a more generic term; i.e., if one has the *ability* to deal with abstract materials he may also (but need not necessarily) have the *skill* necessary for structural-stress analysis in an engineering firm.

individual is a member of the organization. When a person declines organizational membership, he may be seen as withholding his resources from it, and no individual-organization interaction is possible apart from the brief encounter which may be necessary to decide not to interact. (As will be seen in Chapter 5, this encounter itself may be viewed in the present framework. The period of individual-organization interaction may be very short in such cases, but it still appears to follow the principles which will be explicated below.)

While there clearly are upper limits to the amount of skill and the amount of energy a person can contribute to the organization, the individual generally has more discretionary control over the amount of energy he expends in his work activities than he does over the skill level he brings to bear on his work. For practical and research purposes it usually is not necessary to determine the upper limit of the individual's energy. The reason is that most organizational activities involve the use of substantially less than the total amount of energy a person has available. There are some exceptions to this generalization (e.g., the combat soldier who becomes physically exhausted after days in the field, or the air-traffic controller who "burns out" after several weeks of twelve-hour days), but ordinarily the average person's energy resources will be more than adequate for most jobs. With respect to skills, on the other hand, it is quite possible for an individual to be placed in a position that exceeds his currently developed capacities. Since he cannot easily or quickly raise them voluntarily, the organization often takes steps to determine this upper limit of skills in advance of hiring.

Dynamics of the Organization-Individual Interaction

We have suggested that organizations can be seen as providing individuals in the organization with (1) expectations and (2) resources, and that individuals provide the organization with (1) needs and goals—which can be viewed as their *demands* on the organization—and (2) skills and energies—their *resources*. These contributions are summarized in Figure 4-1.

As indicated by the arrows in the figure, the separate demands of individuals and of organizations serve to tax the resources of the other. That is, the communicated expectations of organizations place requirements on the skills and energies of individuals, while the needs and goals of individuals call on certain organizational resources for their fulfillment. It is clear that, if the individual-organization relationship is to be maintained over the long term, both the individual and the organization must find some responsiveness in the other to their own requirements. Thus, if an individual is unable (through inadequate use of skill or energy) to meet the basic, minimal

Figure 4–1 Summary of contributions to individual-organization interaction.

expectations of him by the organization (e.g., showing up at work with reasonable frequency and spending some time in the vicinity of the work station), then it would be expected that the representatives of the organization would seek termination of the individual's membership. This example deals with an employing organization; the same process holds for voluntary organizations as well—but rather than an active decision to terminate on the part of organizational authorities, the individual may simply be allowed to "slip away" with a gradual decrease in the tendency of organizational members to reinvolve the individual. An analogous process operates for individuals: if a person finds that membership in an organization is totally inimical to the satisfaction of his needs or the achievement of his goals, then his interest in maintaining membership and involvement will decrease.

To summarize, then, it is proposed that the degree to which organizations value and seek to perpetuate the contributions of their members varies directly with the extent to which these contributions fulfill the expectations that the organization has of the individual. And, by the same token, the degree to which individuals value and seek to maintain membership in organizations and involvement in organizational activities varies as a direct function of the degree to which they find that such membership and involvement serve to satisfy their own personal needs or facilitate the achievement of their goals. [It should be noted that the model of individual-organization interaction proposed here has much in common with the "inducements-contributions" theory of March and Simon (1958), and with the "exchange" theories of Homans (1961) and of Barrett (1970).]

IMPLICATIONS FOR PERSONAL AND ORGANIZATIONAL EFFECTIVENESS

There are a number of ways in which the resources and demands of individuals and organizations may show relatively good or poor fit with one another. In this section we examine the implications of several resource-demand fits for the overall effectiveness of the individual-organization relationship.

1 *Individual skills and energies are not adequate to meet organizational expectations, and organizational resources are not adequate to fulfill individual needs and goals.* This is a generally dismal situation, and one that is unlikely to persist for very long. The individual is not up to meeting organizational expectations of him, nor is the organization capable of offering resources which, in other circumstances, might serve as an inducement for the individual to upgrade his skills or energies to a satisfactory level. Termination of the relationship between the individual and the organization clearly is predicted—and indeed usually will occur before actual membership in the organization is negotiated. An example of this state of affairs might involve an individual with good clerical skills (but poor interpersonal skills) who is seeking a job where he can develop his aptitude to work with numbers. If the job he were seeking was that of a receptionist in a public relations firm, we can be reasonably certain that neither the organization nor the prospective employee would be interested in pursuing the possibility of employment very far.

2 *Individual skills and energies are not adequate to meet organizational expectations, but organization resources are adequate to fulfill individual needs and goals.* There is somewhat more potential in this situation than in the first one, but it is up to the individual to realize that potential if he can. An example would be an employee of very low ability who found a particular organization highly attractive and stimulating—but who was not able to meet the performance standards of the organization. Since the organization did meet the personal needs and goals of the individual, we might predict that he would, say, study after work hours in order to boost his skill level to a point at which he could meet the minimal expectations of the organization—and thereby be allowed to remain an employee. The degree to which the individual would try to improve his skills, of course, would be expected to vary as a function of the degree to which the resources present in the organizational environment could in fact satisfy his important personal needs and goals.

3 *Individual skills and energies are adequate to meet organizational expectations, but organizational resources are not adequate to fulfill individual needs and goals.* This condition represents perhaps the classic case of the disaffected employee—he can do the work, but he can find little in it that is personally rewarding. An example is the assembly-line worker making weld after weld in exactly the same way on identical automobile fenders as they pass by. To the extent that the individual has personal needs and goals (e.g., increasing his technical competence) which require more from the organization than the opportunity to weld repetitively and be paid

for it, then this particular individual-organizational relationship will represent a poor fit from the point of view of the employee.

It would be expected that individuals would leave the organization under these circumstances, except when one (or more) of three conditions exist: First, the employee might stay if he feels that he has a reasonable possibility of bringing about sufficient changes in the organization or his role in the organization to increase the personal payoff of his membership. This might be the case, for example, if the employee believes that by staying on and "taking it" for a few months or years he eventually can be promoted to another position in which it will be possible for him to fulfill better his personal needs or goals.

Second, the employee would be expected to stay if he had no better alternatives—e.g., if the labor market were especially unfavorable for individuals with his set of skills, if he could not make as much money elsewhere, or if the trauma associated with resigning were sufficiently severe that the negative consequences of staying were the lesser of two unfortunate possibilities.

And third, the individual would be expected to persist to the extent that he had, over time, become "locked into" the organization because of the accumulated worth of one or two organizationally provided resources. A frequent example is the company retirement program, which can represent a severe loss to the individual if he leaves after he has accumulated a substantial retirement investment. Many of the individual's needs and goals may be continually frustrated by membership in the organization in such cases, but accepting those frustrations may represent less of a loss to the individual than accepting the loss of the accumulated benefits which would be the case if he resigned. The second and third of these reasons for staying often combine to leave an individual in an unfortunate position without many viable alternatives—for example, when an employee gets a job during a time of labor surplus, finds that he is not prospering in the work but cannot leave because of the scarce job supply, and much later (when the job market "opens up") finds that he cannot leave because of a loss of accumulated financial benefits.

When the individual stays in a personally unsatisfactory organizational situation for either of the two latter reasons (i.e., no better alternative is available, or he has become locked in), there is little reason to expect that the individual will be motivated to try to do an especially good job within the organization—since his only personal stake in the organization is to remain a member of it. The first reason for staying which was suggested (to try to change the organization, or to get promoted within the organization to a better position) can in some circumstances lead to strong positive work motivation, since the individual may believe that he will be able to get moved from his dissatisfying job more quickly if he does in fact do good work consistently while he occupies the personally unsatisfactory position.

One of the long-term effects of membership in an organization in which one is not fulfilling his personal needs or goals is a possible change in those needs or goals themselves. That is, if an individual stays as a welder or stamp-licker long enough, the needs and goals which were present when he began work on the job may decrease in importance and he may become, if not actually happy in his work, at least passively accepting of it as his lot in life. To the extent that this process is taking place on a widespread basis in contemporary society (and, as will be seen in Chapter 10, there is some evidence that this may in fact be the case for many lower-level jobs in industrial organizations), then this particular type of misfit between organization and individual may have some rather profound implications for the long-term changes which take place in the society itself.

4 *Individual skills and energies are adequate to meet organizational expectations, and organizational resources are adequate to fulfill individual needs and goals*. At first glance, this combination appears to be ideal for both the individual and the organization: the individual is competent to meet the expectations that the organization has for him, and resources are present in the organization which are sufficient to satisfy the individual. The fact of the matter, however, is that the relationship between the individual and the organization is only *potentially* a mutually healthy and satisfactory one. The possibility still remains, even though all resources are adequate, that organizational demands and individual needs or goals may be in conflict.

Consider, for example, an employee who has strong social needs, and who works on a job with several other like-minded employees assembling complicated electronic devices. The employee is highly skilled, and the organization has strong expectations for very careful and high-quality work. It is clear that (1) the individual skills are adequate to meet the organizational demands for high quality and that (2) the resources are present in the organization to satisfy the employee's personal needs—i.e., other people who also are strongly motivated to engage in meaningful social relationships. Yet it is also clear that either the organization or the individual is going to have to "give" somewhat in this situation, in that the demands of each are to some extent incompatible with the demands of the other. If the employee is to maximize satisfaction of his personal needs within the organization, his attentiveness to his work will suffer, and in all probability so will his quality level. If the expectations of the organization for especially high quality work are met, then the employee's opportunity for meaningful social encounters will decrease and his personal satisfaction will suffer. The point is that *even though all the required resources are present in the organizational setting for meeting the demands of both the organization and the individual*, it often is impossible for individual and organizational outcomes to be jointly and simultaneously maximized.

There are two general ways to remedy this conflict and increase the chances that the needs of both the organization and the individual will be met. First, a kind of "psychological contract" (Levinson, 1965) can be established, in which both the individual and the organization are dependent upon meeting the demands of the other in order to obtain their *own* needed resources. That is, the individual may choose to meet organizational demands to the degree that the organizations makes available to him the resources he needs to fulfill his personal needs and goals. And, at the same time, the organization may elect to provide these resources to the individual only to the extent that the individual meets the expectations that the organization has of him.

In the example given above, an arrangement might be worked out so that employees would be given frequent breaks from work when the equipment they assembled was error-free. The employees could use this time for social interaction—thereby satisfying their needs—but the availability of the time would depend upon their doing high-quality work. The organization would have its demands for high-quality work met—but at the cost of providing explicitly social time for the employees so that they would no longer want or need to divert their attention from the work to engage in social activities while actually on the job.

It should be noted that in bargains of the type discussed above, both the organization and the individual are settling for less than an optimal state of affairs; each is, in effect, giving up something to obtain resources which are more centrally important. In the above example, the organization is giving up having the employees on the job all of each workday—and is undoubtedly losing some amount of production quantity by doing so—but is gaining especially high quality in that work which is done. And the individuals in the example are relinquishing the chance to talk on the job throughout the day—but are gaining the chance for more relaxed periods in which they may devote all their attention to social matters.

Another example of this type of bargain or contract—and one that is perhaps especially typical of contemporary business practice—is the use of piece-rate pay incentive plans. These plans pay individuals in direct proportion to the amount of acceptable work that the individuals produce. The demand of the organization is for the individual to turn out large quantities of work; the resource which is made contingent upon the individual's meeting this demand is money. And, to the extent that money is instrumental for the satisfaction of employee needs, the procedure can and does work—i.e., the employee can choose to use his skills and expend his energy primarily to meet the expectations that have been communicated to him in order to receive the additional money. This example also illustrates that something is usually relinquished by one or both of the parties of a mutually contingent exchange in order for the bargain to work. Unfortunately for those who advocate widespread use of pay incentive plans, there is evidence that the satisfactions which must sometimes be relinquished by the employee for incentive plans to work (e.g., the feeling of personal control and autonomy in one's work) are in some cases sufficiently important to employees that they become unwilling to participate fully and honestly in the plans. This, of course, can negate any advantage of the plans to the organization and may lead to a long-term deterioration of the individual-organization relationship itself. (Pay procedures and their effects are discussed in detail in Chapter 12.)

A second general possibility for optimizing the outcomes of the individual-organization interaction is to attempt to design the organizational environment so that both the individual and the organization can maximize the degree to which their respective demands are met—without having to compromise or relinquish important personal outcomes in the bargain. This optimal state of affairs can come about *when one party to the organization-individual interaction obtains his needed resource in the process of meeting the demands of the other party*—and vice versa. An example of this situation might involve a highly skilled repairman, who likes nothing better than the feeling he gets when he fixes a piece of complicated equipment quickly and elegantly. If the expectations of the organization in which this repairman works is that he do quick and elegant work, and if the organization provides the repairman with many complicated jobs on which he can use his valued skills and abilities, then the demands and resources of the individual and the organization should be mutually reinforcing. The repairman can achieve his personal goals *best* by working hard and effectively to meet the demands that the organization makes of him. And the organization can achieve the highest fulfillment of its expectations simply by providing the worker with an ample supply of complicated, challenging jobs. Each party to the interaction in this case does in effect what it prefers anyway, and the other party to the interaction prospers as a consequence.

Other ways of discussing this type of individual-organization interaction are in terms of the "congruence" of the goals of individuals and of organizations (McGregor, 1960, 1967); in terms of the "integration" of the individual and the organization (Argyris, 1964); or as a "fusion" process between individuals and organizations (Bakke, 1950). Whatever the terminology and conceptual frame of reference, the message is similar—namely, that it sometimes is possible for both individuals and organizations to prosper by virtue of their relationship with one another. Yet it should be noted that it often is quite difficult to realize a genuinely mutually satisfactory relationship in real-world organizations. Indeed, in most situations one or both parties of the interaction will be required to relinquish some important valued outcomes in order to maintain the viability of the individual-organization relationship.

There are a number of different routes which may be taken to maximize the mutually reinforcing aspects of the relationship and to minimize the losses that the parties to the relationship must assume. These steps will be discussed in greater detail in subsequent chapters; they involve the ways people are selected for and placed in organizations (see Chapter 5), the way the work itself is designed (see Chapter 10), and the nature of the supervisory and control practices (see Chapters 9 and 14), to name only a few. In point of fact, of course, nearly all organizational practices affect in one way or another the nature of the individual-organization interaction, and therefore all must be considered in any full-fledged attempt to achieve meaningful congruence of the goals of an organization and the goals of its members.

IMPLICATIONS FOR UNDERSTANDING BEHAVIOR WITHIN ORGANIZATIONS

In the previous pages we have examined four major types of relationships between individuals and organizations, and have discussed some of the circumstances under which the outcome of those relationships are likely to be satisfactory to both parties. We now turn to some general implications of this material for furthering our understanding of organizational behavior.

The Experienced Organization

The mailroom clerk in the New York headquarters of the telephone company undoubtedly views that organization differently enough from the way the president of the company views it that an outsider would have difficulty understanding that the two individuals were describing the same organization. And the janitor of the Meadville, Pennsylvania, central telephone office would surely have yet another quite different perspective.

The reason for disparate views of the organization by members at different levels in the hierarchy, or with different functional specialties, is simply that few individual organization members see very much of the *whole* organization. The janitor may have to formulate his entire experience of the organization solely on the basis of the night foreman—whom he sees once each evening, two operators who work the evening shift, the physical premises of the organization, and the company magazine. In other words, the individual's "organizational horizon" is quite limited. The horizon of the company president is rather more extensive—but it still is limited in important ways because of the impossibility for him to maintain contact with the entire company. Some chief executives try to widen their views of their organizations by actively seeking out contacts with employees representing a diverse number of hierarchical and functional positions. The fact of the matter is, however, that most of the impact of organizations on their members—be they presidents or janitors—comes jointly from the people the members associate with in the course of their organizational activities and from the tasks they do. Indeed, it is doubtful that *anyone* in even a small organization has a good personal "feel" for the organization as a whole. The limited horizon of any particular individual in an organization—and the limited influence that "distant" parts of the organization can have on that person—are illustrated in Figure 4-2.

This does not deny that organizations in some sense exist. In Chapter 3

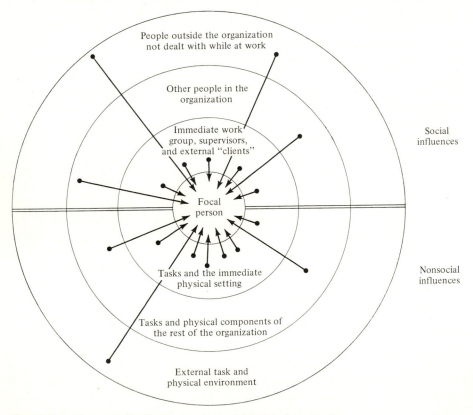

Figure 4–2   Sources of influence on the individual in the organization.

we have suggested several definitional criteria which we are willing to use to understand what organizations are and what they are not; we have no wish to engage in a philosophical discussion at this juncture about the existence of human organizations. Instead, our intent is to emphasize that, even though very large numbers of people may be members of the same organization, in fact they experience that organization differently—and, importantly, the determinants of their experience or perception of the organization are physically or functionally "close" to themselves. It follows, therefore, that when we speak of the impact of the characteristics of organizations on individual organization members, we must speak in terms of the impact of people or things with which the individual comes into personal contact. Thus, if we want to understand the behavior of the janitor, we don't research what the company president says to his vice-presidents (or to an outside researcher); instead, we look at what the janitor's foreman says to the janitor—including what the janitor's foreman says about what the president says about company policy.

Bridging Levels of Analysis The implication is that for developing full understanding of the behavior of organization members, we should prefer variables which reflect aspects of the organization which are available to the experience of the individual (such as communicated expectations about performance from supervisors) rather than more remote and abstract characterizations of the organization (such as "the number of hierarchical levels" or "average supervisory span of control"). To understand the impact of these latter types of variables requires that several intermediate causal links be specified between the variables themselves and the individual behaviors of interest.

Such more abstract and general variables are, of course, often very valuable as summary indices, and they may be useful in developing and testing general predictions about organizational behavior. The point is that in order to develop *understanding* of a specific phenomenon of interest, we need first to understand the immediate causes of that phenomenon, and then look to the question of how those first causes are related to summarizing concepts at a more molar or abstract level. This, of course, would lead one gradually through several "levels of analysis" in considering the phenomenon—from its most immediate (and also most molecular) causes, to the most remote (and also most abstract and general) causes (cf. our earlier discussion of levels of analysis in Chapter 3).

Thus, when we speak of the communicated expectations an individual receives from an organization and examine how those expectations interact with the resources and the personal needs of the individual (as in Figure 4-1), we must take care to note that those expectations necessarily arise from the environment as it is experienced by the individual himself. This includes, of course, expectations which come from virtually any aspect of the organization with which the individual has direct contact—peers, subordinates, the technology with which he works, and so on. The point is simply that for understanding individual behavior in organizations we must attend to causal factors present in the organization *as it exists for the particular organization members of interest.*

Individual Appraisal of the Organization   Even if it were possible to locate two individuals in an organization who, by virtue of holding nearly identical positions, were exposed to highly similar patterns of stimuli in the course of their organizational activities, it is doubtful that they would experience the nature of the expectations placed on them (and the resources available to them) in very similar terms. There are at least two reasons for this. First, the quantity of stimuli available to any given organization member is substantially greater than he is capable of dealing with in the course of his everyday activities in the organization—and as a result individuals must somehow restrict the number of stimulus items they attend to. Since different people use different rules for reducing the number of stimuli they experience, there will be a diversity of perceptions of what the organization *is* and what expectations are being sent from the organization to the individual—even for those people who occupy the same or similar formal positions in the organization.

Second, as pointed out in Chapter 2, individuals selectively distort stimuli they encounter in the organizational environment as a function of their personal needs, values, and goals. Communicated expectations from the organization in particular are likely to be distorted, as individuals cognitively redefine these expectations to increase the degree to which they are personally acceptable to themselves.

Conclusion   The net effect of all of the above is that the organization as it is experienced by a particular member can be—and often is— substantially different from the organization as it is experienced by someone else. In particular, the demands of the organization as experienced by members often will be quite different than the "objective" demands which are communicated to those members. Any adequate analysis of individual behavior in organizations must account for such objective-subjective discrepancies if full understanding of the determinants of behavior in organizations is to be aspired to. Fortunately, this does *not* imply that all analyses of organizational behavior ought to be done on an idiographic or idiosyncratic basis, looking at only one person at a time. The characteristics of individuals which are important in determining the difference between the objective organization and the one that is experienced are likely to be reasonably similar in many cases for members occupying similar positions in any given organization. Thus, all the apprentice tool-and-die makers at Ferris Metals occupy roughly the same organizational position—and therefore the objective stimuli which reach them from the organization probably are relatively similar. Further, these individuals sometimes will have relatively similar needs, values, and goals regarding their membership in the organization. To the extent that this is the case, it is possible to make generalizations about the effects of organizational inputs on employee behavior—so long as the characteristics of the employees to which these generalizations apply are explicated with care.

The Impact of the Individual on the Organization

The framework presented in Figure 4-1 makes explicit an important assumption which will guide treatment of organizational behavior throughout this book, namely, that causation flows in both directions in individual-organization relationships—from the organization to the individual *and* from the individual to the organization. The great bulk of the research literature in organizational behavior, however, has dealt only with the first half of the equation. Numerous research programs have probed the effects on individual behavior of various kinds of reward systems, selection and classification procedures, leadership styles, job designs, training programs, and so on. Only recently have researchers and managers begun to realize that this is only half the story—that individuals may influence patterns of organizational functioning as much as organizations influence individual behavior.

An Example: Supervisory Behavior Consider, for instance, the research literature on supervisory behavior (discussed in more detail in Chapter 14). Traditionally, this research has focused on the effects of various leader personalities or managerial styles on individual and group performance. Many studies have been done which examine how subordinate productivity and satisfaction differ for supervisors who have a "considerate," employee-centered style versus those who have a "structuring," task-oriented style. A number of interesting relationships have been found between such style dimensions and the behavior and attitudes of employees. Almost invariably these relationships have been interpreted as if the leadership styles *caused* the employee reactions.

Recently, however, this interpretation has been called into question, as a number of studies have shown that a substantial proportion of the variation in leadership style is itself determined by the behavior of the people being supervised—and that leader styles are not nearly so consistent across time as once was thought. It appears, for example, that when subordinates are cooperative and competent, leaders tend to use a "considerate" style, but when subordinates are uncooperative and incompetent, leaders tend to engage in considerably more directive or "structuring" activity (cf. Rosen, 1969; Lowin & Craig, 1968). Obviously, in this case, organization members are influencing the behavior of the organization (as represented by its formal agents, the managers) at least as much as the organization is influencing its members.

A Social Process   Such findings clearly call for research approaches which (1) explicitly acknowledge the two-way causality between individuals and organizations, and (2) involve concepts and a methodology which can deal with ongoing interpersonal exchanges in organizations—i.e., exchanges which are heavily social psychological in nature. Use of social psychological concepts and methodology for research on organizations is called for on other grounds as well. It has been argued that the organization *is* for any given member the set of people and things with which he has direct knowledge. Assuming that the member's immediate organizational environment is heavily populated by other people (which, for most organizations, is a relatively safe assumption), it follows that when we talk about the impact of the organization on the individual we really mean, in large part, the impact of a certain set of other people (some of whom will be designated formal agents of the organization as a whole) on organization members of interest. And, similarly, when we speak of the impact of the individual on the organization we mean, in large part, the impact of the organization member on those other individuals with whom he has immediate contact—again, prominently including those who are formal agents of the organization. But the process, in both directions, is an explicitly social one, and therefore one which must be conceptualized and analyzed in terms of a *two-way* flow of social influence.

A MODEL OF INDIVIDUAL PERFORMANCE
IN ORGANIZATIONS

Thus far in this chapter we have presented a very general paradigm for understanding individual-organization interaction (Figure 4-1), and we have examined some of the implications of the approach implied by the paradigm for research and thinking about organizational behavior. In this section we attempt to combine these ideas with the views of individuals and organizations presented in the preceding two chapters. To accomplish this, a general model of individual performance in organizations has been developed, which is intended to illustrate the ongoing dynamics of individual-organization interaction.

The model is outlined in Figure 4-3. The top part of the diagram shows

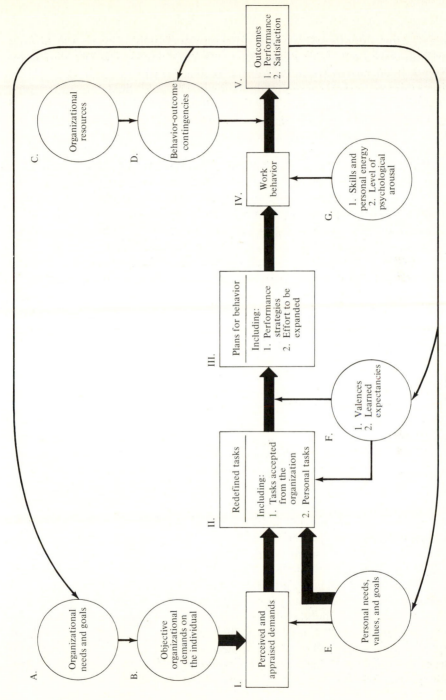

Figure 4–3 A model of individual performance in organizations.

A. Organizational needs and goals

B. Objective organizational demands on the individual

I. Perceived and appraised demands

II. Redefined tasks

Including:
1. Tasks accepted from the organization
2. Personal tasks

III. Plans for behavior

Including:
1. Performance strategies
2. Effort to be expanded

IV. Work behavior

V. Outcomes
1. Performance
2. Satisfaction

C. Organizational resources

D. Behavior-outcome contingencies

E. Personal needs, values, and goals

F. Valences
1. Learned expectancies

G. 1. Skills and personal energy
2. Level of psychological arousal

organizational contributions to the performance process, and the bottom part indicates the contributions of the individual performer. The behavioral process itself moves from left to right across the diagram; it begins with a perception of the organizational demands by the individual, and ends with a set of personal and organizational outcomes which result from individual work behavior. In the material which follows, we will examine briefly the behavioral process as it moves through six separate but related states. Throughout our discussion, we will refer back to the case of Eric and Kipsy, described in Chapter 1, to illustrate the workings of the model.

Stages in the Performance Process

Stage I: Perception and Appraisal of Organizational Demands

The process of work behavior can be instigated by the organization (through its agents—usually managers) communicating to the individual some expectations or demands regarding the work behavior of the individual (circle B in the figure). As noted in Chapter 3, these demands necessarily develop from the essential nature of work organizations: that is, from the goals of the organization; and from the needs organizations have to achieve coordination among members, to differentiate among the functions individuals perform, and to encourage behaviors which will enable the organization to maintain its continuity through time (circle A). The organization for which Eric and Kipsy worked placed high value on having clearly defined functions and close coordination among those functions. This resulted in pressures on Eric for his unit to be able to respond quickly and accurately to the needs of salesmen for information; and Eric translated that pressure to Kipsy and the other clerks as a demand for regular, on-time attendance, quick telephone responses, and high accuracy.

As noted in Chapter 2, however, when an agent of the organization communicates an objective demand or expectation to an individual, it must be perceived and appraised before the individual can act upon it. Such demands can be (and often are) distorted unconsciously at this stage to render them more personally acceptable or meaningful to the receivers— that is, the demands are made to fit with the performer's needs and values (box I and circle E). Thus, early in her career, Kipsy overinterpreted certain organizational demands, and concluded that Eric and the organization really wanted her to show high levels of personal initiative and responsibility. As she gradually learned that such was in fact *not* the case, her appraisals of organizational demands took on a decidedly different tone; namely, she interpreted many of them (e.g., the "increase efficiency" program) as an attempt by Eric to exploit the workers. As her own needs and values vis-à-vis the organization changed, so did the way she perceived and appraised the objective demands the organization made on her.

Stage II: Task Redefinition After an individual has perceived and understood (or appraised) an organizational demand, he may elect to redefine it before accepting it as a personal task that he intends to do (box II). Again, this redefinition process—which is more conscious and deliberate than the process of perception and appraisal discussed above—depends upon the personal needs, values, and goals of the individual performer. Someone who has strong growth needs, for example, might *not* redefine an organizational demand that he take a day away from his regular duties and try to think up a new and more effective way of going about the job. Someone who has low growth needs but high social needs, on the other hand, might well redefine that demand so that it required him only to spend the day talking informally with his coworkers about any thoughts they had about the job.

The tasks that a person accepts for himself do not, of course, all originate from the organization. In addition—and as a function of the personal goals of the individual—a person may himself generate some tasks that he intends to carry out as part of his activities in the organization. For example, as Kipsy found that she could not gain adequate personal satisfactions only from doing organizationally specified tasks, she began making up and performing personal tasks (such as generating the list of helpful hints for dealing with salesmen). These tasks grew directly from her own needs for taking initiative and for doing things which tapped her valued personal skills and abilities.

Sometimes the demands experienced from the organization and those generated by the person himself will be mutually reinforcing (as in cases of congruence between the individual and the organization, discussed earlier in the chapter; Eric's first weeks on the job reflect such a congruence). Other times the two sets of demands will be mostly independent of each other— i.e., the individual can achieve his personal goals in the course of his organizational activities without compromising his ability to meet organizational demands. And sometimes the two sets of demands will be in direct conflict—i.e., when it is not possible to respond adequately to both organizationally specified and personally chosen tasks, as in the case of Kipsy after a few months on the job.

It often develops that an individual receives (and finds acceptable) several different demands from different agents of the organization. In such cases, the individual must somehow choose which demands he will accept and which he will ignore, and is said to be in a state of "role conflict" (cf.

Kahn et al., 1964). (When the conflict is between organizational and personal demands, it is termed "person-role conflict" by Kahn et al.) In either case, the individual must weigh the personal costs and payoffs he believes to be associated with accepting, rejecting, or redefining the various demands on him, and come to a conclusion regarding which tasks he actually will attempt to perform.

Critical in making this decision, of course, are the expectations the individual has about the nature of the consequences of accepting versus rejecting each of the demands which he is experiencing, and the valence the individual has for those outcomes (circle F). Following the general expectancy theory of voluntary choice described in Chapter 2, it is proposed that the individual in a conflict situation will elect to reject (or, at least, to substantially redefine) those demands which have the lowest expected payoff for himself. Thus, if an individual must choose between undertaking a relatively onerous task requested by the boss, or engaging in a relatively pleasant activity that he personally prefers, the degree to which he will elect to accept the organizational task probably will depend upon his expectation about the likelihood of receiving negative outcomes if he ignores it.

Stage III: Developing a Behavioral Plan   Once the individual has determined what he is going to attempt to do in the course of his organizational activities, he then must develop a plan for how he will actually behave. For most organizational tasks, the individual has some latitude in how he will perform his tasks, in particular regarding (1) the performance strategy he will use—i.e., the direction of his task-relevant activities, and (2) the amount of effort he will expend in his work—i.e., the intensity of those activities (cf. Chapter 2). Once again, the particular plans the individual develops can be analyzed in expectancy-theory terms, as a function of the expectancies he has for the outcomes associated with each plan, coupled with the valences of those outcomes (box III and circle F).

When Kipsy made up her list of what she wanted—and the likelihood of improving her situation if she stayed on the job—she was developing a behavioral plan about her career strategy in terms very close to the language of expectancy theory. And when she communicated to Eric what happened when a person worked hard on the job ("backaches and frustration") she was verbalizing certain beliefs which subsequently led her to adopt a strategy of "getting by" and a lowered level of effort expended at work.

Stage IV: Behaving   Actual work behavior emerges in rather straightforward fashion from the behavior plan (box IV). Work behavior is, of course, moderated and limited by the skills, energy capacities, and level of psychological arousal of the performer (circle G). Even a well-executed plan of attack on some organizational task is doomed to failure if the person does not have the skill or the energy to carry it off, or if his level of psychological arousal is not appropriate for effective work behavior (cf. Chapter 14).

Stage V: Obtaining Outcomes   Work behavior leads to some set of outcomes—both performance outcomes (such as work quality and quantity) and personal outcomes (such as satisfaction), as shown in box V. Outcomes are jointly determined by the work behavior of the individual and by the task and organizational contingencies which are relevant to the performance situation (circle D). These contingencies are characteristics of the situation which determine what kinds of outcomes result from various patterns of work behavior. Sometimes, for example, the organizational reward structure will be such that high-quantity work results in high pay; in other cases, the quality of the work may determine pay. Or, for some types of jobs, individuals will obtain growth-need satisfactions when they do especially good work; for other jobs, the personal outcome obtained from working hard will be only a feeling of tiredness. It is clear that in Kipsy's case her expectancies about the consequences of working hard and effectively on the information clerk job were based precisely on the objective behavior-outcome contingencies which characterized that job. That is, it was objectively true that hard work led more to experiencing backaches than it did to feelings of personal accomplishment and increased feelings of self-worth, that pay was objectively related to tenure and not to performance, that effective work did not result in promotion, and so on.

The degree to which such behavior-outcome contingencies are clear-cut, reliable, and visible varies from organization to organization, and from resource to resource. For example, pay (an important and ubiquitous organizational resource) may be based solely on tenure in the organization (as in Kipsy's case), or on almost minute-to-minute performance effectiveness (as in the case of some piecework incentive plans). And even when pay is based on performance, the way that pay is administered can dramatically affect the degree to which individuals perceive and understand the contingency between what they do and what they get (cf. Chapter 12). The same is true for virtually all other resources under organizational control.

The major point is that for most organizational resources, there is *some* set of behavior-outcome contingencies which determine when those resources become available to the individual. Some organizations attempt to capitalize upon this fact by making their resources contingent upon behaviors which are desired of organization members (and by making sure the members perceive these contingencies); others tend more to just "let things happen," and thereby fail to capitalize upon the motivational potential of organizational resources.

Finally, it should be noted that the outcomes obtained as a result of work behavior represent a test of the individual's earlier expectancies about the organization and the environment (circle F). At stages II and III, the individual made decisions regarding what he was going to do in his work activities and how he was going to go about it—based substantially on his perceptions of the expected consequences of those behaviors. The outcomes the individual obtains permit him to determine the degree to which those expectancies about behavior-outcome contingencies were realistic.

Stage VI: Feedback   As indicated in Figure 4-3, the outcomes which result from work behavior feed back to *both* the organization and the individual. Future demands on the individual by the organization are affected by the degree to which performance outcomes meet the needs and goals of the organization, and the nature of the behavior-outcome contingencies which govern the provision of organizational resources also may be altered by management on the basis of the work outcomes which emerge. Thus, as Eric learned that his organizational unit was not performing adequately in his early weeks on the job, he took various steps designed to correct the situation. These steps involved changes both in the objective demands placed on the individuals (e.g., the prods to increase efficiency) and in certain behavior-outcome contingencies (e.g., by assigning supervisors to watch the employees closely—and presumably reprimand and reward them as appropriate—for three hours a day).

Clearly the learned expectancies of the individual are affected by the outcomes he receives, as noted earlier. It is also true, moreover, that the *needs and values* of the individual may gradually be changed as a consequence of outcomes received. As noted in Chapter 2, for example, the level of desire an individual has for higher-order need satisfactions is strongly affected by the degree to which lower-order needs are satisfied. If an individual receives, on a more or less continuous basis, outcomes which are satisfying of his lower-order needs, his need level would be expected gradually to rise (circle E). This ultimately could result in his being *un*willing to accept simple tasks which previously were done as a matter of course, because no longer would he hold the expectation that doing those tasks would lead to personally valued outcomes. If, on the other hand, the individual is *never* given the opportunity to experience higher-order need satisfactions (even though he may have a high desire to do so), he may gradually lose that desire and become "locked into" a pattern of work behavior in which personal growth is neither sought nor valued (Kornhauser, 1965; Walker & Guest, 1952). If Kipsy were to remain in her present job for a long period of time (perhaps because she was unable to find acceptable alternative employment), we might expect to observe precisely such a long-term deterioration of her own need or desire for higher-order need satisfactions.

Conclusion

The model of individual performance in organizations presented and discussed above is at a very general level of analysis. Its intent is to provide an overview of the major *classes of variables* which affect individual behavior in organizations, and to show in general terms how those classes of variables interact to determine the behavior of individuals in organizations.

In particular, the following organization-level variables were emphasized in the model:

1 The objective demands, expectations, and requirements placed on individual organization members by agents of the organization as a whole. These were seen as deriving from the overall goals of the organization, and from the necessity in any social system to attempt to influence individual behavior so that large numbers of people operate in concert to obtain the overall goals (cf. circles A and B in Figure 4-3).

2 The resources controlled by the organization (circle C), and the behavior-outcome contingencies established by the organization which specify the circumstances under which these resources are made available to individual organization members (circle D).

The following individual-level variables were emphasized:

1 The personal needs, values, and goals of the individual (box E). These variables were seen as influencing *(a)* the way in which organizational demands are experienced by the individual, *(b)* the likelihood that organizational demands will be deliberately redefined by the individual before execution, and *(c)* the nature of the personal tasks or goals the individual will set for himself in the course of his organizational activities.

2 The valences the individual has for various organizational outcomes, and the expectancies he has learned about the circumstances under which he will and will not receive various outcomes (circle F). Valences, of course, are yet another reflection of the personal needs and values of the individual, but applied specifically to outcomes which can be obtained at work. Expectancies are more cognitive in nature, and are subject to considerable revision on the basis of the individual's on-going work experience in the organization.

3 The level of the individual's skill, the amount of personal energy available to the individual, and the level of psychological arousal the individual experiences at work (circle G). These all are characteristics of the

person which directly affect the work behavior he actually exhibits. These variables tend not to be under the immediate voluntary control of the individual, and therefore are viewed as moderating the degree to which his behavioral plans are actually realized.

Finally, it should be noted that the model is explicitly cyclic and systemic in nature: the actions of individuals and of organizations continuously feed back upon and influence each other. This often results in a quite stable social system, which has its own unique identifying characteristics. Sometimes such systems are healthy and growing; sometimes they are stagnant and decaying. In subsequent chapters we will attempt to identify some of the factors which are crucial in determining whether growth or decay is dominant in work organizations—factors that, it is hoped, can be used as "handles" for initiating changes which can prompt growth-producing processes on the part of—and for the benefit of—*both* individuals and organizations.

REVIEW AND DISCUSSION QUESTIONS

1   Give examples of "psychological contracts" that you are a party to in other than work organizations (e.g., family, church, social clubs, etc.).
2   What is meant by individual-organizational fit? Does the lack of fit have any consequences for the organization in terms of effectiveness and efficiency of operations?
3   Discuss the plights of Kipsy and Eric (Chapter 1), using individual-organizational fit as a basis.
4   What is meant by the term task-redefinition? What, if any, are the consequences of task-redefinition for the individual and the organization?
5   There are feedback loops in the model shown in Figure 4-3. What implications do these feedback loops have concerning the "correctness" of either the expectancy theory or the behavioristic theory of motivation (both theories were described in Chapter 2)?
6   In the class for which you are reading this book, analyze your own behavior, using the model shown in Figure 4-3 as a basis.

Part Two

The Development of Individual-Organization Relationships

Choice Processes: Individuals and Organizations Attracting and Selecting Each Other

The earlier chapters have stressed that both individuals and organizations have objectives or goals that they try to attain. The search for a fit between the goals of a particular individual and the goals of a particular organization typically begins with the selection process. Individuals seek a work organization where they can fulfill their goals, and organizations try to hire people who can help them reach their objectives. Individuals usually do this by gathering information about a number of organizations, deciding which one is most likely to help them fulfill their needs, and then attempting to get a job with that organization. Organizations do this by trying to attract large numbers of competent applicants and then selecting those who are most likely to be successful in the organization.

ATTRACTION AND SELECTION AS SEEN BY INDIVIDUALS AND ORGANIZATIONS

Perspective of Individuals

People gather information about organizations from a number of sources. They read literature put out by organizations, they talk to their friends or other people who know something about organizations, and they visit organizations and go through the selection process. On the basis of the information they obtain, people *form attitudes about the attractiveness* of occupations, organizations, and jobs. They *form opinions about how likely they are to gain entry* into the different occupations, organizations, and jobs. They then make choices. Sometimes individuals sequentially choose a career, an organization, and a job, but often they don't. Frequently they decide on a job and an organization at the same time. Later in this chapter we will explore just how individuals use the information they gather to make their choices. From the individual's point of view, however, the selection process is not simply a matter of choosing a job in a given organization; it is also a matter of behaving in a way that will lead organizations to offer him a job. An individual usually tries to obtain several job offers in order to increase his chances of finding the "right" job. He tries to do this by exhibiting during the selection process behavior that attracts organizations. This may mean, for example, conducting himself in a certain way during a job interview, preparing a résumé in a particular manner, or filling out a test in the way that he thinks an organization would like to see it completed.

The two things that the individual is trying to accomplish in the selection situation—attracting the organization and evaluating the organization—may at times come into conflict. There are a number of things he could do which might make him more attractive to the organization, but which would make it difficult for him to find out what he would like to know about the organization; e.g., presenting his values as in line with those of the organization. Similarly, there are many things the individual might do which would increase his information about the organization while decreasing his attractiveness to it; e.g., asking in an interview detailed questions concerning how much various managers are paid.

Job applicants differ substantially in the degree to which the choice process is mainly an information-gathering attempt as contrasted with an attempt to attract the organization. Although there is little relevant research here, it would seem that high self-esteem, a good labor market, and a number of job offers are factors that would lead the person to be more concerned with information gathering than with attracting. This would seem to have obvious implications for the hiring practices of organizations. For example, under conditions where the individual is not trying to attract the organization, he will be less likely to tolerate selection procedures that produce high stress and provide little information about the organization (e.g., certain kinds of tests).

Perspective of Organizations

From the point of view of the organization, the choice process is not simply a matter of gathering the information it needs for carrying out selection. It is also a matter of attracting the kind of applicants that the organization wants. Selection can never be very effective unless a relatively large pool of good applicants try to obtain a job and those people who are offered jobs actually accept them.

By far the greatest amount of research on choice processes has been done on determining how organizations can select those people who will be best for them. Numerous instruments (e.g., tests, interviews, weighted application blanks) have been developed to help organizations determine before employment how well individuals will perform a given job. Selection devices are considered to be valid if they can actually predict how effectively a person will perform a job once he is hired. Determining the validity of a selection instrument, therefore, requires a specification of what constitutes effective and ineffective performance in a given job. In one sense this requires that someone translate the goals of the organization down to the level of performance on a particular job and say what kinds of behavior on the job are needed for the organizational goals to be accomplished (see the means-goal discussion in Chapter 3). As will be discussed in Chapter 11, this is often difficult to do.

An interesting example of the relationship between organizational goals and the employee attraction and selection activities of an organization is provided by a series of studies by Argyris (1954) and Alderfer (1971). In the earlier study, it was noted that the selection, promotion, and recruitment policies that were being used tended to lead the organization (a bank) to be staffed by "right type" managers who were characterized as being nonaggressive and avoiders of conflict and competition. A consultant pointed out to the organization that this type of person might not be the "right type" of person to help the bank achieve its goals of growth and profitability. Apparently management agreed, because they changed their selection and recruitment practices so that they would hire more aggressive, competitive, and better-educated individuals. As the later report (Alderfer's) indicates, they seem to have been successful in making some changes in the organization by altering their selection and recruitment program. The recruitment or attraction process had to be changed because previously this "new type" did not even apply for the jobs (presumably because they did not see it as an organization where they could fulfill their needs), and the selection process also had to be changed because under the old system, even if a new type had applied, he would not have been hired. This is a good example of the self-selection process (individuals deciding where to work) and the organization-selection process seemingly keeping away those persons the organization needs most.

Many organizations spend large amounts of money on recruitment in order to attract the kind of people they want to hire. This attraction process is, of course, not independent of the selection process since what goes on during the selection process influences the attractiveness of the organization. A recent study (Alderfer & McCord, 1970), for example, points out that the way in which the selection interview is conducted directly influences the probability that a person will take a job with a company. In this study it was found that job applicants were more attracted to organizations when interviewers were perceived as taking a personal interest in them and where potential careers were discussed with them.

Because the selection process does influence the attractiveness of working for organizations, organizations are faced with a difficult dilemma when considering which selection procedures to use. They need to design a system that both attracts the right applicants and provides all the information that the organization needs to make intelligent selection decisions. The problem is that many approaches that are helpful in attracting people have questionable validity from a selection point of view. The kind of interview suggested by the study mentioned above provides a good example of one such selection device. Further, some devices which produce good selection information can affect the applicant's view of the organization negatively. Certain kinds of tests are good examples here. Often they are valid, yet they make the organization which gives them less attractive to the applicant. Other examples are stress interviews and simulations of the toughest parts of the job.

There also seems to be a limit on the amount of information an

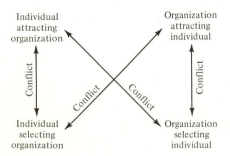

Figure 5–1 The attraction-selection situation.

organization can collect without driving the applicant away. Many individuals simply will not tolerate all the testing, interviewing, etc., that an organization might want to do in order to gather enough information upon which to base its selection decision. To an extent, the organization is always faced with balancing its desire to attract people with its desire to gather valid selection data. The typical interview is a microcosm of these competing desires. Part of the time the interviewer is in the role of attracting an applicant, and part of the time he is in the role of trying to evaluate the applicant.

Individual-Organization Conflicts

So far we have pointed out that during the individual-organization attraction-selection situation, four separate processes may be taking place. The conflict arrow in Figure 5-1 between individuals attracting and individuals selecting illustrates that the two objectives individuals often try to accomplish (i.e., selection and attraction) are in conflict. The arrow between organizations selecting and attracting illustrates that the same is true for the objectives of the organizations. These are not the only conflicts that occur in the selection-attraction situation, however. In fact, they may be the least important.

As shown in the figure, the individual's desire to *attract* the organization and the organization's desire to *select* among individuals are often in direct conflict. In order to make good selection decisions, organizations need valid and complete information about individuals. This, of course, can and often does come into conflict with the individual's desire to make a favorable impression in order to attract the organization. How the individual and the organization cope with this conflict strongly affects the selection process. The same point can in fact be made about the conflict between the individual's desire to *select* among organizations and the organization's desire to *attract* individuals. Individuals need complete, valid information about organizations in order to evaluate them; and organizations feel that if they give out negative information about themselves they will become less attractive to the individuals they would like to hire. Thus, whenever an organization attempts to attract an individual and the individual considers whether or not to join the organization, conflict will be present and it will influence the selection process.

The remainder of this chapter will consider the two *individual* processes of attraction and selection and the two *organization* processes of attraction and selection, in turn. However, in discussing these processes the emphasis will be on how the operation and effectiveness of each of them are influenced by the operation of the others.

INDIVIDUALS ATTRACTING ORGANIZATIONS

Individuals do many things to make themselves appear attractive to organizations. Most of the things they do involve "management" of the impression they create not by presenting false data about themselves but by emphasizing the positive aspects of their experience, skill, and aptitudes (Goffman, 1959). The care many job applicants take in preparing a résumé is, for instance, a classic example of the operation of impression management. They pay great attention to developing a favorable-looking résumé. Strengths are emphasized, weaknesses omitted. Job applicants also carefully select their list of references so that they will receive the most favorable reference letters possible. Let us, then, consider in more detail some of the selection methods that organizations use, and look at them from the point of view of what individuals can do as well as what they actually do in order to try to make a favorable impression.

Tests

Ability and aptitude tests are by far the most commonly used tests for selection purposes, and the desire of individuals to look good rarely affects their usefulness. The reason for this is that the construction of the tests is based on the assumption that, ordinarily, everyone will try to do as well as he can on them. They are like school tests in that a good score can be obtained only by performing well. However, because of the nature of the tests, not everyone does equally well. Even though everyone tries to present himself in the best light on these tests, differences will appear in scores because individuals differ in how well they can perform when trying to do their best. The person who, for example, has an IQ of 100 may want to perform so that he will look as if he has an IQ of 140. However, because of the nature of the test and his response capabilities, he won't be able to do it.

The desire of individuals to look good in the selection situation is a serious problem when so-called typical performance tests, such as personality and interests tests, are used. It is a problem because these types of tests rely for their validity on people attempting to give accurate self-descriptions of their normal or typical behavior. If individuals respond to tests in terms of what they think is wanted rather than in terms of what they are like, these tests may not be valid predictors of job performance.

Many typical performance tests were developed for use in clinical and counseling situations where it was reasonable to assume that the person completing the test was seeking help and was motivated to give a valid self-description and honest answers. This is not a reasonable assumption in many employment testing situations, and several studies have shown that when given specific instructions to make a high score job applicants can do it (Borislow, 1958; Bridgman & Hollenbeck, 1961). Two other studies (Kirchner, 1961, 1962) indicate that faking does take place in actual testing situations. In one study salesmen were tested before and after they were hired, and their scores on one of the most commonly used typical performance tests (The Strong Vocational Interest Blank) were found to be lower after they were hired. In the other study, applicants scored higher than did people already on the job, suggesting they were altering their self-descriptions somewhat in order to obtain the job.

A word of caution is in order here. Just because a test score can be controlled deliberately by the test taker does not mean that it is invalid as a predictor of job performance. It is quite possible for a test to be susceptible to faking and still be valid. One reason for this is that people differ in the way that they think tests should be answered in order to attract organizations, and thus some will deliberately answer it one way and others another way. One person might think the organization is looking for a conservative, unaggressive type, while the other may think it wants just the opposite. Thus, even though two people are trying to look attractive to the organization, they may end up with quite different scores. These scores actually could predict performance for no other reason than that they are a measure of the perceptiveness of the individual about what the organization wants— in short, a measure of the person's ability to correctly diagnose an organizational situation. To the extent that personality and interest tests do measure something like this, they could be valid even when their scores can be purposely altered by the persons taking them; however, the evidence would seem to suggest that often they are not accurate predictors of job performance (Guion, 1965).

Interviews

The interview is the most widely used selection device, and there is clear evidence that job applicants can influence their attractiveness by how they manage the interview. It has been demonstrated that the more interviewers talk, the more favorably they are inclined toward the job applicant (Mayfield, 1964). There also are data that show that interviewers are much more influenced by unfavorable information then by favorable information (Webster, 1964). Additionally, of course, such factors as dress and appearance can influence the favorableness of the interviewer's judgments. What all this suggests is that the thoughtful job applicant can often significantly influence his attractiveness to an organization by behaving in certain specific ways.

To the extent that the applicant, in order to appear attractive to the organization, behaves in an untypical manner in an interview, he is behaving in the same way as the person who tries to look good on a personality test. Both are more concerned with attracting the organization than with presenting a true picture of themselves. Experienced interviewers are, of course, very much aware of the motivation and opportunity for interviewees to present a misleading image of themselves in the hope of appearing more acceptable to the organization. Many interviewers, furthermore, claim they can tell when an interviewee is in fact trying to do this. However, the evidence on the validity of interview judgments (Mayfield, 1964) would suggest that perhaps they are not as good at this as they believe themselves to be.

Application Blanks

Another frequently used selection instrument that is potentially manageable and subject to individuals' providing only selected information about themselves is the application blank. There are some spectacular cases on record of people who have developed completely fictitious backgrounds (including university degrees, etc.) in order to obtain jobs that they wanted. More common, of course, is applicants' providing distorted information on their application blanks concerning their previous jobs, reasons for leaving their past job, age, etc. Just how frequently this kind of distortion takes place is suggested by a study (Weiss and Dawis, 1960) that compared biographical data given by applicants with the actual factual data. Table 5-1 shows some of the results of this study. As can be seen, applicants produced a large amount of inaccurate information. For example, 21 percent gave erroneous information about their educational background, and 22 percent distorted the amount of their pay on their previous job.

It would be dangerous to generalize from the small sample used in this study to other populations and to assume that this much distortion of biographical information typically takes place when people apply for jobs. But this evidence does suggest that it can occur and that it probably does in some cases interfere with the organization's making valid selection decisions.

Conclusions

So far we have focused on how individuals respond to tests, interviews, and application blanks in order to attract organizations. Similar behavior also occurs when other selection devices are used. This behavior in many cases makes it more difficult for organizations to gather valid information upon which to base their selection decision, and can be harmful to both the

Table 5–1 Comparison of Validity of Interview Information

Item	N	% with invalid information
Age	91	10
Sex	91	0
Marital status	91	15
Education	91	21
Veteran status	91	4
Nature of disability	91	10
Age at disablement	48	33
Received assistance	91	55
Job title	49	24
Job duties	49	10
Hours	49	16
Pay	46	22
Length of employment	48	29

Source: Adapted from Weiss and Dawis, 1960.

individual and the organization. Unwise selection decisions can decrease organizational effectiveness and can put employees in stressful and demanding positions for which they may not be prepared. Still, the behavior occurs. Why does it occur? Because for many individuals there is a conflict between their desire to get the job and the organization's desire to make a correct selection decision. For some individuals (those who have the traits and capacities that the organization wants), there is no conflict between their goals and those of the organization as far as the selection process is concerned. However, for others the conflict is present and hence the behavior is present even though in the long run it may not be functional for either the individual or the organization. The problem, of course, is that often the individual doesn't realize this, or he is willing to settle for the short-term rewards that simply obtaining the job will bring.

INDIVIDUALS CHOOSING ORGANIZATIONS AND JOBS

How do people process the vast amount of information that they gather about an organization and the job it offers so that they arrive at a decision about which organization to join? The expectancy-theory model presented in Chapter 2 suggests an answer to this question. It indicates that people's tendencies to perform an action are influenced by their beliefs concerning whether they can perform the action, by their beliefs concerning the consequences of doing it, and by the attractiveness of the outcomes associated with doing it. In the case of a person considering whether or not to try to obtain a particular job in a particular organization, this answer means it is important to look at the kinds of outcomes the person sees associated with holding that job and the value he places on these outcomes. The prediction is that the person will choose the job which he feels will result in the best set of outcomes accruing to him. The net attractiveness of the job is not, however, the only thing that influences which job a person will choose.

If the attractiveness of a job was the only factor that influenced which job a person chose, everyone would be trying to obtain a few highly desirable jobs. This doesn't happen, and the explanation for it is suggested by the first factor in the motivation model. It is, in effect, a reality factor which indicates that people will not be motivated to obtain a job in an organization if they see no probability of getting it. Thus, no matter how attractive a job may be to a person, he will not try to obtain it unless he feels that there is some probability of success. Because of this, many people try to obtain jobs that in their eyes are not the most attractive ones. This does not mean, however, that people will always abandon their most preferred job just because they feel it is difficult to gain entry to it. As long as a person believes that there is some probability that he can obtain the position, he may be motivated to try to get it. The model does suggest two conditions that will lead a person to try to obtain a job that he feels is very difficult to enter: First, the job must be *much* more attractive to him than any other, and second, his second- or third-choice jobs must also be seen as difficult to obtain. When these conditions exist, then it is likely that he will try to obtain the job which is most attractive to him.

Evidence to Support Job-Choice Model

There is a small amount of research directly relevant to this model of job choice. For example, in a study of job choice (Vroom, 1966), students were asked to rate the jobs they were considering in terms of their perceived instrumentality for the attainment of fifteen goals. The students were also asked to rank the goals in terms of their importance. The data showed that the students were most attracted to those organizations that were seen as being instrumental for the attainment of their most important goals (similar results have also been reported by Wanous, 1972), and they actually joined these organizations a few months later when it came time to leave school.

Unfortunately, there are very few other studies that include data which can be used to test directly the approach presented here about how people make job choices. Much of the research that has been done has looked at the effects of economic variables (on turnover and labor supply), and it has not dealt with the psychological processes that underlie the job-choice decision. Still, this research is of interest, and several of its findings do seem to fit particularly well with the approach to explaining job choices described in this chapter (Organization for Economic Cooperation and Development, 1965; Yoder, 1962). These data show that—

1   Organizations which pay higher than average wages seem to be the ones best able to attract and retain high-quality labor.
2   Turnover is high in organizations where wages are low relative to other companies in the area.
3   The stimulus to leave a company is greatest when all the other employees seem to be making more money.
4   Turnover is low in times of recession or depression.

The first three of these findings all point out that people tend to gravitate toward higher-paying jobs, particularly if the higher-paying jobs are local and highly visible. Such findings are perfectly interpretable in terms of the model, since they all show that people are choosing jobs that they perceive to be best for achieving one goal–pay. If it is assumed that the obvious differences between working as an X in organization Y and working as an X in organization Z are typically very small, it would follow that even small differences in wages may often have a great influence on people's decisions about where they will work. This could be true even for people who don't value money very highly, if the one clearly visible difference between working for two organizations is the salary.

The tendency for people to take jobs which offer the greatest number of rewards they value leads one to expect that people who value money will almost always gravitate toward high-paying jobs. This holds whether individuals are choosing a job for the first time or whether they are presently employed and are choosing between their current job and a job in another organization. The only thing that would prevent this from happening would be the low-paying organization's offering important rewards that the high-paying organization did not match.

The fourth finding mentioned above illustrates that a reality factor operates in job choices. Turnover is undoubtedly lower in times of recession because people realize that although jobs in another organization may be higher paying, there is a low probability of getting one. Thus, they decide to hold onto the job they have.

Gathering Job-Choice Information

Not much is known about how individuals gather information about organizations and jobs. It is possible, however, to make some inferences based on research done in other areas. First, it seems likely that individuals do not gather all the information they could. There is in most cases a large number of sources of information about a particular job or organization. Company ads, company recruiters, former and present employees are among the most obvious sources of information. If a person were to search out all the information that is available, not only would the search be time-consuming but the person would undoubtedly suffer from information overload. In short, it seems reasonable to assume that in this search process, as in many others, people end up satisficing rather than optimizing, both because they don't consider all the alternatives and because they don't have complete information about the consequences of all the alternatives (Simon, 1954).

Second, it seems likely that individuals attach varying degrees of credibility to information that reaches them through different channels. It has been frequently shown that there is a strong source credibility effect such that information from some sources is accepted and acted on much more readily than is information from other sources. What are the sources of information about jobs that generally are given the highest credibility? Unfortunately, there is relatively little research evidence on this; however, some educated speculation based upon a recent study of college graduates is possible (Sorensen, Rhode & Lawler, 1973). Advertisements seem to have low credibility as do statements made by recruiters and employment agencies. What sources, then, do have some credibility? Statements made by present and past employees and by teachers. These seem to have the highest believability, particularly where the present or past employee is a personal friend of the person considering the job and is seen as an unbiased source of information.

Reports by employees can be a double-edged sword in the sense that they can both help attract and help drive away potential employees. One advantage of having a satisfied work force, therefore, would seem to be that they are likely to influence others to try and join the organization, thus improving the number and perhaps quality of the applicants. On the other hand, having a large number of dissatisfied and bitter present and past employees could present real problems for an organization that is trying to attract new employees. Not only are the present employees likely to say negative things about the organization, they are likely to be believed. Thus, the future quality of the organization's work force can be seriously impaired.

ORGANIZATIONS ATTRACTING INDIVIDUALS

Basic to a good selection program from the organization's point of view is a large supply of qualified applicants. Without a favorable selection ratio (a large number of applicants per position to be filled), no selection program whether it uses tests, interviews, or other means to select its employees is of value. Not only are large numbers of applicants needed but the right kind of applicants are needed. Attracting people who clearly are not the kind the organization wants and who thus will not be selected, or the kind that will quit within a short period, is not functional from the point of view of the organization.

Stated another way, the ideal recruitment program draws in large numbers of qualified applicants who will take the job if offered it and who will remain with the organization for a long period of time. At the same time it allows intelligent self-selection to take place so that it does not attract those people whom the organization does not want. Presumably it does not attract them because it gives them enough valid information to decide that they shouldn't try to join the organization. Attracting qualified people who do not stay on the job is dysfunctional from the organization's point of view because this kind of turnover uses up money, time, and resources. Attracting unqualified people is costly because they have to be processed and ultimately rejected, frequently resulting in their forming a negative impression of the organization.

There has been relatively little research on just how organizations go about attracting members and on the effectiveness of various approaches. Particularly missing is research on what kinds of expectations various attraction efforts build up in job applicants. It is clear that organizations do a number of things to attract job applicants—advertise, visit schools, provide bonuses to current employees for recruiting applicants who are subsequently hired, and the like. Most of these types of recruiting are directed toward impressing on people the specific rewards that are associated with holding a particular job. Organizations often also invest in general image-building activities that are typically designed to picture the organization as an exciting, dynamic, high status, and progressive outfit. Presumably this kind of advertising also serves to attract job applicants because it creates the perception that certain rewards will be associated with joining the organization.

It is interesting to note that little of the recruiting effort that organizations put forth to attract people seems to be directed toward pointing out the negative aspects of working for the particular organization or the negative aspects of a particular job. The recruiting efforts usually point out only the positive side. Witness the advertising in college newspapers designed to attract graduates. For many years such advertisements stressed security, pay, and promotion opportunities. Now they tend to stress challenge and the opportunity for personal growth. Organizations have thus switched to stressing different kinds of rewards (presumably because they think this is what will attract today's students), but they still talk mainly about the positive aspects of the job. There is evidence to indicate that this approach—of emphasizing or overemphasizing the positive aspects of prospective jobs to applicants—contributes to subsequent problems because it leads to inaccurate expectations concerning which rewards can and cannot be received on a job. Several studies have shown that when compared with job applicants who are given an unrealistic job preview, those who receive a realistic one show higher job-satisfaction scores and lower turnover rates after they are on the job (Wanous, 1972, 1973). This suggests that organization-attraction approaches which are based on creating an unrealistic set of expectations are functional for neither the individual nor the organization.

ORGANIZATIONS SELECTING INDIVIDUALS

A large number of instruments and approaches are used by organizations in order to help them decide whom to hire. Almost every organization handles this process differently. The most commonly used devices are interviews, psychological tests, and biographical data and application blanks. Less commonly used are such devices as graphology and situational tests. The value of all these devices rests on their ability to predict job performance, that is, their validity. Let us turn to a discussion of some of the more commonly used instruments and to a consideration of the research on their validity. At the end of this discussion we will also consider the impact of these devices on the perceived attractiveness of working for an organization which uses them.

Interviews

Almost every employee that is hired by an organization today is given some type of interview. The nature of these interviews varies widely, as does their validity.

Psychologists have generally looked upon the selection interview with considerable mistrust:

> The personnel interview continues to be the most widely used method for selecting employees, despite the fact that it is a costly, inefficient, and usually invalid procedure. . . . It is almost always treated as the final hurdle in the selection process. (Dunnette & Bass, 1963)

Where has the mistrust of the selection interview come from? It has a long history. In one of the first studies concerned with the interview (Scott, 1915), six personnel managers interviewed thirty-six applicants for sales jobs. The results of this study showed that there was virtually no agreement among the evaluations made by the personnel managers. Numerous other studies have followed this first study, and most of them show relatively low agreement among different interviewers when they evaluate the same interviewee. This low agreement among interviewers (interrater reliability), of course, means that interviewers have a great deal of difficulty in deciding who should be hired. Stated in other terms, selection decisions that are based solely on interview judgments usually have proved to be invalid (Blum & Naylor, 1968). The reasons for this are contained in a summary of the results of a number of studies (Mayfield, 1964; Valenzi & Andrews, 1973). Basically, it has been found that—

1   In an unstructured interview, material is not consistently covered.
2   When interviewers obtain the same information, they are likely to weigh it differently. What is positive information to one interviewer may turn out to be negative to another.
3   Interviewers have great difficulty in reliably and validly assessing traits other than intelligence or mental ability.
4   Interviewers in unstructured interviews tend to make their decisions early in an interview, that is, before all the information is in.
5   Interviewers give more weight to negative information than to positive information.

Other research shows that interviewers evaluate applicants against a stereotype of what the ideal applicant is like, and that different individuals have different stereotypes (Hakel & Hall, 1970). It also appears that such context factors as the quality of preceding applicants affects the favorableness of an interviewer's rating (Wexley et al., 1972). Given these findings, it is hardly surprising that the typical unstructured selection interview is invalid. It appears that the interviewer in this situation operates as a poor information processor. He collects unsystematic and incomplete data and weighs it according to an often invalid stereotype. He then combines it into an often invalid prediction. The process is pictured in Figure 5-2. It is not hard to understand why interviewers vary in the kind of information they collect. The interview is an interactive process. The behavior of each person influences the behavior of the other. Studies have shown, for example, that in a two-person situation, agreement by one person encourages the other person to express more opinions (Verplanck, 1955). As a result of the influence process that occurs in an interview, no two interviews are alike even though the interviewer is the same.

Should organizations use interviews in the selection process? Probably. First, they can be important in attracting people. Few people will go to work for an organization unless they receive a job interview. There also is evidence that judgments based upon an interview *can* in some cases be valid predictors of job performance. For example, in a study of stockbrokers

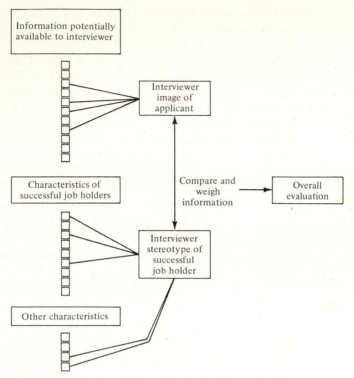

Figure 5-2 Interviewer information-processing model.

(Ghiselli, 1966a), interview judgments could predict fairly accurately who would survive on the job for three years. The previously cited review of interview studies (Mayfield, 1964) suggests some of the factors that frequently distinguish a valid from an invalid selection interview:

    1 The use of a trained professional interviewer who is familiar with the job and organization for which the applicant is being considered

    2 A fairly high degree of structure in the interview so that a high percentage of relevant material is brought out

    3 Providing interviewers in advance with knowledge of what information, given by applicants in connection with particular jobs, should be considered as favorable or unfavorable

    4 The major thrust of the interview clearly being focused on gathering selection information rather than on attracting the applicant

    5 The interview judgment being treated as just one piece of information that is combined (using a statistical predictor model) with the results of tests, etc., when the final selection decision is made

    6 The use of multiple interviewers, either in series or in the same interview

Thus, it appears that under certain circumstances interviews can contribute to the validity of the selection process. However, it is important to note that this is likely to occur under a set of rather specific conditions, conditions which typically do *not* exist when the interview is used for selection purposes.

Psychological Tests

In discussing the validity and usefulness of tests, it is important to keep in mind the distinction between tests of maximum performance and tests of typical performance. Tests of maximum performance have, almost without exception, proved to be the best predictors of job performance. However, for many jobs tests of typical performance have been shown to be completely unrelated to actual job performance. Maximum performance tests, on the other hand, have usually been shown to be the best single predictors of performance for most jobs.

Two recent surveys have been made of the ability of psychological tests to predict job performance (Ghiselli, 1966b; Guion, 1965), and they are in basic agreement. Table 5-2 is taken from one of the reviews (Ghiselli, 1966b) and it presents the validity coefficients for a number of different types of tests as measured by the correlation between test scores and job performance. The validity coefficients that are presented represent average correlations and are based on a number of different jobs. None are high (anything over .50 would be considered quite high), but this is not surprising since they represent averages and thus are probably pulled down by the fact that the tests were used in some situations where they were not appropriate. It is also obvious that the interest and personality types of tests show the lowest validity coefficients.

Before it is assumed that personality and interest tests never work, it is important to look at the data for sales jobs. They are presented in Table 5-3 and show that such tests predict performance quite well while ability tests correlate negatively with performance (high performance associated with low ability). This fact is important because it suggests that personality and interest tests have potential, even though that potential has so far been largely unrealized. In this context, the following comment by Gustad (1956, p. 324) seems appropriate: "Across the front of each test and each manual, there should be stamped in large, red letters (preferably letters which glow in the Stygian darkness of the personality measurement field) the word EXPERIMENTAL."

The extensive research on psychological tests can be summarized by noting that they can play an important role in the selection process when the job under consideration demands an ability or aptitude that is differentially distributed in the population (i.e., people have the ability or aptitude in varying degrees). Stated in other terms, if it is a question of determining

Table 5–2 Comparison of Validity Coefficients for Training and Proficiency Criteria by Type of Test (Ghiselli, 1966*a*)

Type of test	Mean validity coefficient		No. pairs of coefficients
	train.	prof.	
Intellectual abilities	.35	.19	38
Intelligence	.34	.21	16
Immediate memory	.23	.15	5
Substitution	.27	.23	4
Arithmetic	.42	.15	13
Spatial and mechanical abilities	.36	.20	28
Spatial relations	.38	.19	13
Location	.24	.17	6
Mechanical principles	.41	.24	9
Perceptual accuracy	.26	.23	15
Number comparison	.25	.24	4
Name comparison	.24	.29	3
Cancellation	.58	.19	1
Pursuit	.18	.17	4
Perceptual speed	.30	.27	3
Motor abilities	.18	.17	24
Tracing	.18	.15	4
Tapping	.15	.13	6
Dotting	.15	.14	4
Finger dexterity	.16	.20	7
Hand dexterity	.24	.22	2
Arm dexterity	.54	.24	1
Personality traits	.05	.08	2
Interest	.05	.08	2
All tests	.30	.19	107

whether a person can do or can learn to do the job, that is, whether the person has the ability to carry out the job or the aptitude to learn to do it, tests can be of substantial help. Tests can, for example, measure whether people have the finger dexterity to assemble electronic instruments and whether they have the intelligence to solve engineering or accounting problems. <mark>What tests don't seem to be able to measure very well is whether the person who has the skills and abilities *will* try to perform the job well.</mark> Providing information on motivation is, of course, just where personality and interest tests might help, but the data suggest that existing tests do not predict motivation very well in most instances.

Biographical Data and Application Blanks

Application blanks that ask for minimal amounts of information from applicants have been used for a long time. Typically they are not scored in any systematic manner and represent only one of a number of sources of data about applicants. The results are usually combined subjectively by the

Table 5–3 Validity Coefficients for Proficiency in Sales Occupations (Ghiselli, 1966*a*)

	Sales clerks Prof.	Sales- man Prof.	All sales occupations Prof.
Intellectual abilities	$-.10^d$	$.31^d$	$.18^e$
Intelligence	$-.10^d$	$.33^d$	$.33^e$
Immediate memory	$-.08^b$		$-.08^b$
Substitution	$-.16^a$		$-.16^a$
Arithmetic	$-.12^b$	$.26^c$	$.18^d$
Spatial and mechanical abilities		$.07^b$	$.07^b$
Spatial relations		$-.02^a$	$-.02^a$
Mechanical principles		$.16^a$	$.16^a$
Perceptual accuracy	$-.05^d$	$.21^b$	$-.02^d$
Number comparison	$-.14^b$	$.21^b$	$.01^b$
Name comparison	$-.15^b$		$-.15^b$
Cancellation	$.02^c$		$.02^c$
Personality traits	$.35^d$	$.27^e$	$.30^e$
Personality	$.35^d$	$.24^d$	$.28^d$
Interest	$.34^c$	$.31^d$	$.31^a$

[a] Less than 100 cases.
[b] 100 to 499 cases.
[c] 500 to 999 cases.
[d] 1,000 to 4,999 cases.
[e] 5,000 to 9,999 cases.
[f] 10,000 or more cases.

person making the hiring decision with information that is collected from other sources. However, this is not the only way this kind of biographical data is handled. In some organizations substantial amounts of information are collected and an objective scoring procedure is used to analyze the data.

Recently so-called weighted application blanks have been developed for a number of occupations. (The term "weighted application blanks" refers to those forms in which answers to specific items are assigned certain predetermined scoring weights based on their relation to a particular criterion of performance or employment stability.) Some of these blanks have achieved fairly high validity, although it is often not clear why they predict as well as they do (Asher, 1972; Fleishman, 1961; Guion, 1965). Traditionally, these blanks focused on such things as marital status, amount of education, school and community activities, skills, pay on previous jobs, and physical traits. Recently they have often included items in such areas as (1) individual achievements, (2) family experiences, (3) status changes—moving up or down in social status, (4) cultural experiences, and (5) other social and economic experiences. In some instances these longer forms have been shown to be valid predictors, but as will be discussed later in this chapter, they, like many personality and interest tests, often seem to represent an undesirable invasion of people's privacy.

In summary, biographical-data forms can be and often are valid predictors of job performance and job tenure; however, from an analytical standpoint the reasons for such validity are not always obvious. To a great extent the use of biographical blanks is based on the assumption that past behavior is the best predictor of future behavior. This is a reasonable assumption in certain circumstances, of course; however, it would be helpful if better theoretical explanations could be developed to explain why in a given situation particular items predict. This would provide cues to which items might predict across a number of different types of situations, and could suggest how to construct additional useful items.

Situational Tests and Simulations

Work-sample tests have long been used with considerable success for selecting people for certain jobs. They typically simulate the conditions of a job as nearly as possible and then systematically measure the applicant's performance during a short period of time. Typing tests and stenographic tests were among the first examples of these kinds of tests. Recently much more complex simulations and situational tests have been developed. In many tests, the work setting is not precisely duplicated; rather, the person is placed in a situation where he has to solve the same type of problem that is present on the job. During World War II the Office of Strategic Services

(OSS, 1948) developed a series of such tests for selecting spies. They were given to the applicant at a remote location during a week-long assessment session. The tests involved situational tests of leadership and simulations of capture and questioning by the enemy. Because of the nature of the actual job, it was difficult to determine how valid these procedures were for selecting agents. Nevertheless, they did lead to the development of some interesting selection devices for managers. One of the most popular of these is the "in-basket," a technique for simulating some of the decisions a manager has to make during a work day. In its most frequently used version, the job applicant is given a series of letters, memos, etc., and asked to deal with them in a short period of time. The way he handles them is quantitatively scored and an evaluation of his performance developed.

Another situational test that has been used is the leaderless group discussion. Here a group of applicants is put together and asked to discuss a broad problem or topic. They are evaluated by observers on their effectiveness during the group discussion. Both the in-basket and the leaderless group discussion have been shown to have some validity for selecting managers.

One of the most interesting recent developments in the selection of managers, the assessment center, is in effect a three-day situational test not unlike the OSS program. Its use was pioneered by the American Telephone and Telegraph Company, and it is presently used in many companies. Assessment centers are typically used to decide who should be promoted in organizations and as an aid in counseling individuals with respect to their career development needs. Most assesment centers utilize a number of situational tests which are scored by higher-level managers and psychologists who observe the individual's performance. The manager-observers frequently become quite involved in the assessment-center operations and, as a result of their participation, understand the meaning of the results which are produced by the center. A considerable amount of data has been collected on the validity of the centers, and the results are encouraging (Campbell et al., 1970). They seem to do better in predicting future managerial success than traditional paper and pencil tests do. Unfortunately, little research has been done to determine if they are effective as an approach to career counseling.

The use of situational tests and job simulations is in many ways the ultimate method of determining the "can do" aspect of job performance, since they require the person to perform the same behavior that is needed on the job. In many cases, therefore, it is realistic to assume that, if the person can perform the behavior in a job-simulation situation, he can do it in the real-job situation. However, situational tests do have some weaknesses. First, there are questions about how the applicant who is confronted with this kind of selection process will react. It is not clear whether it increases or decreases the attractiveness of working for the organization (if he is an applicant). It probably has no effect in the case of typing tests and many simulations, but this may not be so for some of the stressful simulations that managerial applicants are put through.

Second, it is not clear to what extent the situational test approach can be used to measure the "will do" aspect of job performance. It is not safe to assume that because the person is motivated to perform well under test conditions he will also be motivated to perform well under job conditions. In fact, a good case can be made for the point of view that job-performance motivation and motivation during a situational test probably are only moderately related since the psychological climate, the rewards, and the time span are so different.

Finally, it should be noted that it is more difficult to use simulations and situational tests when applicants do not know how to perform the job and where substantial training is needed. A typing test can be used to select among trained typists, but it is not too helpful in selecting potential typists from among untrained people. The more training that is required, the greater the difference that usually exists between performance on a selection instrument and performance in the job situation. In other words, the more the test or instrument tries to measure some underlying ability or trait and the less it mirrors the work situation, the lower the predictive validity of the test. When an underlying ability is measured, an extra link is added; instead of testing for actual job behavior, the abilities that are needed for the job behavior are being tested and these are one step further away from job performance. In short, under certain conditions situational tests and simulations can be quite helpful, but they are not a panacea.

Limits on the Validity of Selection Instruments

In the 1930s, it was pointed out that no selection instrument was likely to be developed that would come close to predicting job performance perfectly. As we have seen from our review of selection instruments, this statement still appears to be true. One obvious reason for this is the difficulty of measuring job performance. It typically has been measured by having superiors rate their subordinates' performance. This method of measurement produces data that often are themselves unreliable and highly subjective. Thus, imperfections in the criteria of performance set a ceiling on how well any selection instrument can predict performance.

There is, however, a second reason why selection instruments are limited in their ability to predict performance. In the discussion of the selection devices in this chapter, it was pointed out that all of them are much better at measuring the "can do" (ability) than at measuring the "will do" (motivation) aspect of performance. After individuals have been tested, interviewed, etc., the organization usually has a good idea who can do the job, and they can eliminate people who cannot do the job. This is a contribution to good selection and leads to an improvement over simple random selection. However, it does not allow for anywhere near perfect prediction of performance because it still is not possible to forecast whether the person will try to perform the job well or not. As long as this cannot be determined accurately, validity coefficients will remain low even if performance can be measured reliably and accurately. Figure 5-3 illustrates this point. It shows that a person needs both ability and motivation to perform well. Selection as presently done can identify those people who do not have the ability (boxes 1 and 2), but it usually does not identify those people who perform poorly because of low motivation (box 3); and thus selection is far from being a highly perfected process.

Why is a job applicant's motivation to perform once he takes the job so difficult to predict? Largely because, as was stressed in Chapter 4, behavior at work is a function of both the person and the organizational environment. A person's motivation is influenced by his needs (which are changing) and by the way he feels he can obtain outcomes which satisfy them. The environment a person is in can influence both of these factors. All that can be easily measured during the selection process is the person's needs, and in many instances this is difficult to measure. To predict motivation, an assessment of the kind of beliefs the person is likely to develop concerning the relationship of performance to outcomes is required. Additionally, there is a necessity for an assessment of the job situation which focuses on the rewards which are present in the job situation and on how they can be obtained.

As a simple example of the interaction of the environment and the

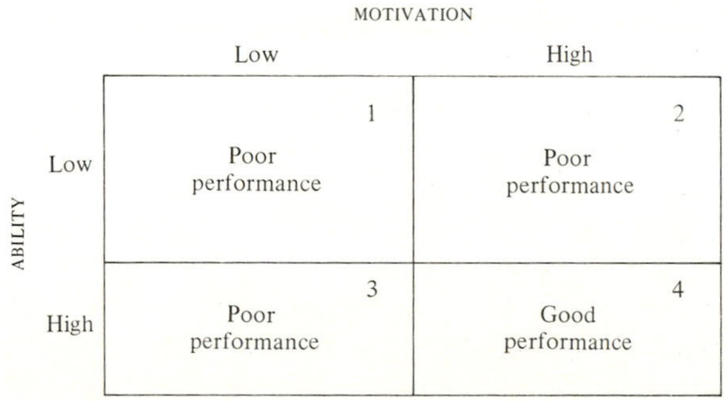

Figure 5-3 Relationship of ability and motivation to performance.

person, consider the possible effect of a company having or not having a piece-rate pay incentive system. Piece-rate pay systems make a major difference in the climates of organizations since they influence the kind of group pressures that exist, the style of supervision that exists, and the reward expectancies of the employees. All of these need to be measured and considered if the performance of an individual worker is to be predicted since they influence motivation. In addition, it is necessary to know how the worker responds to group pressure, how concerned he is about earning money (e.g., large family, mortgage payments, etc.), and a number of other factors. The person who is not concerned about joining a group and who strongly needs to earn money may be highly motivated in an organization that has a pay incentive system, while he might not be at all motivated in an organization where there is no pay-performance relationship but where there is a high degree of team spirit.

Until recently little work was done on the measurement and exploration of variables which meaningfully describe the organizational environment. Jobs, for example, were typically measured only in terms of the activities they require people to perform. Psychological characteristics of jobs—such as how much challenge they provide and how boring they are—were ignored; yet as will be explained in Chapter 10, these are among the most important aspects of any job. Some systematic efforts are being made now to develop instruments that do measure the job environment. For example, a questionnaire has been developed that measures organization climate on six dimensions: support, managerial structure, new employees' concern, general satisfaction, employee independence, and conflict (Schneider & Bartlett, 1968). A similar instrument has been developed to measure employee preference for different climates. The assumption, which is supported by some data, is that where individual preferences fit with the actual climate, turnover will be lower and performance will be higher.

The use of biographical data represents a possible way to obtain information about how people function in different environments. Biographical data do at least provide clues on how people have in the past responded to some environments. They are seldom used, however, in conjunction with an organization-climate analysis. It is usually assumed that if a person has performed well in a similar climate he probably will also perform well in the new one. But what is a "similar" environment? Self-selection can also help here if the person has a clear image of what the climate of the new organization is like. He may be able to decide himself whether or not he will function well in a particular climate. Unfortunately, applicants often do not get enough such information to make this decision intelligently.

Gains and Costs Associated with Selection Programs

Selection programs are expensive to run. They require the time of relatively highly paid professionals, and the resources used are often expensive. It is, therefore, important to consider just how great a contribution selection can make to improving organizational effectiveness. The research which has been done shows that the value of a selection program depends on three things: the validity of the program, the selection ratio (number of applicants to number of openings), and the difficulty of the job. Unless the validity coefficients are high (this seldom happens), and the selection ratio is high (this is usually only true for desirable jobs), and the jobs are difficult (often true of higher-level jobs), selection programs tend to produce only small increases in organizational effectiveness. An obvious implication is that under many conditions selection cannot have a major impact on organizational effectiveness and, as a result, it is often not worthwhile for organizations to have extensive and expensive selection programs.

Legal and Ethical Problems in Selection

The selection programs of many organizations and in particular the tests that are used in these programs have been under considerable attack in the last ten years. During the mid-sixties subcommittees of Congress held hearings that were concerned with psychological testing. The hearings focused on invasion of privacy, and a number of witnesses pointed out that psychological tests (particularly personality and interest tests) seriously violate individual privacy by asking questions about such areas as personal preferences, religion, and family affairs. Figure 5-4 presents a sample of the facetious test items suggested by a newspaper columnist and illustrates the ridicule to which testing was subjected. The tests were defended on the basis that people's feelings and attitudes about these matters are good predictors of behavior in jobs. In short, it was argued, the items were valid predictors, so why not use them?

The simple and totally empirical answer that some test items predict—no matter how irrelevant they might seem to work situations—did not seem to satisfy everyone. Perhaps the most important thing these hearings did was to raise the basic issue of what information can be properly collected for the sake of selection. Often it is assumed that if a selection instrument is valid and will not drive too many people away, it should be used. This seems highly debatable, however. Unfortunately, no really definite rules or guidelines have ever been developed to say what instruments should be used for selection. It is clear, though, that there are questions and instruments which

1   When I was younger, I used to tease vegetables.

2   Sometimes I am unable to prevent clean thoughts from entering my head.

3   I am not unwilling to work for a jackass.

4   I would enjoy the work of a chicken flicker.

5   I think beavers work too hard.

6   It is important to wash your hands before washing your hands.

7   It is hard for me to say the right thing when I find myself in a room full of mice.

8   I use shoe polish to excess.

9   The sight of blood no longer excites me.

10   It makes me furious to see an innocent man escape the chair.

11   As a child, I used to wet the ceiling.

12   I am aroused by persons of the opposite sexes.

13   I believe I smell as good as most people.

14   When I was a child, I was an imaginary playmate.

Figure 5-4   Personality tests: A columnist's parody.

might be valid and which might not keep away applicants but which still should not be used in a selection program.

Perhaps even more complex than the invasion of privacy issue is the equal-employment-opportunity problem. It has been known for a long time that many of the psychological tests which are used for selection purposes show sex and race differences. Because of this, serious questions have been raised about the degree to which selection devices unfairly discriminate against job applicants who are minority group members. Such questions can best be answered for a given selection instrument by determining how valid the selection device is as a predictor of job performance. There are, however, problems in determining the validity of selection devices. There is research to show that selection instruments can be valid predictors of job performance for one group of applicants but not for another (Lopez, 1966; Humphreys, 1973). A particular selection device may, therefore, have some validity when all applicants are considered but upon further examination may prove to be invalid in the case of a particular minority group. One solution in such a situation is to use different selection instruments for different groups of applicants. Such a procedure, however, could become extremely costly if different instruments were needed for each of a number of minority groups. Furthermore, the problem is immensely compounded if each selection device is valid only for a narrow range of jobs. The whole area of selection in relation to minorities is obviously critically important to our society, yet it is exceedingly complex.

It seems clear that the legal and social climate in the United States is such that, if organizations are going to use such selection devices as tests and interviews, they will have to invest more in research on the devices. No longer can organizations simply buy a standardized test, administer it, and be comfortable in the knowledge that their use of the device will not be challenged. All this means that the costs of selection will go up, and before too long they may be too high for many organizations in relation to their contribution to organizational effectiveness. It is possible, therefore, that in the future organizations will, after a rough screening, offer applicants a job on either a random or a first-come, first-served basis.

ORGANIZATION-INDIVIDUAL CONFLICTS AND THEIR CONSEQUENCES FOR SELECTION

Our discussion of the choice process has emphasized that both the individual and the organization are concerned with attracting and selecting. It has also stressed that individuals and organizations often feel they have conflicting goals in the selection process. Given the complexity of the process, it is not surprising that misperceptions develop and that poor decisions often are made. Both sides contribute to this. The individual contributes when he presents himself in an unrealistic manner because he assumes that he is better off having a particular job than not having it. The organization contributes when it presents itself in a misleading way in order to attract individuals. There is, of course, a real question whether in the long run either the individual or the organization profits when one attracts the other because of misrepresentations—no matter how honestly motivated. When the individual is misled, it may cause him to choose a job that he will not find satisfying. The consequences typically are turnover and absenteeism, behavior which is functional for neither the individual nor the organization. When the organization is misled, it may hire someone who cannot adequately perform the job. This decreases organizational effectiveness and often results in the organization eventually dismissing the individual. Obviously neither the individual nor the organization benefits.

Given that both could profit why don't both parties provide more open and accurate information during selection? One reason is that the selection situation typically gets defined as a competitive situation. In order for genuine communication to exist, it would have to be seen as a problem-solving, counseling situation where the individual and the organization trust each other and sit down together to decide whether the job is right for the individual and the individual is suited to the organization.

The ideal situation would look quite different from the one which typically exists. The organization would describe the job it has to offer in realistic terms, pointing out both the satisfactions and the frustrations that the job presents. It might present the results of job attitude surveys carried out with people in the job. If relevant, the individual might be given a chance to interview job holders. Tests would be administered and the individual would be presented with the results to help him decide whether he wants the job. He would be told how likely people with his scores are to succeed on the job. The individual, on the other hand, would present as accurate a picture of himself as he could. He would talk openly about his strengths and weaknesses, and he would respond to selection instruments as candidly as possible.

What is needed for this to happen? Organizations would have to give up some or all of their selection decision-making powers to the individual, and they would have to accept the fact that it is not functional to attract people on the basis of unrealistic expectations. Only if the individual feels the information he provides will be used fairly in evaluating him will he be likely to enter into a counseling relationship with the organization. If organizations continue making hiring decisions in a unilateral manner, individuals will continue to question whether it is to their advantage to be utterly forthright in the selection situation. Giving up some of their selection powers is a big step for organizations to take, and therefore it is not one that is likely to be taken easily or quickly. However, it is also one that, as was noted earlier, organizations may be forced to take because of legal and social pressure to abandon present selection methods.

REVIEW AND DISCUSSION QUESTIONS

1   What types of conflict arise in the attraction-selection process? Is such conflict beneficial or harmful to (1) the individual and (2) the organization?
2   In the selection-attraction process Kipsy (Chapter 1) might have avoided what for her turned out to be a rather unpleasant state of affairs. How might she have done so?
3   What mechanisms does the individual use to attract organizations he desires to work for? What are some of the likely consequences of using such mechanisms for (1) the individual and (2) the organization?
4   What is meant by "impression management"? What role does impression management play in individuals attracting organizations? Does the management of impressions serve to invalidate the selection process? Have you observed this in your own experiences?
5   What efforts are made by organizations to attract individuals? Should the mechanisms used to attract individuals vary as a function of the type of job for which candidates are being sought?
6   A test that perfectly measures an individual's ability to do a job may not be an accurate predictor of his performance on the job itself. Why? Does this suggest that testing is not very useful?
7   What factors determine the success of an organization's selection program?

8 What kinds of tests can be faked? Does this mean they are invalid?
9 Interviewers are often poor information processors. What is meant by this statement?
10 What kinds of tests are usually the best predictors of job performances?

Chapter 6

Adaptation Processes: Individuals and Organizations Learning to Accommodate to Each Other

Once the individual and the organization have chosen each other—as discussed in the previous chapter—the usually complex and often difficult adaptation period begins. The new employee and the organization must mutually learn to adjust to each other. In some instances the "marriage" settles down into an easy, comfortable relationship. In others, there is an abrupt separation that leaves scars with both parties. In between these two extremes are the remaining majority of cases of individual-organization adaptation: flexible accommodations that result in a never-ending series of compromises—the individual never completely obtaining all he wants from the organization, and the latter never fully utilizing him for its own purposes. Yet, each has the chance to gain something from the continuing interaction.

The nature of this relationship has been characterized as a sort of "psychological contract" (Levinson et al., 1962). By this term is meant "a series of mutual expectations of which the parties to the relationship may not themselves be even dimly aware but which nonetheless govern their relationship to each other" (p. 21). Additionally, it is noted that "neither party to the transaction, since the transaction is such a continuing one, fully knows what it is he wants over the length of the psychological contract, though each acts as if there were a stable frame of reference which defined the relationship" (p. 37). In other words, both the individual and the organization, at the time they formally link up when the new employee comes to work, bring with them certain sets of expectations. These anticipations and attitudes then continue to change and evolve as the individual remains longer with the organization. They never become fully and formally defined, and hence there is always present the element of surprise and the possibility of disconfirmation of previously held perceptions. Thus both the frustrations and the stimulations enter into the individual-organizational adaptation processes.

The key to understanding individual-organization adaptation is the fact that it is two-way. The individual gives up a certain amount of his freedom of action when he joins an organization. As part of the psychological contract he implicitly agrees that the organization will have some legitimate demands it can make on him (e.g., requiring a certain number of hours of work per week), which have the effect of limiting his alternative behaviors. The organization, however, also actively aids and abets the shaping of the individual's behavior to its needs and does not leave it to chance. This is the influence process labeled "socialization." It is as if the organization were "putting its fingerprints on people" (Schein, 1968). Simultaneously, however, the new employee will be attempting to exert influence on the organization in order to gain additional personal satisfaction. This reciprocal process can be referred to as "individualization." Both processes go on all the time, and the nature and extent of one will interact to alter the course of the other. Ordinarily, the situation can be likened to a so-called nonzero sum game in which neither process dominates the other to a 100 percent degree. Occasionally, however, socialization can swamp individualization (as in extreme examples of the "organization man" syndrome), or individualization shatters socialization (as when one man so dominates an organization or a unit within it that it is completely made over to his image). In such circumstances, the reciprocal processes deteriorate into a zero sum game.

In the next two sections of this chapter, we will take a detailed look at socialization and at individualization. The section following will examine the psychological situation that exists at the point of entry of the new employee into the organization, and the nature of the specific expectations that each has about the other. The last section of the chapter will deal with the critical initial employment period when the adaptive processes undergo their most severe strain.

SOCIALIZATION
Nature and Importance of Organizational Socialization

Socialization, as defined by social scientists, refers to "the whole process by which an individual, born with behavioral potentialities of an enormously wide range, is led to develop actual behavior which is confined within a much narrower range—the range of what is customary and acceptable for him according to the standards of his group" (Child, 1954, p. 655). The concept, of course, has been particularly prominent for some time in the analysis of the impact of cultural factors on the personality development of individuals. More recently, scholars concerned with organizations have found it useful to apply the socialization concept to these particular social entities. Thus, the phrase "organizational socialization" has been employed to mean "the process of 'learning the ropes,' the process of being indoctrinated and trained, the process of being taught what is important in an organization or some subunit thereof" (Schein, 1968, p. 2). This learning, as Schein notes, is "defined as the price of membership."

In considering the process of organizational socialization, it is necessary to keep in mind its *continuous nature.* It begins even prior to the time the individual enters an organization, because the family, the school, other social institutions, and peers provide information concerning the values and norms of employing organizations. It continues and becomes sharply intensified when the individual enters the organization, but it does not stop there. It goes on—when he is transferred or changes jobs, gets promoted, or joins another organization. In effect, "the behaviors appropriate to an organizational position are not acquired once and for all when the position is assumed but are learned and relearned throughout the length of a career" (Caplow, 1964, p. 169).

The importance of socialization, from both the point of view of the organization and the individual, cannot be overestimated. This has been emphasized by Schein, one of the major investigators of the phenomenon in organizations:

> The process is so ubiquitous and we go through it so often during our total career that it is all too easy to overlook it. Yet it is a process which can make or break a career, and which can make or break organizational systems of manpower planning. The speed and effectiveness of socialization determine employee loyalty, commitment, productivity and turnover. The basic stability and effectiveness of organizations therefore depends upon their ability to socialize new members.(1968, p. 2)

Phases of the Socialization Process

The organizational socialization process involves three basic phases: prearrival, encounter, and change and acquisition. We shall examine each of these briefly.

1 **Prearrival:** The individual arrives at a new organization or a new position within an organization with an already existing set of values, attitudes, and expectations. While in many ways the new situation will be quite ambiguous for the new arrival (as we shall discuss in a later section), he nevertheless typically does not appear on the scene as a completely blank slate. He has been through an educational system, he has had various forms of contact with different kinds of work organizations (as part-time employee, customer, etc.), and he has been recruited for this specific organization—or has chosen to apply to work for this organization on the basis of some information about it acquired from friends, relatives, or employment agencies. He thus comes to the situation with an existing perceptual picture about the organization and (in many cases) about the job.

The degree of comprehensiveness and accuracy of such perceptions will, of course, vary widely from one individual to another. In some cases, the picture is hazy or virtually nonexistent, as is illustrated by a quote from one of the respondents (a tabulating-machine operator) in a study of a utility company. When asked how he came to join the company, this man said: "It was more by accident than anything else. I went to the [state] employment service. They asked if I was interested in IBM or if I had any experience. I said I hadn't, but they sent me down here on Thursday . . . and I started the next Monday. I guess they were hard up for help" (Levinson et al., 1962, p. 24). Another respondent (a junior accountant) in the same study indicates a somewhat more developed set of expectations: "I had come to town looking for a job. Several people from the local high school were working here in. . . . I went to the [state] employment service and found nothing there, so I took the phone book and picked what seemed to me to be the most likely companies and went around to them one by one. I was looking for companies where a person could get ahead and Midland was one place I stopped in the process of doing that" (1962, p. 25).

One can contrast these cases with that of, say, a college graduate with an MBA degree from a prestigious university who has been aggressively recruited and who has received offers from half a dozen companies. This person will have a highly developed set of expectations—many of them probably not very accurate—concerning the organization he decides to join. In any event, though, the point is that people entering an organization or a job bring with them a set of cultural baggage that they have acquired previously, and some of it will be highly relevant and specific to the organization. Thus, a given organization's socialization process does not construct a brand-new individual, so to speak, but rather attempts to reconstruct him.

2. **Encounter:** Immediately at the point of entry into the organization, the individual's existing set of attitudes and his behavioral predispositions encounter those which the organization desires or values. Sometimes, of course, this encounter can take on the appearance of a head-on clash. More typically, it involves a pattern of day-to-day experiences in which the individual is subjected to the reinforcement policies and practices of the organization and its members. Basically, the organization has three reinforcement tactics available to it:

a. Reinforcement and confirmation: The positive reaction by the organization to actions or attitudes exhibited by the newcomer. It can be assumed that in most employment situations there will be at least some minimal degree of congruence between the individual's existing behavioral tendencies on arrival and those that the organization prefers. Thus, frequently, the organization will find that there are a number of areas of the new person's work behavior where it can reinforce what the individual has brought to the situation.

b. Nonreinforcements: These organizational reactions are to be distinguished from negative reinforcements (see item *c* following); they refer, in effect, to the organization's ignoring or not giving definite positive approval to something the individual has said or done. An example would be the new employee's attempts to be particularly gregarious with his immediate work colleagues. Their lack of especially positive response may signal to the individual that this specific type of behavior is not a preferred way for getting along well in the new situation. Consequently it might be expected, according to behavioral principles, that the individual's high level of gregarious activity would diminish somewhat over time through this nonreinforcement.

c. Negative reinforcements: these reactions are responses by the organization (or its members) that are interpreted by the individual as definitely punishing—i.e., they result in a level of behavior below that which existed before the act occurred. This would be illustrated in a situation where a new employee used a piece of equipment before he was given official sanction and where he subsequently received a reprimand from his superior.

It must be emphasized that any of the three types of responses can be either unplanned or deliberate on the organization's part. That is, the organization through its members can react to something the newcomer has done in such a way that it results in, say, a positive feeling on his part, yet the organization members providing the reaction may be quite unaware that they have administered a reinforcement. Similarly, of course, many of the reactions will be definitely deliberate, with the calculated purpose in mind to support or modify the newcomer's behavior. Either way, the effects are the same: the newcomer feels strong pressure to adopt certain modes of behavior—some of which he may have brought with him—and to change others.

Since the encounter phase of socialization can bring considerable discomfort to the individual, its success—from the organization's point of view—involves two factors which are "not always under the control of the organization" (Schein, 1968, p. 5). One of these is the initial level of motivation the new employee has at the time of entrance. If the level is high, the individual is then willing to put up with a high rate of nonreinforcing or even punishing actions by the organization's members. A good example would be someone who wants to join an elite organization (e.g., a professional football team) where the various rewards of employment are potentially quite large. If the level of motivation tends to be low, however, even mild socialization attempts by the organization may result in the new employee's decision to leave. Thus, the organization will need to take into account the value of the new member and his motivation level, in deciding how far to go in deliberate planned socialization attempts.

The second factor tending to influence the success of early socialization attempts concerns the extent to which the organization can use inducements and constraints in keeping the individual attached to it. On the positive side, the organization can hold out the possibility of certain kinds of specific rewards (e.g., bonuses) that will be available to the individual only if he lasts a certain amount of time with the enterprise. On the negative side, the organization can attempt to enforce legal, material, or moral sanctions (e.g., "if you leave now, we would not be able to give you a satisfactory recommendation to any other place of employment"). Some of these tactics, depending upon aspects of the situation, will have the effect of holding the person in an otherwise undesirable situation, and in this case he may become quite resistant to much of the attempted socialization.

3. **Change and acquisition:** As a result of the early socialization encounters—what Schein labels the "unfreezing" process—it is likely that the individual will change to some degree in the directions favored by the organization. He will thus go through the third socialization phase, an acquisition phase, in which he proceeds to learn and develop modified ideas and behavior. Caplow (1964) has provided a list of four of these acquisition requirements:

  a. *A new self-image:* In effect, this involves the individual's new perception of himself that results from his interaction with his organizational role. As the result of all his organizational experiences he acquires a view of himself that may or may not be greatly divergent from that which he had before entry. We may speculate that the degree of change will be directly proportional to the severity and extent of the organization's attempted socialization efforts and the uniqueness and visibility of the particular role he occupies, and inversely related to his age and degree of previous work experience. Caplow notes that "once developed, the self-image is not easily changed . . . and the self-image of a fully socialized member mirrors the entire organization, although not always perfectly" (1964, p. 170).

b. New relationships: This acquisition requirement "always involves something more than the development of new relationships; it also requires the abandonment of old ones. . . . There is always the awareness that becoming what one is now means forgetting what one was before" (Caplow, 1964, p. 171). Furthermore, as Caplow points out: "The extent and importance of the old relationships that are to be abandoned usually determine what kind of socialization process is necessary. In those cases in which socialization takes a drastic form, the severity of the experience is explained not so much by the difficulty of learning the new part as by the difficulty of forgetting the old" (1964, p. 171). It is those present organization members involved in the incoming employee's new relationships who transmit the organization's norms and who thus, in effect, determine when the individual has acquired the "proper" socialized role. They indicate this by the degree to which they accept the newcomer and allow him to enter into their existing network of interactions.

c. New values: The individual undergoing the socialization process acquires values the organization considers appropriate by first receiving information about them, then by accepting them, and finally by internalizing them. Of course, with respect to specific values, the socialization process may stop at any of these three steps; thus, for example, the individual working in a retail merchandising company learns that it values quantity over quality, and he accepts this as a necessary feature of this particular organization but never really internalizes this organizational value as part of his own basic values. As with other attributes associated with his organizational role, the new employee learns that some values are much more central and crucial to the enterprise than others, and a criterion of successful socialization (from the organization's perspective) is whether he can make such distinctions.

d. New modes of behavior: Finally, of course, not only will the individual modify to a greater or lesser degree his self-image, his relationships, and his values but also he will be likely to acquire new sets of behaviors. Indeed, some of these will be absolutely essential to his chances of remaining with the organization and obtaining some of its rewards. Schein (1971) and others have distinguished among three kinds of role behaviors in terms of their necessity for acquisition: (1) *Pivotal:* those role behaviors the organization considers so essential that without their adoption by the individual he will not be considered a minimally adequate performer. For example: for an inspector, carrying out quality-control tests. (2) *Relevant:* behavior modes considered by the organization to be desirable but not absolutely necessary. Presumably, the more of these the individual acquires the greater his chances for success within the organization. Even without demonstrating all of them, however, he can become an accepted member and can continue with the organization. For example: for an airline flight attendant, talking about the airline in favorable terms to passengers. (3) *Peripheral:* role and organizational behaviors that are not seen as necessary nor even particularly desirable but which would be permitted to be exhibited and which might eventually become relevant behaviors in the eyes of the organization. For example: for a typist, conversing with fellow workers about the organization's personnel practices.

The Organization's Methods of Promoting Socialization

All organizations—whether work organizations, religious orders, prisons, or whatever—have available a variety of possible means to promote the socialization of new and continuing members. Some of these specific methods are more feasible for certain types of organizations than for others, as, for example, hazing in a military academy. Thus, certain of the methods become the preferred modes of socialization in particular organizations while other methods become deemphasized or ignored. In general, however, there are a limited number of types of socialization methods that are most commonly used in organizations that employ people. These would include the following (Caplow, 1964).

Selection   While this might tend to be an overlooked method in any analysis of socialization because it occurs prior to the person's entry into the organization, it nevertheless is a widely used and often powerful means of assisting the total process. Therefore, some of the aspects of the organization's choice process that were discussed in the last chapter are directly relevant to a consideration of socialization. Everyone can think of work organizations with which they are familiar that use selection as a major method of ensuring the "right" type of behavior among their employees. The danger to the organization in putting too much emphasis on selection as a means of socialization, however, is that it may screen out some of the very qualities that would be most useful to it at the same time that it permits desired qualities to filter through. Consequently, the organization must be especially careful to weigh the costs and benefits of this particular method.

Training This method is, of course, one of the organization's major and most explicit socializing instruments. (Because it occupies such an important place in individual-organization interactions, it will be given extended treatment in the next chapter.) Ostensibly, organizations use training to develop the necessary technical and task skills that the employee will need to know to carry out his job. In this sense, they are facilitating socialization of new modes of behavior—direct, job-related activities. In addition, however, training programs of organizations also have an impact on the other socialization goals of modified self-images, new relationships, and new values—what has been referred to as "adaptive" skills (Fine, 1967; Dunnette et al., 1973). In some instances, organizations will make these other socialization objectives quite explicit in training (e.g., "this is our agency's policy on this issue"). In other cases, however, the adaptive-type skills are not directly emphasized in training and it is up to the individual to detect what is proper (i.e., attitudes and behavior likely to lead to organization rewards) and what is not. Those who are more successful in ferreting out such cues, which may be quite subtle, often will already have gained an advantage over their new fellow employees. Success or accomplishment demonstrated in training often affects a person's organizational career well beyond the specific training period.

Apprenticeship "Apprenticeship is a preferred mode of socialization in systems in which the values to be communicated are as important as the accomplishments" (Caplow, 1964, p. 173). The method involves the organization's delegation to one of its members the responsibility for socialization of specific newcomers. The organization member thus is to serve as a model to be emulated by the new arrival. The practice in modern-day organizations is a carry-over from the days of craft guilds when the beginner was apprenticed to the master craftsman. In contemporary organizations, apprenticeship may be either explicit and formally acknowledged, or it may be of an indirect and implicit kind. In a number of latter instances, the newcomer's assignment to work with an old-timer is not designated as an apprenticeship relationship as such, but that is often the way it works out in practice, depending, of course, on the leadership and followership characteristics of the two individuals involved. Because apprenticeship is not an especially efficient method of socialization where large numbers of people are involved, its use in many organizations tends to be restricted to particular situations involving unique or highly crucial jobs.

Debasement Experiences This method (called "mortification" by some social scientists) refers to dramatic experiences the individual undergoes that have the effect of detaching him from his previous attitudes and ways of thinking about himself and substituting a more humble self-view that will permit easier application of organizational influences. Some of these experiences are accidental, but others involve deliberate planning and implementation by the organization. A classic example from a nonemployment situation is, of course, traditional fraternity hazing. From a work setting, a striking illustration of one of these deliberate debasement experiences (labeled "upending experiences") is provided by Schein (1968, p. 5):

> [In an engineering company] a supervisor had a conscious and deliberate strategy for dealing with what he considered to be unwarranted arrogance on the part of engineers whom they hired. He asked each new man to examine and diagnose a particular complex circuit, which happened to violate a number of textbook principles but actually worked very well. The new man would usually announce with confidence, even after an invitation to double-check, that the circuit could not possibly work. At this point the manager would demonstrate the circuit, tell the new man that they had been selling it for several years without customer complaint, and demand that the new man figure out why it did work. None of the men so far tested were able to do it, but all of them were thoroughly chastened and came to the manager anxious to learn where their knowledge was inadequate and needed supplementing. According to this manager, it was much easier from this point on to establish a good give-and-take relationship with his new man.

Anticipatory Socialization This method involves the individual's developing a strong identification with a group to which he does not yet belong. In the context of the work organization, this would refer to a new or continuing employee adopting the values and styles of behavior of some other—usually higher level—group of members. Examples would be the younger manager who aspires to the upper echelons of executives, or the person who wants to be among the "in" group of his peers. The greater the extent of anticipatory socialization, especially if the groups identified with it are central to the running of the organization, the easier it is for the organization to influence the individual. One can, of course, think of the reverse of anticipatory socialization where the new member directly rejects the norms and practices of the longer-tenured members. This would be exemplified by those we label as "young Turks." Where this kind of situation exists, socialization is impeded and the organization may have *its* values altered rather than vice versa.

Trial and Error   One of the most common forms of socialization, trial and error is proof that there is a great deal of nonprogrammed, nondeliberate learning of organization mores by the novice. Since most organizations that employ people cannot exercise 100 percent control over the work experiences of the individual, they must depend on trial and error as a useful means of socialization. They know that the newcomer in the daily course of events will encounter a number of situations from which he can learn as he tries different forms of behavior. While such a method of socialization may not be as systematic as, say, training or apprenticeship, it is also considerably less costly to the organization.

INDIVIDUALIZATION

Socialization has been covered at some length because it is a process that social scientists have been studying and analyzing for some time. Individualization, the reciprocal process that goes on simultaneously in employee-organization adaptation, has received much less specific attention. It is, however, no less important.

As we have stressed at the beginning of this chapter, at the same time that an organization is attempting to put its distinctive stamp on the individual, he in turn is striving to influence the organization so that it can better satisfy his own needs and his own ideas about how it can best be operated. This is what is meant by the term individualization—which has also been called "personalization" (Bakke, 1953) or "innovation" (Schein, 1968). Regardless of whatever label one wishes to attach to it, the process is as essential to the organization as is socialization. Without individualization there would be very little of what John Gardner has called "organization renewal." The enterprise, if people did not pursue individualization attempts, would tend to become locked into a particular *modus operandi* encompassing an unchanging set of beliefs and norms. While this might be effective in the short run, the environment in which organizations operate is much too dynamic for this kind of rigidity to lead to success over the long run. Thus, individualization, aside from its functional properties for the psychological well-being of the employee, has potential survival value for the organization.

In part, of course, the character of the single employee's individualization initiatives will be in response to the depth and character of the organization's socialization attempts. Some individuals will find it difficult to exert their unique qualities because of the severity and extensiveness of the socialization process—as in so-called total institutions such as prisons or mental hospitals (Goffman, 1961). Even in certain business-type firms employees will often need to spend a great deal of effort if they are to maintain a sense of individuality amid a host of socialization influences. It should be observed, however, that given the wide range of personal characteristics of those entering an organization—despite possible elaborate screening procedures—there will be some individuals who will exhibit very little in the way of individualization and others who will show a considerable amount of this behavior. That is, while the organization's socialization methods have a decided impact on individualization, they do not totally determine it.

The range of individualization-type reactions to socialization have been roughly classified into three major types (Schein, 1968):

1. *Rebellion:* This extreme type would include the individual who rejects all the organization's values and norms and who thus pushes his individualization to such extremes that it cannot be ignored. The usual outcome of this individualization process is that the person either is dismissed by the organization or is successful in bringing profound change into the organization. Another possible outcome, however, is that the organization will co-opt the individual—that is, give him some position of responsibility which is so attractive to him that he becomes a defender rather than an attacker of the existing norms and values.

2. *Creative individualism:* This type of response to socialization involves a person's acceptance of the pivotal or absolutely essential (from the organization's standpoint) norms and values, but rejection of many of the relevant or peripheral ones. This, presumably, would be the most successful form of individualization for both parties—the employee gains by exerting some influence on the total collective body (or some subunit of it), and the organization gains by an infusion of fresh ideas and possibly more effective modes of performance. However, as Schein points out, "to remain creatively individualistic in an organization is particularly difficult because of the constant resocialization pressures which come with promotion or lateral transfer. With each transfer, the forces are great toward either conforming or rebelling. It is difficult to keep focused on what is pivotal and retain one's basic individualism" (1968, p. 10).

3. *Conformity:* This type, the complete opposite of rebellion, involves the individual's acceptance of all the organization's norms and values, even its most peripheral ones. While at first glance it might seem to some members of the organization that this is the most desired type of socialization outcome, evidence of the "organization man" variety tends to indicate that in the long run it is a far from optimal situation for the organization. In such cases, the organization may have won a type of Pyrrhic victory.

It must be kept clearly in mind that these three types are merely three points on a continuum, and the members of a given organization are likely to fall all along this continuum. The differences among organizations, of course, involve the *distribution* of individuals from rebellion through creative individualism to conformity. It can be hypothesized that the more the distribution approximates a normal curve with most of the employees in the middle section between the two extremes, the more likely it will be a healthy organization. However, it is often hard for both the individual and the organization to discern when a person is exhibiting enough individualization to contribute something new and valuable to the total collectivity, on the one hand, and when he is going so far in this direction, on the other hand, that he is in danger of tearing down a reasonably well-functioning system.

One other aspect of individualization that should be mentioned is that its impact is likely to be greater toward the middle or latter part of a person's career with an organization rather than in the early stages (Schein, 1971). Accordingly, one might think of a set of scales in which the balance is tipped decidedly toward the organization when a man is in his initial years with it, with the balance shifting—not at all for some, gradually for others, and quickly for a few—toward the individual as time passes. Whether, in his very last years with an organization, the balance shifts again back to the neutral point for an individual will depend on a number of factors including, particularly, how far he has risen toward its upper reaches. All of this should remind us that a discussion of socialization and individualization cannot be separated from a consideration of organization careers—a topic relevant to the next chapter.

THE SITUATION WHEN THE NEW EMPLOYEE ENTERS AN ORGANIZATION

When a brand-new employee enters an organization to begin work, it is somewhat like a late arrival joining a party where he knows only a few people. The party has been in progress for some time. The people already present have established certain sets of comfortable relationships. Suddenly, the invited newcomer is thrust into their midst. He is an unknown quantity to many of them. They, in turn, are largely strangers to him. Each side, but particularly the newcomer—who must adapt to a number of people, while they need adjust only to him—feels some sense of ambiguity. Each, however, will also have some expectations. The person who has invited the newcomer has told him how great the party will be and how much he will like the activities and new friends he will meet there. Of course, the newcomer also realizes that something will be expected from him in return—that he will have to enter into the festivities in a lively manner and contribute to the success of the party. Likewise, a few of those already present may have heard great things about the newcomer and will be expecting him to live up to his advance billing. Others, perhaps, may have a strong sense of skepticism, even hostility, directed toward this new arrival who just might upset the already smoothly functioning party. We can see, then, that for both the newcomer and the members of the party already present, the entry situation presents attractive possibilities but is also fraught with potential problems. Accordingly, the new arrival may have wildly unrealistic expectations of how good things will be, or he may be overcome by anxieties about how well he will fit in; the other party-goers, on the other hand, may expect too much from the newcomer or they may try to give him a hard time to see if he really deserves to join their group.

Although the above analogy cannot be pressed too far, it does serve to illustrate some of the aspects of the situation that pertain when a new employee enters into an organization. From the individual's point of view it is a time of stress, anxiety, and hope. From the organization's standpoint, it is a time of great opportunity to exert influence on an employee. For the remainder of this section we will examine some of the expectations that each holds at this time concerning the future relationship.

Expectations of the Individual

Self-initiated Recruitment   The nature of the expectations about the organization that the new employee will bring with him at the time of entry will depend a great deal upon the extent of the prior recruiting relationship (Chapter 5). In the case of the typical rank-and-file employee, the recruitment will probably have been largely self-initiated in that the individual has sought out the organization. Depending upon general economic conditions and the specific condition of the organization, the effort to bring about hiring may be mostly on the part of the individual. In such a circumstance, the would-be employee has endeavored to convince the organization that it should employ him, and the organization has not had to build itself up as a particularly desirable place to work. This would imply that the individual would not have exceptionally favorable or unrealistic expectations concerning how well he will be treated by the organization (and its members). It would also imply that most of his thoughts at entry would focus on how well *he*—not the organization—will measure up to requirements.

The kinds of tensions or anxieties often found when a person enters an organization under the above circumstances have been described in a study of some 400 newly hired machine operators (Gomersall & Myers, 1966). These individuals had been hired for semiskilled jobs but were not required to have had any relevant past experience. Interviews and questionnaire data revealed that most of these workers experienced anxieties of three types: (1) the "unpredictable and sometimes threatening" aspects of the new job situation, (2) anxieties relating to off-the-job situations, such as family and financial problems, and (3) tension related to the desire to do a competent job and demonstrate individual self-expression. The investigators interpreted the first two types of anxieties as depressants on performance during the first months on the job, and the latter type as a potentially positive force helpful to adequate performance. The combined amount of anxiety clearly seemed to be interfering with the operators' ability to learn the new job quickly and to cope effectively with the situation. (In the next section the steps that were taken to overcome the problem in this particular manufacturing company will be outlined.)

Organization-initiated Recruitment   When the recruiting relationship is reversed, with the organization taking aggressive steps to entice the individual to join, different kinds of expectations on the part of the newly hired are created. Many of these expectations will be quite unrealistic—that is, cannot be fulfilled by the organization—because the recruiters or hiring officials have felt it necessary to picture the organization in overly positive terms in order to motivate the individual to decide to join. This can happen with certain categories of nonmanagement workers whose particular skills may be in short supply; however, it occurs most vividly with the college graduate being recruited for potential management jobs.

The relatively high level of expectations on the part of some college graduates who have been vigorously recruited has been documented by a number of investigators (e.g., Schein, 1964; Dunnette, Arvey, & Banas, 1973; Campbell, 1968; Bray, Campbell, & Grant, 1974). For example, the expectations, in relation to reality, of managerial recruits in one large company were characterized in the following way:

> The findings strongly suggest that the young manager goes through a process of adjustment and change during the early years of his career. His attitude toward the company becomes less favorable, and his optimistic expectations are toned down considerably. Examination of case histories indicate that the "negative" changes are realistic ones. For example, it is not uncommon in our samples to find a fairly large percentage of the recently hired college graduates expressing sincerely and with conviction that they expect to become officers of the company. After a year or two of reality testing in the organization, expectations become more realistic. The same point can be made about attitudes toward the company. Some of the new recruits entering the first job of their managerial career have extremely positive views of the company. Their attitudes would be considered very idealistic . . . in a well managed company. (Campbell, 1968, p. 11)

Similar reports come from other organizations: "The bright picture that [these men] hoped for and expected at the time they accepted employment with the company simply failed to materialize" (Dunnette, Arvey, & Banas,

1973); ". . . there were significant differences . . . between a recent graduate's expectations and his actual job experiences during the first three months. . . . A number of new engineers found themselves in situations quite different from what they had expected. . . . [These] difficulties resulting from their original expectations undoubtedly reduced their development and effectiveness during this period" (Harris, 1968, p. 27).

Creating More Realistic Expectations   It is clear that the expectations held by some newly hired employees can sometimes be so unrealistic that definite morale, turnover, and related problems are created once the person begins to experience the actual job situation. One question, therefore, is whether the organization can or should endeavor to generate more realistic expectations. Although this is a problem that has not received extensive research attention, there are at least two investigations that provide some suggestive findings in this area.

One study was carried out in the insurance industry (Weitz, 1956). On the basis that repeated attitude surveys of already-employed agents showed that those who had received more accurate information about the job of the agent were less likely to leave it for some other type of work, one company prepared a new recruiting booklet designed to give a more down-to-earth view of the job and some of its less glamorous duties. The previously used booklet had emphasized only the positive aspects of the job. The new one pointed out these, but also was quite explicit about some of the problems and frustrations that might be encountered. For example, in one section the booklet described sample situations that the typical agent frequently faces:

> An Agent spends several hours preparing a sound insurance program for a family . . . only to be turned down during the second interview.

> An Agent pays a call on a prospect to discuss insurance, only to be subjected to uncomplimentary . . . even though unwarranted . . . remarks about salesmen.

The booklet containing these and similar descriptions of aggravations was distributed to some fifty agencies, while another matched group of fifty agencies continued to use the old hard-sell recruiting booklet. The findings showed that just as many applicants were recruited with the new as with the old booklet (therefore, it did not cut down on the number of applicants desiring to try out such a job), yet the percentage of men still on the job after six months was 71 percent for those exposed to the new "realistic" booklet and only 57 percent for those getting the regular hard-sell treatment. Thus, there was a substantial increase in the six-month survival rate for those exposed to the realism approach.

A somewhat similar type of study, though in a nonemployment setting, was reported by Macedonia (1969). This research was carried out on candidates for appointment to the United States Military Academy. Similar to the life insurance industry study, a new booklet giving a more realistic picture of first-year life at West Point was sent to a random sample of appointees, while no such booklet was sent to a matched sample. It was found that a significantly greater percentage of those receiving the booklet accepted appointments to the academy and in addition survived the first year compared with the no-booklet group.

Both of the above studies indicate that the process of individual-organization adaptation may be facilitated if the organization can take steps toward altering expectations of entrants to bring them more into line with the reality they will face in their new jobs or roles. It is particularly interesting to note that in both instances the presentation of some straight-forward facts about the organization during recruiting did not impair the attraction of recruits to the organization and even aided the entrant's later survival in the new situation. The lessons learned from these studies may be important for the many organizations that do not seem to be aware of the problems that may be created by recruitment practices that artificially inflate expectations—expectations which cannot possibly be met by the real-life organizational environment.

Expectations of the Organization

As previously noted, just as the individual has a set of hopes, anxieties, and expectations about his job and the organization at entry, so does the organization have a reciprocal set of expectations. These expectations may or may not be totally positive, depending again on the circumstances of recruitment. If the person to-be-hired seeks out the organization and applies for a job, the organization may have minimal expectations about the new employee's chances of working out successfully. If, on the other hand, the organization has had to recruit the new person actively, it may be expecting more of him than he can demonstrate, especially in the very early period on the job. Thus, organizational expectations may turn out to be just as unrealistic as are some individual expectations.

It is well to keep in mind that the expectations of those with whom the newcomer will work may be different from the expectations of those who recruited him. The latter's anticipations will usually be quite positive—after all, they are the ones who spent the effort in getting the person to join the organization, and they are the ones who were influential in the organization's decision to hire him—while the former, the potential colleagues, will often hold much dimmer views. In fact, if they perceive the new person to be a threat to their own security and their established relationships to one another and the organization, they may convert their expectations into active hostility. In a sense, this would be a kind of organizational anxiety, manifested by some of its members, that is analogous to the anxiety that the newcomer has when he starts work. The individual at entrance fears that he may fail, and his future colleagues fear that he may be too successful.

Another point to bear in mind concerning the organization's expectations is that they apply not only to how well the individual will perform in his new job but also to how well he will adapt to the organization and its customs and culture. That is, the organization ordinarily will hold definite expectations concerning the socialization process in terms of what end results are desired. The newly hired individual will be expected to adapt to pivotal values and norms, and will be encouraged to adhere to other less crucial ones that serve to reinforce the prevailing psychological climate within the organization and enhance its image outside. The specific level of early job performance may thus not be as important to the organization as some of these other less tangible socialization objectives.

It seems reasonable that an organization would hold its most detailed and well-developed expectations for those entering individuals who represent the highest-cost resources. For many organizations, this would be the new college graduate. In this connection, Schein (1964), in his research on the organizational socialization experiences of this group, has summarized the stereotyped view that many members of business companies hold toward the newly hired graduate at the time of his entrance into the organization:

> He is "overambitious and unrealistic in his expectations regarding the possibilities of advancement and increased responsibility."
> He is "too theoretical, idealistic, and naive to be given an important initial assignment."
> He is "too immature and inexperienced to be given much responsibility."
> He is "too security conscious and too unwilling to take risks."
> He is "unwilling to recognize the difference between having a good idea and the process of selling the implementation of that new idea."
> He is "potentially a highly useful resource. . . ."

While this is what many members of the organization expect the entering college graduate to be like, the organization also has, according to Schein, some definite ideas concerning what it expects from him:

> "Competence to get a job done . . ."
> "Ability to accept organizational realities . . ."
> "Ability to generate and sell ideas . . ."
> "Loyalty and commitment [to the organization] . . ."

"High personal integrity and strength . . ."
"Capacity to grow . . ."

Whether anyone, college graduate or not, could live up to such expectations is debatable. The point is, however, that organizations usually do have a well-developed set of expectations for some new arrivals, particularly those seen as representing potentially quite valuable additions to the membership. If these are set too low, the individual may not perform up to his potential. If they are set unrealistically high, they may serve to hinder the adaptation process and eventually drive the person away from the organization. Either way, the organization has not benefited from its investment in the individual, and he in turn has not gained very much for the time and effort he has given to the organization. Just as inappropriate individual expectations may breach the psychological contract, so can inadequate or unrealistic organizational expectations.

THE CRITICAL INITIAL EMPLOYMENT PERIOD

Available evidence is nearly unanimous in indicating that the very early employment period—the first year or even the first few months—is crucial to the development of a healthy individual-organizational relationship (Herzberg, 1957; Schein, 1968; Dunnette, Avery, & Banas, 1973; Gomersall & Myers, 1966; Berlew & Hall, 1966). It is in this initial period of contact that the two sets of expectations—those of the individual and those of the organization—come into direct confrontation, surrounded by a flow of work realities that neither can control completely.

One primary indication of the stressful nature of the early employment period is the relatively high (compared to later time periods) rate of avoidable employee turnover. One study of rank-and-file workers, for example, found that the quit rate was 491 percent higher for those with less than one year's service than for those who had been employed for longer than a year (Brodman & Hellman, 1947, cited in Herzberg, 1957). The turnover situation for college graduates in management-type jobs is apparently not much different. It is reported (Schein, 1968) that in one sample of such employees 50 percent had changed jobs within three years of graduation, 67 percent within four years, and 73 percent within five years. This kind of evidence appears to indicate that the individual-organization adaptation process has broken down in a relatively high percentage of cases, with consequent costs to both parties.

Impact of the Job Environment

One of the major factors affecting individuals' adaptation to organizations during the very early employment period is the kind of immediate environment or climate that surrounds the job (Porter & Steers, 1973). This job ecology is composed of a number of elements, such as the organization's orientation and induction tactics, the receptivity of fellow workers, the rules and regulations, the attitudes and skills of the supervisor (a factor so important that it will be discussed separately), the morale level of the work group, and so forth. All these elements combine and impinge on the newcomer who is, as we have noted, attempting to make sense out of an ambiguous and possibly threatening situation.

Some newly hired employees, because of their own adaptive skills or because of the relatively benign character of the job climate, will adjust fairly rapidly and will quickly come to terms with this environment. Others will eventually adapt, but it will be a slow, tortuous process. Still others will not be able, or will not want, to cope and thus will become part of the first year turnover statistics. In most job environments there will be some elements which would be difficult for the organization to change—without great cost or the possibility of creating new problems—in order to help the slower-adapting individuals. Examples would include the alteration of basic regulations or the attempt to persuade present workers to be friendlier to new employees. However, there are other elements, such as orientation programs and job instructions, that are much more under the control of the organization and which can be altered to improve the probabilities of successful individual adaptation. A good illustration of such an approach by an organization to provide positive aid for adaptation is contained in the previously cited article by Gomersall and Myers (1966).

As will be recalled, these researchers were concerned about the relatively high amounts of anxiety that seemed to be present when newly hired machine operators (mostly females) were in their first weeks on the job. After obtaining questionnaire and interview data to provide a picture of the nature and extent of the problem, they undertook an experiment. The experiment involved a control group that was oriented and instructed about the job in the usual manner, and an experimental group that was given a new type of introduction to the work.

Members of the control group received the two-hour personnel-department briefing about insurance, parking, hours of work, company regulations, and the like. Then, as was customary, each girl was introduced to "her friendly but very busy supervisor, who gave her further orientation and job instruction." Typically, these instructions might proceed as follows:

> Alice, I would like you to take the sixth yellow chair on this assembly line, which is in front of bonding machine No.14. On the left side of your machine you will find a wiring diagram indicating where you should bond your units. On the right-hand side of your machine you will find a carrying tray full of 14-lead packages. Pick up the headers, one at a time, using your 3-C tweezers and place them on the hot substrate below the capillary head. Grasp the cam actuator on

the right-hand side of the machine and lower the hot capillary over the first bonding pad indicated by the diagram. Ball bond to the pad and, by moving the hot substrate, loop the wire to the pin indicated by the diagram. Stitch bond to this lead, raise the capillary, and check for pigtails. When you have completed all leads, put the unit back in the carrying tray.

Your training operator will be around to help you with other details. Do you have any questions? (Gomersall & Myers, 1966, p. 66)

Naturally, most of the new hires were "overwhelmed" by such instructions but did not wish to upset or irritate the "polite and friendly supervisor" by saying they did not understand. Since the newcomer thus, ordinarily, did not ask many questions concerning the instructions, she was immediately placed at a work station and would try to learn by watching nearby workers. They, being too busy with their own work, were not of much help, and so these members of the control group exhibited the typical anxiety of the new arrival to this job environment.

The experimental group received quite a different introduction to the work. After also listening to the personnel department's briefing, "they were isolated in a conference room where they could be 'initiated' by [a few of] their peers. They were told there would be no work the first day, that they should relax, sit back, and have a coke or cigarette, and use this time to get acquainted with the organization and each other and to ask questions" (p. 66). During the remainder of the day, questions by the new girls were encouraged, and four major points were stressed by the specially selected older workers assigned to assist in this orientation: (1) "Your opportunity to succeed is very good": trainees were shown learning curves and other evidence indicating that 99 percent of all new hires had the necessary skills to learn the job. (2) "Disregard 'hall' talk": the new workers were forewarned of the typical "hazing" [peer-group socialization] that would take place and which often consisted of completely unfounded rumors and other information designed to scare them about the job and their chances of success. (3) "Take the initiative in communication": emphasis was placed on the fact that supervisors expected new workers to ask questions and would not be offended by them. (4) "Get to know your supervisor": briefings were given about the specific personality and characteristics of the supervisor to whom they would be assigned—e.g., ". . . strict, but friendly . . . hobby is fishing and ham radio operation . . . tends to be shy sometimes, but he really likes to talk to you if you want to. . . ."

As a result of this unique orientation to the work and job culture the experimental group reached the organization-established level of competence for the job some four weeks before the control group members, and similar results were replicated by later groups of new employees who received the experimental type of orientation. In essence, anxiety appeared to be reduced much faster than was normal with new hires, and this allowed them to concentrate their energies and alertness on the job to a greater extent than had been possible under the usual procedures. It is likely that the lessons learned from this experiment, would have great applicability in many other kinds of work organizations, as long as each organization or unit introduced modifications appropriate to their particular work situation. In any event, it seems evident that some of the negative aspects of the work environment's impact on the new employee can be lessened, if attention is directed toward understanding the definition of the situation as it would appear from the newcomer's perspective.

Impact of Job Duties

It is in the area of job duties that the new employee may experience the greatest discrepancy between his expectations and organizational reality (Porter & Steers, 1973). As we have seen from the previous section, many employees at entry will have overly optimistic views about what the new job will provide in the way of challenge, interest, and promotional opportunities. These exceptionally high expectations set the stage for initial disappointment and frustration. However, the problem does not lie solely with the expectations. A good portion of the early disenchantment can in many instances be attributed to the anemic quality of the job assignments.

Interesting evidence on the interplay of expectations and initial job duties in producing dissatisfaction is provided in a study of some 1,000 recent college graduates hired by a large manufacturing company. The graduates were surveyed to find out how they felt their first job assignment measured up to their expectations (Dunnette, Arvey, & Banas, 1973). Only about half of those in the sample were still with the company after three years, all the others having left it for a different organization. All respondents were asked to describe both what they had expected when they joined and what the first job was like. The findings are given in Figure 6-1. It can be seen from the figure that the continuing employees and those who left reported similarly: their first job largely failed to meet expectations. Furthermore, it failed to meet expectations in precisely those areas (with the exception of salary) that they considered to be most important: opportunity to use own abilities, feelings of accomplishment, chance to perform interesting work, and the opportunity to advance. Although this study does not allow us to allocate the proportion of responsibility for the men's feelings to their own expectations as opposed to the nature of their first job experiences, it is reasonable to assume that the latter played a role. This organization, like many others, apparently had not taken steps to bring the

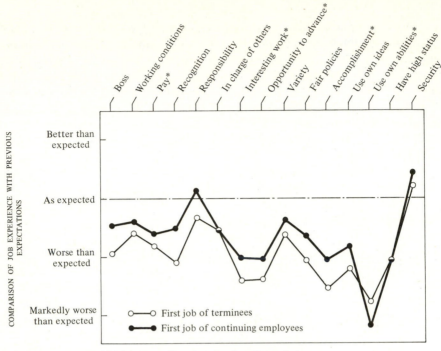

*Job features stated most important by college graduates.

Figure 6-1 Discrepancies between previous job expectations and actual job experiences for both terminees and continuing employees in their first job assignments; based on a sample of 1,000 college graduates hired by a large manufacturing company. (Adapted from Dunnette, Arvey, & Banas, 1973. Reprinted by permission of the publisher from *Personnel*, May/June 1973, © by AMACOM, a division of American Management Association.)

job challenges up to the expectations, or to try to influence the expectations down to the level of the initial job assignments. It can be hypothesized, of course, that a combination of both approaches would be the best means of reducing these expectation-reality discrepancies.

The potential that effective organization actions have to reduce the possible early disenchantment of those employees entering with high expectations is illustrated by the results from studies of two organizations in which the same questionnaire instrument was utilized. It was designed to measure employee expectations to determine whether good performance would lead to favorable organizational and supervisory responses, and hence was intended to show the strength of employees' "motivational force" to perform well (Porter et al., 1971). In Company A, college graduates were actively recruited and then, when arriving to begin employment, were placed in job positions based on the needs of particular departments or units at that specific point in time. Thus, by chance, some of the new employees received especially challenging assignments with exceptionally good supervisors, while others received less exciting assignments coupled with average supervisors. In Company B the newly hired college graduates had been similarly actively recruited. However, their first nine months in the organization were spent in specially selected job assignments that were coordinated by handpicked training supervisors. Thus, early organization experiences were carefully preplanned and received direct attention from highly competent supervisors.

The differences in the motivational force scores for the two groups across their first twelve months with their organizations are shown in Figure 6-2. Even though the new hires in Company A started off—the first day on the job—with somewhat lower expectations, their expectations showed a significant drop between the first day and twelve months. This contrasts with Company B, where a quite steady high level of expectations was maintained across the one-year period. Of course, there are a number of possible reasons for these different results between the two groups (the Company A sample consisted of men in engineering-type jobs, while the Company B sample consisted of men in the merchandising field), but it is highly probable that the drastically different nature of their first-year job assignments accounted for much of the difference in the two trends shown in Figure 6-2.

The positive effects that are possible from particularly challenging first-year jobs have been demonstrated in another research study (Berlew & Hall, 1966). The careers of some sixty junior executives were followed for their first five years in a large utility company. The major question investigated was whether the degree of job challenge a man faced in his first year on the job correlated with later performance and success. The evidence

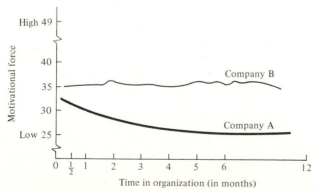

Figure 6-2 Contrasting changes in motivation to perform well during the first twelve months on the job for newly hired employees in two organizations. (Adapted from Porter, et al., 1971.)

strongly confirmed that this was so. Those who were fortunate enough to be given relatively demanding jobs in their early organizational careers seemed to be better prepared to cope with later job assignments. The researchers interpret this finding as suggesting that an entering employee—at least in management—who is given initially challenging job duties will tend to internalize high standards and positive job attitudes. These high standards and positive attitudes in turn will influence the organization to give him increasing opportunities to continue to demonstrate his competence, which consequently will allow for the receipt of a high level of organizational rewards. On the other hand, an entrant who is placed on a relatively easy first job will not have a chance to experience success (since he will not get much credit for doing such jobs well) and to develop high performance standards; in such cases, he may turn his attention to attempts to receive external work incentives rather than being strongly motivated by internal-type rewards of accomplishment and self-fulfilment. It appears, therefore, that organizations—by the way in which they structure initial job assignments and duties—have the opportunity to play an important role in helping prospective managers develop internalized motivation.

Impact of the Supervisor

Equally as important as the meaningfulness of the duties of the first job assignment is the quality of supervision the new employee receives in his first few months in an organization. To the new hire, the supervisor *is* the organization. If he is good, the organization is usually viewed favorably. If he is ineffective in working with the newcomer, the organization itself is seen negatively. As obvious as this point seems, it is surprising how often companies ignore its implications. Their inattention to this situation is manifested in two ways: a failure to select particularly qualified supervisors for assignments to units hiring the highest percentage of new employees, and a failure to prepare supervisors adequately for the special problems likely to be encountered in dealing with new employees.

Supervisor Selection and Assignment Organizations must consider many factors in deciding where to place particular supervisors throughout the total enterprise. Thus, those supervisors who might be most useful in working with new employees are not always available for assignment to these job situations. However, to the extent that the organization does have some latitude in which to select supervisors to work with entering employees, some traits will be more critical than others. For example, the most technically skilled supervisors may not be the most appropriate ones to work with newcomers. These supervisors may be quite impatient with anyone undergoing the learning process, and they would be better suited to working with experienced rather than new employees. More appropriate qualities to consider in supervisor selection for this kind of assignment may include the motivation to be a trainer-teacher and the ability to project a helping rather than a punitive attitude. Above all else, the most important criterion would appear to be a high degree of personal security such that the supervisor will not feel threatened by either the failure or the marked success of the person he is developing on the job. This kind of personal quality on the part of the supervisor would aid the new employee in developing his own identity in the organization and in handling the dependence-independence conflict that all subordinates must face and resolve. By securing a good match between the new employee (especially one who has been costly for the organization to recruit and hire) and his first supervisor, the organization will have taken a major step in the promotion of effective individual-organization adaptation.

Supervisor Training While careful selection of appropriately qualified supervisors to work with new employees will greatly assist the individual in getting through the critical first few months on the job without undue mishaps, it is not a complete solution to the problem. Often, as has been mentioned, the organization will be unable to make desirable supervisory assignments for the new-employee situation because of other factors that must be considered. Thus, many entrants are placed with supervisors not specifically selected for their abilities to handle the newcomers' problems. The organization must in that case rely on training supervisors to be better prepared for this assignment.

The question then arises as to the nature of the training. For supervisors who will be assigned new college graduates, Schein advocates three goals:

> 1 Heighten the supervisors' awareness of the difficult problems which they and the new man will face.
> 2 Provide an opportunity for supervisors to share with one another their insecurities, concerns, and problems . . . and likewise their successful ideas and experiences.
> 3 Create relationships among supervisors which would make it possible for them to consult with one another as a means of obtaining help in dealing with new and unusual problems. . . . (1964, p. 76)

While these are presented as goals for the training of supervisors who will encounter college graduates hired for management-type jobs, they seem equally applicable for supervisors of new employees in rank-and-file jobs.

An interesting and novel approach to the training of supervisors who themselves are new to a particular job situation—and who will have to deal with both new and experienced employees—was tried in one manufacturing company (Gomersall & Myers, 1966): experienced operators trained the supervisors! This was accomplished by having pairs of operators instruct a new supervisor on such matters as the problems usually faced by the new supervisor and the way his role was viewed by the operators. This kind of approach suggests that recently hired employees who have just gone through the critical entry period may be able to assist in training supervisors to handle the brand-new employee.

Expectations of the Supervisor   Much has been written lately about the applicability of Pygmalion-type approaches to developing lower-echelon members of social units (e.g., Rosenthal & Jacobson, 1968; Livingston, 1969; Rosanthal, 1973). (Recall the well-known line in Shaw's *Pygmalion* uttered by Eliza Doolittle: "The difference between a lady and a flower girl is not how she behaves but how she's treated.") There does seem to be some general evidence from a number of sources that if the person in the supervisory or teaching position has positive expectations concerning how well the subordinate can perform, and if these expectations are communicated or made known to the subordinate, his performance may actually be facilitated. This might be labeled the constructive application of self-fulfilling prophecies. Of course, there are some potential dangers here if the expectations that are communicated are too high for a new employee to reasonably meet; in this situation, increased frustration and dissatisfaction, rather than enhanced performance, may result. Also, if the subordinate perceives these stated expectations to be insincere or just a gimmick, the situation will deteriorate rapidly. Therefore, the application of this approach needs to be made with some caution. Nevertheless, it should be clear that whatever expectations the supervisor has for the newcomer will be influential in his progress, and thus the individual will probably be aided more in his adaptation to the new work situation by receiving positive rather than negative supervisory expectations.

COURSE OF ADAPTATION PROCESS OVER TIME

The adaptation process obviously does not stop once the employee has "survived" the critical first months in an organization. It persists, in one form or another, over the remaining time he spends with the organization. While the process may be most painful for both the individual and the organization at the time of entry and immediately thereafter, it may continue to be quite salient for both as time goes on and as the individual transfers from one job to another or moves up from a lower to a higher echelon. The course of the individual-organization adaptation process can therefore be analyzed from the perspective of the individual's organizational career movements through the organization. Two processes are involved in this shaping of the individual's career in the organization. First, there are the organization's attempts to develop the individual so that he will be capable of performing effectively in the jobs that have to be carried out if the organization is to obtain its goals. Second, there are the individual's efforts to develop a career that will help him reach his goals. How these two processes operate and how they influence individual-organization adaptation over time will be considered in the next chapter.

REVIEW AND DISCUSSION QUESTIONS

1 What is meant by "organizational socialization"? What examples can you provide from your own organizational experiences?
2 What is meant by "individualization"? Identify and explain the major types of individualization behaviors.
3 Contrast organizations you are familiar with on the basis of (1) the degree to which they socialize their members and (2) the degree to which individualization occurs in the organizations.
4 What steps might be taken to facilitate the induction of new organizational members? Is it always desirable from the standpoint of the individual and the organization to make the transition from nonmember to member an easy one? For example, should the induction of an assembly-line worker in an auto plant, a first-level supervisor in an insurance agency, and a demolitions expert on a Special Forces team take place in identical ways?
5 How can rewards and punishments (i.e., positive and negative reinforcers) be used by an organization in the socialization of new members?
6 What is likely to occur if a new employee's expectations are not met during his early encounters with an organization?
7 What steps might an organization take to create "realistic" expectations on the part of prospective employees?
8 Analyze the plight of Kipsy (Chapter 1), using the material presented in this chapter as a framework.
9 What conditions determine the degree to which either an individual's coworkers or his supervisor will be effective in socializing him?

Chapter 7

Developmental Processes: Individuals Developing Careers and Organizations Developing Individuals

In the previous two chapters emphasis was placed on how individuals and organizations select each other and initially adapt to each other through socialization and individualization. Neither the selection process nor the adaptation process ends, however, after the individual has joined the organization and has been working there a few months or even years. Individuals continue to consider the possibility of working for other organizations, and thus they continue to make membership decisions. Organizations, for their part, have to decide who to retain, who to promote, who to transfer, etc., and thus they continue to make selection and placement decisions. Organizations and individuals also continue to adapt to each other and to influence each other. Individuals try to develop careers within organizations and organizations try to influence the development of individuals. The efforts of individuals to develop careers and of organizations to develop individuals go on simultaneously and substantially influence each other. Such efforts form the focus of the present chapter.

PEOPLE AS RESOURCES

For many jobs in organizations it is relatively simple to find someone who can and will perform the necessary tasks. For other jobs it is quite difficult since it requires a person who has had years of training and experience of a very particular kind. This is usually true of the top-level jobs in any organization. It is also typically true that these are the very jobs where successful task performance is necessary if the organization is to survive.

Staffing an organization adequately is not simply a matter of having all jobs filled by people who presently are capable of doing them competently. The environment in which organizations exist is always changing, and the skills that are needed to carry out a job one day may not be the right skills at some point in the future. This means that the occupants of jobs either have to develop new skills to keep pace with the changing job demands, or the organization has to replace the person with someone who has the needed skills. Finally, most organizations have life spans that exceed the career of any individual; thus, prospective successors must be available to fill in when job holders retire, change organizations, or are promoted. It is obvious, therefore, that the long-term effectiveness of an organization depends on its developing an adequate supply of people who are prepared to fill the jobs that will exist in the future.

People are a unique kind of resource and often prove difficult to develop, maintain, and utilize. They have their own career objectives, and these may or may not fit the organization's short- and long-range plans. People can be developed through various kinds of training and other experiences, and once they are developed they increase in value both to the organization that has developed them and to other organizations. Unlike other assets, they rarely can be sold and they can decide to leave the organization at any time, thus forcing the organization to write off all its investment in them. Efforts to develop them may fail either because the people are incapable of developing in a given way or because the development was poorly planned or administered. People also often develop and increase in value on their own. Sometimes this occurs as a result of job-related experiences, but often it results from other experiences. Most people want to utilize their skills and abilities, and if they cannot they may leave the organization. Unlike many physical assets, human assets cannot be easily stored or put on the shelf for future use. The organization that trains someone to be the next president may find that the person will leave if he has to wait too long to become president. In a sense, human resources are perishable resources that can be cultivated and that have to be used at the right time.

Many organizations have recognized the importance of preparing people to fill the positions that will be vacant at some future date. They carry on numerous, often diverse, activities designed to develop people so that they will be ready to fill the positions. Many of these activities will be discussed in the remainder of this chapter. The effectiveness of what they do is very much determined, however, by how these activities fit with the career objectives and goals of the people who are being developed. Just as it is obvious to the organization that it must prepare for its future staffing needs, it is obvious to many members of the organization that in the future there will be opportunities for them to develop their careers in ways which will satisfy their goals.

When there is a convergence between the individual's career goals and the organization's development plans, an effective integration of the individual and the organization can take place. The individual will be motivated to develop the skills and abilities necessary to take on new jobs and tasks, and the organization will be inclined to provide the individual with the type of development opportunities he needs. Thus, the organization's desire to develop people and the individual's desire to develop a career need not be forces that operate in opposition to each other. In fact, they can be mutually reinforcing processes.

When there is a lack of convergence between the individual's career goals and the organization's development plans, however, poor individual-organization integration develops, and the results are organizational ineffectiveness and employee dissatisfaction. The literature on careers and development, in fact, suggests that they often do operate in opposition (see, e.g., Sofer, 1970; Campbell, Dunnette, Lawler, & Weick, 1970). There are a number of reasons why this seems to happen. These reasons have their bases both in the way organizations handle their development programs and the way individuals try to develop their careers. Thus, we need to consider both how people develop their careers in organizations and what organizations do to develop people.

INDIVIDUALS DEVELOPING CAREERS

Basic to our understanding of how individuals develop careers in organizations are some of the points made in Chapter 2 about the nature of people. There it was stressed that individuals are goal-oriented and that they develop a perception of their skills and abilities through their attempts to perform certain tasks. As has already been stressed, their career and organization choices are strongly influenced by the kinds of needs they have and by the image they develop of themselves. These same factors also play an important role in determining how individuals pursue their careers in whatever organization they join. A person's self-image and his goals can in turn be influenced by his job, since it can be such an important source of need satisfaction and a basic part of his own identity.

Schein's Organization Model

Schein (1968, 1971) has proposed a set of concepts and variables to describe career movement in an organization. It focuses on "the career as seen as a set of attributes and experiences of the *individual* who joins, moves through, and finally leaves an organization . . . and the career defined by the *organi-zation*—a set of expectations held by individuals inside the organization which guide their decisions about whom to move, when, how, and at what 'speed'" (Schein, 1971, pp. 401–402). One of the key elements in Schein's model is his conceptualization of the structure of the organization *as it pertains to individuals' careers*. This way of looking at organizations is diagrammed in Figure 7-1. As can be seen, Schein finds it useful to conceive of the organization's structure as a "cone," where career movement can proceed along three dimensions:

> Vertically: increasing or decreasing one's rank in the organization
> Radially: increasing or decreasing one's centrality in the organization
> Circumferentially: changing one's function or area in the organization

It is possible for a given move in a person's career to represent a change on one, two, or all three of these dimensions. An individual's aspired and his actual career may involve many moves or very few. If, for example, his long-term goal is to become a vice-president of personnel, he may try to hold a number of different jobs in order to acquire the experience he thinks will be required for the position. Thus, during his career, he may make job changes that involve only radial or circumferential movement; but, of course, these moves are being made only because they all seem to be necessary steps in achieving the ultimate goal—vertical movement.

Especially important in Schein's model is the notion that movement along these dimensions corresponds to crossing *boundaries* that exist within the organization. Thus, when one moves vertically, he crosses *hierarchical boundaries,* and when one moves circumferentially, he crosses *function (departmental) boundaries.* Boundaries can, in turn, be thought of as varying in (1) number, (2) degree of permeability, and (3) type of filtering properties they possess. Presumably, on the average, the larger the organization and the more tightly structured it is, the greater will be the number of boundaries, the less will be their permeability, and the more elaborate their filtering properties.

It is the character and properties of the various types of boundaries that determine how easy or difficult it is for the individual to arrive at where he wants to be in an organization. Some organizations have highly permeable

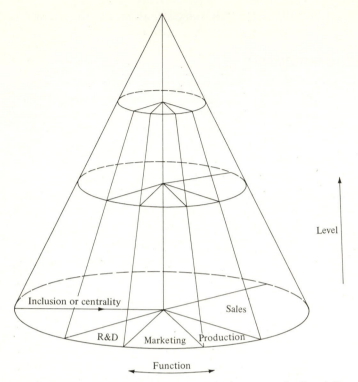

Figure 7-1 A three-dimensional model of an organization (after Schein, 1971).

external inclusion boundaries in that they are not very choosy in their selection process but have highly impermeable interior inclusion boundaries that make it difficult to remain a permanent part of the organization. Other organizations, which put a premium on careful selection but expect those they do take in to stay with the organization, will have the reverse, i.e., a relatively impermeable external inclusion boundary but permeable ones in the interior.

Organizations also differ on their hierarchical boundaries. A "tall" organization with many levels of management in relation to total number of employees will probably make it fairly easy to pass from one echelon to another, but the number of echelons is so great that the individual may have the feeling that he is a long way from the top. So-called flat organizations would be likely to make the echelon-to-echelon boundaries less permeable. The different types of boundaries can also be compared with one another in terms of how they filter; functional boundaries, for example, may emphasize specific competencies, while inclusion boundaries might filter more on the basis of such factors as company politics, adherence to organization norms, and the like.

Individual Career Orientations

Just as organizations differ in the kind of career movement opportunities they present to individuals, individuals differ in how they develop their careers, and in their goals and aspirations. This point is clearly made by some of the research on how individuals develop their careers. An interesting study on a group of some 200 English blue-collar workers showed that they tended to see their jobs and their careers quite differently than upwardly mobile managers who are so often considered when careers in organizations are discussed (Goldthorpe et al., 1968). These blue-collar workers, most of whom were unskilled, saw their relationship with their employers as strictly a financial one in which they did the work in order to be able to do other things off the job. Few were attracted to the idea of promotion; in fact, most only wanted to continue to be paid well for doing the same job. As is shown in Table 7-1, only 10 percent had done anything to increase their chances of promotion. These workers simply did not see promotion as something that would provide them with greater need satisfac-

Table 7-1   Action Taken in Regard to Becoming a Foreman

	Craftsmen (N = 56)	Setters (N = 23)	Process workers (N = 23)	Machinists (N = 41)	Assemblers (N = 86)	All (N = 229)
	Percentage					
Have never thought seriously of becoming a foreman	71	74	70	93	67	74
Have thought seriously of becoming a foreman but have taken no action	18	22	17	5	17	16
Have applied for, enquired about a foreman's job	9	0	13	2	9	7
Have taken other action —e.g., attended training courses	2	4	0	0	6	3
Totals	100	100	100	100	99	100

Source: Goldthorpe, et al., 1968, p. 121.

tion, nor did they see holding a management job as particularly congruent with their self-image. They wanted more leisure and less stress in their lives, and becoming a manager was not seen as likely to provide these. Interestingly, the workers who most saw their jobs in purely "instrumental" terms—i.e., saw them only as a means to gain extrinsic rewards—were those who held lower-status jobs than those held by their parents.

Another study has presented data from a limited sample of employees and suggests that in the United States, too, work may not be the central life interest for at least some blue-collar workers (Dubin, 1956). It concludes that "for almost three out of every four industrial workers studied, work and the work place *are not* central life interests." There is other evidence, however, which indicates that many people are, in fact, identified with and committed to their work. For example, in one study that asked employees whether they would continue to work even if they had enough money so that it was unnecessary, 80 percent of a large sample said that they *would* continue working (Morse & Weiss, 1955).

Two recent studies—one of managers (Sofer, 1970) and one of priests (Hall & Schneider, 1973)—also provide evidence that some employees demonstrate very strong interest in their careers. The managers in the first study were quite concerned with promotion and did a number of things to make themselves look more promotable. Their chief complaint seemed to be that their organization was not using their skills and abilities adequately. The priests similarly reported that particularly in their early careers they were underutilized. They also pointed out that promotion to pastor was too slow in coming. They, like the managers, were strongly identified with their careers, such that their careers were an important part of their total identity. They were like the people who, when asked by Maslow (1968) what they would be if their work roles were changed, responded: "I can't say. If I weren't a [doctor, manager, etc.], I just wouldn't be me."

One interesting question, in this connection, is: *To what* are employees committed? A number of investigators (e.g., Bennis et al., 1958; Kornhauser, 1962; Gouldner, 1958a; 1958b; Hinrichs, 1964; McKelvey, 1969) have been concerned with the issue of professional commitment versus organizational commitment. Indeed, this has come to be called the "cosmopolitan-local" dimension, with the former term representing someone strongly concerned about his professional or occupational group, while the latter represents someone intensely involved in the employing organization. Early research seemed to indicate that individuals were *either* cosmopolitans or locals, but more recent research indicates that it is possible for some individuals to be both or neither. There also is research which suggests that individuals who are cosmopolitan but not locals show the highest turnover rate (Sorenson, 1967).

What is not well understood at the present time is *how* organization commitment can be facilitated. In some cases where the individual has been intensely recruited and then has made a definite decision to work for a particular organization, commitment may be extremely high at the very beginning of the person's career in the organization (Porter, Crampon, & Smith, 1972). Here, the task of the organization is to maintain this already high level of commitment. In other circumstances, individuals may arrive with lower levels of commitment but increase in their identification as they continue their association with the organization. Such a situation was found in a study of forest rangers, where identification with the forest service increased with increasing job tenure, but was not strongly related to changes in position within the organization (Hall, Schneider, & Nygren, 1970). In this case, the individuals seemed to experience a closer relation between their values and those of the organization as they continued their career within it, and this led to increased identification.

> Much that happens to a professional forester tends to tighten the links binding him to the organization. His experiences and his environment gradually infuse into him a view of the world and a hierarchy of preferences coinciding with those of his colleagues. They tie him to his fellows, to the agency. They engender a "militant and corporate spirit," an organized "self-consciousness," dedication to the organization and its objectives, and a fierce pride in the Service. (Kaufman, 1960, p. 197)

Overall, then, it appears that people vary widely in their career perspectives on at least three dimensions: (1) the degree to which they are involved in and identified with their work organization, (2) the degree to which they are involved in and identified with the occupational or professional group of which they are a member, and (3) their mobility aspirations. Although these dimensions are undoubtedly related, they are not perfectly correlated, as is shown by the large number of people who identify with their work organizations but who are not upwardly mobile (Tausky & Dubin, 1965).

Determinants of Career Orientations

How do people develop such different career orientations as those found in the studies on careers? This can be explained only by looking both at the experiences that people have long before they begin their work life—when their self-concept is developing and their perceptions of different occupations are developing—and at the kind of work experiences they have.

Childhood Experiences   Research carried out in England has provided data on how childhood experiences influence individual careers (Carter, 1966). This research stresses the strong impact of social class on the kind of self-image individuals develop and on their perception of different kinds of careers. Four such social classes are identified: (1) "traditional respectable families," (2) "newly affluent families," (3) "solid work class families," and (4) "the roughs." Members of the first two classes raise their children to aspire to high-level jobs and communicate to them that blue-collar jobs are beneath them. The working-class parents "do not think in terms of moving up the social scale significantly." They are mostly semiskilled and unskilled workers, and they teach their children that their jobs are respectable and ones the children should take. The "roughs" also have no aspirations for their children and, in fact, teach their children that work is distasteful. "These children are ready-made for the 'dead end' jobs."

Similarly, in the United States research has shown the strong impact that childhood experiences can have on the career orientations of minorities (Liebow, 1967; Goodale, 1973). As the investigations point out, the kinds of experiences minorities have can cause them to develop self-images in which they see themselves as incapable of holding meaningful jobs and as not valuing the kinds of rewards that work can provide.

Job Experiences   Although childhood experiences influence people's self-concepts and their career aspirations, a number of researchers have pointed out that what happens to individuals once they join an organization also has an impact on them. There is considerable evidence that people are constantly revising their career objectives. As was mentioned in the previous chapter, the kind of initial job the person holds can have an important effect on his career plans and on his commitment to a particular organization. There it was stressed that jobs differ in the degree to which they provide people with the opportunity to experience psychological success or, in terms of our discussion in Chapter 2, the degree to which they provide the person with the opportunity to satisfy his needs for self-actualization, competence, and achievement.

The presence or absence of tasks that provide the person with an opportunity to experience psychological success can be a crucial influence in determining how a person's career will develop. People who hold jobs that do not provide them with the opportunity to experience feelings of psychological success are essentially cut off from the opportunity to satisfy many of their needs on their jobs. The discovery that they cannot satisfy certain needs may change their perceptions of the rewards available in that type of job and lead them to change jobs, occupations, or organizations if it is important to them that they receive these rewards. Alternatively, it may cause them to psychologically withdraw from the job and look for their satisfactions elsewhere. Thus, it has been argued (Argyris, 1957) that jobs which do not provide the opportunity to satisfy higher-order needs will cause people to become apathetic and disinterested, place a high value on extrinsic rewards (e.g., pay), fight the organization and defend their self-concept through the use of defense mechanisms. This, in fact, may partially account for why the workers in the English study mentioned earlier (Goldthorpe et al., 1968) expressed attitudes of noninvolvement.

People who hold jobs which allow for the experience of psychological success, also seem to change their career orientation as a result of what happens to them on the job. There is evidence that when people do actually experience success their commitment to the organization increases as does their view of their competence. This leads them to reformulate their long-term career plans in line with their better-developed conception of their ability to function in a work setting. However, just because a job is designed so that a person can experience psychological success is no guarantee that the jobholder will experience it. In fact, holders of jobs that are high on autonomy and challenge may experience failure because their performance does not live up to other people's performances or the goals they set for themselves. This is particularly likely to happen where there is direct competition among a number of people doing the same job and where performance is visible and easily measured. The experience of failure, like the experience of success, can have a strong impact on individuals' perceptions of their ability to function competently in a particular environment. This in turn can cause them to rethink the career paths they have chosen and to alter them so that they are more in line with their new conception of their skills. Experiencing failure can also lead to reduced job involvement and to attempts to experience desired satisfactions when off the job.

In summary, just as it is reasonable to postulate that some individuals will get onto a success cycle where they will set tougher and tougher goals, achieve them, and raise their self-perceived competence, it is reasonable to assume that other people will get locked into a failure-withdrawal cycle. This can lead them to set lower and lower goals and finally to withdraw from the situation. Thus the kinds of jobs that a person holds can alter his career goals, both in the direction of increasing his commitment to his original set of goals and in the direction of causing him to change his career path.

Other Influences The kind of job a person holds is just one of the things that may change his career goals once he has begun work. He may as a result of working find out more about himself and about the rewards associated with different jobs. He may, for example, find out that certain jobs pay more than he thought and as a result he may try to get one of them. He may find out as a result of nonwork activities that he has certain skills which he didn't know about before he started work. This knowledge may lead to seeking out occupations where these skills can be utilized. He may also become aware of jobs that he never heard of before he came to work and decide that they offer a good mix of the kinds of outcomes he desires. Finally, the individual may change the values he places on different outcomes and because of this change his career aspirations.

Career Stages

It has been suggested that a person may alter his career orientation as he passes through different time periods in his life. One psychologist (Super, 1957) suggests, for example, four stages: (1) exploration of various career possibilities (between ages 15–25), (2) establishment of oneself in an occupation (25–45), (3) maintaining one's own in an occupation (45–65), and (4) decline or reduced work involvement (65 and older). Maslow, likewise, proposed that the levels in his hierarchy of needs may unfold at different points in the life cycle. During the adult years, ego and autonomy needs should be the most important as the person tries to grow and advance in his career. Presumably, as the person moves into the middle and end of his career, he should become more concerned with self-actualization.

In conjunction with his model presented earlier, Schein (1971) defines the structure of careers as a "set of basic stages which create transitional and terminal statuses or positions." The career for Schein, then, consists of movement from one stage to another, a sequence of boundary passages. The various stages posited by the model are shown in Table 7-2, along with Schein's hypothesized psychological and organizational processes.

Very little data have been collected to test the idea of career stages, and what there is sometimes is contradictory. Thus, at this point, it is difficult to reach any firm conclusions about the types of stages that people go through and the concerns that dominate during each one. Particularly open to question is the issue of whether people go through certain stages regardless of the kinds of experiences they have. It seems unlikely that movement through different periods is simply a matter of some sort of basic maturation process that is common to all people. In many ways it is unfortunate that more is not known about the whole concept of career stages since such information might help us to understand one of the influences that causes people to change their career orientations. At the moment, all we can conclude is that the career stages concept seems to be descriptive of what happens in some people's careers but that the concept does not explain fully why people change their career paths, and it is not descriptive of all people because here—as in other areas—large individual differences exist.

Table 7-2 Basic Stages, Positions, and Processes Involved in a Career

Basic stages and transitions	Statuses or positions	Psychological and organizational processes: transactions between individual and organization
1. Preentry	Aspirant, applicant, rushee	Preparation, education, anticipatory socialization
Entry (transition)	Entrant, postulant, recruit	Recruitment, rushing, testing, screening, selection, acceptance ("hiring"); passage through external inclusion boundary; rites of entry; induction and orientation
2. Basic training, novitiate	Trainee, novice, pledge	Training, indoctrination, socialization, testing of the man by the organization, tentative acceptance into group
Initiation, first vows (transition)	Initiate, graduate	Passage through first inner inclusion boundary, acceptance as member and conferring of organizational status, rite of passage and acceptance
3. First regular assignment	New member	First testing by the man of his own capacity to function; granting of real responsibility (playing for keeps); passage through functional boundary with assignment to specific job or department
		Indoctrination and testing of man by immediate work group leading to acceptance or rejection; if accepted, further education and socialization (learning the ropes); preparation for higher status through coaching, seeking visibility, finding sponsors, etc.
Promotion or leveling off (transition)		Preparation, testing, passage through hierarchical boundary, rite of passage; may involve passage through functional boundary as well (rotation)
4. Second assignment	Legitimate member (fully accepted)	Processes under no. 3 repeat
5. Granting of tenure	Permanent member	Passage through another inner inclusion boundary
Termination and exit (transition)	Old timer, senior citizen	Preparation for exit, cooling the mark out, rites of exit (testimonial dinners, etc.)
6. Postexit	Alumnus emeritus, retired	Granting of peripheral status

Source: Adopted from Schein (1971).

Multiorganization and Multioccupation Careers

Increasingly, people seem to be planning on, and actually having, careers that involve multiple organizations and even multiple occupations. More and more organizations are reporting relatively high turnover figures for many different kinds of employees. Studies of college graduates indicate that five years after graduation at least 50 percent of them have changed organizations and some have decided to take up a new occupation. Studies of nonmanagement employees show that in many jobs turnover runs more than 50 percent in the first year. Some of the turnover may be unavoidable in the sense that it represents people taking jobs in which they plan to stay only a short time. An accountant, for example, may take a job with one of the large public accounting firms, merely to learn from the training and experience the firm offers and in order to become a certified public accountant. Thus, his first job might be nothing more than a stepping stone that he intends to stay on for only a short period of time.

Much of the turnover that organizations experience probably is controllable in the sense that it stems from people becoming dissatisfied with how their careers are developing. For one reason or another, the job they have taken isn't providing them with the rewards or outcomes that they expected, and they decide to try a job in another organization because they perceive it as more likely to satisfy their needs. Part of this type of turnover could be reduced by organizations if, as was suggested in Chapter 5, they were to give people a better idea of what was in prospect for them before they took the job and if they were to do a better job of providing people with the rewards they want (Porter & Steers, 1973).

Not all of the turnover that is caused by employee dissatisfaction is controllable, however, since some of it is due to changes that take place in the employee. As has been shown in this and the previous chapter, people do change the kinds of goals they set for themselves, and they do change their concepts of how capable they are of functioning well in a particular environment. When this happens they often find themselves in organizations that no longer are able to provide the things they want. Part of the turnover thus is due to the kinds of success and failure experiences the person has in trying to function in the organization. Repeated failure experiences may convince the person that his abilities do not fit the demands of the organization, and this may cause him to leave. Finally, the kinds of socialization influences (Chapter 6) that are acting on him may affect how well he fits into the organization.

In summary, career changes can be precipitated by (1) changes in the needs and goals of the person, (2) changes in the person's perception of his competence to function effectively in various situations, (3) changes in the skills necessary to function effectively in a given occupation, (4) a decrease in the person's ability to function well in a given occupation because of the effects of age (e.g., professional abilities), and (5) changes in the person's perceptions of the outcomes that are available in different occupations.

Career Management Strategies

Several studies have considered the kinds of career strategies used by managers who aspire to upward mobility. Table 7-3 presents the strategies a number of British managers reported using (Sofer, 1970). As can be seen, improving qualifications was the most frequently mentioned strategy. The second most frequently mentioned strategy was choosing jobs that were stepping stones. A study of American executives also points to the importance of the stepping-stone job strategy in executives' career strategies (Glickman et al., 1968). This research additionally identifies a number of other strategies that managers use in order to advance their careers. The "hitch your wagon to a star" principle is one that was frequently mentioned and indeed the authors suggest that an analysis of the promotions people got indicates that it is often effective. Taking on risky assignments, solving major crises ("crises create heroes"), and acquiring a special competence which is unveiled at an appropriate time were other frequently used approaches.

Sponsors   Other research has pointed out that getting the right sponsor can be an important way for an individual to further his career (Glaser, 1968; Martin & Strauss, 1956). In this approach the protégé may

Table 7-3 Distribution by Mentions of Perceived Career Strategies*

	Autoline	Novoplast	Both
Wait	6	9	15
Do job well	14	8	22
Make it easy to leave	4	1	5
Improve one's knowledge of the firm	4	1	5
Improve one's qualifications	19	16	35
Improve interpersonal relations	13	12	25
Change content of job	3	2	5
Get out of dead-end job	7	10	17
Choose jobs that are stepping-stones	10	17	27
Ask for move or explanation	9	9	18
Leave for another company	5	9	14
Other	2	4	6
Total Respondents	40	41	81

*Multiple responses.
Source: Sofer, 1970, p. 245.

complement his superior by being strong in an area where the superior is weak; he may serve as a detail man, advisor, hatchet man, or information gatherer. A particularly powerful sponsor may have a cluster of proteges surrounding him, and a skillful upwardly mobile manager may have several sponsors. The success of the whole system depends on the sponsor's being promoted and on his ability to carry his protégés along with him. Apparently this system works often enough, since "top management echelons of many companies are made up of interlocking chains . . . certain powerful sponsors and their adherents" (Martin & Strauss, 1956, p. 109).

Agility and Playing It Safe   A different and perhaps more cynical view of how people get ahead in organizations is presented by Mills (1951). According to his rather controversial point of view, the stress is on agility rather than ability, on " 'getting along' . . . rather than what you know. . . . But the most important single factor is 'personality,' which commands attention . . . by charm . . . force of character, or . . . demeanor. . . . Getting ahead becomes a continual selling job. . . . You have a product and that product is yourself" (Mills, 1953, pp. 260–265).

Many of the same points are made in the book *The Organization Man* (Whyte, 1955), which describes how young managers try to avoid taking controversial positions and how they present the correct "organization man" outward appearance in order to get ahead. What research there is, however, suggests that at least in business organizations this approach does *not* necessarily lead to promotion and advancement (Porter & Lawler, 1968). The data, in fact, suggest that people who behave in just the opposite way from that described by Mills and Whyte are promoted. Thus, we must be careful not to accept the rather stereotyped descriptions of Mills and Whyte about how people advance in large organizations. Still, it may be because the stereotype is a widely accepted one that many individuals follow it in the hope it will further their career.

The Nonupwardly Mobile Employee   Nonupwardly mobile employees manage their careers just as do upwardly mobile managers. Rather than drawing attention to themselves and acquiring new skills, they seem to adopt safety-first strategies. They tend to spend their time keeping attention focused away from themselves, protecting themselves with such things as "just in case files" and following rules and regulations to the letter.

On the surface it may not be obvious that the employee who takes no risks and does not extend himself in his work is motivated by the same process as is the employee who takes risky assignments and tries to perform exceptionally well. However, at a deeper level of analysis they are both following a strategy that they feel is congruent with their career goals. Their goals are different, and for this reason they are behaving differently. But this does not negate the fact that both have career goals that reflect their needs, self-image, and perceptions of the rewards that are available in different jobs and that both are behaving in a way that they feel will help them obtain their career goals. For one, playing it safe is the way he feels he can best achieve his career goals (e.g., keeping a good-paying but not too demanding job), while for the other, taking chances is the way he feels he can achieve his career goals (e.g., becoming a top executive).

Mixtures of Orientations within Organizations It might seem that organizations would prefer to have members who are oriented toward mobility because they presumably are more motivated to perform their jobs effectively. However, a desire for upward mobility does not always lead to higher motivation since good performance is not always seen as the way to be promoted. Furthermore, in terms of organizational effectiveness, the best orientation for a particular employee very much depends upon the man-power needs of the organization and the kind of career the organization is planning for the individual. Just as it can cause problems (e.g., turnover) when an organization doesn't promote someone who aspires to upward mobility, it can cause problems when it does promote someone who does not aspire to upward mobility. Thus, from an organization's perspective, the problem is to staff the organization with the right mixture of people. Having too many upwardly mobile people can cause problems, just as having too few. Failing to identify those who can be and want to be developed can also cause problems. How organizations try to develop employees is the subject of the next section of the chapter.

ORGANIZATIONS DEVELOPING INDIVIDUALS

Training costs have risen to a point where, along with the costs of salaries and material, they have come to represent one of the major financial costs that organizations incur (Campbell et al., 1970). Since no organization can function effectively unless it is staffed by employees who have the skills that are necessary to perform the jobs, it is not hard to understand why organizations invest so much in training. As we shall see, however, there are many problems associated with using training as a way of assuring that the members of an organization have the necessary skills. Skill acquisition is a complex psychological process that can be difficult to manage.

According to the approach presented in Chapters 2 and 4, if organizations are to influence performance, they must influence at least one of the following: the employee's motivation or his response capabilities. Stated simply, influencing them and, as a result, performance is a matter of identifying the changes that are needed and of picking the correct training experience for the individual who is to be trained. Although it is simple to state in general terms what needs to be done if training is to be effective from an organization's point of view, it is often not clear how to convert these general statements into specific actions that an organization can take. Thus, training programs often prove difficult to run and are a source of frustration in many organizations. Further, in many instances it is not apparent that they contribute appreciably to the effectiveness of the organization. It is obvious that it is important to provide a training program that fits both the characteristics of the people who are to be trained and the behavior that is to be influenced. But which kind of program is best for which type of learning, given the nature of the people to be trained?

Types of Development Programs

A large number of training and development programs exist that are designed to affect each of the determinants of performance: motivation and capability. Perhaps the greatest number of these programs have been developed to influence the person's response capabilities, but a number do exist that are designed to affect motivation. Some, such as job-rotation programs and T-groups, seem to be designed to influence both determinants of performance but most are designed to influence just one. Thus, training programs can be differentiated by how they try to change employees' performance. They can be further differentiated on the basis of the answers to these four questions:

1   Who is participating? Managers? Workers?
2   Where is it taking place? On the job? Away from the organization?
3   What kind of material is being taught? Cognitive, interpersonal, motivational, etc.?
4   How is it being taught? Lecture, reading, teaching machines, simulations, etc.?

Probably the most typical programs for managers are those that involve lower-level managers, take place at a company training center, and teach cognitive material about different aspects of the supervisory job by using the lecture method. Even more common than these training programs are ones designed for nonmanagement employees in order to teach them the basic cognitive and behavioral skills (e.g., welding, accounting, typing) they need to do their jobs. For a long time, the rarest program was one that involved the top levels of management, focused on interpersonal issues, and was taught by analyzing the behavior of the participants. However, this has changed dramatically since the T-group approach has become popular, and now it has become an accepted thing for corporation presidents to take a week off from work in order to go to a T-group held especially for executives.

There are literally thousands of different kinds of training and development programs, ranging from T-groups to closed-circuit TV courses, on new developments in engineering. This, of course, is an interesting commentary on the degree to which organizations are committed to training. However, it also serves to stress the range of things an organization can do to make a given individual a more effective performer. Just deciding that a person will perform his job better if he knows more about accounting (increase his response capabilities) is not enough; decisions have to be made about how, when, and where it will be taught and whether teaching him accounting represents the best investment of the organization's money.

It would simplify things greatly if it could be stated that certain types of training programs generally are effective in influencing certain types of performance (e.g., for top management, in the laboratory, teaching motivation, using lectures), while others generally are not (e.g., for the worker level, on the job, teaching cognitive material, using teaching machines); but research simply does not exist upon which to base such conclusions. In fact, only a few of the many types of training have been subjected to extensive research:

> By and large, the training and development literature is voluminous, non-empirical, non-theoretical, poorly written, and dull. As noted elsewhere, it is faddish to an extreme. The fads center around the introduction of new techniques and follow a characteristic pattern. A new technique appears on the horizon and develops a large stable of advocates who first describe its "successful" use in a number of situations. A second wave of advocates busy themselves trying out numerous modifications of the basic technique. A few empirical studies may be carried out to demonstrate that the method "works." Then the inevitable backlash sets in and a few vocal opponents begin to criticize the usefulness of the technique, most often in the absence of data. Such criticism typically has very little effect. What does have an effect is the appearance of another new technique and a repetition of the same cycle. (Campbell, 1971, pp. 565–566)

Faced with this lack of comprehensive research, it is obviously difficult for an organization to make intelligent decisions about which types of individual development it should carry out. What research there is suggests that the effectiveness of a given program depends very much on the characteristics of the organization which uses it. The research also suggests that when certain conditions are met, training is likely to be more effective than when they are not. These conditions are worth discussing in detail because they highlight the complex behavioral issues that arise when training and development are considered.

Identifying Behavior to Be Taught

Historically the emphasis of psychologists has been on the so-called principles of learning. These principles are given a prime place in the major texts on training (see, e.g., Bass & Vaughan, 1966; McGhee & Thayer, 1961). They emphasize how the material is to be taught, stressing the advantages of such matters as spaced over massed learning and the role of reinforcement. All too often this emphasis on the principles of learning has obscured the issue of *what* is to be taught. It has been suggested that the principles of learning should be placed in a secondary role and that primary consideration should be given to an intensive analysis on training content (Gagné, 1962). Typically total performance on a job can be analyzed as performance on a number of tasks which are relatively distinct from one another. Looked at this way, the basic procedure in training design is to identify these separate tasks and what makes for successful performance on them. The next step is to teach the employee how to perform each task in a way that will facilitate transfer when the whole job has to be performed. This approach suggests that people interested in training should spend time analyzing jobs and tasks and looking at the behaviors that lead to successful performance on each task. Only then should many of the things that traditionally have been focused on by trainers be considered (e.g., how to present material, where to hold sessions, etc.).

Unfortunately, only a few studies have followed this approach. In one study that did, data were collected from customers on what they felt was desirable behavior on the part of the salesclerks (Folley, 1969). Over two thousand situations where critical behavior occurred were studied and used in developing a training program. In contrast to this are many training programs that are based upon trying to make managers change their managerial styles toward being more democratic or participative. These courses often fail to change behavior because after the sessions those who attended often still do not know how they should behave in a given situation even though they know the principles of democratic management (Campbell, 1971).

Generally speaking, most training programs that are run by organizations are not based on a careful analysis of the kind of behavior required for effective performance on the job. Even if organizations were willing to do this type of analysis, it is not clear that it can always be done. There has been very little research on how it can be done, and as a result few practical methods are available. Those that do exist demand a considerable amount of time per job and most large organizations have hundreds of different jobs.

Still, one must ask whether it is more costly to do the kind of analysis that is necessary on each job, or to run training programs that are not tied to behavior.

Assessing the Trainee

Once it has been determined what kind of behavior is desired, then and only then is the organization in a position to assess the individual who is to be trained. Two important questions need to be asked about the individual. *First,* does he need the training? To answer this question, an organization must know whether the individual does in fact fail to behave in ways that he should if he is to perform effectively.

The most obvious and available source of information about the kind of performance an employee is capable of is the superior of each employee. Thus, superiors often are asked to make training recommendations for their subordinates and to deal with the issue of training in their annual or semiannual performance appraisal sessions. The problem is that superiors often are poor assessors of the kinds of training that their subordinates need. This seems to be particularly true when the subordinate is a potential top-level manager and the superior isn't (Schein, 1964). Further, performance evaluation sessions often are poor places in which to discuss training needs because the subordinate is on the defensive and usually concerned about the size of a raise he may obtain (Meyer, Kay, & French, 1965). One solution to these problems that has been tried is for the organization to assign to a staff specialist the development responsibility for its high-potential people. Another is to have superior-subordinate sessions that are concerned only with talking about training needs. Finally, some of the procedures that now are used to assess people's abilities and motivation for the purpose of making selection and promotion decisions (e.g., tests, assessment centers) can be used to spot areas where training and development work is needed.

The employee who is to be trained represents another available and potentially valuable source of information about his own performance. Unfortunately the individual is often not motivated to give valid data. The training situation is very similar to the selection situation in this respect. The individual often feels that admitting his own performance inadequacies will hurt him in terms of promotion and pay increases, and this prevents him from giving the valid data which is needed for training purposes. It is also true that individuals often have an incorrect perception of their performance ("incorrect" in the sense that it differs from the perception of other qualified observers) and because of this they are not necessarily a valid source of data (Lawler, 1966).

There is one type of information, however, that is often available only from the individual—information about his career orientation. As will be discussed further in Chapter 11, it is difficult for organizations to obtain this type of information, but it is vital if the development plans of the organization are to coincide with those of the individual. Without it the organization is likely to end up planning a career for the individual which doesn't fit what he wants, with resulting negative consequences for both parties. Unnecessary turnover, unfulfilled expectations, inappropriate training, unwanted promotions, and job dissatisfaction are some of the negative consequences.

If it is determined that the individual needs to learn the behavior that is taught in a training course, then a *second* issue arises: Will the individual be able to profit from the training experience? Here the issue of whether he has the necessary aptitude to learn new responses is important if the training is designed to increase the person's response capabilities. If the program is designed to influence his motivation, questions about how committed he is to his present beliefs and needs are important.

In theory, at least, it is possible to ascertain in advance of training some indication of the extent to which an individual will profit from it. Such information, however, is not always easy to obtain. (The assessment-center approach discussed earlier in Chapter 5 represents one recently developed method for collecting such information.) Although a number of tests exist that can be used with some success in predicting whether employees can benefit from training sessions that emphasize cognitive material, they are not as effective in predicting whether the individual will be able to learn from sessions designed to teach new styles of interpersonal relations (e.g., T-groups).

In a different realm, there are motor-skills tests available which will predict how much individuals can profit from most kinds of manual skills training. Figure 7-2 illustrates a case in which many of those individuals who didn't respond to training were identified in advance by tests. It shows the percentage of air force cadets eliminated from flight training at each test score level (Dubois, 1947). High-scoring trainees obviously had a much greater chance of graduating from the training program. Thus, if an organization is willing to make the effort, it is possible to determine in advance if individuals can profit from some types of training and development experiences.

Trainee's Felt Need to Learn and Develop

Unless the individual who is to be trained and developed is motivated to learn the new behavior that is being taught, he will not be likely to learn it. This is not to say that learning is impossible in the absence of motivation. Learning theorists have shown that some learning can take place even

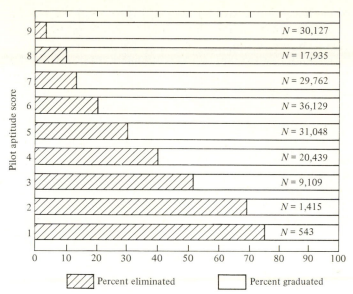

Figure 7-2 The elimination of cadets from elementary flight training based on pilot aptitude scores (after P. DuBois, 1947).

though a felt need to learn is not present (Cofer & Appley, 1964). It is clear,
however, that more learning will take place when the person is motivated to
learn. On the basis of the model presented in Chapter 2, it would seem that a
high motivation to learn will be present if the person sees that learning a new
kind of behavior will lead to his being better able to obtain the rewards he
desires from his job. Often when organizations regard development and
training as a one-way decision-making situation (the organization developing
the individual), rather than as a situation where the individual and the
organization meet to plan jointly the individual's career, this kind of
perception does not exist. In the one-way decision situation, there is a
limited chance for the individual to make his career goals known and to
shape the training to them. The one-way situation also does not encourage
individuals to explore the reasons for the training. Thus, the training often
seems less relevant to the individual's goals.

Conflicts between what is being taught in training courses and what the
individual feels is needed if he is to further his own career can also develop
when training programs teach behavior that will not lead to success in the
organization. The recent emphasis on training managers to be participative
and to use democratic practices provides a good example of this problem.
Many of the organizations that have sent managers to courses that advocate
participative management simply are not organizations where this style of

management is likely to lead to such goals as promotion and high pay. Many managers who go to training programs under these circumstances realize this, and, if they are desirous of obtaining these goals they are not motivated to learn what is being taught—much less to behave differently on the job.

A large amount of research has shown that people often don't see their own behavior as others see it, and because of this they don't see the training programs they are sent to as relevant to their needs. Some training programs try to take this problem into account by first giving the person some data on his present competence level. T-groups often do this by building in at the beginning what they call an "unfreezing" experience—i.e., candid feedback on one's present behavior. Math courses do it by giving the person a test. The expectation is that these data will create a motivation in the person to learn and experiment with new behavior. Organizations can also influence the individual's motivation by sharing with him the data they have that indicates he needs to change his behavior in a particular way. Furthermore, as suggested earlier, they can have the individual participate in the decision concerning the kind of training he gets. This should help to reduce the problem since he is not likely to agree to go to a program unless he feels the need for it.

A parallel can be drawn here between the organization-individual relationship and the doctor-patient relationship. Both the organization and the doctor can make diagnoses and prescriptions, but the individual does not have to accept them, and unless they are accepted they are useless. Thus, it is important that an organization share its data with the individual and involve him in the training decision where it is possible. Often organizations are faced with tough decisions in just this area. First, there is the problem of what kind of information to share with the person, and, second, there is the problem of what to do if the person does not recognize the need for the training. Should they defer the training program, or send the person and risk its being a waste of time and money?

In short, organizations need to develop people, but people only respond to learning and development experiences when they feel the need for the learning and development. Unfortunately, people often don't see the same need as the organization does, and thus the organization has the problem of influencing the person to see the worth of the training it feels he needs. The organization can do this by sharing its data with the person and by getting him more involved in planning his own training and development program.

Learning

Once it has been determined what behavior is to be learned, that the individual needs to learn it, that he can learn it, and that he feels the need to learn it, there are a number of principles of learning that can be used to help facilitate training. A review of the literature on learning (Bass & Vaughn, 1966) suggests that a training program should do the following five things if it is to maximize learning:

1 Provide for the learner's active participation

2 Provide the trainee with knowledge of results (feedback) about his attempts to improve

3 Provide a meaningful integration of the learning experience so that the trainee can transfer the new behavior to the job situation

4 Provide some means for the trainee to be reinforced for appropriate behavior

5 Provide for practice and repetition in a situation that is similar to the job situation

It is beyond the scope of this book to review the literature on learning in detail. It is appropriate here, however, to point out that there is material in this literature which can help organizations design training programs in ways that will facilitate learning. When what is known about learning is combined with various modern training methods, the organization has available a wide range of approaches that can be brought to bear on a training problem. Thus, there is no need for a training program to fail because the person is unable to learn the new behavior, if the preconditions (ability, motivation, analysis of what is to be learned) for learning have been met.

Recently there has been a decided move on the part of many organizations to bring culturally disadvantaged persons into the work force. Although experience with this type of training is not yet extensive, it seems that the principles of learning stated above can be particularly helpful in designing programs for such training. Some specific changes apparently need to be made in the programs, but the basic principles should still apply. For example, rewards that work well in training middle-class whites do not always work well in training disadvantaged minority individuals. Thus, although the general principle of rewarding correct behavior holds, the specific way behavior has been rewarded may have to be changed. Similarly, the rewards that are offered may have to be more closely tied to the desired behavior and more frequently given if culturally disadvantaged employees are to learn (Porter, 1973). It may also be desirable to experiment with giving rewards as people get closer and closer to the correct behavior rather than waiting for the totally correct behavior. Both of these last two approaches are a basic part of the "behavior modification" approach to training which has stemmed from the work of Skinner (1948).

One final point needs to be made about learning that is designed to be used in organizations. It is not enough to perform the new behavior at the end of training; overlearning is necessary in many cases if the individual is to use what he has learned after he leaves the training situation. Some psychologists have referred to this as the need for refreezing. What this means is that the new behavior has to become an integral part of the individual's behavior and part of his self-concept. For this to happen, overlearning may be necessary so that the new behavior becomes almost automatic. Refreezing is often facilitated by having the individual try the behavior in a number of different conditions or, if it is a behavior that is to be used in only one situation, by having him try it out under conditions that simulate the job conditions. Frequently, these steps are not taken and, as a result, the new behavior is not seen as a natural job behavior.

Support on the Job

Many training programs have failed to change the trainee's on-the-job behavior because he does not feel that the new behavior will be rewarded if and when he demonstrates it on the job. Refreezing can help here, but it may not be enough if the trainee feels that the new behavior will not be accepted and rewarded in the day-to-day work environment. The key person is the superior. If he does not reward and support the new behavior of his subordinates, it is likely to be quickly dropped. One of the early studies on the impact of supervisory training on job behavior showed this quite clearly (Fleishman, 1953). Immediately after the training session, a check showed that, as they had been taught, the supervisors were showing more consideration toward their subordinates. However, a check six months later showed that the supervisors were behaving as they did before the training. The reason: Their superiors did not reward them for their new behavior. Since then a number of studies have reported the same phenomenon. One study (Argyris, 1970) shows that the behavior learned in training is often not so much forgotten as it is stored away for use at an appropriate time. Executives who had been in interpersonal training sessions were studied, and it was found that when they were working on their jobs they did not use what they learned in the T-group. However, when they were in a group that had been through a T-group, they used their learning. Thus, it seems clear that what is learned in training must be rewarded and sanctioned on the job if it is to be used.

Career Planning

Although the emphasis so far has been on the role of specific training programs in developing people, this is only part of the story. It is crucial to remember that employee development in the broader sense is a function of a long series of job and training experiences. It is also important to remember that these experiences are cumulative and that they influence each other.

Since each person has a unique set of background experiences, the same training program is likely to impact upon different people in a different manner.

As Schein's cone model illustrates, there is a large number of moves that a person can make in most organizations and, as our discussion of different training programs indicates, there is a large number of different kinds of training a person can receive. However, people have only limited amounts of time in their work life, and thus the number of moves they can make is limited as is the number of training programs they can attend. This raises questions about what sequence of experiences is best as well as questions about just what experiences need to be included. Sequencing can be important, because having one experience may make the person more or less ready to learn from another. But perhaps the most difficult problem is deciding what experiences need to be included in the total package. This is particularly difficult when a person is being prepared for a top-level job: "In order for a man to come up through the ranks to become a top executive of a large corporation, he must move up fast. . . . This accounts . . . for many of the stresses experienced by the individual and the organization in the management development process" (Glickman et al., 1968). It also accounts for the rapid movement of some managers in organizations. A typical career of a manager who is headed for the top of a large organization involves holding most jobs less than two years and moving to key parts of the cone described earlier.

The fact that individuals have their own career goals and plans makes career planning difficult because it creates the possibility of individual-organization conflicts. There is surprisingly little research on how organizations should and do go about managing peoples' careers. As was pointed out, most research is still at the stage of determining whether a particular kind of training experience is worthwhile. Research has yet to progress to studying the effects of different sequences of experiences and to ascertaining whether one type of training is better given before or after another type. This is not surprising since these are much more difficult topics upon which to do research than is measuring the effectiveness of a given training experience.

Still, if career planning is ever to progress beyond the hunch and intuition stage, knowledge of the impact of different career tracks is needed. At this point in time relatively few organizations seem to be making any effort to systematically plan the careers of their employees. One interesting exception, however, is professional baseball teams. They carefully plan the careers of their players. They move them from team to team in the minor leagues, always trying to bring them to the point where they will have the skill to help a major-league team. In a sense they are trying to see that the young player always has a job that is challenging but not overwhelming. Many other organizations could learn something from this strategy.

Our discussion so far points clearly to the conclusion that it is important to look at the training and job experiences people have in organizations as related parts of a total career experience. This means that for organizations to accomplish their development goals, they must take a long-term, integrated approach to developing each individual. A review of the conditions which were said to be necessary for training to be effective can provide some additional cues as to how organizations might do effective career planning. Three of these conditions probably have to be present if adequate career planning is to take place: (1) First, it is important to determine how the person should behave when he reaches the jobs for which he is being prepared. This means that a good analysis of the jobs for which the person is being developed must be made. (2) Similarly, it is important to determine whether the person has the capability to develop the kinds of behaviors that will be needed for the career plan. Typically, this would mean that the organization should do some testing of its members or in some way gather systematic data on their response aptitudes. (3) Finally, it is crucial that the organization try to determine whether the individual feels the need to learn the behaviors that will be needed, and whether the career plan that the organization is considering is congruent with the individuals' own plan.

CAREER DEVELOPMENT AND INDIVIDUAL-ORGANIZATION INTEGRATION

At the beginning of the chapter it was pointed out that individuals tend to set long-term career goals concerned with their own development and that organizations need to develop people. This can create a situation of high individual-organization integration, where the individual's goals are congruent with the organization's goals, and where—because of this—the individual aids the organization in obtaining its goals and the organization aids the individual in obtaining his goals. This type of goal integration can and does happen. It happens, for example, when the individual desires to reach the top of the organization, and the organization has identified him as a top executive and sets out to develop him with that in mind. It also happens when the individual simply wants to stay in his present job and when the organization needs people to do that job and does not see the person as someone who should be developed for an upper-level position.

However, as has been pointed out throughout the chapter, there is not always a high degree of integration between the individuals' career goals and the organization's efforts to develop its members. Organizations often try to develop individuals in ways they do not desire, and perhaps more often they fail to develop individuals in ways that they see as furthering their career goals.

There are a number of factors that can lead to a low degree of convergence between the individual's career goals and the development plans of the organization. First, and perhaps most basic, there are often fewer positions available than there are people who desire them. It is not uncommon to find more people aspiring to high-level positions in an organization than there are such positions. The inevitable result is that some people simply will not achieve their career goals. From the organization's point of view this can lead to such dysfunctional consequences as turnover and low motivation. From the individual's point of view this can mean the experience of psychological failure. Some of this type of poor individual-organization integration would seem to be inevitable in a society where most organizations are (to an extent, at least) hierarchical, and getting to the top has associated with it a large number of privileges. One thing organizations can do to solve this problem is to improve the lower-level jobs so that they will be more rewarding, and a second is to control through the selection process the number of people in the organization who aspire to higher-level jobs. The latter solution, however, has a number of potential disadvantages (e.g., too few people with initiative) associated with it.

Second, organizations often see their development activities as a one-way process—as something they do to the person. This can result in organizations' developing people for jobs that individuals do not see as congruent with their career goals. Sometimes this occurs when the organization decides to develop a person for a job that is at a lower level than the individual would like to attain, but it also occurs because the organization tries to develop the person for a job that is above what he would like to obtain. Some of these problems might be eliminated if the individual and the organization were to plan jointly the individual's career path. As was pointed out earlier joint planning and decision making between the individual and the organization is more likely to lead to convergence between the individual's career goals and the organizational developmental plans than is one-way decision making, although joint planning is no panacea. It will not, for example, solve those problems which are brought about by large differences in how a person's capabilities are viewed. It may, however, prevent some of the problems which are caused by miscommunication.

Because the development process is handled in most organizations as a one-way process, a great deal of miscommunication does seem to take place, about both the kind of development organizations have in mind for people and the kind of career aspirations people have. It is not uncommon to find that employees have no idea why they are being transferred to a new job, while the organization sees the move as a needed part of their development for top management. The opposite also occurs frequently. Moves that the organization sees as having no significance are seen by the individual as indicating that he has been picked for further advancement. Although in the short run this type of misperception may not be dysfunctional, in the long run it can be.

Finally, poor assessment of the individual often is responsible for low convergence between the individual's career goals and the organization's development plans for the individual. In any individual-organization assessment situation, research suggests that both the individual and the organization are often wrong in their assessments. When either overestimation or underestimation by the organization occurs, it can lead to problems for both parties. It can, for example, lead to very capable people not being developed. It can also lead to people being put into jobs they cannot handle.

Individuals can and do both overestimate and underestimate their capabilities. The research evidence (e.g., Lawler, 1967), however, suggests that they are more likely to make overestimations rather than underestimations. This can lead to a problem which occurs in many organizations: individuals setting career goals that are much higher than the organization sees them capable of achieving, which in turn can lead directly to high turnover, dissatisfaction, and feelings of frustration.

THE INDIVIDUAL-ORGANIZATION LINKAGE

Chapters 5, 6, and 7 have followed the development of the individual-organization relationship from its beginning through the development of an individual's career in an organization. It has been stressed that individuals and organizations are continually adapting to each other. In the case of many individuals, this adaptation breaks down and the individual leaves the organization. However, not all terminations are an indication that the adaptation process has broken down. We can categorize the termination act under one of the following four headings: (1) voluntary individual-initiated turnover: the employee decides that he will leave the organization, even though this decision is not forced on him by his personal circumstances or by the organization; (2) involuntary individual-initiated turnover: personal circumstances (e.g., family illness) force him to make a job change, even though he might wish to stay and the organization would continue to employ him; (3) involuntary organization-initiated turnover: the organization is forced for economic or other reasons to reduce the number of its employees, and they must discharge an otherwise satisfactory worker; (4) voluntary organization-initiated turnover: the organization decides to dismiss the individual because of some perceived inadequacies in the individual. Only in the first and fourth cases are we reasonably sure that the adaptation process has broken down. (However, even in the first case, it may be that it is the attractiveness of a new job, rather than the unattractiveness of the present organizational circumstances, that causes a person to terminate.) Nevertheless, voluntary turnover statistics provide us with some information about clear failures of the adaptation process. But, what of the reverse? How can we tell whether adaptation has been highly successful rather than merely barely adequate?

The fact that the individual continues to work for an organization cannot be taken as proof that he and the organization have learned how to get along well together, so that he receives a high level of individual satisfaction and the organization receives a high level of performance. If a person stays with an organization, it also does not necessarily mean he is identified with it or is strongly committed to it and its objectives. It may merely mean that the individual does not have available a more attractive alternative job. Thus, we must analyze the individual-organization linkage in considerable detail if we are to determine its adequacy for both parties.

The research that has been reviewed thus far in this book shows that the nature and form of the individual-organization linkage which develops is a function of the characteristics of both parties. It has been stressed that the linkage depends upon the abilities, needs, and goals of the individual; the nature of the selection process; the initial socialization experience in individual encounters; and the kind of career and development plan the organization has for the individual. In the remaining chapters of this book we will discuss a number of other factors which influence the nature of individual-organization linkages, including the design and structure of organizations, the nature of jobs, the appraisal and reward systems, and the kinds of interpersonal and social relationships which exist. All these factors must be considered if we are to determine the adequacy of any particular individual-organization relationship.

REVIEW AND DISCUSSION QUESTIONS

1 How can boundary passages be used to describe an individual's career history in an organization?
2 What sorts of events might precipitate career changes in an individual's life?
3 Describe the various strategies individuals might use to develop their careers. Should an individual restrict himself to the use of only one strategy?
4 What implications does the concept of career stages have for the way an organization contributes to the "building of careers"? How do the stages relate to the organization's objectives?
5 Why do people differ in their career orientations?
6 How can the design of jobs affect the career aspirations of individuals?
7 How can the learning that takes place in a training situation be maximized?

8 Even though an individual may learn quite well the material presented in a training program, his use of this material may not take place once the individual returns to his job. Why?

9 How can an individual's motivation to learn from a training program be increased?

10 Why was it stressed that training programs and job changes should be viewed as parts of an integrated human resources development program?

Part Three

Influences on Work Behavior: Structural Factors

Chapter 8

Organization Design: Context Factors

Among the many influences on the work behavior of individuals in organizational settings, none is more important or more pervasive than the design of the organization itself. By "organization design" we mean primarily the particular arrangements of the structural factors that constitute the basic form and nature of the organization. We should note, however, that the term "structure" is being used in a broad sense: it not only includes the anatomical outlines of the organization—such as its size, shape, number of levels and spans of control—but it also encompasses the basic operating features such as the degree of specification of activities, the extent of concentration of authority, and the types and degree of severity of controls. All these factors together constitute the designs of organizations—designs that are shaped by both forces and events beyond the control of the organizations themselves and by the deliberate decisions of those who control the resources of the organizations.

In this and the next chapter we will be concentrating on the two organizational characteristics (Chapter 3), differentiated functions and intended rational coordination, that pertain to the methods used to accomplish collective goals. Some organizations utilize sharply defined and specified functions or activities, while others purposely encourage broad and rather loosely defined functions. Some organizations attempt to develop a highly planned coordination of activities and relations, while others seem to deemphasize this kind of coordination and depend more on a loosely coupled and relatively unprogrammed style of integration of different functions. The key questions that arise are these: What seem to be the causes of these different approaches to organization design? And, does it make any difference in individual behavior and organizational performance whether one kind of design is used instead of another? These kinds of issues will be the focus of this and the following chapter.

FACTORS INVOLVED IN THE DESIGN OF ORGANIZATIONS

The key factors involved in organization design are those that (1) are primarily contextual and causal, (2) describe or summarize the structural features that are created, and (3) represent the dependent indices of behavior. It cannot be stressed too strongly, however, that the designation of particular variables as causal and other variables as dependent is partially arbitrary. This is because the design of organizations involves an extremely complex interplay of variables, each of which can function as both a cause and a result of another variable. In other words, the variables in the design of organizations do form a system, but it is a system that does not permit the isolation of unequivocal cause-effect relationships.

The Complexity of Causal Relationships

Let us take as an example the following chain of variables: a "context" factor such as a particular production technology, an "anatomical dimension" such as a particular concentration of authority, and a "behavioral consequence" such as a particular level of intragroup conflict. Ordinarily, for a given organization, we might suppose that the particular technology helped determine the organization's size, that the size in turn necessitated a specified type of authority structure, and that the authority structure that was imposed on the organization's members resulted in a certain amount of intragroup conflict. However, it is entirely reasonable to conceive of other forms of the causal chain. For example, the degree of intragroup conflict led to some innovative product ideas which in turn simultaneously changed the technology; or changes made in the organization's authority structure resulted in a decreased need for the services of certain members, which

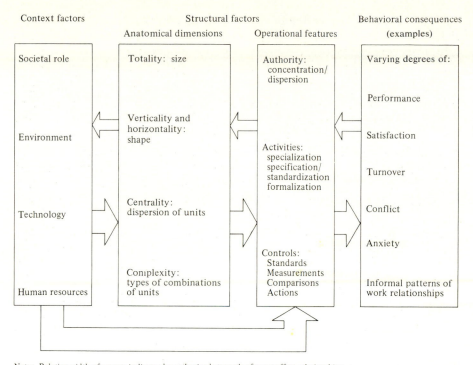

Note: Relative width of arrows indicates hypothesized strength of cause-effect relationships.

Figure 8–1 Factors involved in influencing the design of organizations.

affected the organization's size, which in turn resulted in greater employee satisfaction, and so on. The point is that it is possible to designate the most likely or most predominant causal chains of factors involved in organization design and at the same time recognize that each variable or factor can have a reciprocal effect on the others. It is the challenge of attempting to understand the underlying complexity of the system of these relationships that must be emphasized.

A Proposed Categorization of Design Variables

Despite the difficulties and limitations of trying to classify variables unambiguously as contextual and structural, we have done so for the purposes of analysis in this and the next chapter. Our categorization is depicted in Figure 8-1, where we show context factors influencing operational features, which in turn produce behavioral consequences. Figure 8-1 also shows, however, that we are considering a set of anatomical-type dimensions as intervening between context and operational characteristics. The rationale for this is that we believe that such factors as the size or shape of the organization affect the linkage between context and operational features and also have their own independent effects on activities, authority, and controls. To take just one example, which will be elaborated on in the next chapter, consider organization size: the nature of the environment and the technology of an organization may well be major factors in determining its size, which in turn will influence, say, the number of rules and regulations that it has. However, it is also possible for two organizations to be operating in essentially the same environment and with the same type of technology and yet be of different sizes. Consequently, if size were related to the number of rules, regulations, etc., we would say the effect is independent of the context features. Thus, the points that are being stressed so far are four:

   1 Context factors can affect operational features independently of anatomical features.
   2 Anatomical features of structure are partially but not totally determined by context factors. (They are also affected by other factors such as deliberate decisions of management, chance or "historical accidents," and so forth.)
   3 Anatomical features can have effects on operational features of structure—and hence on behavior—that are in part independent of context factors.
   4 Causal sequences can also go from behavioral consequences back to structure, and from structure back to context (as indicated by the small arrows from right to left in Figure 8-1). However, the primary causal sequences are hypothesized to go from context and structure toward the behavior of individuals and groups.

   Throughout the discussion in Chapters 8 and 9, one additional and very important point should be kept in mind: Different individuals will respond to a given organization structure in potentially diverse ways. For one thing, as was emphasized in Chapter 4, it is not the objective structure or design that people respond to but the *experienced* structure. Hence, there can never be a one-to-one correspondence between an objective structural feature and a particular type of behavior. Also, the general notion of individual differences extends specifically to *differences in preferences* concerning structure; in fact, preferences for more or less highly structured work conditions are often quite salient for many employees. Consequently, organizations ordinarily cannot expect to find uniform reactions to designs that appear to incorporate "inherently good" features.
   In the remainder of this chapter we will examine contextual factors relating to organization design. This will provide a necessary foundation for

our discussion in the following chapter of the direct impacts of design features on the behavior of organization members. By "context," we mean the sets of circumstances or factors that are more or less external to the organization's basic structure and functioning. These are factors that impinge on the organization from beyond its boundaries but which extend into and through the fundamental fabric of the organization. Thus, they are contextual or external only to the extent that the organization itself has limited control over the degree and extent of their impact. This is not to say that a given organization cannot alter its context somewhat—such as changing its technology or importing a different set of human resources—but rather that the main course of influence runs from context to organization rather than the reverse.

The contextual factors of the organization which we will consider include (1) the societal role or function of the organization; (2) its environment—economic, social, legal; (3) the basic technologies it utilizes; and (4) the quality and characteristics of its human-resources input. All of these are considered crucial contextual factors because they are so pervasive and because they are presumed to be influential in affecting the design of organizations.

SOCIETAL ROLE

The function or functions that an organization fulfills in the society at large would appear to have a strong impact on organization design, particularly at the time that the organization is formed. The organization's societal role can be broadly considered to include its original charter and its primary objectives. It is the variable that we usually refer to when we talk about different "types" of organizations—e.g., elementary schools, manufacturing companies, public welfare agencies, newspapers, volunteer charitable organizations, organized crime syndicates, and the like.

The function or role of organizations in society has been particularly stressed as an important variable by sociologists (e.g., Parsons, 1956; Selznick, 1949, 1957). Indeed, a well-known typology of organizations has been put forth by Blau and Scott (1962) that especially emphasizes organizations' societal role. These two sociologists have suggested that organizations can be grouped or classified on the basis of *cui bono*—who benefits. Using the criterion of "prime beneficiary" they posit four basic types of organizations:

"Mutual benefit" (primarily benefiting the membership)
"Business concerns" (benefiting the owners)
"Service organizations" (benefiting the clients)
"Commonweal organizations" (benefiting the public at large)

Mutual benefit
    County medical association
    County political party
    Farm cooperative (2)
    Farmers' federation
    Labor union organization (2)
    Local religious organization (2)
    Private country club
    Religious-fraternal organization
    State church organization (2)
    Trade association

Service
    Civil rights organization
    Delinquent reformatory (2)
    Insurance company
    Juvenile detention center (2)
    Parochial school system
    Private hospital
    Private school
    Private welfare agency (2)
    Public school system (2)
    Religious service organization
    State psychiatric hospital
    State school
    University (2)

Business
    Bank (2)
    Hotel-motel (2)
    Manufacturing plant (8)
    Marketing organization (2)
    Newspaper (2)
    Private television station
    Public transit firm
    Public utility
    Quarry
    Railroad
    Restaurant (2)
    Retail store (3)
    Trucking firm

Commonweal
    City recreation department
    Educational television station
    Fund-raising agency
    Governmental regulative agency (2)
    Law-enforcement agency
    Military supply command
    Municipal airport
    Post office
    State hospital
    State penal institution (6)

Figure 8–2   Seventy-five organizations classified according to the Blau-Scott typology. (Source: Hall et al., 1967)

With each type of organization goes a major problem to be faced: internal democracy for mutual benefit organizations, efficiency for business concerns, a professional structure for service organizations, and a bureaucratic structure for commonweal organizations. An example of how seventy-five organizations were classified on the basis of the Blau–Scott typology is provided in Figure 8-2 (Hall et al., 1967).

Attempts to formulate typologies of organizations on the basis of their societal functions have been criticized on several counts. For one thing, some organizations could easily be put into at least two categories on the who benefits criterion: "A public school, for example, benefits both the client group, i.e., the students, and the public-at-large. . . . Mass media organizations, such as television stations or newspapers, present a similar problem. The owners are the primary beneficiary, but the public-at-large also benefits in a less direct, but still important way" (Hall et al., 1967, pp. 119–120). A more serious problem with such typologies, however, is pointed out by Perrow (1967), who appropriately calls attention to the fact that there may be as much variation among organizations within types as between types. As he says, "The variations within one type of organization may be such that some schools are like prisons, some prisons like churches, some churches like factories, some factories like universities, and so on" (p. 204). Essentially, this point is analogous to the biological distinction between phenotypes and genotypes. The Blau and Scott classification scheme focuses on the more obvious phenotypical differences among organizations in terms of their societal function, while empirically organizations may be more appropriately grouped together on less obvious characteristics.

Despite some of the logical and empirical difficulties in constructing typologies of organizations on the basis of their societal role, it nevertheless seems clear that this is a factor that will to some degree help shape the underlying designs of organizations. Even though one school may not necessarily be very similar to another school, the fact that they are both involved in teaching students, rather than, say, collecting taxes or selling furniture, will be likely to influence the types of activities performed, the degree of authority exercised, and the nature of control that is employed. Whether this factor is more important in influencing organization design than are other contextual factors is, however, an open question. Evidence collected to date from a wide variety of sources would suggest it is not. At thesame time this factor clearly cannot be ignored.

ENVIRONMENT

The immediate operating environment of organizations is another contextual factor that exerts singular influence on their basic design. By "operating environment" we are referring to the set of conditions outside the organization that have a direct impact on the day-to-day functioning of the organization. The two related dimensions of the environment that appear to be the most salient ones for affecting the basic designs of organizations are (1) the environment's relative stability versus its instability and (2) the environment's relative simplicity versus its complexity. These aspects have been found to be strongly correlated with the nature and amount of structured relationships existing within organizations.

In general, as we shall relate below, researchers have tended to find that relatively stable and simple environments seem to permit, and indeed encourage, the development of highly structured organizations with strong controls and tightly specified duties for job incumbents—in a word, so-called "bureaucratic" organizations. On the other hand, environments which have many rapidly changing elements, and which involve a large component of uncertainty and unpredictability, tend to lead to more fluidly designed organizations that deemphasize structured relationships and rely more on informal nonspecified-in-advance arrangements for coping with operating problems.

Furthermore, and perhaps most important, there is some evidence to indicate that if an organization's design is not commensurate with the salient features of its environment, it may be less effective. That is, if the environment is highly dynamic and turbulent, the hierarchical, bureaucratically structured organization appears to be at a disadvantage. Similarly, however, if the immediate operating environment is essentially simple and has a slow rate of change, the highly structured organization appears to have an edge over the more loosely structured and less rigidly controlled one. The reasons for this involve a number of factors to be considered on the following pages, but the import of the findings to date is clear: different types of environments require different types of organization designs for effectiveness.

Burns and Stalker Study

Let us take a look at two of the more important studies that have been particularly concerned with the relationship of environment to organization design. One of these was reported by Burns and Stalker (1961) who studied some twenty manufacturing concerns (some being parts of larger corporations) in Scotland and England. These investigators were especially interested in the types of structure and management practices that developed in relation to the rates of change in the markets for the firms' products and in technological innovations. They conducted their research through in-depth interviews with supervisors and managers and through observation. Although this research project lacked systematic measuring devices—and its findings must be judged in that light—the total information obtained enabled the researchers to discern two distinct types of systems of management, which they labeled "mechanistic" and "organic." The former seemed particularly characteristic of stable environments and was described as follows:

> In mechanistic systems the problems and tasks facing the concern as a whole are broken down into specialisms. Each individual pursues his task as something distinct from the real tasks of the concern as a whole, as if it were the subject of a sub-contract. "Somebody at the top" is responsible for seeing to its relevance. The technical methods, duties, and powers attached to each functional role are precisely defined. Interaction within management tends to be vertical, i.e., between superior and subordinate. Operations and working behavior are governed by instructions and decisions issued by superiors. This command hierarchy is maintained by the implicit assumption that all knowledge

about the situation of the firm and its tasks is, or should be, available only to the head of the firm. Management, often visualized as the complex hierarchy familiar in organization charts, operates a simple control system, with information flowing up through a succession of filters, and decisions and instructions flowing downwards through a succession of amplifiers. (p. 5)

By contrast, where market and technological environments were rapidly changing, the organic system appeared predominant:

Organic systems are adapted to unstable conditions, when problems and requirements for action arise which cannot be broken down and distributed among specialist roles within a clearly defined hierarchy. Individuals have to perform their special tasks in the light of their knowledge of the tasks of the firm as a whole. Jobs lose much of their formal definition in terms of methods, duties, and powers, which have to be redefined continually by interaction with others participating in a task. Interaction runs laterally as much as vertically. Communication between people of different ranks tends to resemble lateral consultation rather than vertical command. Omniscience can no longer be imputed to the head of the concern. (pp. 5–6)

With these descriptions, one might conclude that organic designs are always superior to mechanistic ones. (Indeed, even the two terms, mechanistic and organic, seem to imply this.) Burns and Stalker, however, are insistent that such a conclusion is incorrect and that the nature of the environment must be taken into account:

We have endeavored to stress the appropriateness of each system to its own specific set of conditions. Equally, we desire to avoid the suggestion that either system is superior under all circumstances to the other. In particular, nothing in our experience justifies the assumption that mechanistic systems should be superseded by organic in conditions of stability. (p. 125)

Lawrence and Lorsch Study

Another major study that reaches essentially the same conclusion is one by Lawrence and Lorsch (1967). These investigators studied firms in three industries—plastics, packaged foods, and standardized containers—that differed in the nature of their operating environments. Firms in the plastics industry were confronted with a constant necessity for technological innovation, and hence managers in these firms were faced with environments that had high degrees of uncertainty and unpredictability. By contrast, the environment for the container industry firms was highly stable, and competition centered on service and product quality rather than product innovation. The packaged food firms operated in an intermediate-type environment—one that was more stable than that of the plastics firms but less so than that of the container manufacturers.

Utilizing standardized questionnaires and interviews with managers, Lawrence and Lorsch focused their attention on the nature of the environment and its relation to the degree of *differentiation* among departments within the same firm, and on the degree and type of *integration* required across departments within the firms. "Differentiation," as they defined it, referred to "the difference in cognitive and emotional orientation among managers in different functional departments," while "integration" was defined as "the quality of the state of collaboration . . . among departments. . . ."

The results of this study indicated that dynamic and complex environments require considerably more differentiation among departments within an organization than do relatively stable and simple environments. Thus, the firms in the plastics industry exhibited more differentiation than those in the foods industry, which in turn had more differentiation than the container companies (see Table 8-1). But the more interesting point is that the nature of the environment of the plastics firms seemed to cause a much greater premium to be placed on the proper degree of differentiation than did the environment of the container firms. This can be seen in Table 8-1, where the degree of differentiation between the high- and low-performing plastics organizations was clearly greater than that between the high- and low-performing container companies. Apparently, the fast-changing and diverse environment in an industry like plastics required the achievement of a necessary amount of differentiation for organizational success, whereas the relatively stable environment of the container firms did not force this kind of requirement in organization design in order for a firm to be highly effective.

Not only does the environment pose demands upon the organization in

Table 8-1 Average Differentiation and Integration across Three Environments*

Industry	Organization	Average differentiation	Average integration
Plastics	High performer	10.7	5.6
	Low performer	9.0	5.1
Foods	High performer	8.0	5.3
	Low performer	6.5	5.0
Containers	High performer	5.7	5.7
	Low performer	5.7	4.8

*Higher differentiation scores mean greater differences. Higher integration scores mean better integration.
Source: Lawrence & Lorsch, 1967, table IV-6, p. 103.

terms of appropriate degrees of differentiation but also, as Lawrence and Lorsch emphasize, it necessitates designs that can achieve integration across departments so that they will function as a total organizational system. The requirement for integration is present in all environments, whether changeable or stable. What is most important is that this integration be of sufficient quantity and of an appropriate kind.

In each of the three environments studied, the more effective organization achieved a greater degree of integration (as shown in Table 8-1). In addition, however, the structural methods of integration utilized by the three effective organizations differed: in the dynamic environment of the plastics industry, the better-performing organization utilized a formal integrating department. The nature of the environment appeared to demand an explicit integrating device to prevent the highly differentiated departments from working at cross-purposes. The effective food-products company used individual integrators, while the high-performing but not highly differentiated container firm used the least complex device, namely, direct managerial contact through the chain of command. In these latter cases, the more predictable environments did not appear to force effective organizations to develop elaborate and expensive mechanisms for integrating different units. In fact, the researchers found that the low-performing container firm had designed a special integrating department into its structure, but "there was no evidence that the integrating unit was serving a useful purpose." This would indicate that this organization's design was not completely compatible with the fundamental nature of its operating environment.

Applicability to Other Kinds of Organizations

While both of the studies we have been describing, the one by Burns and Stalker and the one by Lawrence and Lorsch, have been confined to samples of industrial manufacturing organizations, it must be stressed that the characteristics of the immediate operating environment are critical to organization design no matter what institutional realm we are considering—whether it be a business company, a government bureau, or some other kind of organization employing people. Surely, a federal agency set up in the 1960s to deal with some aspect of modern urban problems faces a more turbulent and changing environment than, say, a unit created many years ago to deal with problems that have gradually receded or at least stabilized over time. This difference, in turn, can be assumed to have an effect on the basic outlines of the agency's structure and operating design. The point is that the dimensions of environmental simplicity-complexity and stability-change can affect all comparisons of organization designs, regardless of whether the system is producing a product for profit or a service for the general welfare.

TECHNOLOGY

Probably the most controversial contextual factor presumed to have a relationship to organization design is technology. Technology also happens to be a factor which was generally ignored for many years in analyses of the design and structure of organizations but which lately has generated a considerable amount of discussion and research (e.g., Thompson & Bates, 1957; Thompson, 1967; Burack, 1967; Udy, 1959; Dubin, 1958; Harvey, 1968; Perrow, 1967; Woodward, 1958, 1965; Hickson et al., 1969). The controversy stems from the question of the degree of dominance of this single factor over all other factors (whether contextual or structural-anatomical) in determining the basic operating structure and characteristics of organizations. On the one hand, there are those who believe technology is the preeminent influential variable and who hold that "we cannot expect a particular relationship [among variables] found in one organization to be found in another unless we know these organizations are in fact similar with respect to their technology" (Perrow, 1967, p. 203). On the other hand, many writers on management, particularly those holding so-called "classical" management viewpoints, have "striven to put forward principles which would apply irrespective of task and technology" (Hickson et al., p. 379). As we shall report later, the research evidence tends to show definite linkages between technology and structure, but linkages which are not always unequivocal and not always strong and overriding.

Definitions of Technology

Before one can hope to proceed very far in attempting to ascertain the effects of technology on organization design, the problem of defining technology must be faced. As might be imagined, definitions abound, but most seem to focus on some notion approximating the following: the techniques used by organizations in work-flow activities to transform inputs into outputs. Or, to put it another way, "the technology of organizations is the 'who does what with whom, when, where, and how often'" (Chapple & Sayles, 1961, p. 34).

Although technology can be subdivided into various components such as operations technology, knowledge technology, etc., most of the research and analytical focus has been on the "operations technology" aspect, and that will be our usage of the term here. Of course, it must be emphasized that technology is a term that is applicable to all types and kinds of organizations, not just industrial or manufacturing. All organizations, whether production-oriented or service-oriented, are presumed to involve individuals in some sort of activities that result in the transformation of "things" (requests, raw materials, people, communications, symbols, etc.) coming in into things going out. The fact that some of these techniques and activities deal with less tangible objects in no sense obviates the necessity to consider the technology of the operations used to deal with them.

Typologies of Technology

Considerations of technology and its effects often involve the problem of how to classify various "types" of technology. Writers on the subject have proposed several different typologies, although none of them have been completely adequate for a wide variety of situations and uses. An example of one of the more widely cited typologies is that of Thompson (1967), who has proposed a three-way classification:

>   1   *Long-linked Technology:* Characterized by serial interdependence of a number of different operations, and illustrated by a mass-production assembly line.
>   2   *Mediating Technology:* Characterized by processes that join together otherwise independent elements of a system, such as customers and clients, and illustrated by employment agencies, banks, and the post office.
>   3   *Intensive Technology:* Characterized by the usage of a variety of techniques to solve a particular problem or bring about a change in some key object, and illustrated by general hospitals and construction companies.

Other technology typologies have been proposed that are somewhat more limited in scope in that they tend to be applicable primarily to production-type organizations. One such typology (Perrow, 1967), for example, focuses on a routine-nonroutine dimension. The bases for determining the degree of routineness of technology in this classification system are two: (1) "the number of exceptional cases encountered in the work" and (2) "the nature of the search process undertaken by the individual when exceptions occur," or the degree to which the search involves analyzable or unanalyzable problems. Another classification system (Harvey, 1968) utilizes the dimension of "technical diffuseness–technical specificity," with diffuseness defined as the number of product changes per unit of time.

As the reader can see, in general these latter approaches to technology typologies describe a more or less generalized continuum:

> Simple — complex
> Routine — unusual
> Stable — changeable

A different sort of typology that is perhaps more amenable to research purposes, yet at the same time definitely limited only to production

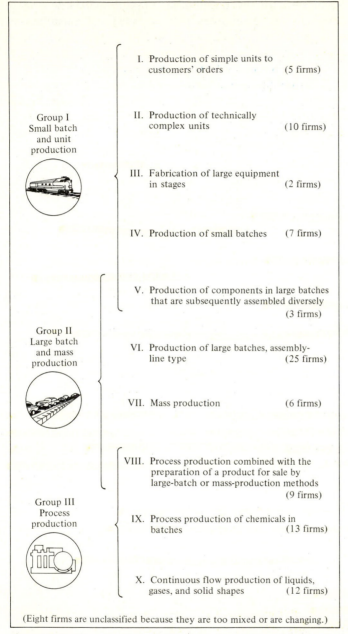

I. Production of simple units to customers' orders (5 firms)

II. Production of technically complex units (10 firms)

Group I
Small batch
and unit
production

III. Fabrication of large equipment in stages (2 firms)

IV. Production of small batches (7 firms)

V. Production of components in large batches that are subsequently assembled diversely (3 firms)

Group II
Large batch
and mass
production

VI. Production of large batches, assembly-line type (25 firms)

VII. Mass production (6 firms)

VIII. Process production combined with the preparation of a product for sale by large-batch or mass-production methods (9 firms)

Group III
Process
production

IX. Process production of chemicals in batches (13 firms)

X. Continuous flow production of liquids, gases, and solid shapes (12 firms)

(Eight firms are unclassified because they are too mixed or are changing.)

Figure 8–3 Classification of 100 firms by system of production, according to Woodward. (Source: Woodward, 1958)

organizations, is that advanced by Woodward (1958, 1965). It has been utilized by Woodward in her extensive research (discussed in more detail below) and has influenced other investigators in their research on organizations. Essentially, Woodward uses a threefold categorization system based on techniques of production: small batch or unit production, large batch or mass production, and continuous process production. Each of these categories in turn can be subdivided into more narrow categories as illustrated in Figure 8-3. The categories in this system are viewed as being arranged on a scale of "technical complexity," meaning "the extent to which the production process is controllable and its results predictable" (1958, p. 12). The use of the term "complexity" to designate the upper end of the continuum can of course be challenged, since "this sequence [dimension] could be viewed as a move toward technical simplicity rather than complexity. It is, after all, the frequent emergence of problems calling for innovation that characterizes unit rather than process production" (Harvey, 1968, p. 249). Despite such criticisms, Woodward's typology has been, as we have noted, quite influential in the field of organization study.

At this point, we can move from a discussion of the nature and types of technology to an examination of two large-scale research projects that have investigated the relationship of technology to organization structure. The first was conducted in the 1950s by Woodward with results that have had a strong impact on organization theory. The other was carried out in the 1960s by Pugh and his associates. Interestingly, both sets of researchers conducted their investigations on firms in Great Britain, though the latter research project has recently been extended to include data collected in other countries. We shall take up the Woodward findings first, since they had some influence on the later work of Pugh and his colleagues.

Woodward Studies

This large-scale research project involved a detailed analysis of the structure of 100 firms in southeast England. All were manufacturing companies, and most were quite small: about 40 percent of the enterprises employed less than 250 people, about 40 percent employed between 250 and 1,000, and only 20 percent employed more than 1,000. Data were collected by a variety of means (interviews, company records, etc.), not only on structural indices (e.g., ratio of managers and supervisors to total personnel) but also on the relative success of the firm in its type of industry.

The Woodward team first attempted to relate the structural features of the organizations to their size, but found little or no such relationship. (Note, however, as we have mentioned, the range of organization size was rather limited and was concentrated toward a large number of small firms.) They

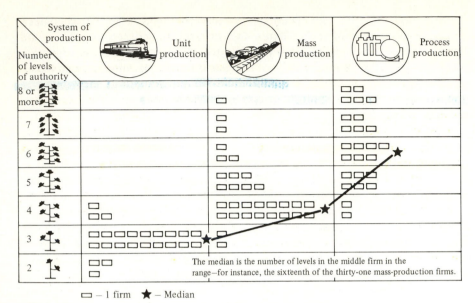

The median is the number of levels in the middle firm in the range—for instance, the sixteenth of the thirty-one mass-production firms.

▢ – 1 firm   ★ – Median

Figure 8-4 Number of levels of authority in relation to system of production, in Woodward study. (Source: Woodward, 1958)

then devised the categorization scheme described above that was based on the technology employed by each firm. When they grouped their firms into three primary categories of technological process—unit, mass, process—they found a number of interesting relationships, such as the following:

   1   Levels of authority: increased with technical complexity (see Fig. 8-4)
   2   Ratio of managers to total personnel: increased with technical complexity
   3   Labor costs: decreased with technical complexity
   4   Span of control of first-level supervisor: increased from unit to mass and then decreased from mass to process (see Fig. 8-5)

   The most intriguing aspects of Woodward's data, however, and the findings that have caused the most attention of organization theorists, concern the relationship of technology to structure and that in turn to organizational success. As Woodward put it, "It was found that the figures relating to the organizational characteristics of the successful firms in each production category tended to cluster around the medians for that category as a whole, while the figures of the firms classified as below average in success were found at the extremes of the range" (1965, p. 69). This is illustrated in Table 8-2, which details the results concerning span of control of the first-level supervisor. Here it can be seen that there was a marked tendency for successful firms in each category to cluster about a particular size of span of control, with the less successful firms seeming to have either a too small or a too large span for their particular technology. The crucial import of this type of finding is summed up by Woodward: "The fact that organizational characteristics, technology, and success were linked together in this way suggested that not only was the system of production an important variable in the determination of organizational structure, but also that one particular form of organization was most appropriate to each system of production" (1965, pp. 69–71). This type of finding strongly reinforces the conclusions derived from the studies of Burns and Stalker and of Lawrence and Lorsch that were mentioned earlier in this chapter.

Related to this kind of finding was the Woodward team's additional important observation that the administrative or operational procedures that typified each firm varied by the type of technology. At what Woodward calls the "top and bottom of the technical scale" (i.e., unit and process firms) there was a tendency toward fewer rules, controls, and definitions of duties, and more flexibility in interpersonal relations and delegation of authority,

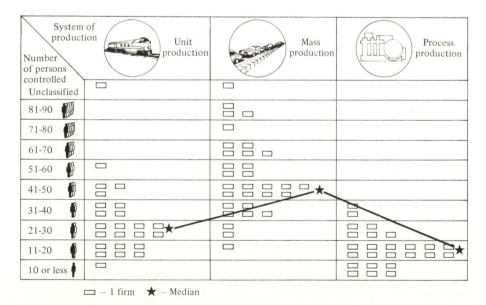

☐ – 1 firm   ★ – Median

Figure 8–5 Span of control of first-line supervision in relation to system of production in Woodward study. (Source: Woodward, 1958)

Table 8-2 Average Span of Control of First-Line Supervisors Analyzed by Business Success

Production system	Less than 10	11 to 20	21 to 30	31 to 40	41 to 50	51 to 60	61 to 70	71 to 80	81 to 90	Un-classi-fied	Median	Total
Unit and small batch												
All firms	1	6	8	4	3	1	—	—	—	1	23	24
"Above average" in success	—	—	4	1	—	—	—	—	—	—		5
"Below average" in success	1	1	—	—	2	1	—	—	—	—		5
Large batch and mass												
All firms	—	1	2	5	9	4	5	1	3	1	49	31
"Above average" in success	—	—	—	—	3	2	—	—	—	—		5
"Below average" in success	—	1	1	1	—	—	—	1	2	—		6
Process												
All firms	6	12	5	2	—	—	—	—	—	—	13	25
"Above average" in success	1	5	—	—	—	—	—	—	—	—		6
"Below average" in success	1	—	1	2	—	—	—	—	—	—		4

Source: Woodward, 1965, table IV, p. 69.

compared to the middle-range mass-production firms. Furthermore, firms in a given technological category that deviated from this general pattern tended to be less successful. Thus, for example, it appeared to these researchers that the most successful large batch or mass-production firms were those which *did* emphasize tight controls, high specification of duties, etc., and which in general typified the embodiment of classical management principles—i.e., they were "bureaucratic"- type organizations. If a firm in this category tended toward flexibility and informality, it tended to be less successful. On the other hand, rigid and rule-bound unit and process firms tended to be less successful than more flexible and human-relations-oriented firms. All of this again appears to support the idea that there are not only appropriate structures but also ways of operating that are specific to particular types of technologies. Woodward summarized her findings by using the organic-mechanistic terminology of Burns: "Successful firms inside the large batch production range tended to have mechanistic management systems. On the other hand, successful firms outside this range tended to have organic systems" (1965, p. 71).

One other aspect of Woodward's commentaries on her findings deserves mention, particularly in relation to the notion of organization design. In a more intensive analysis of twenty firms in her sample, she found that in each of the three types of technologies there were different relationships among the various functions pertaining to the manufacturing cycle. The three sequences that the researchers felt characterized the firms were the following:

Unit: marketing → *development* → production
Mass: development → *production* → marketing
Process: development → *marketing* → production

Not only were the sequences different across the three types of organizations but as Woodward and her colleagues note the "relative importance of the various functions was also related to the system of production" (1965, p. 126). (Note the italicized functions in the sequences above.) Hence, in unit or small batch firms development seemed to be the most critical activity; in mass-production firms the major problems revolved around pushing back the technological limits on production; and in process firms, where technology permitted the rapid and continuous output of material, the key function was marketing. This kind of finding implies that the nature and relative importance of individual-organization interactions will be highly affected by which function is most crucial for a firm, and this in turn appears to be in large part determined by the firm's basic technology.

Pugh–Hickson Studies

It is easy to see from the gist of Woodward's conclusions that she tends toward a technological determinism point of view. In fact, she states that "formal organization depends more on technical considerations than is generally realized, and . . . any tendency to divorce it further ought to be resisted" (1965, p. 77). A somewhat different perspective, however, emerges from the more recent empirical research of another group of English researchers (Pugh, Hickson, and colleagues).

This research team, as part of a much larger project, studied the technological characteristics of forty-six firms (thirty-one manufacturing companies and fifteen service organizations) (Hickson et al., 1969). They attempted to measure such aspects of technology as the degree of automa-

Table 8-3 Distribution of Sample of 46 Diverse Organizations on Scale of Workflow Integration for Operations Technology.

Score	Organization	No. of organizations (N = 46)	Score	Organization	No. of organizations (N = 46)
17	Vehicle manufacturer	1	—	Mechnical handling truck manufacturer	—
16	Brewery	—	—	Engineering tool manufacturer	9
—	Food manufacturer	2	10	Vehicle metal components manufacturer	—
15	Two food manufacturers	—	—	Carriage manufacturer	—
—	Packaging manufacturer	3	—	Local authority water department*	3
14	Local authority baths department*	—	9	Component manufacturer	—
—	Metal components manufacturer	—	—	Nonferrous metal processing	2
—	Metal goods manufacturer	3	8	Toy manufacturer	1
13	Metal goods manufacturer	—	7	Local authority civil engineering department*	1
—	Metal components manufacturer	—	6	Insurance company*	—
—	Vehicle tire manufacturer	—	—	Omnibus company*	—
—	Vehicle electrical components manufacturer	—	—	Local authority transport department*	—
—	Glass components manufacturer	—	—	Government repairs factory	4
—	Vehicle metal components manufacturer	—	5	Research division*	1
—	Commercial vehicle manufacturer	7	4	Civil engineering firm*	—
12	Metal components manufacturer	1	—	Savings bank*	2
11	Two metal components manufacturers	—	3	Cooperative chain of retail stores*	—
—	Printer	—	—	Chain of shoe repair stores*	2
—	Component manufacturer	—	2	Local authority education department*	—
—	Metal goods manufacturer	—	—	Department store*	2
—	Abrasives manufacturer	—	1	Government inspection department*	—
—	Domestic appliances manufacturer	—	—	Chain of retail stores*	2

*Service organizations (N = 15).
Source: Hickson et al., 1969, table 7, p. 385.

tion of equipment, the rigidity of the work flow, the specificity of evaluation of operations, and the interdependence of work-flow segments. Through intercorrelations of various measures of these variables, the researchers concluded that they were all features of a more general factor that could be labeled "work flow integration." Across all forty-six organizations they found a wide range of scores on this composite variable as shown in Table 8-3, where high scores indicate greater integration of work flow (i.e., greater automation of equipment, interdependence of operations, etc.). These technology scores were then related to various measures of organization structure, of both the more anatomical type utilized by Woodward (span of control of first-level supervisor, ratio of supervisors and managers to total personnel, etc.) and the more operational type, such as specialization of activities and standardization of operations. The results, in general, showed weak relationships to structural indices. This finding is, of course, in contrast to that of Woodward.

In an attempt to reconcile the apparent discrepancy between their results and those of Woodward, the Pugh–Hickson research team undertook a more detailed analysis of their data. In particular, they found that one aspect of their findings did coincide with Woodward's results, namely, the curvilinear relation between type of technology and span of control of first-level supervisor, where the largest spans are found in mass-production-type enterprises, with smaller ones in both the unit and batch firms. Additional features of the Pugh–Hickson data showed that certain "job counts" of types of employees on the job floor—such as the proportion in inspectional jobs, the proportion in maintenance jobs, etc.—did relate to Woodward's classification of types of technology. These latter findings, coupled with attention to the fact that Woodward's sample included mostly small firms while their own sample had a higher percentage of larger companies, led the Pugh–Hickson group to conclude the following: "Structural variables will be associated with . . . technology only where they are centered on the work flow. The smaller the organization the more its structure will be pervaded by such technological effects; the larger the organization the more these effects will be confined to variables such as job counts of employees on activities linked with the work flow itself, and will not be detectable in variables of the more remote administrative and hierarchical structure" (Hickson et al., 1969, pp. 394–395).

In essence, the conclusion just cited implies that the effects of technology on organizational design cannot be considered separate from the effects of the size of the organization. The Pugh–Hickson team's hypothesis is that if organizations are small, technology will be critical to structure and design; and if organizations are large, the impact of technology will tend to be confined to the structure of operations at the level of the rank-and-file employee. Such a hypothesis has not yet been adequately documented by sufficient research, but it does provide a promising way to think about how technology can have an impact on the design of organizations. It also is able to incorporate the general thrust of the stimulating results obtained in Woodward's research on technological effects.

How Important Is Technology?

In concluding this section on technology we need to return to the key controversial issue that we said dominated discussions of technology in relation to organization design. This is the issue of "technological determinism"—the extent to which technology by itself *causes* organizations to be structured and operated in certain ways. Our review of the research evidence has shown that it does have some relationship to certain features of structure. But it is particularly difficult to estimate how many of the structural features have been caused by technology, how much technology has been the effect of structure, and, especially, how much other factors have affected or caused both the nature of the technology and the design of organizations. With respect to this latter point, it cannot be emphasized too strongly that individuals in organizations are not helplessly dependent upon the particular existing technology. While it may be difficult to change certain features of technology in a given organization, it is not impossible. Actions can be taken by individuals to change the technology and make it responsive to human choice. [This is basically the theme of those who advocate a "sociotechnical systems" approach to organizations (Cooper & Foster, 1971), but their approach has dealt mostly at the microlevel of jobs and small work groups.] In any organization, technology can be made to function as both a dependent and an independent variable. To say that technology plays an important role in affecting organization design does not preclude its being considered something that in itself can be changed and altered.

HUMAN RESOURCES

A final contextual factor that will be considered in relation to organization design is one that has not received great attention so far but one which is highly important in many instances, namely, the modal characteristics of the human resources employed by the organization. In other words, What types of people does an organization have working for it? The nature of this human input is surely as critical in many cases as is the technology in determining how an organization is currently designed and how it might be redesigned for the future.

Abilities, Skills, and Experience

In Chapter 2 we discussed the "nature of individuals," emphasizing particularly the notion of individual differences. These differences relate to several types of variables, but especially to abilities and skills and to needs and personality characteristics. With respect to skills and abilities of the work force, two dimensions are critical for organization design: their mean level and the degree of their dispersion.

Mean Level If an organization is composed of employees who have a very high mean level of skill—as evidenced, say, by experience in jobs requiring a high degree of skill and by considerable amounts of appropriate formal education—then it is presumed that the nature of the structural-operational features of the organization should take cognizance of this. To be more specific, if employees tend to be especially skilled and well educated, it is likely that a high degree of formal specification and standardization of activities, and the imposition of close and severe controls, would result in an inefficient use of human resources, both from the organization's standpoint and from the individual's standpoint. Resulting behavior could be presumed to be characterized by performance much lower than potentially possible, frustration, and perhaps overt expressions of resentment against the organization. This is recognized by some organizations, particularly those employing scientists and professionals, where activities are not highly specified, authority is widely dispersed (because each employee is to some degree an "expert"), and controls are not rigid. However, many other organizations that also employ individuals with high skill levels fail to take this factor into account and are designed as if their employees constituted a low level of human resources when actually their potential is much greater .

Similarly, of course, it is possible for organizations to "misdesign" in the other direction and structure their operations as if they have a work force of high skills and ability when in fact this is not the case. That is, a structure that assumes too high a level of skills and abilities can potentially be as frustrating and dissatisfying to the individual as the reverse. Such a situation seems, on the basis of the general literature on organizations, to be a less common occurrence than the former, but it is not unknown. Also, some (e.g., Miles, 1965) would argue that it is better for organizations to err on the side of expecting too much rather than too little from their employees because "self-fulfilling prophecies" will operate and individuals will strive to meet the levels of performance expected of them. (This is often referred to as the "Pygmalion" effect.)

Distribution   Not only is the mean level of abilities important, but so also is their degree of distribution or dispersion throughout the organization. Two different organizations may have work forces that average the same degree of experience, abilities, skills, etc., but one of them may have individuals high in these qualities widely scattered throughout the organization while the other may have them concentrated in one unit or section (e.g., as in an R&D laboratory). For both organizations to adopt the same kind of structural-operational features of design would appear to be inappropriate. The enterprise with the greater dispersal of high skill and experience levels might be more likely to take advantage of them in a more organic rather than mechanistic structure. On the other hand, the organization with a narrow dispersal might well adopt an organic form for the unit containing most of the people with high-level abilities and skills, but a more mechanistic form for the majority of units in the organization. When considering how to utilize the skills and experience of work forces, the concept of distribution appears to be at least as crucial as the concept of average or mean level.

Needs and Personality Traits

Individuals who come to work for an organization differ in their needs and personality traits as well as in their capabilities. This, as we indicated, is another aspect of the human-resources contextual variable that is highly likely to influence the effectiveness of an organization's design. Not every individual will need or want a wide latitude of decision making with very flexible and informal procedures that require much from him and relatively little in the way of direct supervision. Likewise, there are many other individuals who will not desire to be parts of rigidly structured operations. But it is not just a matter of how individuals differ in their needs, say, for achievement or affiliation. It is also a matter of how they differ in their characteristic modes of behaving and in their own views of themselves. These kinds of regularities, commonly referred to as personality traits, also have an impact on the effectiveness of different types of organization design for the person and for the organization. We can hypothesize that if individuals have strong needs for independence and self-realization and have relatively high self-confidence, they will prefer organic-type organizations and will do better in them. Individuals who have less of these traits can be presumed to fare better in a relatively more highly structured organization.

Actual versus Perceived Characteristics

In all these considerations of the nature of the human-resources input into organizations, we must be constantly alert to the distinction between actual and perceived abilities and characteristics of individuals. Many organization designs seem to be affected not by the objective measures of the traits and capabilities of employees but by the assumptions that organization leaders make about them. This is essentially the message that McGregor has provided in his classic *The Human Side of Enterprise* (1960). If one is a manager or leader, it is not what subordinates are actually like that guides his actions but rather what he *thinks* they are like. Hence, if those who influence organization design consider their work force to be composed of individuals with relatively low abilities and capacities for self-direction, they are likely to urge designs that tend toward the highly structured and rule-oriented type, regardless of how high the level of abilities might actually be if objectively measured. On the contrary, if individuals with very strong needs for self-actualization are major determinants of certain design features, they are likely (if not cognizant of this point) to influence organizations in the direction of loose structure and controls on the assumption that everyone else is like themselves. (Strauss, 1963, has an especially good discussion of this point.) Thus, when we are considering the impact of human resources on the design of organizations, we need to take into account the perceived resources as well as the actual ones.

One additional aspect of human resources as a contextual variable in relation to organization design merits attention. This is the notion that the quality and nature of human resources, as of technology, can be thought of as a dependent as well as an independent variable. Organization leaders who feel that their particular design is necessary because of the other variables in the situation (e.g., technology, environment, etc.) may be able to bring about a greater congruence between their human resources and their organization through changing their input into the organization labor force rather than changing the degree of structure of their organizations. Many organizations (as pointed out in Chapter 5) seem to recruit and hire on a very narrow basis and hence obtain a work force that is not particularly compatible with the organization's fundamental way of operating. If an organization, for example, exists in a very turbulent and uncertain environment, it might well consider hiring not just the technically best personnel (especially when the "best" may not be very much better than the average) but rather those who would be adaptable to, and even might "enjoy," such an environment. In this way, organization design, human resources, and other contextual variables could all be brought into line in an advantageous way. In any event, it is clear that the human resources of an organization offer an opportunity as well as a challenge in constructing organizations that will meet the needs of individuals as well as the collective units themselves.

This section on human-resources inputs concludes our discussion of the basic contextual factors that influence organization design. The stage is now set to look at the central core of design considerations, namely, structural factors, as they affect the behavior and performance of organization members.

REVIEW AND DISCUSSION QUESTIONS

1 How do the various contextual factors influence the way in which an organization is designed?
2 Are some of the contextual factors more important than others in influencing organizational design?
3 The stability of the environment in which an organization operates is thought by some to affect the degree to which the organizations are structured. Is this a reasonable position to take?

4 Contrast mechanistic and organic organizations, focusing on their structural features. In what types of environments would each of these two "ideal types" be most appropriate? Why?

5 An organization as a whole may have a mechanistic structure. Would this preclude the existence of subunits within the same organization with organic structures? What does this suggest concerning the accuracy with which organizations can be classified as *either* organic or mechanistic?

6 How important are the studies of Woodward for the design of organizations?

7 How is the notion of "work-flow integration" related to the "environmental stability" idea? Would one be likely to find a highly "integrated" work flow in a rapidly changing environment?

8 According to Pugh and Hickson, the effects of technology on organization design will vary as a function of the organization's size. Explain why this should be so.

9 What influence, if any, does the variable nature of human inputs (in terms of personality, ability, attitudes, etc.) have on organization design?

Chapter 9

Organization Design: Structural Factors

It will be recalled that at the beginning of the last chapter we pointed out that the structures of organizations could be thought of in terms of both their anatomical dimensions and their more operational features. (Refer back to Figure 8-2 that outlined the relationships among factors involved in organization design.) In the present chapter we will consider both facets of structure in detail and then will conclude with a brief overview of the probable impact of these and the contextual factors on behavior within organizations. In all instances it should be kept in mind that we are not attempting to catalog every conceivable variable that might affect the design of organizations. Rather, we will be concentrating on the ones that we and others consider to be among the more influential variables that must be taken into account in achieving an understanding of organization design and its behavioral effects.

ANATOMICAL DIMENSIONS

In Chapter 8 we noted (see p. 223 and Figure 8-1) that the anatomical dimensions of organizations can be considered as intervening links between contextual factors and operational features; in addition, however, we also stated that these anatomical-type variables can have effects on basic operational features that are independent of contextual factors. Or, to put this another way: individuals in organizations are affected by the factors (e.g., environment, technology) that cause a particular size or span of control or degree of decentralization, but their behavior can also be directly affected by the fact that many other people work for the organization, or by the fact that their boss supervises only a few people, or by the fact that their unit is closely tied to the headquarters unit of the organization. The major issue, however, is the degree of influence these types of variables have on the overall functioning of organizations and the behavior of employees within them.

Totality: Size

By far, the totality or size dimension of organizations is the most widely researched anatomical variable. It is visible and tangible, and intuitively it "seems" important to both social scientists and to employees. But size, more than any other anatomical variable, also illustrates the issue just mentioned above: is it really influential or is it merely some sort of masking-type variable that evaporates when examined closely to reveal the "real" causal variables?

Size Is Not a Simple Variable   Before attempting to answer this question with the available evidence, it may be well to sound a cautionary note concerning the use of the term "size." At first glance, it would appear to be a deceptively simple variable if one is willing to specify the referent (e.g., number of employees, amount of assets, etc.). However, organization researchers have been rather casual in their use of the term (assuming that for most purposes it is being confined to a measure of the number of employees) in describing their findings, for they often have not made clear whether the "units" are total organizations, major subunits, or even smaller subunits.

Frequently it will become a very sticky matter to designate the appropriate units for comparison on a size basis. Should, for example, a company that is part of a conglomerate composed of a number of relatively autonomous companies be considered a total organization or a major subunit? Could it be compared, in size, to a totally independent company? Or, to take an example from a different realm: Is the Department of Labor part of a larger organization (the federal government) or is it an organization in its own right. Or, what about the Bureau of the Budget? Should it or can it be compared with a bureau that is part of one of the departments, or with one of the so-called independent commissions such as the Federal Communications Commission? These are knotty questions to which there are only arbitrary answers. It is only necessary to keep in mind that researchers often have not concerned themselves with these precise distinctions, and this lends difficulty to interpreting conclusions concerning the effects, or lack of effects, of size.

Studies of organization size tend to fall into two categories: those that relate size to other characteristics of the organization, particularly the ones we have labeled "structural-operational" features such as degree of specification of job duties, and those that relate size directly to various indices of individual attitudes and behavior such as job satisfaction, turnover, and job performance.

Size in Relation to Other Organizational Characteristics   Turning to the first category of studies of size, we find clearly conflicting evidence. Several major studies, particularly those of Woodward (1958, 1965) and Harvey (1968), failed to find any meaningful relationships of size to other structural and operational variables of organizations. However, the distributions of sizes sampled in both of these studies tended to be weighted heavily toward the very small end of the scale. Thus, there is considerable doubt that the full range of organization sizes was adequately sampled.

The Pugh–Hickson research, already referred to in the previous chapter, sampled a somewhat broader range of sizes and did find significant relationships of size to other measures of organization structure. (It should be noted in passing that these researchers classified size as a context rather than an organizational structural variable. Although this makes some sense, we feel it overemphasizes the independent-variable quality of size and underemphasizes the fact that size also can be thought of as a dependent-type variable.) This research team found that size was strongly correlated with a composite measure of "structuring of activities" that included variables such as specialization of roles, standardization of functions, and formalization of procedures. From their findings, the investigators hypothesize that "an increased scale of operation increases the frequency of recurrent events and the repetition of decisions, which are then standardized and formalized. . . . Once the number of positions and people grows beyond control by personal interaction, the organization must be more explicitly structured" (Pugh et al., 1969, p. 112).

Although the available evidence (including other studies not cited here) is not clear-cut about the relationships of size to other organizational variables, it does appear to point to some limited impact of size *if* (1) the range of sizes being considered is great enough and (2) the other variables in the relationship tend toward measures of bureaucratic-type operations. The direction of the relationship, where there is one, seems clear: larger size tends to be related to a more mechanistic, bureaucratic mode of operation. Whether size "causes" this to occur is still an open question, since all these studies involved essentially correlational rather than experimental data. Nevertheless, there is a presumption that organization size can be thought of as a causal type of anatomical dimension.

Size in Relation to Individuals' Attitudes and Behavior The relationships of size to individuals' attitudes and behavior have been investigated in a vast array of studies. Most of these studies, however, have made comparisons across different sized subunits of larger organizations rather than across independent total organizations. Many, in fact, as can be seen in Table 9-1, involved comparisons of relatively small units such as work groups and departments. Nevertheless, Table 9-1 shows some relatively definite trends of relationships between subunit size and several of the "dependent" variables. Larger-sized subunits clearly seem to be related negatively to job satisfaction and to the individual's tendency to stay on the job by not being absent and not terminating his employment. Indeed, the studies relating size to these three indices of employee behavior—job satisfaction, absenteeism, and turnover—show remarkable consistency in comparison with almost any other category of studies dealing with organizations and organizational behavior.

The weight of the evidence would seem to make a strong indictment against large-sized subunits, both from the individual's point of view and from the organization's standpoint. However, several qualifications to this conclusion need to be added. First, as Table 9-1 shows, the relationships of subunit size to two other indices of behavior—accident rates and productivity—are definitely equivocal, with some studies finding that large size is disadvantageous, others that it is advantageous, and still others that the size–behavior relationship is curvilinear rather than linear. Second, most of these studies involved rank-and-file employees, and thus it is not clear how size affects supervisory or managerial attitudes and behavior. There is some evidence, for example, insofar as job attitudes are concerned (Porter, 1963a; 1963b; 1964), to indicate that there may be some interaction between size and level of management: lower-level managers were more satisfied if they worked in smaller companies, but upper-level managers were more positive about their jobs if they were employed by larger organizations. At least, it appeared that there were no clear-cut overall advantages for smaller-sized organizations as far as managers and their feelings about their jobs were concerned.

Finally, there is the problem referred to previously of trying to distinguish among types of subunits in analyzing the effects of size. Simply put:

Table 9-1   Studies of Relationships between Organization Subunit Size and Job Attitudes and Job Behavior

Attitude or behavior studied	Investigators	Type of subunit considered	Relationship found*
Job satisfaction	Talacchi (1960)	Factories	Negative
	Kerr, Koppelmeier, & Sullivan (1951)	Departments	Negative
	Indik & Seashore (1961)	Departments	Negative
	Katzell, Barrett, & Parker (1961)	Departments	Negative
	Campbell (1952)	Work groups	Negative
	Worthy (1950)	?	Negative
	Indik & Seashore (1961)	Automobile dealerships	Zero
Absenteeism	Revans (1958)	Gas works	Positive
	Revans (1958)	Factories	Positive
	Revans (1958)	Factories	Positive
	Acton Society Trust (1953)	Factory	Positive
	Baumgartel & Sobol (1959)	"Plants" (airline locations)	Positive
	Research Council for Economic Security (Baumgartel & Sobol, 1959)	Plants	Positive (?)
	Hewitt & Parfitt (1953)	Departments	Positive
	Indik & Seahore (1961)	Departments	Positive
	Kerr, Koppelmeier, & Sullivan (1951)	Departments	Positive
	Metzner & Mann (1953)	Work groups (blue-collar)	Positive
	Argyle, Gardner, & Cioffi (1958)	Work groups	Curvilinear
	Metzner & Mann (1953)	Work groups (white-collar)	Zero
Turnover	Indik & Seashore (1961)	Automobile dealerships	Positive
	Kerr, Koppelmeier, & Sullivan (1951)	Departments	Positive
	Mandell (1956)	Departments	Positive
	Argyle, Gardner, & Cioffi (1958)	Work groups	Zero
Accidents	Revans (1958)	Mines (Britain)	Positive
	Revans (1958)	Factories (Britain)	Positive
	Revans (1958)	Departments (Asia)	Positive
	Revans (1958)	Mines (U.S.A.)	Curvilinear
	U.S. Department of Labor (Revans, 1958)	Factories (U.S.A.)	Curvilinear
	National Safety Council (Revans, 1958)	Factories (U.S.A.)	Negative
Labor disputes	Cleland (1955)	Factories	Positive
	Revans (1958)	Mines	Positive
Productivity	Katzell, Barrett, & Parker (1961)	Company divisions	Negative
	Indik & Seashore (1961)	Departments	Negative
	Marriott (1949)	Work groups	Negative
	Revans (1958)	Mines	Curvilinear
	Revans (1958)	Retail stores	Curvilinear
	Herbst (1957)	Retail stores	Curvilinear
	Indik & Seashore (1961)	Automobile dealerships	Zero
	Argyle, Gardner, & Cioffi (1958)	Work groups	Positive

*A positive relationship indicates a trend for the attitude or behavior to become more frequent as size increases. A negative relationship indicates a trend for the attitude or behavior to become less frequent as size increases. A curvilinear relationship indicates a trend for the middle-sized subunit to exhibit the greatest or the lowest frequency of the attitude or behavior.

Source: Porter & Lawler, 1965, table 2.

A typical worker is a member of at least three organization subunits: a primary work group, a department, and a factory or office. Although the evidence indicates that large-sized subunits are associated, for example, with high absenteeism, it is impossible to know on the basis of past studies if it is large size in the primary work group, department, or factory that is crucial in this relationship. . . . Investigators have failed to control for variation in the size of the other types of sub-units of which an individual is a member while they are studying the effects of size of one type of unit. (Porter & Lawler, 1965, p. 39).

Perhaps a conclusion such as the following might be warranted with the present state of our knowledge concerning the impact of size, especially as it relates to employee attitudes: "An increase in the total size of an organization—with the consequent technological advantages of large-scale operation—will not necessarily reduce the morale and job satisfaction of employees as long as intra-organization work units are kept small" (Porter, 1963b).

Verticality and Horizontality: Shape

An anatomical dimension that is beginning to receive more attention in recent years (e.g., Meltzer & Salter, 1962; Porter & Lawler, 1964; Porter & Siegel, 1965; Kaufman & Seidman, 1970) is that of "shape," that is, the number of levels in an organizational hierarchy in relation to the size of the organization. An organization with many levels in relation to its size would be termed "tall" and would thus have a small *average* span of control (number of subordinates reporting to a given supervisor), while an organization with few levels in relation to its size would be designated as one with a "flat" structure.

Classical management theorists (e.g., Fayol, 1949; Urwick, 1935) have generally advocated small spans of control and hence (by implication) tall organization shapes. The presumed advantages were that a superior could have closer control over subordinate performance and thereby achieve better coordination among the different parts of the organization. Vigorous disagreement with this viewpoint has been put forth by others (e.g., Worthy, 1950; Soujanen, 1955) who advocate larger spans and flatter structure. Typical of this alternative point of view is the statement that "flatter, less complex structures, with a maximum of administrative decentralization, tend to create a potential for improved attitudes, more effective supervision, and greater individual responsibility and initiative among employees" (Worthy, 1950, p. 179).

Research Findings What has the empirical research shown with respect to this issue? Again, as might be expected, the available data are not clear-cut. One aspect of the findings, however, does seem indisputable: the shapes that exist, particularly the size of spans of control at the lowest level of supervision, show some relationship to the type of technology characteristic of the organization. Both the Pugh–Hickson and the Woodward studies show, for example, that the average size of the existing span of control at the foreman level is much larger in large batch and mass-production firms than it is in small batch or process-type organizations. Furthermore, as we have previously pointed out, Woodward claims that for each type of technology those firms closest to the modal span of control are the most successful economically. This clearly would imply that there is not an optimum span of control at lower organization levels that is suitable for all types of organizations. (House and Miner, 1969, in a review of the literature on span of control, also arrive at the same conclusion.) We can further presume that not only technology but other contextual variables, particularly the skill and ability levels of operative personnel, will also play a large role in determining appropriate spans of control at the lower levels of the organization.

Research findings relating more to the shape of the total organization (i.e., the average span of control across all levels) follow the same kind of pattern. That is, there is some evidence (e.g., Woodward, 1958; Hickson et al., 1969) to indicate that the total number of levels in the hierarchy may be related to the degree of technical complexity characterizing the organization. However, the relationships are not strong and the samples of types of organizations studied are limited. Also, data from a different type of sample, federal government agencies, showed that a pyramidal type of shape existed for line components of the organizations, but not for staff personnel (Kaufman & Seidman, 1970). This highlights the fact that there can be different shapes within the same organization, and that it may not always be appropriate to talk about "the" shape of the total organization.

Research relating shape of structure to attitudes of employees has been sparse, but it so far fails to confirm beliefs (such as that of Worthy, 1950) that one shape is definitely superior to another. For example, findings from a study of some 700 scientists (Meltzer & Salter, 1962) did not show attitude differences between those working in flat versus tall organizations. Studies of managers both in United States and foreign firms (Porter & Lawler, 1964; Porter & Siegel, 1965) tended to indicate that when managers were working in firms larger than 5,000 employees they were more satisfied with their jobs if they were in tall structures, whereas the reverse results were true for managers working in small organizations. In this connection, the following reasoning suggests why one might expect such an interaction between size and shape:

> In a small organization problems of coordination and communication do not tend to be severe, simply because the organization is small. Thus, in a small organization there would be little advantage in a tall structure and, in fact, since it tends to amplify the disadvantages associated with tight managerial control, a

tall structure probably is a liability in a typical small organization. In large organizations, on the other hand, problems of coordination and communication are complex. Thus, for large organizations a taller type of structure may be needed to overcome these problems and allow managers to supervise their subordinates more effectively. (Porter & Lawler, 1965, pp. 44–45)

Clearly, this kind of emphasis on a possible interaction effect points to a conclusion that seems appropriate to anatomical-type variables: Whatever effects any specified variable may have, they are probably strongly conditioned by the simultaneous existence of other such variables: "Organizations appear to be much too complex for a given variable to have a consistent unidirectional effect across a wide variety of types of conditions" (Porter & Lawler, 1965, p. 48). Thus, while it is satisfactory for descriptive purposes to discuss such variables one by one, we must keep in mind that they probably interact together to produce their effects.

Centrality: Dispersion of Units

"Centrality" is a structural-type variable that has a variety of meanings and consequently presents severe difficulties in studying it for purposes of research. As one pair of writers has put it with respect to the decentralized end of the dimension: "Decentralization is several things to different people. There are those who view it entirely in terms of decision-making; others see it from the standpoint of geographical dispersion of plants and installation; and still others approach it as a philosophy of corporate life, a set of organization values with sociological, psychological, and spiritual facets" (Pfiffner & Sherwood, 1960, p. 190). The first and third uses of the term in this comment really involve more operational features of organizational design and consequently will be covered in the next section. The other use of the term, geographical dispersion, is relevant to a consideration of the structural anatomy of organizations, but it may be a relatively superficial aspect in many instances.

While it is difficult to define structural centrality unambiguously, it seems apparent that this is a dimension worth consideration and investigation. We are using the term to mean the presence or absence of separate operating units, whether or not they are geographically dispersed. Ordinarily, "separate" will mean geographically dispersed, as in a multifactory company or a multibranch bank, but this is not an absolute prerequisite. What is essential is whether or not the employees and managers in the organization *perceive* it to be an organization with separate operating units or, on the contrary, whether they think of it as one single organization. The questions for organizational design revolve around the consequences of such dispersion, if it is present, on operational features such as specification of activities, types of control, and concentration of authority. Research evidence (e.g., Porter & Lawler, 1965) is insufficient to provide any firm conclusions in this regard, but it seems obvious that with more structural decentralization, managers and leaders of organizations face more complex problems in bringing about coordination of the organization as a whole. Whether it will necessarily lead to more or less specification of activities, more or less concentration of authority, etc., is moot at this point.

Combinations

In recent years, a number of organizations, particularly those dealing with aerospace and military weapons production, have utilized structures that are not easily analyzable along typical anatomical dimensions such as number of hierarchical levels, etc. These types of structural arrangements are referred to by a variety of terms such as "project management," "program management," "task forces," etc. The essence of these structures is that they involve units that cut across segments of both the vertical and horizontal dimensions of the organization. (See Figure 9-1 for an example of a matrix-type structure.) Hence, the term "matrix" has commonly been applied to structures that include a number of projects, programs, or task forces.

Reasons for Matrix Designs Such structures have come about because "the pressures of accelerating technology and short lead times have made it necessary to establish some formalized managerial agency to provide overall integration of the many diverse functional activities" (Kast & Rosenzweig, 1970, p. 194). Matrix forms of structure, where lateral relationships are emphasized relatively more strongly than vertical superior-subordinate interactions, permit the organization to mobilize diverse resources to concentrate their efforts on a specific target outcome (which usually has a specific target date for completion). They are advocated as a means of overcoming the difficulties encountered in more typically structured organizations in cutting across intraorganizational boundaries to achieve some integrated result. Matrix structures thus attempt to utilize the resources of the specialist without paying the typical penalties of high degrees of specialization where coordination problems become magnified.

Advantages and Disadvantages of Such Designs Organizations and individuals involved in structures featuring a matrix design gain both advantages and disadvantages. From the organization's standpoint, where highly identifiable unique projects are part of the organization's work, this form of structure seems to permit greater focus of resources on meeting the

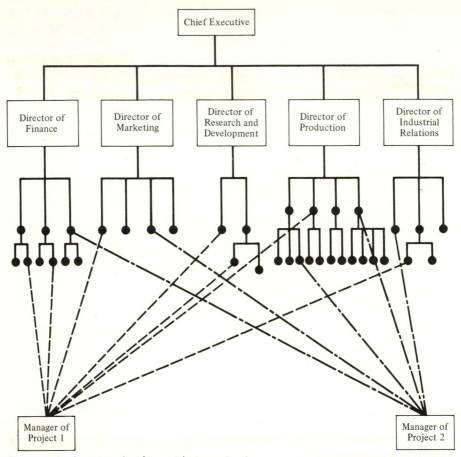

Figure 9–1   An example of a matrix-type structure.

specified target outcomes. On the other hand, there may be problems of integrating across projects and integrating the projects with other ongoing work of the organization.

From the perspective of the individual, such an arrangement permits him to keep his attention directed on tangible performance outcomes. He can, perhaps, more easily see how his actions at any given moment will be instrumental to some final outcome. This is often a comfortable feeling. Conversely, however, what he gains in this kind of clarity of objective he may lose in increased ambiguity concerning reporting (i.e., superior-subordinate) relationships. He may find himself with responsibilities both to his project manager and to his functional area (e.g., engineering, marketing, etc.) superior. While this situation per se does not seem to involve inevitable problems or conflicts as envisioned by traditional management theorists, it can be disconcerting and anxiety-arousing to some individuals. (Here again, the importance of the nature of the human-resource context variable is critical in analyzing the likely effectiveness of a particular kind of organizational design.) Furthermore, such structures are likely to be quite fluid and involve a "temporary" quality, as Bennis (1966) points out. This can be seen by some individuals as providing great challenge and stimulation, and by others as creating unnecessary frustration and anxiety.

In short, although the matrix type of organization has been in effect for a relatively limited period of years, it would appear to offer some clear-cut advantages over more traditional structures. However, it also appears that if organizations uncritically adopt this kind of structure regardless of the other parameters of their context, they may find that they have not realized any appreciable gains and may have indeed incurred a whole set of new problems. A matrix structure offers an attractive alternative organization design, but it is not a universal answer to every design problem.

OPERATIONAL FEATURES

In the preceding section we examined the more anatomical or skeletal dimensions of organization structure. In this section we will look at the more operational or functional features of structure and design. As will be recalled from Figure 8-1, we conceive of both contextual variables and anatomical dimensions as playing major roles in affecting the nature of operational features of the design of organizations. These operational variables are, in turn, presumed to influence various aspects of individual performance and behavior in organizational settings.

We have chosen three particular structural-operational variables for discussion because both the theoretical and research literatures seem to identify them as among the most important defining characteristics of organization design. Interestingly, these three features—authority, activities, and controls—also are roughly analogous to the three basic elements that can be present in any job: planning, doing, and evaluating. Thus, we can think of this kind of linkage between organization design and job design (which will be covered in detail in the next chapter) as a correspondence that ties together the macro aspects of design with the micro.

As we proceed through an analysis of each of these three operational features, it is advisable to keep in mind that each of them can be somewhat independent of the others (as Hall, 1963; Pugh et al., 1968, have stressed in their empirical studies). Thus, for example, an organization that exhibits a high degree of concentration of formal authority in the hands of a few people at the top is not necessarily also characterized by a high degree of specification of activities (Pugh et al., 1969). Of course, in a given organization there can be a strong degree of relationship among these three features, but this is not a necessary requirement. All organizations have some type of authority, some type of activities, and some type of control; but the particular form of one of these variables does not automatically dictate the form of the other variables. We will return to this point in the last section of this chapter because it is a fairly crucial one in any overall consideration of organization design.

Authority Structure

This operational feature of structure refers to the locus and degree of dispersion of decision making within the organization. It addresses itself to the question of what part of the organization, or who in the organization, can determine the nature of the activities of the members of the organization and can commit the resources of the organization to certain courses of action. It is related, obviously, to the usual use of the dimension centralized-decentralized in describing how organizations typically operate. It is also related to the notion of a specified hierarchy or chain of command.

The dimension of authority structure that distinguishes one organization from another is whether authority is concentrated among a small group of individuals at the very top of the structure, or whether it is widely dispersed among a number of different echelons and units such that these units and individuals have a relatively high degree of autonomy. Organizations of the first type have been labeled more bureaucratic or mechanistic, while the latter have been labeled more adaptive or organic.

Empirical data collected by Pugh and his colleagues on forty-six organizations tend to show that those organizations toward the bureaucratic end of this dimension frequently are not simultaneously high with regard to another major bureaucratic-type feature, namely, structuring or specification of activities (Pugh et al., 1968). Indeed, from the findings of their data, these researchers distinguished between two types of organizations in this regard: "personnel bureaucracies" that have a high concentration of authority but a relatively low degree of activity structuring, and "work-flow bureaucracies" or organizations that show the reverse pattern. The personnel-bureaucracy type seemed to be characterized by a higher percentage of service-type and governmental organizations when compared with the so-called work-flow bureaucracies. Of course, these researchers also found some organizations that were high on both dimensions and others that were low on both (Pugh et al., 1969). In any event, the point to keep in mind is the one we referred to earlier, namely, that organizations with a high concentration of authority do *not* necessarily exhibit other excessive bureaucratic-type features.

The important issue concerning the variable of the locus and dispersion of authority in relation to organizational design is: How necessary is it for organizations to have high concentration of authority and low degrees of individual and unit autonomy? The answer would seem to be strongly tied to the nature of the contextual variables and, perhaps to a lesser extent, the nature of the anatomical variables. As aptly summed up in a recent review of the relevant literature: "The degree to which the authority structure should be hierarchically differentiated in order to maximize task accomplishment seems in many cases to be a direct function of an appropriate match between the nature of the task and the availability and dispersion of relevant human skills to accomplish the task" (Friedlander, 1970, p. 117). The nature of the environment can also be added to task and human skill factors as a critical factor in determining an appropriate authority structure. To quote the same review again, "In environments which are relatively stable, where problems and functions can be effectively programmed, and where the skills for this programming are centrally and authoritatively located in the organization, an hierarchical authority structure is superior" (p. 118).

Taken together, these factors point to a major conclusion: The more that an organization faces a stable environment, deals with familiar and relatively simple tasks, and contains a work force in which only a small number of individuals at the top possess long experience, technical skills, and a strong desire to exercise discretion in making decisions, then the more a high degree of concentration of authority located at the top of the organization seems appropriate. If, on the other hand, the organization generally faces an unpredictable and constantly changing environment, involves many complex tasks, and contains a work force in which skills and experience are fairly broadly dispersed, a more widely distributed system of authority would seem to be called for, with a consequent greater degree of autonomy for individuals and units at lower levels in the hierarchy. At least, this seems to be the general thrust that can be drawn from the research that we have available at this time. Future research will undoubtedly cause us to add qualifications to this conclusion even if it does not result in basic changes in it.

Activities Structure

The ways in which employee activities are structured constitutes a second major feature of the operational aspects of organizational design. This dimension refers to the degree of "specificity (or precision) of role prescription" (Hickson, 1966). It focuses, in other words, on *how* activities are to be carried out and whether there are standards, rules, procedures, etc., which circumscribe the individual's discretion in this respect. It is closely akin to such concepts as the division of labor and task specialization.

Elements of Activities Structure The detailed research findings of Pugh, Hickson, and colleagues indicate three specific aspects of operational features form an overall dimension labeled "structuring of activities" (Pugh et al., 1968). These are (1) "specialization"—the degree to which tasks and duties are subdivided within the organization, (2) "standardization"—the degree to which procedures and rules are specified for carrying out tasks, and (3) "formalization"—the degree to which the procedures and rules exist in written form. The researchers found these three characteristics appearing together, such that if an organization exhibited a considerable amount of one element it also was high on the other two variables. The three elements thus provide a sort of concrete definition of this major dimension of the operations-structure nature of organizations that can be applied to a variety of enterprises whether they are primarily manufacturing or service-oriented.

Causes and Effects of Activities Structure The most important influence of all on the degree of structuring of activities may well be the discretionary decisions made by those in positions of authority in the organization (Child, 1972). In other words, relating back to the basic "technological-imperative" issue we discussed in the previous chapter, neither technology nor size completely dictates how much standardization, specialization, formalization, etc., must exist in an organization. Within limits, the structuring of activities is modifiable and subject to voluntary determination by those who make the decisions in the organization.

If the degree of activity structuring is not completely determined by factors and events beyond the control of those in the organization, the question then becomes one of "how much structure" is desirable. Interestingly, theorists seem to have converged on this single feature of organizations—the amount of role or activity structuring—as the key one in differentiating organizations (Hickson, 1966). The strong focus on this dimension is shown in the accompanying table (9-2) (from Hickson, 1966), where the various terminologies used to describe the ends of this dimension are identified. The "structural analysts" have described the dimension, the "structural designers"—mostly classical management theorists—have advocated the higher-specificity end, and the "structural critics"—often called "modern organization theorists"—have prescribed the lower-specificity end.

The activities structure dimension has been the object of much analysis and prescription because of the direct consequences that seem to result from whether or not activities are highly specified and structured. This situation is summarized in another table (9-3) (also from Hickson, 1966). Those who advocate high degrees of specificity see the advantages as basically "bringing order out of chaos" and preventing wasted effort by organization members. Those who prescribe less structuring of activities see the advantages in terms of greater member creativity, commitment, and motiva-

Table 9-2   The Terminologies Used by Various Students of Organization Structure for Specificity of Role Prescription

Students of organization structure	Terminologies for specificity (or precision) of role prescription	
	Higher specificity	**Lower specificity**
Structure analysts (sociologists and administration theorists)		
Weber	Traditionalistic, bureaucratic	Charismatic
Burns and Stalker	Mechanistic	Organic (or organismic)
Barnes	Closed system	Open system
Whyte	Formalized	Flexible
Hage	High formalization (standardization)	Low formalization
Crozier	Routinized	Uncertain
Gordon and Becker	Specified procedures	Unspecified
Thompson	Overspecification	Structural looseness
Litwak	Weberian	Human relations
Janowitz	Domination: manipulation	Fraternal
Frank	Well defined (and overdefined)	Underdefined
Simon	Programmed	Nonprogrammed
Presthus	Structured perceptual field	Unstructured
Bennis	Habit	Problem solving
Structure designers (management writers)		
Taylor	Scientific task determination	Personal rule-of-thumb
Fayol ⎫ Urwick ⎬ Brech ⎭	Clear statement of responsibilities	Personalities predominant (rather than intended design)
Brown	Explicit authority and accountability	Undefined roles and relationships
Structure critics (social psychologists)		
Likert	Authoritative	Participative
McGregor	Theory X	Theory Y
Argyris	Rational organization	Self-actualization

Source: Hickson, 1966, table 1, p. 227.

tion. The table also shows, however, that still others, who are not necessarily in favor of specification, see some other potential disadvantageous results of low degrees of structuring.

As can be appreciated, the "how much structure" question engenders

Table 9-3 Consequences of Specificity of Role Prescription

Higher specificity	Lower specificity			
Reduces confusion	More motivating	More innovating	Result: anxiety	Result: power conflict
Taylor	Likert	Burns and	Presthus	Crozier
Fayol	McGregor	Stalker	Burns and	Gordon and
Urwick	Argyris	Thompson	Stalker	Becker
Brech	Barnes	Frank		Litwak
Brown	(Bennis)	Bennis		
Weber		Hage		

Source: Hickson, 1966, table 2, p. 233.

considerable controversy. Both the classical management theorists and the human-relations-oriented "modern" organization theorists tended to ignore parameters of the situation and context, such as human-resource skills, nature of the task, etc. Here again, the most recent research seems to point away from an "all or none" conclusion, and instead supports the notion that no single degree of activities structure will be appropriate for all organizations nor even for all units within the same organization. When skills and expertise are low, the technology involves standardized materials and routine tasks (and, thus, the technology itself integrates the work flow); and when the environment is relatively stable and predictable, advantages may be gained with relatively greater activity structuring. When individual skills and abilities are high and widely dispersed, the technology requires coordination and interdependence across diverse units; and when the environment is dynamic and unpredictable, the advantages for both the individual members and the organization may accrue to relatively lower degrees of role and activity specification. Specification in all situations seems unwarranted. Analysis of the context and other situational factors seems highly desirable and advisable.

Control Structure

Control structures constitute the third major component in the operational design of organizations. If the authority structure determines what is to be done in an organization, and activities structure determines how plans are to be carried out, a third set of mechanisms—the control structure—is necessary for determining whether actions meet objectives. This organizational design feature also completes the analogy to the plan-do-control cycle of elements in job design.

The concept of control involves the notion of regulating. In order for any control system to be effective in regulating, whether it is an organizational control system or a simple mechanical control device, four basic elements must be present: (1) standards or specified objectives, (2) sensing or monitoring devices to measure the current performance of the individual or system, (3) comparing devices to determine whether the current state of the system is close enough to the planned state, and (4) effectuating or action devices to correct any deviant performance and return it to the preset standards.

Each of these four elements that make up control systems generates a set of important questions for organizational design (Lawler, 1975). Thus we can ask:

1 Standards:
  Who sets them?
  How high or realistic are they?
  How explicit are they?
2 Sensing:
  Who acts as the sensor?
  Is the individual job incumbent involved in the sensing process?
  What activities or behaviors are monitored?
3 Comparing:
  Who does the comparing?
4 Effectuating:
  What methods are used to bring action in line with standards?
  What kinds of rewards are provided for keeping performance up to standards?
  What kinds of penalties are administered for failure of performance to meet standards?

The important point is this: The ways in which these kinds of questions are answered in specific organizational situations often determine the degree of acceptance or rejection of controls by employees and the degree to which the controls will increase or decrease their motivation to meet organizational objectives. We shall return to some of these questions shortly, but first it will be useful to look at some of the typologies that have been proposed for classifying controls and control systems.

Typologies One organization theorist, Etzioni (1961), classifies organizations according to the broad type of controls they utilize, which results in certain patterns of member compliance. Three major types of organizations are thus identified by Etzioni:

1 *Coercive.* Organizations that use force or coercion to control the behavior of lower-level members. Such organizations would include prisons, armies, certain types of hospitals, etc.

2 *Utilitarian.* Organizations that use remuneration as the basis for control of members. In such organizations individuals provide their services

in exchange for monetary inducements the organization has to offer. This type of exchange involves the individual's subjecting himself to certain kinds of control in order to obtain the "rewards" desired from the organization. Examples, of course, include most business and governmental organizations, in fact, almost any kind of organization where the use of the term "employee" is appropriate to designate members.

3 *Normative.* Organizations that use moral controls to influence the behavior and actions of members. Examples would include religious organizations, political parties, voluntary associations, etc. The use of such "moral controls" depends upon members having a positive and highly committed orientation to the organization.

Etzioni's system can be compared with other typologies of organizations, such as that of Blau and Scott (mentioned in the previous chapter). One difference between these two widely cited typologies is that the Blau–Scott approach has the organization as the dependent variable, whereas the Etzioni scheme has organizations as the independent variable with the type of control structure as the dependent variable (Hall et al., 1967). In any event, it is clear that the Etzioni system places great emphasis on controls as a basis for distinguishing among different kinds of organizations. As with other organizational typologies, however, unequivocal classification is difficult, since many organizations seem to contain elements of all three types of controls.

There are various other ways to categorize types of controls and control systems used in the kinds of organizations that are the focus of this book—i.e., organizations that employ people. For example, one can classify control systems on the basis of their content—whether they deal with (1) administrative, (2) financial, or (3) production-performance matters. Or, they can be viewed in terms of their purpose: (1) providing top management with information necessary for long-range planning, (2) providing management with information necessary to apply motivational leverage to employees to meet or exceed performance standards, and (3) providing individual employees with direct feedback during ongoing performance on their job (Lawler, in press).

An additional interesting method for classifying control systems has been developed by Woodward as a result of her investigations of the relationship of technology to organization structure (Woodward, 1970; Rackham & Woodward, 1970). Her classification approach is based on two dimensions: whether the controls are personal or impersonal, and whether they are unified in a single system or exist in multiple form. This approach is diagrammed in Figure 9-2. Woodward believes that "the normal process of industrial and technical development would move a firm [from condition 1 to condition 4]" (1970, p. 30). The small entrepreneurial firm would have highly

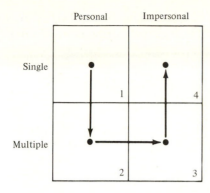

Figure 9–2 A proposed classification of types of control systems. (Source: Woodward, 1970)

personalized individual control by the owner-manager. As such a firm grew larger, the necessity for multiple methods of personal control would emerge, and these then would be succeeded by the conversion of the personal into the mechanical and hence multiple mechanical controls. Finally, from Woodward's perspective, if the firm's technology becomes highly sophisticated and automated, then a single integrated mechanical control system will evolve. Her own research indicates that unit and small batch firms fall mostly into box 1 in Figure 9-2, and process-type firms fall into box 4. The large batch and mass-production firms, on the other hand, appear to be distributed over the four categories, although they tend to be found more in types 2 and 3. Woodward interprets this distribution for mass-production firms as reflecting the fact that in this kind of technology, "management is much less restricted in its choice of control mechanisms." Their technology and size are too advanced for type 1, yet the technology is not so highly developed that it permits the single integrated mechanical system.

Dysfunctions of Control Structures   There would appear to be little dispute that organizations need some kind of control structure if they are to operate effectively. Thus, the potential advantages of control systems are fairly obvious. However, they also carry the seeds of self-produced disadvantages, such as: (1) the engendering of rigid, "bureaucratic-type" job behavior, (2) the provision of invalid data, and (3) outright resistance to controls (Lawler, 1975). Let us look briefly at each of these in turn.

The commonly used term "bureaucratic behavior" refers to a type of reaction to controls that frequently occurs regardless of the type of organization (i.e., it clearly does not apply only to governmental agencies). It is behavior that is characterized by excessive conformity to particular controls such that the individual meets those standards but fails to contribute to overall organizational objectives. This was termed a type of "goal displacement" in Chapter 3, and it results in behavior that is functional for the individual—he "looks good"—but is not necessarily functional for the total organization. In effect, means toward objectives become ends in themselves.

A good example of this type of dysfunction of controls is provided by Blau (1955) in his description of the operation of an employment agency in a state government:

> An instrument intended to further the achievement of organizational objectives, statistical records constrained interviewers to think of maximizing the indices as their major goal, sometimes at the expense of these very objectives. They avoided operations which would take up time without helping them to improve their record, such as interviewing clients for whom application forms had to be made out, and wasted their own and the public's time on activities intended only to raise the figures on their record. Their concentration upon this goal, since it was important for their ratings, made them unresponsive to requests from clients that would interfere with its attainment. (p. 43)

A second type of dysfunction that can result from control procedures concerns the provision of invalid data into the system. Such data are of two types: data concerning what can be accomplished and data concerning what has been accomplished. Examples of the former include the proverbial duels between some production employees and time-study staff personnel, wherein the worker attempts to convince the rate setter that the job can be performed at only a certain speed when in fact it is possible to do it much faster (Whyte, 1955). The budget estimates that various units provide in setting an overall organizational budget can also be sources of invalid data concerning what is possible and achievable in an organizational system (Argyris, 1951, 1964; Hofstede, 1967). Examples of invalid data about what has actually occurred in a situation range all the way from incidents involving rank-and-file workers on pay incentive plans (e.g., Roethlisberger & Dickson, 1939) to managers involved in providing data for management information systems (e.g., Argyris, 1971; Mumford & Banks, 1967; Pettigrew, 1970).

The reasons why control systems can result in such instances of invalid data being generated and placed into use by the organization are varied. In some cases it can be due to the desire to get lower standards set; in others, the motivation may be to disguise performance levels that do not meet standards, or even to discredit the particular control system itself. Still another reason may be that the organization demands data that are not readily available in valid and reliable form, yet the employee feels compelled by the system to provide them (Lawler, 1975).

Resistance to control systems is a commonly cited event in the behavioral literature on organizations. The primary cause advanced for this resistance is that controls have the potential to threaten individuals' opportunities for need satisfactions. There are several specific reasons why such concern is very real and often justified from the point of view of the employee: for one thing, measurement may be much more precise than before, and this may be seen as threatening to feelings of security if one's performance is to be held to narrowly acceptable levels of outcome. Furthermore, this more accurate and comprehensive measurement may include aspects of performance that were not hitherto taken into account. An example of a new-type control system, coming into some vogue, that results in greater inclusion of performance indices is "human asset accounting" (Likert & Bowers, 1969; Brummet, Flamholtz, & Pyle, 1968), in which managers may now be held accountable for preserving the value of the human assets under their jurisdiction. Under this system managers would be measured on variables (e.g., rates of turnover among experienced personnel) that they heretofore might have ignored with some impunity in order to obtain high ratings on the other variables (e.g., monthly sales) on which they traditionally had been evaluated (Rhode & Lawler, 1973).

A second reason that control systems may appear threatening to need satisfactions of employees is that when they are introduced they have the potential for altering the social structure of the organization, thereby affecting the relationships among employees and the relative power and status of different units. Regardless of objective reality in such situations, it is likely that some individuals and groups will feel that they can only lose by the new arrangements.

Still another reason why individuals may feel threatened by control systems is that they can, under some circumstances, decrease individuals' opportunities for intrinsic need satisfaction. This is especially likely to occur if the control system deprives the individual of certain discretionary decision making about how he is to carry out his job duties. Thus, the individual may feel that the controls take away any feeling of being an "expert" in his own particular job. In effect, they can increase his feelings of dependence on the organization and its procedures and decrease his feelings that he can exercise some degree of self-direction and self-control.

In this discussion of resistance to controls and some of the probable causes behind it, a certain caveat must be entered; namely, the existence or introduction of controls does not automatically result in resistance. Indeed, as we will discuss below, a great deal depends on the nature of the controls, how they are implemented, and who administers them. The point is that not all controls are resisted, and often employees are positive rather than negative toward them. This would be expected to be especially true for those who feel that the control measures will highlight their own good performance, and for those who may feel the need for more structure in their jobs. In addition, if controls provide the individual with feedback about his performance—almost everyone likes to know "How am I doing?"—this can be a positive aspect for many people if it is not also accompanied and outweighed by other negative features of the system. It is probably safe to assume that most employees in most organizations will have ambivalent attitudes toward control systems—seeing some degree of threat but also recognizing that both the individual and the organization can gain something from them.

Factors Affecting Reactions to Control Structures   In a recent extensive review of the literature concerning control systems in organizations (Lawler, 1975), a number of factors were identified that seemed to be crucial in determining the success or failure of various types of controls such as budgets, incentive pay systems, management information systems, and the like. We will briefly summarize some of these more important factors by referring to the four elements of control structures:

Factors relating to Standards   The most obvious aspect of standards that is likely to affect employees' attitudes and behavior concerns how high or difficult the standards are. Clearly, if standards are set too low, individuals will be prone to disregard them and not be affected by them. However, it does not follow that organizations will therefore gain the most by setting extremely high standards. If the standards are too high, they can be perceived as unrealistic by those who are expected to meet them; and this in turn can engender hostility and resistance, both overt and covert, to them. Psychological research on motivation would seem to indicate that moderately high standards offer the best climate for effective control systems.

The degree of difficulty or the level of standards cannot, however, be separated as an issue from the question of who sets them. Research would tend to indicate that if the individuals who will be impacted by the standards feel that they have not had some opportunity to help determine them, they are much less likely to be motivated to try to meet them. In other words, standards are less likely to be accepted if they are seen as being unilaterally set, especially if those who set the standards are not seen as particularly qualified to do so by those who are expected to adhere to them.

One other factor relating to standards that can influence reaction to them relates to their degree of clarity. Clarity, of course, is something of a two-edged sword in that if there is a great deal of ambiguity in the standards, individuals are likely to find ways to meet the "letter" but not the "spirit" of them, but if they are too precise (as we have previously noted) they may be resented for not providing reasonable leeway for variations in performance (Miles & Vergin, 1966). Research points to clarity of standards as a desirable objective, as long as it does not also include unnecessary precision and inflexibility.

Factors relating to Sensing   Here, the two key aspects that seem to affect employee reactions concern the degree of inclusiveness of control measures and the degree of their objectivity. The more the individual feels that aspects of his performance are not being measured which he feels should be, the less likely he is to have confidence in the sensing or measuring devices of control systems. On the other hand, if the measurements include items that the employee feels are misleading indicators, this will also decrease his confidence in the monitoring system. Thus, the narrowness or width of measurements can be critical to their acceptance. Similarly, the more the measurements can eliminate subjective elements (such as the boss's informal notion of what's good performance), the more likely it is that the employee will feel the measurements can be trusted. Greater trust in turn is likely to lead to less resistance.

Factors relating to Comparing   A crucial aspect of this phase of control appears to be whether the process involves the employee himself or whether it is entirely in the hands of an "outsider" (i.e., a superior or staff man). (It should be stressed that we are not implying that the outsider personally has to make the comparison between actual and expected performance—the physical comparing in many cases may be done entirely mechanically, as with a computer—but rather that the comparison data go *only* to the outsider.) Research indicates that the more the individual is excluded from the comparison process, either never seeing the data concerning the degree of his adherence to standards or only seeing it long after someone else has seen it, the more likely he is to feel alienated from the control system. Controls that involve the employee himself in the determination of whether he has met expectations seem to provide the strongest motivation for maintaining performance at such levels. This is an aspect of control systems that would seem fairly easy to incorporate into most situations, yet it is often overlooked when control structures are being designed.

Factors relating to Effectuating   The critical aspects of this final stage in control processes seem to be the degree to which the individual is allowed to make his own corrections and, especially, the degree to which the measurement data are used to reward and penalize employees. When the employee is given a chance for self-corrective action before external pressures are brought to bear, there seems to be more acceptance of the system and more motivation to meet standards. The denial of this opportunity through the short-circuiting of the system around the employee often engenders resentment that is not inherently necessary in the situation.

The most crucial characteristic of the effectuating phase of controls concerns the uses to which the organization puts the information. If the information is used mainly or only for administering rewards and penalties, this makes the particular control extremely salient in the eyes of the employee. This is not necessarily bad, of course, because it can serve to emphasize what behavior is desired and what is not. Attaching rewards and penalties to control systems can thus positively influence motivation. On the other hand, it can lead to less desirable consequences such as an over-emphasis on narrow, short-run, and easily measured aspects of performance to the detriment of broader, more long-run organizational objectives. Furthermore, excessive emphasis on certain control measures can increase the likelihood and temptation for invalid data to be put into the system. In short, if the uses of the data tend to be for self-feedback and for organizational planning rather than merely for administering rewards and penalties, it will be easier for the organization to gain acceptance of the controls. Nevertheless, this issue of the relationship of control systems to reward systems is so complex that we will devote a whole chapter (Chapter 12) to a comprehensive consideration of reward practices.

In concluding this section on factors affecting reactions to control structures, it is important to point out that individual differences cannot be ignored. A given control system may be reacted to quite positively by a majority of employees but negatively by others. Often, such reactions may seem relatively independent of the particular characteristics of the systems themselves. This is because sometimes the characteristics of individuals may be the major source for reaction variance.

Individual difference factors appear to play an especially strong role in determining the effectiveness of using participation in the setting of standards and self-control to keep performance in line with these standards. More specifically, participation and strong reliance on self-control seem contraindicated when self-esteem and need for achievement are low and the person is high on authoritarian tendencies. Since most people are not at either extreme on these dimensions, this indicates that organizations and individuals will be generally positive toward control systems that do not exclude opportunity for participation and self-control but which also do not rely totally on these methods.

IMPACTS ON BEHAVIOR

At various points throughout the earlier portions of this and the previous chapter we have discussed some of the relationships between contextual and structural factors on the one hand and behavioral consequences on the other hand. Here we will attempt to provide an overview of the impacts of organization design on behavior.

In this connection, several conclusions have emerged from the material we have reviewed. These would include the following:

1 Contextual factors partially determine organizational design and hence behavioral consequences, but there is still considerable latitude for those in positions of power in organizations to exercise options in design and thereby have some choice in influencing the behavior that will be exhibited in organizations.

2 There is no single organizational design that will have positive effects on behavior for all types of individuals and in all types of environmental and technological contexts. Furthermore, different parts of organizations appear to require different designs.

3 There are some combinations of context and structure that appear to be more beneficial than others to both the organization itself and its employees.

Let us briefly consider each of these conclusions:

If one thing seems clear from our analysis of the research and theory dealing with organization design, it is that designs are totally and irrevocably determined by neither a single contextual factor nor any particular combination of factors. An organization's social function, its technology, and the status of its human resources, say, are *all* influential and provide some kinds of constraints in limiting design options, but they do not in themselves reduce these options to zero. Those who control an organization's resources thus have a certain amount of "strategic choice" (Child, 1972) in deciding what kinds of designs they want, and this means they have a choice in influencing the predominant types of behavior that will be characteristic of individuals in the organization. By the same token, though, organization design is not so pervasive that the individual himself does not also have some degree of discretion concerning how he chooses to perform and interact with others in the organization.

Our second conclusion—that no single type of organization design will have universally positive effects on behavior across all individuals and in all types of contexts—seems well documented. In recent years there has been, as we noted earlier, a trend for many social scientists concerned with organizations to prescribe organic and relatively unstructured types of design as definitely preferable in terms of their impacts on individual and group behavior—e.g., more organizational commitment, higher levels of motivation, more innovative behavior, and the like. Such ideas are the reverse of the prescriptions offered by traditional management theorists. On the basis of presently available evidence (e.g., the reviews of Strauss, 1963; Leavitt, 1962; Lawrence & Lorsch, 1967; Friedlander, 1970; and such research projects as those by Woodward, 1958, 1965; Burns & Stalker, 1961; Lawrence & Lorsch, 1967; Morse & Lorsch, 1970) unqualified prescriptions of any sort appear to be unjustified. While, as we have seen, certain designs can bring about many of the positive effects on behavior that have been claimed, they also can lead to mediocre performance, frustration, anxiety, and conflict. This is especially so if the designs do not seem adapted to the particular types of tasks and employees that are present in the organization. Thus, one type of design seems no more a universal solution than another type.

It also seems necessary to state a corollary of the above conclusion: For organizations of any size and complexity, it is unlikely that there is one type of design that will have equally effective positive impacts on behavior in all parts of the organization. Thus, in many situations, multiple structures seem called for rather than a single structure applied across diverse parts and groups (as was so well demonstrated in the Lawrence & Lorsch, 1967, research). There is no reason, for example, why upper levels must be structured in the same manner as lower levels, or staff departments in the same way as line departments.

Finally, we come to the conclusion that there are some combinations of context and structure that appear to be more beneficial (e.g., producing feelings of psychological success for individuals and better performance for organizations) to both employees and organizations than other arrangements. These have been highlighted by several investigators (e.g., Friedlander, 1970; Lawrence & Lorsch, 1967; Morse & Lorsch, 1970; Burns & Stalker, 1961). Basically their ideas embody what Lawrence and Lorsch label a "contingency" approach, and reduce to the following:

Organic, low-structured, nonbureaucratic-type designs are most effective when:
Individuals have relatively high skills, widely distributed.
Individuals have high self-esteem and strong needs for achievement, autonomy, and self-realization.
The technology is rapidly changing, nonroutine, and involves many nonprogrammable tasks.
The environment is relatively dynamic and complex.

Mechanistic, high-structured, more bureaucratic-like designs are most effective when:

Individuals are relatively inexperienced and unskilled.
Individuals have strong needs for security and stability.
The technology is relatively stable and involves standardized materials and programmable tasks.
The environment is fairly calm and relatively simple.

Lest anyone be tempted to conclude that these involve invidious comparisons, let him be reminded that not all employees are highly skilled and experienced, not all individuals want high degrees of freedom and autonomy in work situations, not all technology involves highly intricate tasks, etc. The trend over time may well be in this direction, but at present there is still so much variation across organizational situations on all these dimensions that sophisticated analysis continues to be required for achieving appropriate designs. Furthermore, one must bear in mind (as Pugh, Hickson, and colleagues, and Hall, have shown) that organization structures and designs tend to be multidimensional rather than completely unitary. It is therefore extremely difficult to bring about high or low structure in all respects. Perhaps, for the people who have to work in these organizations, this is just as well.

REVIEW AND DISCUSSION QUESTIONS

1 What are some of the indices that might be used to specify the size of an organization? What are the problems associated with each of these indices?
2 Even if one could accurately determine size, the prediction of organizational behavior using such an "objective" measure of the organization might not necessarily be improved. Why?
3 What are the major relationships that have been found in previous research between size and: (1) attitudes and (2) behavior of employees? What do these relationships imply as far as the design of organizations is concerned?
4 How do matrix organizational forms differ from the more "traditional" organizational forms? What are their advantages *and* disadvantages?
5 Under what circumstances would an administrator be likely to strurcture his organization along mechanistic lines? What circumstances would lead to the development of a more organic organizational structure?
6 What is the relationship, if any, between concentration of authority in an organization and the stability of the environment in which it operates?
7 As Table 9-3 indicates, there appears to be a high degree of convergence among organizational theorists on the use of role specificity as a dimension on which organizations vary. Why do you think so many "authorities" on the subject have written about this particular dimension?
8 To what degree, if any, will the type of control structure in an organization influence other organizationally relevant variables (e.g., authority structure, activities structure, etc.)?
9 Etzioni's typology (p. 263) is based on the control structure predominantly used by an organization. Is it possible for subunits within an organization to have control structures that deviate greatly from the predominant organizational control structure? Would it be wise to design an organization with control structures that vary from one subunit to another?
10 Control systems are designed (ideally) to produce what might be termed "organizationally functional" consequences. Explain how *dys*functional consequences may result from the use of controls.

Chapter 10

The Design of Work

As shown in Chapters 8 and 9, the way organizations are designed and the kinds of structures used to guide and control activities within them can have a considerable effect on how they function. In this chapter, we focus on one particular structural issue, namely, the design of the work done by individual organization members. As will be seen, the way jobs and tasks are designed may be one of the most substantial influences on the work motivation and productivity of individuals in organizations.

The chapter begins with a historical overview of managerial thought about how work "should be" structured. Discussion then turns to a set of general issues about job designs which must be resolved if an "optimal" strategy for structuring work is ever to be achieved. On the basis of these issues and the state of current knowledge about them, a new approach to work design is proposed which is intended to maximize the likelihood that individuals will become intrinsically motivated on their jobs. Finally, some of the interrelationships between the design of jobs and the design of larger organizational units are reviewed, and some suggestions are made for optimizing the fit between people, their jobs, and the organizational context in which work takes place.

MANAGERIAL PHILOSOPHIES OF WORK DESIGN

Before the turn of the century, the problem of work design could be dealt with on a more or less ad hoc basis—the cobbler-entrepreneur who had to manage the design, production, and marketing activities of himself and three fellow cobblers could afford to be reasonably casual about how the work was structured and tasks were allocated.

But as mass-production technology increasingly replaced individual craftsmen, and as organizations continued to grow in size, problems emerged. Inefficiencies in the use of expensive machines cut into organization productivity; so did nonuniform work procedures and practices. It soon became clear to managers and engineers that if the promise of the new industrial era were to be realized, a more systematic approach to the design of work activities was needed. The stage was set for the emergence of scientific management.

Scientific Management

Developed and evangelized at the turn of the century by Frederick W. Taylor, "scientific management" was nothing if it was not scientific. The design of tasks and jobs was central to the notion of scientific management, as illustrated in the following quotation from Taylor's *Principles of Scientific Management (1911):*

> Perhaps the most prominent single element in modern scientific management is the task idea. The work of every workman is fully planned out by the management at least one day in advance, and each man receives in most cases complete written instructions, describing in detail the task which he is to accomplish. . . . This task specifies not only what is to be done but how it is to be done and the exact time allowed for doing it. And whenever the workman succeeds in doing his task right, and within the time limit specified, he receives an addition of from 30 per cent to 100 per cent to his ordinary wages. These tasks are carefully planned, so that both good and careful work are called for in their performance, but it should be distinctly understood that in no case is the workman called upon to work at a pace which would be injurious to his health. (p. 59)

The principles underlying the scientific management approach to work design may be summarized (in terminology relevant to the approach) as follows:

1 The work to be done should be studied scientifically to determine, in quantitative terms when possible, (a) how the work should be partitioned among various workers for maximum simplicity and efficiency and (b) how each segment of the work should be done most efficiently. Such analyses specified, for example, the exact weight and size of shovels which should be used for handling various kinds of material, and the exact spacing of rest breaks for maximum workday productivity.

2 Employees selected for the work should be as perfectly matched to the demands of the job as possible. Workers must, of course, be physically and mentally capable of the work, but care should be taken as well to ensure that they are not *overqualified* for the job. For example, in discussing the kind of man needed to handle pig iron, Taylor (1911, p. 59) argued:

> Now one of the very first requirements for a man who is fit to handle pig iron as a regular occupation is that he more nearly resembles in his mental make-up the ox than any other type. The man who is mentally alert and intelligent is for this very reason entirely unsuited to what would, for him, be the grinding monotony of work of this character. Therefore the workman who is best suited to handling pig iron is unable to understand the real science of doing this class of work. He is so stupid that the word "percentage" has no meaning for him, and he must consequently be trained by a man more intelligent than himself into the habit of working in accordance with the laws of this science before he can be successful.

3 As suggested by the latter portion of the above quotation, employees should be trained very carefully by managers to ensure that they perform the work exactly as specified by the prior scientific analysis of the work. In addition, many planners and supervisors are kept near the worker to make certain that he is in fact performing the work exactly as he is supposed to, and that there are no distractions or activities which the worker must attend to other than productive work itself. The work of the supervisors is subdivided into functional specialties just as was the case for the workman himself. For example, in discussing shopwork, Taylor specifies seven different supervisors (whom he calls "teachers") who are constantly on the floor available to help and guide the working employee; these are the "inspector," the "gang boss," the "speed boss," the "repair boss," the "time clerk," the "route clerk," and the "disciplinarian."

4 Finally, to provide motivation for the employee to try to follow the detailed procedures and work practices which are laid out for him and constantly enforced by supervisors, a substantial monetary bonus should be established to be paid upon successful completion of each day's work.

The scientific management approach was highly controversial at the time it was introduced, but it gradually came to be accepted by a large number of managers, engineers, and industrial psychologists. Indeed, it spawned a whole new technological and research culture aimed at providing the kinds of skills and data necessary for successful implementation of the scientific management philosophy. There have been, for example, massive research efforts aimed at describing and analyzing jobs to provide a systematic basis for selecting, training, evaluating, and compensating employees. New occupational groups have emerged as a result of the scientific management approach, e.g., the "methods engineers," who plan the most efficient means of accomplishing work from a technological perspective, and the "time and motion analysts," who study in detail the specific operations which must be carried out by a worker and establish time standards for each work segment. Line managers have given increased attention to ways that work can be simplified and standardized, and even today, more than half a century since the introduction of scientific management, its principles continue to strongly influence the way work is arranged and jobs are designed in many organizations.

Some Unexpected Consequences

As the scientific management approach gained popularity early in the century—and as, at the same time, mass production and automation became increasingly pervasive—fundamental changes in the makeup of jobs were being made throughout society. More and more jobs came to be highly routine and simple to perform, repetitive and monotonous, and largely out of the control of the worker. In effect, workers became servants to machines and methods rather than vice versa.

The assembly-line job illustrates the consequences of this trend in fairly extreme form. Many assembly-line workers performed (and still perform) identical operations (such as making a single weld on an automobile) over and over again hundreds of times during a single working day. The job is simple, it is engineered so as to be both standard and technologically highly efficient, and it is repetitive in the extreme. Further, all control of the work is out of the hands of the employee: his supervisors establish and enforce the methods he is to use, and the assembly line itself, moving constantly and not always slowly, controls the pace of the work.

As assembly-line jobs and other simple, repetitive jobs increased in number, more and more employees were required to fill these kinds of jobs. Hiring was not a significant problem for most organizations, however, since the skill levels required for acceptable performance on the repetitive jobs generally were quite low. Taylor's warning against hiring people who were *overqualified* for the jobs they were to perform often was ignored in many organizations: any worker who was qualified for a job got a job, and, when there were many job applicants from whom to choose, the more generally educated and skilled tended to be hired.

Unfortunately, it turned out that many employees did not like working on routine, simplified jobs, and some employees did not like it intensely. In addition to complaints from employees and from their supervisors about the jobs, empirical studies began to appear in the management literature which suggested that absenteeism and turnover as well as employee dissatisfaction often increased when the jobs were oversimplified and routinized.

As far back as 1924, a study of several simplified jobs (in which a complete work cycle took less than one minute) found that employees on these jobs frequently were bored and, apparently in response to their boredom, they took unauthorized breaks from their work whenever possible (Vernon, 1924). Thirty-five years later the findings of a series of employee attitude surveys carried out in a nationwide retail organization showed that both employee morale and productive output were lower in jobs which were highly segmented and simplified (Worthy, 1950). A large-scale study, carried out in the 1950s, of the reactions of over 1,000 assembly-line workers to their jobs at an automobile plant found quite high levels of absenteeism, turnover, and job dissatisfaction among employees with repetitive, machine-paced assembly-line jobs (Walker & Guest, 1952). Recent unpublished data from a large automobile manufacturing plant supports the earlier findings: turnover among assembly-line workers at this plant was reported by company management to be over *100 percent* in a single year.

A verbatim record of the way one employee in the 1952 (Walker & Guest) auto assembly-line study described his job and his reactions to it is presented in Figure 10-1. This description, which provides considerable insight into the psychological dynamics of working on an assembly-line job, is paired in the figure with a report of conditions at a new, "state-of-the-art" automobile plant which began operations at Lordstown, Ohio, in the early 1970s.

The Job-Enlargement Revolution

Faced with an apparently rising tide of dissatisfaction, absenteeism, and turnover among employees with highly simplified jobs, a number of researchers and company managers concluded in the late 1940s and early 1950s that the trend toward simplification and routinization of work had gone too far. One of the businessmen who reached this conclusion was Thomas J. Watson, Sr., founder of IBM. The story is told (and may in fact be true) that Mr. Watson, while walking through one of IBM's manufacturing plants, came upon a milling machine operator who was standing idly beside his machine waiting to start it. The operator informed Mr. Watson that he was not allowed to set up his machine or inspect the output from it, but only to actually operate the machine. On further questioning he indicated that he felt he was quite competent to perform the setup and inspection operations. Taken aback by the inefficiency of this segmentation of work activities, and probably empathizing with the frustration that the worker must have felt, Mr. Watson is reported to have strongly suggested to local management that machine operators be allowed to perform the full milling operation—including machine setup and inspection. The suggestion was accepted by plant management (albeit quite reluctantly—since it was directly counter to prevailing notions about how to design work for optimum efficiency) and later was expanded upon. The ultimate result was both a substantial cost savings for the company (since the need for inspectors and setup men decreased almost to nothing) and a substantial increase in employee productivity and job satisfaction (Walker, 1950).

Soon a large number of similar "job-enlargement" experiments were underway around the country. Typically when a job was experimentally enlarged, employees would be given responsibility to set up and inspect their own work, to make decisions about methods and procedures to be used, and within broad limits to set their own work pace. Often the net effect was that jobs which had been simplified and segmented into many small parts were simply put back together again and made the responsibility of individual workers.

An illustrative case of an early job-enlargement effort was one involving workers assembling a small centrifugal water pump used in washing machines (Kilbridge, 1960). Prior to job enlargement, the pumps were assembled by six operators on a conveyor line, with each operator performing a particular part of the assembly. Each worker spent about 1/2 minute on each pump, and total pump assembly time was about 1 3/4 minutes. The job was changed so that each worker assembled an entire pump, inspected it, and placed his own identifying mark on the pump. In addition the assembly operations were converted to a "batch" system in which each worker had more freedom to control his work pace than had been the case under the conveyor system. The investigator reported that after the job had been enlarged, total assembly time decreased to about 1 1/2 minutes, quality improved, and important cost savings were realized.

Numerous other jobs have been experimentally enlarged in the last decade, and those experiments which have been reported in the research literature generally have been described as successful (cf. Ford, 1969; Davis & Taylor, 1972; Walters & Associates, in press). Indeed, by the early 1970s, the popular media had turned the "blue-collar blues" into an issue of national concern, and job enlargement showed all the signs of turning into a national fad.

Life on the Assembly Line—around 1950

My job is to weld the cowl to the metal underbody. I take a jig off the bench, put it in place and weld the parts together. The jig is all made up and the welds are made in set places along the metal. Exactly twenty-five spots. The line runs according to schedule. Takes me one minute and fifty-two seconds for each job. I walk along the line as it moves. Then I snap the jig off, walk back down the line, throw it on the bench, grab another just in time to start on the next car. The cars differ, but it's practically the same thing. Finish one—then have another one staring me in the face.

I don't like to work on the line—no man likes to work on a moving line. You can't beat the machine. Sure, maybe I can keep it up for an hour, but it's rugged doing it eight hours a day, every day in the week all year long.

During each day I get a chance for a breather ten minutes in the morning, then a half-hour for lunch, then a few minutes in the afternoon. When I'm working there is not much chance to get a breather. Sometimes the line breaks down. When it does we all yell "Whoopee!" As long as the line keeps moving I've got to keep up with it. On a few jobs I know, some fellows can work like hell up the line, then coast. Most jobs you can't do that. If I get ahead maybe ten seconds, the next model has more welds to it, so it takes ten seconds extra. You hardly break even. You're always behind. When you get too far behind, you get in a hole—that's what we call it. All hell breaks loose. I get in the next guy's way. The foreman gets sore and they have to rush in a relief man to bail you out.

It's easy for them time study fellows to come down there with a stop watch and figure out just how much you can do in a minute and fifty-two seconds. There are some things they can see and record with their stop watch. But they can't clock how a man feels from one day to the next. Those guys ought to work on the line for a few weeks and maybe they'll feel some things that they never pick up on the stop watch.

I like a job where you feel like you're accomplishing something and doing it right. When everything's laid out for you and the parts are all alike, there's not much you feel you accomplish. The big thing is that steady push of the conveyor—a gigantic machine which I can't control.

You know, it's hard to feel that you are doing a good quality job. There is that constant push at high speed. You may improve after you've done a thing over and over again, but you never reach a point where you can stand back and say, "Boy, I done that one good. That's one car that got built right." If I could do my best I'd get some satisfaction out of working, but I can't do as good work as I know I can do.

My job is all engineered out. The jigs and fixtures are all designed and set out according to specifications. There are a lot of little things you could tell them, but they never ask you. You go by the bible. They have a suggestion system, but the fellows don't use it too much because they're scared that a new way to do it may do one of your buddies out of a job.

Life on the Assembly Line—in the Early 1970s

The Vega workers (at the new Lordstown, Ohio assembly plant) are echoing a rank-and-file demand that has been suppressed by both union and management for the past twenty years: HUMANIZE WORKING CONDITIONS.

Hanging around the parking lot between shifts, I learned immediately that to these young workers, "It's not the money."

"It pays good," said one, "but it's driving me crazy."

"I don't want more money," said another. "None of us do."

"I do," said his friend. "So I can quit quicker."

"It's the job," everyone said. But they found it hard to describe the job itself.

"My father worked in auto for thirty-five years," said a clean-cut lad, "and he never talked about the job. What's there to say? A car comes, I weld it. A car comes, I weld it. A car comes, I weld it. One hundred and one times an hour."

I asked a young wife, "What does your husband tell you about his work?"

"He doesn't say what he does. Only if something happened like, "My hair caught on fire," or "Something fell in my face."

"There's a lot of variety in the paint shop," said a dapper twenty-two-year-old up from West Virginia. "You clip on the color hose, bleed out the old color, and squirt. Clip, bleed, squirt, think; clip, bleed, squirt, yawn; clip, bleed, squirt, scratch your nose. Only now the Gee-Mads have taken away the time to scratch your nose."

A long-hair reminisced: "Before the Go-Mads, when I had a good job like door handles, I could get a couple of cars ahead and have a whole minute to relax."

I asked about diversions. "What do you do to keep from going crazy?"

"Well, certain jobs like the pit you can light up a cigarette without them seeing."

"I go to the wastepaper basket. I wait a certain number of cars, then find a piece of paper to throw away."

"I have fantasies. You know what I keep imagining? I see a car coming down. It's red. So I know it's gonna have a black seat, black dash, black interiors. But I keep thinking what if somebody up there sends down the wrong color interiors—like orange, and me putting in yellow cushions, bright yellow!"

"There's always water fights, paint fights, or laugh, talk, tell jokes. Anything so you don't feel like a machine."

But everyone had the same hope: "You're always waiting for the line to break down."

Figure 10–1 Life on the assembly line: Around 1950 and in the early 1970s. (Sources: R. H. Guest, "Men and Machines: An Assembly-line Worker Looks at His Job," *Personnel*, May 1955, p. 6; and B. Garson, "Luddites in Lordstown," *Harper's Magazine*, June 1972, pp. 68–69.

CURRENT ISSUES IN WORK DESIGN

How, then, *should* jobs be designed in contemporary organizations? The brief history of thought, research, and practice reviewed above seems to lead simultaneously to two contradictory conclusions. On the one hand, the principles of job design derived from scientific management—i.e., simplifying and segmenting work into small, tightly defined pieces—apparently can lead to improvements in job performance, at least in the kinds of settings researched by Taylor and his associates. Yet, on the other hand, the more recent job enlargement experiments—in which jobs were made more demanding, more complex, and less tightly defined—also are reported as successful in improving productive effectiveness.

The fact of the matter is that few data presently are available which are helpful in evaluating the sometimes contradictory results of studies of job design. Many research findings about the effects of different types of work design are based on one-shot case studies of changes made in a single job in a single organization. Further, the studies have addressed almost exclusively production jobs in industrial organizations, and have little direct applicability to the design of other types of work—such as managerial, professional, and service activities. Thus, while the studies have been provocative of thought and encouraging of further experimentation, they have added little in the way of cumulative *systematic* knowledge about how the design of jobs makes differences in on-the-job performance and attitudes.

Most contemporary organizational psychologists probably would argue that job enlargement is more right than wrong, and the principles of job design derived from scientific management are more wrong than right. Yet these arguments would of necessity be based mainly either on personal values or on rather tangential research evidence, for solid research data on fundamental issues relevant to how work should be designed have only very recently started to become available.

In the sections to follow we will discuss several questions that we believe are central to the development of fuller understanding of the design of work, and then we will propose a conceptual framework which may be useful in organizing and extending knowledge in the area.

What Criteria Should Be Used in Evaluating Job Designs?

The Efficiency Criterion The traditional criterion used to evaluate most job-design experiments has been some form of "work efficiency." It has been argued that more efficient jobs will lead to lower labor costs, which will in turn lead to increased organizational effectiveness. And, from a purely rational, technological perspective, a good case can be made that when jobs are simplified and routinized, efficiency should go up and labor costs go down. Simple jobs can be filled with relatively simple people. It is easier and less expensive to recruit an unskilled worker off the street than it is to locate a highly skilled individual. Further, simple jobs can be learned very quickly, decreasing the need for expensive training programs and training staffs. Since training is not an important problem, it also becomes economically feasible to interchange workers among different jobs as day-to-day staffing needs change. Finally, many standardized and special-ized jobs—especially in industrial organizations—have the additional ad-vantage that they can be mechanically paced. Presumably this should create conditions under which production can be made quite predictable and consistent, since the rate of production is determined by the speed at which the machine runs, and machine speed is controlled by management.

The kinds of considerations outlined above are all relevant and im-portant in making decisions about the general impact of job designs—and, indeed, when such considerations are taken by themselves they strongly imply that standardized, simplified jobs are likely to be optimal for organiza-tional effectiveness. But these considerations also very much reflect an "engineering" orientation to the design of work. This is not coincidental: Taylor, the founder of the movement toward simplified and routinized jobs, was himself an engineer, and most work-design changes carried out in this country since the inception of scientific management have been done by industrial "methods" engineers.

Problems with the Efficiency Criterion   What is omitted when job design is examined strictly from an engineering viewpoint, of course, is the impact of the job on the human being who must perform it. The assumption frequently has been made that the responses of people to their work can be programmed and controlled just as can the technology involved. By machine pacing and close supervision, it has been argued, human variability can be made negligible.

The research literature suggests that the above view grossly underesti-mates several factors: (1) the intensity of the reactions of some workers to highly simplified and routinized work, (2) workers' ingenuity in fighting back when they are unhappy, and (3) the costs of these responses to the organization. Research data reviewed earlier (e.g., Walker & Guest, 1952) strongly indicate that at least some workers are very unhappy when they have no control over what happens on the job, when their work has little variety or challenge for them, and when the work is so simplified and segmented that it has little or no intrinsic meaningfulness to them. Em-ployees may behaviorally deal with such dissatisfactions in a variety of ways—some which have little impact on organizational effectiveness, and others which are quite detrimental to the smooth, effective functioning of an organization.

Studies as far back as the 1920s (e.g., Vernon, 1924) found that workers on short-cycle, repetitive jobs tended to change their posture or adjust their seating position frequently while on the job. Many automobile drivers will engage in analogous behaviors, such as slapping the face, singing, or flexing various muscles, to deal with monotonous driving conditions. These activities have the effect of introducing at least a token level of variety into work activities and probably serve merely to keep the worker awake at no real cost to the organization.

Other ways of dealing with a routine, repetitive, simplified job are not so innocuous. The phrase "throwing a monkey wrench in the works" is based in reality: many supervisors of assembly-line jobs can tell some horror stories about how employees have sabotaged the line by just this means. While managers sometimes attribute such destructive behavior to a "lack of responsibility" or to "psychological problems" of the employees, those who have had to man lower-level jobs during strikes have found—much to their surprise—that they were engaging in some of the same behaviors for which they had previously condemned their subordinates.

A less destructive but also dysfunctional way that some employees deal with disenchantment with their jobs is to stay away from work relatively frequently or to resign and find work elsewhere (cf. Porter & Steers, 1973, for a recent review of relevant studies). High employee absenteeism and turnover can be extraordinarily costly to an organization. For example, if too many workers leave, even minimal training costs begin to become significant, and expenses of recruitment, selection, payroll accounting, and supervision all increase as well. When absenteeism is high, a large float of extra employees must be maintained on a standby basis to man the jobs. In addition, high absenteeism usually means that employees are likely to use up all or most of their paid sick-leave time. The result is a relatively smaller return to the organization for dollars spent on wages.

Combining Efficiency and Satisfaction   Costs such as those discussed above rarely have been considered in organizational decision making about how work should be designed. Yet these costs easily could more than offset the engineered savings which are expected to accrue from simplified, standardized jobs. Thus, in making evaluations of various ways of designing work it seems imperative that criteria involving human satisfaction and adjustment to the work be considered in addition to engineering and technological assessments of potential work efficiency. That is, neither a grossly inefficient job which makes employees joyously happy nor a highly efficient job which is dissatisfying and frustrating to employees is likely to be facilitative of long-term organizational effectiveness.

An optimal state of affairs, of course, would be a job which was designed so that an employee could gain important personal satisfactions in direct proportion to the degree that he worked efficiently and effectively toward the goals of the organization (cf. Chapter 4). If jobs could be so designed, it might be possible to have simultaneously both high productive efficiency for the organization and high personal satisfaction for employees.

To create the conditions under which such a mutually beneficial state of affairs might be possible, however, it surely would be necessary to know something about how different people react to different kinds of jobs. Further, to the extent that differences among people are in fact important in understanding workers' responses to their jobs, it would also be necessary, in staffing jobs of various kinds, to have some coherent strategy for dealing with differences among workers. It is to these issues that we now turn.

How Are Individual Differences Dealt with in Designing Jobs?

Taken collectively, individual employees represent the single most valuable resource an organization can have, and simultaneously the source of some of the most vexing problems that an organization must face. And the very reason that individuals can be such an important resource is the same reason that they can present such frustrating problems; namely, every individual is different in some ways from every other individual—in terms of abilities, needs and goals, and strategies for responding to stimuli in the organizational environment.

In designing jobs, organizations necessarily (although sometimes implicitly) make some assumptions about the people who will perform the jobs—and employ some strategy for dealing with potential differences in the way people respond to their jobs. As will be seen below, such strategies can range from ignoring individual differences, or attempting to suppress them, to designing jobs and assigning people to them so that the differences among people are capitalized upon toward increased organizational effectiveness.

The Costs of Suppressing Individual Differences Some researchers and managers, especially those sympathetic to a "scientific" approach to management, argue that differences among people are an anathema to smooth organizational functioning. The argument, in somewhat extreme form, is that work should be designed in such a way that the idiosyncrasies of individual employees will have little or no opportunity to disrupt the ongoing functioning of organizational activities. Operationally, this means that the worker should have as little personal discretion in what he does on the job as possible.

This approach may be implemented in a number of different ways. For example, by preparing careful analyses of jobs and descriptions of work procedures it is possible to supply each employee with highly detailed specifications of exactly what he is to do on the job and how he is to do it. And, by supervising workers very closely, it is possible to enforce these prescriptions to a degree. When mechanical pacing of jobs is technologically possible, even more consistency in the activities of various workers can be obtained. Finally, by using powerful monetary incentives which are contingent upon strict adherence to prescribed procedures, voluntary suppression of individual differences can in some cases be literally "bought" from an employee, at least for a time.

In practice, however, it has been found that attempting to suppress individual differences among employees is not a viable long-term strategy. Differences among people invariably show themselves, even when the situation is tightly constrained. Research evidence discussed earlier in this chapter shows that many individuals react quite negatively to a loss of discretionary control over their work activities and that they find ways to assert themselves in their work even when, as on the assembly line, such individuality theoretically is not possible.

Placement as a Strategy for Dealing with Individual Differences

One way that organizations may avoid the negative consequences of having to try to suppress individual differences is by carefully selecting employees and placing them in jobs where they will fit well. Indeed, in outlining the principles of scientific management, Taylor was quite emphatic in recommending that individuals who are assigned to a particular "scientifically" designed job should be carefully selected so that they are neither underqualified nor overqualified for it.

Consistent with Taylor's recommendation, a large amount of research in traditional industrial psychology has been aimed at finding ways to obtain good matches between the skills required for various jobs and the abilities of prospective employees (see Chapter 5). There is no question but that the sophisticated testing and placement procedures which have been developed over the years have contributed greatly to the productive effectiveness of many organizations. It should be noted, however, that the "test and select" approach to dealing with individual differences treats the a priori design of jobs as "given" and deals only with finding people who are qualified to work on the jobs. The actual design of jobs is left to methods engineers or to company managers; the organizational staff responsible for developing and administering the personnel selection program typically has little or nothing to say about how jobs might be designed in such a way that employees would be more likely to find their work motivating and satisfying rather than tedious and frustrating.

The Importance of Personal Needs and Goals   The tests and selection procedures which typically are used in industrial and business organizations tend to focus primarily on the *ability* of employees to perform the work at adequate levels, with little or no attention given to the more personal psychological needs or goals of the prospective employee. It is very possible, for example, that two prospective employees, both qualified to do the work, would differ greatly in the degree to which performing a particular job would be a personally satisfying and rewarding experience. Traditional selection procedures would miss this important difference entirely. It might turn out, for example, that a worker with strong needs for personal growth and development would be selected for an assembly-line job (where his needs most likely would be frustrated) over a second worker of perhaps lower aptitudes who would experience the performance of routine, repetitive operations as highly satisfying.

Both the adherents of the traditional scientific management approach to job design and the more recent evangelists of job enlargement have tended to deny either the existence of differences among employees in job-relevant needs and goals, or the importance of these needs and goals in determining how a person reacts to his work (cf. Chapters 2 and 4). This is not to suggest, however, that those who persist in the scientific management tradition and those who advocate job enlargement make even approximately similar assumptions about the needs and goals which characterize "typical" employees in organizations. The point is only that advocates on both sides of the fence have implicitly (and occasionally even explicitly) denied the existence and the importance of what might be called the "second" class of individual differences.

In actuality, the assumptions about people which may be inferred as characteristic of the two points of view are markedly different. In Chapter 2 several assumptions about people which underlie the Theory X and Theory Y approaches to management were presented and discussed. It appears that the fairly pessimistic view of people implicit in Theory X would fit well a scientific management approach to job design, whereas the more optimistic view implied by Theory Y would be congruent with the position of those who argue that job enlargement will tend to be facilitative of organizational effectiveness.

It probably is not a coincidence that the proponents of the two approaches to job design have, more often than not, carried out their experiments on populations of workers having characteristics congruent with their respective assumptions about people. Recall, for example, that Taylor described the typical worker selected for one of his first successful tests of the scientific management approach (handling pig iron) as "so stupid and so phlegmatic that he more nearly resembles in his mental make-up the ox than any other type" (1911, p. 59).

Taylor and his followers did later on, of course, introduce their approach to job design in settings populated by somewhat more capable workers and characterized by somewhat more challenging work. Such experiments apparently did not work as well as did those which involved quite low-level employees. And, as the scientific management approach gained popularity and became widespread, the number of reported problems with employee morale, absenteeism, and turnover did in fact increase. Apparently what was an appropriate kind of job for some employees turned out to be highly inappropriate for others—and unfortunately for Taylor it appears that there are relatively few workers in this society for whom his job-design proposals, strictly interpreted, would work exceptionally well.

Those who have experimented with job enlargement have encountered a set of difficulties analogous to the problems which eventually came to plague the house of the managers with a "scientific" persuasion. Some of the major successes of job enlargement have been conducted in organizations (e.g., IBM, AT&T) that tend to employ personnel who might, on the whole, be expected to be responsive to a chance to show individual initiative and to take personal responsibility for a meaningful piece of work. But as has been pointed out in a review of research on job enlargement (Hulin & Blood, 1968), there also are a large number of job-enlargement experiments in which results are ambiguous. The idea that enlarged jobs are universally better than simple jobs is not, the review concludes, justified by research data.

Toward a More Realistic View of Jobs and Individual Differences

A large-scale study of the relationship between job characteristics and employee reactions was carried out in the mid-1960s in an effort to provide more systematic data than heretofore had been available on how differences in jobs affect employees (Turner & Lawrence, 1965). As it turned out, the research also provided some significant and unexpected insights into the ways different groups of people are affected by different types of jobs.

The researchers developed measures of six "requisite task attributes" which, on the basis of existing research literature and an a priori conceptual framework, were expected to relate positively to employee satisfaction and attendance. The attributes are (1) variety, (2) autonomy, (3) required social interaction, (4) opportunities for social interaction, (5) knowledge and skill required, and (6) responsibility. Scores on each of the six dimensions were obtained for forty-seven different jobs by observations in the field and interviews with employees and supervisors. When the authors examined the relationships among the six requisite task attributes, they found that they were very closely interrelated. Therefore, a summary measure was derived, called the Requisite Task Attribute Index (RTA Index). This summary index was used in ascertaining the relationships between the nature of jobs and worker satisfaction and attendance.

The authors' expectations that employees working on jobs which were high on the RTA Index would have higher job satisfaction and lower absenteeism (an expectation that would have supported the point of view espoused by the advocates of job enlargement) were not fully supported. Instead, it appeared that the expected relationships held *only for workers from factories located in small towns.* For workers in urban settings, reported satisfaction was less when jobs were high on the RTA Index, and the RTA Index was unrelated to absenteeism for these urban workers. It was argued by the investigators that the obtained differences were substantially modified by differences in the cultural backgrounds of employees.

Additional data on the importance of subcultural factors in determining how workers will respond to the way their jobs are designed are provided in another investigation (Blood & Hulin, 1967). The researchers proposed that alienation from the traditional middle-class work norm* is an important factor in moderating the relationship between job characteristics and worker responses. When employees hold values which are congruent with this norm (as might be expected of the small-town employees in the Turner and Lawrence study), then more complex and demanding jobs would be expected to be responded to positively. When, however, employees are alienated from this work norm (as might be expected more frequently of workers in urban settings), then the relationship between job level and positive behavioral responses and feelings would be expected to be reversed.

Reanalysis of previously collected data from approximately 1,300 blue-collar workers in factories spread throughout the Eastern United States provided general support for the predictions. For example, the correlations between job level and work satisfaction ranged from approximately −.50 (for workers in the most "alienated" community setting) to +.40 (for workers in the community where people would most likely be expected to accept middle-class work norms).

Data from these studies are sufficiently compelling that the generality of the strong hypothesis that enlarged jobs lead to improved satisfaction, attendance, and performance on the job must be called into serious question. Instead, it seems clear that enlarged jobs may be optimal for the performance of some workers, and simplified jobs more appropriate for others.

This conclusion reinforces the notion that it is important for organizations to have explicit strategies for dealing with differences among individual workers when designing jobs and assigning people to them. Moreover, it would appear that such strategies must incorporate the personal needs and values of workers as well as their skills and abilities, if a genuinely good match between a worker and his job is to be achieved.

How Do Jobs Affect Employees?

Any adequate strategy for matching people and jobs must surely be based on a solid understanding of the mechanisms by which jobs make differences in

---

*The middle-class work norm is defined as "a positive affect for occupational achievement, a belief in the intrinsic value of hard work, a striving for the attainment of responsible positions, and a belief in the work-related aspects of Calvinism and the Protestant ethic" (Hulin & Blood, 1968, p. 48).

the feelings and behavioral responses of employees at work. Only as we understand *how* jobs make differences can we develop understanding of which characteristics are critical in influencing employee reactions and which are less relevant. And, of course, any attempt to match people and jobs requires some specification of the appropriate dimensions (of both the employees and of their jobs) on which the matching is to be done.

An unfortunate characteristic of the research literature which currently exists on job design is that it focuses almost exclusively on industrial jobs—and especially on production jobs in industrial organizations. Any truly general understanding of jobs and their effects must deal as well with a wide variety of job types (e.g., service jobs, professional jobs, self-generated jobs). In the pages to follow, we will propose three different mechanisms by which jobs can affect people. While most of the examples which will be used will involve production jobs in industry, reflecting the emphasis of previous research, our intent is that the proposals be more generally applicable to a broad range of jobs. Nevertheless, no claim to exhaustiveness is made; there undoubtedly are ways that jobs make differences in addition to those proposed below, and there are particular types of jobs for which our analysis will have limited applicability. What is claimed, however, is that the three mechanisms discussed here, taken together, are likely to account for considerable variance in the responses of most workers to their jobs.

Affecting the Physiological Activation of Individual Employees

Psychologists have for many years been interested in the conditions which induce a state of physiological activation in organisms and in the behavioral and affective consequences of being activated at various levels (see Chapter 2; also Berlyne, 1967). Recently attempts have been made to use basic knowledge about activation to understand the effects of task characteristics on the work behavior of individuals in organizations.*

Activation theory can be helpful, for example, in understanding the ways people behave on highly repetitive jobs—and the reasons why certain behavior patterns develop. In Figure 10-2, we quote a description (Scott, 1966) of some of the behaviors which people engage in when working on jobs which provide minimal activation. The figure shows how employees adapt (sometimes with dysfunctional consequences for organizational effectiveness) to a chronic state of underactivation.

This theory also is relevant, of course, to jobs which stimulate the individual to excessively high levels of activation. Relatively less research

---

*The psychological counterpart of physiological "activation" is usually termed "arousal." The latter term is used in Chapters 13 and 14 where we talk about social influences on the individual, but in the present context where the emphasis is primarily on the physiological reactions to task stimuli, we use the term "activation." It is understood that the two terms are closely related.

has been carried out on such jobs, however, in large part because relatively few jobs exist in contemporary society which provide the worker with too much activation. A well-known example of such a job is that of the air-traffic controller who must constantly deal with extraordinarily large amounts of constantly changing and highly meaningful stimulation as he shepherds high-speed aircraft along often crowded airways.

While activation theory clearly has much to offer researchers and managers interested in job design, two thorny problems must be dealt with before the theory can realize its full potential and gain applicability to real-world job-design problems. First, means must be developed for *measuring* levels of activation in meaningful terms and for determining the optimal level of activation for different individuals. Without such data it will remain impractical to use activation theory in predicting or changing employee reactions to their jobs except in a very gross fashion—i.e., in situations where it is clear that most employees are enormously overstimulated or understimulated by their jobs.

A second problem concerns ambiguities about the processes by which individuals adapt to *changing* levels in stimulation. Apparently individuals' levels of activation decrease markedly as a function of familiarity with a given stimulus situation, but after a period of rest re-presentation of the same stimulus situation will once again raise the level of activation. More complete understanding of the waxing and waning of activation in various circumstances could have many implications for job-design practices—for example, the practice of job rotation. Those who advocate job rotation claim that if an individual cycles through several jobs, each of which would be monotonous and boring if he remained on it for long periods of time, his work motivation can be kept reasonably high. If, through additional research on activation theory, data can be developed which indicate how activation levels can be kept high through planned stimulus change, the theory will be able to contribute substantially to increasing the usefulness of the practice of job rotation. If, however, it turns out that there are general and inevitable decreases in activation level over extended periods of time regardless of the way different tasks and rest periods are cycled, the long-term usefulness of job rotation plans would seem to be limited.

Establishing Conditions for Individual Need Satisfaction or Goal Achievement Depending on how the work is arranged, jobs can provide various kinds of opportunities for employees to satisfy important needs or achieve important goals while at work. For example, on some jobs there may be opportunities for workers to satisfy social needs; on others, personal growth needs; on others, material needs.

The point is that jobs can affect behavior to the extent that they are

Activation theory anticipates a number of behavioral outcomes in tasks which require the constant repetition of a limited number of responses to stimulation which is configuratively simple and temporally unvarying.

As the individual becomes familiar with the surroundings and learns the responses required in the repetitive task, a decline in activation level is expected. With continued exposure at the task site. . . . (this) may lead to a decrement in performance. If the activation level falls below the characteristic norm, the individual will experience negative affect and will attempt to increase impact. If he is prevented from engaging in impact-increasing behavior, the result is a continuous decline in performance. When confronted with these circumstances, the individual may temporarily or permanently leave the task situation if these alternatives are readily available. If the individual is successful in increasing stimulus impact, the result would be an increase in the activation level and positive affect which is postulated to occur with shifts in activation toward the characteristic level. The quality or quantity of performance, or both, may then be sustained or restored to its original level depending upon the nature of the impact-modifying behavior.

It may be noted that any of a wide range of behaviors may be utilized to increase activation level. Additional cortical stimulation resulting from thoughts of an anticipated hunting trip or the recall of a recent encounter with a sexual partner may offset a decline in activation level. The individual may increase proprioceptive stimulation and thus sustain activation level by stretching, alternating positions, or otherwise varying his position at the task site. Leaving to visit the water fountain, another department, or the rest room not only

Figure 10–2 Activation theory and task behavior. (Source: Scott, 1966, pp. 15–16)

designed so that *achievement of satisfactions or goals is dependent upon some specifiable pattern of employee behavior.* Thus, following the expectancy-theory view of individual motivation (see Chapter 2), if an employee believes that generally desirable outcomes for himself will be more likely to result from engaging in behavior X than in behavior Y on the job, it is expected that he will in fact be more likely to try to engage in behavior X.

The way jobs are designed can substantially determine the degree to which various kinds of behaviors will in fact lead to desired outcomes for particular types of employees—and therefore the extent to which such behaviors will be exhibited by these employees. Consider, for example, a hypothetical employee who is primarily motivated to obtain social satisfactions. Though we are oversimplifying him for the sake of the example, assume that this man loves to participate in interesting conversations and that he usually feels best about himself when he finds he has been helpful or stimulating to another person through social interaction.

Imagine that this man works on a manufacturing job making small electrical fixtures at a circular table with five other employees. Further

increases proprioceptive stimulation but results in greater stimulus variation. Social activity including conversation with fellow employees, the development of complex group relationships, gambling, and horseplay also introduces variation which may serve to increase activation level.

It is obvious that much of the impact-increasing behavior which is described above and which is generally available to the individual is extrinsic to the task and may be incompatible with task performance. If the impact-increasing behavior is incompatible with task performance, we have the possibility of sustained activation levels and "high morale" but low performance. If it does not interfere with task performance, we have the possibility of successful adaptation to a repetitive task.

The individual may also introduce variation into the task itself. In a wide variety of work activities, individuals, when confronted with a repetitive task of long duration, may be observed dividing the total task into discrete units and then responding until each unit is completed. The experience seems to be pleasant and associated with a feeling of reduced effort—this type of variation is probably most effective where the individual can arbitrarily set intermediate goals, can obtain immediate feedback regarding progress as responding continues, and can be reasonably certain of a change in activity such as a rest period when the goal is reached. This is only one example of what must be a wide variety of ways of increasing functional variation by modifying the task itself. If the individual is successful, the effect may be to sustain activation level over a long period of time in which case there is the possibility of continued high performance and moderately high morale in what is otherwise a repetitive task.

assume that the work is fairly simple, demanding only minimal skill and attention and thereby providing considerable opportunity for conversation while at work. It would be predicted that this employee and others similar to him would (1) have good attendance on the job, (2) tend to have relatively long tenure on the job, and (3) have adequate (but certainly not especially high) levels of performance. Since the job is structured so that the employee can satisfy his strong social needs while at work, he probably would find work an attractive place to be—thus the prediction of low absenteeism and long tenure. Moreover, since the task is not demanding, he would be able to maintain an adequate level of performance without losing the chance to engage in social activities. There is no incentive in the way the work is designed for this employee to try to perform at especially high levels.

Now assume for a moment that the job were a much more complex and difficult one, which constantly required the employee to give his full attention to the work and to use all his job-relevant skills to maintain even minimal levels of performance. Still assuming that our hypothetical employee is primarily motivated to achieve social satisfactions, predictions about his job-relevant behaviors would not be as optimistic. He probably would experience considerable conflict between trying to maintain adequate levels of performance and trying to engage in relatively incompatible activities aimed at satisfying his social needs. As a result, he might tend to (1) spend too much time in social activities and thereby perform poorly on the job, (2) spend the majority of his energies performing the complex task and letting his social needs go mostly unsatisfied, or (3) try somehow to balance the inherently incompatible task and social activities. For either of the last two possibilities it would be expected that the employee would become highly frustrated on the job, would be dissatisfied, and might well respond to the dissatisfaction by being absent from work relatively frequently or by resigning from the job to find more personally acceptable work.

Finally, assume that the same person held a job as a customer service representative for a public utility, in which his duties consisted mainly of answering telephone calls from customers and dealing with the problems they presented. In this situation, it would be expected that the employee would show both very high levels of performance and, at the same time, high job satisfaction, good attendance, and long tenure with the organization. Such a job would be nearly optimal for our hypothetical employee: he could, while on the job, satisfy his personal needs best by working hard and well toward the goals of the organization, i.e., by being as helpful as possible to the customers who call in for assistance. Moreover, the harder and more effectively he worked on the job, the more he would be able to satisfy his own needs and achieve his personal goals.

The point of the above example is that, for this particular employee and for other employees with similar needs, *the way the work is designed* very strongly determines both the kinds of behaviors most likely to be engaged in and the satisfactions experienced with the work. And again, it becomes very clear that what happens on the job is a joint function of the conditions for satisfaction which are created by the job design *and* the kinds of needs or goals which are of major importance to the employee.

As a final example of the same principle—but dealing with different kinds of needs and different job-design factors—consider young, highly skilled employees who are very much oriented toward being promoted and otherwise "making it" in the organization. Imagine that these are young female accountants working for an auditing firm and that their jobs might be designed in one of two ways. First, it might be that they would work in auditing teams in which a group of employees together audit the accounts of a firm (spending a good deal of time on site at the customer firm) and produce a single team report. Alternatively, it might be possible to design the work so that in addition to the team report each individual employee would have a certain set of responsibilities which were hers and hers alone. Given our assumptions about the personal goals of these particular employees, it would be expected that individual effort and performance might be considerably higher in the second design than in the first—since upper management would have the opportunity to see and evaluate each individual's own job performance rather than a single team report in which the differential contributions of individuals would not be visible. (It might also develop, of course, that the second job design would induce higher levels of covert competitiveness among the employees. If extreme enough, dysfunctional consequences of such competition might more than offset the increments in performance expected to result from designing the work so that each employee had the chance to show her individual capabilities to upper management.)

To develop organizational job-design practices based on the general approach described above requires the development of—

1 A means of describing the dimensions of jobs which will create various kinds of opportunities for individual need satisfaction and goal achievement.

2 A means of describing the differences among people in terms of relevant needs and goals.

3 A conceptual framework which specifies how people with various needs and goals will in fact respond to jobs with different characteristics in ways which increase organizational effectiveness.

In a subsequent section of this chapter we draw on the basic framework proposed in Chapter 4 in an attempt to specify how jobs might be structured to increase the chances that employees will become internally motivated to do high quality work. At this point, however, let us turn to a third way that jobs can affect employee behavior on the job.

Affecting the Needs and Goals of Employees Themselves   In the section above, it was suggested that jobs could affect employee behavior by creating conditions in which employees could satisfy personal needs or achieve personal goals by engaging in particular on-the-job behaviors. What is proposed here is that jobs can *affect need and goal states themselves.* And, of course, if this is so, the ways employees react behaviorally and affectively to various kinds of job designs will be importantly—albeit indirectly— affected. For example, if the hypothetical employee discussed previously were affected by his job in such a way that he *no longer valued* social activities, then everything that was predicted about his behavior in the various job situations described would become invalid.

There are compelling research data available which establish that tasks and jobs can affect important needs, goals, and motives of individuals on both short- and long-term bases. Indeed, most need theorists and researchers agree that many important needs, goals, and motives are *learned* by individuals throughout their lifetimes, and that performing various kinds of tasks and experiencing the consequences of performance substantially affect subsequent need and goal states.

In a major line of research relevant to the present discussion, McClelland (1951, p. 466) has defined a motive as "a strong affective association, characterized by an anticipatory goal reaction and based on past association of certain cues with pleasure or pain." Thus, if in his previous work history, an individual has found that he experienced a good deal of pleasure (or pain) while working on some particular kind of task, that affective state would become conditioned (in the Pavlovian sense) to the cues which were present at the time of the experience. (By "cues" are meant simply those stimuli in a situation which can serve as "signals" to the person.) In subsequent situations in which those cues were again present (as would be the case in performing the same task again or in performing a different but similar task), the prior affective state would be reactivated on a very small scale. This reactivated affective state would serve as an incentive for the individual to engage in behaviors which, based on previous experience, he believed would lead to the previously rewarding state of affairs (or avoid the previously punishing state of affairs).

One important function that tasks and jobs can serve, then, is to *provide cues which serve to reactivate previously learned motives*—i.e., to arouse needs in the work situation. Thus, for example, if an individual has learned that when he is faced with a task of moderately high difficulty he experiences positive feelings about himself when he succeeds, a need to achieve will tend to be aroused when he finds moderately strong difficulty cues present in a subsequent task. And, to the extent that the individual also has learned that he is most likely to succeed on such tasks when he puts a good deal of effort into his performance activities, it would be expected that he would in fact work very hard on the new task to maximize the chances that he would once again obtain positive feelings about himself.

The present point of emphasis is that tasks and jobs which employees deal with in real-world organizational settings are *not* likely to be motivationally neutral. Instead, they provide cues which, through the past experience of the employees, serve to temporarily arouse or depress various need states. And arousal or depression of a need state should importantly affect the degree to which employees respond behaviorally to opportunities in the work environment to satisfy that need state.

This mechanism may have been operating, for example, in a recent study which examined the performance of research and development scientists when faced with various kinds of "job pressures" (Hall & Lawler, 1970). They found that when the researchers experienced pressures to (1) do especially high quality work and (2) assume responsibility in their work for the general financial well-being of the organization, overall performance was higher. It may be that for highly skilled employees doing organizationally relevant research these two kinds of pressures served as cues which aroused needs for work achievement. Since the researchers had jobs which provided them with considerable autonomy in their work and personal responsibility for it, they may have been able to achieve important satisfactions of achievement needs by working hard and effectively toward the research goals of the organization.

Research evidence also exists which shows that experience on a task or job may affect the *long-term* need or goal states of employees—in addition to the more temporary arousal of needs by cues in the task (discussed above). For example, one study varied the degree to which collective and in-terdependent task behavior was required of research subjects (Breer & Locke, 1965). An effect of working on tasks requiring interdependent behavior was a fairly substantial change in the subjects' measured values regarding the value of collective endeavors in a wide variety of situations. Presumably such subjects, in subsequent tasks, would respond more readily than previously to opportunities to engage in performance activities with other people. Since the data were collected in the laboratory, however, the degree to which such observed changes were in fact enduring is open to question. Even if (as would be expected) the attitudinal effects of participat-ing in such an experiment did not persist, the implication of the results is that more prolonged and intense task experience could in fact alter the personal orientations of the participants on an enduring basis.

A case in point is provided in a study of automobile workers in Detroit (Kornhauser, 1965). In this research, the reactions of a large number of employees who worked on low-level, routine, repetitive jobs were compared with those of a demographically similar group of company employees whose jobs were more complex and more under control of the workers themselves.

The findings showed that individuals who worked on the lowest-level jobs tended to exhibit a diminishing amount of initiative regarding work activities, and that they had less of an active orientation toward life and toward their career. In addition, they showed less personal ambition and less desire for personal growth. One worker, for example, when asked whether he would "push hard to change things in your life" responded: "I quit pushing, I guess. There's a time when I did but the last 8 or 10 years I sorta slowed down (he was 42 at the time);I guess I just got tired of trying to get somewhere and you don't" (p. 241). The researcher took pains to demon-strate that his findings regarding such reactions were in fact due to the job experience of the workers rather than to some pattern of a priori personal characteristics, and his case for attributing the effects to job experiences is a convincing one. He concludes: "Factory employment, especially in routine production tasks, does give evidence of extinguishing workers' ambition, initiative and purposive direction toward life goals" (Kornhauser, 1965, p. 252).

Summary   We have suggested above that the way jobs are structured potentially can affect the reactions of people to their work in at least three ways. These three mechanisms are:

1 Jobs can affect the level of activation of employees and thereby influence (a) their cognitive and motor capabilities to adequately perform the work and (b) their affective reactions to the work. At either very high or very low levels of activation, performance efficiency is likely to be disrupted (through cognitive and motor disorganization at high activation, and through lack of attentiveness and responsiveness at low activation).

2 Jobs can provide incentives for individuals to obtain satisfaction of important needs (or to achieve important goals) by engaging in particular on-the-job behaviors. This mechanism would appear to have considerable potential for developing long-term motivation of employees. First, it offers the possibility that jobs can be designed so that the employee will be best able to obtain need satisfactions or achieve his goals by engaging in behaviors which are facilitative of organizational effectiveness. It may be possible, therefore, to develop means of *simultaneously* satisfying employees and achieving organizational goals through job design. In addition, to the extent that employees develop work "strategies" based on their perceptions of what leads to personally desirable job outcomes, the motivational advantages accrued through this mechanism will tend to persist through time and perhaps even generalize to other, similar job or task situations.

3 Jobs can affect the need and goal states of employees directly, thereby indirectly influencing the kinds of opportunities for need satisfactions or goal attainment that employees seek out. These effects can be either short-term or long-term in their impact. In the case of short-term effects, cues embedded in the task or work situation can serve to arouse motives from their normal levels and thereby provide additional incentives for employees to engage in need-satisfying behaviors. From the long-term effects, employees can *learn to value* various kinds of outcomes (e.g., success at a difficult task, collective endeavors) through continuing on-the-job experiences.

JOB DESIGN AND INTERNALIZED WORK MOTIVATION

In the preceding pages, the general mechanisms through which jobs can make differences in the individual's work attitudes and behavior have been explored. We turn now to the more specific and more practical question of how jobs might be designed to maximize employee attendance, job performance, and satisfaction through motivational mechanisms that are *internal* to the person.

The Herzberg Two-Factor Theory

One approach to this question which has had a major impact on contemporary organizations in recent years is Herzberg's two-factor theory of satisfaction and motivation (cf. Herzberg, Mausner, & Snyderman, 1959; Herzberg, 1966). In essence, the theory proposes that the primary determinants of employee satisfaction (distinguished in the theory from the determinants of *dis*satisfaction) are factors intrinsic to the work that employees do—i.e., recognition, achievement, responsibility, advancement, personal growth in competence. These factors are called "motivators" because employees are presumed to be motivated to obtain more of them, for example, through good job performance. Dissatisfaction, however, is seen as being determined by a separate set of factors which are extrinsic to the work itself. These aspects of the work environment are called "hygiene factors" and include company policies, supervisory practices, working conditions, salaries and wages, and interpersonal relationships on the job. Thus, the Herzberg theory suggests that a job should enhance positive work motivation and employee satisfaction to the extent that it provides opportunities for employees to achieve, to gain recognition and responsibility, to advance in the organization, and to grow in competence.

The theory has stimulated a great deal of empirical research, some of which has been designed to test the conceptual validity of the theory and some of which has assessed the usefulness of the implications of the theory for redesigning jobs. Of particular note in the latter regard is a series of generally successful job-enlargement studies performed throughout the American Telephone and Telegraph system which were based on principles derived from the Herzberg theory (Ford, 1969).

The theory has gained wide acceptance among managers throughout the country. The reasons are not difficult to discern: the theory is simple, providing only two categories (motivators and hygiene factors) in which all aspects of the job and the work situation can be placed, and the theory makes good intuitive sense to many managers who have had personal experience with jobs in which motivators are mostly absent.

Unfortunately, a number of researchers have been unable to provide empirical support for the major tenets of the Herzberg two-factor theory (see, for example, Dunnette, Campbell, & Hakel, 1967; Hinton, 1968; King, 1970; for analyses favorable to the Herzberg position, see Herzberg, 1966; Whitsett & Winslow, 1967). In particular, data have been presented which suggest that the original division of aspects of the work place into motivators and hygiene factors may have been largely a function of a methodological artifact. Contrary to the expectations of the theory, a number of researchers have provided data which indicate that both satisfaction and dissatisfaction can derive *both* from intrinsic job factors and from extrinsic "surround" factors. All things considered, the general conceptual status of the theory must be considered highly uncertain.

Aside from the difficulties in obtaining consistent empirical support for the original two-factor dichotomy, problems on the conceptual level arise when one attempts to use the theory to understand how jobs should be designed for optimal work effectiveness and employee satisfaction. The implementation of the theory in the AT&T studies (Ford, 1969) assumes that the presence of the motivating conditions (i.e., recognition, achievement, etc.) can potentially motivate *all* employees. And indeed, such an assumption is not inconsistent with published statements of the theory; it appears in fact that the theory has not yet been elaborated to specify the way in which characteristics of workers interact with the presence or absence of the motivators in affecting worker performance and satisfaction—or even if such an interaction is to be expected. Data reviewed at several points throughout this chapter have suggested strongly that the characteristics of workers *must* be considered if the impact of job design on worker affective and behavioral responses is to be fully understood. (It may be that unmeasured interactions between employee characteristics and job characteristics are part of the reason that the job enlargement studies conducted at AT&T were not always successful; unfortunately, data are not available in the report of the AT&T research which would allow testing of this possibility).

Finally, the theory in its present form does not specify how the presence or absence of the motivating conditions can be measured for existing jobs. This makes specific tests of the theory in ongoing organizations very difficult to perform, and also makes it difficult to generate unambiguous predictions from the theory about the effects of various kinds of changes being contemplated for existing jobs.

Because of the conceptual and empirical difficulties which have developed around the Herzberg theory, and especially considering the need to take explicit account of individual differences in needs and goals in designing work, an alternative conceptual approach may be called for. The outlines of one possibility will be developed below.

Jobs and Individuals: A Conceptual Framework

It was suggested in Chapter 2 that various events or outcomes that occur in organizations are valued by employees to the extent that they satisfy personal needs or facilitate the achievement of personal goals. In addition, it was proposed (and indeed is a theme throughout many discussions in the book) that the likelihood that an employee will engage in some given pattern of behavior is enhanced to the degree that he believes engaging in that behavior will provide him with outcomes he values. It follows, then, that to the extent that conditions on the job can be arranged so that employees believe that they will be most likely to obtain valued outcomes by working hard and effectively toward organizational goals, the work motivation of employees should be enhanced.

What kinds of outcomes are likely to be valued by employees in contemporary organizations in this country? Most lower-level needs (e.g., physical well-being, security) often are reasonably well-satisfied for contemporary workers, and therefore cannot be expected to serve as motivational incentives except under unusual circumstances. This is not the case, however, for certain "higher-order" needs (e.g., needs for personal growth and development, or for self-actualization). Further, as was suggested in Chapter 2, a person may experience higher-order need satisfactions on a continuing basis without the desire for additional satisfactions of these needs diminishing. It would appear, therefore, that opportunities for higher-order need satisfaction could serve as powerful incentives on a long-term basis for many employees in contemporary organizations.

It may be possible to specify a set of "job characteristics" which will provide employees with higher-order need satisfactions to the extent that they work hard and well toward organizational goals. In particular, the work of behavioral scientists (e.g., Lewin, Dembo, Festinger, & Sears, 1944; Argyris, 1964) suggests that individuals may experience higher-order need satisfaction *when they learn that they have, as a result of their own efforts, accomplished something that they believe is personally worthwhile or meaningful.* Thus, in more concrete terms, such satisfactions should be obtained when an employee works effectively on a job which (1) provides feedback about what is accomplished, (2) allows him to feel personally responsible for a meaningful portion of the work, and (3) provides outcomes which are intrinsically meaningful or are otherwise experienced as worthwhile. The harder and better an individual *who is desirous of higher-order need satisfactions* works on a job with these characteristics, the more likely he will be to obtain higher-order need satisfaction. Further, as he gains experience on the job, the greater incentive there will be for him to continue to perform effectively. Let us now examine in somewhat more detail those job characteristics which may establish conditions for internal motivation of people who desire higher-order need satisfactions.

The Characteristics of Motivating Jobs   It appears that four of the requisite task attributes proposed by Turner and Lawrence (1965) (and discussed earlier in this chapter) may be useful in operationalizing the general job characteristics proposed above. These attributes are specified

below, in the context of a more detailed discussion of three basic characteristics of "motivating" jobs.

1 *The job must allow a worker to feel personally responsible for a
meaningful portion of his work:* What is accomplished must be through the
individual's own efforts; he must realize that the work he does is his own and
he must believe that he personally is responsible for whatever successes and
failures occur as a result of his work. This does not mean, of course, that
feelings of personal responsiblity for work outcomes cannot occur in team
projects; all that is required is for team members to feel that their own
efforts are important in accomplishing the task at hand.

The dimension *autonomy* (as specified by Turner and Lawrence) would
seem to tap the degree to which workers feel personal responsiblity for their
work. In jobs high on measured autonomy, workers will tend to feel that
they "own" the outcomes of their work; in jobs low on autonomy, a worker
may feel that successes and failures on the job are more often due to the
good work (or to the incompetence) of other workers or of his superior.

2 *The job must provide outcomes which are intrinsically meaningful or
otherwise experienced as worthwhile to the individual:* If an employee does
not feel that his efforts make much difference to anybody, himself included,
it is unlikely that he will feel especially good if he works effectively. It
clearly is not possible to indicate for *people in general* what kinds of job
characteristics will be likely to provide outcomes seen as meaningful and
worthwhile. People simply differ too much in the kinds of things they value
for any statement of such generality to be made. It is possible as an example,
however, to provide some specifications in this regard for individuals who
have high desires for higher-order need satisfactions.

There are at least two ways that work can come to be experienced as
meaningful for employees with relatively high desires for higher-order need
satisfaction. The first is that the employee's job be a sufficiently "whole"
piece of work that he can perceive he has produced or accomplished
something that makes a difference to other people. In other words, the job is
high on *task identity.* Jobs high on task identity are characterized (according
to Turner & Lawrence, 1965, p. 157) by (a) a very clear cycle of perceived
closure—the job provides a distinct sense of beginning and ending of a
transformation ("doing something") process, (b) high visibility of the
transformation to the worker, (c) high visibility of the transformation in the
finished product, and (d) a transformation of considerable magnitude. For a
worker who has strong needs for developing and using his competence, a job
with such characteristics generally would be expected to be experienced as
highly meaningful and worthwhile.

A second way work can come to take on personal meaning to an
individual desirous of higher-order need satisfactions is for his job to require

him to use a variety of valued skills and abilities—perhaps regardless of the broader significance of what is done. For example, a strongly motivated duffer feels good when he hits a good tee shot, even though the broader significance of this event is open to question. His golfing skills are on the line when he steps to the tee, those skills are important to him, he performs well—and that in itself is enough.

Jobs high on the dimension of *variety* would be expected to provide opportunities for workers to experience this kind of meaningfulness on the job, since high-variety jobs typically tap a number of different skills which may be important to the employee. Working on high-variety jobs may be personally meaningful to well-motivated employees through a process analogous to that which makes golf meaningful to the duffer. It should be noted, however, that only variety which does in fact challenge the employee will be expected to be experienced as meaningful for those with desires for higher-order needs; screwing many different sizes of nuts on many different colors of bolts, if this could be considered variety, would not be expected to be perceived as meaningful.

3 *The job must provide feedback about what is accomplished:* Even if the two general conditions discussed above are met, an employee will not experience satisfaction of his higher-order needs when he performs effectively unless he obtains some kind of *feedback* about how he is doing. Such feedback may come from doing the task itself, but it also may come from some other person such as an esteemed coworker, a supervisor, etc. The crucial thing is that it be present in a form that is believable to the worker.

In summary, then, it appears that individuals who desire higher-order need satisfactions will be able to obtain satisfaction of these needs when they perform effectively on jobs which are high on *autonomy, task identity, variety,* and *feedback.* And the harder and better one performs on a job which is high on these dimensions, the more satisfaction one is likely to feel.

It should be emphasized that the above conclusion holds *only* for individuals who care about obtaining higher-order need satisfactions from their work. The individual who works solely to "make a buck" would not be expected to be motivated by a job high on the four dimensions specified above. Instead, he might be more likely to perform effectively on, say, a nonchallenging, routine job with bonus pay for high production. Therefore, we come to a key question: Is the "typical" employee in contemporary organizations one who does desire higher-order need satisfactions, or is he likely to respond only to the dollars on the paycheck? There is substantial evidence (see Chapter 2) that large numbers of employees *do* seek higher-order need satisfactions from their work and that money is by no means the only important outcome in the work environment of most employees.

What is worrisome is that there are good reasons to believe that experience on jobs designed according to the scientific management approach can, in the long run, serve to orient employees away from desires for higher-order satisfactions and toward monetary and other existence-level satisfactions. Consistent with the third mechanism by which jobs can affect behavior and attitudes (discussed earlier in this chapter), it would appear that when work is designed so as to ensure that an employee cannot reasonably hope to obtain higher-level personal satisfactions from his work, he will eventually come to devalue these satisfactions. The data on automobile assembly-line workers (Kornhauser, 1965) appear to support this view.

A Test of the Theory   In a study designed to test the ideas set forth above (Hackman & Lawler, 1971), data were collected from some 200 employees of a telephone company. The primary purposes of the research were to determine (1) the overall relationships between job characteristics and employee work attitudes and behavior, and (2) whether or not the reaction of an employee to his work is dependent on the particular kinds of satisfactions he values. Thirteen different jobs were assessed on the four "core" dimensions discussed above (autonomy, task identity, variety, and feedback), and the strength of desire for higher-order need satisfactions of employees working on these jobs was assessed. Level of desire for higher-order need satisfactions was measured by asking employees how much they would like to obtain relevant kinds of personal outcomes from their work (e.g., feelings of personal growth and development, feelings of accomplishment, etc.).

The average employee in the company was found to be fairly high in self-described desire for higher-order satisfactions (the overall average was 6.01 on a seven-point scale, which is high even assuming a moderate amount of social desirability impact on the questionnaire responses). Therefore, it was expected that across all employees there would be a positive relationship between the four core job dimensions and employee work motivation, satisfaction, performance, and attendance. The expectation was confirmed: in general, the "better" an employee's job (in terms of the core dimensions), the more positively he responded to it, both in attitudes and behavior. Of special interest is the fact that when jobs were high on the core dimensions, employees reported having higher *intrinsic motivation* to perform well. That is, employees indicated that when they performed well on such jobs they experienced positive internal feelings; and when they did poorly, they felt badly. On jobs which were low on the core dimensions, they tended *not* to have such feelings.

Consistent with the conceptual framework outlined above, then, it appears that jobs high on the core dimensions establish conditions whereby some workers can obtain personally rewarding experiences by doing well on the job. The data suggest, moreover, that "doing well" as interpreted in the job context has much more to do with high-*quality* performance than with producing large quantities of work. The core dimensions do not relate either to internal pressures for high-quantity production or the actual quantity of work produced. This fits with the notion that employees with strong higher-order need strength feel positively when they have accomplished something that they feel is meaningful; it is not unreasonable that such workers would see doing high-quality work as a much more meaningful accomplishment than simply turning out large quantities of work.

The researchers also tested the degree to which the predicted interaction between employee need strength and reactions to jobs could be empirically demonstrated. Correlations between job characteristics and the dependent variables were computed separately for (1) those employees whose measured strength of desire for higher-order need satisfactions was in the top one-third of the distribution of scores for all employees in the study and (2) those employees whose scores were in the bottom one-third of the same distribution. As expected, the relationship between job characteristics (in terms of the core dimensions) and employee performance, satisfaction, and attendance was substantially higher for subjects in the top one-third of the distribution of need-strength scores than for subjects in the bottom one-third. The actual correlations obtained for four measures of employee reactions to their work are shown in Table 10-1.

Table 10-1 Moderating Effect of Growth Need Strength

	Correlations between perceived job complexity and employee reactions	
	Employees with high growth-need strength	Employees with low growth-need strength
Level of internal motivation	.54	.23
Quality of performance (rated by supervisors)	.23	.02
Satisfaction with opportunities for personal growth and development on the job	.57	.16
Satisfaction with the feelings of worthwhile accomplishment obtained from the job	.59	.32

Source: From Hackman & Lawler, 1971, p. 279.

In sum, the results strongly suggest that *only* workers with reasonably high strength of desire for higher-order need satisfactions (i.e., growth, obtaining feelings of accomplishment, etc.) will respond positively and productively to the opportunities present in jobs which are high in meaning, autonomy, complexity and feedback. These results are not very helpful, of course, in understanding or dealing with the work motivation and performance of employees who have little desire for higher-order satisfactions; the problem of designing work appropriate for such employees will be dealt with briefly in the next section of this chapter.

THE DESIGN OF WORK AND THE DESIGN OF ORGANIZATIONS

The theory and the data summarized in the previous section reinforce once again the need to know something about *both* the nature of jobs and the characteristics of people if one is to make predictions about performance and attitudes of employees on the job. And, of course, both kinds of data appear to be quite necessary if a good match between jobs and employees is to be achieved in organizational settings.

How can such matches be accomplished? Certainly one approach is to continue to collect data on characteristics of workers about how they may react to jobs with different characteristics, and then to carefully *select and place* employees on the basis of these data. Such a strategy—assuming reasonable prospects for implementation—could be expected to lead to at least some improvements in the motivation, satisfaction, and tenure of employees beyond the levels which have resulted from the practice of using only skill and ability data for purposes of selection and placement.

Flexibility in Job Designs? But a somewhat more "radical" approach also may have merit. Traditionally, the design of jobs has been considered pretty much inviolate; people have been selected and perhaps crunched a bit to fit into existing jobs, but jobs have only rarely been changed to be better fits for the people who work on them. If a degree of flexibility in how jobs are designed and defined could be achieved by organizations even while the customary flexibility in selecting and placing people were retained, organizations would have considerably more latitude for change and adjustment in trying to achieve a situation in which workers would have the greatest opportunity and incentive to perform effectively in their work.*

Such a strategy as that suggested above could, unless adopted and

---

*The use of job redesign as a general technique for organizational change is dealt with in Chapter 15 and will not be probed further here.

implemented with great care, result in a good measure of organizational chaos—everyone's job would be different from everyone else's, and rational coordination within the organization (see Chapter 3) could be severely affected, to the detriment of overall organizational effectiveness. Indeed, even to begin to implement an approach to job design similar to the one suggested above would appear to require a good deal of skill and resilience on the part of an organization. The implication is, therefore, that the way organizations structure and staff jobs may be very intimately tied to the way the organization itself is structured, the nature of interpersonal relationships within the organization, and the usual patterns of organizational functioning. It is to this general issue that we turn in concluding this chapter.

Evidence from one large organization (Alderfer, 1967) indicates that there is a strong interaction between the way jobs are structured in an organization and the nature of interpersonal relationships between superiors and subordinates. (Similar evidence was also found in a later study by Lawler, Hackman, and Kaufman, 1973.) Although employees working on relatively complex jobs (including jobs which recently had been enlarged) reported that they were more satisfied with the opportunities they had to use their personal skills and abilities than were employees working on less complex jobs, they also reported substantially more *dis*satisfaction with "respect from superiors." The researcher suggested that one reason for the decay in superior-subordinate relationships when jobs were made more complex is that such jobs are intrinsically more difficult to supervise and performance on them is more difficult to evaluate. Unless supervisors are able to deal effectively with evaluation problems (in the organization studied, they apparently were not able to), relationships between managers and subordinates might be expected to deteriorate.

The Impact of Organizational Structures   These results suggest that the way jobs are designed can have important implications for the kinds of managerial and organizational competences which are necessary for effective organizational functioning. The interaction between job-design variables and organizational characteristics operates in reverse direction as well: the way an organization is structured appears to set functional limits on the latitude it has in determining how its jobs may be designed. Consider, for example, an organization which is designed and which operates according to the principles of classical Weberian bureaucracy. [It will be recalled from Chapter 8 that such organizations are termed by Burns and Stalker [1961] as "mechanistic" systems, and that they tend to be "tall," with power and authority centralized at the top, and with clearly defined and enforced organizational rules and procedures.]

The options realistically open for such organizations in designing jobs appear to be quite restricted. Mechanistic systems could not, for example, enlarge jobs in what has been called a "vertical" direction without disrupting the rational coordination of the organization. The reason is that when jobs are vertically enlarged, workers are given authority and responsibility to make a maximum number of their *own* decisions about how they do their work, the pace they set, and (to a more limited extent) the goals they establish for their performance. In a mechanistic system these kinds of decisions are clearly the responsibility and the prerogative of management. Employees are the doers and in no sense the decision makers or the planners.

"Horizontal" enlargement of jobs might be attempted in mechanistic organizations, since horizontal job enlargement is restricted to expanding the scope of the job content—e.g., by giving the employees added duties which would increase the variety of their work. But even horizontal enlargement would, in a mechanistic system, have to come about through the chain of command and could not occur at the instigation of individual employees (except, of course, in the unlikely instance in which an employee suggestion for horizontal enlargement went up through the chain of command, was approved, and came back down again in a form similar to the original suggestion). It would appear that mechanistic organizations would tend to reinforce jobs designed according to the principles of scientific management—systematically segmented and simplified jobs with little autonomy or decision making required of employees, and great consistency in the work done by all employees on the same job. Thus, to some extent any move to enlarge jobs, either horizontally or vertically, might be expected to be resisted by such organizations.

The alternative form of organizational design, "organic systems," tends to be decentralized and relatively "flat" in shape, with the individuals at lower levels given the option of managing or performing the work in ways that are not necessarily consistent with what is being done in other parts of the organization—so long as the overall goals of the organization are well served by the variations (Chapter 8). It would appear that organic systems would tend to reinforce jobs which are enlarged in both the horizontal and vertical directions. Such organizations should have the capability to design jobs in a number of different ways throughout the system without introducing organizational chaos. In addition, organic organizations should be much more able to adjust job designs to *individual* needs on either a temporary or semipermanent basis than would be the case for mechanistic organizations.

Predicted Relationships among Organizational Designs, Job Designs, and Individual Needs Although it has been argued above that jobs designed according to the principles of scientific management are likely to be more congruent with a mechanistic organization (and that enlarged jobs are likely to be more congruent with an organic organizational design), such congruence is not by any means an immutable law. Both simple jobs in organic organizations and enlarged jobs in mechanistic organizations are observed in practice.

In Figure 10-3 some of the expected consequences both of congruence and incongruence between organizational design and job design are set forth. Since the characteristics of individual employees (especially the strength of their desires for growth need satisfaction) have been shown

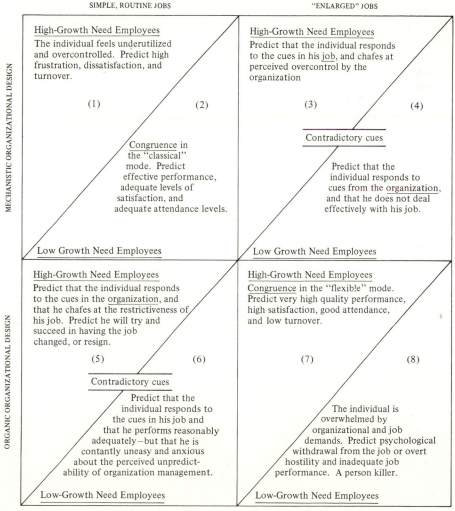

Figure 10–3 Predicted relationships among illustrative types of organizational design, job design, and employee characteristics.

(earlier in this chapter) to be very important in determining how people react to their work, individual differences are included in the figure as well. The figure is, in essence, a $2 \times 2 \times 2$ table, with the defining factors being (1) organizational design—organic versus mechanistic, (2) job design—simple and routine versus enlarged, and (3) individual need strength—high growth needs versus low growth needs.

Two cells in the figure reflect general congruence: (1) cell 2—mechanistic design, simple and routine jobs, and low growth need employees and (2) cell 7—organic design, enlarged jobs, and high growth need employees. For both of these cases, generally adequate performance and satisfaction are predicted, with expectations somewhat higher for cell 7 (organic-enlarged-growth). Cells 1 and 8 are the opposites of each other: in cell 1 an individual with high growth needs is faced with an entirely constraining situation as regards both his job and his organization; in cell 8 an individual with low growth needs is faced with a wide-open set of opportunities that he would, in all probability, have no idea how to deal with. Thus, it is predicted that individuals in cell 1 will feel underutilized, frustrated, dissatisfied, and probably will leave the organization; individuals in cell 8 would be expected to feel overwhelmed by organizational and job demands, and would have great difficulties adapting to the work situation.

Cells 3 through 6 are characterized by contradictory messages: the job provides one set of cues to the worker, and the organization itself provides a second and contradictory set of cues. The prediction (which is not based firmly on existing theory or data) is that individuals will tend to respond to and act in accordance with *those cues which are congruent with their own need states*. Thus, high growth need individuals will tend to respond to cues provided by their jobs in cell 3 and to organizational cues in cell 5; low growth need people will tend to respond to the organization in cell 4 and to the job in cell 6. In none of these cases, however, would fully adequate performance on the job be expected, nor would it be predicted that employees would be well satisfied with their work. The reason is that in every case in cells 3 through 6, contradictory cues are present about what kinds of behavioral strategies are appropriate, and dealing with this conflict undoubtedly will tend to frustrate the achievement of high on-the-job performance and the development of genuine satisfaction with the work environment.

It should be stressed, of course, that the "types" of people, organizational designs, and job designs presented in Figure 10-3 are to some extent caricatures of the real world: pure types of any of the three simply do not exist. It is more useful and valid to think of the cells in Figure 10-3 as end points on a continuum rather than as meaningful types in themselves.

And, finally, it should be emphasized as well that the predictions included in the cells of Figure 10-3 are just that: predictions. Data are presently available only to support the predictions in cells 1, 2, and 7; in particular, no research attention has been given to the cells in which contradictory messages are experienced by employees. Thus, the validity of the formulation remains open to question; its reason for inclusion here is to emphasize one last time, as we conclude our discussion of work design, the enormous importance of the interdependencies between the characteristics of individuals, the characteristics of jobs, and the characteristics of the organizations in which the work is done.

REVIEW AND DISCUSSION QUESTIONS

1 What are the likely consequences of designing jobs with only one criterion in mind—efficiency? Consider both functional and dysfunctional outcomes.
2 In what way are the Theory X and Y assumptions of McGregor related to job design?
3 In what ways do job designs influence employees' work-related attitudes and behavior?
4 What does "activation theory" have to do with the design of jobs? Can jobs be designed so that the worker is "overactivated" and his performance is less than it might be if the activation level were decreased somewhat? How likely is it that a typical worker would be "overactivated" on the job? That is, are jobs typically designed so that the activation level is too high?
5 Explain how job design factors influence the needs that individuals satisfy on a job. Can an individual's needs be modified as a result of job experiences? How?
6 What constraints do organizational structure variables place on the way jobs are either designed initially or redesigned?
7 How does job design (vertical and horizontal dimensions) relate to the Burns and Stalker mechanistic-organic continuum (discussed in Chapter 8)?
8 Examine Figure 10-3. What are the implications of this model for organizational activities in the areas of personnel selection and placement?

Part Four

Influences on Work Behavior: Organizational Practices and Social Processes

Chapter 11

Evaluating Work Effectiveness

With an organization structured and its jobs designed, the next issue that must be dealt with is the evaluation of the work effectiveness of the individuals who hold these jobs. In a very real sense, the performance of everyone in an organization is constantly being appraised—by the person himself as well as by his superiors, peers, and subordinates. Evaluation is an inevitable consequence of the way organizations are structured and jobs are designed. The assignment of responsibility to particular individuals for the performance of certain tasks makes the assessment of how an individual performs both possible and necessary. It makes it possible because it identifies the results for which the person is responsible. It makes it necessary because in order to operate, complex, differentiated organizations need information on how well jobs are being performed.

Much of the evaluation that takes place in organizations is informal, but some of it becomes part of the formal performance evaluation systems that are present in many organizations. Ideally, formal evaluation systems utilize valid data in order to determine how well an individual is performing his job.

Information of this type then forms an important input to organizational reward (the subject of the next chapter) and planning systems. In this chapter the focus is on examining why and how organizations conduct formal appraisal programs and on understanding how individuals react to them.

ORGANIZATIONAL AND INDIVIDUAL GOALS IN PERFORMANCE EVALUATION

Both organizations and their employees have certain goals or aims they wish to achieve as a result of performance evaluation. As will be seen, in some cases such objectives are compatible, but in other situations they are in conflict. We will first examine the organization's goals, then the individual's, and then consider the possibilities for conflicts.

The Organization's Goals

Performance evaluation is an important element in the information and control systems that operate in most complex organizations. In Chapters 3 and 9 it was emphasized that in order to operate, a control system needs data on what is occurring, and it needs a way of correcting or adjusting performance when its sensors indicate it is needed. In most organizations the performance appraisal process is designed to both facilitate information exchange and influence performance. That is, it is designed to provide the individual and the organization with data about what is going on, and it is designed to be a medium through which the organization tries to influence the behavior of individuals. Table 11-1 (from Spriegel, 1962) shows the functions performance appraisal serves in 357 firms. As can be seen, in many organizations it serves multiple purposes, some of which are basically information exchange and some of which are designed to influence performance.

It was pointed out in Chapter 7 that organizations are increasingly becoming aware that they have to plan and program the development of their human resources just as they do their economic resources. This would seem to explain the data in Table 11-1, which shows that career development and assessment are the most frequent purposes for which appraisal is done. People have to be prepared to fill the many expected and unexpected job vacancies that are constantly occurring in organizations. This is simply too important a process to be left to chance. Not having someone ready to fill an important job can be just as costly as not having the money to expand the organization's physical plant. People, unlike other resources of an organization, can grow, and their growth and development can be managed.

Table 11–1   Purposes for Which Appraisal Is Used

Purpose	Number of firms
Counseling	300
Promotion	298
Training and development	265
Considering retention or discharge	240
Salary administration or merit increase	237
Bonus payments	54
Profit-sharing payments	14

Source: Spriegel (1962, p. 82).

However, as was also stressed, if organizations are going to make intelligent development decisions, they need to be able to identify who needs development and what kinds of development they need. This type of information is often not readily available, just as a general catalog of the human resources in an organization is not readily available. Data from the performance evaluation system can help to pinpoint who might be good candidates for development and just what kind of development experiences might be best for them. Thus, one reason organizations appraise performance is that they need the information it yields in order to plan, coordinate, and administer training and development programs.

Basic to the effective functioning of any organization is the ability to influence the motivation of its members. The performance appraisal process is often used by organizations as a way of influencing intrinsic and extrinsic work motivation. In Chapters 2 and 4 it was emphasized that the manner in which valued rewards are given has an important influence on motivation. The giving of such rewards as promotion and pay increases is often tied to the results of performance appraisal sessions in the hope of creating the belief that good performance leads to desired rewards. Employees are also given feedback on their performance during appraisal sessions, and, as was noted in the previous chapter, under certain conditions this can lead to intrinsic motivation. Finally, some performance appraisal sessions also include goal setting on the part of the subordinates—a process also designed to motivate behavior.

Both the training and counseling function and the performance motivation function of the performance appraisal process are important to the very existence of organizations. Thus, it is not surprising that most organizations have performance appraisal systems. However, the two functions of performance appraisal situations can conflict with each other. Appraisal for motivation tends to focus on objective evaluation of the employee in relation to other employees. Appraisal for development tends to focus on strong and weak spots of performance from the point of view of how overall performance can be improved and what the implications are for the employee's career. In addition to calling for different discussion emphases, appraisal for reward purposes and appraisal for counseling purposes produce different, somewhat competing motivations in the individual who is being appraised.

Individuals' Goals

Just as the organization has certain goals that it tries to accomplish through the performance evaluation process, so does the individual. A number of social psychological theories have pointed out that individuals want and seek out feedback about their performance (e.g., Festinger, 1954; Pettigrew, 1967) since it helps them learn more about themselves. The performance appraisal situation represents an opportunity to get such feedback, and thus individuals often have as a goal obtaining information which will help them evaluate their own performance and learn how they are progressing in their own development. If their performance compares favorably with others, then people tend to satisfy their needs for competence and psychological success; if it does not, they tend to experience failure, and the feedback is often difficult to accept.

When the performance evaluation process is crucial in determining the extrinsic rewards an individual will receive, employees have a very direct reason for wanting to be favorably evaluated. Thus, they often do what they can to present themselves and their performance in the best possible way during the performance evaluation process. They tend to deny problems with their work and to emphasize the most favorable parts of their performance. In short, the individual very naturally tries to present his performance in the best light in order to obtain the valued rewards that led him to join the organization in the first place.

There is an obvious potential conflict, however, between the two goals the individual has in the performance appraisal situation. Only if the individual provides complete information—even if some of it is not favorable to him—is he likely to receive the valid feedback on his performance that he needs if he is to grow and develop. However, giving complete data about his performance is often not the best thing for the individual to do if he hopes to obtain the extrinsic rewards he desires. Thus, in the performance evaluation situation the individual often has conflicting objectives. On the one hand he wants to look as good as possible in order to maximize his extrinsic rewards, while on the other he wants accurate and helpful feedback about his performance (Meyer, Kay, & French, 1965).

Individual-Organization Conflicts

The discussion so far has emphasized that the individual and the organization both have several goals in the appraisal situation. It has also emphasized

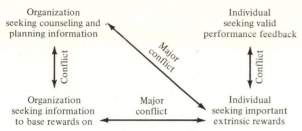

Figure 11–1 Conflicts in performance appraisals.

that these goals are sometimes in conflict. This is shown in Figure 11-1 by the arrow between the two individual level goals and the arrow between the two organization level goals. The major conflicts in the performance appraisal situation, however, are those shown by the arrows connecting the individual's goal of obtaining rewards and the two goals of the organization. The reason for these conflicts is simply that to accomplish its purposes the organization needs complete and valid data about the nature of the individual's ability and performance, yet it often is not in the best interest of the individual to provide such data. The conflict then is over the exchange of valid information. As long as the individual sees the appraisal process as having an important influence on the rewards he receives, the potential for this conflict will be present. In the case of the good performer, the conflict is negligible because the individual *wants* to provide sound data; but in the case of the poor performer, it is bound to be substantial.

PROBLEMS IN PERFORMANCE EVALUATION
Superior and Subordinate Ambivalence

Given the conflicts that are present in the performance appraisal process, it is not surprising that superiors and subordinates both often have ambivalent feelings about participating in it (Hall & Lawler, 1969). From the superior's point of view, being in the position of evaluating someone's performance and giving feedback is not very pleasant. Many superiors feel that the performance appraisal process puts them in the position of "playing God." Further, most supervisors are not trained to handle the kind of interpersonal issues that arise when a subordinate's performance is being evaluated. As a result, particularly when the feedback is negative, unpleasant interpersonal situations develop which the supervisor cannot handle effectively. On the other hand, most superiors recognize the importance of doing performance evaluation. They feel an obligation to give feedback to their subordinates, and they recognize that this is one way they can influence their subordinates' behavior. Thus, superiors tend to feel that performance evaluation is something they should do, but they also are hesitant to face the uncomfortable interpersonal issues that may arise when it has to be carried out.

As has already been stated, subordinates want the feedback that the performance appraisal process yields. They may, however, be very ambivalent about receiving it, particularly if they feel it is likely to be negative. This concern about obtaining negative feedback may be compounded by the subordinates' doubts about the superior's ability to give the feedback effectively. Subordinates don't want just any kind of feedback; they want constructive feedback that will help them reach their goals. The discomfort the superior experiences often is communicated to a subordinate so that both feel even more uncomfortable about being in the performance evaluation situation. Finally, subordinates also frequently experience some stress because of their conflicting desires for valid feedback and for extrinsic rewards.

Because both superiors and subordinates have ambivalent attitudes about performance appraisal, a phenomenon called the "vanishing performance appraisal" occurs in many organizations. When interviewed separately, subordinates report that they have not had a performance appraisal session for several years, while superiors report they hold regular performance appraisal sessions (Hall & Lawler, 1969). Further investigation typically reveals that the superiors at some point in time have talked in rather general terms with the subordinates about their performance. The superiors consider this to be a performance appraisal session, but the subordinates do not and wonder why they are not getting the kind of feedback they want. It is not hard to see how this kind of behavior on the part of the superiors can occur, given their mixed feelings about holding these sessions. It is also not hard to understand why what constitutes an acceptable appraisal session for an anxious superior might not provide the kind of information a subordinate wants.

Dysfunctional Consequences

Because of the conflicts that exist in the appraisal situation, performance appraisal programs often fail to accomplish the objectives of both the individual and the organization. They frequently end up causing many of the same dysfunctional consequences that other control systems produce (mentioned in Chapter 9).

Subordinate Defensiveness McGregor (1957) has pointed out that because appraisals tend to have both administrative (salary and promotion) and developmental purposes, they tend to place the superior in the incompatible roles of judge and counselor. The act of judging a subordinate tends to elicit defensiveness so that those people who need development the most have trouble hearing about the kind of development they need. As McGregor notes the superior usually finds that the effectiveness of the communication is inversely related to the subordinate's need to hear it (1957).

Studies have presented some data which support the point that subordinates tend not to "hear" criticism (Meyer, Kay, & French, 1965). When presented with a long list of criticisms, subordinates tend to remember only the first few. The rest are never heard because the subordinates are busy thinking up arguments to refute the first few criticisms that are presented. Research also suggests that, rather than serving as a stimulant to more effective behavior, criticism can have a negative effect on future performance. The most common outcomes of a critical (i.e., negative evaluation) performance appraisal are defensiveness and deteriorating performance. Thus, rather than serving as facilitators and motivators of good performance, many performance appraisal sessions tend to have just the opposite effect; they decrease performance. Ironically, they are especially likely to have this effect when they are conducted with the people who need help the most—the poor performers. This is a particularly devastating comment on the appraisal process since one of the most important reasons for doing it is to correct performance that is substandard and dysfunctional from the organization's point of view.

Invalid or Misleading Data   Other critics of the performance evaluation process have pointed out that it also often fails to produce valid data about employee performance levels. Study after study has shown that the typical performance evaluation ratings done by a superior tend to be suspect (Campbell et al., 1970; Anderson et al., 1973). For example, when he is asked to rate his subordinates on a number of traits, the ratings show a "halo effect" such that a given subordinate tends to be rated the same on all traits. There are data which suggest that peers' ratings are often more accurate than superiors' ratings, but they are seldom used (Lawler, 1967). It has also been shown that some superiors tend to rate everyone high and others tend to rate everyone low, which further serves to reduce the accuracy and usefulness of performance ratings. Thus, one reason why performance evaluation ratings often are not useful is that superiors frequently are poor raters and evaluators, but this is far from the only reason.

There are a number of examples in the behavioral science literature of employees giving invalid data about their performance. For example, the classic Western Electric studies (Roethlisberger & Dickson, 1939) point out how employees manage the kind of production reports that go outside their work group. The employees studied were on a pay incentive plan, and they wanted to show a consistent daily production figure. They did this by not reporting what they produced on some days and reporting things as having been produced that never were produced on other days.

A number of researchers have documented that subordinates sometimes present false assessments of what is possible in terms of future performance. Frequently, subordinates intentionally lead superiors to believe that low levels of performance are reasonable, when in fact much higher ones are possible. The kinds of behaviors, for example, that some workers go through in order to mislead their superiors and the industrial engineers assigned to study their jobs have been well documented (e.g., Whyte, 1955). The following quote illustrates one worker's way of dealing with a performance measurement system and the time-study man who ran it.

"You got to outwit that son-of-a-bitch! You got to use your noodle while you're working, and think your work out ahead as you go along! You got to add in movements you know you ain't going to make when you're running the job. Remember, if you don't screw them, they're going to screw you! . . . Every movement counts! . . ."

"Remember those bastards are paid to screw you," said Starkey. "And that's all they got to think about. They'll stay up half the night figuring out how to beat you out of a dime. They figure you're going to try to fool them, so they make allowances for that. They set the prices low enough to allow for what to do."

"Well, then, what the hell chance have I got?" asked Tennessee.

"It's up to you to figure out how to fool them more than they allow for," said Starkey.

"When the time-study man came around, I set the speed at 180. I knew damn well he would ask me to push it up, so I started low enough. He finally pushed me up to 445, and I ran the job later at 610. If I'd started out at 445, they'd have timed it at 610. Then I got him on the reaming too. I ran the reamer for him at 130 speed and .025 feed. He asked me if I couldn't run the reamer any faster than that, and I told him I had to run the reamer slow to keep the hole size. I showed him two pieces with oversize holes that the day man ran. I picked them out for the occasion! But later on I didn't have to change gears—And then there was a burring operation on the job too. For the time-study man I burred each piece after I drilled and reamed, and I ran the burring tool by automatic feed. But afterwards, I let the burring go till I drill 25 pieces or so; and I just touched them up a little by holding them under the burring tool." (Whyte, 1955, pp. 15–16)

Another example of how employees, if so motivated, can provide invalid performance data is described below:

In one case, a group, who worked together in assembling a complicated and large sized steel framework, worked out a system to be used only when the rate setter was present. They found that by tightening certain bolts first, the frame would be slightly sprung and all the other bolts would bind and be very difficult to tighten. When the rate setter was not present, they followed a different sequence and the work went much faster (Gardner, 1945).

Such instances of employees giving misleading performance estimates is certainly not confined only to the lower levels in organizations, but it often takes different forms at the higher levels.

Managers often provide invalid data when they are asked to give budgetary estimates (Argyris, 1951; Hofstede, 1967). They usually tend to ask for much larger amounts than they need, because they assume that their budget requests will be cut; and, in order to get the budget they need, they feel they must come in with a high initial budget figure. However, in instances where a low budget estimate is needed in order to get a budget or project approved, a low one may be submitted. The bargaining process they go through is similar to the one that goes on between the time-study man and the worker who is on a piece-rate plan or work standard plan. The time-study man and the superior both try to get valid data about what is possible in the future, and the employees who are subject to the control systems give invalid data and try to get as favorable a standard or budget as they can.

How frequently do employees consciously provide invalid or misleading data when standards and budgets are being set? It is impossible to come up with any hard figures, but the research on standard setting suggests that it happens most of the time when piece rates are being set (Lawler, 1971). There is less evidence with respect to how often it occurs in setting budgets, but what there is suggests it happens much of the time there too. In this situation, as in the standard-setting situation, low trust often exists. And when low trust exists, people are likely to conceal data or to communicate invalid data (Mellinger, 1956; Zand, 1972).

Bureaucratic Behavior   Performance appraisal systems like most control systems can produce rigid bureaucratic behavior that is dysfunctional as far as the goals of the organization are concerned. They can bring about such behavior because people who are subject to them behave in whatever ways will help them look good on the measures that are taken of their activities. In many cases this is a functional outcome, but in others it is not. It is those cases in which it is not functional that have "caught the eye" of some researchers, and there are a number of examples of this phenomenon in the literature. The example of the operation of an employment agency of a state government (Blau, 1955) was considered in Chapter 9. Another example is the situation faced by plant managers in the Soviet Union (Berliner, 1961). They typically are placed on a production-based pay incentive plan and are given unreasonably high production goals on the assumption that this is best for the overall economy.

The bonus system is an effective device for eliciting a high level of managerial effort, but in the context of excessively high production targets, it induces management to make certain types of decisions that are contrary to the intent of the state. The production of unplanned products, the concealment of production capacity, the falsification of reports and the deterioration of quality are the unintended consequences of the system of managerial incentives. . . . The incentives that motivate managers to strive for the fulfillment of their production targets are the same incentives that motivate them to evade the regulations of the planning system. Because of the tightness of the supply system . . . managers are compelled to defend their enterprise's position by overordering supplies, by hoarding materials and equipment and by employing expediters whose function it is to keep the enterprise supplied with materials at all costs, legal or otherwise (p. 369).

FACTORS INFLUENCING THE OUTCOMES OF PERFORMANCE EVALUATIONS

The preceding discussion of the dysfunctional consequences of performance evaluation should not obscure the fact that it has the potential to lead to a number of positive outcomes for both the individual and the organization. It *can* produce valid performance data, which can be used as a basis for rewarding employees, for long-range planning, and for training and development activities. It *can* motivate ineffective employees to improve their job performance. It *can* increase the level of both intrinsic and extrinsic motivation that is present in the employees who are appraised. It *can* provide employees with constructive feedback that will help them correct and alter their own behavior. Finally, it *can* lead to a clearer definition of the subordinate's job, and to a higher level of agreement between the superior and the subordinate about what constitutes acceptable job performance. The critical question therefore is: What factors determine whether the net effect of evaluation will be negative or positive? Fortunately, this question can be answered fairly well. It is possible to state with some certainty what the crucial factors are, and how they affect the kinds of outcomes that will be produced by performance evaluation.

Activities versus Results

The work effectiveness of any individual can be evaluated from two perspectives. It can be looked at in terms of the activities the person performs and the inputs he makes (e.g., swinging a bat at a baseball in a particular way); and it can be looked at in terms of the results of that activity or the outcome it produces (e.g., a batting average of .302). Performance evaluation systems can and do focus on only results, only activities, or some combination of the two. The research evidence on performance evaluation suggests that focusing on results produces quite a different impact than focusing on activities or on a combination of the two (Tosi, Rizzo, & Carroll, 1970).

Focusing on either activities or results to the exclusion of the other produces undesirable consequences because it causes individuals to emphasize that which is measured to the exclusion of that which is not measured. This follows from the model presented in Chapter 2, which emphasizes that people will try to perform well in those areas in which they are evaluated, particularly if the evaluation will determine whether or not they receive important rewards. A system which focuses on only results often motivates employees to behave in ways which are dysfunctional from the point of view of organizational effectiveness but which assure good scores on the measures. For example, salesmen who are evaluated on the basis of sales results sometimes get their sales in ways that produce customer ill will and that lead to high costs (e.g., promising quick deliveries which cannot be made). A system which focuses on only results also often fails to provide the type of data which is needed to counsel and develop individuals. For this to be done effectively, information is needed on *why* the person did or did not achieve the desired results. Knowing how well a person has performed in terms of results is important because it indicates whether or not development is needed, but it often does not indicate what kind of development is needed.

An appraisal approach which measures only the activities the person engages in and how they are engaged in obviously fails on a number of counts. It tends to motivate activities rather than accomplishment. For example, a system which measures salesmen only on how many calls they make and on how polite they are is likely to motivate the salesmen to be very courteous and to make a high rate of calls, but it may not motivate them to sell. The study of the government employment office cited earlier provides another example of the kind of behavior which develops when measures are activities-oriented. From the point of view of development, activities measures can be helpful. They provide a necessary but not sufficient basis on which to do developmental-type counseling. They are incomplete because they fail to signal clearly who needs counseling, and they do not leave room for the person who accomplishes things by engaging in nonstandard activities. An activities-only measurement system would identify the successful nonconformist as an individual who needs to be changed.

Our discussion so far leads to one conclusion: Any performance measurement system which is to meet the objectives of the individual and organization must measure both activities and results. In short, it must be inclusive of all the behavior and results which need to be performed and achieved. If it is not, there is likely to be rigid bureaucratic behavior, short-term results maximization, or the failure to perform certain important functions. Such inclusive evaluation is not always an easy thing to do, however. In some jobs it is difficult to measure results in a quantifiable, objective way (e.g., a personnel job). In some it is difficult to measure activities, particularly from the point of view of how they are carried out. Inevitably the measurement systems which are used end up being subjective, and for these to operate trust must be present. However, this does not negate the point that both results and activities need to be measured.

Types of Measures

Probably the single most important determinant of the effectiveness of any evaluation process is the type of measure that is used. It is crucial whether a person is appraised on the basis of a list of evaluative adjectives or on the basis of some more direct measure of his behavior and accomplishment.

Traditional Trait Ratings In the past, most organizations asked superiors to rate subordinates on a number of personality or performance traits. Figure 11-2 is an example of this type of rating form. However, there has been a definite movement away from using the trait-rating approach. More and more organizations are appraising employees against specific performance objectives. The data in Table 11-2 suggest that this trend is likely to increase. As will be discussed later, the increasing use of the objectives-oriented approach seems to be a response to the many criticisms that have been leveled against the trait-rating approach.

Trait-rating measures are particularly likely to lead to defensive reactions on the part of the person who is being appraised. When an employee is told that he has been rated low on a trait such as "responsibility," his reaction is to think of all the times he behaved in a responsible manner and to present these to the evaluator, or to argue with the evaluator about what constitutes responsible behavior. This kind of reaction is not likely to produce behavior change or to provide further valid data.

The major problem with trait ratings is that they are not sufficiently tied to concrete behavior. A great deal of research shows that evaluative, nonbehaviorally related feedback tends to produce defensiveness and rigidity (Meyer, Kay, & French, 1965). Telling a person that he is low on responsibility does not tell him how he should change his behavior. All it tells him is that his present behavior is not acceptable, and people do not react well to this kind of feedback. Because trait ratings are not tied to behavior, it is difficult to set goals and objectives for the future, and this serves to reduce the motivational potential of the process. The motivational potential is further reduced by the fact that it is difficult to tie rewards to specific behaviors. Thus, discussion involving traits rarely leads to better job

PERSONAL SKILLS	RATING	COMMENTS (IF DESIRED)
Articulateness		
Diagnostic ability		
Has a proprietary interest		
Takes calculated risks		
Generates good new ideas		
Gets things done		
Decisive		
Plans and prepares		
Follows up and expedites		
Promotes own ideas		
Communicates effectively		
Creativity		
Accurate		
Scientific integrity		
Makes and meets commitments		
Relationship with boss		
Relationship with associates		
Relationship with subordinates		
Relationship with outsiders		
Leadership		
Tenacity		
Self-development/own initiative		
Develop subordinates		
Managerial judgment		

Figure 11-2   A trait-rating form.

definition or to productive superior-subordinate communications. It is also obvious that trait ratings do not form a good basis upon which to plan developmental activities. How do you train someone to be more responsible?

Trait ratings are also difficult to do and tend to produce invalid data for several reasons. Superiors tend to dislike rating their subordinates on traits such as responsibility (Campbell et al., 1970). Further, they have

Table 11-2   How 141 Companies Appraise Managers, 1964

Type of Appraisal	Present use, percent			Future emphasis, percent		
	None	Little	Much	Less	Same	More
Trait appraisal	26	28	46	24	63	13
Appraisal against specific objectives	39	38	23	2	49	49

Note: Columns do not add to 100 percent because some companies use more than one type of program.
Source: Wickstrom (1964, p. 126).

trouble defining and discriminating among the various traits. Subordinates too tend to dislike trait ratings because they fail to provide the kind of feedback that they want.

Single Global Ratings   Instead of having superiors rate their subordinates on a number of separate traits, many organizations simply ask for a single rating of overall job performance. Such ratings can be done validly by many superiors. There is, for example, evidence that separate raters agree when they assess the performance level of a given performer. Such ratings have additional advantages: (1) an employee is compared with his peers and thus relative standing is apparent; (2) a global rating includes a number of behaviors and thus tends to be rather inclusive; and (3) superiors are willing to make such ratings. Because of their advantages, global ratings are often useful as one basis for making raise and promotion decisions.

How helpful are data from this kind of global rating in providing subordinates with useful feedback and in forming the basis for developmental counseling? The answer would seem to be not very helpful, because like trait ratings they are far removed from actual behavior. In fact, one of their advantages from the organization's point of view is that they are global summaries of many pieces of behavior. Because they are global summaries, they can be helpful in making certain kinds of personnel decisions (e.g., pay and promotion decisions); however, because they are global, they do not provide behavior-related feedback to those people who are evaluated. They, like trait ratings, often produce defensiveness on the part of the person who is evaluated. They also do not tend to produce better job definitions, greater motivation, or well-defined training objectives. The reason for this is their failure to deal with behavior. In order to improve job definitions, specific behaviors need to be discussed. In order to produce increased motivation, specific behavioral objectives need to be set, and rewards tied to their achievement. In order to plan developmental programs, it is necessary to identify those behaviors which are missing or are being performed poorly by the person. Global performance ratings do not relate directly to behavior and because of this do not contribute to motivation, job definition, or development planning.

Subjective global ratings of performance are particularly likely to produce negative reactions on the part of individuals when the trust level in an organization is low. Figure 11-3 illustrates this point by showing that, when trust is high, relatively subjective measures can be used but when it is low they cannot. When trust is low and they are used, subordinates tend to become defensive and to reject the evaluations. They do not try to change their behavior when they are poorly evaluated, and they do not believe that good performance will be rewarded.

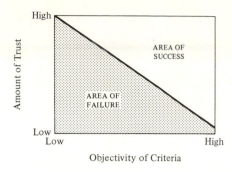

Figure 11-3   Relationship of trust and the objectivity of performance criteria to success of appraisal.

Behaviorally Anchored Ratings   Some researchers have suggested that ratings can be improved if the rating scales include behavior observations (Campbell et al., 1970). Figure 11-4 presents a behavior-rating scale that was developed by Dunnette et al. (1968) for department managers in retail stores. The research done so far does indicate that scales of this type can yield better ratings and they can lead to clearer job definitions. Still, they may not give individuals the kind of specific behavior-related feedback they need for development, and they may not provide them with motivating objectives to try for in the future.

Objectives-oriented Ratings   In recent years, programs stressing management by objectives (MBO) have provided an alternative to the various rating approaches. They typically involve superior and subordinate agreement on specific performance objectives and on how achievement of these objectives is to be measured. This is usually done as part of an overall organization development and improvement program, and the effectiveness of MBO for this purpose will be discussed in Chapter 15. Here the focus will be on the effects of evaluating employees on the basis of agreed-upon objectives.

The arguments that can be mustered in favor of evaluating people in terms of agreed-upon measures of results are persuasive (see e.g., Meyer, Kay, & French, 1965; Drucker, 1954; Odiorne, 1965). Setting specific goals and objectives for future performance should lead to increased motivation and performance since, as was noted earlier, goals can motivate behavior. Superiors should be better able to rate whether subordinates did or did not perform acceptably since it is a matter of determining whether an agreed-upon goal was reached. The validity and reliability of the performance ratings that are obtained should increase since the bases of performance ratings are more explicit and objective. Since it is possible to talk about specific accomplishments, subordinates should be less defensive and better able to measure their own performance. People tend to be less defensive

Could be expected to exchange a blouse purchased in a distant town and to impress the customer so much that she would buy three dresses and three pairs of shoes.

Could be expected to smooth things over beautifully with an irate customer who returned a sweater with a hole in it and turn her into a satisfied customer.

Could be expected to be friendly and tactful and to agree to reline a coat for a customer who wants a new coat because the lining had worn out in "only" two years.

Could be expected to courteously exchange a pair of gloves that are too small.

Could be expected to handle the after-Christmas rush of refunds and exchanges in a reasonable manner.

Could be expected to make a refund for a sweater only if the customer insists.

Could be expected to be quite abrupt with customers who want to exchange merchandise for a different color or style.

Could be expected to tell a customer that a "six-week-old" order could not be changed even though the merchandise had actually been ordered only two weeks previously.

Could be expected to tell a customer who tried to return a shirt bought in Hawaii that a store in the States had no use for a Hawaiian shirt.

Figure 11–4 Department manager job behavior rating scale for the dimension "handling customer complaints and making adjustments." (Source: Dunnette et al., 1968)

when the discussion centers in a minimally evaluative way on their accomplishments than when they are given feedback in terms of highly subjective personality traits. Finally, since specific behaviors are involved, the discussion should contribute to the superior's and the subordinate's better understanding of each other's jobs.

Although it may sound at this point as if we are arguing that by using objective results-related measures most organizations can solve their performance evaluation problems, we aren't. No system will ever do this because of the many conflicts which are present in the performance evaluation situation. It is true, however, that, as a general rule, they are superior to the traditional trait-rating approach. It is not clear, though, that they are always superior to the kind of rating approach shown in Figure 11-4. There are many jobs for which it is extremely difficult to develop objective performance measures. In these cases, global or behaviorally anchored ratings may prove to be more useful.

It is frequently overlooked that objectives measures are not always helpful when promotion and pay decisions have to be made, because they frequently do not produce the kinds of comparisons between people that are most helpful in making these decisions. Objectives are supposed to be set according to how difficult they are for a given person to accomplish. Thus, it is possible for two people to accomplish their objectives and for them to be performing at vastly different levels. The question then arises as to how these individuals should be evaluated for the purpose of giving a pay raise or promotion.

Table 11-3 summarizes what has been said so far about the various approaches to measuring performance. It shows that objectives-oriented performance measures tend to be the best on an overall basis, although the approach does have the "comparison" problems mentioned above. Both the behaviorally anchored and the single global rating have some merit, but also have a number of deficiencies. The traditional trait-rating approach seems least defensible, yet it continues to be used in a number of organizations.

The Degree to Which Measures Can Be Influenced

Performance measures vary in the degree to which they can be influenced by the behavior of the person whose performance is being evaluated. An individual's reaction to being evaluated and rewarded on the basis of a particular measure is very much determined by how much he feels he can affect the measure by his job behavior. As was explained earlier, for motivation to be present the individual has to feel that his effort influences his reward level. In the situation where performance measures are not seen as influenceable, there is little chance of the person seeing a connection

Table 11-3 Evaluation of Four Approaches to Measuring Performance

	Traditional trait rating	Single global rating	Behaviorally anchored ratings	Objectives oriented evaluation
Acceptability to superior and subordinate	Poor	Moderate	Good	Good
Counseling and development information	Poor	Poor	Moderate	Good if it includes activities measures
Salary and reward administration	Poor	Moderate to good	Good	Moderate
Motivation based upon goal setting	Poor	Poor	Poor	Good
Clarify nature of job	Poor	Poor	Moderate to good	Good

between his effort and his rewards. Further, when measures which are felt to be noninfluenceable are used, people frequently become resentful to the extent that they are willing to tamper with the measures so that they will produce invalid data which will help the person achieve his personal goals.

In practice, it is not a question of some measures being influenceable and some not. It is a question of degree. Most measures are to some degree influenceable. Profits, for example, are influenced by factors over which a manager has no control, but they are also influenced by things over which he may have considerable control. As a general rule, measures of activities are more influenceable than are measures of results. Regardless of whether activities or results are being evaluated, however, it is important to determine how influenceable the various measures are in a given situation. Only if this is done will it be possible to predict the consequences of using the measures. There is no firm answer to the question of how influenceable a measure should be. It is clear, however, that as measures become less influenceable they tend to produce more dysfunctional consequences.

The Difficulty of Goals

When the performance evaluation process involves the setting of goals or standards, a critical issue is how difficult the goals are seen to be. Perceived goal difficulty has a strong impact on the degree to which valid data can be obtained and on employee motivation. Too difficult goals can lead to invalid data and on occasion can encourage bureaucratic-type behavior. When employees feel the performance goals which are set for them are unreachable or virtually impossible to obtain, they tend to either give up or distort the system in order to make it appear they have reached them. The example cited earlier of the Russian plant managers shows how a system can be distorted. First, invalid data can be sent through the evaluation system in order to make performance look better. In the Russian example, reports were falsified and production capacity hidden. Second, dysfunctional activities can be carried out in order to achieve the difficult goal. This is precisely what happened in the Russian example, where such dysfunctional actions as hoarding materials were undertaken in order to achieve a high productivity level.

Goals which are seen to be too difficult can also end up motivating poor performance. When faced with very difficult goals, individuals often engage in a kind of implicit bargaining with organizations. They restrict their performance so that it falls well below the goals in order to convince their organization that the goals are much too difficult. Of course, it is also the case that goals which are too easy to obtain can have a negative effect on performance. Research has shown that when individuals are given goals that are too easy they tend to perform poorly because they are content simply to achieve these low goals.

Much of the experimental work on achievement motivation stresses that it is highest on tasks that participants see as moderately difficult (Atkinson, 1964). Apparently, when people who have strong achievement needs are performing a task that they see themselves as having about a 50:50 chance of completing successfully, good performance on the task becomes especially attractive to them. It is attractive to them because it becomes associated with feelings of achievement and competence. This suggests that standards and goals which are seen as moderately difficult to achieve will produce the highest levels of intrinsic motivation. One implication of this finding—if achievement motivation is to be emphasized—is that budgets, production standards, and other performance goals should be set so that the employees have about a 50:50 chance of reaching them.

Three studies have considered the relationship between the perceived difficulty of obtaining a given budget level and the motivation of people to achieve that budget (Stedry, 1960; Stedry & Kay, 1964; Hofstede, 1967). Basically, all the studies suggest that intrinsic motivation is most likely to be present when standards or budgets are set that have approximately a 50:50 chance of being obtained. Very difficult goals seem to have a positive effect on performance *only* when they are accepted. Easy goals seem to have little positive effect on intrinsic motivation because, even if they are accomplished, performance is still rated as poor. These studies must be interpreted cautiously, however, because they are all based on limited samples of situations and people. Furthermore, the results of these and other studies show that goal difficulty is only one determinant of motivation. In fact, our previously discussed model (Chapter 2) suggests that extrinsic motivation may be highest when easy goals are set. It is not going too far to say, however, that intrinsic motivation is aided when moderately difficult goals are set and that if too difficult goals are set, serious dysfunctional consequences can occur.

Time between Appraisals

If performance appraisals are either too far apart or too close together, the feedback may be meaningless to the person, and the generation of invalid data may be encouraged. On any job it takes a certain amount of time for the impact of an individual's actions to show up in a measurable form. This fact has been utilized by Jaques (1961) to develop a measure labeled "time span of discretion." It is defined as the time it takes for substandard performance to show up. In some jobs the time span is very short, perhaps only a few minutes, while in others it is several years. As might be expected, the time span of discretion tends to be much longer for higher-level management jobs than it is for lower-level jobs. Problems can develop when the time between performance evaluation sessions is either much longer or much shorter than is the time span of discretion.

When the time between performance evaluation is shorter than the time span of discretion, problems are created because it is difficult to evaluate the performance of the jobholder. Any measures that are taken will be seen as premature and as not accurately reflecting the individual's performance. Any personnel or other decisions that the organization might make on the basis of these measures could be quite wrong; and, in fact, by waiting a while longer the results might look very different. Premature performance measures simply are not a good basis upon which to make pay, promotion, or development decisions. Problems are also created, however, when the time span of discretion is much shorter than the interval between performance appraisals. In this situation individuals tend to see the feedback as irrelevant to their present performance, and they experience a lack of feedback during the period between appraisals. It is also difficult for the organization to clearly relate rewards such as pay to performance, because there is inevitably a long separation between the performance and the pay change.

Subordinate Participation

Traditionally, the performance appraisal process has been seen as a super-ior-active–subordinate-passive situation (Wexley et al., 1973; White & Barnes, 1971). The superior let the subordinate know where he stood, and thus the superior was active in the process; the subordinate, on the other hand, was to "find out" about his performance and therefore was a passive but attentive listener. Since the appearance of the "classic" article by McGregor in 1957, however, this view of how the process should take place has been more and more frequently questioned. McGregor suggested that the subordinate should take an active role in establishing performance goals and in appraising his progress toward these goals. This view has been echoed by subsequent writers: "The individual establishes performance targets for each of his responsibilities for the forthcoming period. . . . He meets with his superior to discuss his target program. . . . The superior and the subordi-nate meet at the end of the period to discuss the results of the subordinate's efforts to meet the targets he had previously established" (Kindall & Gatza, 1963, p. 157).

Why should there be subordinate participation in the performance appraisal process? Most writers who have argued for participation have also argued for appraisals being done on the basis of goal setting and not on the basis of traits. Participation can help in setting meaningful, motivating goals and standards. It is not necessary if trait ratings are done. The subordinate-passive view is highly congruent with the trait-rating approach since there is little the subordinate can contribute to his own appraisal. Thus, the argument for participation is tied to the argument that appraisals should be based upon meaningful, mutually agreed-upon goals.

The presumed advantages of having appraisals based upon goals include greater motivation, less defensiveness, and better data upon which to base training and development decisions. If these advantages are to be realized, however, the subordinates must be committed to the goals or objectives that are set, and they must feel the goals are reasonable. Participation can help produce real subordinate commitment to goals and standards. There is a large amount of literature which supports the view that when most subordinates are given the opportunity to participate in deci-sions, they tend to be more committed to those decisions. The decisions become "their" decisions, and they are more motivated to see that the decisions work out. Apparently, the self-esteem and feelings of competence of the subordinates become involved, and they feel badly if a decision they make turns out poorly. The same thing can occur when subordinates participate in setting their own goals. They feel a sense of "ownership" of the goals, and their feelings of self-esteem and competence become more closely tied to their attempts to achieve the goals.

Participation can also be helpful in establishing reasonable goals. Subordinates frequently have important unique information about the level at which the goals should be set. This point is clearly illustrated in situations where workers outsmart time-study men in getting piece rates set. Further, there are many technical and managerial jobs where the subordinate simply knows more about the job than the superior does. As was pointed out previously, goal difficulty is an important influence on motivation. There is always the danger that unilaterally set goals may be set unrealistically easy or hard because the superior lacks information about where they should be set. In many cases this can be corrected by having the subordinates be involved in the goal setting. If an open and trusting relationship exists, they often are willing to contribute the information they have so that reasonable goals can be set. Of course,if basically good relationships do not already exist between a superior and his subordinates, then attempts to have them participate in the goal-setting process by contributing pertinent information are likely to fail.

Subordinate participation need not be limited solely to the goal-setting aspect of the appraisal process. Subordinates can also participate in deciding how performance will be measured and in evaluating their own performance relative to the goals. Here, too, they are likely to have information that the superior does not have, and because of this they can contribute meaningfully to the evaluation process. In addition, they are much more likely to feel that they have been fairly appraised if they are given an opportunity to make inputs to the process. This is particularly important if the results of the appraisal are to be used to determine directly their pay and promotion prospects.

Subordinates do not always respond positively to the opportunity to participate in goal-setting and performance evaluation sessions. Particularly when budgets and piece rates are set, they sometimes try to get goals set for themselves that are easily achieved; and, when their performance is being discussed, they sometimes are motivated to present only the positive aspects of their performance. Others apparently simply prefer to be told what to do because they find participation to be uncomfortable. One study (Meyer, Kay, & French, 1965), in fact, found that managers who were not used to participation usually worked best when goals were set for them. It may be that if individuals are given practice in meaningful participation in goal setting, they will eventually prefer this approach despite any initial reluctance. So far, however, there is no evidence to support this point, but there is evidence which suggests that most people do prefer to participate (Wexley et al., 1973).

Poor communication—whether intended or not—and the resultant setting of inappropriate goals represent a major problem for all performance appraisal systems that emphasize subordinate involvement. There is no simple way to prevent this from happening. It is clear that the superior has a major responsibility to try to see that it does not happen, thus he must take an active role in the process even when subordinates are asked to participate actively in it. It is also clear that communication problems are most likely to occur when the results of the appraisal will influence the reception of important rewards.

Relationship of Appraisal to the Reward System

A number of writers have argued that salary actions should be separated from the appraisal process, because when they are discussed they dominate all else. It was noted earlier in our discussion of the individual-organization conflicts which are present during appraisal that the individual's desire for rewards conflicts with the organization's need for valid data. Thus, it is not surprising that it is difficult for a superior and subordinate to discuss meaningfully at the same time such matters as salary, developmental needs, past performance, and future goals. This creates a problem with respect to pay or for that matter any important extrinsic rewards. On the one hand, if an outcome is to be a significant motivator of performance, it must be closely tied to performance. This can only be done well if a performance appraisal program exists which measures performance validly and makes explicit the pay-performance connection.

On the other hand, when reward decisions are tied into the performance appraisal process, a number of negative things seem to happen (as mentioned earlier in the chapter). The subordinate's stance toward the process changes. Suddenly it is a contest in which he has to present himself in the best possible light to get a raise, be promoted, or whatever. He has to make himself look good on those measures that will determine his rewards. In some cases this may lead to the kind of rigid bureaucratic behavior that was described earlier. In other cases it may lead to the subordinate's providing invalid data about the performance he is capable of doing so that his objectives will be set low (Whyte, 1955). In still others, it may lead to the subordinate's producing invalid data about how he has performed so that he will "look good." Making the discussion of the distribution of important rewards a direct part of the appraisal process often leads to defensive reactions when constructive criticism is intended, and it becomes difficult to plan training and development activities. Because of the defensiveness that is produced and because of the difficulty of setting moderately difficult goals when rewards are tied into the appraisal system, it is also difficult to create those conditions which lead to intrinsic motivation.

Why base extrinsic rewards on the results of performance appraisal systems? The answer is quite simple: Only by relating rewards such as pay to good performance is it possible to generate strong extrinsic motivation. Motivation based on extrinsic rewards is often functional for an organization. Although we talk about rigid bureaucratic-type behavior being dysfunctional, it is important to remember that in many cases this kind of behavior is just what is wanted by the organization (e.g., on many lower-level, repetitious jobs). (Whether it *should be* desired by the organization is another question.) Many parts of some organizations are designed to function well when people behave in relatively rigid, predictable, repetitious ways. The problem is that on some occasions other kinds of behavior are required.

What is the answer? Must an organization choose between having extrinsically motivated employees and having intrinsically motivated, nondefensive employees? To some extent probably yes, but actions can be taken to minimize the negative effects of tying extrinsic rewards to the outcomes of the performance appraisal process. Some of them have already been mentioned. They include having employees participate in the evaluation process, the development of objective measures, and the setting of moderately difficult goals. Another is to operate two somewhat separate appraisal systems: one to handle extrinsic rewards; the other for development, training, and intrinsic-motivation purposes.

The issue of how much to separate or combine the various appraisal functions is a crucial one. The range of alternatives seems to be from having all the functions of the appraisal system built into the same session to having completely separate appraisal systems. Either of these extremes would appear to be unsatisfactory to both the individual and the organization. When everything is combined into a single system, it has been demonstrated that many important things tend to get neglected (e.g., development and training). Having completely separate systems ignores the natural spillover from one to the other. One possibility is to have relatively separate sessions, i.e., sessions separated by time, for the different functions. If development discussion sessions are held after the reward decisions have been made and communicated, it may be possible to talk about development needs without salary too strongly lurking in the background. The developmental sessions should provide the individual with a chance to get feedback on his performance in a relatively nonevaluative setting and provide him with the opportunity to plan his growth and development. These are functional outcomes for both the individual and the organization. At best, achieving these outcomes is no easy task.

OUTCOMES FROM THE APPRAISAL PROCESS: CONCLUSIONS

This chapter began by pointing out the important conflicts which exist among the objectives organizations and individuals would like to accomplish in the performance appraisal process. It should be obvious that because of the conflicts rarely are all the goals of the individual and the organization achieved in this realm. In fact, unless organizations carefully structure their programs to evaluate work effectiveness, none of their goals may be achieved. The research evidence conclusively establishes that performance appraisal is difficult to do because of the important psychological processes which are present when evaluation takes place. What can individuals and organizations realistically expect, then, to get out of a performance appraisal program? The answer to this question depends very much on how it is done. If it is done correctly, it might accomplish many of the objectives they both would like it to.

But what does doing a performance appraisal correctly mean? Research suggests that it means:

1 Measures are used that are inclusive of all the behaviors and results that should be performed.

2 The measures used are tied to behavior and as far as possible are objective in nature.

3 Moderately difficult goals and standards for future performance are set.

4 Measures are used that can be influenced by an individual's behavior.

5 Appraisals are done on a time cycle that approximates the time it takes the measures to reflect the behavior of the persons being evaluated.

6 The persons being evaluated have an opportunity to participate in the appraisal process.

7 The appraisal system interacts effectively with the reward system.

If both the individual and the organization benefit when appraisals are done in this manner, why aren't they always done this way? There are a number of reasons! First, it is simply very difficult to do appraisals this way. It is time consuming, and it takes a large commitment on the part of both superiors and subordinates. Second, they require a certain kind of organizational climate if they are to be done. They cannot work well in a traditional authoritarian-type organization. Many organizations do not have the kind of open, trusting climate that is required to do them. Third, many superiors are not trained to do these kinds of appraisals, which involve giving meaningful and helpful feedback, setting goals participatively, and the like. Finally, there is the understandable ambivalence about appraisal and evaluation which both superiors and subordinates share.

REVIEW AND DISCUSSION QUESTIONS

1 Consider the various purposes of performance appraisal shown in Figure 11-1. Taking these purposes two at a time, consider the compatibility of each such pair.

2   How might the conflicts in performance appraisal you found in answering
    question 1 be resolved so as to satisfy simultaneously both the individual and the
    organization?
3   The "vanishing performance appraisal" phenomenon was mentioned in this
    chapter. What are the likely consequences of this phenomenon for the individual
    and the organization? Does this suggest the need for mandatory formal perform-
    ance appraisal sessions?
4   What steps can be taken by the appraiser to minimize defensiveness on the part of
    the individual appraised in evaluation sessions?
5   Compare and contrast the various rating schemes (e.g., trait, global ratings,
    behaviorally anchored ratings, etc.) in terms of their utility as appraisal mechan-
    isms.
6   What factors account for the relationship between goal difficulty and motivation?
7   Is there a relationship between the "time span of discretion" notion and the
    proper timing of feedback about performance? What is it?
8   Employees have at times been allowed to (1) set their own goals and (2) evaluate
    the degree to which they have reached such goals. What are the potential benefits
    that the organization might derive from allowing individuals such discretion? Are
    there disadvantages? Can "participative" techniques be utilized successfully with
    all types of employees?
9   Why should performance appraisal be separated from appraisal concerned with
    salary actions? How much separation is possible?

Chapter 12

Rewarding Work Effectiveness

Once work effectiveness is evaluated, then it can be rewarded. This leads us, in turn, to one of the most important features of work organizations: the power they have to give individuals extrinsic rewards. These rewards are allocated to individuals by organizations for many reasons and in different ways. Sometimes, as was noted in the previous chapter, they are given differentially on the basis of the results of performance evaluations. When this occurs, it strongly influences the nature of the evaluations. At other times, the same rewards are given to everyone who qualifies as a member of the organization.

The more obvious extrinsic rewards that most organizations can and do give include pay, promotion, more interesting work, and a large number of status symbols and fringe benefits. In this chapter we are concerned only with extrinsic rewards such as these—tangible rewards that can be directly given by the organization. In several of the other chapters we have dealt with intrinsic, intangible rewards such as feelings of competence and self-actualization. In the case of intrinsic rewards, all the organization can do is create conditions (e.g., particular job designs) that make it possible for the individual to experience them. In the end the individual must reward himself. Extrinsic rewards, on the other hand, differ in two important ways: they must be given to the individual or he must obtain them, and they are tangible and potentially visible to others.

In this chapter we focus on how the way extrinsic rewards are distributed affects both the individuals who receive them and the organizations that give them. The major emphasis is placed on the rewards of pay and promotion because they are given in all work organizations, they typically are the most valued of the extrinsic rewards that organizations give, and they have been subjected to the most research. With few exceptions, what is said about the effects of pay and promotion practices can be said about the effects of similar practices involving any extrinsic reward. Thus general principles about how individuals react to different extrinsic reward practices and about the advantages to organizations and individuals of distributing rewards in certain ways can be developed by focusing on a few extrinsic rewards.

THE ROLE OF EXTRINSIC REWARDS: THE ORGANIZATION'S PERSPECTIVE

Why do organizations give extrinsic rewards? Perhaps the simplest and most valid answer to the question is to motivate people to behave in ways they would not otherwise behave. In order to function effectively, most work organizations need people to do tasks that in the absence of extrinsic rewards they often would not do. Basically, organizations use extrinsic rewards to motivate three kinds of behavior: membership, attendance, and performance. People simply do not casually join organizations, as was pointed out in Chapter 5; they have to be motivated to do it. Organizations often have to compete for members, and one way they compete is by offering more extrinsic rewards than competitors do. Partially separate from the joining and membership maintenance decision is the attendance decision. Membership does not guarantee regular attendance. Many people maintain membership in organizations but do not regularly attend organizational functions—it is one thing to accept an assembly-line job; it is quite another to show up regularly to work on it. Since for most organizations having employees who attend regularly is important, they sometimes give extrinsic rewards (e.g., financial bonuses) for attendance. Finally, although attendance is a necessary condition for acceptable performance, it is not a sufficient condition for it. Thus, many organizations also try to use extrinsic rewards in order to motivate performance.

THE ROLE OF EXTRINSIC REWARDS:
THE INDIVIDUAL'S PERSPECTIVE

The models presented in Chapters 2 and 4 are helpful for understanding how individuals react to the reward practices of organizations. These models stressed that the impact of a particular outcome (e.g., an extrinsic reward) on motivation is determined by both how attractive it is and what one has to do to obtain it. The more attractive a reward, the more it can motivate people to behave in certain ways in order to obtain it. It was emphasized in Chapter 2 that there are large individual differences in how much value individuals attach to the different outcomes that are available. For example, research suggests that for some people pay clearly is first in importance, while for others it is not very important. Extrinsic rewards are also important to different people for different reasons; for example, pay is important to some people because it buys food, to others it is important because it symbolizes success and positive feedback. In addition, it was stressed in Chapter 2 that the value people place on outcomes changes over time, so that what is valued now by a person may *not* be valued at a later time by the same person. There is evidence, for example, that as some people accumulate more money, pay becomes less important to them.

Organizations have relatively little control over the value people place on extrinsic rewards. This is largely a function of the person's needs. The organization can, however, influence what employees have to do in order to obtain the rewards. Individuals react to the offering of important rewards by doing what is required in order to attain them. Thus, how an organization *distributes* rewards has a very important influence on the behavior of individuals. Stated simply, *organizations tend to motivate the kind of behavior they reward*. Thus, one effective way to understand the behavior of individuals in an organization is to look generally at how rewards are given in the organization and specifically at what individuals have to do to obtain the rewards they value.

Finally, it was also pointed out in Chapter 2 that individuals seek many outcomes and that they have affective reactions to whether or not they receive the outcomes they desire. These reactions tend to generate feelings of satisfaction and dissatisfaction, and they affect a person's willingness to join a union, to look for another job, and to come to work. It was also argued in Chapter 2 that individuals do not simply want more extrinsic rewards; rather, they want what they feel is a fair level of reward. Thus, depending upon how it is perceived by the employee, an organization's reward system may or may not motivate the kind of behavior it was designed to motivate; and the employees may or may not be satisfied with the rewards they receive from it. Whether employees are highly *motivated* or not will depend on how attractive the rewards are and what the employees feel they have to do to obtain the rewards. Whether employees are *satisfied* or not will depend on how much in the way of rewards they receive relative to how much they feel they should receive.

At this point it should be obvious that the reactions of individuals to extrinsic rewards are complex. However, they can be understood if the points made in Chapters 2 and 4 are kept in mind as we consider the effects of reward systems that have been designed to motivate membership, attendance, and performance.

REWARD SYSTEMS AND MEMBERSHIP

Motivating the best people to join and remain members of an organization is not simply a matter of paying everyone a high salary. Offering high levels of extrinsic rewards may attract many people to the occupations and to the organizations that offer the rewards, but it will not guarantee either their continued membership or their attendance. It also will not necessarily attract those people who have the most to contribute.

Occupational and Organizational Choice

If we consider first the issue of occupational choice, the evidence which was reviewed in Chapter 5 shows that individuals' choices are strongly influenced by how obtainable the rewards they value are in different occupations. Thus, it is not surprising that extrinsic rewards can influence occupational choice such that people who value money highly tend to choose business occupations. In one study (Rosenberg, 1957) an extrinsic reward index was developed which measured the degree to which people value outcomes like money. Information collected from nearly 4,000 students showed that those choosing business occupations consistently scored highest on this index. Other studies have shown that students see business as providing the greatest economic returns (Lawler, 1971).

Evidence in Chapter 5 also showed that in organizational choice, like occupational choice people choose positions in which they feel they can obtain the rewards they value. It seems safe to conclude, then, that organizations can attract members by offering high extrinsic rewards. However, it is also important to note that they will not attract a random sample of the population. They will tend to attract those people who value the extrinsic rewards they offer. Thus, if they pay high salaries, this will attract people who tend to value high pay. This may be functional, particularly if the organization is prepared to use pay to motivate performance; but it also can be expensive and dysfunctional.

Remaining with an Organization

Just as extrinsic rewards can be used to get individuals to join an organization, they can and are used to motivate individuals to remain as members of an organization. Satisfaction with extrinsic rewards does clearly influence employee turnover. Figure 12-1 shows the usual results of the different kinds of reward dissatisfaction. As the figure shows, dissatisfying outside comparisons tend to produce turnover. This means that by paying high wages it is possible to reduce turnover. The issues involved in using extrinsic rewards this way are complex, however, and, as will be seen, this use of extrinsic rewards can lead to dysfunctional as well as functional consequences.

Intraorganizational Equity   Attracting and holding employees with high extrinsic rewards can raise problems of intraorganizational pay equity. People can feel fairly paid with respect to the outside world and yet feel unfairly paid if they think there are other people who contribute less to the organization than they do but receive similar or more rewards. This type of situation is not likely to lead to turnover, but it is sure to lead to feelings of resentment and to high levels of political activity.

Problems of intraorganizational equity are often created when high pay is given to new employees in order to attract them to the organization. In the past, for example, computer programmers were often brought into an organization at very high wages because of conditions dictated by the labor market. This caused many current employees to feel inequitably treated, not because they were underpaid relative to the market for their own skills but because they felt that within the organization they were underpaid relative to the newly hired computer programmers. The result was not turnover, but it was dysfunctional complaints and dissatisfaction.

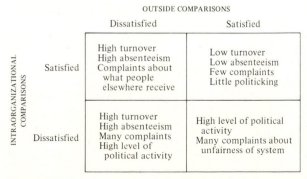

Figure 12–1   Consequences of different types of reward dissatisfaction.

Holding Employees Only by Extrinsic Rewards   An organization that retains its employees largely or only by giving extensive extrinsic rewards can end up with a group of apathetic, uninvolved workers. The situation of the automobile assembly-line worker provides a good example (Walker & Guest, 1952). He makes more money than he can anywhere else (often a dollar an hour or so more), and so he stays on the job. However, he typically dislikes the work, is not attached or committed to the organization, and is often a poor worker because he does not find performing well to be rewarding. In extreme cases he even engages in sabotage and other dysfunctional behavior in order to relieve his boredom. This type of individual-organization relationship can hardly be viewed as healthy for either party.

Effects of Different Distributions of Extrinsic Rewards   Depending upon how they are distributed, extrinsic rewards can even hold the wrong people in the organization. Most organizations have only a limited ability to give pay and other extrinsic rewards; thus, they must make some difficult decisions about how to allocate the extrinsic rewards they can give among the various employees in the organization. One strategy is to concentrate on giving everyone similar-sized raises to keep their salaries in line with the marketplace. Another is to distribute the money systematically according to performance or some other criterion. These strategies can have a significant and quite different impact on who stays with the organization.

Giving essentially across-the-board raises does not mean that everyone will be equally satisfied with his raise. Quite to the contrary, it means that poor performers will be relatively better satisfied than the good performers. Poor performers tend to feel they deserve less in the way of rewards, and thus they react more favorably to a given pay raise than do good performers (Porter & Lawler, 1968a). Further, the outside job market tends to be better for good performers than for poor ones. By giving everyone similar raises, organizations may end up putting their poor performers above the market and their good performers below it. This makes the good performers ripe candidates for higher-paying jobs in other organizations and locks in the poor performers because they cannot afford to take jobs elsewhere.

Effects of Deferred Extrinsic Rewards   Such extrinsic rewards as stock options and deferred-pay plans are often used by business organizations to attract and hold managerial talent. Like high salaries, they attract a certain kind of person, and because of this, their use raises the same kinds of problems that are involved when high salaries are used. There is one important way, however, that the stock option and deferred-bonus plans differ from the simple practice of paying high salaries. This approach postpones payment for present performance to some time in the future. A good example of this is the kind of bonus plans used by some automobile companies. A manager earns a performance bonus based upon his year's work, but this bonus is paid to him over the next five years. After the individual has been in the organization for a few years, he is owed bonus money for several previous years' performance; and for higher-level managers, this may amount to thousands of dollars. All the manager has to do to receive this money is to remain a member of the organization. Clearly, this creates a strong financial motivation for him to stay with the company. Much the same situation can develop with stock option plans, since the receipt of the stock usually depends upon a manager's staying with the company.

There has been very little research on the effectiveness of deferred-compensation and pension plans, but it is reasonable to assume that they probably do lock many employees into organizations. In some organizations this is even referred to as the "golden padlock." The real question from the point of view of organizational effectiveness, however, concerns who is locked in. There are some indications that these plans may lock in the wrong people. They may retain only the less effective and less desirable employees. As has been illustrated time and again, when one organization wants a good employee from another organization badly enough, it is willing to pay off or buy out any bonuses, retirement, or stock options that he might have built up in his current firm. However, rarely is a competing organization willing to buy out the options of a poor performer, even though they may be somewhat less than those held by a good performer. Thus, the poor performer is in no position to leave an organization, while the good performer is, just as he would be if there were no plan to lock him in. Thus, these plans, as is the case where everyone's salary is kept high, can create a situation in which voluntary turnover may still take place among the good performers, while the desirable voluntary turnover of poorer performers is sharply reduced.

Nonbusiness organizations are less likely to try to retain their employees by using such extrinsic rewards as pay. They do, however, use such status symbols as titles and large offices. From the point of view of retention, giving everyone a large office or other status symbols can have the same negative effects as giving everyone a pay raise or stock option, if the status symbol is important.

Who Is Satisfied with His Extrinsic Rewards?

Our discussion of the use of extrinsic rewards to motivate membership raises some interesting issues about satisfaction with extrinsic rewards. Specifically, it raises the question of what organizations can do to influence satisfaction with extrinsic rewards and the question of who should be satisfied with their extrinsic rewards. The greater individuals perceive their inputs and contributions to be, the more they feel they should receive in extrinsic rewards. However, individuals differ in how much they feel different kinds of inputs should be weighted in determining rewards. For example, a research study indicates that managers tend to feel that their pay should be based on their performance and on those nonperformance input factors in which they excel (Lawler, 1966). Those managers who had been with an organization a long time thought that seniority should be an important determinant of reward level; those who were well educated thought that education level should be, and so on. There is evidence that some individuals tend to value their inputs more highly than others do. For example, as was pointed out in the last chapter, most individuals think they are above-average performers. Not surprisingly, most individuals also feel they should be paid highly in comparison to other members of the organization.

Because of the differences that exist among individuals in their view of what should determine reward level, and the tendency of individuals to overvalue their inputs, it is impossible for any organization to create a reward system that will satisfy everyone with their intraorganizational reward comparisons. Every system is bound to attach less importance to some inputs than a particular group of individuals thinks is fair and to value some individuals' inputs less than they value them. It is possible, however, for an organization to decide to have all members highly rewarded in comparison with the outside world and thereby have low turnover. However, organizations typically lack the resources to reward everyone highly enough to assure they will all be satisfied. Thus, organizations are often forced to decide who will be satisfied with their rewards.

An organization may be most effective if it contains some employees who are very much satisfied with their extrinsic rewards, a large group who are above average in their satisfaction, and a third group who are dissatisfied. This kind of variation in satisfaction will contribute to organizational effectiveness, however, only if careful control is maintained over who is dissatisfied and who is satisfied. Stated most simply the best performers must be the most satisfied and the worst performers the least satisfied. The reason for this should be evident; dissatisfied employees quit their jobs, are absent more, etc. It is far better to risk losing poor performers through turnover than to risk losing good performers. What is really being stated here is a strategy of investing in the good performers in order to hold them in the organization while minimizing the investment in the poorer performers.

To create this kind of positive relationship between satisfaction and performance, it is necessary to tie large differences in rewards directly to performance so that the good performer will receive more than the poor performer. The good performer must receive significantly more because he sees himself as having higher inputs, and it requires more rewards just to have him as satisfied as the poorer performer. But, if he is to be retained, he should not be "just as satisfied" as the poor performer; he should be more satisfied. If he does not receive greater rewards, a negative relationship between satisfaction and performance will exist; and the people most likely to leave the organization will be the good performers because their dissatisfaction is higher and their job opportunities greater.

An analysis of the relationship between satisfaction and performance in an organization can provide some important insights into the effectiveness of its reward system (Porter & Lawler, 1968b). A strong positive relationship between satisfaction and performance indicates a reward system that is functioning in a way that rewards good performance. On the other hand, a zero relationship or a negative one (i.e., the best performers being least satisfied) can indicate that turnover in the organization is likely to be centered among the better performers rather than the poorer ones.

REWARD SYSTEMS AND ATTENDANCE

There is no question that absenteeism is a major problem in many organizations (Porter & Steers, 1973). It disrupts schedules, creates the necessity of overstaffing, and reduces productivity. Absenteeism reflects the fact that employees have to be motivated—intrinsically or extrinsically—to go to work; they do not just show up automatically. They decide whether or not to go to work by comparing the perceived consequences of that activity with the perceived consequences of such alternative behaviors as going hunting, shopping, sleeping, or looking for another job. Employees will be motivated to go to work only when they feel that this behavior will lead to more positively valued outcomes and fewer negatively valued outcomes than any alternative behavior they consider.

Individuals do consider extrinsic rewards when they are debating whether or not to go to their job, but extrinsic rewards are only one of many influences. Employees are often absent even though it means less pay, lost promotion opportunities, and not seeing their friends at work. Frequently, this is because these rewards simply are not that important to the individual. Unless an extrinsic reward is at least somewhat important, it will not play a role in determining job attendance. Extrinsic rewards may also not influence job attendance because the person sees no connection between going to work and getting them. It is unlikely that anybody could feel that there is no overall relationship between attendance and rewards such as pay and promotions, but it is perfectly possible to feel that the relationship on any given day is nil. That is, a person may well feel that he will get the same amount of pay whether he goes to work on a particular day or not. In such a situation, pay will not influence his job attendance decision for that day, even though pay is important to him.

Punishments for Not Attending

Punishment in the form of dismissal and penalties for excessive absenteeism is used by many organizations to motivate attendance. The idea is to tie negatively valent outcomes to absenteeism, thereby increasing the relative attractiveness of coming to work. This approach can increase attendance; however, it is often limited in its effectiveness by four factors. First, for many employees, union contracts often strictly limit the kind of penalties that organizations can give out. Second, particularly in times of full employment, punishments such as dismissal are not feared by employees and thus are not very effective. Third, punishments such as dismissal can only be used once, and thus they are inflexible. Fourth, punishment can lead to turnover, which is very expensive.

Specific Rewards for Attendance

There is surprisingly little research on the way different reward and punishment systems affect absenteeism. A recent study does, however, provide strong support for the view that rewards can influence attendance (Lawler & Hackman, 1969). A company that had been experiencing high absenteeism among part-time janitorial employees installed a plan which was developed participatively in three work groups. It offered a cash bonus to workers who showed up regularly. Figure 12-2 shows that the bonus plan did lead to higher job attendance, thus illustrating the importance of tying pay to the kind of behavior that is to be motivated.

Further data from the study illustrate a second important point about pay plans. The pay plan that was participatively developed by the groups involved in the study was imposed upon two similar work groups elsewhere in the organization. The findings indicated that the plan was not as effective where it was imposed as where it was developed. The other groups saw the plan as more of a management tool to get them to come to work, which, of course, it was. These data emphasize that the mechanics of a pay plan alone do not determine its success. Success is also very much influenced by how it is introduced, the degree to which it is accepted, the workers' initial experience with it, and the superior-subordinate trust level in the organization.

In a follow-up study of the bonus plan, data were collected on the impact of the plan after one year (Scheflen, Lawler, & Hackman, 1971). In two of the three groups where the plan had been participatively developed, it

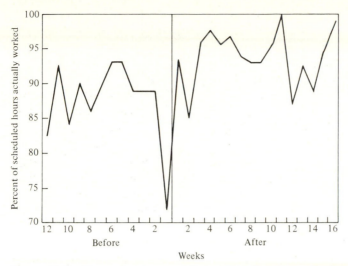

Figure 12-2 Mean attendance of the participative groups for the twelve weeks before the incentive plan and the sixteen weeks after the plan. (Attendance is expressed in terms of the percentage of hours scheduled to be worked that were actually worked.) (Source: Lawler & Hackman, 1969.)

had been discontinued by management. Figure 12-3 shows what happened when the plan was discontinued. Attendance dropped significantly, indicating that the plan did have an effect on attendance. In the other participative group (where the plan was not discontinued), attendance remained high even though the plan had been in effect for a year.

In summary, then, organizations can influence attendance behavior by tying extrinsic rewards to coming to work and by tying penalties to being absent. How individuals respond to the efforts of organizations to motivate attendance is determined by a complex set of factors. These include the value the individuals place on the outcomes that are involved and the connection they see between their attendance behavior and the outcomes.

Organizations can significantly influence the connections their employees perceive between attendance and certain outcomes by the installing of reward and penalty incentive systems and by their structuring of the work situation. As will be discussed further in the next two chapters, organizations also can do things that encourage or inhibit the formation of social groups which in turn provide the individual with certain rewards (e.g., friendship) for being at work. The physical work environment can play an important role, as can job-rotation policies and the issue of whether individuals are allowed to choose with whom they work.

Organizations have limited influence on the values individuals place on

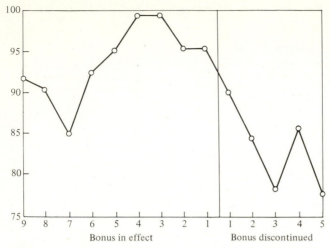

Figure 12–3   Mean attendance of two participative groups for the nine weeks before the plans were ended and for the first five weeks after they were ended. (Attendance is expressed in terms of the percentage of hours scheduled to be worked that were actually worked.) (Source: Scheflen, 1971.)

the outcomes that can be used to motivate attendance. They can change the amount of the outcomes and the types of outcomes, but they have little influence over the value an individual places on a given amount of a particular outcome. Finally, because significant individual differences exist in how people value extrinsic rewards, any attendance incentive system that involves only a single reward will not motivate all employees.

REWARD SYSTEMS AND JOB PERFORMANCE

There is little question that extrinsic rewards can be used to motivate job performance. It is also quite clear what conditions must exist if they are to motivate job performance: they must be important, and they must be clearly tied to the type of performance that is to be motivated. However, motivating performance by using extrinsic rewards is not simply a matter of selecting an important reward and linking it to performance. If it were, then piece-rate incentive plans, would be much more effective than they have proven to be. Because of the complexities and problems involved in utilizing extrinsic rewards as motivators, in some cases using them may actually be more dysfunctional than functional. But before we decide when they should be used, let us consider in more detail the conditions that determine whether they will motivate performance.

The Correct Reward or Penalty

The motivation model presented in Chapter 2 pointed out that rewards must be important if they are to be effective in motivating performance. The research that has been done on the importance of rewards suggests that promotion and pay are the most highly valued extrinsic rewards most organizations have to offer. However, the research also suggests that there are large individual differences in the degree to which these rewards are valued. For some people money is not very important, and, as was noted in Chapter 7, for some people promotion is something to be avoided. Thus, in deciding which rewards to use, an organization has to be careful to consider individual difference factors. Otherwise, it may end up trying to motivate people with rewards they do not value.

Both pay and promotion have certain advantages and disadvantages as rewards. Using pay as a reward can be quite expensive since large amounts of money are needed to motivate some people. An organization must be willing and able to give certain employees large raises and/or bonuses if pay is to motivate performance. Many nonbusiness organizations simply cannot do this because they lack the resources or because their policies prohibit it. Even if organizations are willing to spend large amounts of money, pay may not be very important to certain employees and therefore it is not a major source of motivation. For example, in one factory where time off the job was more important than money a pay incentive plan failed; but when the employees were told they could go home after a certain amount of work was done, productivity increased dramatically.

One of the advantages pay has as a reward is that it can be given on a group basis or an individual basis and it can be given in widely differing amounts. Unfortunately, promotion is not such a flexible reward. It is hard to give on anything but an individual basis. Also, promotion can only be given when old positions are open or new ones created, although it can be held out as an incentive at all times. Thus, an organization that relies on promotion as its major reward can get into difficulty because of its low flexibility.

Pay and promotion are not the only rewards that can be used to motivate performance. Certain status symbols and prizes can be tied to good performance as can special privileges such as that of leaving early. In addition, of course, supervisors can give approval and praise to those who perform well. The effectiveness of any of these rewards as motivators of performance depends upon whether they are important and whether they can be tied to performance. The problem with many of them is that they sometimes are not important to employees (e.g., praise from a disliked boss) and are difficult to relate specifically to performance (e.g., status symbols).

Performance can also be motivated by penalties and sanctions. Dismissal is a real threat to many people; and if people believe they will be fired for poor performance, it may be a significant motivator—at least for bringing performance up to some minimally adequate level. The problem with it is that it can only be used once with each person and that the threat of it may produce undesirable side effects. For example, many managers develop "just-in-case files" whose sole function is to protect them against the charge that they have performed poorly. The threat of dismissal can produce other self-protective and defensive behaviors that are not necessarily functional (e.g., risk avoidance). Other sanctions like reprimands and criticism from the boss can also be tied to poor performance in the hope of making it unattractive. Again, these can work only if they have a negative valence. The problem is that they often do not. In fact, situations can develop where they have a positive valence. In certain work groups, being criticized by the boss may be more positive than negative. It can lead to increased status in the work group if the group has an antimanagement value system.

Effective Performance Evaluation

As discussed in the previous chapter, an organization must have an effective performance appraisal system if it is to use extrinsic rewards to motivate performance. For any reward to be a motivator, it must be tied to performance; and for this to happen, performance must be measured. In fact, it must be measured very well if people are to *perceive* a relationship betweeen their performance and their rewards. The measures must meet all the criteria that were mentioned in the last chapter (e.g., responsive, objective, inclusive, etc.), and they must be accepted by the people in the organization as valid measures of their behavior. If they are not generally thought to represent appropriate measures of behavior, then it will be difficult for the perception to develop that performance and rewards are related.

Reward System Openness

Secrecy about management pay rates seems to be an accepted practice in many organizations. However, organizations typically do not keep secret how other extrinsic rewards are administered. They do not keep promotions or who gets certain status symbols secret; in fact, they publicize these things. Why then do they keep salaries secret, and what are the effects of keeping them secret? It is usually argued that the pay of individuals is kept secret in order to increase pay satisfaction. Presumably secrecy increases satisfaction because if employees knew what other employees were earning, they would be more dissatisfied with their own pay. This may in fact be true in organizations where the pay system is chaotic and cannot be rationally defended, but it is not clear that it is better to keep pay information secret when it is being well administered. In fact, there is evidence that keeping it secret may increase dissatisfaction and make it more difficult to use it as a motivator.

One of the findings that has consistently appeared in the research on pay secrecy is that managers tend to have incorrect information about the pay of other managers in their organization (Milkovich & Anderson, 1972). Specifically, there is a general tendency for them to overestimate the salaries of managers around them. For example, in one organization that was studied the average raise given was 6 percent, yet the managers believed that it was 8 percent; and the larger their own raise, the larger they believed other people's raises were (Lawler, 1971). This tended to *increase* pay dissatisfaction because the managers felt other managers at their level were making more than they were. It also had the effect of wiping out much of the motivational force of the differential reward system that was actually operating in the company. Almost regardless of how well the individual manager was performing, he felt that he was getting less than an average raise. This problem was particularly severe among the high performers, because they believed that they were doing very well but received only an average reward. They did not believe that pay was in fact based upon merit. This was ironical since their pay *did* reflect their performance. However, what actually existed did not matter as far as the motivation of the managers was concerned; they responded to what they thought existed.

There is another way in which pay secrecy may affect motivation. As was stressed in Chapter 10, accurate feedback about work quality can be a stimulus to good performance. People work better when they know how well they are performing in relation to some meaningful standard. For a manager, pay is one piece of performance feedback. High pay means good performance; low pay is a signal that he is not doing well and should improve. When managers do not know what other managers earn, they cannot correctly evaluate their own pay and the feedback implications of it for their own performance. Since they tend to overestimate the pay of subordinates and peers, and since they also overestimate the raises others get, the majority of them consider their salary to be lower than that of others and, because of this, they receive negative feedback. Moreover, although this feedback suggests that they should change their work behavior, it does not tell them what type of changes to make.

In summary, an organization that wishes to use pay or any extrinsic reward as a motivator of performance must decide how much information it should release about how the rewards are distributed. For many rewards this is not a difficult decision because the rewards are by their nature visible to all (e.g., promotion), but in the case of pay it can be a difficult decision. Many managers prefer to have their pay kept secret, and organizations usually do not want to be in the position of having to defend the salaries that are paid to their managers. Thus, significant pressure exists that encourages secrecy. However, unless information about salaries is released to members of the organization, it is difficult to establish that higher-than-average pay is obtainable by those who perform especially well.

Making pay information more open will not automatically establish the belief that pay is based upon merit or ensure that people will get accurate performance feedback. All it can do is clarify those situations where pay actually *is* based upon merit and where this fact is not obvious because salaries are not accurately known. For example, an organization was studied that had a merit-based plan and pay secrecy. At the beginning of the study the data collected showed that the employees saw only a moderate relationship between pay and performance. Data collected after the company became less secretive about pay showed a significant increase in employees' perceptions of the degree to which pay and performance were related (Lawler, 1971). The crucial factor in making this change to openness successful was that pay was in fact actually tied to performance. Revealing salary data where pay is not tied to performance will only serve to emphasize more dramatically that it is not, thereby further reducing the power of pay to motivate.

Management Style and Reward System Must Fit

The reward system of an organization must fit the management style of the organization if it is to work effectively. Consider for a moment the suggestion that salary information be made more widely known within an organization. In the kind of organization that generally adopts an open or participative approach to management, this practice should develop naturally. As employees begin to participate more in evaluating themselves and others, they will gradually come to know other employees' salaries as well as the general pay structure of the organization. On the other hand, a policy of salary openness is incongruent with an autocratically run organization. Salary openness demands trust, frank discussions of performance, and justification of salaries. None of these are likely to occur in an authoritarian type of organization. Collaborative superior-subordinate performance appraisal is another practice that may be necessary if rewards are to be clearly tied to performance. It too is likely to fit well with a participative but not with an authoritarian style of management. Similarly, a high level of superior-subordinate trust is needed if valid performance appraisals are to be done in the absence of objective measures. This seems to develop best where a history of participative decision making exists (Lawler & Cammann, 1972).

What kind of extrinsic reward plan will work in an organization run on traditional lines? The evidence suggests that the more "objectively" based the plan, the more likely it is to be successful. Plans that tie rewards to "hard" measures, such as quantity of output, profits, or sales, and thus require a minimum level of trust, stand a much better chance of succeeding in the traditional organization than approaches which depend on joint goal setting and so-called "soft" (i.e., subjective) criteria. Piece-rate pay plans that are administered in a consistent and fair manner and have rates that are set fairly work sometimes. So do sales bonuses for salesmen and profit sharing plans in small organizations. But where trust is low, these plans seldom reach their full potential.

The most severe problems for traditional organizations occur in jobs where there are no hard criteria for measuring performance and where trust and participation are needed if extrinsic rewards are to act as an incentive. Here the traditionally managed organization has difficulty in getting rewards to work as a motivator because the conditions are not suitable. For example, nonbusiness organizations often lack the hard criteria that are present in business organizations (e.g., sales or profits), and when they also lack the trust that is necessary if subjective criteria are to be used, they are in a poor position to use pay as a motivator.

In summary, it has been argued that one of the factors which influences the type of reward plan an organization can successfully use is the management style that exists in the organization. For illustrative purposes, organizations characterized by an open, organic style of management were contrasted with those characterized by a more authoritarian or mechanistic approach. Ironically, the potential for using extrinsic rewards to motivate performance seems to be greater in the former than in the latter despite the fact that the authoritarian approach has typically put more stress on the importance of using extrinsic rewards to motivate performance.

Other Performance-Outcome Connections

In addition to the performance-reward association they are intended to affect (i.e., good performance leads to desirable rewards), extrinsic reward systems often affect the perceived relationship between performance and other outcomes. Perhaps the most obvious example of this point is provided by the effects of pay incentive plans. There is considerable evidence that when workers are placed on piece-rate plans, restriction of output often results because the incentive plans unintentionally cause a number of negative outcomes to be associated with good performance. In the Western Electric studies, for example, a rigidly enforced output restriction system was found to be in force. Workers who exceeded the quota could expect to receive a "bing" (punch on the arm) and to be rejected and degraded by the other members of the group. More recent studies (Collins, Dalton, & Roy, 1946; Dalton, 1948; Dyson, 1956; Roy, 1952; Whyte, 1955) have provided a great deal of additional evidence to support the point that production restriction is not uncommon and that it comes about because negative outcomes like social rejection and interpersonal sanctions are administered to high performers by other employees.

On the surface it seems that the existence of output restriction in incentive pay situations indicates that employees are not highly motivated by money, since they appear to be earning less money than the pay system allows. In fact, many writers have argued that the restriction phenomenon shows that employees are more concerned about obtaining social than economic outcomes, since the group seems to be able to force individuals to make less money as the price for group acceptance and support.

Several studies have tried to determine why norms against high productivity develop (Hickson, 1961; Viteles, 1953). The data from these sources suggest that workers often feel that high productivity will lead to negative economic consequences. In one study, 30 percent of the workers felt that high production would lead to higher production quotas, 11 percent felt that it would result in lower piece rates, and a smaller percentage thought that higher productivity would result in no change in wages. Another study (Opinion Research Corporation, 1949) showed that workers also feared that if they responded to wage incentive plans by producing a great deal they might work themselves out of a job. Thus, there is evidence from attitude surveys that beliefs about economic factors may cause some of the production restriction which occurs. This is not, however, to suggest that social sanctions are not real and important causes of the restriction (see Chapters 13 and 14). It is merely to suggest that they may have an economic basis and that they may be effective only when combined with certain economic realities and beliefs. The following description of a researcher's experiences while working on a piece-rate job provides a different kind of evidence, but it too suggests that fear of rate changes is an important basis for production restriction:

From my first to my last day at the plant I was subject to warnings and predictions concerning price cuts. Pressure was heaviest from Joe Mucha, day man on my machine, who shared my job repertoire and kept a close eye on my production. On November 14, the day after my first attained quota, Joe Mucha advised:

"Don't let it go over $2.25 an hour, or the time study man will be right down here! And they don't waste time either! They watch the records like a hawk! I got ahead, so I took it easy for a couple of hours."

Joe told me that I had made $10.01 yesterday and warned me not to go over $1.25 an hour. He told me to figure the setups and the time on each operation very carefully so that I would not total over $10.25 for one day, or $1.31 an hour.

Jack Starkey defined the quota carefully but forcefully when I turned in $10.50 for one day, or $1.32 an hour.

Jack Starkey spoke to me after Joe had left. "What's the matter? Are you trying to upset the applecart?"

Jack explained in a friendly manner that $10.50 was too much to turn in, even on an old job. "The turret-lathe men can turn in $1.35, but their rate is 90 cents, and ours 85 cents."

Jack warned me that the Methods Department could lower their prices on any job, old or new, by changing the figure slightly or changing the size of the drill. According to Jack, a couple of operators (first and second shift on the same drill) got to competing with each other to see how much they could turn in. They got up to $1.65 an hour, and the price was cut in half. And from then on they had to run that job themselves, as none of the other operators would accept the job. (Whyte, 1955, p. 23)

Figure 12-4 (Lawler, 1971) presents an explanation of why production restriction develops which is consistent with the survey data which have been gathered as well as with the above example. It suggests that when a piece-rate incentive is installed in a situation where mistrust exists between management and employees, the employees will develop beliefs to the effect that high productivity will lead to negative economic consequences. These beliefs in turn will lead to the creation of informal pressure groups in which employees seek to protect their economic interests by using social means to control other employees' production. It also suggests that these beliefs will destroy any perception that high production leads to high pay. The net result is that the individual worker will see more negative than positive outcomes associated with high productivity and consequently will restrict his production.

Extrinsic reward systems can also create a strong connection between performance and outcomes that are not part of the formal reward system. For example, there is evidence that when group-pay plans like the Scanlon Plan are installed, this happens. The Scanlon Plan gives a bonus to everyone

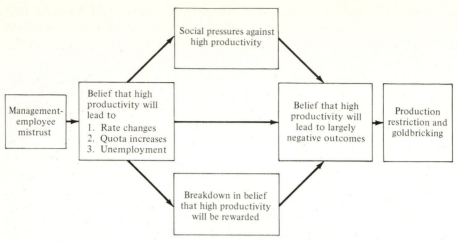

Figure 12-4 Causes of production restriction and goldbricking.
(Source: Lawler, 1971.)

in a plant based on the overall effectiveness of the plant, so that when someone performs effectively everyone profits financially. Sometimes this leads employees to encourage their fellow workers to perform effectively, and it can lead to good performers' enjoying high status. Thus, employees see a positive connection between high production and being accepted and respected—just the opposite of what often happens in piece-rate situations. Plans such as the Scanlon Plan, however, are far from being perfect motivators since, as will be discussed next, they do a poor job of relating individual pay to individual performance.

Different Approaches to Relating Rewards to Performance

Once it is decided to relate a particular reward or set of rewards to performance in order to produce extrinsic motivation, the question of how to do it becomes crucial. Organizations often have merit promotion plans, suggestion award programs, technical ladder-promotion systems for researchers, and a host of other programs designed to relate nonfinancial rewards to performance. But these are less visible than the many pay incentive plans that have been designed to relate pay to performance. Literally thousands of pay plans have been designed. By looking at some of them, we can get a good view of the issues involved in actually relating extrinsic rewards to performance.

An evaluation of a number of pay plans in terms of how successful they have been in producing motivation illustrates the impossibility of developing an extrinsic reward system that is strong in all respects. Table 12-1 lists different types of plans and provides a general effectiveness rating for each plan on three separate criteria (Lawler, 1971). The plans are categorized according to the type of financial reward they give (salary increase or bonus), according to whether the rewards are given on an individual or group basis, and according to how performance is measured. First, each plan is evaluated in terms of how effective it is in creating the perception that pay is tied to performance. In general, this perception develops only when an individual's behavior directly, quickly, and clearly influences his pay. Second, each plan is evaluated in terms of how well it minimizes the perceived negative consequences of good performance. This criterion refers to the extent to which the approach eliminates situations where social ostracism and other negative consequences become associated with good performance. Third, each plan is evaluated in terms of whether it contributes to the perception that important rewards other than pay (e.g., recognition and acceptance) stem from good performance. The ratings range from +3 to −3, with +3 indicating that the plan has generally worked well in terms of the criterion and −3 indicating that the plan has not worked well. A 0 rating indicates that the plan has generally been neutral or average.

Table 12–1 Ratings of Pay Incentive Plans

Type of plan		Performance measure	Tie pay to performance	Minimize negative side effects	Tie other rewards to performance
Salary reward	Individual	Productivity	+2	0	0
		Cost effectiveness	+1	0	0
		Superiors' rating	+1	0	+1
	Group	Productivity	+1	0	+1
		Cost effectiveness	+1	0	+1
		Superiors' rating	+1	0	+1
	Organizationwide	Productivity	+1	0	+1
		Cost effectiveness	+1	0	+1
		Profits	0	0	+1
Bonus	Individual	Productivity	+3	−2	0
		Cost effectiveness	+2	−1	0
		Superiors' rating	+2	−1	+1
	Group	Productivity	+2	0	+1
		Cost effectiveness	+2	0	+1
		Superiors' rating	+2	0	+1
	Organizationwide	Productivity	+2	0	+1
		Cost effectiveness	+2	0	+1
		Profit	+1	0	+1

Source: Lawler, 1971.

Linking Pay to Performance A number of trends appear in the ratings presented in Table 12-1. Looking just at the criterion of tying pay to performance, we see that individual plans tend to be rated highest, while group plans are rated next, and organizationwide plans are rated lowest. This reflects the fact that in group plans to some extent and in organizationwide plans to a great extent, an individual's pay is not directly a function of his *own* behavior. The pay of an individual in these situations is influenced by the behavior of others with whom he works and also, if the payment is based on profits, by external market conditions.

Bonus plans are generally rated higher than pay raise and salary increase plans. Under bonus plans, a person's pay may vary sharply from year to year in accordance with his most recent performance. This does not usually happen with salary increase programs, since organizations seldom cut anyone's salary; as a result, pay under salary increase plans reflects not recent performance but performance over a number of years. Consequently, pay is not seen to be closely linked to immediate job behavior. Bonuses, on the other hand, typically do depend on recent behavior, and so if someone performs poorly, it will have a definite short-term effect on his pay. A person under the bonus plan cannot perform poorly for a year and still be highly paid, as he can under the typical salary and merit-pay program that does not cut salaries.

Finally, approaches which use objective measures of performance are rated higher than those which use subjective measures. In general, objective measures enjoy higher credibility; that is, employees will often grant the validity of an objective measure, such as sales or units produced, when they will not as readily accept the validity of a superior's rating. Objective measures such as sales volume and units produced are visible to all; and thus, when pay is tied to them, it is often much more visible than when it is tied to a subjective, nonverifiable measure, such as a superior's rating. Overall, then, individually based bonus plans which rely on objective measures produce the strongest perceived connection between pay and performance. However, even they can do poorly if, as was noted earlier, a low trust level exists and the employees fear rate changes or job loss.

Minimizing Negative Consequences The ratings with respect to the ability of pay programs to minimize the perceived negative consequences of good performance reveal that most plans are regarded as neutral. That is, they neither contribute to the appearance of negative consequences nor help to eliminate any which might be present. The individual bonus plans do receive a negative rating on this criterion, however. This negative rating reflects the fact that piece-rate plans often lead to situations in which social rejection, layoff, and running out of work are perceived by individuals to result from good performance. Under a piece-rate system, the perceived negative consequences of good performance may cancel out the positive motivational force that such plans typically generate by tying pay closely to performance.

Linking Nonpay Rewards to Performance   With respect to the final criterion for pay plans, tying nonpay rewards to performance, the ratings are generally higher for group and organizationwide plans than for the individual plans. As was noted earlier when the Scanlon Plan was discussed, under group and organizationwide plans it is generally to the advantage of everyone for an individual to work effectively. Thus, good performance is much more likely to be supported by other employees, although it is not always. Just as in the case of individual plans, when mistrust is high and the employees fear rate changes, they will not only not praise peers who are high producers; they will punish them.

It should be clear from this short review that no one pay plan is a panacea for an organization's motivational problems, since no one type of pay program is strong in all areas. Thus, no organization probably ever will be completely satisfied with its approach because any given approach will have problems associated with it. As might be expected, a national survey of company personnel practices showed that there was widespread dissatisfaction with current pay systems and that many companies were considering changing their pay plans (Campbell et al., 1970).

Just as there is no one pay plan that perfectly ties pay to performance, there are no perfect plans or programs for tying any extrinsic rewards to performance. It is true, however, that some plans are better for certain kinds of organizations than are others. For example, a plan effective in motivating performance in a small organization often is not effective in a large one. The Scanlon Plan, for example, has been shown to work in small, democratically managed organizations but not in large, more autocratically managed ones. The reason for this is that it relies on employees' suggestions and an organizationwide bonus. In a small organization, even with an organizationwide bonus, individuals can see some relationship between their performance and their pay, while in a large organization they cannot. This example serves to illustrate the point that to understand the impact of any reward system it is crucial to consider both the nature of the plan *and* the nature of the organization in which it operates.

Should Organizations Relate Rewards to Performance?

At this point it should be obvious that there are conditions under which differentially distributed extrinsic rewards probably should not be used to motivate performance because the dysfunctional consequences outweigh the positive ones. We have already mentioned a number of conditions which must be present for rewards to motivate performance, but it is worth summarizing them here: (1) important rewards can be given, (2) rewards can be varied widely depending upon the individual's current performance, (3) meaningful performance appraisal sessions can take place between superiors and subordinates, (4) performance can be objectively and inclusively measured, (5) information can be made public about how the rewards are given, (6) trust is high, (7) superiors are willing and able to explain and support the reward system in discussions with their subordinates, and (8) the plan will not cause negative outcomes to be tied to performance.

If many of these things do not exist or cannot be done, it is better not to use differential extrinsic rewards as motivators. Merely adopting some of the practices that are necessary if rewards are to be really effective motivators (e.g., openness) or putting them into an organization where the conditions are not right (e.g., where good superior-subordinate relations do not exist) may only make the situation worse.

REWARD SYSTEMS IN PRACTICE: A COMPROMISE

In practice most organizations try to use the wide array of rewards and punishments they have available to accomplish a number of purposes. For example, in trying to motivate performance they may offer pay increases, promotion, approval from the supervisor, and higher status to the good performer while threatening the poor performer with criticisms, reprimands, and even dismissal. Often, however, they end up accomplishing few or none of their purposes because the rewards members receive are influenced by a number of factors including seniority, attendance, and performance. It is a rare organization that gives rewards strictly on the basis of performance or any other single measure. The result of this is that employees are often not sure what does determine the rewards they receive.

Even in organizations that claim to have merit pay programs, pay is not consistently related to performance. For example, one study found a negative relationship between amount of salary and performance as evaluated by superiors (Svetlik, Prien, & Barrett, 1964). Another study of seven organizations found that managers' pay is relatively unrelated to superiors' performance evaluations (Lawler, 1964). Other research (Haire, Ghiselli, & Gordon, 1967; Brenner & Lockwood, 1965) shows that the size of raises managers get from one year to another often are not related. If the companies were tying pay to performance, the lack of correlation would mean that a manager's performance in one year was completely unrelated to his performance in another year. This assumption simply does not fit with what is known about performance; a manager who is a good performer one year is very likely to be a good performer the next. Thus, we must conclude that the companies studied were not linking pay directly to performance. Apparently, pay raises were distributed on a close-to-random basis, or the criteria for awarding raises were frequently changed. As a result, recent raises were often not related to past raises or to performance.

Overall, then, the evidence suggests that many organizations do not consistently pay for performance and that pay is influenced by many nonperformance factors. The same is probably also true for the way other extrinsic rewards are administered. Promotions certainly are not always given to the best performers and, as was noted earlier, there are good reasons for this. It is important to promote those people who will do well in higher-level jobs, and these may or may not be the persons who have performed best in a lower-level job. Thus, promotion systems like pay systems often end up compromising the motivational potential because promotions are made on the basis of a number of criteria.

One reason why rewards are not closely related to performance in organizations may be that some employees object to basing rewards upon performance. Employees obviously can have some influence on how rewards are administered in organizations. They are not passive responders to the reward system. They do not simply try to figure out how rewards are distributed and then behave in whatever ways will lead to the rewards. They often are active in trying to influence the kind of policies that are set as well as how they are implemented. Thus, if a significant number of employees object to the idea of basing rewards on performance, one would expect that organizations would tend to avoid doing it.

Do employees think rewards should be based upon performance? The research suggests that, particularly at the management level, employees favor having their pay based upon their performance. Two studies have measured managers' attitudes toward how their pay should be determined, and both show that managers prefer to have their pay based upon performance (Andrews & Henry, 1963; Lawler, 1967). Most managers reported that performance should be the most important determinant of their pay but that in fact it was not. There was a consistent tendency across all organizations studied for a large gap to exist between how important managers felt performance was in determining pay and how important they felt it should be. This gap between what "should be" and what "was" reflects the inability of the companies to develop pay plans that fit the needs of employees. It also indicates that at least at the managerial level the failure of organizations to tie pay to performance does not stem from deep philosophical objections to the principle.

Studies done among blue-collar workers to determine their preferences with respect to pay plans do not show overwhelming acceptance of merit-based plans. The studies are somewhat difficult to interpret, however, since many of them asked for reactions to specific pay plans, such as piece-rate plans, rather than to the general idea of merit-based pay. Even though they show less acceptance of the idea of merit-based rewards systems, workers do seem to favor the idea (Lawler, 1971). Thus, it seems unlikely that the failure of many organizations to base rewards on performance can be explained by the resistance of their nonmanagement employees to the idea. What, then, is the probable explanation? The answer seems to lie in the points made in Chapter 11 about the difficulty of measuring performance and in the tendency to reward such behaviors as attendance and continued membership.

CONCLUSION

In the final analysis, each organization has only a limited quantity of rewards, and how they are given out determines who will come to work for the organization, who will continue to work for it, how hard people will work, and what the attitudes of the employees will be toward it. The giving of extrinsic rewards represents an investment in people, and, therefore, a crucial issue in any organization concerns how this investment is made. Because of this, one effective way to understand an organization is to look at how the extrinsic rewards it has to offer are distributed among its members.

REVIEW AND DISCUSSION QUESTIONS

1   What are the strengths and weaknesses of piece-rate pay systems?
2   The same "reward" may be highly regarded by some individuals and considered insignificant by others. What factors account for such differences?
3   What factors influence the "desirability" of a given reward?
4   Some rewards (e.g., a bonus paid to an employee who submits a money-saving suggestion to an organization, or publication of a person's name in the organization's newspaper for some effort "above and beyond the call of duty") may have demotivating consequences to individuals. Why? (Hint: Consider the social milieu in which the individual operates.)
5   Why do rewards for organizational membership do little, if anything, to motivate above-average performance?
6   Employees can in many instances be "tied" to an organization (i.e., motivated to maintain organizational membership through the use of extrinsic rewards). Are there any long-run problems associated with an organization "paying to keep its work force"?
7   How is the motivational impact of rewards affected by the length of time interval between an employee's performance (especially when it is exceptionally good)

and the receipt of those rewards? What does this suggest about the payment schedules (once a week, once a month, etc.) most organizations use?

8 What methods might a manager use to reward attendance? How effective are these in the long run?

9 Should payroll data be kept secret for managerial employees in an organization? Why? What policy should a company follow concerning the secrecy of compensation information on hourly employees? Why?

10 Compare and contrast the various incentive plans (Table 12-1) in terms of their effectiveness in motivating performance.

11 Why is it argued that everyone should not be satisfied with the level of his extrinsic rewards?

12 Why do norms against high productivity develop?

13 Why is it difficult to use pay as a motivator in an autocratically run organization?

Chapter 13

Social Influences on Organization Members

The other people we work with in an organization can profoundly affect our thoughts and behaviors in that organization. Ultimately, the effectiveness of the organization itself can be strongly influenced by the nature of the interpersonal activities which take place within it. In this chapter, we will discuss the ways other people can have an impact on the work attitudes, beliefs, and behavior of an individual. Then, in the next chapter, we will examine how these social processes can directly affect the work *effectiveness* of individual organization members and of the organization as a whole.

A few examples from the research literature may help point up the substantial effects that a person's relations with his coworkers can have on his own attitudes and behavior at work. Probably the most widely known study of groups in organizations was performed at the Hawthorne plant of the Western Electric Company in the late 1920s (Roethlisberger & Dickson, 1939: summarized in Homans, 1950). This research program, which original-ly was intended to assess the impact of working conditions (e.g., lighting, rest pauses, etc.) on the productivity of employees, showed such conditions to be clearly less important in influencing the behavior of individual workers than were various psychological and social conditions which developed. Of particular importance was the existence or emergence of a group "identity" on the part of many of the employees who participated in the research. As a consequence, group norms were formed which specified what was and was not appropriate on-the-job behavior, and these norms strongly affected the behavior of individual workers—sometimes they were supportive of high work productivity, sometimes not.

In another "classic" study (Coch & French, 1948), workers were found to be much more accepting of a change in work practices when they had participated (either directly or through representation) in the planning of the changes. Apparently participation facilitated the acceptance of the new procedures as a *group* goal, which was thereafter enforceable by the group. When participation was by representation, there was an initial fall-off of productivity, suggesting that it took longer for individual workers to understand and/or accept the new procedures when they personally were not directly involved. It is important to note, however, that in all conditions (i.e., direct participation, participation by representation, and no participation) the changes led to a marked decrease in the amount of variation in the productivity of individuals in each group. Thus, the change itself seemed to have led to an increase in the degree to which productivity norms were group-defined and group-enforced. In the participation condition, these norms were for higher production; in the no-participation condition, they were for lower production; and in the representation condition they resulted in a slow movement toward higher production.

A case study (Newcomb, cited in Golembiewski, 1962, pp. 223–224) shows how group norms can have an especially strong effect on the quantity of work of an individual employee. In this instance, the group had established a production norm of 50 units a day, but one particular worker wanted to produce more than 50 units a day. Her attempts to do so were so successfully discouraged by her peers in a variety of ways that her output finally fell below the 50-unit norm. Subsequently, the work group was broken up so that she no longer worked with the employees who had established and enforced the 50-unit norm. Her output soon *doubled*—providing striking evidence of the effects of group norms on member behavior.

The examples given above deal mainly with the effects of group norms on individual group members. The Tavistock studies of coal mining (Trist & Bamforth, 1951) generated important data on the role of the work group by examining what happens when existing work groups are broken up. Initially, coal miners worked together in small groups (usually from two to eight miners) in which there was high interdependency among members—and high cohesiveness among them both on and off the job. Partly because of the very real dangers involved in doing the work, there was a good deal of emotional closeness among group members. A technological change (i.e., shifting from a "shortwall" to a "longwall" method of removing coal) required that the existing groups be recomposed into larger work units of forty and fifty men. Each of the new groups worked under a single supervisor, but the workers were often widely separated from one another while working in the mines. Although a great deal of work interdependence was required (indeed, a mistake or poor performance by an individual miner could substantially decrease the productivity of the entire unit), existing interpersonal relationships on the job were severely disrupted. Productivity deteriorated following the change of procedures, with the employees reporting heightened feelings of indifference and alienation from their work, and ultimately a norm of low productivity developed—apparently at least partly as a means of coping with the emotional and technological difficulties which were encountered.

Such problems are not, of course, an unusual consequence of a major technological change. The negative impact of the change apparently was heightened in this case, however, because exactly those social units which could have been most helpful in achieving personal readjustments by individual workers (i.e., the existing cohesive work groups) were themselves done away with as part of the change. The employees were, in effect, left without a social "anchor"; and a number of powerful negative consequences resulted both for the organization and for the individuals themselves.

THE NATURE OF DISCRETIONARY STIMULI

Why is it that groups seem to have such a pervasive and substantial impact on the behavior and attitudes of individuals in organizations? One highly useful way of approaching a general response to this question is to note that groups control many of the stimuli to which an individual is exposed in the course of his organizational activities. "Stimuli" are defined simply as those aspects of an individual's environment which potentially can be attended to or noticed by him and which can affect his behavior. Thus, by making certain stimuli available differentially and selectively to the individual group member, others in the group can help determine the nature of "social reality" for that individual and thereby influence his beliefs, his attitudes, and his behavior. This point is critical for understanding all the material we will be presenting in this and the next chapter: without the benefit of groups (i.e., other people), it is difficult for the average person to arrive at meaningful interpretations of changes or events which take place in the organizational setting.

Stimuli which can be transmitted selectively to individual group mem-

bers at the discretion of their peers will be called "discretionary stimuli" (Hackman, 1975). Such stimuli can include messages of approval or disapproval, physical objects, money, instructions about (or models of) appropriate behavior, and so on. All that is necessary is that the group have discretionary control over which members are and are not exposed to various stimuli.

This chapter reviews the ways groups use discretionary stimuli to affect members of groups in organizations. In particular, we examine the following major topics:

1 Why groups send discretionary stimuli. Before considering the effects group-generated stimuli can have on members, the conditions or circumstances which prompt groups to initiate such stimuli are briefly reviewed.

2 The impact of discretionary stimuli on group members. This section examines how group-generated discretionary stimuli affect four general characteristics of individuals which have special importance for understanding individual behavior in organizational settings (refer back to Chapters 2 and 4): (a) the beliefs individuals have about "reality": (b) the preferences, attitudes, and values held by individuals; (c) the level of motivational "arousal" of individuals; and (d) the job-relevant knowledge and skills of individuals. As will be seen in the following chapter (Chapter 14), each of these four classes of variables has important consequences for understanding the effects of groups on the work effectiveness of group members.

3 Group norms and member deviance from them. This section shows how the development and enforcement of group norms is the most efficient and direct way groups can control the behavior of their members. The conditions under which individuals can and cannot successfully deviate from group norms also are examined.

Then, in the following chapter, the material presented in this chapter will be applied to the particular problem of individual work effectiveness in organizations: the ways in which groups can facilitate (or impair) individual effectiveness will be discussed, as will various organizational practices aimed at improving work effectiveness by changing the nature of social relationships in organizations. Particular attention will also be given in the following chapter to the effects of leadership practices on individual and group behavior.

WHY GROUPS INITIATE DISCRETIONARY STIMULI

To Educate and Socialize

Influencing group member attitudes, beliefs, or behaviors is the primary purpose of some groups—such as religious study groups, political education groups, physical fitness clubs, and so on (Cartwright & Zander, 1968, p. 141). In such cases, the group serves explicitly as a socializing agent for its members. Sometimes this is at the request of the member ("Educate me"), and sometimes it is not ("I'll put up with this nonsense because it's part of being a member of the XYZ group, but that's sure not the main reason I'm here."). In either case, groups primarily oriented toward the education or socialization of their members rely heavily upon discretionary stimuli to bring about the desired changes (cf. Chapter 6). Such stimuli typically are dispensed quite selectively, contingent upon the current level of "progress" of each group member, and may provide the members with information, with rewarding stimuli for "correct" ideas or behavior, or with punishments for being "incorrect."

To Produce Uniformity

Even when member socialization is not a major purpose of a given group, however, there still are numerous occasions when groups take the initiative in assigning discretionary stimuli to their members. Group members often believe, for example, that a high level of uniformity among members is necessary or appropriate for group goal attainment, and use their control of discretionary stimuli to achieve such uniformity. It often is useful, for example, for a work group to have uniform procedures for dealing with frequently encountered tasks so that members can reliably predict the behavior of other members and thereby achieve a reasonable level of coordination and efficiency. Further, it may be important for group members to hold similar beliefs about the external environment, especially if the group must respond as a unit to that environment (e.g., as when management issues a new set of "rules and regulations").

Groups may, however, seek uniformity for purely "maintenance" reasons—i.e., keeping the group intact and functioning as a unit, independent of task-related activities (Cartwright & Zander, 1968, p. 142). Too much individualistic or idiosyncratic behavior on the part of a few members, for example, can threaten the very survival of a group, as can unresolved disputes among members regarding what the group should try to achieve and how it should proceed toward its goals. Perhaps reflective of a collective uneasiness about such dangers is the seeming ethic among members of intact groups to try to achieve a consensus among all members on any matter of consequence—falling back on majority rule only as a second-best way of proceeding.

To Produce Diversity

Apparently contrasting with the pressures toward uniformity discussed above is the tendency for groups to use discretionary stimuli to help create and to maintain *diversity* among members. In particular, a number of different member roles emerge in most groups, and these roles may become organized into a fairly complex and well-differentiated structure. As used here, the term "role" refers simply to expectations which are shared by group members regarding who is to carry out what types of activities under what circumstances (cf. Thibaut & Kelley, 1959, Ch. 8).

In a new group, differentiation typically takes place first between those who will assume leadership roles and those who will be followers, and between those who will specialize in task activities and those who will perform group maintenance functions (Slater, 1955; Bales & Slater, 1955; Thibaut & Kelley, 1959, Ch. 15; Gibb, 1969, especially pp. 268–271).* As group members gain experience in working together, additional role differentiation may take place in both the task and maintenance domains. For example, a highly elaborated division of labor among members may emerge, complete with "subleaders" responsible for several classes of task activity (cf. Biddle & Thomas, 1966, Pt. VII). Group maintenance functions may be highly differentiated as well; for example, one member (often the group wit) may be expected to reduce the level of interpersonal tension when it gets dangerously high, another may be responsible for providing encouragement and support when activities begin to drag, a third may provide social reinforcement to members who work especially hard or effectively on the group task, and so on (cf. Whyte, 1943).

As a group gains a history and its pattern of activities becomes more stable, the role assignments of individual members often become well defined and resistant to change. When change is attempted by a member, the group may use its control of discretionary stimuli to keep the existing role structure intact. It should be noted, however, that such resistance presupposes general satisfaction with the existing role structure by most group members; when consensus is low, a great deal of "jockeying" for position may ensue.

The apparent need of group members for a well-defined role structure and for predictable behavior by role incumbents is sometimes strikingly illustrated in groups where some members have *formally* defined roles (i.e., roles assigned by the parent organization, such as "supervisor" or "inspector"). Normally the existence of formal roles should short-cut much of the process of role differentiation in a group. For example, in an organizational work group with an assigned supervisor or foreman, the leadership role is both defined (at least in part) and occupied on an a priori basis. But when an assigned leader refuses to fulfill his role according to the expectations of group members, serious disruption of the group process invariably takes place.

---

*The distinction between task and maintenance functions is quite similar to the distinctions made between "internal" and "external" systems (Homans, 1950) and between "task" and "socio-emotional" roles (Bales, 1953).

For example, one can imagine the distress expressed by group members when the assigned leader of a "seminar on executive management" for military officers chose not to perform the executive functions expected of him and instead asked the group members to organize their own learning experiences (Mills, 1967, Ch. 6). Similar distress may be experienced initially by the subordinates of a manager who returns home from an off-premises T-group or executive development seminar with a new and unexpected way of enacting his formal leadership role (Argyris, 1962, Ch. 10). Finally, difficulties are experienced by group members when they and their formal leader agree on the *definition* of the leader's role but group members feel that the leader is not performing the role in a satisfactory manner. In such cases, an informal or "shadow" organization often is formed within the group which has its own set of differentiated roles and which may complement the formal role structure or compete with it (Roethlisberger & Dickson, 1939).

In summary, it appears that group members have a strong tendency to create differences among themselves and then to regularize and stabilize these differences over time. And, furthermore, research evidence (cf. reviews by Sarbin & Allen, 1968, pp. 503–504; Collins & Guetzkow, 1964) suggests that such internal organization, *when it is task-appropriate and accompanied by high role clarity,* can facilitate both group effectiveness and member satisfaction.

The issue may be even broader than that. Systems theorists (e.g., F. H. Allport, 1955, p. 475) have argued that *all* systems exhibit a basic tendency toward disorder and disorganization (entropy) which must be controlled if the system is to survive. Applied to groups, this principle suggests that *both* uniformity *and* structured diversity may be essential for maintaining the viability of the group as a social system. In this context, the striving of a group for *diversity* among members parallels its pressures toward *uniformity:* both processes, although superficially contradictory, reflect a tendency toward organization, order, and predictability. By judiciously controlling the discretionary stimuli at its command, a group should be able to move simultaneously toward uniformity and diversity—e.g., by inculcating a common set of work values among members while generating a task-appropriate division of labor among them, or by creating a common set of beliefs about the external environment while spawning a number of different functional leadership roles.

THE IMPACT OF DISCRETIONARY STIMULI ON GROUP MEMBERS

Group-individual relationships in organizations often are discussed simply as a process in which the individual *conforms* in some degree to group expectations in exchange for social acceptance from his peers. The main behavioral dilemma for the individual is seen as whether or not to conform, and the primary resources of the group are seen as social acceptance and rejection.

It is the purpose of the present discussion to make clear that group-individual relationships in organizations are considerably more complex than that. As noted already, groups send discretionary stimuli to their members for many different reasons and have a diversity of resources (not just social acceptance) to offer. Similarly, as discussed in Chapter 2, members use their group memberships to serve a variety of personal needs, and they can be affected by group-supplied discretionary stimuli in many different ways—some of which have nothing whatever to do with behavioral conformity. The dynamics of these effects are examined in the sections to follow.

It should be noted at the outset, though, that in our discussion of discretionary stimuli we will talk of things that groups *do* vis-à-vis their members; e.g., the group sanctions a member for exceeding the group production quota. The implication of such statements is *not* that groups act as intact units, consciously and deliberately planning and executing behaviors in the same ways that individuals do. To take such a position would be reifying the concept of groups in a way that is not congruent with the way groups actually operate. Instead, we talk about "group behavior" vis-à-vis group members merely as a shorthand way of referring to the behavior of other people with whom individual organization members have meaningful and continuing contact. We could just as well refer to his "peers" or his "role set" (i.e., those who send him role expectations) in this regard (Katz & Kahn, 1966); we use the term "group" because it is convenient, and because much of the research literature having to do with the effects of peers (or "role partners") on organization members is conceptualized and discussed using group terminology.

Let us turn now to the effects groups have on members through group control of discretionary stimuli. We will treat separately, and in turn, effects on (1) beliefs about the group and the environment; (2) preferences, attitudes, and values; (3) motivational arousal; and (4) job-relevant knowledge and skills.

Shaping Beliefs about the Group and the Environment

Relying only on their own senses and experiences, individuals in an organization can obtain neither a very complete nor, in many cases, a very accurate view of their environment. Individuals are, therefore, substantially dependent upon their work groups for obtaining information about that environment.

Many groups are only too happy to fill that need. To the extent that all group members have the same general perceptions of, and beliefs about, the environment, the likelihood of internal disagreements and dissention among members is somewhat lessened. Most groups are not very competent in handling overt disagreements among members. Indeed, group members often consider it a mark of their success as a group when they have done away with the appearances of internal disagreements and maintained instead a comfortable feeling of consensus and togetherness—even if that feeling was obtained by glossing over some very real differences among members.

As a result of this tendency to move away from interpersonal discomfort, many groups tend to generate substantial pressure for uniformity of beliefs among members. The pressure is likely to be particularly evident (1) when there is turbulence in the environment of the group and members have a strong need for social reassurance and (2) when new members join the group—since the perceptions and beliefs of these new members may turn out to be divergent from the existing shared views of veteran group members.

An example of how groups can use discretionary stimuli to maintain shared beliefs when not all is well in the environment is provided by a study of an organization in which cliques of older men met regularly to reassure each other about just how unfortunate things were in the organization (Burns, 1955). Various organizational features (e.g., the bonus system, formal communication procedures, and so on) invariably were discussed in deprecating terms. Groups of younger workers, on the other hand, had quite a different assessment of organizational reality. While they did not necessarily endorse the features deprecated by their older colleagues, they did tend more frequently to view them as challenges—as aspects of the system to be improved upon or to be overcome. In both cases, group members were actively involved in providing information about the organization to their fellows which served to preserve the protective "social reality" of the group.

The pressure toward belief uniformity when new members join a group is evidenced in the following exchange observed in a work setting. In this case, a new group member was present during a conversation between two veteran members. The main topic of the conversation was the frustrations the veterans had experienced recently at the hands of management. The discussion ran its course without either participant appearing to notice the presence of the new employee. Questioned later, one of the veterans admitted that the conversation had been informally "staged" and that its main purpose was to help the newcomer learn that it was "useless to suggest any changes in how things are done here, because management never pays any attention"—which indeed represented the existing views of the work group. This interaction probably had a substantial impact on the beliefs of the new member, simply because his lack of personal experience in the organization made him heavily dependent upon his work group for information about the organization.

The pressure toward uniformity of belief in a group may sometimes be functional for the group. It does provide a kind of social reassurance regarding one's beliefs which many individuals desire, and it can provide the basis for effective concerted action in those task groups where unanimity of view is essential to carrying out the work of the group. But such pressure almost certainly is dysfunctional when the beliefs shared about the environment have been obtained by stamping out genuinely different points of view among members. In such cases perspectives which, if explored, could contribute importantly to the work of the group may never be considered at all (cf. Maier & Solem, 1952; Janis, 1972).

Beliefs and the Behavior of Group Members   Groups clearly cannot and do not attempt to provide members with information about all aspects of "reality." Those beliefs which are mostly irrelevant to the actual *behavior* of group members (and therefore unlikely to be disruptive to the group itself in any way) are generally overlooked by the group. It is doubtful, for example, that a group would bother much with member beliefs about the total number of employees in the organization, with member perceptions of the color of the plant walls, and so on. Instead, communication of information is likely to be rather intensely focused on two general issues (cf. Chapters 2 and 4):

1   What rewards and punishments are present in the environment, and who controls them?
2   What behaviors lead to these rewards (and avoid the punishments)?

Both of these aspects of reality are of immediate relevance to the behavior and outcomes of individual group members. Therefore, they are of considerable importance both to the individual (because he would like to maximize his gain and minimize his pain) and to the group (because if the individual goes off half-cocked on the basis of the "wrong" information, he may mess things up for everybody). Thus, it would be expected that the characteristics of the *supervisor* of the group would be the focus of a great deal of information sharing by groups members—since the boss is *both* someone who is a direct source of rewards and costs *and* someone who can control the contingencies regarding what behaviors lead to what outcomes. Similarly, the pay and promotion system of the organization, the peculiarities of equipment used on the job, and, of course, the nature of the work group itself all would be the topic of communications designed to affect the belief states of individual group members.

When group members continually reinforce their common views on some matter (as, for example, in the groups of older men described by Burns), those views can become quite immune to change—even when they no longer accurately reflect objective reality. It is not uncommon, for example, for members of a work group to persist in believing that management will "lower the rate" if members produce over standard in a piecework incentive system (e.g., in the Hawthorne studies—discussed in Chapter 12). Neither assurances from management nor objective guarantees to the contrary are likely to dent the beliefs (or change the behavior) of an individual member in such a group, so long as members continue to reinforce each other's views about the nature of the "system." Instead, it would seem that before a management-introduced system could work in such a situation the nature of social reality would have to change: the group would have to abandon beliefs such as "hard work only hurts the working man in the long run around here."

Observation as a Source of Beliefs   The above discussion has emphasized stimuli which are communicated directly from the group to individual members—whether at the initiative of the group or in response to a request from the member. It should be noted as well that group members can use the group to obtain information about reality in another, more subtle, way: namely, by observing other group members in action, seeing the results of that action, and on the basis of these observations drawing *inferences* about the nature of the group and its environment. The group still has some control over such inferences, but by and large it is much more difficult for a group to "fake" its actual behavior than it is, say, to communicate a slightly distorted view of reality to a member verbally. This is especially the case for information having to do with the sources of rewards and costs in the environment and for the behaviors which lead to these outcomes. Regarding these aspects of the environment (which, indeed, are those that the member is most likely to be attending to), other group members can attempt to mislead the observer but only at the risk of negatively affecting their own level of outcomes.

There also are some traps, however, for a member who relies heavily on personal observations of the group as a strategy for learning about the environment. For example, what works for some group members (e.g., those with high status) may backfire when tried by a new member or one with low status. A member who bases his behavior on beliefs about reality gleaned solely from observational data, therefore, runs a high risk of behaving in a personally maladaptive way. In practice, most group members draw simultaneously upon several kinds of information—including observations—to gain understanding of the environment. When there is consistency across both data sources and time, a group member should be able to make attributions about reality with considerable confidence (Campbell, 1961; Heider, 1958) and safely base his behavior upon those attributions.

Conditions for Accepting Group-supplied Information about Reality The degree to which group members *accept* stimuli from the group in formulating their own views of the nature of reality varies considerably in different circumstances. There is a vast literature within the "conformity" tradition in social psychology regarding the conditions under which acceptance occurs (Allen, 1965; Kiesler, 1969, Chs. 10 and 11; Tajfel, 1969, pp. 347–357), and the evidence suggests that member acceptance of group-supplied data about reality is a function of the following three interrelated factors:

Characteristics of the Environment To the extent that the targets of a member's perceptions or beliefs are ambiguous or unclear, his reliance on the group for information about those targets increases (e.g., Asch, 1951; Wiener, 1958). This suggests that in organizational settings individuals should be especially dependent upon group-supplied information for help in understanding the *social* environment—including sources of social rewards and behavior-outcome contingencies which are controlled by groups or by individuals—since the social environment characteristically is more ambiguous and obscure than is the physical environment.

Characteristics of the Perceiver To the extent that an individual feels poorly qualified to assess the environment for himself, he will rely more heavily on the group for information about it (e.g., Kelley & Lamb, 1957; League & Jackson, 1964). Such low personal confidence can be either a relatively enduring characteristic of the person or a momentary state induced by recent failures to perceive or accurately assess the environment. The degree of influence of the group on member beliefs about the environment, then, should vary substantially from time to time as the situation changes and as the member's self-perceptions change.

Characteristics of the Group Ignoring, for the moment, the self-confidence of the member, it is likely that he will tend to accept group-supplied data about reality to the extent that he perceives the group as being a credible (competent, successful, trustworthy) source of information (e.g., Rosenberg, 1961; Kelman, 1950). Again, such perceptions may be either relatively enduring ("This is an awfully competent group; I'd better listen to what they say.") or transitory ("They were right last time, so I guess I should hear them out this time."). Finally, it should be noted that the greater the unanimity of views of group members, the more an individual will accept information provided by the group—probably at least in part because unanimity increases the perceived credibility of the group in the eyes of the member (e.g., Asch, 1955; Allen & Levine, 1971).

Changing Preferences, Attitudes, and Values*

Numerous studies have documented that the groups of which a person is a member can have potent effects on his attitudes and values. A good example is provided by a rather unique study (Lieberman, 1956) of the attitudes of a number of unionized manufacturing workers over a period of almost three years, during which time the group membership of many of the workers changed dramatically. During the first year of the study, twenty-three workers were promoted to foremen, and thirty-five workers were elected union stewards. Then, some time later, eight of the new foremen were returned to the worker role (because of cutbacks associated with an economic recession) and fourteen of the union stewards returned to the worker role (because they chose not to run again in union elections or ran and were defeated).

The attitudes of the workers were assessed before any changes took place, after the initial round of changes, and again after some of the workers had reverted to their original roles. The focus of the research was on worker attitudes toward management, toward the union, and toward two different reward systems—one espoused by the union and one by management. In essence, the research was a naturally occurring field experiment in which the groups the workers belonged to were changed once—and then, for some of the subjects, changed again back to the original state of affairs.

It was found that workers who were promoted to the job of foreman became markedly more promanagement (and more critical of the union) after they had assumed their new role. When some of these workers subsequently were moved back to the worker role, their attitudes eventually reverted to those they previous had held. Foremen who remained in that role did not show this decrease. The responses of these two groups of foremen to specific questions about the organization and the union are shown in Table 13-1.

Results for workers who became union stewards were somewhat less clear. Following election to the union steward role there was some change in the prounion-antimanagement direction, but it was not so strong as that for

*As used here, a "preference" refers to a choice by an individual regarding which of a finite number of stimuli or alternatives he likes best; an "attitude" is simply the amount of positive or negative affect an individual has for some person, thing, or concept; and a "value" is the amount of positive or negative affect an individual holds regarding some abstract ideal or end-state. The three concepts are grouped here because they all reflect an individual's affect toward something; they differ mainly in generality and in level of abstraction.

Table 13-1 Effects of Entering and Leaving the Foreman Role on Attitudes toward Management and the Union

	Workers who became foremen and stayed foremen ($N = 12$)			Workers who became foremen and were later demoted ($N = 8$)		
	(W) 1951	(F) 1952	(F) 1954	(W) 1951	(F) 1952	(W) 1954
% who feel Rockwell is a good place to work	33	92	100	25	75	50
% who feel management officers really care about the workers at Rockwell	8	33	67	0	25	0
% who feel the union should not have more say in setting labor standards	33	100	100	13	63	13
% who are satisfied with the way the incentive system works out at Rockwell	17	75	75	25	50	13
% who believe a worker's standard will not be changed just because he is a high producer	42	83	100	25	63	75
% who feel ability should count more than seniority in promotions	33	58	75	25	50	38

Source: From Lieberman (1956), as adapted in Proshansky & Seidenberg, 1965, p. 490.

the workers who became foremen. Also, those who returned later to the worker role tended not to revert to their previously held attitudes.

The changes both for those who became foremen and for those who became stewards involved shifts in the groups with whom the individuals were associated—and thus changes in the source and nature of the attitude-relevant stimuli to which the individuals were exposed. If it is assumed that groups of supervisory personnel tend to exchange stimuli (and encourage views) which are more promanagement and antiunion in orientation than do groups of workers, then the observed changes in attitudes for new foremen (and the later changes of these attitudes back again for those who reverted to the worker role) make good sense.* Further, it seems reasonable to expect that the observed changes would be less for workers who became union

*It should be noted, however, that the nature of the *jobs* of the workers in this study changed as well; it is likely that changes in job-supplied stimuli also were partly responsible for the attitude changes observed. In the particular setting where the research took place, the stimuli supplied in doing the new job probably reinforced those supplied by the new work group; this would not necessarily be true in other settings.

stewards—simply because becoming a steward involves a much less significant change in group membership for an operative employee than does
becoming a foreman. A union steward still tends to maintain close contact
with the worker group, augmented by contact with other union stewards and
some higher union officers.

The study we have been describing would seem to provide good
inferential data for demonstrating how one's group memberships can affect
his own attitudes and values—how, as we stressed before, groups help
determine social reality. Yet there also is evidence available which suggests
that *mere* membership in a given group is not sufficient for realizing affective
or attitudinal changes—even if the individual is exposed to discretionary
stimuli from that group on a more or less continuous basis. A well-known
field experiment carried out on college students in the 1930s is a good case in
point (summarized by Newcomb, 1952).

The research focused on the political attitudes of students during their
four years at a small college in New England and found that most students
developed a more "liberal" stance as a result of their experiences at the
college. Since a liberal point of view was dominant among students and
faculty at this particular college at that time, it can be argued that the group
membership of the students somehow affected their own attitudes and
values regarding political matters. Yet as Newcomb notes, there were
some students for whom the modal changes did *not* take place; these
students, it turned out, were ones who (for various reasons) had not
accepted their membership group (i.e., students and faculty at the college) as
a positive point of reference for their own attitudes. In some cases, the
college group was actively rejected and served as a *negative* point of
reference (i.e., students tended to adopt values or attitudes in opposition to
the dominant views at the college). In other cases, the predominant group
was merely not accepted, and the college environment apparently had little
impact on the political attitudes of these students one way or another. These
latter students invariably had some other group of which they were members
(often the family) which they maintained as the point of reference for their
political attitudes.

Data consistent with the above findings are provided in a later study
(Siegel & Siegel, 1957)—also in a college environment. A group of students
expressed an interest in living in prestigious "row houses" (former sorority
houses), and these students tended to score high on the Ethnocentrism-
Fascism (E-F) scale—which reflects a decidedly "conservative" set of
values. Only some of these students were able actually to move into row
houses (because of logistic problems); the others were assigned to less
prestigious dormitories. After one year, three groups had emerged: (1) row
house occupants, for whom the row house group was both a membership

and a reference group; (2) dormitory occupants who still wanted to move to a row house—i.e., students for whom the row house was a reference group but not a membership group; and (3) dormitory occupants who no longer wanted to move to a row house—i.e., students for whom the row house was neither a membership group nor a reference group. The E-F scale scores of the first group (membership *and* reference group) remained quite high; the scores of the second group (reference but not membership group) showed only a slight drop; and the scores of the last group (neither membership nor reference group) dropped very substantially.

These types of findings confirm the notion that the groups of which one is a member can indeed have a powerful impact on one's attitudes and values—but only if that group is *accepted* as a relevant point of reference for those attitudes and values. Those in the New England college study who remained conservatives during their four years at the college never accepted the college as a valid reference group; and those subjects in the second study who ceased using the "row" as a point of reference—and presumably accepted instead the more liberal dormitory group as a reference group—changed their values to a less conservative orientation.

Mechanisms for Group-generated Attitude Change   In conclusion, three general mechanisms will be suggested by which groups can, over time, influence the affective states of their members. Each of the mechanisms, to be effective, requires that the target member *accept* the group (or stimuli provided by it), and each should be considerably more potent over an extended period of group membership than in the short term.

Mechanism 1: Changing Behavior, with Affective Changes Following   A group often is able to directly influence the behavior of selected members simply by making group-controlled rewards contingent upon the members' engaging in the behavior deemed desirable by the group. As the individual finds himself exhibiting the behavior—especially when the behavior tends to become habitual—his attitudes are likely to become more and more consistent with it. Consider, for example, a work group which subtly coerces one of its members to engage in dishonest behaviors aimed at subverting the attempts of the group's supervisor to increase the rate of production. It would not be surprising in this case to find the attitude of the worker toward the supervisor gradually changing in the negative direction. Over time, his attitude toward the supervisor would become increasingly consistent with the behaviors that he was exhibiting vis-à-vis the supervisor.

Two general explanations have been offered for the pervasive tendency for behavior and attitudes to become consistent over time: "dissonance reduction" (Festinger, 1957) and "self-attribution" (Bem, 1965). The former explanation, in brief, is that an individual experiences a state of tension or dissonance when he finds himself doing things that are inconsistent with his attitudes and beliefs; if he cannot conveniently rid himself of this tension by changing or terminating the behavior, he may change his attitudes or values to bring them into line with that behavior. The self-attribution hypothesis leads to nearly identical predictions but from a different theoretical perspective. This hypothesis suggests that an individual observes himself engaging in a behavior and, in attempting to explain why he behaves as he does, he attributes to himself an attitude which would be an appropriate *reason* for the behavior. For example: "I seem to work very hard and very long hours—therefore I must really like my work."

In each case, however, the more the group explicitly coerces the individual to engage in the behavior by using very potent rewards or punishments, the *less* substantial the affective change of the individual. One feels little dissonance when he engages in a slightly aversive behavior for a very large reward; one does not have to look to his own attitudes to find a *reason* for that behavior—the extrinsic reward suffices, and attitude change is unlikely. This is probably part of the reason that the Chinese Communists' attempts to use group methods to brainwash prisoners during the Korean war were less than completely successful: the coercion to "confess and repent" was so strong that many prisoners were able to attribute their acquiescence to the demands of their captors to the group-supplied rewards and punishments rather than to any genuine change of their own values (cf. Schein, 1956).

When, however, a group is able to provide relatively *subtle* coercion to obtain the behavior (e.g., "Come on, everybody else is doing it, don't be a laggard!"), substantial affective changes may result. Yet it also should be kept in mind that unless the individual *values* the rewards controlled by the group, he is unlikely to go along with the group, and this mechanism for obtaining affective changes in group members will lose its power.

Mechanism 2: Changing Beliefs, with Affective Changes Following   Attitudes tend to be based upon the *beliefs* individuals hold about the attitude object—and the affect an individual associates with the object may be changed by changing the beliefs he holds about it (Fishbein, 1967; Rosenberg, 1956). A worker might, for example, have positive feelings toward labor unions—and base those feelings on beliefs that unions lead to better pay for workers, keep managements from exploiting workers, and in general contribute to a healthy national economy. If (as in the case of the Lieberman study) that worker became a member of management, he probably would be subjected to stimuli which would weaken the strength of his beliefs and, perhaps, introduce others in their place—for example, statements or opinions that unions hinder industrial progress, that union officials often are corrupt, and so on. To the extent that the worker's new group is effective in changing the content and/or the strength of the beliefs he holds about unions, his overall feelings toward labor unions is likely to change as well. Since (as discussed previously) groups often can powerfully influence the beliefs of their members, this mechanism probably is one very important means by which a person's group membership influences his preferences, attitudes, and values.

A second version of mechanism 2 has to do with the beliefs the group member holds about *himself*. When an individual is in an unusual situation or other circumstances in which his confidence regarding his attitudes and affective reactions is not high, he may turn to other members of the group for purposes of self-evaluation and comparison (cf. Latane, 1966). If that comparison reveals that the individual's attitude is inconsistent with that of the other group members, he may (perhaps without conscious choice) change his feelings to be more consistent with those of his peers. For example, an individual who was uncertain about whether or not he really liked a speech by a visiting government official reported experiencing much more positive feelings about the speech when, at its conclusion, his friends spontaneously gave the official a lengthy standing ovation.

For either version of mechanism 2 to be effective, of course, it is essential that (1) the beliefs of the group member—whether about the environment or about his own attitudes and feelings—be open to change and (2) the group be valued by the individual and/or seen as a source of trustworthy data about the environment or about the "appropriate" affective response to it. Thus, mechanism 2 is likely to be much more potent in influencing the attitudes and values of new and/or low-status group members than of those who are more experienced or self-confident.

Mechanism 3: Direct Change of Affect   A substantial body of literature is available showing that by judicious control of the positive or reinforcing stimuli which are at the command of the group, it should be able to "condition" the attitudes of group members regarding some person, object, or concept. In the study of students at the small New England college, for example, Newcomb found that the most popular students tended to be of a liberal persuasion. When other students were in the presence of these students, therefore, it is likely that they often were exposed simultaneously to social reinforcement (i.e., attention from someone who was admired) *and* to liberal political viewpoints. It is possible that such conditioning of student attitudes is part of the reason for the change observed among many students at this college.

Concluding Comment on the Three Mechanisms   The three mechanisms for group-generated attitude change, which are shown graphically in Figure 13-1, have been discussed above separately. It is likely, however, that in most real-life situations they act in close concert. As mentioned

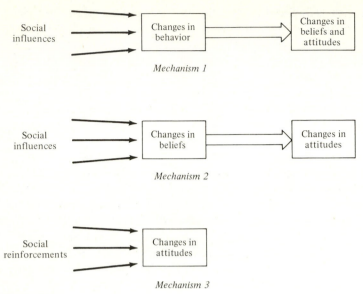

Figure 13-1 Three mechanisms for group-generated attitude changes.

before, for each to be effective it is necessary for the individual to *value* what the group has to offer and, in that sense, to be dependent upon the group for the satisfaction of his own needs. A group member who is very much his "own" person (i.e., has low social needs) or who has plenty of alternative groups where he can satisfy his needs is not likely to find his preferences, attitudes, or values very much influenced by the group.

But when the group *is* of importance to the individual, the stimuli which are supplied by it can—and often do—have a great deal of impact on the person's likes and dislikes. Although the stimuli responsible for such effects are very much under the control of the group, it often is the case that substantial changes in attitudes or feelings may be realized without either the individual or his fellow group members being fully aware of what is happening or how it is happening. If a group were to set out deliberately to use its control over discretionary stimuli to change the attitudes of one or more members who were dependent upon the group for personal satisfactions, the amount of change realized could be very large indeed.

Arousing Motive States

The discretionary stimuli supplied by a group can increase (or decrease) both the general level of psychological "arousal" of group members and the particular motive states that members experience in the group setting. As will be seen below, these effects can come about simply because of other group members *being there*—and making their presence known to the target individual—or because of the specific content of the stimuli provided by the group. In the paragraphs to follow, we will examine separately how group-supplied stimuli can (1) increase the arousal of individual group members, (2) decrease their arousal and anxiety, and (3) cue particular motive states of group members.

Increasing Arousal   It has sometimes been proposed (e.g., Zajonc, 1965) that the *mere presence* of other people can increase the level of arousal of individuals in performance-relevant situations. In recent years, however, a number of researchers have questioned whether it is the *mere* presence of others which increases arousal or the presence of others who are in some specified relationship to the individual. In general, it now appears that the presence of other people can and does increase the level of arousal of an individual—but only when the other people are in an evaluative (or potentially evaluative) relationship vis-à-vis the individual (e.g., Cottrell et al., 1968). Thus, one would not expect that a worker's arousal would be much affected by being in a large room where a number of other people also were working—unless, as often happens, the worker had reason to believe that the other people might be assessing his rate or quality of output. If among the other people were members of management who were responsible for *evaluating* the performance of the worker, his arousal could rise very high.

Decreasing Arousal and Anxiety   Although at first glance it may seem contradictory to the material discussed immediately above, there also is available in the research literature good evidence that merely being in the presence of other people in many cases *reduces* a person's level of anxiety and arousal. A number of researchers have shown that individuals who are highly aroused (especially when the arousal is due to fear) actively seek out others and prefer to spend their time in a group rather than alone.

In general, such findings fit well with those showing that under external stress, group members often seek out each other and develop new or heightened feelings of closeness or cohesiveness. When, for example, a natural disaster strikes or threatens a community, individuals show levels of mutual support, reassurance, and cooperation that previously were unknown. Similar phenomena often (but not always) occur when the survival of a work group (or even of an organization) is threatened from an external source—including another group or organization (cf. Sherif, 1965; Klein, 1971).

In summary, then, it appears that in some circumstances being in a group can serve to increase one's level of arousal and anxiety; and in other cases, group membership can help decrease experienced upset. The research evidence suggests, in particular, that when the individual has reason to believe that other group members will provide negative or explicitly evaluative (and, therefore, possibly negative) stimuli to him, his level of arousal increases; when he expects the stimuli to be positive (e.g., reassuring or fear reducing), arousal decreases. These effects are based largely on research in which a person is (or expects to be) merely in the presence of other people; as yet, few studies have examined what happens to a person's level of arousal as a function of actual social interaction in groups. It would be expected that the arousal-increasing and arousal-decreasing effects of the group should be considerably magnified when the other group members provide the individual with discretionary stimuli which confirm his expectations—whether those expectations have to do with the possibility of being socially evaluated or with the possibility of being comforted and reassured. The effects of such changes in level of arousal on individual performance effectiveness are discussed in the next chapter.

Cuing Member Motive States   In Chapter 10 it was shown how the cues present in a person's task or job materials could arouse or depress his strength of desire for various outcomes—such as social affiliation, achievement, and so on.

The stimuli provided by other group members often have similar effects. For example, if the climate of a given work group is one of social acceptance and interpersonal warmth, any member of that group is likely to encounter a goodly number of cues which will arouse his motives for social affiliation. If the climate is characterized more by a high task orientation and performance-related activities, on the other hand, the individual will tend to experience, instead, cues which are likely to arouse the strength of his own motives for achievement and accomplishment.

The existence of such cues in group settings probably represents one reason why it is often so difficult to change the norms and activities which take place in ongoing groups in work organizations: that is, the activities themselves provide cues which maintain the motivation of the members to engage in that type of activity—which increases the likelihood of the activity continuing, and so on, in a self-perpetuating cycle.

Increasing Job-relevant Knowledge and Skills

We turn now to the final type of impact of group-supplied discretionary stimuli to be considered—namely, how such stimuli can be useful to group members in gaining the knowledge and skills they need to perform their jobs or fulfill their organizational roles. The group is of considerable importance in learning *how* to behave in organizations for several reasons. Personal trial-and-error learning of a new skill or behavior pattern is, in many cases, very inefficient. The help of other group members often permits an individual to short-cut his learning process and to lessen the personal risks involved in learning. Indeed, there are many skills and role behaviors which probably are impossible to master without the active involvement of other people— for example, learning how to manage part of an organization or learning how to operate a sophisticated piece of equipment. In his book *The Making of a Surgeon*, William Nolen describes numerous ways in which the fledgling surgeon is completely dependent upon other members of his medical team in developing the capability to execute surgical procedures with even minimal adequacy.

In general, the group can assist members in developing their skills and role behaviors in three ways: (1) by direct instruction, (2) by providing feedback about behavior, and (3) by serving as models of correct or appropriate behavior.

Direct Instruction   By itself, direct instruction is probably useful only for the most simple skills and behaviors. Simply being *told*, for example, how to drive a car or how to perform an appendectomy is not sufficient to master such skills. Nevertheless, the importance of direct instruction in skill and role learning should not be underestimated, especially for new members of groups or organizations. If the group elects to withhold direct instruction from an individual, his adaptation can be severely impaired: not knowing how to do something as simple as processing a request for paper clips through the bureaucracy can be highly stressful for a new employee. Thus, while direct instruction is not *sufficient* for an individual to develop needed skills and behavior patterns, it often is a necessary part of such learning— and does represent an important resource held by the group, which may be provided or withheld from a person at the group's discretion.

Feedback   Feedback from other group members can serve two major functions for a group member: it can provide him with information, identifying which behaviors are "right" (or appropriate) and "wrong" (or inappropriate) in carrying out one's job or role; and it can provide him with reinforcement, rewarding "right" behaviors and punishing "wrong" ones. Both functions can, of course, increase a member's job-relevant knowledge and skill.

Informational feedback, in the form of other members' responses, has been shown in laboratory investigations to affect both learning and memory. Feedback which is primarily rewarding or punishing in impact also has been shown to affect skill learning and role behavior (cf. Bandura, 1971; Berger & Lambert, 1968; Walters & Parke, 1964). Perhaps of special interest in this regard is research showing how it is possible to *change* the role of a given group member by selectively reinforcing certain of his behaviors (e.g., Bavelas et al., 1965; Sarbin & Allen, 1968a). In one such study, for example, reinforcing feedback from high-status group members was shown to increase the level of participation of initially recalcitrant group members, and there was some tendency for negative feedback to decrease the participation of members who initially were highly verbal (Sarbin & Allen, 1968a). Unfortunately, very few studies of the role of feedback in skill or role-behavior learning have been conducted using groups of adults in the context of ongoing groups or organizations.

Modeling   One of the most pervasive ways a group can be helpful to individual members in role and skill learning is through the provision of models. The need for models is often very great—especially for complex tasks and roles, some of which may be impossible to learn adequately in the absence of a concrete model.

The earliest analyses of modeling and imitative learning (e.g., Miller & Dollard, 1941) focused on situations in which the learner simply "matched" the behavior of a model. It was shown, for example, that an observer who watched a model engage in some behavior and be rewarded for it would engage in the same behavior if he also was motivated to obtain the reward. If he was then rewarded, the new behavior would become established in his repertoire.

Although learning through matching clearly is one way people use others in developing skills, it is not the whole story. In addition, individuals can acquire quite robust symbolic representations of new activities by *observing* models—in addition to the simple stimulus-response associations required for matching behavior (Bandura, 1971). Thus, learning through modeling can occur without immediate reinforcement of the new behavior, and such learning can be stored away for use much later by the individual. Reinforcement, then, can be viewed as a condition which may *facilitate* learning from models (because reinforcement—or anticipated reinforcement—can lead to increased attention to the model and retention of what he does) but not as a necessary condition for such learning. It should be kept in mind, of course, that reinforcement directly controls when the newly learned behaviors actually will be *performed* after they have been learned—regardless of how those behaviors were acquired.

Summary   The individual is substantially dependent upon the group for gaining the knowledge and skills he needs to perform his job adequately. However, little controlled research has yet been done which illuminates how this process takes place in organizational contexts. The processes of skill and role learning may be of special interest in work organizations because of the *complexity* of the skills and role behaviors required of many organization members. The more complex a job or role, the more likely an individual is to perform inadequately if left to his own devices—and also the more likely he is to need *all three* of the aids a group can provide to learn it well (i.e., direct instruction, feedback, and model provision). This, of course, makes the individual heavily dependent upon the group in precisely those cases when the risk of failure for him is greatest. It would be expected, therefore, that the amount of power and influence a group has over an individual should be very great when the individual is attempting to obtain knowledge about how to perform a complex new job or role. In such circumstances, the capability of the group to influence the member in *other* ways—such as obtaining behavioral or attitudinal conformity from him on matters not immediately relevant to the task at hand—also should be especially great.

Little attention has been given above to the use of the group as a site for increasing the job-relevant knowledge and skill of members *above* levels minimally required for adequate performance. Many interpersonal "training groups" are explicitly designed so that group members can effectively use one another as resources in increasing their competence in *interpersonal* behavior (cf. Chapters 7 and 15). Interestingly, it generally is assumed in the T-group movement that direct instruction can be of little help in learning new interpersonal skills; the focus instead is on members' providing each other with information-full feedback about their behavior and models of alternative ways of behaving. Apparently important to whatever success such groups might achieve is the development of a climate within the group which is minimally threatening—thereby allowing and encouraging members to freely experiment with new interpersonal behaviors.

To the extent that such a group climate is, in fact, necessary for the development of new interpersonal skills in a group, one would have to be substantially pessimistic about the usefulness of most existing groups in ongoing organizations as sites in which group members could experiment with and learn radically new ways of behaving. Indeed, most groups in contemporary organizations seem instead to be characterized by very little experimenting, little risk taking, and high interpersonal competitiveness (Argyris, 1969)—conditions which would not likely be conducive to members' effectively using each other to learn genuinely innovative patterns of behavior.

DIRECT EFFECTS OF GROUPS ON MEMBER BEHAVIOR: GROUP NORMS

In the previous sections, we have examined how group-supplied discretionary stimuli can affect various psychological and informational states of group members. Change in the actual behavior of group members was viewed as a typical (but indirect) consequence of changes in the beliefs members hold and in their attitudes and skills. It also is true, of course, that a member's behavior can be affected *directly* by the discretionary stimuli controlled by his fellows; indeed, one of the most generally accepted principles of psychology is that the behavior of a person can be shaped effectively by someone who is in control of stimuli which are valued (or disvalued) by the target person.

Since most groups do, in fact, have many resources which are valued by group members, member behavior can be directly affected by the rewards (and punishments) which are administered by the group contingent upon the actions of the individual. Such effects must, however, take place on a highly individualistic basis. That is, when other group members wish a particular person to engage in some behavior, they must use their control of discretionary stimuli in such a way that the individual comes to realize that it is in his personal best interest to comply with the behavioral demands of his peers.

Such a process, while powerful, can consume a great deal of the time and energy of group members and thus is not a very efficient means of coordinating their activities—especially if the group is moderately large. Therefore, most of the regulating of group member behavior typically takes place through behavioral *norms* which are created and enforced by group members. Indeed, norms are so pervasive and powerful in groups that it has been suggested that "it is only in imagination that we can talk about a human group apart from norms" (Davis, 1950, p. 53).

This section focuses on the nature of group norms and their effects on member behavior. In particular, we will examine (1) the structural characteristics of norms, (2) what happens when someone deviates from a norm, and (3) the conditions under which individuals are and are not likely to comply with group norms. In the paragraphs which follow immediately below, we specify several of the major characteristics of group norms which guide the subsequent discussion.

1 *Norms are structural characteristics of groups, which summarize and simplify group influence processes.* Although numerous definitions and conceptualizations of norms have been proposed, there is general agreement that a norm is a *structural* characteristic of a group, which summarizes and highlights those processes within the group which are intended to regulate and regularize group member behavior. Thus, norms represent an important means of short-cutting the need to use discretionary stimuli on a continuous basis to control the behavior of individual group members.

2 *Norms apply only to behavior—not to private thoughts and feelings.* Although some writers speak of the effects of group norms on member attitudes and beliefs, norms are treated here as being exclusively relevant to the actual behavior of group members. This usage does include verbal

behavior, and so what a member *says* he believes or what he *says* his attitude is can be very much under the normative control of the group. It should be emphasized, however, that such behavioral compliance does not necessarily reflect the true private attitudes and beliefs of group members. As pointed out earlier in this chapter, group-supplied discretionary stimuli can indeed affect one's private attitudes and beliefs—but the process is considerably more complex and subtle than merely coercing a member to *say* he agrees with the stance of the group on some matter.

3 *Norms generally are developed only for behaviors which are viewed as important by most group members.* Norms generally develop only for behaviors which otherwise would have to be controlled by direct and continuous social influence (Thibaut & Kelley, 1959). While this implies that only those behaviors viewed as most important in the eyes of group members will be brought under normative control, it does not mean that normatively controlled behaviors are necessarily *objectively* the most important to the group. Some businesses, for example, even today have a norm that one should wear a hat when he leaves the building; it is doubtful that hat-wearing behavior is objectively important to the group, but the fact that most members *believe* it to be important is sufficient cause for the norm to be developed and enforced.

4 *Norms usually develop gradually, but the process can be short-cut if members wish.* Norms about behavior typically develop gradually and informally as members learn what behaviors are, in fact, important for the group to control and what discretionary stimuli seem most effective in regulating the occurrence of those behaviors. It is possible, nevertheless, for groups to consciously short-cut the process of norm development. If for some reason group members decide that a particular norm would be desirable or helpful, they may simply agree to institute such a norm suddenly by declaring that "from now on" the norm exists. Someone might say, for example, "We seem to interrupt each other a lot in this group; let's agree [i.e., have a norm] that nobody talks until the other person is finished." If the group as a whole agrees with this proposal, then one might observe marked differences in the social interaction within that group thereafter.

5 *Not all norms apply to everyone.* Finally, it should be noted that norms often do not apply uniformly to all group members. For example, as is discussed in detail later, high-status members often have more freedom to deviate from the letter of the norm than do other people—that is, they build up so-called idiosyncrasy credits. Also, groups will at times form a norm which applies only to one person (or to a small subset of persons) within a group. In such cases, we may speak of the norms as representing the *roles* of the person(s) to whom the norms apply (Thibaut & Kelley, 1959, pp. 142–147).

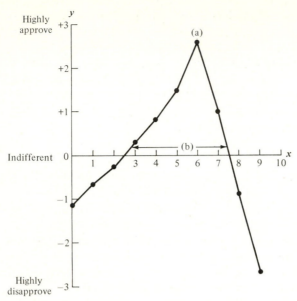

Figure 13-2 Schematic representation of the Return Potential Model (RPM) of normative structure. The ordinate is an axis of evaluation; the abscissa is an axis of behavior. (Adapted from Jackson, 1965, p. 303.)

A Model of Group Behavioral Norms

An elegant conception of the structure of group norms has been proposed by Jackson (1960, 1965, 1966). The model, which focuses on the distribution of potential approval and disapproval others feel for various behaviors which might be exhibited in a given situation, can be represented in two-dimensional space: the ordinate is the amount of approval and disapproval felt, and the abscissa is the amount of the given behavior exhibited. A "return potential curve" can be drawn in this space, indicating the *pattern and intensity* of approval and disapproval associated with various possible behaviors. An example of a return potential curve is shown in Figure 13-2.

The "return potential model" (RPM) can be used to describe any situation in which a group norm serves to regulate the behavior of group members. To apply the model, one would obtain from group members (or infer from observations of behavior in the group) the amount of approval or disapproval associated with various behaviors and, from these data, plot a return potential curve. The curve in Figure 13-2, for example, might reflect the norms of a group regarding the amount of talking an individual member does during a group meeting. Both too little and too much talking, in this case, would be disapproved—but the intensity of the disapproval is stronger for someone who talks too much than for someone who talks too little. (The units of behavior in the example in Figure 13-2 are arbitrary; in practice, the abscissa would be scaled using units appropriate to the behavior in question.)

A return potential curve can, theoretically, assume any shape. In a formulation similar to that of Jackson, March (1954) suggests three basic types of norms: the unattainable-ideal norm, the preferred-value norm, and the attainable-ideal norm. The unattainable-ideal and attainable-ideal norms are depicted as return potential curves in Figure 13-3; the preferred-value norm is of the general type shown in Figure 13-2. In essence, the unattainable ideal norm connotes "the more the better"; thus, among a group of scholars, the more insightful one's contributions are the better; or on a football team, the more tackles made the better. The preferred-value norm is often characteristic of the approval and disapproval felt by members of a work group regarding the productivity of individual members: too little output is disapproved—but so is too *much* output. An example (from March, 1954) of the attainable-ideal norm might involve a football team in possession of the ball on the opponents' 20-yard line. A halfback will earn increasing approval as he carries the ball increasing distances—up to 20 yards. After that, he will have made a touchdown and can gain no further approval: 25 yards are no better than 21. There are, of course, many other possible curves which would be descriptive of other types of group norms.

The RPM is a useful device for thinking about norms and can be especially helpful in making systematic one's observations of normative behavior in an organization. It is possible, for example, to generate objective

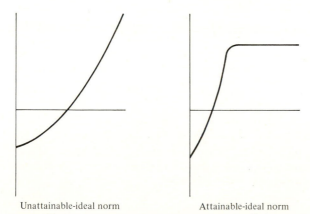

Unattainable-ideal norm   Attainable-ideal norm

Figure 13-3   Unattainable-ideal and attainable-ideal norms (March 1954) shown as return potential curves.

measures of norms using the model, and Jackson (1965, 1966) suggests (and provides computational formulas for) five such measures:

1 The Point of Maximum Return: the point on the behavior dimension which generates the highest level of approval from others. (Point *a* in Figure 13-2.)

2 The Range of Tolerable Behavior: the segment of the behavior dimension which is *approved* by others. (Indicated by *b* In Figure 13-2.)

3 The Potential Return Difference: the amount of approval versus disapproval associáted with norm-regulated behaviors—indicating the relative emphasis on rewards versus punishments in regulating member behavior.

4 Intensity: the overall strength of approval and disapproval associated with norm-regulated behavior—indicating the amount of affect associated with the norm, regardless of whether that affect is predominantly positive or negative in direction.

5 Crystallization: the degree of consensus among group members regarding the amount of approval or disapproval associated with each point on the behavioral dimension.

The RPM has been utilized in research in a number of group and organizational settings, both for understanding the internal dynamics of ongoing groups and organizations and for making comparative studies of different social systems (Jackson, in press). In addition to its obvious uses for research on the effects of various organizational practices aimed at changing the social climate of work groups, the RPM has considerable potential for making *diagnoses* of the normative state of affairs within a given group—as a first step in a change program involving diagnosis, feedback, and action. Through the RPM it should be possible to help group members see, objectively and in simple terms, what the group norms actually are and how they may be guiding behavior in ways that are unrealized or unintended—which should provide an impetus for group-generated changes.

Deviance from Group Norms

In an analysis of the reasons for the Bay of Pigs fiasco undertaken by President Kennedy and his advisers in 1961, Janis (1972, Ch. 2) quotes Arthur Schlesinger explaining why he had not pressed more urgently his objections to the developing plans:

> In the months after the Bay of Pigs I bitterly reproached myself for having kept
> so silent during those crucial discussions in the Cabinet room, though my

feelings of guilt were tempered by the knowledge that a course of objection would have accomplished little save to *gain me a name as a nuisance.* I can only explain my failure to do more than raise a few timid questions by reporting that one's impulse to blow the whistle on this nonsense was simply undone by the circumstances of the discussion. (Schlesinger, 1965, p. 255, italics added)

It is not difficult to understand how Schlesinger might have come to hold the above views, given the following event:

At a large birthday party for Mrs. Robert Kennedy, the Attorney General, who had been constantly informed about the Cuban invasion plan, took Schlesinger aside and asked him why he was opposed. The President's brother listened coldly and then said, "You may be right or you may be wrong, but the President has his mind made up. Don't push it any further. Now is the time for everyone to help him all they can." (Janis, 1972, Ch. 2)

Communicating with the Deviant　The "treatment" given Schlesinger illustrates how groups can use their control of discretionary stimuli to bring into line members who are behaving contrary to group norms. A number of research studies document that when a group member expresses a view which deviates from that of the group, his fellow members do increasingly direct communications toward him (e.g., Schachter, 1951; Emerson, 1954; Berkowitz & Howard, 1959). The researchers interpret this communication as reflecting attempts to move the member back into congruence with the group norm. Sometimes the stimuli provided may be material or physical rather than verbal. For example, the practice of "binging" (i.e., hitting someone forcefully on the upper arm) has been described as an effective means used by work group members to correct the behavior of a worker who is violating the group norms about production quantity (cf. Homans, 1950).

It may be recalled from earlier in the chapter that a *role* in a group can be described in terms of special behavioral norms which apply specifically to the role occupant(s). Thus, it is not surprising to find that a member who deviates from his role in the group (e.g., a leader who quits leading) encounters reactions which are similar to those observed when someone violates a general group norm. Unfortunately, experimental research which focuses on the reactions of groups to this type of deviance is scarce.

The literature on role conflict, however, offers some relevant insights. For example, research on interrole conflict suggests that when a person deviates from his role (even if the reason is to fulfill another equally legitimate role), discretionary stimuli may be applied swiftly by his peers to enforce the expectations associated with the first role. A similar process often ensues when an individual encounters intersender conflict—i.e., when conflicting expectations are sent from different sources regarding appropriate behavior for the occupant of a single role. The essence of role conflict (and the crux of the problem for the role occupant) in either case is that the individual is confronted with discretionary stimuli aimed at changing his behavior *regardless* of how he actually behaves. Because he cannot please all role senders at once, the individual experiences conflict. (The effects of such conflict and the ways individuals react to it are discussed by Kahn et al., 1964, and by Sarbin & Allen, 1968).

Rejection of the Deviant   When a member persistently deviates from what is acceptable to his fellow group members (either by his expressions of attitudes and beliefs or by his overt behavior), he becomes vulnerable to rejection by the group. In other words, the application of discretionary stimuli intended to persuade or pressure the deviant to change will persist for only so long, whereupn the other members may "change the composition of the psychological group" (Festinger, 1950). A number of studies provide support for the hypothesis that a persistently deviant member tends to be rejected. In general, however, research results suggest—and informal observation of groups in operation provide some confirmation—that rejection of a member is viewed as a fairly serious step for a group to take, and may be administered by a group only when all else has failed or when the deviant is seen as completely incorrigible (e.g., Sampson & Brandon, 1964).

Yet there may be another reason why groups apparently are so hesitant to cease communicating with a deviant and to reject him with finality. It has been argued that the group *needs* the deviant—and therefore cannot really afford to eliminate him completely (Dentler & Erikson, 1959). Group norms, for example, may become more explicit and more clearly understood by group members as a result of their observation of various deviant behaviors and the consequences which ensue. In addition, because deviants are observed to receive negative outcomes from the group, the incentive value of conformity may be enhanced as a result. Moreover, the process of dealing with deviant members may help the group clarify its own boundaries and gain a better sense of what is distinctive about the group and central to its identity—and what is not.

In a number of ways, then, deviant members can contribute positively to the stability of the group and to the maintenance of its identity. As a consequence, the role of the deviant often becomes institutionalized within the group, and group members will strongly resist any trend toward complete elimination of a deviant member (Dentler & Erikson, 1959, p. 102). While this particular perspective does not purport to handle all the dynamics of a group's response to deviance, it does suggest one important and frequently overlooked set of reasons why groups may be reluctant to respond to deviance by immediately rejecting the member who deviates.

Some Determinants of Member Compliance with Group Norms

Group members tend to behave in accord with the norms of the group in two general cases:

Case 1. The norm-specified behaviors are congruent with the personal attitudes, beliefs, and prior behavioral dispositions of the group members. In this case, there is no conflict between the individual and the group; the member would tend to behave in norm-congruent ways anyway. It should be noted, however, that the reason group members are predisposed toward compliance with the norm in such cases may be that the group has long ago done an effective job of inculcating in the individual attitudes and beliefs which are consistent with the norm.

Consider, for example, a work group that enforces a norm of not communicating very much or very openly with members of management. A member who has been in that group for some time may have come to genuinely believe that "managers can't be trusted—they'll use what you tell them to exploit you whenever they can." The group would not need to pressure this member into compliance with the norm; the more subtle and continuing influences of the group on his attitudes and beliefs over time would have rendered such direct pressure unnecessary.

Case 2. It is frequently the case, however, that the behaviors specified by a group norm are *not* consistent with the personal attitudes or beliefs of one or more members. In the example described above, a recent college graduate just joining the work group would be unlikely to hold an antimanagement set of beliefs and attitudes—and therefore would not be likely to comply with the group norm if left entirely to his own devices. Whether or not the member does in fact comply with the group norm in such cases depends upon two conditions:

1   Pressures to comply must be sent from the group and sent strongly enough to be experienced and understood by the target individual.

2   The target individual must value the rewards (or devalue the sanctions) controlled by the group sufficiently that he is willing to be guided by the wishes of the group, rather than by his own predispositions or by pressures he may experience from other groups.

In the paragraphs to follow, we will list several factors which affect the degree to which these two conditions are met.

Noticeable Pressures to Comply Must Be Sent by the Group   The degree to which discretionary cues will be sent to the target individual strongly enough to attract his attention depends both upon (1) who the target individual is and what his role is in the group and (2) the characteristics of the group and the nature of the deviant behavior in question.

1 Some members can get away with deviance more readily than others. It has been suggested (Hollander, 1958, 1964) that group members can earn "idiosyncrasy credits" during the course of their experience in a group. When held in sufficient numbers, these credits permit a member to exhibit some deviant behaviors without incurring the pressures or sanctions usually applied to members who violate a group norm. Group members generate "idiosyncrasy credits" mainly by being "good group citizens"—that is, by generally conforming to the expectations of the group and by contributing effectively to the attainment of group goals. Thus, new group members should not have a balance of "idiosyncrasy credits" to draw upon and therefore should not have much freedom to deviate early in their tenure. Consistent with this prediction, it has been found that new members of a work group were expected to conform more closely to group production norms than were workers who had been group members for some time (Hughes, 1946). Members who have attained high status in the group also would be expected to have a substantial balance of "idiosyncrasy credits" (Hollander, 1961). And, as would be predicted, research evidence suggests that higher-status members are able to be more resistive to conformity pressures than are their lower-status peers (e.g., Harvey & Consalvi, 1960).

2 Some groups send more pressures to comply than do others—and even in the same group, some deviant members will be sanctioned more severely than others. In general, research literature suggests that a group will tend to send more pressures to conform to group norms when (a) group members are strongly motivated to achieve uniformity within the group (Festinger, 1950); (b) the norm in question is of high importance or relevance to the group; and (c) the behavior in question is deviant from the norm to an especially noticeable extent (Mudd, 1968).

Alternatively, in terms of the Jackson RPM of norms, it might be predicted that pressures sent to group members to comply with norms should be especially strong (a) when the norm is of *high intensity*—i.e., when group members hold strong feelings of approval or disapproval contingent upon norm-congruent behavior; and (b) when the norm is *highly crystallized*—i.e., when there is substantial agreement among members about the amount of approval or disapproval associated with each possible behavior relevant to the norm.

The Stimuli Used to Enforce the Norm Must Be Valued by the Target Member(s)   The second general condition which must be met for an initially recalcitrant member to comply with group norms is for the rewards of compliance (or sanctions for noncompliance) to be sufficiently potent that the individual comes to *want* to change his behavior. Thus, the more a member personally needs or desires those resources over which the group has control, the more likely he is to go along with group norms.

As noted throughout this chapter, groups generally have control over many affectively powerful stimuli. Therefore, a group typically has a variety of means to add considerable "punch" to the pressures it places on group members for compliance to group norms. It should be noted, however, that the group need not always actually use the stimuli under its control to obtain member compliance; merely having the member know that the group has the potential to administer such stimuli often is quite sufficient. One does not need to be struck down by a bolt of lightning to know the fear of God. It also is true, on the other hand, that when a group is not present in a given situation (or when responses of group members are made in private), behavioral compliance decreases—presumably in part because the capability of the group to apply rewarding or punishing stimuli to the members in such circumstances is lessened (Kiesler, 1969, Ch. 11; Allen, 1965, pp. 145–146).

Previous research has focused on the use of *interpersonal* rewards and punishments as a means of gaining member compliance to group norms. Little attention has been given to the use of material rewards, the provision of information as a reward, or the provision of access to external rewards. The emphasis on interpersonal rewards and sanctions should not restrict the generality of research findings in the area substantially, however, since interpersonal stimuli are probably the most widely used means of obtaining norm compliance in groups and interpersonal rewards and punishments are highly potent for most people.

The not-surprising conclusion from such research is that, in general, the more an individual is attracted to a group (or the more he has a personal need for the social rewards controlled by the group), the more he conforms. Thus, as would be expected, compliance tends to be very high in highly cohesive groups—where members presumably care a great deal about being together and about continuing their mutually satisfying social interaction. Further, there is evidence that group members who do not much need or care about the social rewards which can be provided by their fellows (for example, very high-status members, or very low-status members who are not committed to remaining in the group) often conform less than other group members.

It should be emphasized, however, that the relationship between a member's need for rewards controlled by the group and his conformity to the group assumes that "other things" are constant. Other things never are. By and large, it has been found that when the individual has a high *personal* stake in the task situation—i.e., he has something else he may value as much or more than the potential rewards or punishments he may receive or forgo in the group—he shows less conformity to group norms.

CONCLUSION

Most broadly viewed, this has been a chapter about social influence processes which take place in organizations—and especially how those processes affect what employees think, feel, and do at work. We have elected to discuss these processes in terms of the stimuli which are provided by the groups of which individuals are members—using the concept of "group" very loosely to refer to all those people with whom a person has meaningful and continuing contact in the organization.

Our general conclusion is that the people with whom one works in an organization can—and often do—have rather substantial effects not only on behavior but on how one thinks and feels as well. In the next chapter, we examine some specific implications of this material, particularly as it applies to the *effectiveness* of individual and group behavior in organizations.

REVIEW AND DISCUSSION QUESTIONS

1 Is high work group cohesiveness always desirable from the standpoint of an organization's attempts to achieve its major goals? Why?

2 From your own experience in organizations, give examples of group activities involving the use of discretionary stimuli aimed at (a) socialization, (b) achieving uniformity, and (c) achieving diversity.

3 What can the practicing manager do to ensure that organizational members receive the "right" types and amounts of group-supplied discretionary stimuli? Should he even try to do this?

4 How may group-supplied discretionary stimuli be used in the prevention of organizational "entropy"?

5 Describe the various methods that groups might use to bring about "group-generated" attitude change. How effective are these methods? What factors influence the effectiveness of the various methods?

6 What is the relationship between organizational roles and norms? Can a role exist in an organization without norms?

7 How can Jackson's RPM model be used to describe (model) the behavior of work group members in organizations? Take, for example, the "productivity norm" as a theme for discussing this.

8 In what ways can a group influence the perception of organizational "reality" by its members? What factors influence the degree to which group-supplied information about "reality" is accepted by group members?

9 In what ways can groups influence the arousal or anxiety states of group members? What is the practical importance of this?

10 Much of the theory that now exists in the area of group processes has resulted from the analysis of behavior of individuals in one group in a laboratory. In the "real world" individuals have membership in many groups. How applicable is the theory from studies of individuals in artificially created (laboratory study) groups to groups in the "real world"?

Chapter 14

Social Influences on Work Effectiveness

In the previous chapter, we examined in some detail how groups and other members of a person's role set can exert influence on individuals in organizations. We now take a more specific focus and analyze how such social influences relate to work *effectiveness* in organizations. The chapter begins by looking at some conditions within groups themselves that limit or enhance their ability to be able to bring about an impact on an individual's effectiveness at work. The second part of the chapter deals with the means by which groups can affect the individual employee's work performance. Particular stress is placed here on the notion that the nature and degree of such social influences depend crucially on the type of work being performed and thus on the demands that the work makes on the person. The final section narrows to an analysis of a particular form of social influence that is likely to have especially strong consequences for the work effectiveness of the individual: namely, leadership.

CONDITIONS WITHIN GROUPS THAT MODERATE THEIR IMPACT ON WORK EFFECTIVENESS

Before proceeding to consider (in the next section) the ways that groups can influence the work effectiveness of individuals, we should first take into account certain conditions within groups that can affect how much and what kind of impact they will have. Uppermost among these are a group's characteristic reactions to deviance and the degree of cohesiveness that exists within the group.

Deviance and Group Effectiveness

The experimental work on how groups react to members who engage in behaviors which are inconsistent with group norms (described in the previous chapter) reveals a fairly primitive type of group process. Caricatured a bit, the process operates as follows: Uniformity, conformity to norms, and adherence to one's role is the rule. When someone steps out of line, other members provide him with potent doses of discretionary stimuli designed to persuade or coerce him back to "normal." This pressure continues until the would-be deviant (1) gives in and ceases expressing his deviant thoughts or exhibiting his deviant behavior; (2) is psychologically or bodily rejected by the group or becomes institutionalized by the group as the "house deviant"; or (3) finally convinces the other group members of the rightness of his thoughts or the appropriateness of his behavior.

The more the group has control of discretionary stimuli which are important to group members, the more it can effectively eliminate most appearances of deviance on the part of its members. The members, in such circumstances, may faithfully behave in accord with their roles in the group, refrain from violating group norms, and express their endorsement of the "right" attitudes and beliefs. And from all visible indicators, at least in the short term, everything seems well with the group.

Dysfunctional Aspects of Eliminating Deviance from Group Norms

It can be argued, however, that this pattern of dealing with deviance is highly dysfunctional for the long-term effectiveness of a group, for at least two reasons (Hackman, 1975). First, if members comply primarily because of the application of pressure from the group (or the expected application of that pressure), the result may be public compliance *at the expense of* private acceptance and personal commitment to what is being done (cf. Kelman, 1961; Kiesler, 1969, pp. 279–295). And when a group is heavily populated by individuals who are saying and doing one thing but thinking and feeling another, high effectiveness in the long haul is unlikely.

Second, to the extent that a group uses its control of discretionary stimuli to swiftly extinguish any signs of deviance, it loses the opportunity to explore the usefulness and ultimate validity of the very attitudes, beliefs, norms and roles it is enforcing. For example, if compliance to a given norm about work behavior is enforced so effectively that deviance from that norm virtually never occurs, the group will be unable to discover whether that norm is actually helpful or detrimental to the achievement of the goals of the group. In essence, it may be that an unexamined norm is not worth enforcing—at least if high group effectiveness is aspired to in the long run.

Despite these and other dysfunctions of excessive pressures against deviance, the research literature suggests that groups have a strong tendency to stamp out (or at least sweep under the rug) behaviors which are not congruent with traditional standards of acceptability in the group. Apparently groups rarely attempt to work through the more basic problems of why people deviate from the group, what the consequences of such deviance for the group are, and how deviance can be most effectively dealt with for the good of both individual members and the group as a whole. This style of social behavior is consistent with the observation of Argyris (1969) that most groups in contemporary society operate according to what he calls "Pattern A" interpersonal rules. In a Pattern A world, conformity takes precedence over experimentation, intellective and cognitive matters drive out feelings and emotionality, and interpersonal behavior is characterized more by diplomacy, mistrust, and caution than by interpersonal openness, trust, and risk taking.

Consider, for example, the suggestion (Dentler & Erikson, 1959; discussed in the previous chapter) that groups often "institutionalize" the deviant and resist attempts to explicitly reject deviant individuals. It is doubtful that this phenomenon reflects a conscious and deliberate decision by group members that the group would be best served by retaining the deviant in the group and using his behavior to help maintain the boundaries and equilibrium of the group. Instead, it is more likely that group members simply find themselves unable and unwilling to handle the emotional and interpersonal issues which invariably are involved in carrying off an overt rejection of one of their number. By gradually defining a role of deviance for the member in question, the problem of the deviant's behavior can be defused in the short term, without the necessity of surfacing issues which are "out-of-bounds" in a Pattern A world. The fact that there may be some functional payoffs for the group as a consequence of the deviant's membership in the group, then, is more a happy coincidence than the outcome of a conscious and deliberate decision by the group.

Although there are some instances (such as that described above) in which Pattern A interpersonal behavior can lead to apparent solutions to problems which might be difficult for the group to deal with directly, Argyris argues that Pattern A behavior is *not* facilitative of group effectiveness in the long run. For generating short-term solutions to "easy" task and interpersonal problems (e.g., How can we get member C to shut up so we can get back to work on the task?), a Pattern A solution may be fine, but for more basic and more important problems (e.g., How can we more effectively deal with and learn from our individual and collective failures?), Argyris suggests that it will be difficult or impossible for groups operating according to Pattern A rules to obtain valid data and generate lasting solutions.

Even so, it is not difficult to understand why groups persist in handling deviance essentially according to Pattern A rules. The reason, in brief, is the same one proposed for why groups sometimes develop institutionalized roles for deviants—namely, it is emotionally quite stressful and difficult for group members to deal openly with core questions of conformity, deviation, and interpersonal relationships in a group. Indeed, research (Bion, 1959; Argyris, 1969) suggests that it may be impossible for a group to break out of a traditional pattern of interpersonal behavior without outside professional assistance. Even with such assistance, it may take a great deal of time and effort before a group can overcome the basic assumptions which guided its early behavior and develop into an effective and truly interdependent work group (Bion, 1959). When a group becomes able to make more open and conscious choices about the use of those discretionary stimuli under its control to deal with issues of conformity and deviance, the long-term effectiveness of the group should be greatly enhanced.

Why High Group Cohesiveness Can Be Dysfunctional

In general, as the cohesiveness of a work group increases, the overall level of member conformity to the norms of the group would also be expected to increase—for two different but mutually reinforcing reasons: First, as was shown in the discussion of group norms in the last chapter, there tend to be stronger group-generated pressures toward uniformity and conformity in groups which are highly cohesive than in groups which are not (cf. Festinger et al., 1950). And second, group members are likely to value especially strongly the interpersonal rewards which are available in highly cohesive groups—precisely because of the strong positive feelings members have for one another in such groups. Therefore, group members are unlikely to risk losing those rewards by ignoring or defying pressures to conform to group norms. And, in fact, research evidence confirms that conformity is especially high in cohesive groups (cf. Tajfel, 1969, pp. 334–347; Lott & Lott, 1965, pp. 292–296; Hackman, 1975).

The problem is that conformity to group norms which occurs in highly cohesive groups may *not* be functional for group or individual productivity. Indeed, cohesiveness may be strongly dysfunctional for effectiveness in some situations for several reasons, which are discussed below.

Deviance Is Dealt with Ineffectively   As noted previously, groups tend in general to stamp out deviant behavior on the part of individual group members—rather than use such deviance to increase either the learning of individual group members or the capability of the group as a whole to respond effectively to a changing or turbulent state of affairs. Since pressures toward uniformity are highest in highly cohesive groups, the risk of quick and ill-considered elimination of all appearances of deviance in the group also are likely to be highest in cohesive groups—even though exploration of such deviant behaviors might actually be helpful to the group in the long run.

Norms Are Strong, but Their Direction May Be Negative   While it is generally true that cohesive groups are able to effectively control members such that their behavior closely approximates that specified by the group norm, the *direction* of the group norm itself (i.e., toward high versus low performance) has been found to be unrelated to the level of cohesiveness (Schachter et al., 1951; Berkowitz, 1954; Seashore, 1954; Darley et al., 1952).

For example, in several studies (e.g., Schachter et al., 1951; Berkowitz, 1954) conditions of high versus low cohesiveness and high- versus low-productivity norms were created by experimental manipulation. It was found that member productivity was indeed closer to the group norm in the high- than in the low-cohesiveness groups—for both the high- *and* the low-production norms. There have been similar findings in industrial situation using survey techniques (Seashore, 1954). In this study of over 200 work groups in a machinery factory, no correlation was found between cohesiveness and productivity—but, as would be expected, when cohesiveness was high, the amount of *variation* in the productivity of group members was low, and vice versa.

Groupthink May Develop   One of the seeming advantages of having a great deal of uniformity or conformity in a group is that members do not have to deal with the thorny interpersonal problems which can arise when members behave in nonuniform ways—e.g., when each member of a work group is allowed to select his own level of production and the levels selected turn out to vary a good deal from member to member. This "group-maintenance" function of uniformity may be especially important to members of highly cohesive groups, since members of such groups typically value strongly the rewards controlled by their fellows—and would be particularly upset to receive negative interpersonal reactions from them.

It has been suggested, however, that as a group becomes excessively close-knit and develops a strong feeling of "we-ness," it becomes susceptible to a pattern of behavior known as "groupthink" (Janis, 1972). Among the several symptoms of groupthink are an excessive concern with maintaining uniformity among members, a marked decrease in the openness of the group to discrepant or unsettling information (from sources either inside or outside the group), and a simultaneous unwillingness to examine seriously and process such negative information if it ever is brought to the attention of the group.

These social processes may often serve immediate group-maintenance functions and help perpetuate the warm and cohesive feelings which characterize the group. In addition, however, they result in an increased likelihood that the group, in a spirit of goodwill and shared confidence, will develop and implement a course of action which is grossly inappropriate and ineffective. It has been shown (Janis, 1972), for example, how the groupthink phenomenon may have contributed substantially to a number of historical fiascoes planned and executed by groups of government officials (e.g., the Bay of Pigs invasion and Britain's appeasement policy toward Hitler prior to World War II).

Should Cohesiveness Be Avoided?

It might appear from the above discussion that high cohesiveness of groups in organizations is something that should be avoided—to minimize the possibility of enforced low-production norms in work settings or the likelihood that groupthink-like phenomena will develop among decision makers. Such a conclusion would be a very pessimistic one: low cohesiveness among members of work groups or decision-making groups would indeed lower the possibility of obtaining the negative outcomes mentioned but also would require that the positive potential of cohesive groups be forgone as well—such as the increased capability of such groups to regulate behavior so as to *increase* the attainment of group and organizational goals.

The question, then, becomes how the norms of highly cohesive groups can be changed such that they encourage careful examination of the task environment (including negative or unsettling information which may be present), exploration of interpersonal issues which may be impairing group performance, and high rather than low levels of group and member productivity. Although presently little is known about what factors affect the kinds of norms developed by work groups in organizations (cf. Vroom, 1969, pp. 226–227), two general approaches to the problem are discussed briefly below.

Fostering Intergroup Competition One frequently espoused tactic for developing simultaneously high work-group cohesiveness and commitment to organizational goals can be referred to as the "best damn group in the whole damn organization ploy." Many managers realize that if they can get their subordinates, as a group, to experience themselves in competition with other groups in the organization, a kind of team spirit often develops which results in high group cohesiveness and great member commitment to be the "best" in whatever it is that defines the competition. And, in fact, there is considerable research evidence that when groups enter into competitive relationships with other groups, internal cohesivensss and high individual task commitment do increase—often dramatically (cf. Sherif, 1965).

The problem is that such intergroup competitiveness often actually works against the best interests of the total organization in the long run. For example, in the interest of "winning," information which really should be shared *among* groups for optimal organizational functioning often is withheld—and at times even misinformation is communicated up and down the line in a way intended to make sure that "our group looks best" (cf. Chapter 9). The pervasive line-staff and interdepartment (e.g., sales versus production) conflicts in contemporary organizations often reflect exactly this type of intergroup competition.

One common means of attempting to overcome such problems of dysfunctional intergroup competition within organizations (while maintaining high commitment within groups) is to introduce or make especially salient a superordinate goal which all groups share. Research evidence does support the idea that a superordinate goal can reduce or eliminate hostilities between groups (Sherif, 1965). And, in fact, many business organizations use the idea of the superordinate goal in their attempts to get employees in diverse groups to pull together for the good of the organization as a whole—for example, by prominently posting the number of trunkets sold this month by one's own company versus the number sold by the chief competitor. The problem, of course, is that it is not likely that a lower-level employee who hates his job and feels he is grossly and unfairly underpaid is going to *care* very much about whether or not his own organization is ahead in the trunket-selling competition—regardless of the attempts of the company employee-relations department to make that competition an organizing theme of the company.

Basing Cohesiveness on Task rather than Social Rewards It may be that one of the major reasons for the failure of many cohesive groups to work as effectively as they might toward group and organizational goals has to do with the basis of the cohesiveness itself—i.e., the reasons why the group members have a strong desire to stick together.

In virtually all the research which has been discussed here, cohesiveness was based upon the *interpersonal rewards* present or potentially present in the group. The "stake" of most group members in such situations, then, would be to refrain from behaviors that might disrupt the interpersonal satisfactions which are obtained from group membership. The control of the group over its members in such cases rests largely upon its capability to provide or withhold such valued social satisfactions. In the groupthink situation, for example, such control results in interpersonal strategies characterized by lessened vigilance for new and potentially disruptive information, acceptance of the views of "high-status others" as the doctrine of the group, and suppression of any interpersonal unpleasantries—all of which can severely impair the work effectiveness of the group.

If the basis for the cohesiveness were a shared commitment to the *task* of the group (instead of a commitment to maintaining the interpersonal rewards received in the group), the picture might change considerably. The criterion for when to accept information and direction from others in the group, for example, might change from something like "Will questioning what is being said by the leader risk my being rejected or ridiculed by the group?" to "Will such questioning contribute to our succeeding in the task?" Conformity, then, should remain high in such groups, but the norms to which conformity is enforced would focus on facilitating the group's task performance activities rather than on maintaining interpersonal comfortableness. This change in orientation also would bear on the question of the *direction* of norms for individual production in work groups: if one of the major reasons for the cohesiveness of the group were a shared commitment to succeeding in the task, then that commitment should in most cases lead to group norms oriented toward high rather than low task effectiveness.

Data generally supportive of this view are provided by several experimental studies (e.g., Back, 1951; Thibaut & Strickland, 1956). In one such experiment (Back, 1951), three types of cohesiveness were induced in dyads: cohesiveness based on (1) personal attraction, (2) the prestige of being a group member, and (3) the task itself. The first two bases of cohesiveness are, of course, primarily interpersonal in nature, and led to predictable patterns of social interaction. In the "personal attraction" condition, for example, group members tended to make the interaction into a longish, pleasant conversation and to resent any rejection of an influence attempt; in the "prestige" condition, members tended to take few interpersonal risks and acted very cautiously—focusing more on their own behavior and its possible interpersonal impact than on the group task. In the "task" condition, however, group members tended to ignore interpersonal issues and to work intensely and efficiently to complete the task activity.

The problem in attempting to develop task-based cohesiveness in real-world work groups is twofold. First, many tasks (and perhaps most production tasks) in organizations are not such as to generate genuine group commitment. Instead, the reverse may often be true: the task may be so uninteresting that the group accepts as an alternative a task of "getting" management or of avoiding hard work. In such cases, the power resident in the group cohesiveness may be exceptionally dysfunctional for organizational goals. Second, it is quite difficult, even for objectively important tasks, for group members to overcome their orientation to interpersonal rewards and rejections. The group of Kennedy advisors during the Bay of Pigs crisis, for example, certainly had an important task; but the heavy investment of each member toward remaining a member of the high-status, high-prestige group apparently was so strong that "not rocking the interpersonal boat" overwhelmed "doing the task well" as a behavioral criterion for most group members.

Thus, while there appears to be much to be said for the development of tasks which can provide a strong positive basis for group cohesiveness, few guidelines for designing such tasks currently exist. The crux of the problem, it seems, is to create conditions such that the rewards from genuinely shared task activities become as salient and as attractive to group members as are the more skin-surface interpersonal satisfactions, which, unfortunately, currently typify relationships within most "cohesive" groups in organizations.

WAYS GROUPS INFLUENCE INDIVIDUAL WORK EFFECTIVENESS

Now we are in a position to turn to the question of *how* groups can in fact have an impact on how hard and how well their members work. It may be recalled from Chapters 2 and 4 that the major direct determinants of the work behavior of organization members can be summarized in terms of four major classes of variables:

1   The job-relevant knowledge and skills of the individual
2   The level of psychological arousal the individual experiences while working
3   The performance strategies the individual uses doing his work
4   The level of effort the individual exerts in doing his work

The two latter factors were shown in Chapter 2 to be substantially under the voluntary control of the individual, as part of his "behavioral plan" for performing his job; the first two factors were viewed as being much less under the control of the individual and therefore as moderating the degree to which his behavioral plans actually are realized.

Which (or which combination) of the four classes of variables can contribute substantially to increased individual work *effectiveness*, of course, very much depends upon the nature of the task or job being performed. On a routine and simple clerical job, for example, where the sole performance criterion is quantity of acceptable output, only effort is likely to be of real importance in influencing measured work effectiveness. On a more complex job, where there are many ways to go about performing it (e.g., most managerial jobs), the performance *strategies* used may critically influence effectiveness. For yet other jobs, arousal and/or the job-relevant skills of the individual may be critical.*

Thus, to analyze the diversity of group and social influences on individual work effectiveness, it may be useful to examine group effects separately on each of the four summary classes of variables listed above. Moreover, the implication of this view is that when one is attempting to assess the impact of the work group on an individual's performance effectiveness, he need deal with only those variables which can, in fact, exert a significant influence. If effectiveness in a given situation is responsive to differences in skill, then the impact of the group on the ways an individual's skills are developed and used must be examined; if the job is such that different performance *strategies* can influence performance effectiveness, the impact of the group on the strategies used by an individual must be assessed; and the same reasoning follows for effort and for arousal.

Group Influences by Affecting Member Knowledge and Skills

Performance on many tasks and jobs in organizations is strongly affected by the job-relevant knowledge and skills of the individuals who do the work. Thus, even if an employee has both high commitment toward accomplishing a particular piece of work and a well-formed strategy about how to go about doing it, the implementation of that plan can be constrained or terminated if he does not know how to carry it out, or if he knows how but is incapable of doing so. While ability is relevant to the performance of jobs at all levels in an organization, its impact probably is somewhat reduced for lower-level jobs. The reason is that such jobs often are not demanding of high skill levels. Further, to the extent that organizational selection, placement, and promotion practices are adequate, *all* jobs should tend to be occupied by individuals who possess the skills requisite for adequate performance.

---

*The characteristics of tasks or jobs which identify which classes of variables are of most importance in determining work effectiveness have been termed "critical task contingencies", i.e., those contingencies which specify what behaviors are critical to effective or successful performance for the job in question. Depending upon what the critical task contingencies are for a given task or job, it is possible to determine on an a priori basis which variables must be dealt with in any attempt to improve performance effectiveness on that job. This notion is developed more completely by Hackman (1975).

Discussion in the previous chapter focused on how groups can improve the job-relevant knowledge and skills of an individual through direct instruction, feedback, and model provision. For jobs in which knowledge and skill are important determiners of performance effectiveness, then, groups can be of help. Nevertheless, the impact of groups on member performance effectiveness by improving member knowledge and skill probably is one of the lesser influences groups can have—both because employees on many jobs tend already to have many or all of the skills needed to perform them effectively and because there are other sources for improving skills which may be more useful and more potent than the work group, such as formal job training programs and self-study programs.

Group Influences by Affecting Member Arousal Level

It was shown in the last chapter how a group can substantially influence the level of psychological arousal experienced by a member—through the mere presence of the other group members and by those others sending the individual messages which are directly arousal-enhancing or arousal-depressing. The conditions under which such group-promoted changes in arousal level will lead to increased performance effectiveness, however, very much depend upon the type of task being worked on (Zajonc, 1965).

In this case, the critical characteristics of the job have to do with whether the initially *dominant task responses* of the individual are likely to be correct or incorrect. Since the individual's output of such responses is facilitated when he is in an aroused state, arousal should improve performance effectiveness on well-learned tasks (so-called performance tasks) in which the dominant response is correct and needs merely to be executed by the performer. By the same token, arousal should impair effectiveness for new or unfamiliar tasks (learning tasks) in which the dominant response is likely to be incorrect.

As noted in the previous chapter, it has sometimes been argued that the *mere* presence of others should heighten the arousal of individuals sufficiently for the predicted performance effects to be obtained. However (as also previously discussed), the evidence now seems to indicate that the *mere* presence of others may not result in significant increases in arousal. Instead, only when the other group members are—or are seen as being—in a potentially evaluative relationship vis-à-vis the performer are the predictions confirmed (cf. Zajonc & Sales, 1966; Cottrell et al., 1968; Henchy & Glass, 1968).

Groups can, of course, increase member arousal in ways other than taking an evaluative stance toward the individual. Strongly positive, encouraging statements also should increase arousal in some performance situations—for example, by helping the individual become personally highly committed to the group goal, and making sure he realizes that he is a very important part of the team responsible for reaching that goal. What must be kept in mind, however, is that such devices represent a double-edged sword: while they may facilitate effective performance for well-learned tasks, they may have the opposite effect for new and unfamiliar tasks.

What, then, can be said about the effects on performance of group members when their presence (and interaction) serves to *decrease* the level of arousal of the group member—as, for example, when individuals coalesce into groups under conditions of high stress? When the other members of the group are a source of support, comfort, or acceptance to the individual (and serve to decrease his arousal level), it would be predicted that performance effectiveness would follow a pattern exactly opposite to that described above: the group would impair effectiveness for familiar or well-learned performance tasks (because arousal helps on these tasks, and arousal is being lowered) and facilitate effectiveness for unfamiliar or complicated learning tasks (because in this case arousal is harmful, and it is being lowered).

The relationships predicted above are summarized in Figure 14-1. As the group becomes increasingly threatening, evaluative, or strongly encouraging, effectiveness should increase for performance tasks and decrease for learning tasks. When the group is experienced as increasingly supportive, comforting, or unconditionally accepting, effectiveness should decrease for performance tasks and increase for learning tasks. And when no meaningful relationship at all is experienced by the individual between himself and the group, performance should not be affected. While some of these predictions have been tested and confirmed in small group experimental settings, others await research.

Even that research which has focused on these relationships has not been designed or conducted in actual organizational settings, and the findings must be generalized with caution. It is clear, however, that individuals in organizations do use their group memberships as a means of achieving more comfortable levels of arousal. Individuals in high-pressure managerial jobs, for example, often find that they need to gather around themselves a few trusted associates who can and do provide reassurance and continuing acceptance when the going gets especially tough. This, presumably, should help reduce the manager's level of arousal and thereby increase the likelihood that he will be able to come up with *new and original* ways of perceiving and dealing with his immediate problem. If the theory is correct, however, this practice should not facilitate performance of the more "routine" (i.e., well-learned) parts of his job.

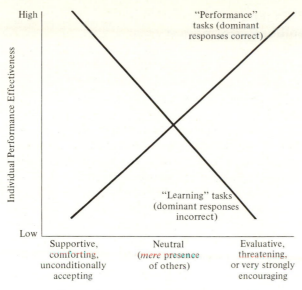

Figure 14-1   Individual performance effectiveness as a function of
type of task and experienced relationship to the group.

It is well known (cf. Chapter 10) that overly routine jobs can decrease a worker's level of arousal to such an extent that his performance effectiveness is impaired. It seems quite possible, therefore, that the social environment of workers on such jobs can be designed so as to compensate partially for the deadening effects of the job itself and thereby lead to an increment in performance on well-learned tasks.

Finally (as discussed in a subsequent section), the supervisor probably has a more powerful effect on the level of arousal of a worker than any other single individual in his immediate social environment. By close supervision (which usually results in the worker's feeling more or less constantly evaluated) supervisors can and do increase the level of arousal experienced by workers. While this may, for routine jobs, have some potential for improving performance effectiveness, it also is quite likely that the worker's negative reactions to being closely supervised ultimately will result in his attention being diverted from the job itself and focused instead on ways he can either get out from "under the gun" of the supervisor or somehow get back at the supervisor to punish him for his unwanted close supervision.

Group Influences by Affecting Level of Member Effort and Member Performance Strategies

The level of effort a person exerts in doing his work and the performance strategies he follows are treated together here because both variables are largely under the performer's *voluntary* control.

Direct versus Indirect Influences on Effort and Strategy

Throughout this book we have used a general "expectancy theory" approach to analyze those aspects of a person's behavior in organizations which are under his voluntary control. From this perspective, a person's choices about his effort and work strategy can be viewed as hinging largely upon (1) his *expectations* regarding the likely consequences of his choices and (2) the degree to which he *values* those expected consequences. Following this approach, it becomes clear that the group can have both a direct and an indirect effect on the level of effort a group member exerts at his job and on his choices about performance strategy.

The *direct* impact of the group on effort and strategy, of course, is simply the enforcement by the group of its own norms regarding what is an "appropriate" level of effort to expend on the job and what is the "proper" performance strategy. We previously discussed in some detail how groups use their control of discretionary stimuli to enforce group norms, and thereby affect such voluntary behaviors. Thus, if the group has established a norm about the level of member effort or the strategies members should use in going about their work, the group can control individual behavior merely by making sure that individual members realize that their receipt of valued group-controlled rewards is contingent upon their behaving in accord with the norm.

The *indirect* impact of the group on the effort and performance strategies of the individual involves the group's control of information regarding the state of the organizational environment outside the boundaries of the group. Regardless of any norms the group itself may have about effort or strategy, it also can communicate to the group member "what leads to what" in the broader organization, and thereby affect the individual's *own* choices about his behavior.

For example, it may be the case in a given organization that hard work (i.e., high effort) tends to lead to quick promotions and higher pay; the group can influence the effort of the individual by helping him realize this objective state of affairs. Similarly, by providing individual members with information about what performance strategies are effective in the organization, the group can indirectly affect the strategy choices made by the person. Whether high quality of output or large quantities of output are more likely to lead to organizational rewards, for example, is information that the group can provide the individual with to assist him in making his own choices about work strategy.

Moreover, as shown in the last chapter, groups can affect the *personal preferences and values* of individual members—although such influences tend to occur relatively slowly and over a long period of time. When such changes do occur, the level of desire (or the valence) individuals have for various outcomes available in the organizational setting will change as well. And as the kinds of outcomes valued by the individual change, his behavior also will change to increase the degree to which the newly valued outcomes are obtained at work. The long-term result can be substantial revision of the choices made by the individual about the effort he will expend and the performance strategies he will use at work.

It should be noted, however, that such indirect influences on member effort and performance strategy will be most potent early in the individual's tenure in the organization (cf. Chapter 6) when he has not yet had a chance to develop through experience his own personal "map" of the organization. When the individual becomes less dependent upon the group for data about "what leads to what" and "what's good" in the organization, the group may have to revert to direct norm enforcement to maintain control of the work behavior of individual members.

In summary, the group can and does have a strong impact on both the level of effort exerted by its members and the strategies members use in carrying out their work. This impact is realized both directly (i.e., by enforcement of group norms) and indirectly (i.e., by affecting the beliefs and values of the members). When the direct and indirect influences of a group are congruent—which is often the case—the potency of the group's effects on its members can be quite strong. For example, if at the same time that a group is enforcing its *own* norm of, say, moderately low production, it also is providing a group member with data regarding the presumably *objective* negative consequences of hard work in the particular organization, the group member will experience two partially independent and mutually reinforcing influences aimed at keeping his rate of production down.

Effort, Strategy, and Performance Effectiveness   What, then, are the circumstances under which groups can improve the work *effectiveness* of their members through influences on individual choices about level of effort and about strategy? Again, the answer depends upon the nature of the job. Unless a job is structured so that effort level or performance strategy actually can make a real difference in work effectiveness, group influences on effort or strategy will be irrelevant to how well individual members perform.

Strategy: In general, groups should be able to facilitate member work effectiveness by influencing strategy choices more for complex jobs than for simple, straightforward, or routine ones. The reason is that on simple jobs, strategy choices usually cannot make much of a difference in effectiveness; instead, how well one does is determined almost entirely by how hard one works. On jobs characterized by high variety and autonomy, on the other hand, the work strategy used by the individual usually is of considerable importance in determining work effectiveness. By helping an individual develop and implement an appropriate work strategy—of where and how to put in his effort—the group should be able to substantially facilitate his effectiveness.

Effort: In the great majority of organizational settings, most jobs are structured such that the harder one works, the more effective his performance is likely to be. Thus, group influences on the effort expended by members on their jobs are both very pervasive and very potent determiners of individual work effectiveness. There are, nevertheless, some exceptions to this generalization: the success of a complicated brain operation, for example, is less likely to depend upon effort expended than it is upon the strategies used and the job-relevant knowledge and skills of the surgeon.

When either effort or strategy or both are in fact important in determining performance effectiveness, the individual has substantial personal control over how well he does in his work. In such cases, the degree to which the group facilitates (rather than hinders) individual effectiveness will depend jointly upon (1) the degree to which the group has accurate information regarding the task and organizational contingencies which are operative in that situation and makes such information available to the individual and (2) the degree to which the norms of the group are congruent with those contingencies and reinforce them.

Participation   One management practice which in theory should contribute positively to meeting both of the above conditions is the use of group participation in making decisions about work practices. Participation has been widely advocated as a management technique, both on ideological grounds and as a direct means of increasing work effectiveness. And, in fact, some studies have shown that participation can lead to higher work effectiveness (e.g., Coch & French, 1948; Lawler & Hackman, 1969). In the present framework, participation should contribute to increased work effectiveness in two different ways.

1 Participation can increase the amount and the accuracy of information workers have about work practices and the environmental contingencies associated with them. In one study (Lawler & Hackman, 1970), for example, some groups themselves designed new reward systems keyed on coming to work regularly (a task clearly affected by employee effort—i.e., trying to get

to work every day). These groups responded both more quickly and more positively to the new pay plans than did groups which had technically identical plans imposed upon them by company management. One reason suggested by the authors to account for this finding was that the participative groups simply may have understood their plans better and had fewer uncertainties and worries about what the rewards were (and were not) for coming to work regularly.

2 Participation can increase the degree to which group members feel they "own" their work practices—and therefore the likelihood that the group will develop a norm of support for those practices. In the participative groups in the study cited above, for example, the nature of the work-related communication among members changed from initial "shared warnings" about management and "things management proposes" to helping members (especially new members) come to understand and believe in "our plan." In other words, as group members come to experience the work or work practices *as under their own control or ownership*, it becomes more likely that informal group norms supportive of effective behavior vis-à-vis those practices will develop. Such norms provide a striking contrast to the "group protective" norms which often emerge when control is perceived to be exclusively and unilaterally under management control.

We can see, then, that group participative techniques can be quite facilitative of individual work effectiveness—but only under certain conditions:

1 The topic of participation must be relevant to the work itself. There is no reason to believe that participation involving task-irrelevant issues (e.g., preparing for the Red Cross Bloodmobile visit to the plant) will have facilitative effects on work productivity. While such participation may indeed help increase the cohesiveness of the work group, it clearly will not help group members gain information or develop norms which are facilitative of high work effectiveness. Indeed, such task-irrelevant participation may serve to direct the attention and motivation of group members *away from* work issues and thereby even lower productivity (cf. French, Israel, & Ås, 1960).

2 The objective task and environmental contingencies in the work setting must actually be supportive of more effective performance. That is, if through participation group members learn more about what leads to what in the organization, then it is increasingly important that there be real and meaningful positive outcomes which result from effective performance. If, for example, group members gain a quite complete and accurate impression through participation that "hard work around here pays off only in backaches," then increased effort as a consequence of participation is most unlikely. If, on the other hand, participation results in a new and better

understanding that hard work can lead to increased pay, enhanced opportunities for advancement, and the chance to feel a sense of personal and group accomplishment, then increased effort should be the result.

3 Finally, the work must be such that increased effort (or a different and better work strategy) objectively can lead to higher work effectiveness. If it is true—as argued here—that the main benefits of group participation are (1) increased understanding of work practices and the organizational environment and (2) increased experienced "ownership" by the group of the work and work practices, then participation should increase productivity only when the *objective determinants of productivity are under the voluntary control of the worker*. There is little reason to expect, therefore, that participation should have a substantial facilitative effect on productivity when work outcomes are mainly determined by the level of skill of the worker and/or by his arousal level (rather than effort expended or work strategy used) or when outcomes are controlled by objective factors in the environment over which the worker can have little or no control (e.g., the rate or amount of work which is arriving at the employee's station).

Implications for Diagnosis and Change

This section has focused on ways that the group can influence the performance effectiveness of individual group members. While it has been maintained throughout that the group has a substantial impact on such performance effectiveness, it has been emphasized that the nature and extent of this impact centrally depends upon the characteristics of the work being done.

To diagnose and change the direction or extent of social influences on individual performance in an organization, then, the following three steps might be taken.

1 An analysis of the task or job would be made to determine which of the four classes of variables (i.e., skills, arousal, strategies, effort) objectively affect measured performance effectiveness. This might be done by posing this analytical question: "If skills (or arousal, or effort, or strategies) were brought to bear on the work differently than is presently the case, would a corresponding difference in work effectiveness be likely to be observed as a consequence?" By scrutinizing each of the four classes of variables in this way, it usually is possible to identify which specific variables are objectively important to consider for the job. In many cases, of course, more than one class of variables will turn out to be of importance.

2 After one or more "target" classes of variables have been identified, the work group itself would be examined to unearth any ways in which the group was blocking effective individual performance. It might be determined, for example, that certain group norms were impeding the expression

and use of various skills which individuals potentially could bring to bear on their work. Or it might turn out that the social environment of the worker created conditions which were excessively (or insufficiently) arousing for optimal performance on the task at hand. For effort and strategy, which are under the voluntary control of the worker, there are two major possibilities to examine: (a) that norms are enforced in the group which coerce individuals to behave in ineffective ways or (b) that the group provides information to the individual members about task and environmental contingencies in an insufficient or distorted fashion, resulting in their making choices about their work behavior which interfere with task effectiveness.

The return potential model (RPM) (discussed in Chapter 13) might prove to be a useful tool in making such diagnoses. It provides a direct means of assessing group norms relevant to member effort and work strategy—and in addition can be adapted for use in assessing worker perceptions of what the organizational "payoffs" are for various work behaviors.

3 Finally, it would be useful to assess the group and the broader social environment to determine if there are ways that the "people resources" in the situation could be more fully utilized in the interest of increased work effectiveness. That is, rather than focusing solely on ways the group may be blocking or impeding performance effectiveness, attention should be given as well to any unrealized *potential* which resides in the group. It could turn out, for example, that some group members would be of great help to others in increasing the level of individual task-relevant skills, but these individuals have never been asked for help. Alternatively, it might be that the group could be assisted in finding new and better ways of ensuring that each group member has available accurate and current information about those task and environmental contingencies which determine the outcomes of various work behaviors.

The point is that the people who surround an individual at work can facilitate as well as hinder his performance effectiveness—and that any serious attempt to diagnose the social environment in the interest of improving work performance should explicitly address unrealized possibilities for enhancing performance as well as issues for which remedial action may be required.

What particular organizational changes will be called for on the basis of such a diagnosis—or what techniques should be used to realize these changes—will, of course, largely depend upon the particular characteristics of the organization and of the resources which are available there. The major emphasis of this section has been that there is *not* any single universally useful type of change or means of change—and that, instead, intervention should always be based on a thorough diagnosis of the existing social, organizational, and task environment. Perhaps especially intriguing in this regard is the prospect of developing techniques of social intervention which will help groups see the need for (and develop the capability of) making such interventions *on their own* in the interest of increasing the work effectiveness of the group as a whole.

LEADERSHIP: A PARTICULAR FORM OF SOCIAL INFLUENCE

In any social or group environment, there is one particular agent of influence who often has a disproportionate impact on the individual: the leader. He can operate either in congruence with the work group or instead of it, but regardless of which set of circumstances exists he exerts his influence in ways that are fundamentally the same as those used by groups (and which were discussed previously). He simply is more likely to have more powerful influence than the typical group member on the work of a given employee. It is for this reason that the question, What makes for effective leadership? has pervaded the thinking of researchers and managers alike for many years.

While there has been a plethora of definitions of leadership and of theories of leadership effectiveness (cf. Gibb, 1969; Fiedler, 1971), we will restrict our discussion to what we believe to be the major issues involved in understanding how leaders can *behave* in organizational settings to increase the effectiveness of the individuals and groups for which they are responsible.

Trait versus Situational Approaches to Leadership

Early research on leadership effectiveness was dominated by the "trait versus situation" controversy. Some scholars, following Carlyle's dictum that "the history of the world is the history of great men," searched for the definitive set of traits which would differentiate between those people who were and were not capable of effectively leading people. Other scholars attempted to understand the characteristics of situations which, they claimed, would thrust any man who was in the right place at the right time into an effective leadership role.

Neither the trait nor the situational approach resulted in a major advance in understanding the nature of effective leadership. We still have no adequate "theory of situations" which is useful in understanding the leadership process, for example, even though a number of early studies did point up the importance of situational considerations in determining what kinds of leadership behaviors would be effective. The ultimate situationist position—i.e., that given adequate understanding of the situation, different individuals should be virtually interchangeable in leadership roles—has, however, by now been abandoned by most students of the leadership process.

The efforts of the "trait" researchers have yielded long lists of individual difference characteristics which have been shown to correlate with effective leadership performance. Included in these lists are traits such as self-confidence, intelligence (but not *too* much intelligence), sociability, ambition, perseverance, will, and, of course, height. Unfortunately, as several reviewers of these studies have pointed out, the magnitude of the correlations between these traits and actual group or subordinate effectiveness generally is so low (e.g., on the order of .10 to .20) that their usefulness in either selecting individuals for positions of leadership or as the basis for a more general theory of leadership effectiveness is extremely limited.

Researchers gradually have come to the conclusion that effective leadership probably represents some *interaction* between the characteristics of the leader himself and the characteristics of the situation (including the kinds of people to be led) in which leadership takes place. While several researchers have attempted to develop "interactional" theories of leadership, only one such theory continues to generate significant research activity.

This is the "LPC" theory of Fiedler (e.g., 1967, 1971). Fiedler has identified one measurable leader characteristic which, he claims, relates consistently to effective leadership—but sometimes positively, sometimes negatively, depending on the situation. This trait, esteem for one's "least-preferred coworker" (or LPC), is predicted to interact with three situational characteristics: the structure of the task, the quality of the leader-member relationship, and the amount of formal "position power" the leader has. Some of the research carried out by Fiedler and his associates has provided support for the complex theory he postulates; other research (e.g., Graen et al., 1970) has not been supportive. Thus, the conceptual and empirical status of the theory remains unclear; the theory, in any case, seems not yet ready to be used for leader selection or training. Probably its greatest strengths are its explicit recognition of the *interaction* between the person and the situation in understanding effective leadership, and its attempt to specify important situational variables (i.e., leader's formal position power, etc.).

Behavioral Styles of Leaders

In the late 1940s and 1950s a new stream of research aimed at understanding leadership and leadership effectiveness emerged—this time focusing not on the personal traits of leaders per se but instead on the behavioral styles which characterized their leadership activities. Examples of the numerous dimensions of leadership style which have been proposed include authoritarian versus democratic; task-oriented versus socioemotional; employee-centered versus production-centered; and so on. (For additional examples, see Sales, 1966; Taylor, 1971; Yukl, 1971; and Gibb, 1969.)

A rather large body of research evidence has accumulated which probes the relationships between various leadership styles and individual or group effectiveness. Some of this research has yielded useful and interesting substantive findings. One series of organizational studies (summarized in Kahn & Katz, 1960), for example, indicated that more effective leaders tend to (1) behave so as to make clear the differentiation of their role from that of the employees—e.g., by refraining from performing the same functions as the rank-and-file worker; (2) spend substantial time in supervisory functions—but not *closely* supervising employee activities on a minute-by-minute basis; and (3) orient their behavior predominantly toward employee concerns—rather than behaving in a more production-oriented or institution-oriented fashion.

Initiation of Structure versus Consideration   Undoubtedly the most ambitious (and in some ways the most successful) example of the behavioral style approach to leadership is the Ohio State series of studies (sympathetically summarized by Fleishman, 1971). This program undertook first to describe the major behavioral dimensions upon which leader style varies and then to determine how these dimensions relate to employee productivity and morale. Two major (and relatively independent) dimensions of leadership style emerged from these researches:

Consideration reflects the degree to which a leader is considerate of the persons led—showing warm personal relationships, trust, willingness to explain his actions, willingness to listen to subordinates, and so on. The consideration dimension does not, however, imply any *laxity* in the behavior of the leader.

Initiation of structure reflects the degree to which the leader himself organizes and defines the superior-subordinate relationship and takes an active, initiating role in determining who does what when.

Unfortunately, recent reviews (e.g., Korman, 1966; Sales, 1966) fail to reveal any substantial *consistent* effects associated with given behavioral styles of leaders nor any consistent trend for one or another style to be particularly effective in terms of individual or group performance—although there do seem to be some tendencies for employee morale to be positively associated with a considerate, employee-oriented style. It appears (as illustrated by a study by House, Filley, & Kerr 1971) that the relationship between leader behavioral styles and employee attitudes and performance is substantially moderated by the characteristics of the organizational setting in which the leadership activities take place.

Questions about the Direction of Causality In general, relationships between leader style and subordinate behavior have been tested by correlational methods; and, when significant correlations have been obtained, it has been assumed that differences in leader style *caused* the associated differences in subordinate behavior. Interestingly, however, evidence recently has become available suggesting that leader behavioral style may, at least in some instances, be more a *consequence* of subordinate behavior than its cause (e.g., Rosen, 1969; Lowin & Craig, 1968; Lanzetta & Hannah, 1969; Farris & Lim, 1969).

In one study (Lowin & Craig, 1968), for example, subjects were led to believe that they were being hired to supervise a "Job Corps trainee" (actually an experimental confederate) who was typing letters for signature by the "office supervisor" (actually the experimenter). The quality of the typed letters was experimentally varied as a manipulation of employee competence, and the behavior of the supervisor toward the "trainee" was carefully monitored and extensively documented. It was found that the supervisor's closeness of supervision, his level of initiating structure, and his level of consideration all varied as a function of the manipulated competence of the subordinate. (In the low-competence condition, for instance, supervisors behaved less considerately, supervised more closely, and were higher in "initiating structure.")

Such findings strongly suggest that the observational studies which have shown relationships between leader behavioral style and employee performance and attitudes may frequently have been interpreted exactly backwards: that is, that leader styles were causing employee reactions, when in fact the employee behaviors and attitudes were influencing the styles of the leaders. It seems doubtful, therefore, that attempts to chart the effects of various behavioral styles of leaders on subordinates can ever provide a *sufficient* base on which to build a general theory of leadership effectiveness—even though the effects of leader behaviors on subordinates undoubtedly will turn out to be one important part of any such theory.

A Normative Theory of Leadership Style Most of the research which has been carried out on leader behavioral styles has been descriptive; that is, the research has attempted to understand and document existing relationships between leader styles and subordinate behavior. An alternative—and explicitly normative—approach to leader style recently has been proposed by Vroom and Yetton (1973). The behavioral style variable of interest to these researchers has to do with the ways leaders involve their subordinates in organizational decision-making processes—ranging from no involvement whatever to full leader-subordinate collaboration in reaching decisions. The model explicitly considers characteristics of the organizational and task environment as moderators of which types of leader styles will maximize organizational outcomes. In particular, Vroom and Yetton identify the following five behavioral styles:

AI   The leader solves the problem or makes the decision himself, using information available to him at that time.

AII   The leader obtains necessary information from subordinates, and then decides on the solution to the problem himself. Subordinates are not involved in generating or evaluating alternative solutions.

CI   The leader shares the problem with relevant subordinates individually, getting their ideas and suggestions without bringing them together as a group. Then the leader makes the decision—which may or may not reflect the influence of the subordinates.

CII   The leader shares the problem with his subordinates as a group, collectively obtaining their ideas and suggestions. Then he makes the decision—which again may or may not reflect the influence of the subordinates.

GII   The leader shares the problem with the subordinates as a group. Together the leader and the subordinates generate and evaluate alternatives and attempt to reach agreement on a solution.

The authors also identify three general criteria of effective decision making in organizations (i.e., the objective quality of the decision; the time required to make it; and the degree to which the decision will be acceptable to subordinates) as well as various attributes of the decision-making situation (e.g., "Do subordinates have the information necessary to generate a high-quality decision"; "Are subordinates likely to be in disagreement about preferred solutions"; and so on). The problem attributes are combined with the decision-making criteria in an elegant flowchart which specifies the most rational decision-making style for a leader to follow in any specified situation. This flowchart is reproduced in Figure 14-2.

While this model is still in the testing stage, initial research suggests that it can be useful both in diagnosing the existing styles of leaders in organizations and as an educational tool for helping managers become more flexible and adaptive in their relationships with subordinates in organizational decision-making situations. It should be reemphasized, however, that the model is explicitly normative in character in that it specifies what leaders *should* do in various organizational circumstances—rather than attempting to summarize what leaders *do* do and what the effects of those actions are.

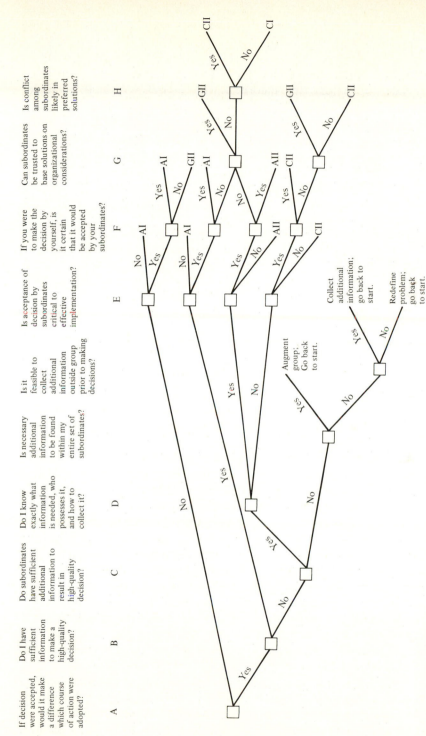

Figure 14-2 Decision process flowchart in the Vroom-Yetton model. (From Vroom, 1973)

A — If decision were accepted, would it make a difference which course of action were adopted?

B — Do I have sufficient information to make a high-quality decision?

C — Do subordinates have sufficient additional information to result in high-quality decision?

D — Do I know exactly what information is needed, who possesses it, and how to collect it?

Is necessary additional information to be found within my entire set of subordinates?

Is it feasible to collect additional information outside group prior to making decisions?

E — Is acceptance of decision by subordinates critical to effective implementation?

F — If you were to make the decision by yourself, is it certain that it would be accepted by your subordinates?

G — Can subordinates be trusted to base solutions on organizational considerations?

H — Is conflict among subordinates likely in preferred solutions?

Thus, if the assumptions in the model about the outcomes which result from various leader behaviors are incorrect, the model will lead to faulty behavioral prescriptions. Even so, the model can be self-correcting: when prescribed behaviors fail to result in effective organizational decision making, then further descriptive research can be undertaken to pinpoint and correct the erroneous assumptions about leader behavior which gave rise to the failure. Over the long term, such an interplay between the normative and the descriptive should improve both the usefulness of normative models and our general level of understanding of the dynamics of leader-subordinate interaction in organizational settings.

Leadership as a Process of Shared Influence

One feature which is common to the trait, the situational, and the behavioral style approaches to leadership is a strong emphasis on the behavior of *the* leader. An alternative approach to understanding leadership is to view it as a *process of influence* which can be (and often is) shared among members of a work group. From this perspective, then, any time an individual influences his fellow group members in the interest of achieving group goals, that person could be said to be performing an act of leadership.

In work groups which have formal or assigned leaders, such persons usually will engage in influential behaviors more frequently than will other group members. Indeed, in most groups the formal leader receives plenty of communication from his subordinates (and from his own boss) that he is *expected* to engage in such behavior—and he may receive sanctions from both his subordinates and his superiors if he does not meet those expectations.

It also is the case that the influence attempts made by the formal leader often will be more powerful and effective than those made by a rank-and-file member of the group. The reason is that formal leaders typically have at their disposal resources which are unavailable to other group members (or available to them in lesser quantities). These resources might include, for example, special information about task or environment contingencies received from the managerial hierarchy of the organization; control over rewards (e.g., bonuses, time off from work) which may be administered to subordinates at the leader's discretion; and, frequently, freedom to deviate from existing group norms or change traditional work practices to move the group in new directions.

Since (as was discussed in Chapter 13) control of information and rewards can significantly influence the beliefs, attitudes, and behaviors of group members, the formal leader should be in a strong position to affect what a group does and how well it does it. The same is true, to a somewhat lesser degree, for *informal* leaders—that is, group members who occupy no formal position of authority in the group but who are perceived by group members as occupying a leadership role. Because of these perceptions of the other group members, informal leaders tend to receive (and send) more communications than other group members—and thereby usually have at their disposal more information about the group and its environment than others do. Also, to the extent that the informal leader is seen as a high-status or popular individual, he should have more control than other members over interpersonal rewards which may be dispensed in the group. Receiving a compliment, for example, from the informal leader of the group is likely to be more rewarding to group members than receiving the same compliment from a lower-status person.

Thus, whether the leader occupies a formal or informal role in the group, he should be able to exert significant influence on the activities of the group. The question remains, however, as to what activities are likely to increase the effectiveness of group and individual performance—and what ones will have no impact (or even a negative impact) on performance effectiveness. It is to this question that we now turn.

Leadership Functions

Following McGrath (1962), we believe that there are two general types of leadership "functions" which must be fulfilled if a group is to be able to achieve its goals effectively over the long term. First, "diagnoses" must be made of the state of the environment and the state of the group to determine what needs to be done (if anything) to keep the group moving in the intended direction. The second function is one of "execution"—i.e., taking specific action to deal with the needs of the group at the time, as revealed by the diagnosis. These two types of leadership functions are discussed below, as they apply both to the internal functioning of the group and to its external environment. It should be kept in mind throughout the discussion that both the diagnostic and the execution functions are continuous (rather than one-shot) activities, as illustrated in Figure 14-3.

Diagnosis   In order for a work group to achieve its goals or perfrom its task effectively, it must be more or less constantly in touch with the external environment. Thus, monitoring the environment is one important leadership function. Of particular relevance for most groups are the demands of the *task* for which group members are responsible. It often is important to determine what kinds of member behaviors are critical (and what behaviors are mostly irrelevant) to effective task performance. Thus, the leader might wish to diagnose the task to determine which of the classes

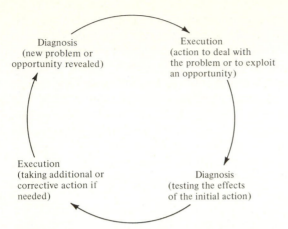

Figure 14-3   The cyclic character of leadership functions.

of variables discussed earlier in the chapter (i.e., skills, arousal level, performance strategies, effort) are likely to be important to task success. On the basis of this diagnosis, the leader would help the group plan how best to use its resources in going about working on the task.

Diagnostic activities are important not only for the external and task environment but for the internal environment of the group as well. Even when an accurate diagnosis has been made of the demands of the task and the environment, the group will experience little success unless it also is able to identify and deal effectively with issues of member coordination and interpersonal relationships within the group itself. Thus, an effective leader will help group members determine what interpersonal problems (and potentials) exist in the group which must be remedied (or can be developed) in the interest of effective group performance.

Finally, diagnostic activities must not focus *solely* on those internal and external states of affairs which exist at the present moment. The long-term viability of most work groups depends as well upon the ability of the group to *forecast* the states the external and internal environments will assume in the future. Thus, effective leadership will involve active search for clues about what problems and opportunities are likely to arise in the future so that effective preparatory action may be taken to deal with those issues when they do in fact develop.

Executing: Internal Actions   The second major type of leadership function involves the actual use of group-controlled resources for taking task-appropriate action on the basis of the needs and goals of the group as they have been diagnosed. In this section we examine executive actions relevant to the internal functioning of the group, and in the next section we turn to executive actions having to do with the external environment.

Creating Conditions An important function of the leader is the creation of conditions within the group that increase the degree to which the group is able to deal directly with both motivational and interpersonal issues that may be interfering with task effectiveness. This almost invariably will involve some discussions of the process of the group itself—a procedure, in many groups, that is counter to existing group norms about what is and is not a legitimate topic for group discussion. Thus, it may be that *only* the leader (who usually has high status and a positive balance of "idiosyncrasy credits") can afford to take the risk of deviation and raise the necessary process issues. If, by such behavior, he can manage to create conditions within the group which allow interpersonal and motivational problems to be discussed and solved *when they are occurring,* he will significantly have increased the capability of the group to respond adaptively to a variety of tasks and problem situations.

Moreover, it should be noted that probably only the leader can establish a norm of genuinely shared leadership—another kind of internal condition which can be highly facilitative of group effectiveness. If someone not in a position of influence were to attempt to move the group toward more sharing of leadership functions, he risks being perceived by his peers as making a grab for power. If the leader himself suggests and encourages shared influence, the suggestion is probably maximally credible—since it is his *own* power that is being offered for sharing.

Taking Direct Action A second type of internal action that a leader can take to improve group functioning is to directly influence group members so that they work both hard and effectively on the group task. The most straightforward (and probably most widely used) means of accomplishing this is to use the rewards and sanctions controlled by the leader to direct and motivate member task behavior. For popular, high-status, or charismatic leaders, merely a nod and a smile may be sufficient to obtain hours and hours of voluntary envelope stuffing and stamp licking. Others, with less personal charisma, must use more concrete or material rewards over which they have control to get subordinates to do their bidding. In either case, the leader is directly and personally rewarding the desired behavior.

There are some serious and very real dangers involved in this leadership strategy. First, when interpersonal rewards are used as a means of motivating group members, the leader runs the risk that at some point in time his subordinates will have "had enough" and his interpersonal favors no longer will serve as a reason for doing what the leader wants. If that happens, of course, the leader's ability to lead the group (in the sense of influencing what happens in the group) will deteriorate substantially. Second, the nature of the *relationship* between the leader and the group members may suffer if he relies too heavily on direct administration of rewards and punishments as a means of motivation. Many writers (e.g., Argyris, 1957; Whyte, 1972) have pointed out the frequently dysfunctional consequences which develop when adults are placed in a highly dependent relationship with someone else whom they must please in order to have valued rewards dispensed to them. Hostility, withdrawal, and even active sabotage are not unknown when the full impact of one's dependence on another for valued rewards is experienced. Thus, if the leader elects to use direct administration of rewards or punishments as a means for shaping member behavior, he must carefully monitor the state of the relationship between himself and the subordinates, lest it "turn sour" as the subordinates become increasingly cognizant of the nature and implications of that relationship.

Executing: External Actions   While many of the leadership functions required for effective group performance have to do with the internal functioning of the work group, there also are important ways in which leaders can operate on the external environment of the group to faciliate performance as well.

Because most leaders have at least some power "upwards" in the hierarchy of the organization, they often are able to create conditions in the broader organization which increase the degree to which group members are capable of and motivated to work effectively toward organizational goals. By using their influence to change organizational selection and training practices (Chapter 5 and 7), for example, leaders should be able to increase the degree to which their work groups are composed of capable, well-trained individuals.

Similarly, by taking external actions to create appropriate job designs (Chapter 10), control systems (Chapter 9), and organizational reward practices (Chapter 12), leaders should be able to create conditions for high and self-sustaining work motivation among their subordinates—motivation which is *not* dependent upon the leader's personally administering rewards and punishments. Thus, rather than directly administering rewards and punishments to motivate subordinates, the leader can attempt to change things in the organization so as to increase the likelihood that people will become *intrinsically* motivated in their work.

Moreover, when connections have been developed in the organization between effective performance and organizational rewards, the leader can reinforce their motivational effects by making these connections very explicit and salient to his subordinates. That is, the subordinates can be helped by the leader to see the positive outcomes which exist in the environment and which can become available to them when they perform well. The "path-goal" approach to leadership effectiveness (e.g., House, 1971; Evans, 1970) focuses explicitly upon the role of the leader in developing and making explicit relationships between employee work behavior on the one hand and the rewards which are contingent upon that behavior on the other hand.

In general, the degree to which leaders can successfully facilitate subordinate performance by creating conditions in the organizational environment depends directly upon the amount of leverage they have with their own superiors, and on the degree of autonomy they have in their own jobs. Moreover, unless a leader himself is *aware* of the ways he can influence subordinate work effectiveness by redirecting organizational policies and practices, this set of leadership functions will not be performed. It is, therefore, unfortunate that so little attention has been given in the management literature to the use of external influence as a potent, albeit indirect, way for leaders to facilitate the work effectiveness of their subordinates.

Conclusion The several "functions" of effective leadership suggested here are diagrammed in Figure 14-4. In our view, such leadership involves several types of activity: monitoring, forecasting, taking direct action to solve problems, creating conditions to head off problems and to exploit opportunities, and so on. Moreover, different leadership functions will be required at different times: sometimes a work group will be suffering through a complex motivational crisis; other times external obstacles may be blocking the task activities of group members; and still other times there may be significant interpersonal tensions which are disrupting the group.

	Internal	External
Diagnosis	Monitoring Forecasting	Monitoring Forecasting
Execution	Taking direct action Creating conditions	Taking direct action Creating conditions

Figure 14-4 Functions of effective leadership. (Adapted from McGrath, 1964)

It should be clear, therefore, that it ultimately is impossible to draw up a set of behavioral specifications for the "perfect" leader. And it should be equally clear that it is impossible for any single leader to perform all the critical leadership functions which invariably arise throughout the life history of a group. Effective leadership, then, seems to us to be characterized mainly by (1) an *awareness* of factors which influence the interpersonal and work behavior of group members, (2) the capability to *diagnose* with sensitivity which of those factors are impairing the effectiveness of the group at any given time—and which are waiting to be developed in furthering group goals; and (3) the willingness and the skill to *share selectively* with group members responsiblity for making those decisions and performing those leadership acts which are necessary to keep the group moving toward its goals.

REVIEW AND DISCUSSION QUESTIONS

1 What is "Pattern A" behavior? In general, is this type of behavior functional or dysfunctional for work organizations? Does the type of organization being considered make any difference (e.g., mechanistic versus organic organizations)?
2 Explain how extremely high degrees of group cohesiveness may work to the disadvantage of the organization.
3 How can the potentially dysfunctional aspects of high group cohesiveness be avoided? That is, how can group effort be channeled toward the accomplishment of organizational goals?
4 Under what conditions will increased group-induced arousal levels lead to higher levels of individual performance? Under what conditions will the same group-induced arousal lead to lower levels of performance?
5 Using the information contained in this chapter as a base, explain how a practicing manager might diagnose and solve a particular organizational problem by influencing group processes.
6 Given enough formal power in an organization, anyone can be a leader. Do you agree or disagree with this statement? Why?
7 Take an administrative problem that you are aware of. Explain how you, as an administrator, would attack this problem. Use the "functions of leadership" outlined in this chapter as a foundation for this discussion.

Part Five

IMPROVING ORGANIZATIONAL EFFECTIVENESS

Chapter 15

Methods of Organizational Change

Organizations that employ people are never completely static, since they are "open" social systems constantly interacting with their various environments. The pace of change will vary from organization to organization, but the fact of change will not. Many changes, of course, will be beyond the control of the organization—but others can be created and guided by the organization. In this and the next chapter, therefore, we turn our attention to some of the major methods and goals of *planned* change in organizations. The specific focus throughout will be on how changes can be made that will ultimately improve the effectiveness of organizations and the well-being of those who work in them.

The intentional change and development activities which we examine draw explicitly on knowledge and methods from the behavioral sciences. This is not to deny that applied expertise from many other areas can also exert great influence on what happens to and in organizations. However, it seems clear that if organizations are going to increase their capacities to withstand the stresses placed on them by dynamic—often turbulent—

environments, planned change will require the extensive use of behavioral science knowledge and techniques.

In the first part of this chapter we review and discuss briefly the diversity of "handles" for making organizational changes—that is, various approaches such as the selection process, the control systems, the design of work, the resolution of conflict, and the like. Each of these can be used as a focal point for planned change. These handles—some of which parallel topics covered earlier in this book—suggest the many different kinds of opportunities open to organizations for making effective changes.

The latter part of the chapter focuses on various critical issues and choices which must be faced by anyone attempting to guide organizational change activities. Such issues include which handle to grasp under what circumstances, whether change proceeds better from the "top down" or from the "bottom up," and whether gradual or radical changes are likely to be more effective.*

In general, there are fewer hard data reported in this chapter than has been the case thus far in the book. In fact, well-documented studies of the process and effects of organizational change are still rather scarce in the research literature. There are many reasons for this state of affairs, not the least of which is the extreme difficulty of collecting valid and consistent data regarding a change process while that process is taking place. Changes always are anxiety-arousing and often are seriously distressing to both individual organization members and the system as a whole. Such are not, obviously, circumstances under which it is a simple matter to collect complete and robust sets of research data. Further, the nature of some change techniques themselves seems to have diverted attention from research. Interpersonal and experiential change procedures, for example, seem often to draw interventionists and participants alike into an increasing investment in the personal and emotional aspects of ongoing events—which can leave little time, energy, or interest for involvement in research on the nature and effects of the intervention activities.

Finally, it should be noted that the *criteria* of change effectiveness frequently turn out to be most elusive creatures. What does it mean to *change* an organization? Is it sufficient for member attitudes to change if

---

*Because of space limitations, we are unable to explore many of the issues important to organizational change in as much detail as we would like. We refer readers who wish for more detailed treatments of the change process to the following sources: for general but detailed overviews of the technology of organizational change, see Beer (1975) and Strauss (in press); for a treatment of the nature of the change process itself—at the individual and group as well as organizational level, see Alderfer (1975); for an inclusive coverage of social intervention strategies, see Hornstein et al., (1971); for a heterogeneous collection of essays and articles on planned change, see Bennis et al., (1969); and for in-depth essays on the "organization development" approach to change, see the Addison-Wesley series of paperbacks on that topic (i.e., Bennis, 1969; Beckhard, 1969; Blake & Mouton, 1969; Lawrence & Lorsch, 1969; Schein, 1969; and Walton, 1969).

behavior does not, or for interpersonal relations among members to change if measures of organizationwide performance do not? There are no easy or clear answers to such questions. For present purposes, we will regard a planned organizational change as having taken place when there are observable differences in what happens within the boundaries of the organization as a consequence of some intervention. Whether such differences ultimately are healthy or unhealthy for organization members or for the organization as a whole will be reserved for discussion in the following chapter (16).

ALTERNATIVE APPROACHES FOR INITIATING CHANGE IN ORGANIZATIONS

Three general sets of handles or approaches for making organizational change can be identified for further consideration: (1) changing the *individuals* who work in the organization, (2) changing specific *organizational structures and systems*, and (3) changing directly the *overall climate and interpersonal style* which characterize an organization. It will become clear throughout our discussion that each of these approaches to initiating organizational change tends to involve different intervention techniques, focus on different short-term goals, and imply different assumptions about what factors are most important in determining what takes place within organizations. Some of the most prominent of these differences are summarized in Table 15-1.

It should be kept in mind, however, that effective programs of organizational change usually involve the simultaneous use of more than one type of approach, and a variety of intervention techniques. Unfortunately, when multiple approaches are used, it usually is quite difficult to be sure exactly which interventions were crucial in causing observed changes and which had negligible (or even negative) effects. In the pages to follow, we review intervention techniques associated with each of the three major sets of handles for initiating changes and provide some perspective on the organizational outcomes which might reasonably be expected from each one.

CHANGING INDIVIDUALS

One obvious means to bring about change in organizations is to change the individual members—their skills and attitudes and, ultimately, their behavior. This can be accomplished in a variety of ways as will be discussed below. The point to be kept in mind when thinking about these types of change approaches, however, is that they are not focused on the individual as the end product of the change process. Rather, such methods should be

Table 15–1 Comparison of Three General Approaches for Initiating Organizational Changes

Approaches for initiating change	Typical intervention techniques	Intended immediate outcomes	Assumptions about the major causes of behavior in organizations
Individuals	Education, training, socialization, attitude change	Improvements in skill levels, attitudes, and motivation of people	Behavior in organizations is largely determined by the characteristics of the people who compose the organization.
Organizational structure and systems	Modification of actual organizational practices, procedures, and policies which affect what people do at work	Creation of conditions to elicit and reward member behaviors which facilitate organizational goal achievement	Behavior in organizations is largely determined by the characteristics of the organizational situation in which people work.
Organizational climate and interpersonal style	Experiential techniques aimed at increasing members' awareness of the social determinants of their behavior and helping them learn new ways of reacting to and relating to each other within the organizational context	Creation of a system-wide climate which is characterized by high interpersonal trust and openness; reduction of dysfunctional consequences of excessive social conflict and competitiveness	Behavior in organizations is largely determined by the emotional and social processes which characterize the relations among organization members.

considered as individually oriented procedures aimed at achieving broader changes in the functioning and effectiveness of the organization. They may or may not have the by-product of helping the individual, at least as seen from his perspective. The extent to which both the individual member and the organization would benefit simultaneously would depend upon how well the needs and objectives of each coincide. Sometimes they will, but this is not a foregone conclusion.

Selection and Termination

The characteristics of the people who work for an organization obviously make important differences in what happens there—and, as discussed in detail in Chapter 5, organizations spend substantial resources attempting to attract and select people who have both the capability and the temperament to carry out their work successfully. Once selection and placement procedures become routinized, however, these procedures tend to persist. As a consequence, the possibility of making changes in organizational functioning by changing recruitment and selection practices tends frequently to be overlooked.

An Example of Change through Recruitment and Selection A good example of this type of change is the study of a bank (Argyris, 1954; Alderfer, 1971) mentioned previously in Chapter 5. It will be recalled that the bank had a tendency to recruit managers who were quiet and noncompetitive and who were quite willing to take orders but uneasy about giving them. The preferences of these individuals ("right types") for security, stability, and predictability had certain definite (and often dysfunctional) consequences for organizational effectiveness—e.g., new sources of business would not be aggressively pursued. Further, the existence of the "right-type" image tended to influence who applied (and who was selected) for management positions at the bank, thereby perpetuating the existing managerial style of the bank. The bank mounted a recruiting campaign to attract management trainees who were more aggressive, risk-oriented, and self-confident. A new management training program was instituted as well, designed to help the trainees ("new types") prepare themselves for positions of responsibility in the bank. The presence of the "new types" in the bank significantly changed how the organization functioned—it became much more oriented to growth and profit potentials—confirming the possibility of achieving organizational change through selection. In addition, however, an intergroup conflict emerged between the older "right types" and the "new types" which created a new and troublesome set of problems for the organization.

In essence, then, the organization was changed through revised recruitment and selection procedures—but the change itself caused problems which previously had not existed. Such unexpected consequences in one part of an organization resulting from planned changes in another part is a theme which will emerge frequently in this chapter. It emphasizes once again the "systems" nature of organizations.

Termination   Just as organizations can be changed by recruitment and selection, so also they can be changed by practices regarding who is encouraged or required to leave the organization. It is possible, for example, for organizations to "de-recruit" individuals by consistently not promoting them or giving them only token increases in pay. In such circumstances, the "target" persons usually understand the message they are being sent and elect on their own to leave the organization if alternative possibilities for employment are open to them. Actual termination or firing of employees takes place more rarely, in part because for most people firing someone is an anxiety-arousing and unpleasant chore. Yet it is true that by systematically eliminating from an organization those individuals who cannot or consistently will not work effectively toward organizational goals, the overall level of organizational effectiveness often can be improved.

Because termination is an unsettling process for the individual and the organization alike, organizational consultants at times are called in for advice about how the process can best be handled. By and large, most such consultants probably would follow a general two-stage procedure for dealing with problems which appear to be rooted in unacceptable employee performance. First, the consultant would explore with the employee and with his supervisors factors in the situation—and in the employee's own behavior—which may be impairing his performance and which are potentially open to change. Then, if such changes were found not to be possible, the consultant could serve as a third party in helping work through the process of termination. It may be the case that, in the long run, the best interests of the organization and the employee are served by the individual not staying in a position to which he is not suited.

Training and Socialization

As was discussed in Chapters 6 and 7, organizations heavily use socialization and training activities—both the formal and informal—to mold and change individuals to better fit the needs of the organization. While some such activities typically are very effective (e.g., informal socialization regarding existing organizational norms and attitudes, and job-skill training at lower organizational levels), their consequences often are essentially conservative for the organization as a whole. That is, new organization members effectively are trained to fit the way things were prior to their joining the organization. This results in the maintenance of consistency and continuity through time, but any incipient tendencies toward change held by the new employees may be stamped out or suppressed.

Trend toward Experiential Training   Organizations which have attempted to use more traditional training and socialization techniques (e.g., company newsletters, lecture-type orientation sessions) typically have not met with much success (Beer, 1975; Campbell et al., 1970). In recent years, however, organizations have turned to other types of training activities in their attempt to bring about organizational change by changing the ways people behave within the organization. By and large, the movement has been away from primarily cognitive and content-oriented approaches and toward more "experiential" training, in which participants are encouraged to learn from often potent emotional and interpersonal events which occur in the training sessions themselves. Dominant among the experiential approaches, of course, is the encounter group (or laboratory training group, or T-group). What typically takes place in a T-group was discussed in Chapter 7, as was the effectiveness of the T-group method in achieving actual change in the behavior of individual group members. In this chapter we will comment only on the degree to which such training (assuming it is successful at least for some individuals in some cases) represents a useful means for achieving broader organizational changes.

The Carry-over Problem   Exponents of change in the human relations movement typically have, as mentioned previously, specified three stages which characterize a successful change program: unfreezing, in which old attitudes, values, and behaviors are decreased in potency; change, in which new ways of thinking, feeling, and acting are learned; and "refreezing," in which the new learnings are stabilized and become a continuing part of the individual's repertoire. It appears that T-groups often succeed in moving individuals through these three stages but that upon returning to the back-home organization from the "cultural island" of the laboratory setting, the new learnings fail to work very well. One reason for this phenomenon is that norms and structures in the organization which reinforce traditional patterns of behavior do *not* change while a manager is away at the T-group. Thus, when he returns to the organization and attempts to behave in accord with his new learnings, he directly contradicts powerful group norms about what kinds of behaviors are appropriate. Quite frequently the existing norms turn out to be more potent than the new perspectives, and the latter gradually are extinguished. The problem is illustrated by one participant in laboratory education who commented that he had indeed changed his diagnosis of "his interpersonal work world and his role in it" but that he saw "no clear connection between his new perceptions and how he translates them into action" (Oshry & Harrison, cited by Strauss, in press).

Overcoming the Carry-over Problem In recent years, T-group practitioners have been quite concerned about the problem of "carry-over" or transfer and have been experimenting with a number of means to deal with it. One way is for organization members to attend laboratory experiences as organization "families" (i.e., people who work in the same organization attend laboratories together so that they can reinforce and support each other when they return home). Another approach is for the entire organization (or for all managers in the organization) to attend laboratories, usually in phases, in the hope that if everybody in the organization changes, the old rules and norms will fade quietly away. However, this approach has not yet been shown to be successful—in no small part because of the logistical chaos often created by trying to run an entire organization through laboratory experiences. A final, and perhaps most promising, approach is the attempt to use T-groups as only *one part* of a broader organizational development program, initiating structural and other changes supportive of the new work attitudes and behaviors at the same time that individual training in interpersonal competence is taking place (Beer, 1975; Beckhard, 1969; Strauss, in press). The experience of one organization in this regard is summarized by Margulies and Wallace (1973) as follows:

> A large organization which had been using laboratory training on a wide scale became suddenly aware of the difficulties in the application of laboratory training to on-the-job situations. Participants reported that the laboratory training was a new and different kind of learning, but that its usefulness in their jobs was vague and ill-defined. In an attempt to deal creatively with this issue the organization experimented with the formation of organizational clusters of participants in laboratory training programs. The clusters were made up of people who did not work directly with one another (that is, either superior, subordinate, or peer relationship), but who *did have potential interfaces* in the pursuance of their organizational tasks. People who wished to take part in a laboratory training session were asked to recruit from 3-5 other persons to make a cluster. For example, one such group was made up of a representative from each of the departments of the Management Systems Division. The departments normally pursued their own special area of interest and rarely collaborated, even when issues cut across all departments.
>
> During the laboratory training sessions time was allotted so that these organizational clusters could meet. Their task was to specifically think through and plan how the application of laboratory learning could be used to enhance their organization's effectiveness. Related clusters also met to provide additional ideas and insights for each other.

In phase 2 of this program the organizational clusters continued to meet after the laboratory training program was completed. Meetings back in the organization were for the purpose of continued planning for the application of what they had learned. Most clusters identified at least one problem area to work on and actually designed and implemented a change intervention for their organization. The cluster turned out to be a useful device for helping organizations transfer laboratory learning to backhome situations. It also emphasized that laboratory training must be followed by other organizational interventions if change is to occur.

Changing Individuals' Motives In closing our discussion of organizational change through training activities oriented toward individual members, a note should be made of a different type of program designed to increase organizational effectiveness by changing the *personal motive states* of top managers. Research by McClelland (e.g., 1965a) has suggested that entrepreneurial activities may be positively associated with a person's measured need for achievement. On the basis of this research, plus a relatively well articulated theory of how motives are acquired (McClelland, 1965b), McClelland undertook to train managers of small companies in India to develop higher levels of need for achievement. Through a variety of training devices, participants in the program were taught to generate high-achievement fantasies, to analyze work situations in achievement terms, to comprehend and internalize the characteristics of high-achievement entrepreneurs, and to work together in achievement-oriented groups. The program (McClelland & Winter, 1969) apparently achieved at least some degree of success. The measured need for achievement of participants increased, and, more important, their behavior in their own organizations became more strongly oriented toward achievement.

One of the major potential strengths of this type of training program is that, if successful, the motivational changes are likely to become self-reinforcing. That is, when a manager learns what it is to experience intrinsic feelings of accomplishment from reaching an achievement goal he has set for himself, he is apt to seek out further opportunities to realize those feelings, which leads to additional achievement-oriented behavior, and so on. It should be noted, however, that such motivational training is likely to be successful only for those individuals who are in fact in a position whereby they can set their own work goals and work toward them with reasonable autonomy. While this clearly is true of a small business entrepreneur (as in McClelland's research in India), it may be much less the case for a "middle manager" in a large United States business or governmental organization. Further, while an achievement training program (like any training program oriented exclusively toward individual organization members) can affect what an individual personally desires and how he behaves, the program does not address those organization level processes which may be crucial in determining whether or not he will be able to carry out his newfound personal intentions.

CHANGING ORGANIZATIONAL STRUCTURES AND SYSTEMS

An alternative to attempting to change the people who make up an organization is to change the structure of the organization itself—or the systems and practices which guide its activities. At its worst, this set of handles for organizational change amounts only to somebody pushing boxes around an organization chart, with nobody else knowing or caring much about it. At its best, this approach can profoundly influence the patterns of activity which take place within organization boundaries—with important consequences for the long-term growth and health of the organization.

Organizational structure was discussed in detail in Chapters 8 and 9. There, two types of structural dimensions were specified. First were "anatomical" dimensions, such as organizational size, shape, centrality, and complexity. Second were "operational" features, such as the authority structure, the arrangement and definition of work activities, and the nature of organizational control systems. We will maintain that distinction here in reviewing opportunities for making organizational changes by modifications of organizational structure and systems.

Anatomical Dimensions

Ordinarily, within an organization only top management can significantly affect the overall "anatomy" of an organization. And, as was noted in Chapter 9, even the control of top management is sometimes "iffy" in this regard—simply because the anatomical structure of an organization is often subject to powerful outside influences, such as the technology and the societal role of the organization. Another problem in attempting organizational change by manipulation of anatomical structure is that the effects of such changes often are quite complicated and diffuse: it is hard to know, for example, just what will happen when an organization experiences a noticeable period of growth or shrinkage.

Size and Shape   For these reasons, manipulation of the overall size of an organization rarely is used as a specific technique for making changes in organizational functioning. The horizontal and vertical "shape" of the organization is subject to some of the same difficulties. Although there is a general feeling among most managers and behavioral scientists that "tall" organizations are more closely associated with traditional or bureaucratic-type organizational practices (and that "flat" organizations are associated with more modern practices), the research literature actually shows no clear-cut advantages of one shape over the other. Manipulation of the shape of the overall organization as a means of affecting internal functioning, then, would seem at best an uncertain change strategy.

Decentralization   More widely used manipulations of anatomical structure for achieving organizational change have focused on the centrality of the structure (i.e., the dispersion of organizational units) and on the arrangement and combination of units within the organization (termed "complexity" in Chapter 9). Decentralization is a widely used means of attempting to increase the autonomy and responsibility of local management for local operations. The expectation is that decentralization will lead to greater overall profitability for the organization, in part because those managers who have closest access to information regarding local operations are given decision-making responsibility (and are held financially account-able) for those operations. There is little direct evidence in the research literature, however, regarding the potency of decentralization as a means of achieving organizational change.

The movement toward decentralization of General Motors as the organization grew in size is often cited as evidence of the success of the technique. In fact, the General Motors experience represents a rather complex and continuing debate between the merits of centralization and decentralization. Alfred P. Sloan, longtime president of the corporation, has described this tension as follows:

> Good management rests on a reconciliation of centralization and decentraliza-tion, or "decentralization with coordinated control." Each of the conflicting elements brought together in this concept has its unique results in the operation of a business. From decentralization we get initiative, responsibility, develop-ment of personnel, decisions close to the facts, flexibility—in short, all the qualities necessary for an organization to adapt to new conditions. From coordination we get efficiencies and economies. It must be apparent that coordinated decentralization is not an easy concept to apply. There is no hard and fast rule for sorting out the various responsibilities and the best way to assign them. The balance which is struck between corporate and divisional responsibility varies according to what is being decided, the circumstances of the time, past experience, and the temperaments and skills of the executives involved. (Sloan, 1964, p. 429)

Matrix-type Structures   Another increasingly popular structural de-vice for change is the use of "task forces," "project teams," and "matrix"

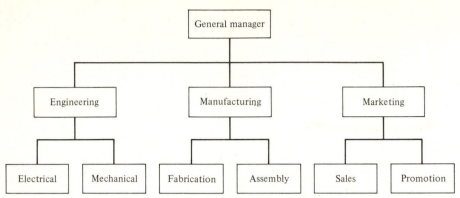

Figure 15-1a The original functional organization of Standard Products.

organizational structures—many of which are designed and staffed for a particular purpose with the expectation that the unit will dissolve when its particular task is completed (Chapter 9). An example of an organization which evolved from a functional to a matrix form (Galbraith, 1971) is illustrated in Figures 15-1*a* and *b*. Figure 15-1*a* shows how the organization (called the Standard Products Company) was originally structured along functional lines: Figure 15-1*b* shows the matrix organization which evolved. The movement toward a matrix organization in the case of Standard Products began not as a planned organizational change but as a result of the organization's inability to coordinate across different functional areas in product development and marketing. Initially cross-functional task forces of middle managers were created to achieve the desired coordination. Later, however, product managers were appointed at the same level in the organization as traditional functional managers to coordinate work on each product line—ultimately resulting in the pure matrix organization shown in Figure 15-1*b*. The matrix organization proved more effective than the traditional functional organization in achieving and coordinating the high levels of technical sophistication required by Standard Products to develop, manufacture, and market its products.

Spatial Arrangements A final anatomical dimension (not discussed in Chapter 9) which can be used to achieve change in an organization is its *spatial* arrangements. Increasingly organizations are attending to (and changing) internal physical and spatial arrangements of people and units as a means of making organizational functioning more effective. The emerging field of "social ecology" has established that the spatial and physical characteristics of a place can strongly affect the ways in which people interact and perform their work (cf. Sommer, 1966, 1967; Steele, 1968); research is now progressing on ways space can be used so as to facilitate the achievement of organizational goals and objectives (Steele, 1973). Although at present there are few firm guidelines for spatial arrangement, as research progresses in this area alteration of spatial arrangements may become an increasingly potent means of changing organizations.

Operational Features

More specific, and therefore more amenable to planned change efforts, are the operational features of organization structure. We will examine structures and systems having to do with (1) authority and decision-making responsibility, (2) work and production flow, (3) standards and controls, and (4) employee performance appraisals and rewards. (The first three of these roughly correspond to the three classes of operational features discussed in Chapter 9.)

Authority Structures   Many theories of organization and many normative prescriptions for organizational change focus centrally on authority —and in particular on the level in the organization at which decisions are

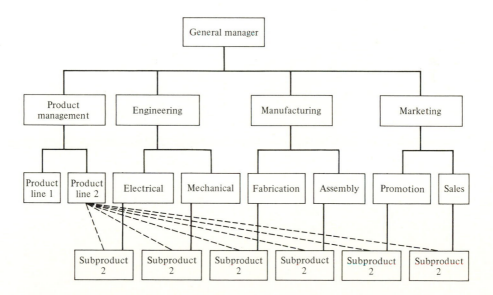

——— Technical authority over the product

——— Formal authority over the product (In product organization, these relationships may be reversed.)

Figure 15-1b   The pure matrix organization which evolved.

made (McGregor, 1960; Argyris, 1964; Likert, 1961, 1967). Normative theorists frequently argue that organizational effectiveness will increase if the authority structure is changed so that decision-making responsibility is "pushed down" to lower organizational levels.

While the research literature confirms the importance of the authority structure as a determinant of organizational functioning, no clear-cut "best answers" have yet emerged. A widely cited study carried out some years ago (Morse & Reimer, 1956) is a good case in point. These researchers gained access to four parallel divisions of a company—two of which had a history of high performance and two of which had a poor performance record. One high- and one low-performing division were assigned to a "participative" condition in which authority was moved lower in the organizational hierarchy. The other high-low pair was assigned to a "hierarchically controlled program" in which close supervision was the rule and the level at which decision making took place was moved *upward*. Results showed some small performance differences between conditions after one year: all divisions increased in performance, and the hierarchical divisions increased slightly more than the participative divisions. Measures of morale, commitment, company loyalty, and the like, on the other hand, favored the participative condition. As the experiment lasted only a year, it is impossible to know whether the observed differences would have persisted and become even more clear-cut or whether events would have occurred within the organization to smooth out the differences between conditions.

In any case, it is clear that alteration of the authority structure does represent one potentially powerful handle for making organizational changes. While most theorists would agree that the objective of any changes in the authority structure should be to increase the likelihood that decisions will be made by those organization members who have both the information and the competence required to make them effectively, it is less clear just what specific structural changes should be made in any given case to achieve this general objective.

Work Structure and Technical Systems   The impact of work design on employee behavior was discussed in detail in Chapter 10. There it was stressed that changes in the structure of work can significantly alter behavior and attitudes in organizations. Experience in a number of organizations, however, has also shown that activities aimed at redesigning jobs and work almost invariably lead to a surfacing of other organizational problems and issues which initially may have been hidden from view. By beginning the process of structural change through job redesign, preexisting problems of supervision, pay, intergroup relationships, organizational subunit structure, and the like often become publicly acknowledged for the first time and therefore amenable to analysis and change. Work or job redesign, then, potentially can open up a full range of issues which provide opportunities for organizational improvement.

There are, nevertheless, still many unknowns regarding the use of job redesign as a means of organizational change. It was noted in Chapter 10 that attempts to enlarge jobs sometimes introduce tensions into the relationships among employees and their supervisors and that therefore any change strategy based on this approach must be able to deal simultaneously with both job and relationship issues. This, typically, is not easy to accomplish. Further, job redesign activities can create dissatisfactions with pay—for example, when a worker feels he is doing more work in an enlarged job for the same pay—and can even have the effect of exacerbating union-management problems (Beer, 1975). Still another problem with job redesign as an approach to organizational change is the fact that at present we have relatively little systematic and controlled experimental data about the effects of various alternative strategies for carrying out these kinds of change activities.

A closely related handle for initiating organizational change is the design of larger-scale technical and production systems which involve more than just a few specific jobs (Bennis, 1966, Ch. 5; Chapple & Sayles, 1961). Enormous changes in the ways organizations function have been wrought by technological advances over the last several decades. Examples include the introduction of computer control of the production process, intricate operations research models for production and inventory control, and sophisticated and automated equipment design. While such advances clearly have affected the work of managers and employees in organizations, it has only been relatively recently—and then not on a very widespread basis—that organizations have explicitly utilized behavioral science knowledge in their design or implementation. One interesting and recent example, where this was the case, illustrates how such knowledge might usefully be brought to bear on situations involving changes in technical and production systems (Walton, 1971):

> A pet food manufacturer decided to expand facilities by building a new plant at another location. The existing plant had been suffering from various symptoms of employee discontent that led to indifferent and "inattentive" performance which in turn was causing problems of waste, product recycling and plant shutdown time. The new plant was planned by a small group of managers using behavioral science consultants and was constructed to take into account employee needs and expectations. The resulting design incorporated such features as:

"Autonomous work groups": Self-managed teams of 7-14 members, in which assignment of tasks to individuals are "subject to team consensus." Such teams also, for example, screen and select new employees to replace any members who leave the team, and in addition are given major responsibility for dealing with manufacturing problems that occur within or between teams.

"Integrated support functions": Such activities as quality control, normal equipment maintenance, and custodial duties are performed by the teams rather than being assigned to separate specialist groups.

"Challenging job assignments": All jobs consist of sets of tasks purposely designed to "include functions requiring higher-order human abilities and responsibilities such as planning, diagnosing mechanical or process problems, and liaison work."

While it is still too early to assess adequately the effectiveness of the above innovative approach to design, initial reports indicate that it has been relatively successful (e.g., as measured by decreases in problems of quality and absenteeism and by the fact that the plant is operated by some 40 percent fewer employees than had been anticipated). Of course, as with any other new design, it also has its share of problems (in this case, some negative reactions to compensation practices, some difficulties for a few supervisors adjusting to their new roles, some occasional exertion by teams of undue influence on individuals, and the like). The point is not that technical system redesign involving behavioral science knowledge is in some way a panacea for the complex problems of organizational change. Rather, it is that technical systems can be changed in such a way that they take into account social and behavioral systems rather than ignoring them—thereby offering a potentially valuable approach to change for both the employee and the organization itself (Trist & Bamforth, 1951; Emery & Trist, 1959; Davis & Trist, 1972).

Control Systems   Relatively little is known about how organizations can be changed through changes in the design of control systems (Chapter 9). While it is well-established that people attend to what is measured and reported out (and especially that which is reported up), few research data are yet available which examine the effects of alternative control-system designs on actual behavior in organizations.

One recent innovation in control-system design that is attracting a good deal of attention and experimentation is the idea of "human asset accounting" (Likert, 1967; Rhode & Lawler, 1973). Basically, human asset accounting makes an explicit link between the human and social processes which take place in organizations and the "results" measures which so often are critical in assessment of managerial performance and in resource allocation decisions. By putting effective management of human resources on the same footing as the management of physical and financial resources, human asset accounting offers some interesting possibilities for significant change of internal organizational priorities.

Reward Systems   Reward systems (previously reviewed in Chapter 12) are, of course, a widely used and potentially powerful means of making changes in organizations. There are large numbers of different salary plans, incentive plans, bonus plans, stock option plans, and so on—many of which have been designed explicitly to orient individual behavior in organizations toward the achievement of organizational goals. In general, it has been shown that reward systems can significantly alter individual work behavior and thereby ultimately change overall organizational effectiveness.

It should be noted that reward systems can have effects on organizational climate as well as on individual behavior. The Scanlon Plan (Lesieur, 1958; McGregor, 1960) type of approach is a good case in point. This plan, in essence, jointly rewards employees and managers on the basis of any labor cost savings that are achieved after the plan is installed. When the plan works, it appears to improve interpersonal relations between managers and workers—and ultimately to generate a more democratic climate throughout the organization—as well as increase individual productivity and organizational profitability.

In general, the plan has been shown to be reasonably effective in organizations of varying size, technology, and initial profitability. Apparently critical to the success of the plan, however, is the development of *genuine* commitment to the plan by both workers and mangers. Thus, the plan tends not to work when either the union or the management group is itself weak or noncohesive and therefore unable to carry its part of the joint responsibility for the success of the plan (Schultz, 1958). In effect, the plan provides a superordinate goal to orient the potential conflict between union and management into mutually facilitative and constructive activities—and for this to occur, both groups must be reasonably strong and cohesive.

It also should be noted that the Scanlon Plan and similar types of incentive programs are unlikely to lead to enduring organizational improvements unless they are entered into for their own sake—and not as a means of coping with some more basic organizational problem, such as pervasive employee hostility toward the work or the pay. Such approaches require not only collaborative activity between workers and managers but a willingness to experiment and risk failure as well. Unless an organization is reasonably healthy at the outset, then, it is likely to experience considerable difficulty in generating the levels of joint commitment and willingness to experiment which are crucial to the ultimate success of these types of collaborative reward systems.

Finally, the role of organizational rewards as facilitators of other planned changes should not be overlooked. Providing employees with substantial increases of pay, for example, might be one way to break through the "trust barrier" which so often prevents organizational change activities from getting off the ground. This is illustrated by a recently reported case (described by Beckhard and cited by Beer, 1975) in which a union was preventing the introduction of new employees task forces aimed at reducing costs. By granting a pay increase at the outset, management reduced employees' concerns about exploitation and thereby gained the cooperation of the union in the cost-saving innovations.

Appraisal Systems   For any reward system to be effective in changing behavior in organizations, it must be paired with a fair and reliable appraisal system which measures the behavior intended to be reinforced by the reward system (Chapters 11 and 12). Appraisal systems have additional potential for changing behavior in organizations, however, which goes beyond their central role as a basis for the effective use of reward systems. As noted in Chapter 11, one feature of any good appraisal system is a clear statement of individual performance goals for the appraisal period, which are discussed and shared between the individual and his supervisor. Since there is evidence that goals which are *accepted* by an individual can increase work motivation (cf. Locke, 1968), appraisal systems can provide the basis for a program of organizational improvement by emphasizing recognition for goal attainment.

Citing the powerful directing influence that goals can have on behavior, several writers have proposed *objective setting* as an important management technique (e.g., Drucker, 1954; McGregor, 1960). Management by Objectives (MBO) (Odiorne, 1965) has become perhaps the most widely used version of this type of approach, and there are now many organizational consultants who prominently employ one or another version of objective-oriented management as a technique of organizational change (Beckhard, 1969, pp. 35–40).

At its best, objective setting can become a genuinely organizational activity—with the goals of top management influencing the goals set by middle managers, which in turn influence the goals set by their subordinates, and so on. (Refer back to the concept of means-end chains discussed in Chapter 3.) At each level of the organization highly specific and concrete goals are set and are heavily influenced by the managers whose behavior will be guided by them. The result, in theory, is high personal commitment by managers at all levels of the organization to work toward achievement of their performance goals. This state of affairs is, unfortunately, often rather difficult to achieve.

The reasons for the difficulty are not hard to understand. One of the strengths of an MBO approach is that goals are made concrete—thereby both permitting objective assessment of performance and providing the opportunity for intrinsic reward when goals are accomplished. It is, however, often quite difficult to formulate concrete goals whose achievement can be reliably measured. There is a tendency for goals to be framed in terms of things that can be counted, which sometimes significantly subverts the original intent of the goal. This is especially troublesome when goals are stated for outcomes which are by their nature somewhat intangible.

An example is the goal of improving customer service. This goal is almost impossible to measure. The possible behavioral consequences of adopting such a goal are spelled out by Levinson (1970, pp. 127–128) as follows:

> There is therefore a heavy concentration on those sub-goals which can be measured. Thus time per customer, number of customer calls, and similar measures are used as guides in judging performance. The *less* time per customer and the *fewer* the calls, the better the customer service manager meets his objectives. He is cutting costs, increasing profit—and killing the business. Worse still, he hates himself.

A second major problem in implementing an MBO-type program is that goals often are "sent" to subordinate managers by their superiors rather than being openly discussed with them and influenced by them. When this happens the level of acceptance of the goal by the subordinate manager is likely to suffer, since his personal needs and hopes may not have been considered when the goal was formulated. Worse, transmitting goals unilaterally from the top down can lead to the setting of unrealistic goals. When a subordinate manager feels his boss is not open to influence about what the goal should be, he may retaliate by withholding information he has (but that the boss does not have) which bears on the likelihood that the goal as formulated is realistic. Then, when the goal subsequently is *not* achieved, he can point to that information as being a "good reason" why the goal was not met. Organizational effectiveness, obviously, suffers when such patterns of behavior develop.

It seems, therefore, that for goals to be both realistic and acceptable to subordinate managers throughout all levels of an organization, an overall climate of mutual influence, trust, and openness of communication may be required. When the climate is such that employees throughout the organization are more oriented toward "looking good" than toward openly discussing their objectives and the problems faced in achieving them, then the approach may merely perpetuate individual defensiveness and competitiveness between groups and across organizational levels.

In sum, an objectives-oriented appraisal approach should work best in organizations which already are relatively well-off; if, however, the organization is characterized by low trust, one-way influence, and distorted communication, goal-setting programs such as MBO will not fix things. Instead, under such circumstances it is more likely that goal-setting activities and associated appraisal systems will rapidly dissipate as they move from the top level of management down through the ranks of the organization—and all the old problems will remain.

DIRECTLY CHANGING ORGANIZATIONAL CLIMATE AND INTERPERSONAL STYLE

In recent years organizational researchers (e.g., Halpin & Croft, 1962; Litwin & Stringer, 1968; Taguiri & Litwin, 1968; Schneider & Bartlett, 1968; Pritchard & Karasick, 1973) have been devoting increasing attention to the concept of "organizational climate." At its simplest, the term refers to the typical or characteristic day-to-day properties of a particular work environment—its nature as perceived and felt by those who work in it or are familiar with it. (Similar terms would include "organizational personality" and "organizational culture.") One can, indeed, readily think of familiar phrases that are commonly used to describe an organization's climate, such as "warm," "fast moving," "impersonal," "open," "stressful," "conservative," etc. These depict, in other words, an organization's *modus operandi*—particularly the quality and style of the interpersonal relations among its members.

Changing the overall climate or interpersonal style which characterizes an organization is the primary objective of many programs of organizational change. This is because climate is so pervasive and its presumed effects so strong. Even when rather specific changes are made, such as modifying the reward system to more closely tie rewards to performance, the intent of management in undertaking the change usually is reasonably broad (e.g., to create a climate supportive of hard work and high productivity throughout the company).

The previous two handles for initiating organizational change (i.e., changing people and changing organizational structures and systems) address the broader issues of climate and style only indirectly. That is, it is assumed and intended that modifications of the people or the structures which compose an organization will, ultimately, affect climate and style—but usually as a long-term consequence of the specific change and not as an immediate change objective.

In this section we examine a group of approaches to organizational change which are intended to *directly* affect and improve the climate and interpersonal style of the organization. In general, the techniques which are reviewed here have been the province of those who call themselves "organizational development" (OD) specialists or consultants. Organizational development has been defined by Strauss (in press) as a set of programs "designed to obtain [organizational] change primarily (or at least initially) through altering attitudes and improving interpersonal relations." A somewhat more specific definition of OD has been proposed by Beckhard (1969, p. 9):

> Organization development is an effort (1) planned, (2) organization-wide, and (3) managed from the top, to (4) increase organization effectiveness and health through (5) planned interventions in the organization's "process," using behavioral science knowledge.

Beckhard then goes on to list several assumptions which would be shared by most OD consultants and which would guide their choices of interventions and activities in an organization (pp. 26–27):

> 1 The basic building blocks of an organization are groups (teams). Therefore, the basic units of change are groups, not individuals.
> 2 An always relevant change goal is the reduction of inappropriate competition between parts of an organization and the development of a more collaborative condition.
> 3 Decision-making in a healthy organization is located where the information sources are, rather than in a particular role or level of hierarchy.
> 4 Organizations, subunits of organizations, and individuals continuously manage their affairs against goals. Controls are interim measurements, not the basis of managerial strategy.
> 5 One goal of a healthy organization is to develop generally open communication, mutual trust, and confidence between and across levels.
> 6 "People support what they help create." People affected by a change must be allowed active participation and a sense of ownership in the planning and conduct of the change.

Obviously, this particular view of OD would encourage the use of many structural and personnel-oriented change techniques in a full-fledged organizational development effort. It is quite specific, for example, about the importance of goal setting and individual skill development as part of any truly general process of organizational development. Most of the activities of contemporary organizational development practitioners, however, can be subsumed by two general approaches, both of which purport to realize direct change in the climate and interpersonal style which characterize an organization:

1   Helping organizations build more effective *teams* of organization members, with special attention to issues of participation and leadership within teams.

2   Helping organizations find new and better means of managing interpersonal and intergroup (e.g., department-department or line-staff) *conflict*, with special attention to creating a climate of collaboration throughout the organization

Interventions of the first type focus on the patterns of interpersonal functioning *within* intact groups of workers or managers; interventions of the second type deal with conflicts which arise *between* groups (or between individuals in different groups). These two classes of intervention techniques are discussed immediately below. This section concludes with a discussion of integrated approaches to organizational development, which aim for changes in the entire organization rather than in specific groups and individuals within the organization.

Team Building

Team building refers to activities oriented toward helping individuals who work together in an organization become effective organizational units. This involves at least two kinds of learning:

1   First, the group is helped to identify and change various group norms and patterns of interpersonal relationships (especially those between a boss and his subordinates) which may be impeding the effectiveness of the group—sometimes unbeknown to its members. It will be recalled from Chapter 13 that group norms and the way information is transmitted within a group can powerfully affect both the attitudes and the behavior of individual group members; in team-building activities, the group is helped to *gain control* over this often implicit process so that barriers to effective functioning are removed, or at least brought to a conscious level as something to watch out for.

2   In addition, most team-development activities seek to help group members learn *new* ways of relating to one another in the organizational context which are likely to be helpful in increasing group effectiveness. That is, it is not sufficient merely to remove barriers and identify problems—in addition, many individuals need to learn *how* to be effective group members. This often involves, for example, learning how to express disagreement without getting into a win-lose argument with the other person; or how to express negative feelings without seeming to condemn; or how to provide leadership without controlling others; or how to tolerate and learn from tensions which exist in the group—rather than immediately seeking for ways to eliminate the tensions as quickly as possible; and so on.

Almost all team-building activities take place with the active assistance of a consultant skilled in working with groups. Also, such activities frequently take place away from the organization (to allow members to place their full attention on the learning to be done) and usually involve a number of meetings—frequently a full day at a time. Team building has been done with many different kinds of groups: existing units under one supervisor; groups of first-line supervisors; groups of technical specialists from different parts of the organization who must, in their day-to-day activities, coordinate with one another; line-staff teams; top management groups and even boards of directors; and, with increasing frequency, temporary task forces or project teams who must learn quickly how to work together effectively—and how to terminate their group when the work is completed.

Team building obviously has many similarities to the use of T-group laboratory training for changing the behavior of individual organization members (discussed earlier in this chapter). The difference between individual-oriented laboratory education and team building is as follows: In individual-oriented training, it is assumed that the learnings gained in the laboratory by a person will affect how he behaves in the organization—and, when many organization members attend laboratories, the interpersonal style of the larger organization ultimately should change. In team building, on the other hand, the focus is on obtaining direct changes in the pattern of interpersonal behavior which takes place *within an intact group from the organization.* Individual group members may, of course, achieve personal learnings in the process, but the emphasis clearly is on improving how members work together, as a unit, in carrying out their organizational activities.

There is a variety of procedures used by organizational development consultants for accomplishing the task of team building. Three general approaches will be reviewed briefly here: (1) the "survey-feedback-discussion-action planning" technique, (2) the "process consultation" approach, and (3) the "interpersonal" approach.

Survey-Feedback-Discussion-Action Planning   In general, this approach involves a consultant's helping the group collect information about the way the group operates at the outset of the team-building process; then his feeding this information back to group members, in a form that will facilitate their understanding of it and ability to discuss it; then exploring by the group (again, with the assistance of the consultant) of some of the implications of the information—often including examining the ways the information is being validated by the process of the group, even as they are discussing the information; and finally, planning for ways the group would like to change its mode of operation, and selecting action steps for getting there from here.

Often useful in the survey-feedback process is a questionnaire or interview for collecting initial data about the state of the group. One instrument which has been widely used for this purpose is the "System 1–System 4" diagnostic questionnaire of Likert (1967). A short adaptation of the questionnaire is shown in Figure 15-2 (Albrook, 1967). In a typical use of the scale, there would first be a brief discussion among group members of the meaning of each of the items. Then each member would complete the scale anonymously, and the ratings would be pooled. Finally group members would be shown the average group score for each scale, and using these results would begin discussion of what the major group problems were and how members might begin to work on these problems.

Process Consultation   Process consultation, as articulated by Schein (1969), involves a very flexible and often ad hoc set of consultative interventions aimed at helping a group (or, more broadly conceived, an organization) understand and do something constructive about its problems. The technique demands a great deal of clinical sensitivity and perceptiveness on the part of the consultant since there is no set of standard procedures to guide his behavior. Indeed, Schein explicitly characterizes process consultation as an essentially "trial-and-error" procedure, with the consultant and the client group working *together* to diagnose the state of the group and to plan what to do on the basis of that diagnosis.

While the process consultant does give feedback to the group, he tends to shy away from highly structured means (such as questionnaires and structured interviews) of obtaining the data he feeds back. Instead, he prefers to observe the group in action in actual work settings, keeping a very "low profile"—at least in the early stages of his consultation. Further, the process consultant keeps closely tuned to the level of sophistication of the group, and refrains in the early stages of his work with a team from making explicitly interpersonal interventions or "process comments," on the grounds that such interventions when made too early can make group members defensive and actually impede the team-development activities. Only later, when signs of readiness appear spontaneously in the group itself, is the consultant likely to suggest the group consider working explicitly on interpersonal issues. (At that time, of course, it may be appropriate for the group to consider moving off-premises and set time aside from its normal working agenda to focus on the interpersonal issues.) In the early stages, then, the interventions of the consultant are likely to have to do with such issues as how the group sets the agenda for its meetings, what the logistical and procedural roadblocks are to effective functioning, and so on. The intent of the consultant is to be of genuine help to the group but not to push it too quickly into sensitive areas.

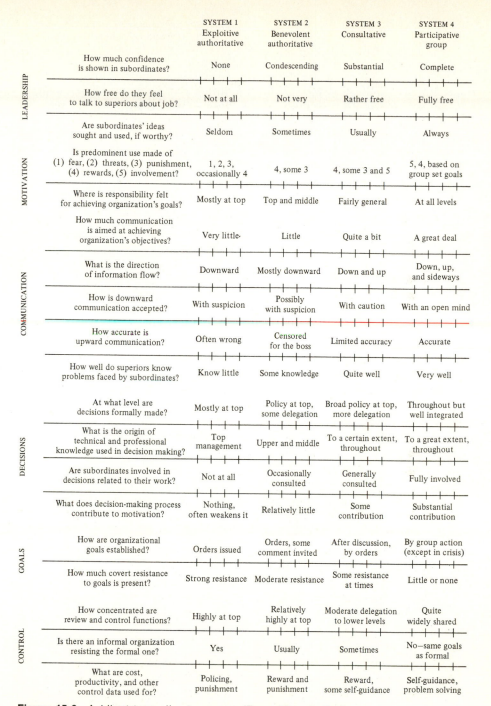

		SYSTEM 1 Exploitive authoritative	SYSTEM 2 Benevolent authoritative	SYSTEM 3 Consultative	SYSTEM 4 Participative group
LEADERSHIP	How much confidence is shown in subordinates?	None	Condescending	Substantial	Complete
	How free do they feel to talk to superiors about job?	Not at all	Not very	Rather free	Fully free
	Are subordinates' ideas sought and used, if worthy?	Seldom	Sometimes	Usually	Always
MOTIVATION	Is predominent use made of (1) fear, (2) threats, (3) punishment, (4) rewards, (5) involvement?	1, 2, 3, occasionally 4	4, some 3	4, some 3 and 5	5, 4, based on group set goals
	Where is responsibility felt for achieving organization's goals?	Mostly at top	Top and middle	Fairly general	At all levels
	How much communication is aimed at achieving organization's objectives?	Very little	Little	Quite a bit	A great deal
COMMUNICATION	What is the direction of information flow?	Downward	Mostly downward	Down and up	Down, up, and sideways
	How is downward communication accepted?	With suspicion	Possibly with suspicion	With caution	With an open mind
	How accurate is upward communication?	Often wrong	Censored for the boss	Limited accuracy	Accurate
	How well do superiors know problems faced by subordinates?	Know little	Some knowledge	Quite well	Very well
DECISIONS	At what level are decisions formally made?	Mostly at top	Policy at top, some delegation	Broad policy at top, more delegation	Throughout but well integrated
	What is the origin of technical and professional knowledge used in decision making?	Top management	Upper and middle	To a certain extent, throughout	To a great extent, throughout
	Are subordinates involved in decisions related to their work?	Not at all	Occasionally consulted	Generally consulted	Fully involved
	What does decision-making process contribute to motivation?	Nothing, often weakens it	Relatively little	Some contribution	Substantial contribution
GOALS	How are organizational goals established?	Orders issued	Orders, some comment invited	After discussion, by orders	By group action (except in crisis)
	How much covert resistance to goals is present?	Strong resistance	Moderate resistance	Some resistance at times	Little or none
CONTROL	How concentrated are review and control functions?	Highly at top	Relatively highly at top	Moderate delegation to lower levels	Quite widely shared
	Is there an informal organization resisting the formal one?	Yes	Usually	Sometimes	No—same goals as formal
	What are cost, productivity, and other control data used for?	Policing, punishment	Reward and punishment	Reward, some self-guidance	Self-guidance, problem solving

Figure 15-2 A Likert-type climate survey. (From Albrook, R. C., "Participative Management: Time for a Second Look," *Fortune*, May 1967, p. 167)

461

Schein argues that the diagnostic activities which the consultant engages in are themselves interventions and that it is artificial for a consultant to attempt to partition his work with a team into separate diagnosis and intervention periods. Instead, he argues that the consultant should be engaged in continuous diagnosis throughout his period of consultation with the group and help group members realize that as they learn to diagnose their team functioning for themselves they have, in fact, gained an intervention skill.

Interpersonal Intervention   This approach, as described by Argyris (1962, 1964), relies heavily on so-called laboratory education or the T-group method. The assumption is that as group members increase their competence in working together as a unit, their team effectiveness will increase —and ultimately the organization as a whole will be helped as well. Thus:

> A group in which there is sharing of feelings, mutual supportiveness and non-evaluative communication is one which develops mutual trust and confidence. As trust develops, individuals in the group are more willing to cooperate, take personal risks in the group and communicate more frequently, accurately, and openly. These conditions enhance important task-related functions of conflict resolution and decision-making. Increased cooperation and group cohesiveness will also lead to higher commitment to group goals and enhance team effectiveness and productivity. It is important to note that the development of effective interpersonal relations does not have the objective of increasing motivation in any intrinsic task-related sense. It does have the very important objective of creating a climate where conflict can be confronted, problems effectively solved, and effective decisions made. (Beer, 1975)

This approach to team building, then, is similar to standard laboratory training programs—except that the groups involved are intact teams, whose members are attempting to increase their interpersonal competence explicitly vis-à-vis each other in the context of their own organizational unit. It is true, nevertheless, that in interpersonally oriented team building, little explicit attention is likely to be given in group sessions to formulating the kinds of group "action plans" which are central to the diagnosis-feedback and the process-consultation approaches. Instead, the consultant serves much more as a facilitator of here-and-now interpersonal learning, and the expectation is that the group itself—as its members increase in interpersonal competence—will ultimately be able to generate effectively all the action plans it needs or wants.

An example of the use of this approach is an attempt by Argyris (1962) to realize general changes in an organization through intensive team-development activities with a group of top managers. As a consequence of team development, the reported values of the managers significantly changed, and they exhibited sharply improved interpersonal competence in their dealings with each other. It also was true, however, that no evidence of organizationwide changes as a result of the team-development activities was found. Indeed, many of the managers reported experiencing considerable frustration when they attempted to apply their new learnings to their interactions with other organization members who had not been a part of their training group.

Conflict Resolution

A second major approach to making direct changes in organizational climate and interpersonal style focuses on the resolution of interpersonal and intergroup conflict.

Conflict, both between people and between groups, is pervasive in most organizational settings for very understandable reasons. Managers in business, for example, often are evaluated explicitly and continuously against their peers as they move up the organizational hierarchy. Whoever "looks best" to higher management gets the nod for promotion, and this state of more or less constant competition can result in conflict which substantially drains both the individuals involved and the resources of the organization.

Similarly, competition between groups in organizations often is structurally encouraged—even if nobody explicitly *intends* to provide such encouragement. There almost always is a "scarce resource" problem in organizations, and different functional and staff groups often find themselves in competition for these resources at budget time. The problem is sometimes worsened when the competing groups are dependent upon each other for meeting their own group goals. An example is the classic conflict between production and sales: sales cannot sell if the product is not of adequate quality and on time; production cannot operate efficiently unless it has accurate, predictable, and complete information about sales prognoses and needs. Finally, functional groups in organizations often are physically as well as organizationally separated, which increases the chances for mutual stereotyping and misunderstanding.

All in all, there are quite understandable reasons for the presence of frequent conflict in organizations. This does not, however, make the frequently negative consequences of excessive conflict (e.g., duplication of effort, withholding information or passing on misinformation, poor coordination, and so on) any less detrimental to the overall health of the organization.

A good deal of energy has been invested by behavioral scientists, therefore, in finding ways to resolve (which is *not* the same thing as reducing to zero) conflict in organizations. ==Three major approaches to conflict resolution are used: process consultation, laboratory exercises, and structural change.==

Process Consultation   Following the general strategy of process consultation (discussed earlier), a consultant often can help the parties to the conflict come into meaningful contact with one another (on neutral territory) and begin a process of dialogue with each other which can lead to possible conflict resolution. As was the case for the team-building application of process consultation, procedures are usually ad hoc, diagnostic activities often serve the function of interventions as well, and a great deal of clinical sensitivity and skill is called for. One skilled consultant on matters of interpersonal conflict (Walton, 1969) has provided the following list of interventions which he has found useful in dealing with conflict:

Initiating agendas for meetings of the parties to the conflict
"Refereeing" the interaction between the parties, and sometimes even providing mild rewards (and punishments) for productive (and counterproductive) behavior by the participants
Restating the views of the parties, making sure they are heard and heard accurately
Helping the parties provide each other with honest and constructive feedback about their reactions to each other
Helping the parties diagnose the reasons for their conflict
Diagnosing (and sometimes attempting to change) the conditions which have caused poor dialogue between the parties
Suggesting specific ways in which discussion between the parties might proceed
Structuring the setting of meetings of the parties to be maximally facilitative of constructive exchange

Laboratory Exercises   A second general type of intervention used in conflict resolution activities (especially for those involving intergroup conflict) is the arrangement of exercises in which conditions are created for the parties to the conflict to learn how they may be misperceiving (and misjudging) the other parties. The intent of such exercises is to set the stage for the parties in conflict to engage in constructive actions to do something about the conflict. Numerous potentially helpful exercises exist, but one of the most popular is described by Blake et al. (1964) and is paraphrased in Figure 15-3.

The general procedure (often modified in various ways as appropriate for particular circumstances) outlined in Figure 15-3 has been fairly success-

1 First, after the two groups have agreed to meet to work on their problems and have arrived at a "neutral" site, each group is asked to meet separately and develop a list of attributes that characterize both itself and the other group. In addition, group members often are asked to predict what the other group will put on its list about their own group.

2 The groups are brought together, and each group in turn presents the list which has been generated. Group members at this stage are asked only to *listen* and to refrain from discussing or explaining items on the lists.

3 The groups then return to private meetings to discuss what has happened thus far and to revise the lists if desired. In addition, group members at this point often are asked to arrange the points of difference between the groups in terms of their priority for action.

4 The groups meet together again, exchange and discuss their revised diagnoses regarding the conflict, and work together to develop a combined list of the most important intergroup problems which require attention.

5 On the basis of their consolidated list of priority items, the combined group, with the aid of the consultant, formulates a set of action plans which lead to the resolution of the conflict—or at least make it manageable and less dysfunctional for group members and for the organization.

6 A follow-up meeting usually is scheduled to monitor the progress of the action steps and to maintain contact between the groups.

Figure 15-3 Steps in laboratory exercises for groups to explore conflicts (based on Blake et al., 1964)

ful in handling certain types of intergroup conflict (Beer, 1975; Beckhard, 1969). In essence, the procedure does four things: (1) it makes public the privately shared views held by members of each group about the other; (2) it provides a supportive setting (i.e., neutral turf and the assistance of an outside consultant) for discussion of differences; (3) it encourages the formulation of explicit action steps to do something concrete about the problem; and (4) it encourages the development of one or more superordinate goals common to both groups. The last item is important since the literature on conflict between groups suggests that having a shared goal is one of the most effective means of moving groups from a competitive to a collaborative relationship.

Structural Changes In some cases, of course, there is no possibility of finding a superordinate goal; that is, the environment of the warring groups is such that it is objectively true that when one group wins, the other loses. Process consultation or laboratory exercises may be helpful to members of the two groups in learning to live with the conflict situation—but the possibility of developing a superordinate goal from the combined discussions is slim at best. In such cases, the interventionist may wish to turn his attention to the organizational context itself to see if the reward structure or the work structure could be changed so that the objective sources of conflict could be minimized or removed. This would involve making structural changes (discussed earlier in this chapter) rather than direct intervention into the climate of the organization (which is the focus of this section); such changes are mentioned here because they represent one important way of attempting to minimize the extent and dysfunctionality of conflict in an organization.

Integrated Approaches

Although some organizational interventionists focus on a single change technique, many consultants have developed more or less integrated strategies for helping organizations improve their climate and their interpersonal style. Typically these include the use of laboratory training, process consultation of some type, and often particular kinds of team or organizational exercises which the consultant has found from experience to be especially useful.

An Example of an Integrated Approach: Grid OD   Probably the most elaborate and well-articulated integrated approach to improving organizational climate and style is the "grid organizational development" program developed by Blake and Mouton (1964, 1969). In essence, the Grid OD approach utilizes a heterogeneity of intervention techniques in a deliberate sequence of phases to move an organization to what is called a "9,9" management style. The "9,9" style is characterized by a climate which has simultaneously high concern for production and for people. This ideal is described by Blake and Mouton (1969, p. 61) as follows: "Work accomplishment is from committed people; interdependence through a 'common stake' in organization purpose leads to relationships of trust and respect." It contrasts the "9,1" style (high concern for production but low concern for people); the "1,9" style (high concern for people but low concern for production); and the "1,1" style (low concern for both people and production)."

The developmental phases specified in a Grid OD program are:

Phase 1   Study of the "managerial grid" (i.e., the two-dimensional array of management styles focusing on concern for people vs. concern for production) by organization members starting with the top management group

Phase 2   Study of the actual behavioral dynamics of the organization, including team development activities for groups within the organization

Phase 3   Study of the inter-group dynamics of the organization with interventions being made in areas where coordination among groups can be improved

Phase 4   Development by top management of an ideal "model" of the organization using a variety of cognitive and data-based inputs

Phase 5   Formation of temporary task forces or project teams to operationalize and begin putting into practice the ideal model which was developed by top management

Phase 6   Measurement of changes which have occurred, stabilization of organizational achievements, and establishment of new goals and objectives for the future

The Grid OD program, then, draws on a variety of procedures and techniques in its approach to improving organizational climate and managerial style—and, as can be seen by following through the six phases, begins with change at the individual level at the top of the organization. From there, it moves down through the organization as a whole. Further, Grid OD explicitly attempts to provide a social and cultural *context* for those parts of the program which are oriented toward individuals; a manager in a Grid OD program who returns to his regular work role after completing training hopes to find that his peers and subordinates support rather than thwart his attempts to implement a new interpersonal style in his relations with them.

Evaluation and Alternatives   So far, relatively few tightly controlled studies have been performed that provide solid data regarding the effectiveness of the Grid OD program in achieving long-term revitalization of organizations. There are, moreover, several a priori reasons for concern about the general usefulness of Grid OD for achieving organizational revitalization. Grid OD shares many of the same difficulties which confront Management by Objectives programs discussed earlier in this chapter. For the long-term success of Grid OD, it is necessary that the program spread downward through the organization—and that managers throughout the organization remain committed to the program through all six developmental phases. If an organization is strong and has a "healthy" climate at the outset of the program, this may be a realistic goal; if not, it is doubtful whether the required level of managerial commitment to the program can be maintained during the considerable time it takes to proceed from Phase 1 to Phase 6. The problem, of course, is that exactly those organizations which need a program of revitalization most are those which are least likely to be able to successfully complete a Grid OD program.

In addition, it is not clear that the prepackaged six phases necessarily represent the best approach to change for all organizations. Rather than begin change with study of the managerial grid, for example, it might be better in many cases to undertake first a thorough diagnosis of the particular problems which are impairing organizational goal achievement. Initial study and change activities could then be focused on possible causes of the problems revealed by the diagnosis. This approach to change could involve a variety of different intervention techniques, depending both upon the nature of the problems identified and upon the structure and climate of the organization at the time.

Consistent with this eclectic model of change is the "open systems" approach proposed by Beer and Huse (1972). These authors argue that change need *not* begin with top management; instead, they suggest that an input-process-output model be used to identify organizational problems and that change start wherever in the organization managers can be found who want change and will support it. Successful change activities, then, will be tried by other managers, and gradually the organization as a whole will be affected.

Such eclectic approaches, however, require sophisticated understanding of exactly what intervention strategies and techniques are likely to be effective in various organizational circumstances. There often are a number of different change tactics which can be used for a given and well-defined organizational problem, and it usually is unclear which approach should be used in a given specific case. It is to this general problem that we now turn.

ISSUES AND CHOICES INVOLVED IN MAKING ORGANIZATIONAL CHANGES

Which "Handle" to Use?

The match between a particular organizational problem and the handle or approach which offers the best chance of improving things sometimes is fairly obvious and straightforward. If employees working on a highly simplified job complain bitterly of boredom and feelings of uselessness, it is entirely reasonable and appropriate to consider job enlargement as a means of attempting to deal with the problem. Or, if line and staff groups which optimally should be working closely together have developed highly negative and unrealistic stereotypes of each other—creating severe problems of coordination and cooperation between the groups—then intergroup consultations would seem very much in order.

The choice of a handle for making organizational change in a given situation is often much more complicated than it might seem, however, for a number of reasons. These reasons, which are discussed immediately below, suggest that decisions about which handle to grab in planning intervention activities may be a much more demanding and complex process than many managers (and not a few organizational consultants) realize.

The Obvious Problem May Not Be the Real Problem It is widely agreed among medical doctors that, while it is important to listen carefully to the "presenting symptom" which has prompted a patient to visit a physician, the problem described by the patient may have little to do with what is really wrong with him. The patient may have chosen symptoms that he somehow feels comfortable talking about as a basis for initiating interaction with the doctor—while holding back the symptoms which are really troubling him until he can "happen to mention" them casually at some point in his discussion with the physician. Alternatively, the patient may be trying very hard to report his full set of complaints accurately—and may succeed in doing so—but his real medical difficulty may be well removed from the immediate physical troubles he experiences. An upset stomach, for example, may ultimately turn out to be a disorder of the nervous system rather than of the gastrointestinal system—with neither the patient nor the doctor realizing this at the outset of the examination.

Very similar phenomena occur in organizations—especially when a manager is seeking help from a behavioral science consultant. The particular problem a manager reports may be that "employees are loafing too much on the job." The manager then asks the consultant to institute a motivational program to repair things. It may be, however, that the actual cause of the difficulty is a flaw in the production process which leaves employees necessarily idle many times a day, or it may be a deliberate strategy employees are using in an attempt to "get" the foreman who they feel (perhaps justifiably) is supervising them far too closely, or it may be any of a number of other problems. The point is that the *apparent* problem should not be accepted too quickly as the problem that actually needs attention, or the behavioral science interventionist may find himself in the business of treating symptoms rather than illnesses.

This issue is of special importance for difficulties which initially appear to be "people problems"—for example, employee laziness, lack of responsibility, hostility toward supervision, and so on. Many managers tend to see such difficulties as rooted primarily in the personal characteristics of the individuals involved (cf. Eric's view of Kipsy in Chapter 1). As a consequence, there is a reliance on intervention techniques which focus on changing people (e.g., training programs, attitude change programs, and so on) as a means of solving the problem. In fact, however, it is equally possible that the real source of the difficulty lies elsewhere—for example, in the kind of supervision the employees receive, the design of their jobs, or the nature of the organizational reward system. This alternative hypothesis deserves especially serious consideration when many of the employees in a given work unit exhibit similar problem behaviors. In such cases, structural or interpersonal handles for initiating change may well provide more leverage in solving the apparent problem than tactics which attempt to directly change the characteristics of individual employees.

The Manager May Be Mainly Interested in Buying an Attractive Change Package   Often various management fads sweep through an organization (or even across the country) like wildfire. The manager who does not have, say, a "management by parsimony" program going somewhere in *his* shop feels quite out of it—and therefore is likely to attempt to find himself a consultant who can run a "parsimony" program and to persuade the consultant that the organization really needs that program. In point of fact, of course, the organization may or may not need the program, but the manager never stops to check that out, and he is apt to be a bit impatient if the consultant should suggest some preliminary diagnostic activities before initiating a program to increase the parsimony of teams of local managers.

The reverse of this phenomenon, of course, is the consultant who has adopted a particular intervention technique focusing on a particular organizational problem as the "answer" to all organizational problems. There are consultants, for example, for whom it somehow invariably turns out that managerial team building is "just what the situation requires"; there are others for whom job enrichment seems always to be just the right change program; and so on.

What is needed—and what happens all too rarely—is some serious *joint* exploration by managers and the behavioral sciences professionals they have called in for assistance regarding (1) what the problem seems to be; (2) how it can be determined whether that problem—or something entirely different—is *really* causing the difficulty; and (3) whether the kinds of skills the particular behavioral scientists have are, in fact, likely to be useful for the problem as it ultimately is jointly defined.

Sometimes, Attacking an Organizational Problem Head On—Even If It Is the Real Problem—Does Not Work   Even in cases when diagnostic activities have confirmed that an apparent organizational problem *is* in fact a core problem (and not merely a manifestation of some more basic difficulty), it may not always be wise to deal with the organizational dysfunctions by attempting to change them directly. This issue has emerged as one of particular concern for problems having to do with organizational climate and interpersonal style (the third general handle for change discussed earlier in this chapter).

There is now some reason to doubt the long-term effectiveness of behavioral science interventions which attempt to deal *directly* with interpersonal "process" problems in organizations (e.g., changing managerial styles, modifying attitudes about superior-subordinate relations, altering the manifest social climate of an organization, and so on). There have been in recent years a number of OD interventions carried out in organizations which have attempted to directly affect social processes and managerial attitudes. However, the number of well-documented instances in which an organization has been substantially "turned around" by interventions which have relied solely (or primarily) on *direct* intervention into interpersonal processes and social attitudes is relatively small.

There are, of course, several alternative explanations for the current paucity of support for the usefulness of direct social interventions. It may simply be that not enough research—or not sophisticated enough research—has been done to substantiate some very real changes which do occur. Or it may be that the state of the art regarding interventions into organizational climate and interpersonal style is not yet adequate to bring about lasting changes.

The possibility also exists, nevertheless, that the *assumptions* which underlie the use of direct interventions into climate and style are deficient—and therefore that it is unlikely that even more sophisticated intervention strategies will be able to effect major changes in the social character of organizations. The two assumptions which need to be questioned are:

1 It is possible to change behavior in organizations by changing individual attitudes and values.

2 Once an individual has learned a new skill or gained a new understanding (in this case, skills and understandings in the domain of interpersonal or managerial behavior), he will more or less automatically use that skill or that understanding in his behavior within the organization.

The first assumption roughly corresponds to the assumption social psychologists held for many years that changes in attitudes will lead to changes in behavior vis-à-vis the attitude object. That assumption gradually is being abandoned by most social psychologists—simply because it is generally unsupported by research data. People rather often behave in ways which are *not* directly consistent with their personal attitudes—and for very good social and personal reasons. An individual may dislike motorcycles, for example, but elect to behave quite to the contrary when he finds himself sharing a gasoline station with a crew of tough-appearing motorcyclists.

The validity of the second assumption is called into question by the distinction learning theorists make between the conditions under which a new behavior is *learned* (i.e., the individual develops the capability to exhibit a given new response or pattern of responses) and the conditions under which the new behavior is *performed.* In brief, research data show that new learnings can occur under a variety of conditions (including, for example, merely watching someone else engage in a behavior that one himself has never done) but that actual performance of the new behavior is controlled rather directly by the reward structure of the performance setting. In other words, we know a lot we do not show, and we *will not* show it until it somehow is in our own best interest to do so.

The implication of the above is that it may be as legitimate to assume that behavior causes attitudes in organizational situations as vice versa. That is, it may *not* be the case that because an individual feels, say, trusting toward another person, he will therefore engage spontaneously in risk-taking behavior vis-à-vis that person. Instead, it may be that the feelings of trust emerge *after* the person has actually engaged in some risk-taking interpersonal behavior—and has found that the experience was a rewarding one.

This, then, implies that change in organizations might well proceed by attempts to *create conditions in which new and desired behavior is likely to be exhibited by organization members*—and found by them to result in personally rewarding outcomes—letting attitudes then follow as they will. What are the characteristics of organizations which might be useful to examine in this regard? They could include: (1) the work structure of the organization—which determines how a considerable amount of the time of individual employees is actually spent; (2) the control structure—which determines what often is attended to by organization members; and (3) the reward structure—which determines what "pays off" in the organization and therefore what the individual is likely to choose to do when he has choices.

The structural makeup of organizations more often than not has been cast in a negative light by researchers and commentators on organizational life. For example, poor job structures can create motivational problems for employees; excessively elaborate control structures can create rigidities in managerial behavior; poor reward structures can create dysfunctional levels of competition among managers; and so on. What is being suggested is that behavioral scientists and managers alike should consider the other side of the structural coin—namely, how structural modifications can be used to elicit and encourage new patterns of *healthy* personal and social behavior in organizations.

Recently organizational consultants have begun to use structural devices as "supports" for ensuring that interpersonal learnings (especially those acquired away from the organizational premises) do not dissipate when the learner returns to his regular organizational duties in his everyday organizational environment. To go one step further, it may be best in the long run to reverse the roles of structural and process interventions. Thus, structural devices could be used to induce and provide objective reinforcement for new behaviors. Process interventions could be used to help organization members (1) better understand and internalize these new behaviors and (2) deal effectively with the interpersonal problems and opportunities which inevitably arise as a consequence of structurally prompted changes in behavior. Since unresolved interpersonal issues can negate the potentially positive effects of structural change, such process work will in most cases be a necessary part of any long-term change effort. It seems doubtful, however, that efforts to change interpersonal processes are either a sufficient way to achieve long-term change or usually the best way to initiate the change process.

The notion of relying more heavily on structural devices for inducing new patterns of behavior in organizations is not original, and there is some scattered support for it in the research literature. The problem, unfortunately, is that we know very little about *how* to use structural changes to influence patterns of interpersonal behavior, to change managerial styles, or to affect overall organizational climate (Argyris, 1971). It is noteworthy, for example, that in our discussion of the three classes of handles for organizational change earlier in this chapter, the material having to do with direct changes in climate and interpersonal style was dominated by discussion of various alternative intervention techniques and strategies. The material on structural change, however, was almost devoid of discussion of technique and procedure. The fact of the matter is, with the exception of change programs based on goal setting (i.e., MBO) and on job redesign (i.e., the job enrichment approach), little technology currently exists which is likely to be useful in planning change through structural modification. Until such time as the technology is developed, the relative merits of change processes dominated by structural versus interpersonal interventions cannot be compared conclusively.

Change Top Down or Bottom Up?

A manager or an interventionist who aspires to full-fledged organizational change must make a choice (as shown in Figure 15-4) about where to start his change activities—at the top of the organization, working down; near the bottom, working up; or perhaps somewhere in the middle, working both ways.

Most interventionists in the organizational development tradition (e.g., Schein, Bennis, Beckhard, Argyris, Blake & Mouton) express in their writings a strong preference for the "top-down" approach. The idea, which is entirely reasonable and justifiable, is that for any OD program which generates internal stresses in the organization to have a chance of survival

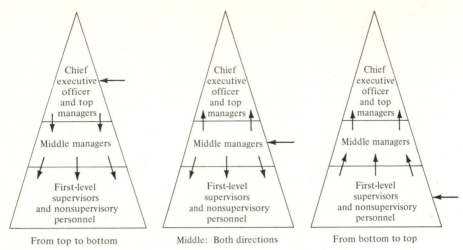

Figure 15-4 Alternative locations for initiating organizational
change.

(and virtually all change programs generate such stresses in one way or
another), the key people in the organization must be knowledgeable about
and committed to the change (Bennis, 1969; Blake & Mouton, 1969).
Further, when the focus of the change activities is the interpersonal
relationships among organization members (e.g., Argyris, 1970), a "top-
down" approach seems imperative to allow the new learnings which are
being gained to be transmitted effectively throughout the organization—and
to provide a necessary climate of support for experimentation with new
patterns of behavior. It is considerably more congruent with traditionally
shared organizational norms, for example, for a boss who has some new
interpersonal learnings under his belt to provide support and encouragement
to a subordinate as he begins the learning process than it is for the
subordinate who "has the message" to help his boss get it.

When change is attempted through modification of organizational
structures and systems, however, it may be easier and more effective to
initiate the changes relatively lower in the organization. Structural changes
which result in desirable outcomes can have "spin-off" effects both laterally
and vertically in the organization, as managers monitor the effects of the
changes in the initial locations where they are tried. Further, those structural
modifications which do not work (or which yield unexpected and negative
outcomes) can be analyzed and altered without major organizational disruption before they are instituted on an organizationwide basis.

The logic of focusing on structural changes in a "bottom-up" change
strategy is consistent with the observation of Argyris (1971) about when it is
appropriate to use structural modifications as a change technique. He

suggests that at lower levels of an organization individuals tend to experience relatively less personal responsibility for their work outcomes or sense of personal causation of those outcomes. He argues that in such circumstances work behavior often may be substantially affected by structural (or externally induced) changes. People at higher levels in the organization, on the other hand, are seen as having higher levels of personal responsibility and causation; for these individuals, interpersonal (or internal) change activities may be most appropriate.

Even change which takes place in the lower regions of an organization and which relies heavily on structural interventions, however, may require substantial support and commitment of key organizational executives. It will be recalled from Chapter 12 how an objectively very successful new pay incentive plan (introduced by external change agents working directly with employees and their first-line supervisors) was terminated by a middle manager soon after the external change agents had ended their personal involvement in the project. Retrospective analysis (Scheflen, Lawler, & Hackman, 1971) revealed that this middle manager had not been brought sufficiently "on board" the project by the organizational consultants; he then demonstrated his lack of support for the project by the relatively risky step of reversing some of the changes even though the reversal was quite costly to the company—and even though the top managers of the company (who had initiated the project) remained quite supportive of the intervention and quite pleased with the results.

Thus, for change at lower levels in an organization to have a reasonable chance to persist, it generally seems necessary to have (1) the support of top management and (2) *either* personal involvement by key middle managers or introduction of a protective top management umbrella over the project for a definite period of time. Such an umbrella often can be provided by top management at the time the project plans are negotiated, but even then it is wise to consult extensively with (if not actually involve in the project) those members of middle management who may have reason to feel that the project is somehow impinging on their own "turf." It should be noted, however, that some organizational scientists (e.g., Beer & Huse, 1972) argue that the full-fledged support of higher management may not always be required. Nevertheless, the role of top management appears critical for effectiveness of most planned change attempts.

Prepackaged Versus Individualized Change Programs

Prepackaged Change   Many changes which are undertaken in organizations come preprogrammed and neatly packaged, and an outside consulting team often is ready and willing to deliver the package and implement it in any available organization. Programs such as Grid OD, MBO, job enrichment, and certain laboratory training programs conducted by the National Training Laboratories can all be introduced into an organization on a fairly straightforward basis. Such programs often are quite appealing to organizational management but not always for the best reasons:

> American companies are suckers for gimmicks. Managers are too anxious to find short-cut solutions to complicated problems, particularly in the area of human relations. Companies try one attractive package after another, just so long as each promises a painless solution to their problems. Human relations, suggestion systems, the open door policy, brainstorming, zero defect programs —all have had their day. Each is tried in turn and then allowed to lapse gradually into oblivion. (Strauss, in press)

This statement may be somewhat too pessimistic regarding the overall potential usefulness of packaged change programs. Such programs *can* have tangible advantages to an organization. They typically have been used in a number of different organizations—which can provide important data to a given organization about what the problems of implementation are and how those problems can be overcome. Moreover, the consultants who administer the programs may be skilled and experienced in their implementation.

The problem remains, nonetheless, that "buying" a packaged change program diminishes the need for organizational management itself to attempt to seriously diagnose and understand the nature of the organizational problems and developmental opportunities which face the organization— and negates the need for management to become personally committed to and involved in the change activities. Many managers deal with the ideas of their subordinates, for example, by asking them to develop a program which then will be presented to a management group for evaluation. Typically, the program is carefully designed by the subordinate to be maximally attractive to the managers and is presented to the management group complete with flip charts and slides. The managers can sit back, watch the presentation as more or less detached observers, and then retire to the conference room and decide either to "buy" or "pass up" the subordinate's program. If they buy, of course, the program clearly is owned by the subordinate—and it is *his* responsibility, not theirs, to make sure it works (or at least to make sure that it *looks* as if it is working; it is, after all, his own career in the organization that potentially is on the line).

This strategy for dealing with subordinates is not noted for its effectiveness in yielding significant and long-lasting changes in organizations. Yet managers often try to deal with outside consultants—including behavioral scientists—in exactly the same way and with exactly the same abdication of their personal responsibility for implementing change programs or for working for their ultimate outcomes. This can make life comfortable for the managers involved, at least in the short term, but it is not likely to lead to meaningful organizational change.

Individualized Change   An alternative to such universal and prepro-grammed change packages are individualized programs which are tailored to fit the specific needs of a particular organization. Individualized approaches to change involve no presumptions by either managers or behavioral scientists regarding what will be required for organizational change to take place or what intervention techniques will be used.

The first step in any individualized program of organizational change is an explicit and extensive *diagnosis* of the current state of the organization. Diagnosis of a sort does, of course, take place when a manager buys a preprogrammed change package: the manager determines by some means the nature of the problem and then assesses the likelihood that the change package will be effective in dealing with the problem. An organizational diagnosis conducted by a behavioral scientist as part of an individualized change program, however, goes far beyond managers' personal definitions of the problem.

There are many different types of data-collection activities which contribute usefully to organizational diagnosis (Beer, 1975; Hornstein et al., 1971; Levinson, 1972). Examples include: systematic interviews or question-naire surveys of managers and employees, observations by a trained consultant of the organization as it normally operates, and special group meetings in which managers are helped by a consultant to explore in depth how the organization currently functions and why it operates that way.

Generally the results of the data-collection activities are compiled and interpreted by the behavioral science professionals and then fed back to the relevant management group so as to reveal as fully as possible the way things are currently in the organization. Based on the diagnosis jointly developed by the managers and the consultants from the survey data, alternative action plans are developed for undertaking planned change to remedy problems identified and to develop opportunities which have emerged from the data-collection activity.

One important role for the behavioral scientist in the diagnostic process is the development of technically adequate data-collection procedures so that the changes which ultimately are made will rest on a solid basis of fact—and not on someone's fantasies or assumptions about what's right and what's wrong with the organization. In addition, the behavioral scientist must help management ensure that *feedback* procedures are adequate for two reasons:

First, it is essential that the people from whom data are collected see that "something is being done" with the data they have provided. Otherwise, their expectations and hopes for change may be built up by the data-collection activity, only to be dashed when "nothing seems to happen" as a consequence. If this occurs, of course, morale can drop sharply, and later changes are likely to be met with increased resistance and a generally defeatist attitude.

Second, by feeding back the results, it is possible to get an additional check on the accuracy of the conclusions reached—and, importantly, to provide all participants who will be involved in the subsequent change activities with a common, data-based set of perceptions about the current state of the organization. Such shared perceptions, when they actually exist, can greatly facilitate the change planning process and reduce the likelihood of conflict among the participants which derives from different assumptions about the way things are in the organization at the moment.

Such diagnostic and feedback activities usually result in a substantially more complete and more sophisticated understanding of the organization than is obtained from initial descriptions of "the problem" by managers. Indeed, very often organizational diagnoses reveal that the managers who originally brought the consultant into the organization may themselves be unknowingly contributing in significant ways to the very problems they hoped the consultant would solve.

In general, the collaborative process of diagnosis and action planning between behavioral scientists and managers increases the likelihood that the individualized approach to change will in fact be "on target" with the real needs of the organization. It also should result in heightened commitment to the actual change activities by organizational management—in major part because they themselves will feel ownership of the change process.

Yet the selection of the most appropriate intervention strategy for any given organization is no easy task, and explicit decision rules about what interventions are most useful in what circumstances are as yet not highly developed. Perhaps the best existing guidelines for instituting a successful individualized change program are those proposed by Argyris (1970): (1) that the intervention be based on *valid and useful information;* (2) that the organization and its members have genuinely *free choice* about the courses of action they elect; and (3) that conditions be created that make it possible for organization members to generate *internal commitment* to the courses of action they do, in fact, follow.

Following these guidelines is a most challenging task for consultants and managers alike. Moreover, individualized change programs invariably require very high levels of personal investment in the change process by managers—as well as a good deal of tolerance for ambiguity, especially in the diagnostic stages. As a result, only organizations which have had some considerable experience in behavioral science methods, or which for other reasons are rather sophisticated and open in their approach to change, are likely to be initially sympathetic to an individualized change program.

Radical versus Gradual Change

Conventional wisdom about change states that the way to *really* change an organization is to bring in a new top executive, give him his head (and maybe a hatchet as well), and let him make the changes he deems necessary. And, in fact, organizations (especially in times of crisis) often use exactly that strategy to achieve change—sometimes unwittingly, sometimes not. What the conventional wisdom overlooks are the *long-term* consequences of unilateral, top-down .change. It may often be the case, for example, that short-term problems are solved quickly, radically, and dramatically by executive action but that the "human problems" of the organization—which very well may have been causal in generating the short-term problem in the first place—are substantially worsened in the process (Blake & Mouton, 1969, pp. 8–9).

The problem with radical and unilateral change, then, is the possibility of creating a negative balance of the human resources of the organization, which can result in a severe backlash in the organization over the long term. The complementary problem for changes which are made very gradually and participatively is that after years of meetings and planning sessions and endless consultations, nothing very striking or interesting has actually *happened* in the organization, and in a spirit of resignation organization members slowly abandon their change activities and settle back comfortably into their old ways.

Finding an appropriate pace for the change to take place—neither too quickly and radically nor too slowly and gradually—is one of the most critical problems of planned organizational change. Trying to set the right pace often poses special problems for organizational consultants—especially those who are based outside the organization. On the one hand, if they suggest or introduce change which moves too quickly or is too radical vis-à-vis a given organization, they risk losing their association with the organization—and therefore any chance they might have to influence the effectiveness of the organization. As one experienced observer (Shepard, 1965) notes in a list of "Rules of Thumb for Consultants," the first task of a consultant is to "stay alive"—one means of which is to peg the level and pace of one's consulting activities in reasonable congruence with the current state of the organization. Similarly, others (e.g., Harrison, 1970; Schein, 1969) explicitly counsel consultants about being careful not to introduce interventions which are at too intense or deep a level for the client organization to be able to handle; and Bennis (1969, p. 71) notes that "in undertaking any planned social change using laboratory training, the core of the target system values must not be too discrepant with the laboratory training values."

The other side of the issue, of course, is that the consultant or change expert can get "seduced" by the existing values of the client system, and ultimately find himself co-opted by that system or even implicitly colluding with it in activities which restrict genuine change. For this reason, it often is useful for consultants to work in groups so that they can maintain an independent point of reference which contrasts with that of the client organization. By this means, additional insurance is provided that the consultant will be more likely to adhere to professional values concerning change recommendations.

In summary, the tension between the readiness of (and capability of) an organization for change and the values and aspirations of the professional change consultant is a continuing problem for which no easy resolutions are available or appropriate. Somehow the consultant must introduce material to the organization which is sufficiently discrepant from the status quo to provide impetus for change—but not so deviant as to be rejected out of hand by organizational managers. That, as most practicing organizational interventionists know very well indeed, is a fine line to walk.

CONCLUSION

In this chapter we have examined both the kinds of handles which are available for making planned organizational change using behavioral science methods and a number of issues which we believe are important in determining the likely success of change attempts.

It should be obvious by now that changing organizations is an enormously challenging task—and that there are no easy answers or surefire techniques for going about the job. Especially critical is the problem of generating a *process of change* which can become self-perpetuating. So long as organizations remain dependent upon interventions introduced from outside their boundaries for dealing with problems or guiding internal development, they will remain incapable (as most contemporary organizations indeed are) of genuine self-renewal. And unless organizations become capable of *self*-renewal, they will continue to merely react to conditions in the external environment rather than anticipate and cope effectively with them.

REVIEW AND DISCUSSION QUESTIONS

1   Is it reasonable to assume that a change strategy aimed at one "target" (e.g., the organization's structure) will have no impact upon other organizational areas (e.g., interpersonal relations among organizational members)? Explain the reason for your answer.

2 Why is structural modification a seldom used organizational change strategy?
3 Should members at all levels in the organization be allowed to participate in the planning and implementation of change? Should such participation be allowed for all types of change? Should participation be equal for managers and non-managers?
4 How do survey feedback, process consultation, and interpersonal intervention differ from one another as change techniques? Can any of these be applied to any given organizational problem, or is each appropriate for a limited purpose or purposes?
5 How do the three major approaches to conflict resolution differ from one another?
6 In Chapter 1 the problems faced by Kipsy and Eric (in a fictitious firm) were described. Assume that you are a management consultant specializing in organizational change. What change techniques would you recommend to help both Kipsy and Eric? Why?
7 What factors influence whether a "top-down" or a "bottom-up" change strategy should be used by an organization?
8 Organizational change efforts might produce some "positive" outcomes even though they fail to bring about the specific change they were initially intended to. Why? (Hint: Does just the *attempt* to make changes have beneficial effects?)

Chapter 16

Goals for Organizational Change and Development

Toward what ends should work organizations be changed and developed? For example, do we want them to be especially efficient producers of goods or services at the possible sacrifice of high job satisfaction for their employees, or do we want them to be very responsive to employees' needs even if efficiency is not increased? Do we want them to be innovative and highly changeable, or do we want them to be relatively stable and predictable? Do we want them to emphasize aggressive competition among members within the organization, or do we want them to try to maximize collaboration and teamwork? These are some of the implicit and explicit questions that form the basis of this chapter. They are not necessarily either-or issues as we have suggested by the way we stated them—organizations presumably can be both productively efficient and capable of providing for employees' needs, at least to a degree, for instance—but they are issues that cannot be avoided.

In the preceding chapter we described and analyzed various methods that have been proposed to help organizations change and develop. However, any such consideration of methods is incomplete unless attention is given to the *direction* of change. Only if one holds that "change for change's sake is good" can the goals of change and development efforts be ignored. Indeed, it is difficult if not impossible to evaluate the effectiveness of different developmental methods unless objectives and goals can be specified.

Any consideration of goals—keep in mind, as we noted in Chapter 3, that goals can be considered as both desired future states of affairs and as constraints—raises the question: Who is proposing the goals? The answer to that question for the purposes of analysis in this chapter is: Those organizational scientists, scholars, and researchers who have been studying behavior in organizations during the past decade or so. Whether one agrees or disagrees with the goals advocated by such "experts," their ideas have been and will be influential, and therefore they merit attention.

CRITERIA FOR EVALUATING CHANGE AND DEVELOPMENT GOALS

As we proceed to consider various types of goals that have been advocated for organizational development, we should beware of the temptation to prescribe the organizational equivalent of "mom and apple pie." That is, it is easy for even experts to fall into the trap of advocating such broad and obviously "good" goals as "excellence," "effectiveness," and "quality," that nobody could possible take issue with them. By the same token, however, they are so diffuse and vague as to be meaningless. They add up to the single prescription: Organizations should be better. Such a conclusion is not really very helpful to those working in, or managing, organizations, yet it often seems to be the main message of some of those who write about organizations.

The nonutility of goals stated in such broad all-inclusive terms highlights the necessity of specifying some criteria by which change and development goals can be evaluated. Let us briefly describe four such criteria that the reader can apply to the various goals that will be discussed later in this chapter.

Operationality

This criterion relates directly to the "mom and apple pie" issue. As brought out in Chapter 3, goals are regarded as operational to the extent that standards exist for determining whether actions lead toward or away from them. Thus, to be operational, goals must be specified precisely enough for someone to tell whether or not they are being achieved. "Organizational excellence," for example, would not seem to fall within the category of operational goals. "Confrontation of conflict," as another example, would seem to be slightly more operational but still not highly so. In fact, most of the goals to be considered in the remainder of this chapter are not per se operational, but the presumption is that most of them could be operationalized for specific situations. Thus, for example, confrontation of conflict could be translated into various tangible activities—such as the percent of meetings in which subordinates felt free to disagree with superiors—that would be regarded as definite evidence that goals were being (or not being) achieved.

Feasibility

This criterion for evaluating change and developmental goals refers to the degree to which they are capable of being achieved. "The elimination of all conflict," for instance, would be regarded as an infeasible goal because of the highly unlikely probability that it could be attained, whereas "the reduction of conflict" would fall within the feasible domain. By itself, of course, feasibility would not be a crucial criterion, because organizations have not advanced very far if all they can do is set many highly feasible but unimportant goals. Thus, this criterion must be considered in conjunction with the other bases for judging developmental goals.

Costs

In any endeavor there are goals that appear highly desirable but which turn out not to be worth the costs involved in obtaining them. This clearly can be the case for certain possible goals of organizational development. For example, the goal of maximum commitment of employees to common organizational objectives often is seen as of utmost desirability from the point of view of the enterprise. Few would doubt its desirability. Nevertheless, the costs of obtaining such commitment, in terms of the resources of the organization that would be necessary to produce it, could outweigh any potential benefits. A much more modest level of commitment might serve the organization almost as well but without the heavy investment of resources (e.g., extensive use of managers' time). In effect, any of the goals proposed for the development of organizations should be subject to some type of "cost analysis." (By this term we do not necessarily mean the same thing as the technical term used by accountants. We mean something broader, wherein consideration is given to the intangible as well as the tangible costs of trying to reach certain goals.) Unfortunately, some behavioral scientists, in their zeal to point the way to improved organizations, tend to leave this analysis much more implicit than explicit.

Consequences

As we have already indicated, it is necessary that goals be capable of being operationalized, that they be feasible, and that they do not represent exorbitant costs. These are not sufficient conditions, however. The final criterion that must be added is the one of consequences or outcomes of goal attainment. This refers to the importance of the goals and thus to the question: "What difference does it make if the goals are met or not met"? It represents the benefit part of a cost-benefit analysis. For example, highly feasible goals may involve too few benefits to justify them, or, conversely, high-cost goals may still be worth pursuing when the benefits are great. This criterion, then, must be combined with the other three in any evaluation of organizational development goals.

It is worth noting, in passing, that consequences of organizational goal achievement may be of three types: (1) intended and positive: these are consequences that were aimed for and which the organization considers to be of benefit to it; (2) unintended and positive: frequently, in pursuing certain goals, highly desirable but unintended consequences will result from goal attainment; these represent outcomes not anticipated but which can be turned to advantage by the organization and those who work in it; and (3) unintended and negative: just as there are unexpected positive outcomes as the result of goal pursuit, so there are sometimes unanticipated negative ones; i.e., new problems are created that were not foreseen. This latter type of consequence is an especially crucial one to keep in mind during our examination of some of the most commonly prescribed goals in the following pages. The reader should constantly be asking himself: If organizations try to reach such and such a goal, are there some disadvantages that might result as well as advantages? Are the disadvantages serious enough to outweigh the predicted benefits?

In the remaining portions of this chapter we will first take a look at some of the typical value assumptions that underlie social scientists' prescriptions for organizations. Such value assumptions are important for understanding the reasons why certain goals are advocated. Following that section, we will examine goals that have been put forth with respect to the behavior of individuals in their organizational roles. (The reader will recall that in Chapter 7 we discussed the concept of individual development in organizations. In the present chapter, we are specifically limiting our consideration to goals that organizations hold for their members if the *organizations* are to develop and change.) The next two sections will deal with goals for the maintenance of organizations and goals for the task performance of organizations. In the final section we will provide a brief overview and consider the question: Have these goals (that have been advocated) been achieved?

TYPICAL VALUE ASSUMPTIONS

Since goals, by their very nature, are statements of what people think *ought* to happen, they are not subject to proof or disproof in the way that statements of fact are. Therefore, in attempting to understand *why* they are being proposed or advocated, it is necessary to examine the values and assumptions that appear to underlie them. In this way, the observer has a better means of interpreting them and a better basis for forming his own stance with respect to them.

In this section, we shall try to summarize what appear to be some of the more typical and important values that underlie the goals for organizational development that are proposed by social scientists who have written on this topic. Unfortunately, such assumptions have not always been stated openly, as was recognized in a recent important article (Tannenbaum & Davis, 1969):

> Perhaps the most pervasive common characteristic among people in . . . organizational development work is their values, and yet, while organizational development academicians and practitioners are generally aware of their shared values and while these values implicitly guide much of what they do, they too have usually been reluctant to make them explicit. (p. 69)

Despite what appears to be the accuracy of this observation, there is nevertheless enough evidence in total to be able to discern a fairly clear-cut set of assumptions that most organizational scientists would subscribe to. (What follows is a distillation of the views of a number of the more important and influential writers on organizational development, including Argyris, McGregor, Likert, Bennis, Schein, Tannenbaum, Davis, and others.)

Individuals Have a Capacity for Growth

As Bennis (1969, p. 37) has observed, those concerned with organizational development hold "generally hopeful" assumptions about people. One particular assumption of this type is that individuals have a *capacity* for growth—that they can make fuller use of their capabilities than they may be demonstrating at present. More explicitly:

> The value to which we hold is that people can constantly be in flux, groping, questing, testing, experimenting, and growing. We are struck by the tremendous untapped potential in most individuals yearning for discovery and release. Individuals may rarely change in core attributes, but the range of alternatives for choice can be widened, and the ability to learn how to learn more about self can be enhanced. (Tannenbaum & Davis, 1969, p. 71)

Most organizational scientists would probably subscribe to this value statement and to its implied corollary: Organizations have not given sufficient recognition to individuals' growth capacities.

Individuals Desire to Grow, Achieve, and Utilize Their Capabilities

This assumption is obviously related to the preceding one, but it is considerably more controversial. Thus, while relatively few people would probably want to question the notion that individuals have the capacity or wherewithal for personal growth, many more might be inclined to challenge the assumption that most individuals *want* to try to develop themselves. They would point to the specific instances where individuals apparently have been given the opportunity to demonstrate growth and achievement and yet have not seemed to take advantage of such opportunities. Those organizational scientists who support the idea that individuals want to grow and achieve would counter, however, that such inferences are incorrect. They would argue that there are many factors in work situations that militate against employees, behaving in ways indicating motivation to develop. Essentially, they would point to inhibitory factors in the day-to-day work situation—such as the absence of recognition for achievement or the requirement to work on tasks that provide little in the way of personally satisfying experiences—that stifle such expression. In effect, the social scientists are saying that the outward absence of obvious attempts of individuals to develop themselves is misleading and that more basic causal factors may reside in the work environment, not in the individual.

Individual and Organizational Goals Can Be Compatible

A crucial assumption for any attempts to change and develop organizations is that the goals of individuals and the goals of organizations need not be incompatible. Such an assumption was at the heart of McGregor's famous Theory-Y approach to management. He labeled this assumption as "the principle of integration," calling it the "central principle of Theory Y." He believed that conditions could be created such that "the members of the organization can achieve their own goals best by directing their efforts toward the success of the enterprise." Of course, he was not assuming that this always or even frequently happened, only that it *could* happen. If it were to happen, he felt that it "demands that both the organization's needs and the individual's needs be recognized." In effect, the assumption that individual needs and organizational goals can be compatible says something about motivation: namely, there is no necessary reason why employees cannot be motivated to pursue organizational objectives. It is assumed they will be so motivated to the extent that they believe they will satisfy their own needs by trying to satisfy the organization's requirements.

The Open Expression of Feelings and Emotions Is Good

The assumption here is that the free and open expression of affect—i.e., feelings and emotions—is both healthy for the individual and beneficial for the organization. This assumption is based on the notion that any individual at work in an organization cannot, even if he wanted to, shed this aspect of his self. He will have feelings and emotions concerning a multitude of facets of his work environment, and the only question is the extent to which these should be allowed to be expressed *at work.* The assumption of many organizational scientists is summed up in the following quotation:

> An individual cannot be a whole person if he is prevented from using or divorced from his feelings. And the energy dissipated to repression of feelings is lost to more productive endeavors. . . . Organizations will increasingly discover that they have a reservoir of untapped resources available to them in the feelings of their members, that the repression of feelings in the past has been more costly, both to them and to their members, than they ever thought possible. (Tannenbaum & Davis, 1969, p.73)

Needless to say, there are many managers, and, indeed, some social scientists, who would challenge this particular assumption. Nevertheless, it is one that is a major underpinning of many current attempts to improve the functioning of organizations.

Collaboration Is Preferable to Competition within Organizations

This assumption does not deny that conflicts are natural to any organization, but it does argue that collaboration should be valued more highly than competition as a way of life within organizations. Thus, it is assumed that the needs of individuals and the goals of organizations will be advanced by attempting to resolve conflicts in the direction of greater collaboration rather than increased competition. This value involves a deemphasis on win-lose solutions to problems between parties within organizations because of their assumed dysfunctional consequences. Here again, this issue has been well summarized:

> A pervasive value in the organizational milieu is competition. Competition is based on the assumption that desirable resources are limited in quantity and that individuals or groups can be effectively motivated through competing against one another for the possession of these resources. . . . Collaboration, on the other hand, is based on the assumption that the desirable limited resources can be shared among the participants in a mutually satisfactory manner and, even more important, that it is possible to increase the quantity of the resources themselves. (Tannenbaum & Davis, 1969, p.79)

The Organization Is an Open and Interdependent System

We have already discussed in Chapter 3 the idea of the organization as an "open" social system. As we pointed out there, one of the basic notions of systems is that of the interdependency of parts. The assumption that organizations are interdependent systems is fundamental to most attempts to change and develop them. It is the recognition that the alteration of any one part or characteristic of an organization (whether the impetus is from within or outside the outer boundary of the organization) will have repercussions beyond that part or characteristic immediately affected. Thus, an effort to clarify organizational objectives, for example, will undoubtedly highlight the existence of certain communication problems that were not heretofore seen as directly connected to the nature of the organization's goal. Or, as another example, the attempt to increase individual self-direction and self-control will be likely to have an impact on superior-subordinate relationships. The assumption of interdependency emphasizes the interlocking nature of different developmental goals for organizations.

The Culture of Organizations Is Critical for the Success of Any Developmental Efforts

As stressed in the previous chapter, it is assumed that change and development activities do not take place in a vacuum. They are always imbedded in some existing organizational climate or "culture"—a set of customs and typical patterns of ways of doing things. The force, pervasiveness, and nature of such modal beliefs and values vary considerably from organization to organization. Yet, it is assumed that an organization that has any history at all has developed some sort of culture and that this will have a vital impact on the degree of success of any efforts to alter or improve the organization. The organizational behavior literature is replete with illustrations of developmental attempts that have failed due to insufficient attention in advance to the prevailing culture. Of course, if these cultures were completely immutable, then no change undertakings would ever be successful. So, the point is not that an organization's culture cannot be modified but rather that if development is to take place, its chances for success will be improved by taking into account the prevailing and dominant norms and values that already exist in the situation. The recognition on the part of the organization's members that there is a predominant "culture" that can be identified is presumed to be a significant factor in facilitating and ensuring the survival of meaningful changes.

GOALS FOR INDIVIDUALS IN THEIR ORGANIZATIONAL ROLES

Having examined some of the typical underlying value assumptions of those who have been prominent in advocating organizational change and development, we are in a position to consider specific goals that have been proposed. Some of these goals pertain much more to aspirations of individuals, especially in terms of their roles as members of organizations. (Needless to say, these goals would also be seen as compatible with individuals' roles as citizens as well as their roles as employees.) Other goals pertain much more to the functioning of organizations as entities. We shall first take up the goals for individuals, in this section, and then proceed to the goals for organizations.

Interpersonal Competence

Organizations are presumed to be able to function better the more interpersonally competent their members are. (Other kinds of competence, such as intellectual or mechanical skills, are obviously also important, but their development is ordinarily regarded as a goal of regular training activities. In this chapter, where we are talking about goals relevant to organizational development, we limit our consideration of competence specifically to the interpersonal sphere.) Competence of this type refers to the ability to deal effectively with an environment populated by other people.

Since one of the more persuasive advocates of the goal of interpersonal competence has been Argyris (1962, 1964, 1970), let us take a look in some detail at certain of his ideas concerning this objective and why he considers it important in relation to organizations. He postulates that there are three "conditions" or requirements for the development of interpersonal competence:

1 *Self-acceptance:* This refers to the degree to which the person values himself in a positive fashion. This feature is especially important in organizational situations because, as Argyris sees it, "The more [an individual] values himself, the more he will tend to value others. . . . He knows that only by interacting with human beings who value themselves will he tend to receive valid information and experience minimally defensive relationships" (1970, p. 39).

2 *Confirmation:* By "confirmation," Argyris means the reality-testing of one's own self-image. That is, "An individual experiences a sense of confirmation when others experience him (or aspects of his self) as he experiences his self" (1970, p. 39). Argyris feels that the more frequently a person receives confirmation, the greater is his "potential to behave competently." Such confirmation is seen as an essential ingredient in developing improved interpersonal relationships.

3 *Essentiality:* This third condition for interpersonal competence is defined by Argyris as one's opportunity to "utilize his central abilities and express his central needs." To the extent that a person works in a situation where only his secondary or peripheral abilities are used he will be deprived of a chance to feel essential. Such deprivation will in turn, according to Argyris, reduce his commitment and contributions to the organization.

In attempting to operationalize the concept of interpersonal competence, Argyris has specified several specific kinds of behavior that he regards as concrete evidence of interpersonally competent behavior. These four types of behavior are listed below and are arranged roughly in order of decreasing frequency of occurrence and increasing potency for contributing to competence—as hypothesized by Argyris and apparently confirmed by his empirical data:

1 *Owning up to,* or accepting responsibility for one's ideas and feelings
2 *Being open* to ideas and feelings of others and those from within one's self
3 *Experimenting* with new ideas and feelings
4 *Helping others* to own up to, be open to, and to experiment with their ideas and feelings (1970, p. 40)

It is likely that most people in organizations—whether managers or rank-and-file employees—would agree with Argyris that interpersonal competence is a desirable goal, both for themselves and for the benefit of the organization. However, legitimate questions can be raised concerning how much interpersonal competence is needed in organizational and work settings and what are the possible costs (human as well as financial) in attempting to raise the level of such competence significantly. For example, one can question whether high levels of interpersonal competence are needed equally throughout the organization. Does each kind of job or position require an equivalent amount? Obviously, there are certain jobs— e.g., labor relations negotiator, first-level supervisor, receptionist—where there is a premium on the quality of one's interpersonal relationships. There may be many other jobs, however, where competence in this realm is desirable but not critical. Thus, both organizations and the individuals who work in them need to face the issue of how much effort they should devote to increasing this capability. As seems apparent, learning to always "own up to one's ideas," or "help others own up to their ideas," is not easy. Time spent in concentrating on developing this type of behavior, however ultimately desirable, is time that is not spent on performance in other spheres. Again, the question is not whether individuals should strive to become more interpersonally competent; the crucial questions are: How much competence is necessary for effective individual functioning? And, where and how does one put in his efforts?

Self-control and Self-direction

This goal is seen as a joint responsibility of both individual members of the organization and the organization as a whole. Primarily, however, many organizational theorists have focused on the organization's role in increasing the *opportunities* for individuals to exercise self-control and self-direction. Their implicit assumptions are that *self*-control and *self*-direction constitute the most effective type of control and direction possible within a human system and that most people have the capacity for such behavior.

The desirability of increasing the organization's reliance on self-control and self-direction in relation to various external types of control, such as the exercise of formal authority, is a cornerstone of McGregor's Theory-Y approach to management. McGregor emphasized that there were clear limitations to the effectiveness of hierarchical authority as a means of control, especially when (1) it cannot be enforced through the use of punishment; and (2) there is the "availability of countermeasures." He makes a convincing argument that both of these conditions are broadly present throughout most work organizations (at least in this country). Thus, there are often many restrictions against the organization's use of punish- ment, and there are effective countermeasures—ranging from strikes to minimally acceptable performance and lack of concern about organizational goals—available to the members of organizations. Therefore, reasons Mc- Gregor, authority must be supplemented by other methods of influence and control, namely, those that involve the individual's own concern about his behavior and performance.

Self-direction and self-control involve the internalization of certain standards and values. From the organization's standpoint, these should be ones that are compatible with the goals of the organization. For this to take place, McGregor states that individuals must see that their own goals can be achieved best by attempting to reach organizational objectives—the principle of "integration" that we referred to earlier in this chapter. Unless individuals have this commitment to common goals, the argument goes, the organization cannot assume that there will be self-control and self-direction and hence is forced to rely on less satisfactory external methods of control. However, to say, as McGregor does, that "people will exercise self-direction and self-control in the achievement of organization objectives *to the degree that they are committed to those objectives*" [italics McGregor's] merely pushes the key question back one step: How does the organization obtain commitment to its objectives? That is a question we will deal with later in this chapter (and have already examined at various points throughout this book). In the meantime, there are two additional questions that can be raised concerning the goal of maximizing self-direction and self-control:

1 Are there certain organizational situations—e.g., "high temptation" positions, such as bank-teller jobs involving the daily direct handling of sizable sums of cash—where the risks of relying exclusively on self-control may outweigh the general desirability of trying to utilize it throughout the organization? Clearly, such risks are often present. The mere fact that there are such specific risk situations, however, does not in itself constitute sufficient reason for abandoning high reliance on self-control and self-direction as an appropriate goal for organizational development. It does, though, at least raise the issue of whether such reliance is appropriate for all conditions.

2 Do all individuals want increased chances to exercise self-control and self-direction? The concept of individual differences has been emphasized throughout this book, and it applies just as much here as elsewhere. Some people may not relish having to make, or take part in, an increased number of decisions, even if such decisions directly concern their own work situations. Some organizational theorists would argue, of course, that the apparent lack of interest of some employees in exercising more self-direction is simply a function of their previous lack of opportunity to experience it on the job. They would contend that managers who refuse to try to increase such opportunities because of their belief that subordinates do not want more chances for self-direction and self-control are only demonstrating the self-fulfilling prophecy: "Since I have not seen them exercise it, I know that they would not want it."

The extent to which people actually do vary in their desire for more self-determination in their work roles is difficult to document conclusively. Typical distributions of individual differences would imply that there is considerable variance in this need or desire as with many others. On the other hand, research in organizations by behavioral scientists seems to indicate that the mean level of this need is well above the level of opportunities provided by the majority of organizations for their employees—including managerial employees.

Individual Growth: Utilization of the Total Person

Earlier in this chapter we stated that two value assumptions of leading proponents of organizational change and development were that (1) individuals have the capacity for growth and (2) they desire to grow. These value assumptions lead directly to a key goal: to bring about this growth and the more complete utilization of "the total person."

The nature of this goal is closely akin to Maslow's concept of self-actualization. As such, it is difficult to operationalize. Bennis has stated the problem succinctly:

> "Self actualization" is a term used rather loosely . . . to explain that an individual will "realize his full potential." It is a fuzzy term, drenched in value connotations both of what people are like and of what they can become. I have as much difficulty seeing concretely the self-actualized man as I do the typical bureaucrat. . . . And when I ask for examples of the self-actualized person, the proponents suggest people like Einstein, Goethe, Spinoza, William James, Schweitzer, Beethoven, and Thoreau. (1966, p. 74)

Obviously, if individual growth, as a goal, is equated with each organizational member's becoming a Goethe or a Schweitzer, then it is infeasible, let alone nonoperational. However, those proposing this goal generally speak in less grandiose terms and talk more about how jobs and career lines can be redesigned to tap more of the individual's present capabilities and bring about increases in these capacities that are reasonably within reach. Again, the notion is that organizations have typically underestimated these capacities and have not focused sufficiently on utilizing them and enhancing them. The argument is that many practices and customs relating to opportunities for individual development can be changed without too much difficulty if organizations (i.e., key managers) are willing to make the assumption of growth.

The intended advantages to the organization in promoting individual growth and the greater utilization of available talents seem readily apparent:

"for most organizations, especially those desiring long-term survival through adaptability, innovation, and change, [fostering individual growth] is an increasing necessity" (Tannenbaum & Davis, 1969, p. 71). However, there may well be created simultaneously some problems that were not anticipated. For example, the organization may have certain sets of rather menial and unglamorous jobs which cannot be economically automated out of existence and yet are essential for the total functioning of the system. If each employee is strongly oriented toward growth experiences and opportunities and has a wide set of high-level capabilities, who will be available to (i.e., want to) do these tasks? That is, it is possible for individuals' growth to outrun the opportunities available to demonstrate this growth.

Or, consider another potential problem: If individuals do enlarge their capabilities considerably—in part because the organization has urged them to do so—will the organization have available adequate means to compensate them financially and otherwise? This is the phenomenon of the "rising level of expectations" that often accompanies growth. In this case, it is an increase in expectations concerning what the organization is going to give in return for the individual's being a much more completely developed person.

From the individual's perspective there is also the problem that if he is called upon to utilize to the fullest his capabilities on the job, he may have little psychic energy left over for other elements in his life space—his family, community service, etc. The father who is too exhausted mentally and physically from his job to be able to spend time with his son (often a manager or executive who has excessive amounts of "growth opportunities" on the job) is hardly an isolated example of this condition. Both the individual and the organization need to ask the question of whether all jobs in organizations must necessarily require the involvement of the total person.

Receptivity to Change

Receptivity to change, as a goal for individuals in organizations, has not been advocated as explicitly as have some of the goals we have just been discussing. However, it seems to be an implicit objective of many organizational development efforts. If individuals feel more comfortable with change, and more readily accept it, the presumption is that the organization as a whole will be better able to cope with the dynamic environment in which it operates.

Increasing employees' receptivity to change involves reducing their feelings of being threatened by it. Such fears or concerns are sometimes irrational, but often they are completely rational or logical because of the experiences that individuals have had in the past when changes have taken place in the organization. The introduction of new time standards for the performance of certain jobs may have been experienced as "speedups," or the introduction of a new boss from outside the organization may have presaged the lopping off of certain subordinates from the payroll. Any change at any time, whether within an organizational setting or outside of it, always has the *potential* for threat to the individual. At the very least he has to learn to adapt to a new set of circumstances. If he has successfully adapted to the prechange situation, he cannot guarantee to himself that he will be able to continue to do so. Thus, it is not difficult to see why change is not always embraced warmly and eagerly by members of organizations.

As with the other developmental goals we have enumerated in this section, the achievement of greater receptivity to change involves efforts on the part of both the individual and the organization. The former will need to learn to live with the notion that change is inevitable and not to assume that every change will necessarily be detrimental. This requires a certain maturity that may be facilitated by various of the methods for organizational change and development that were discussed in the previous chapter. The organization, on the other hand, will need to give attention both to the methods by which it introduces changes and to the possible negative consequences for those who will be affected by the changes. All too often, managers, or those instituting changes, look at changes only from the narrow perspective of how they will benefit the organization. The possibility that some of these changes might at the same time reduce the opportunities for need fulfillment of those lower down in the organization may be deliberately or unintentionally ignored. When this is the case, it should be no surprise that resistance to the changes is exhibited along with a reduction in receptivity to future changes.

The goal of increased receptivity to change seems reasonably attainable in many organizations if some of the conditions reducing the threatening aspects of change can be created. Also, there would appear to be relatively few disadvantages to increasing such receptivity. In other words, the goal seems feasible, not too costly, and generally desirable.

GOALS FOR THE MAINTENANCE OF THE ORGANIZATION

We now shift to consideration of a set of goals that focus on the maintenance of the organization—goals relating to its survival and "health," so to speak. It is these goals that are usually the direct target of the organizational development (OD) methods discussed in the previous chapter. (Goals relating to the task performance of organizations will be taken up in the following section.)

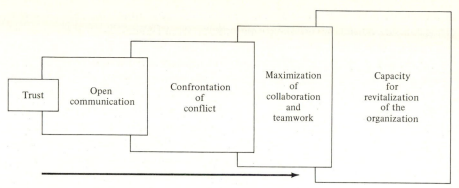

Figure 16-1 Hypothesized sequential and interlocking relation-ships among goals for the maintenance of the organization.

Five maintenance goals will be examined, and it is our view that these goals have a logical relationship to each other, as diagrammed in Figure 16-1. Thus, while each of the goals can be considered by itself, it is also possible to think of some of them as *means* to other of the goals. As Figure 16-1 indicates, developing a high level of trust and an openness of communication are probably necessary first if conflict is to be confronted; in turn, confrontation of conflict seems essential if collaboration and teamwork are to be developed. Finally, all these goals are thought of as preceding the building of the organization's capacity for revitalization and adaptability to change. Such a pictorial representation of the sequencing of goals is not to be taken as a literal set of 1,2,3, . . . steps, but rather as a useful analytical tool to provide a meaningful view of the relationships among the goals.

Development of a High Level of Trust throughout the Organization

A climate of trust, as a goal for organizational development, tends to be somewhat like a combination of the weather and motherhood: it is widely talked about, and it is widely assumed to be good for organizations. When it comes to specifying just what it means in an organizational context, however, vagueness creeps in. Presumably, it means that members of organizations, no matter what their positions, can rely on the integrity of what other members say and do—in short, where there is trust there is the feeling that "others will not take advantage of me." It implies that suspiciousness is absent in interpersonal relationships, and therefore ener-gies do not need to be diverted from productive tasks to nonproductive acts of self-defense. This means that blame, which in turn can generate guilt, is deemphasized and attacks on problems rather than people are substituted in its place. In effect, in organizations where there is high trust, the "games" that people are inclined to play—such as (after Berne, 1964) "now I've got you, you _____"—are supposedly minimized in favor of constructive and nonpunitive reactions to the behavior and ideas of others.

The failure of an organization to create a broad level of trust often revolves around the ways in which it collects and uses information for control purposes (as discussed in Chapter 9). When individuals feel that others will take advantage of them due to the possession of certain kinds of information—especially information relating to individual or group perform-ance—the tendency is to resist the collection of it, or at least to distort it. Such behavior in turn results in even greater pressures and more stringent controls being imposed on the individual, leading to increased motivation on his part to find ways to protect himself. Thus, a vicious circle or "spiral reinforcement pattern" (Zand, 1972) is easily created which makes it extremely difficult to establish or reestablish trust.

Such a "vicious circle" of events is well illustrated in a recent experimental study involving "expectations of trust" as a variable (Zand, 1972). The subjects in the experiment were managers assigned to roles in small problem-solving groups (composed of a "president" and several of his "vice-presidents"). In half of the groups, the managers were "briefed to expect a tendency toward trusting behavior" (on the part of the others in the group), while in the other half of the groups the managers were led to expect "mistrusting" behavior. The findings showed that as the groups worked on their assigned decision-making problem (the subjects did not know they were taking part in an experiment), the high-trust groups displayed increasingly open and constructive problem-solving behavior, while the reverse was true of the low-trust groups. The investigator reported that after the experimental sessions were over, conversation among the low-trust subjects often "showed the high defensiveness and antagonism they had induced in each other" (by their behavior in the experimental situation). For example, the introductory instructions informed the groups that the president would have to leave the meeting after thirty minutes to catch an airplane. In discussions following the meetings, several vice-presidents said "they hoped the president's plane would be hijacked or crash. The president usually retorted that he had decided to dismiss them before the next meeting" (p. 236).

Building a high level of trust *throughout* an organization is probably one of the most difficult and tricky goals to achieve in organizational development. The very structures of complex organizations, involving as they do a myriad of differentiated functions, militate against trust being developed among all units and among all people in a unit. Not everyone can share

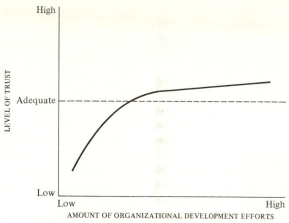

Figure 16-2 Hypothesized relationship between amount of organizational development efforts and the resulting level of trust throughout the organization.

equally the fate of a group or department. Those within it are naturally more concerned than those outside of it. This differential identification with different positions and different units makes it exceedingly hard to establish wide networks of trust. Furthermore, the stresses and strains imposed by the organization's external environment on various of its members pose problems which prevent them from finding the time to devote to a painstaking and patient development of genuinely trusting relationships.

What this suggests is that many organizational change and development efforts will likely be able to increase or improve very low levels of trust up to some moderate or at least minimally adequate level but that the goal of a really high level will prove to be quite elusive. This situation is diagrammed in Figure 16-2, where it is hypothesized that the level of trust fairly quickly reaches an adequate level with minimum developmental efforts but only slowly increases beyond that with greater developmental efforts. It is, nevertheless, crucial that organizations attempt to bring about at least this moderate level of trust because it would appear to be a necessary condition for the achievement of additional developmental goals relating to the maintenance of the organization.

Open Communication

This goal follows naturally the goal of the development of a high level of trust, for without the existence of a general level of trust it is virtually impossible to achieve open communication. This goal also logically precedes the goal of confrontation of conflict, because without open communication it will be difficult for people to bring conflict into the open to be dealt with.

Openness of communication involves, basically, the free provision of accurate information: one party (group or individual) providing facts to another party regardless of what the facts are. It is the willingness of individuals to "say what they mean." Even with the existence of considerable degrees of trust, it is not easy for employees in organizations to develop the habit of open communication. Because of the strong conditioning and reinforcement for being guarded that people receive in many other aspects of their daily life, the mere existence of a feeling of trust in a specific organizational situation does not automatically make it comfortable for a person to open up his communications. He has to "learn" to do this, and like any other learning the process may be slow and at times painful. As with other types of learning, however, the speed of acquisition will be strengthened by the applications of positive reinforcement or rewards. Thus, the organizational development goal of openness of communication translates itself into the goal of providing positive encouragements for openness.

Perhaps even more importantly, the developmental goal of openness also involves reducing the negative or threatening *consequences* for this type of behavior. Nothing will extinguish openness faster than some well-timed instances of unfavorable things happening after a person has communicated in an accurate, open manner. Of course, this does not mean that feedback or responses to open communications are always positive in the sense of being in the direction the person wants to hear. What it does mean is that the responses are nondistorted and that the receiver will not use the information obtained in a way that will harm the sender. In organizations that have achieved a high degree of openness, neither party to the communication process is afraid to give or receive information which may be negative (i.e., "bad news") if it is honest and authentic. The assumption is that communications of this quality strengthen the organization.

There are, of course, several problems connected with the goal of open communication in organizations. For one thing, even with the benefit of various developmental efforts, it still takes a set of rather mature individuals to be at ease with a practice of completely open communication and not to be threatened by it. Some organizations may simply not have a large enough percentage of these types of individuals already in their work force to make the goal a realistic objective. Another problem is that there may be circumstances in the life of organizations when completely open communication may be self-defeating by causing more anxieties and even recriminations than would be the case under somewhat more closed communication. That is, there may be times when individuals would prefer *not* to be open and the organization might actually be more productive, at least over the short run. At any rate, this is an issue that organizations and individuals will need to consider carefully because on the surface it is difficult to argue with the norm of openness.

Confrontation of Conflict

As we have indicated, this developmental goal flows naturally from the goals of trust and openness of communication. When they are absent, or at least not at a high enough level, the organization will not be able to bring conflict into the open in order for it to be confronted. The confrontation of conflict is the opposite of denying its existence, of trying to sweep it under the rug. Since conflicts will occur in any organization, no matter what its goals or management policies, the problem for the organization is to prevent this denial so that the conflicts can be faced and resolved rather than allowed to persist and undermine the performance of individuals and the total system.

Confrontation of conflict is seen as a major step in helping the organization focus its attention on solving its important problems. Particularly if conflicts can be dealt with in their early states, the prospects are improved for keeping them from interfering with the productive work of the organization. Or, to put it another way, early and open dealing with conflict may be one of the most constructive activities an organization can engage in to help itself.

Nevertheless, many individuals and organizations will find that confronting conflict is difficult and painful, as well as apparently expensive in its use of time and resources. It can be justified only if the end results seem to merit it. As two advocates of this approach see it, it "may be time-consuming in the short run but time-conserving over a long term. It permits men to disagree, to work out their disagreements in the light of facts, and ultimately to understand one another" (Blake & Mouton, 1969, p. 67).

Maximization of Collaboration and Teamwork

The confrontation of conflict allows the organization eventually to turn its attention to other more directly task-oriented activities. It lays the groundwork for the development of collaboration and teamwork. The goal of achieving collaboration is perhaps one of the most fundamental of all objectives for those who are concerned with changing and improving organizations. They feel that traditional management approaches have in the past either ignored this point or at least not given it sufficient attention. Such approaches, they feel, have put too much emphasis on individuals as separate units in organizations and also too much emphasis on the virtues of competition among the members of the organization.

The case for deemphasizing competition and increasing the emphasis on collaboration has been well put by Tannenbaum and Davis (1969, p.79):

> A pervasive value in the organizational milieu is competition. Competition is based on the assumption that desirable resources are limited in quantity and that individuals or groups can be effectively motivated through competing against one another for the possession of these resources. But competition can often set man against man and group against group in dysfunctional behavior, including a shift of objectives from obtaining the limited resources to blocking or destroying the competitor. Competition inevitably results in winners and losers, and at least some of the hidden costs of losing can be rather high in systematic terms.
>
> Collaboration, on the other hand, is based on the assumption that the desirable limited resources can be shared among the participants in a mutually satisfactory manner and, even more important, that it is possible to increase the quantity of the resources themselves.
>
> As organizational work becomes more highly specialized and complex, with its accomplishment depending more and more on the effective interaction of individuals and groups, and as the organic or systems views of organizational functioning become more widely understood, the viability of collaboration as an organizational mode becomes ever clearer. Individuals and groups are often highly interdependent, and such interdependency needs to be facilitated through collaborative behavior rather than walled off through competition. At the same time, collaborative behavior must come to be viewed as reflecting strength rather than weakness.

The question that some might raise about this particular goal for organizational change and development is not whether collaboration and teamwork are needed, but rather whether they are needed to the absolute maximum extent possible. Put another way, are there some hidden costs in always attempting to encourage teamwork rather than individual effort? And, indeed, are there times when competition among members within organizations (e.g., as in sales contests) might actually be a virtue rather than a problem to be eliminated? Also, does every person function best in the absence of competition? What appears to be the case, in any event, is that in the past many organizations have not emphasized teamwork and effective collaboration enough, and it is this balance that needs to be redressed. Whether this optimum balance should equal "maximum possible collaboration" is a question that each organization will have to answer in terms of its own specific context.

Capacity for Organizational Revitalization

All the organizational maintenance goals we have discussed so far culminate in the goal of developing a capacity for organizational revitalization. Unless the organization is able to develop this capacity, the achievement of the other goals will not count for much. Thus, a capability for organizational self-renewal is in some senses an ultimate developmental goal.

The primary reason for the great importance attached to this particular goal is, of course, the pressures put on organizations by the ever-changing and increasingly dynamic environments in which they operate. If the environment were essentially unchanging, or at least very slow to change, an organization could develop an effective way to operate and then simply concentrate on preserving this particular *modus operandi* in the face of any internal threats. Indeed, for many years, this is exactly what many business companies and other organizations did. They worked toward perfecting certain specific forms of organizational structure and operations and then exerted considerable effort to prevent any alterations of them. Such an approach appeared to be effective at the time, as long as the environment in which these organizations were operating was essentially stable, but it has increasingly ceased to be effective in recent years when the external environments have become much more changeable and unpredictable.

The goal of developing a capacity for revitalization is the goal of preventing the inevitable decay that will occur without it. As Bennis has phrased the issue: "Growth and decay emerge as the penultimate conditions of contemporary society. Organizations, as well as societies, must be concerned with those social structures that engender buoyancy, resilience, and a fearlessness of revision" (1969, p. 32). Bennis goes on to list four necessary elements in the capacity for revitalization:

> **1** An ability to learn from experience and to codify, store, and retrieve the relevant knowledge.
> **2** An ability to learn how to learn, that is, to develop methods for improving the learning process.
> **3** An ability to acquire and use feedback mechanisms on performance, in short, to be self-analytical.
> **4** An ability to direct one's own destiny.

These constitute a tall set of orders for any organization and certainly must be regarded as abilities that are never fully realized but only approached in various degrees. The problem for most organizations revolves not around decisions of whether they want to develop this set of revitalization abilities, but rather around questions of how to do it. Our discussion in the previous chapter of various techniques and methods for organizational development has indicated some of the possible approaches, but it also has shown that no single method, or set of methods, will guarantee a successful revitalization capacity. The extreme difficulty of attaining the revitalization goal, what Gardner (1965) refers to as the prevention of organizational "dry rot," is matched only by the vital necessity of trying to reach it.

GOALS FOR THE PERFORMANCE OF THE ORGANIZATION

The mere maintenance of organizations—at least those in which people are employed—while absolutely necessary is not a sufficient condition for them to contribute to the welfare of their members and to society. They must also *do* something. That is, they need to be concerned with performance as well as maintenance. It is to goals relating more explicitly to performance that we now turn our attention. In doing so, we should keep in mind that while the distinction between the two types of goals is not always clear-cut and is to an extent arbitrary, it can be useful for analytical purposes by helping us organize our thinking about the overall topic. Furthermore, there are empirical data that suggest that the distinction is meaningful in terms of describing the actual behavior of individuals in organizational-type settings.

The Clarification of Organizational Objectives

Despite the seemingly obvious principle that organizations should have clearly specified objectives, many do not appear to have them. At least, that is often the view of the people who work in a particular organization. Usually it is a situation where the upper echelons *assume* that everyone in the organization knows what its goals are, but where those at the lower levels are in fact in doubt about them. To the extent that this is the case, the performance of the organization falls short of its potential. Without the framework for action provided by clear-cut organizational objectives (French, Kay, & Meyer, 1966; Locke, 1968; Steers, 1973), the activities of individual employees and units would be expected to lack focus and involve wasted or nonproductive effort.

As an organizational development goal, the clarification of objectives involves attention both to *setting* them in the first place and then to *disseminating* them widely throughout the organization. With regard to the first of these two elements, most organizational development specialists would advocate broad participation by a number of parts of the organization. The purpose would be not only to produce better-quality goals but also to gain subsequent acceptance of them (see the discussion of the next goal). Without such participation, stated objectives are likely to be clear only to a small segment of the total organization. Once specified and stated, the organization would need to use its communication channels to convey them throughout the system. Here again, if participation has been reasonably broad during the formulation phase, the communication of them to members is facilitated.

The goal of clearly specified organizational objectives is not as difficult to reach as a number of the other developmental goals we have been considering. Thus, the costs involved and the feasibility do not present undue problems. The major problem is that the leaders of many organizations think they have accomplished this particular goal when in fact it is not seen this way by the rest of the organization. And, of course, in organizations where there is low trust and relatively nonopen communication, feedback of these perceptions to the leaders will be greatly diminished and will allow them to exercise the luxury of a fair amount of self-deception regarding the situation.

Commitment to Organizational Objectives

The clear specification of objectives obviously will not ensure a high level of organizational performance. There usually also needs to be a certain level of commitment to these objectives by the members of the organization. Or, to use the phrase of organizational development practitioners, the objectives should be "'owned' by the entire work force." Also, as we related earlier in this chapter, McGregor sees such a sense of ownership of, and commitment to, objectives as fundamental for ensuring that members will be motivated to exercise self-direction and self-control.

While the desirability of obtaining commitment to common goals is taken for granted by managers, the difficulties in producing it are not. Generally, the approaches advocated by organization theorists such as Argyris, Bennis, and Likert seem to be: Provide tasks that are personally satisfying, and increase the opportunities for each organization member to share in making the decisions that affect his work situation (his task goals, the methods used on the job, etc.). The chief feature of these approaches is that they do not rely on the use of external rewards. The major problem with them, since they involve changing the basic nature of work tasks and changing the level of participation, is that they involve many other elements of the interdependent system. Thus, it is not a simple matter to put into effect practices that are designed to increase commitment of individuals to organizational objectives because in doing so other practices will inevitably be affected. For example, (as pointed out previously in Chapter 10), enlarging and enriching jobs of a set of rank-and-file workers may definitely increase their "feelings of ownership" of the organization's objectives but at the same time may so drastically alter the jobs of the first level of supervision that these jobs in turn have to be redesigned, and so on up the organizational hierarchy. Let us be clear: We are not trying to imply that such consequences are "bad" and therefore are to be avoided. Rather, we are saying that the commonly advocated methods for increasing organizational commitment involve a string of ramifications that will need to be considered in advance, if the employment of these methods is to be successful. To put this another way, the developmental goal of increasing members' commitment to organizational objectives cannot be considered in isolation from other, perhaps equally desirable, goals.

Creation of a Problem-solving Climate

This goal is closely related to several others we have previously discussed, particularly the maintenance goal of openness of communication. The achievement of such openness implies that a climate for problem solving will emerge rather naturally. However, this is not necessarily so, because the content of the open communications may not focus on solving organizational problems, particularly performance ones. Rather, unless such goals are made explicit, the open communications may be directed toward everything except the solving of problems—such as elaborating their symptoms or assigning blame to individuals.

How do we recognize a problem-solving climate when we see one? Argyris (1964) provides us with several relevant criteria. He states that such a climate exists when problems (1) are actually being solved; (2) remain solved once they are dealt with; (3) are solved with minimum expenditures of energy; and (4) are solved with "minimal damage to the continued effectiveness of the problem-solving process" (p. 137).

The creation of such a climate involves the development of a frame of reference or, one might say, a "state of mind" among members of an organization such that they *want* to attack problems. Since problems can often be extremely sticky and nearly intractable, this perspective is not always easy to bring about. Constant and persistent problem solving is hard work! It is likely that the degree to which such a climate is created in an organization is quite dependent upon the attitude and behavior of those at the very top of the organization. If they are perceived by lower-echelon personnel as problem-avoiders or problem-ignorers, a non-problem-solving climate is easily and quickly created. And, once created, it is difficult to replace with a different orientation.

Increased Innovation

The case for increased innovation as a goal for organizational development has been aptly summarized by Katz and Kahn:

The organizational need for actions of an innovative, relatively spontaneous sort is inevitable and unending. No organizational planning can foresee all contingencies within its own operations, can anticipate with perfect accuracy all environmental changes, or can control perfectly all human variability. The resources of people for innovation, for spontaneous cooperation, for protective and creative behavior are thus vital to organizational survival and effectiveness. An organization which depends solely upon its blueprints of prescribed behavior is a very fragile social system. (1966, p. 338)

Little or no innovation would seem to be clearly deleterious both to individual members and to the organization as a whole. But, can organizations be *too* innovative and creative? At first glance, the answer might seem to be definitely "no." More detailed consideration of the question, however, makes it not so simple to answer.

To deal with the issue, it is probably useful to consider two types of innovation: that directed outward from the organization toward its environment (e.g., marketing a new product), and that directed inward toward the organization itself (e.g., instituting a new organizational structure). The former kind permits the organization to keep ahead of its environment, to anticipate changes that might be harder to deal with if the organization had to wait for them to happen. Though maximum innovation in this external sphere would appear to be highly desirable, there are enough examples of organizations overextending themselves by attempting to do too many new things too fast that would indicate that the optimum level is less than the maximum level. With respect to internal innovation, which requires the adjustment of organization members to changes, there would seem to be even more reason for an organization to try to find a rate of innovation that keeps it from being stagnant but which at the same time is not so fast as to disrupt the organization and possibly "tear it to pieces."

More Effective Utilization of Total Organization Resources

Just as increasing the capacity for organizational revitalization could be considered the ultimate maintenance-type developmental goal, increasing the effectiveness of the utilization of their total resources could be considered the ultimate performance-type developmental goal for organizations. It is ultimate in the sense that all other goals seem subsidiary to it. Utilization of a set of resources is at the heart of what an organization is all about.

While this is a goal that is central to the very essence of an organization, by the same token it is also so all encompassing as to be virtually nonoperational. What are the criteria for determining the degree to which an organization is utilizing its total resources? If it is performing at a very high level relative to other similar organizations, or has made great improvements in its performance compared to some previous time period, how is it determined that it could not be doing even better? These are impossible questions to answer, since there is really no way for anyone to know what is the absolute capacity of an organization's resources. Only well-informed guesses can be made as to the probable degree of resource utilization.

Despite the fact that this is a nonoperational goal, it is still a useful one for organizations to have as a developmental objective. The reason is that a goal of this type can function as a type of self-fulfilling prophecy. As long as people think that they can improve an organization so that it will make more effective utilization of its resources, the more likely they are to perform in such a way as to actually bring about greater utilization. Thus, the goal can be functional for organizations. The difficulty in determining whether progress is being made toward it may be one of its most powerful features, but only as long as people *believe* that they are making progress.

OVERVIEW: ARE THESE DEVELOPMENTAL AND CHANGE GOALS BEING ACHIEVED?

Looking back over the goals that have been discussed in the preceding pages, one can ask the question: Are they being achieved in organizations today? The answer for a small minority of organizations employing people would seem to be: "Yes, definitely." The answer for a larger number of such organizations would very likely be: "Yes, to some extent." But, for many organizations, the answer may well be: "No, hardly at all." No empirical body of data exists—either from a single study or from a combination of studies—to indicate conclusively just how well organizations are meeting these goals, or what percentage of organizations have reached a certain degree of achievement.

Perhaps the best way to answer the question of how well these goals are currently being achieved by organizations is to ask the people who work in them. Regardless of what the "true" facts are, it is their perceptions of them that affect their behavior. So, each of us could ask ourselves, based on our own work experiences, "Are the organizations with which I am familiar doing a good job in changing and developing in the direction of these goals?" The collective answer would probably be: "Organizations still have plenty of room for improvement."

REVIEW AND DISCUSSION QUESTIONS

1 Can organizational effectiveness ever be evaluated in other than relative terms? Why?

2 Are there any functional aspects of limiting upward communication?

3 How have the values and beliefs of theorists (e.g., Likert, McGregor, Argyris, Tannenbaum, etc.) mentioned in this and other chapters in the book influenced the organizational development objectives set down in this chapter?

4 Can one assume that the goals for organizational change that have been put forth by organizational theorists are applicable to all types of organizations? (Consider, for example, business organizations, prisons, asylums, the military, voluntary organizations, etc.)

5 What is meant by interpersonal competence? How is it achieved?

6 Assume for the moment that you are in an industrial organization that is operating profitably (according to the profit-and-loss statement). All people in the organization do the work assigned them. Rules and regulations are obeyed. How important is the development of "interpersonal trust" in this organization? Why?

7 How can the practicing manager determine when it is best to use confrontation as a conflict-resolving mechanism?

8 If employees in an organization perform their role-related duties effectively (i.e., they perform according to whatever the existing standards dictate), there is no need to make them aware of the organization's overall goals. Do you agree or disagree? Why?

9 As long as an organization performs at least as well as its competitors with respect to resource utilization, there is little or no need to do better. Do you agree or disagree? Justify your answer.

Chapter 17

Conclusions

A final chapter in a book is ordinarily concerned with taking stock, looking to the future. This chapter will be no exception. Throughout the book we have concentrated on analysis and description rather than on prescription. We have attempted to let the data and concepts speak for themselves. Here, however, we will shift to an expressly personal view of what is, what will be, and what ought to be in organizations. These will be conclusions, specula- tions, and prescriptions that *we* draw from the ideas and facts that we have presented earlier. What follows, then, is a series of statements about the future: What changes we think should take place in the ways organizations function, and the kinds of research that are going to have to be accomplished if it all is to work.

   Our projections and prescriptions are basically optimistic. We firmly believe that life in organizations *can* improve, and we think we know some of the things that will have to be done to bring about such improvements. We also believe that unless organizations take some of the steps we suggest, they will be in danger of becoming flabby and sterile, their effectiveness will often plummet, and people both inside and outside of them frequently will be treated more like objects than like humans with untapped potentials. To reverse this trend is, in our opinion, the major challenge behavioral scientists dealing with organizations will face in the decades to come. It will be no easy task.

THE NATURE AND MEANING OF WORK MUST CHANGE

The Distinction between Work and Nonwork Should Decrease

In the past, work often has had the connotation of a "chore" and nonwork the connotation of "play" or "recreation." In the future, we believe that for many people work should increasingly take on the appearance of nonwork so that they will find it difficult to determine which it is they would *rather* do. That situation exists now for certain categories of employees: top-level managers, professionals, and the like. Many of these people, far from avoiding work or trying to put in as little time as possible on it, have to force themselves (or be forced by others, such as their families) to keep from devoting too much attention to it. One can ask: What is it about these jobs and working conditions that brings about this total commitment to organizational tasks? The answer is that work on such jobs has the characteristics of fun: It is pleasurable, stimulating, changing, and arouses feelings of exuberance. In a word, it is something in which to revel. Nonwork, on the other hand, for these people often seems to suffer by comparison—a pale imitation of the play of work, as it were.

We are not suggesting that in the future most people should prefer to stay at work rather than engage in nonwork activities. What we would hope for, though, is that the changing nature of work and jobs will produce a situation where a much larger percentage of the work force than at present will find their jobs to be attractive rather than aversive. While this may sound as if we are forecasting and advocating a sort of organizational nirvana, we have no illusions about the fact that the trend will be slow or nonexistent in some organizations and in many jobs. Nevertheless, the direction of the trend we want to see is clear: work that takes on the colorings of nonwork, with those organizations in which this takes place earliest and fastest having an advantage in selecting among the best available potential employees. People will *want* to come to work (nonwork) for such organizations.

Research Task A: *Learning more about the ways productive activity in organizations can be made personally challenging and attractive to employees—and how organizations can be changed to provide more such* *opportunities.* As was suggested in Chapter 10, we are just now beginning to understand how work can be designed to "turn on" people. While we can say some things about how particular jobs should be designed to maximize the chances for "intrinsic" work motivation, we know that the total experience of the employee is heavily dependent on other aspects of the work environment as well—the work group, supervision, the physical place where the work is done, and so on. Considerable additional knowledge is needed, however, about how these various aspects of the work setting interact to affect the overall quality of the working experience of the individual.

Research Task B: *Learning about the relationship between work and leisure.* Historically, psychologists interested in organizations focused their attention on measuring individual capabilities, to ensure that people hired for a given job could do the work satisfactorily. At the same time, engineers were designing the technology of organizations for maximum efficiency. The problem, as it was seen then, was how to achieve a good "match" between the system and the people—with the system given clear priority. That often didn't work, in large part because people were turned off—unmotivated—on the jobs they were given. So attention turned to various "extrinsic" factors which could be used to motivate people on their jobs—things like pay, promotions, and supervisory practices. As has been seen in several chapters of this book, extrinsic motivators by themselves are also not sufficient to turn people on to their work—and extrinsic motivators often are administered in ways which yield unintended and unfortunate consequences for both the people and the organizations involved.

So, in recent years, attention has increasingly turned to ways "intrinsic" work motivation can be attained. Routine jobs can frequently be made more challenging and interesting to the people who do them or, where possible, automated out of existence. As that happens, there are going to be more people with better jobs—but also more people with more leisure time on their hands. We know relatively little about the social science of leisure activities or about the relationship between work and leisure. This issue should become one that receives increasing attention from behavioral scientists in the years to come.

The Distinction between "Management" and "Nonmanagement" Should Decrease

Even now there is a widespread blurring of the distinction between that part of an organization called "management" and inhabited by individuals termed "managers," on the one hand, and that part called "nonmanagement" that is occupied by those called "workers" or "rank-and-file employees." One development that has accelerated the trend in this direction, certainly, is the increasing percentage of the work force that is composed of white-collar workers. In previous decades, when the majority of work organizations had many blue-collar employees and only a small group of office employees, it seemed fairly clear who was management and who was not. One could usually tell just by looking. The two groups dressed differently and were located in widely contrasting and (usually) separate work settings. Now, with the rise of service organizations and the great increase in governmental-type agencies, it is not so easy to distinguish visually who is and who is not management. More importantly, it is not so easy to distinguish by other means either, in many office-type situations.

A second development that may decrease the management-nonmanagement distinction is the organization's greater reliance on technical and professional expertise. To take an example, one would often be hard put to determine with certainty whether a highly trained computer programmer were truly "nonmanagement" or not. What is an airline pilot? A surgical nurse in a hospital? A professor in a university? A foreign service officer in the government? To see how the distinction has already faded, try thinking of any of these as a "worker." They hardly occupy a relationship to the top leaders of an organization that is similar to the relationship in the past of a miner to a coal mine owner or of a pig iron handler to a superintendent of a steel mill.

There is one important reason why it is necessary for this developing trend toward a decrease in the management-nonmanagement distinction to continue if organizational life is to improve: Increasing expectations are emerging in all parts of the labor force for individual employees to have a say in how the organization operates insofar as they are directly affected. An obvious factor in these expectations is, of course, the increasing educational level of the average employee. He or she knows more and expects more. These expectations can be met only if a greater percentage of the employees in an organization have some hand in helping to determine where the organization is going and how it is going to get there. This will not make it easier for anyone to "lead" an organization, but it could make it a more exciting and challenging place in which to work. One thing is obvious: Organizations which frustrate these expectations will risk organizational ineffectiveness or worse.

Research Task: *Investigating the impact of new forms of organizations that incorporate innovative conceptions of what "managerial leadership" means and implies.* We need to bring our research and our prescriptions about how organizations "ought" to be run in line with the emerging

realities of employee participation and what could be called the "democra-
tization" of work. Some organizations, both here and abroad, are beginning
to take some interesting steps in this direction. The number of such
imaginative forays into really new and different methods of operating
organizations still seems distressingly small in relation to the size of the
need, however. Obviously, such experiments are risky; and many will not
work out well—they may even make matters worse (at least for a while).
Nevertheless, we believe that attempts along these lines are imperative, as
are the research efforts that should accompany them.

The Role of Trade Unions Should Change Substantially

The trend toward a different type of managerial leadership discussed above
should also extend to trade unions, resulting in a certain amount of turmoil
or upheaval in some of the more traditional unions. Even now, unions are
feeling the impact of problems they have never faced before. In fact, it
appears that we were on the threshold of an important new period in the
history of American unions. In response to these developments, a number of
national union leaders are tentatively "trying on" new issues which may
become part of their contract demands in future negotiations.

Such trends require a substantial change for most unions: moving away
from traditional and almost exclusive emphases on pay, benefits, and work
rules; moving toward an increasing emphasis on responsiveness to the
nonmaterial and more intrinsic needs and desires of their members. The
result will be that many new ideas will become part of union–management
discussions, and union–management cooperation will increase in noneco-
nomic areas. And this, in turn, must result in changes both in the nature of
the day-to-day work experience of the individual and in the dynamics of the
relationships between unions and the management of organizations.

Research Task A: *Developing a better understanding of the dynamics
of unions as organizations.* The organizational behavior field has been
derelict in generating an understanding of unions as organizations. Social
scientists who study and write about organizations have often been accused
of being excessively "management oriented," and it is unfortunately true in
too many instances. It is true partly because that is where support for
research has come from, and that is where it has been easier to gain entry
into organizations. It is true because of the middle-class backgrounds of
many of the researchers. It is also true because unions simply have not been
seen as very interesting organizations for purposes of study. They have been
implicitly regarded by many organizational scholars as merely a necessary

appendage to the total work situation. This is clearly a mistake that should be corrected in the future by some vigorous research efforts.

Research Task B: *Developing new models for the dynamics of union–management relationships.* There is little intellectual excitement today in the field of labor–management relations. Students beginning their study of organizational behavior invariably seem to move toward the supposedly more appealing areas of motivation, leadership, and organizational intervention. That is where the current action is.

However, there is still plenty of action to be had in intergroup phenomena as important and substantively rich as union–management relations. What is needed, we believe, are some forward-looking approaches to the study of such relations, approaches which draw on the developing body of research and theory on the relations between intact groups. The raw materials are there; all that is needed is for a few scholars to put them to work in understanding what goes on at the negotiating table, in the cloak room outside the negotiating room, and (importantly) when the negotiating teams go "back home" to report to their constituents and to receive instructions on what to do next.

Career Paths and Mobility Patterns Should Continue to Loosen

A few years ago the janitor who, by dint of study and hard work, became a computer programmer was worthy of a short article on the back page of the local newspaper. No longer—and even less so in the future, we hope. Competence and good performance should increasingly become the criterion for advancement in organizations. Sexual and racial constraints on mobility and career progression should and will continue to drop, although at a less rapid pace than we would hope for.

At the same time, personal needs and goals should be increasingly recognized as important in hiring, placement, and promotion. As pointed out earlier, organizational personnel practices have historically focused on the "can do" aspects of behavior. The future should see more emphasis on the "will do" and "want to do" characteristics of people. The relationship between a person and the organization he works for should be recognized as much more of a two-way street than is presently the case, and questions of what the individual *wants* from his work experience should come to be seen as a central part of organizational personnel practices.

Research Task A: *Developing measures of the need and motivational characteristics of people which can be used for purposes of selection,* *training, and placement in organizations.* At the same time, measures of organizational climate and of the psychological characteristics of jobs will need to be refined, thereby allowing mutually beneficial "matches" between people and their work to be made.

   Research Task B: *Developing understanding of organizational entry, career change, career progression, and organizational exit as social psychological phenomena.* Traditional research on personnel matters has underemphasized the essentially social nature of the individual-organization relationship. The organization has been the peg board, made up of holes of different shapes and sizes; individuals have been the pegs, to be trimmed and shaped to fit the existing holes or, if that turned out to be too difficult (or if there were lots of pegs around looking for holes to fill), rejected. Sophisticated selection and placement models which focus on individuals' skills and the ability requirements of jobs now exist. Indeed, research on such models may have reached the point of diminishing returns.

   There remains, however, a real paucity of knowledge about the *social* processes involved in selection, placement, adaptation, and career development. Not enough is known, for example, about how individual differences among people moderate the way an individual-organization relationship develops over time or about the ways the social character of the selection, placement, and training practices of an organization affect the individual's reactions to those practices and to the organization as a whole. Relatively little is also known about how organizations can help individuals make better job and career choices.

ORGANIZATIONS SHOULD BECOME MORE ACCOUNTABLE FOR ALL THEIR ACTIONS

We live in a society that is dominated by complex organizations. Most of us are directly tied to an organization for at least eight hours a day, and many of us engage in organized activities evenings and weekends on our own "personal" time. So organizations affect each of us, personally, on a more or less continuous basis. What happens in organizations can and does thrill us, depress us, make us grow, and frequently frustrate us.

   But it doesn't end there. Organizations also determine what our society is like: the cost and availability of consumer goods, the level of air pollution, the ease and safety of travel, the spectrum of available leisure activities, the laws and services provided by our governments, and on and on. If we can improve the functioning of our organizations, many aspects of our lives—at work and at home—will change for the better. But if we cannot get organizations working effectively, responsively, and responsibly, the chances of making any significant changes in the way we live are quite slim.

People are gradually coming to realize the full extent of the impact of organizations. As this happens, we are becoming less and less willing to let organizations operate in whatever way they want to. In a phrase: We are increasingly demanding that organizations, whether they be in the public or private sector, be made *accountable* for their effects on people and on society at large.

The Criteria for Organizational Effectiveness Must Change and Broaden

Traditionally, the success of organizations has been measured by a very limited set of criteria—for example: output, efficiency, profitability (if a business organization). We believe that in the future several major criteria should increasingly emerge as the gauges for assessing the effectiveness of organizations. Those organizations which do not meet these criteria will very likely be coerced to do so, whether by direct legal and governmental controls or by the demands of customers, clients, and employees. Among the criteria that should become of increasing importance are the following:

1 High-quality service, even at the cost of quantity. For years, quantity has dominated the quality of the product or the service rendered as the bench mark for assessing organizational effectiveness. In an economy that may not be growing at such rapid rates as before, quality should emerge as a major index of the effectiveness of an organization.

2 Minimal damage to the environment. Organizations should be required to operate in such a way that natural resources are used as efficiently as possible and that the environment is not damaged by the operation of the organization.

3 Honesty. No longer should the "white lie of advertising" be an accepted practice. Organizations should be required to report honestly the strengths and weaknesses of their products or services and should be able to document the claims made.

4 Positive contribution to the physical and psychological health of organization members. For years the government has attempted to monitor and correct organizational practices which risked the physical well-being of employees. Those efforts will continue, but they should be augmented by activities aimed at assessing the impact of the organization on the *psychological* health and well-being of organization members. No longer, for example, should organizations be encouraged or perhaps even permitted to operate in the technologically most efficient way—*if* it means that the jobs people hold clearly jeopardize them. Organizations, whether they be private or public ones, should also be measured on whether they contribute significantly to individual growth and development.

Research Task: *Developing measures of organizational effectiveness in meeting nonfinancial and other nonefficiency criteria.* It has traditionally been the case that the financial balance sheet told most of what needed to be known about the effectiveness of an organization. As the criteria for assessing effectiveness broaden, new kinds of measures will be required. We will need to measure aspects of organizational functioning which, in many cases, have not even been tracked on a casual basis in years past. And we will have to measure them in such a way that we can make comparisons across organizations and assess their overall "cost" or "benefit" to individuals and to society. What, for example, is the dollar value of a given level of pollution by a steel mill? How much is an increase in the quality of the working life for automobile assembly line workers worth? How is the quality of the working experience to be measured in any case? If we are serious about broadening the criteria with which we assess organizational effectiveness, we must proceed soon with the development and refinement of measures of the criteria we care about enforcing.

Criteria for the Quality of the Working Experience of Individuals Should Broaden

Even as the criteria for measuring the effectiveness of organizations broaden, there should be a corresponding widening of our conception of what the "quality of the work experience" means and implies. In years past, we have been concerned mostly about physical matters: the roof of the mine should not cave in, the eyes should be protected from flying bits of metal, ambient noise and temperature should be kept at tolerable levels.

But recently, as noted above, the psychological impact of work has become recognized as important as well, and we believe that it should become increasingly so in future years. The problem, again, is how to measure the psychological nature and consequences of the work experience. Should we assess organizational practices per se (e.g., job designs), and attempt to eliminate those considered harmful? Or should we attempt to measure the psychological outcomes of these practices (e.g., job dissatisfaction)? Both approaches, of course, have their problems.

Research Task: *Developing multiple measures of the quality of the work experience of organization members.* This is no easy task, mainly because there is something inherently wrong with virtually every single measure. which has been proposed. The solution of the problem may well lie in the simultaneous use of several different types of measures—of both organizational practice and varieties of personal outcomes—in an attempt to "converge" on the best comprehensive estimate of the quality of the experience. Although there are many different measures of job satisfaction now available, considerable developmental work needs to be done before we will have the capability to make multiple assessments of the quality of the work experience with reasonable validity.

ORGANIZATIONS SHOULD BECOME MORE PLURALISTIC AND MORE INDIVIDUALIZED

Currently, conventional bureaucratic-type structures and procedures predominate in the vast majority of organizations in this country—whether they are businesses, schools, hospitals, or government agencies. We believe that this situation is beginning to change, however, and that we may be entering an age of "organizational pluralism" where differences both among and within organizations will be accentuated.

Several factors point in this direction. For one thing, employees are, on the whole, becoming better educated and have more highly developed skills and interests. This alone suggests that organizations will be composed of people with a diversity of tastes—and therefore a variety of preferences for organizational life-styles. No longer do most employees come out of the same mold. No longer are the clerical personnel confined only to white women and the managerial ranks to white males. The increasing prevalence of minorities and women throughout all parts of organizations is a potent factor in the direction of greater pluralism in the ways that organizations structure themselves and carry out their operations.

Additionally, society at large and the general cultural milieu seem more supportive of experiments in organizational forms and practices. The seemingly strong positive values attached to such concepts as "innovation" and "change" (especially if labeled "imaginative change") are likely to encourage managers and leaders of organizations to depart from past ways of doing things in organizations and at least try out new ideas and methods. This does not mean that every change will be subsequently evaluated positively, but it does seem to indicate that there will be a greater willingness to experiment in and with organizations.

These trends, we believe, will make it possible for genuinely new organizational forms to develop. These new forms should make it increasingly possible for people to work individually toward satisfaction of their own personal needs, even as they are working together toward the achievement of common organizational goals.

Individual Differences Should Be Seen in a New Way

Individual differences have always seemed to plague most organizations, especially bureaucratic or mechanistic-type ones. Individuals have been selected because their skills are above the minimum required to do the work. Beyond that, standardized procedures are supposed to ensure that the work will be done, and done essentially the same way, no matter who is filling the slot at the moment or what his personal dispositions are. It never works that way of course. Managers are forever running about putting out brush fires caused by "people problems" and cursing the idiosyncrasies of individuals which always seem to keep the organization from operating as it is designed to.

We believe that individual differences should be looked at in a new way, by managers and behavioral scientists alike, and that the differences should be treated in a new way in organizations. The evidence is increasing that individual differences *moderate* the way people respond to various aspects of organizations and to the practices of organizations. As we have emphasized in the earlier chapters of this book, particular job designs, leadership styles, reward systems, training procedures, and the like simply do not have the same effects for all people who work in an organization. Moreover, it tends to be not only the skills and abilities of the people that make the differences; instead, it is also their personal *psychological* makeup that counts, especially their needs and goals.

This, of course, goes against the dictums of traditionally run organizations: you supposedly cannot run a good organization if everybody reacts differently to everything you do. But everybody does, or at least many do, it turns out; and we believe that individual differences—the much abused old friend of industrial psychologists—is about to gain some significant new respect. For through a new way of looking at individual differences, we believe, lies the potential for innovative and exciting types of "individualized" organizations which accept that people react differently to the same practices and events and that people must be treated differently if both organizational goals and individual needs are to be met.

Research Task: *While the moderating effects of individual differences are becoming increasingly well documented, much more (and much more systematic) research needs to be done on the nature and extent of the observed effects.* It is not enough to know, for example, that different people respond differently to a "democratic" versus an "authoritarian" leadership style; in addition, we need to know exactly what it is about different people that is responsible for the effect and the circumstances under which it does and does not occur. And the same is true for individual difference moderators of responses to various kinds of jobs, reward systems, and so on. The ground has been broken, but there is a good deal of systematic plowing that needs to be done before we can effectively use our new understanding of individual differences in designing and operating organizations.

Organizational Practices Should Become More Individualized

People in industrialized societies are becoming increasingly critical of the lack of individual attention and respect they receive at work. They complain of being mechanized and reject the organizations and societal values that have put them in this position. Organizations built on the principles of universalistic theories such as scientific management (i.e., standardization, specialization, simplification) have contributed to the dehumanization of people.

We believe that many industrialized societies are about to embark on a process of *re*humanization. Universalistic principles will tend to be abandoned. Instead, organizations will increasingly begin to treat each person as an individual and to create internal structures whereby each individual is provided—at least to a large extent—with the setting and climate in which he personally can work best. By "individualizing" organizations, we believe, the chance exists to increase simultaneously both the quality of the work experience for the individual *and* the effectiveness of the organization as a whole.

How can this be done in actual practice? Obviously, nobody knows as yet. We can, however, identify some of the "pressure points" at which individualization would seem likely to be most fruitful. In particular, we believe that the process toward individualizing organizations should begin at those points *where organizational practices have direct and immediate effects on the day-to-day work activities of the individual.* These include:

1 The job itself. Probably the single most potent influence on what a person does at work is his job. As seen in Chapter 10, people with different psychological makeups do indeed respond differently to challenging versus routine jobs. It would seem well warranted, therefore, to try assigning people to different types of jobs (assuming sufficient skill to do the work) partly on the basis of their personal psychological needs and not just their abilities alone.

2 The reward system. People differ substantially in their desires for various types of rewards, and the rewards provided to individuals for good work could be tailored to the preferences of the individuals involved. Some organizations are already providing "cafeteria-type" fringe benefit arrangements, which permit the individual to make up his own benefit package.

3 The work group and the manager. Different people prosper in quite different types of social climates and, by extension, under different leaders. Some prefer a warm, close, supportive social environment; others operate best in a colder, more businesslike setting. Similarly, some leaders operate more effectively when they can be warm and supportive with their subordinates; others operate more effectively in a task-oriented mode. Matching the

preferred styles of leaders and their subordinate groups could create a more comfortable, and potentially more productive, climate for all.

4   Control and feedback systems. Again, people differ in the extent and nature of the feedback they desire and require: Some apparently need almost hour-by-hour feedback; others prefer to work long stretches before finding out how they are doing. It should be possible to design organizational control and feedback systems to provide individuals (including managers) with the type and frequency of information they find most helpful in effectively performing their jobs.

5   Training and developmental procedures. It is well known that individuals differ in the ways they learn best. When an individual is to be given training (whether initial training at the time of hiring or later "developmental" training), his particular learning style could be assessed and he could be provided with a training package that would be maximally enjoyable and facilitative of his learning.

Research Task A: *Developing new models of work design and job choice which give an individual real choice about his work, but at the same time transcend the limits of his aspirations imposed by his previous organizational experiences.* The problem of years of working experience "deadening" an individual is a real one. Is it sufficient merely to create organizational conditions which will lead to a state of current satisfaction, ignoring the fact that a person's hopes and expectations may be significantly lower now than they used to be because of what the organization has done to him? On the other hand, is it legitimate (or even ethical) for an organization to coerce an individual to engage in potentially growth-producing activities if the individual would experience these activities as threatening, anxiety-arousing, and unpleasant?

One argument is that organizations and behavioral scientists *must* take the individual as he exists now and attempt to maximize the quality of the work experience for him in his own, current terms, even if this means ignoring a possible years-long process of dehumanization. The alternative argument is that the organization is at least partly responsible for the way the person is now and that therefore the organization can and should provide the person with opportunities for growth—and make sure that the individual at least "tastes" them. From this viewpoint, the choice should indeed rest with the individual—but only after he has tried out the new kind of work for a while and learned from personal experience what it feels like, even if this makes him tense and unhappy during the trial period.

The dilemma between the two alternatives is a real one, and one for which we see no easy or ethically "pure" answers. Future research on organizational change and job choice should give explicit attention to this issue. It is hoped that such research will yield some new strategies or models which will be used to increase the opportunities individuals have for personal growth at work, with minimum feasible coercion.

Research Task B: *Developing and testing the components of an "individualized" approach to organizational management.* Use of the principles of individualized management would require:

1 Rather complete knowledge of how individual differences moderate employee reactions to organizational practices—an issue discussed earlier in this chapter

2 Valid measures of the individual differences found to be important moderators

3 Revision of selection and placement practices of the organization, so as to provide an individualized "fit" between each employee, his job, and his work group

4 Retraining of organizational management in the concept of the individualized organization, so that those practices under managerial control (e.g., feedback, rewards) could be administered, insofar as possible, on an individualized basis

Obviously, neither contemporary organizations nor state-of-the-art organizational science is "ready" for the individualized organization. What we are ready for, however, are small-scale experiments in which attempts are made to individualize bits and pieces of organizations. Such experiments should both (1) increase our knowledge about how different types of individuals respond to various organizational practices and (2) provide some first steps toward the development of effective managerial strategies for implementing the principle of individualization. The gaps in our knowledge about individual differences and about individualized organizational practices are obviously enormous. We also believe there is a great need to begin to grope for and experiment with new, nonuniversalistic organizational forms.

Throughout this chapter we have been stressing some of the changes we think will and should come about if progress is to be made for individuals and organizations and, indeed, society. Such gains will not be easy; they will require significant adjustments by both employers and employees. Responsibility for improvements in organizational life—improvements that will benefit all parties—will need to be widely shared. Behavioral scientists, for their part, can contribute to advances that will help both those who work in organizations and those who determine their destiny. Of course, as we have pointed out throughout this book, the greatest impact of behavioral science will come about through research and objective analysis. We need to use these research skills, however, not only to evaluate current practices but also to suggest new ways to design work and organizations.

Our readers may not agree with all of our views on the points we have discussed in this chapter, but we hope that they will share with us a commitment to help make organizations better places in which to work and more effective contributors to the general well-being of society.

Bibliography

Albrook, R. C. How to spot executives early. *Fortune,* 1968, **78** (July), 107–111.

Alderfer, C. P. An organizational syndrome. *Administrative Science Quarterly,* 1967, **12,** 440–460.

Alderfer, C. P. Understanding laboratory education: An overview. *Monthly Labor Review,* 1970, **93** (12), 18–27.

Alderfer, C. P. Effect of individual, group, and intergroup relations on attitudes toward a management development program. *Journal of Applied Psychology,* 1971, **55,** 302–311.

Alderfer, C. P. *Existence, relatedness, and growth: Human needs in organizational settings.* New York: Free Press, 1972.

Alderfer, C. P. Change processes in organizations. In M. D. Dunnette (Ed.), *Handbook of industrial and organizational psychology.* Chicago: Rand McNally, 1975.

Alderfer, C. P., & McCord, C. Personal and situational factors in the recruitment interview. *Journal of Applied Psychology,* 1970, **54,** 377–385.

Allen, V. L. Situational factors in conformity. In L. Berkowitz (Ed.), *Advances in experimental social psychology* (Vol. II). New York: Academic Press, 1965.

Allen, V. L., & Bragg, B. W. Effect of group pressure on memory. *The Journal of Psychology,* 1968, **69,** 19–32. (a)

Allen, V. L., & Bragg, B. W. Effect of social pressure on concept identification. *Journal of Educational Psychology,* 1968, **59,** 302–308. (b)

Allen, V. L., & Levine, J. M. Social support and conformity: The role of independent assessment of reality. *Journal of Experimental Social Psychology,* 1971, **7,** 48–58.

Allport, F. H. *Theories of perception and the concept of structure.* New York: Wiley, 1955.

Allport, F. H. A structuronomic conception of behavior: Individual and collective. I. Structural theory and the master problem of social psychology. *Journal of Abnormal and Social Psychology,* 1962, **64,** 3–30.

Anderson, H. E., Roush, S. L., & McClary, J. E. Relationships among ratings, production efficiency, and the general aptitude test battery scales in an industrial setting. *Journal of Applied Psychology,* 1973, **58,** 77–82.

Andrews, I. R., & Henry, M. Management attitudes toward pay. *Industrial Relations,* 1963, **3,** 29–39.

Argyris, C. *The impact of budgets on people.* New York: Controllership Foundation, 1951.

Argyris, C. *Organization of a bank.* New Haven, Conn.: Labor and Management Center, Yale University, 1954.

Argyris, C. *Personality and organization.* New York: Harper, 1957.

Argyris, C. *Interpersonal competence and organizational effectiveness.* Homewood, Ill.: Dorsey, 1962.

Argyris, C. *Integrating the individual and the organization.* New York: Wiley, 1964.

Argyris, C. The incompleteness of social psychological theory: Examples from small group, cognitive consistency and attribution research. *American Psychologist,* 1969, **24,** 893–908.

Argyris, C. *Intervention theory and method: A behavioral science view.* Reading, Mass.: Addison-Wesley, 1970.

Argyris, C. *Management and organizational development: The path from X. A. to Y. B.* New York: McGraw-Hill, 1971. (a)

Argyris, C. Management information systems: The challenge to rationality. *Management Science,* 1971, **17,** 275–292. (b)

Asch, S. E. Effects of group pressure upon the modification and distortion of judgments. In H. Guetzkow (Ed.), *Groups, leadership and men.* Pittsburgh: Carnegie Press, 1951.

Asch, S. E. Opinions and social pressure. *Scientific American,* 1955, **193,** 31–35.

Asher, J. J. The biographical item: Can it be improved? *Personnel Psychology,* 1972, **25,** 251–269.

Atkinson, J. W. *An introduction to motivation.* Princeton, N.J.: Van Nostrand, 1954.

Atkinson, J. W. *Motives in fantasy, action, and society.* Princeton, N.J.: Van Nostrand, 1958.

Back, K. W. Influence through social communication. *Journal of Abnormal and Social Psychology,* 1951, **46,** 190–207.

Bakke, E. W. *Bonds of organization: An appraisal of corporate human relations.* New York: Harper, 1950.

Bakke, E. W. The fusion process. New Haven, Conn.: Labor and Management Center, Yale University, 1953.

Bales, R. F. The equilibrium problem in small groups. In T. Parsons, R. F. Bales, and E. A. Shils (Eds.) *Working papers in the theory of action.* New York: Free Press, 1953.

Bales, R. F., & Slater, P. E. Role differentiation in small groups. In T. Parsons, R. F. Bales, et al. (Eds.), *Family, socialization, and interaction process.* Glencoe, Ill.: Free Press, 1955.

Bandura, A. *Social learning theory.* New York: General Learning Press, 1971.

Barnard, C. I. *The functions of the executive.* Cambridge, Mass.: Harvard University Press, 1938.

Barrett, J. H. *Individual goals and organizational objectives: A study of integration mechanisms.* Ann Arbor: Institute for Social Research, University of Michigan, 1970.

Bass, B. M., & Vaughan, J. A. *Training in industry: The management of learning.* Belmont, Calif.: Wadsworth, 1966.

Bavelas, A., Hastorf, A. H., Gross, A. E., & Kite, W. R. Experiments on the alteration of group structure. *Journal of Experimental Social Psychology,* 1965, **1,** 55–70.

Beckhard, R. *Organization development: Strategies and models.* Reading, Mass.: Addison-Wesley, 1969.

Beer, M. The technology of organizational development. In M. D. Dunnette (Ed.), *Handbook of industrial and organizational psychology.* Chicago: Rand McNally, 1975.

Beer, M., & Huse, E. F. A systems approach to organization development. *Journal of Applied Behavioral Science,* 1972, **8,** 79–101.

Bem, D. J. An experimental analysis of self-persuasion. *Journal of Experimental Social Psychology,* 1965, **1,** 199–218.

Bem, D. J. *Beliefs, attitudes and human affairs.* Belmont, Calif.: Brooks/Cole, 1970.

Bennis, W. G. *Changing organizations.* New York: McGraw-Hill, 1966.

Bennis, W. G. The case study: Introduction. *Journal of Applied Behavioral Science,* 1968, **4,** 227–231.

Bennis, W. G. *Organization development: Its nature, origins, and prospects.* Reading, Mass.: Addison-Wesley, 1969.

Bennis, W. G., Benne, K. B., & Chin, R. *The planning of change* (2nd ed.) New York: Holt, 1969.

Bennis, W. G., & Slater, P. E. *The temporary society.* New York: Harper & Row, 1968.

Berger, S. M., & Lambert, W. W. Stimulus-response theory in contemporary social psychology. In G. Lindzey and E. Aronson (Eds.) *The handbook of social psychology* (2nd ed.) Reading, Mass.: Addison-Wesley, 1968.

Berkowitz, L. Group standards, cohesiveness and productivity. *Human Relations,* 1954, **7,** 509–519.

Berkowitz, L., & Howard, R. C. Reactions to opinion deviates as affected by affiliation need *(n)* and group member interdependence. *Sociometry,* 1959, **22,** 81–91.

Berlew, D. E., & Hall, D. T. The socialization of managers: Effects of expectations on performance. *Administrative Science Quarterly,* 1966, **11,** 207–223.

Berliner, J. S. The situation of plant managers, In A. Inkeles & K. Geiger (Eds.), *Soviet society: A book of readings.* Boston: Houghton Mifflin, 1961.

Berlyne, D. E. Arousal and reinforcement. *Nebraska Symposium on Motivation,* 1967, **15,** 1–110.

Berne E. *Games people play.* New York: Grove Press, 1964.

Berrien, F. K. A general systems approach to social taxonomy. In B. P. Indik & F. K. Berrien (Eds.), *People, groups, and organizations.* New York: Teachers College Press, 1968.

Biddle, B. J., & Thomas, E. J. *Role theory: Concepts and research.* New York: Wiley, 1966.

Bion, W. R. *Experiences in groups.* New York: Basic Books, 1959.

Blake, R. R., & Mouton, J. S. *The Managerial Grid.* Houston: Gulf, 1964.

Blake, R. R., & Mouton, J. S. *Building a dynamic corporation through GRID organization development.* Reading, Mass.: Addison-Wesley, 1969.

Blake, R. R., Shepard, H. A., & Mouton, J. S. *Managing intergroup conflict in industry.* Houston: Gulf, 1964.

Blau, P. M. *The dynamics of bureaucracy.* Chicago: University of Chicago Press, 1955.

Blau, P. M., & Scott, W. R. *Formal organizations.* San Francisco: Chandler, 1962.

Blauner, R. *Alienation and freedom.* Chicago: University of Chicago Press, 1964.

Blood, M. R., & Hulin, C. L. Alienation, environmental characteristics, and worker responses. *Journal of Applied Psychology,* 1967, **51,** 284–290.

Blum, M. L., & Naylor, J. G. *Industrial psychology: Its theoretical and social foundations.* New York: Harper & Row, 1968.

Borislow, B. The Edwards Personal Preference Schedule and fakability. *Journal of Applied Psychology,* 1958, **52,** 22–27.

Bray, D. W. Approaches to management development research. Paper presented at the 70th Annual Meeting of the American Psychological Association, New York, September, 1962.

Bray, D. W. The management progress study. *American Psychologist,* 1964, **19,** 419–420.

Bray, D. W. The management progress study. Paper presented at the 74th Annual Meeting of the American Psychological Association, New York, 1966.

Bray, D. W., Campbell, R. J., & Grant, D. L. *Formative years in business: A long-term A.T.&T. study of managerial lives.* New York: Wiley, 1974.

Breer, P. E., & Locke, E. A. *Task experience as a source of attitudes.* Homewood, Ill.: Dorsey, 1965.

Brenner, M. H., & Lockwood, H. C. Salary as a predictor of salary: A 20-year study. *Journal of Applied Psychology,* 1965, **49,** 295–298.

Bridgman, C. W., & Hollenbeck, G. P. Effect of simulated applicant status on Kuder Form D occupational interest scores. *Journal of Applied Psychology,* 1961, **45,** 237–239.

Brodman, K., & Hellman, L. P. Absenteeism and separation in relation to length of employment. *Industrial Medicine,* 1947, **16,** 219–222.

Brown, J. A. *The social psychology of industry.* Baltimore: Penguin, 1954.

Brummet, R. L., Flamholtz, E. G., & Pyle, W. C. Human resource measurement: A challenge for accountants. *The Accounting Review,* 1968, **43,** 217–224.

Buhler, C. Humanistic psychology as an educational program. *American Psychologist,* 1969, **24,** 736–742.

Burack, E. H. Industrial management in advanced production systems: Some theoretical concepts and preliminary findings. *Administrative Science Quarterly,* 1967, **12,** 479–500.

Burns, T. The reference of conduct in small groups: Cliques and cabels in occupational milieux. *Human Relations,* 1955, **8,** 467–486.

Burns, T., & Stalker, G. M. *The management of innovation.* London: Tavistock, 1961.

Campbell, D. T. Conformity in psychology's theories of acquired behavioral dispositions. In I. A. Berg and B. M. Bass (Eds.), *Comformity and deviation.* New York: Harper, 1961.

Campbell, J. P. Personnel training and development. *Annual Review of Psychology,* 1971, **22,** 565–602.

Campbell, J. P., Dunnette, M. D., Lawler, E. E., & Weick, K.E. *Managerial behavior, performance, and effectiveness.* New York: McGraw-Hill, 1970.

Campbell, R. D. Career development: The young business manager. Paper presented at 76th Annual Meeting of the American Psychological Association, San Francisco, September, 1968.

Caplow, T. *Principles of organization.* New York: Harcourt, Brace & World, 1964.

Carnegie, D. *How to win friends and influence people.* New York: Simon and Schuster, 1936.

Carter, L., & Nixon, M. Ability, perceptual, personality, and interest factors associated with different criteria of leadership. *Journal of Psychology,* 1949, **27,** 377–388.

Carter, M. *Into work.* Baltimore: Penguin, 1966.

Cartwright, D., & Zander, A. *Group dynamics: Research and theory* (3rd ed.) New York: Harper & Row, 1968.

Chapple, E. D., & Sayles, L. R. *The measure of management.* New York: Macmillan, 1961.

Child, I. L. Socialization. In G. Lindzey (Ed.), *Handbook of social psychology,* Vol. II. Cambridge, Mass.: Addison-Wesley, 1954.

Child, J. Organizational structure, environment and performance—the role of strategic choice. *Sociology,* 1972, **6,** 1–22.

Coch, L., & French, J. R. P., Jr. Overcoming resistance to change. *Human Relations,* 1948, **1,** 512–532.

Cofer, C. N., & Appley, M. H. *Motivation: Theory and research.* New York: Wiley, 1964.

Collins, B., & Guetzkow, H. *A social psychology of group processes for decision-making.* New York: Wiley, 1964.

Collins, O., Dalton, M., & Roy, D. Restriction of output and social cleavage in industry. *Applied Anthropology,* 1946, **5** (3), 1–14.

Cooley, C. H. *Human nature and the social order.* New York: Scribners, 1902.

Cooper, R., & Foster, M. Sociotechnical systems. *American Psychologist,* 1971, **26,** 467–474.

Cottrell, N. B., Wack, D. L., Sekerak, F. J., & Rittle, R. H. Social facilitation of dominant responses by the presence of an audience and the mere presence of others. *Journal of Personality and Social Psychology,* 1968, **9**, 245–250.

Cyert, R. M., & March, J. G. *A behavioral theory of the firm.* Englewood Cliffs, N.J.: Prentice-Hall, 1963.

Dalton, M. The industrial "rate-buster": A characterization. *Applied anthropology,* 1948, **7**, 5–18.

Dalton, M. *Men who manage.* New York: Wiley, 1959.

Darley, J., Gross, N., & Martin, W. Studies of group behavior: Factors associated with the productivity of groups. *Journal of Applied Psychology,* 1952, **36**, 396–403.

Davis, K. *Human society.* New York: Macmillan, 1950.

Davis, L. E., & Taylor, R. N. *The design of work.* London: Penguin, 1972.

Davis, L. E., & Trist, E. L. Improving the quality of work life: Experience of the socio-technical approach. Philadelphia: Management and Behavioral Science Center, University of Pennsylvania, 1972.

Dearborn, D. C., & Simon, H. A. Selective perception: A note on the departmental identification of executives. *Sociometry,* 1958, **21**, 140–144.

Dentler, R. A., & Erikson, K. T. The functions of deviance in groups. *Social Problems,* 1959, **7**, 98–107.

Drucker, P. F. *The practice of management.* New York: Harper, 1954.

Dubin, R. Industrial workers' worlds: A study of the "central life interests" of industrial workers. *Social Problems,* 1956, **3**, 131–142.

Dubin, R. *The world of work.* Englewood Cliffs, N.J.: Prentice-Hall, 1958.

Dubois, P. H. (Ed.) The classification program. *AAF Aviation Psychology Progress Research Report No. 7.* Washington: Government Printing Office, 1947.

Dunnette, M. D. *Personnel selection and placement.* Belmont, Calif.: Wadsworth, 1966.

Dunnette, M. D., Arvey, R. D., & Banas, P. A. Why do they leave? *Personnel,* 1973, May-June, 25–39.

Dunnette, M. D., Campbell, J. P., & Hakel, M. D. Factors contributing to job satisfaction and job dissatisfaction in six occupational groups. *Organizational Behavior and Human Performance,* 1967, **2**, 143–174.

Dunnette, M. D., Campbell, J. P., & Helervik, L. W. *Job behavior scales for Penney Co. department managers.* Minneapolis: Personnel Decisions, 1968.

Dunnette, M. D., Hough, L., Rosett, H., Mumford, E., & Fine, S. A. Work and nonwork: Merging human and societal needs. In M. D. Dunnette (Ed.), *Work and Nonwork in the Year 2001.* Monterey, Calif.: Brooks/Cole, 1973.

Dyson, B. H. Whether direct individual incentive systems based on time-study, however accurately computed, tend over a period to limitation of output. Paper read at Spring Conference, British Institute of Management, London, 1956.

Edwards, W. E. The theory of decision making. *Psychological Bulletin,* 1954, **51**, 380–417.

Emerson, R. M. Deviation and rejection: An experimental replication. *American Sociological Review,* 1954, **19**, 688–693.

Emery, F., & Trist, E. L. Socio-technical systems. Paper presented at the 6th Annual International Meeting of the Institute of Management Sciences, Paris, 1959.

Etzioni, A. *A comparative analysis of complex organizations.* Glencoe, Ill.: Free Press, 1961.

Etzioni, A. *Modern organizations.* Englewood Cliffs, N.J.: Prentice-Hall, 1964.

Evans, M. G. The effects of supervisory behavior on the path-goal relationship. *Organizational Behavior and Human Performance,* 1970, **5,** 277–298.

Farris, G. F., & Lim, F. G., Jr. Effects of performance on leadership, cohesiveness, influence, satisfaction, and subsequent performance. *Journal of Applied Psychology,* 1969, **53,** 490–497.

Fayol, H. *General and industrial management.* London: Pitman, 1949.

Festinger, L. Informal social communication. *Psychological Review,* 1950, **57,** 271–282.

Festinger, L. A theory of social comparison processes. *Human Relations,* 1954, **7,** 117–140.

Festinger, L. *A theory of cognitive dissonance.* Evanston, Ill.: Row, Peterson, 1957.

Festinger, L., Schachter, S., & Back, K. *Social pressures in informal groups.* Stanford: Stanford University Press, 1950.

Fiedler, F. E. *A theory of leadership effectiveness.* New York: McGraw-Hill, 1967.

Fiedler, F. E. *Leadership.* New York: General Learning Press, 1971.

Fine, S. A. Three kinds of skills: An approach to understanding the nature of human performance. *Proceedings of the 75th Annual Convention of the American Psychological Association,* 1967, p. 365.

Fishbein, M. A behavior theory approach to the relations between beliefs about an object and the attitude toward the object. In M. Fishbein (Ed.), *Readings in attitude theory and measurement.* New York: Wiley, 1967.

Fiske, D. W., & Maddi, S. R. (Eds.) *Functions of varied experience.* Homewood, Ill.: Dorsey, 1961.

Fleishman, E. A. Leadership climate, human relations training, and supervisory behavior. *Personnel Psychology,* 1953, **6,** 205–222.

Fleishman, E. A. Twenty years of consideration and structure. Paper presented at Southern Illinois University Leadership Conference, April, 1971.

Fleishman, E. A., & Berniger, J. One way to reduce office turnover. *Personnel,* 1960, **37,** 63–69.

Folley, J. D., Jr. Determining training needs of department store sales personnel. *Training and Development Journal,* 1969, **23** (7), 11–17.

Ford, R. M. *Motivation through the work itself.* New York: American Management Association, 1969.

Freeman, H. E., & Giovannoni, J. M. Social psychology and mental health. In G. Lindzey and E. Aronson (Eds.), *Handbook of social psychology* (2nd ed.) Reading, Mass.: Addison-Wesley, 1969.

French, J. R. P., Jr., Israel, J., & Ås, D. An experiment on participation in a Norwegian factory. *Human Relations,* 1960, **13,** 3–19.

French, J. R. P., Jr., Kay, E., & Meyer, H. H. Participation and the appraisal system. *Human Relations,* 1966, **19,** 3–19.

Friedlander, F. The relationship of task and human conditions to effective organizational structure. In B. M. Bass, R. Cooper, & J. A. Haas (Eds.), *Managing for accomplishment,* Lexington, Mass.: Heath, 1970.

Gagné, R. M. Military training and principles of learning. *American Psychologist,* 1962, **18,** 83–91.

Galbraith, J. R. Matrix organizational designs. *Business Horizons,* 1971, **14,** 21–40.

Gardner, B. B. *Human relations in industry.* Chicago: Irwin, 1945.

Gardner, J. W. *Self renewal.* New York: Harper & Row, 1965.

Garson, B. Luddites in Lordstown. *Harper's Magazine,* June, 1972.

Ghiselli, E. E. *The validity of occupational aptitude tests.* New York: Wiley, 1966. (a)

Ghiselli, E. E. The validity of personnel interviews. *Personnel Psychology,* 1966, **19,** 389–394. (b)

Gibb, C. A. The sociometry of leadership in temporary groups. *Sociometry,* 1954, **13,** 226–243.

Gibb, C. A. Leadership. In G. Lindzey and E. Aronson (Eds.), *The handbook of social psychology.* (2nd ed.) Reading, Mass.: Addison-Wesley, 1969.

Glaser, B. (Ed.) *Organizational careers.* Chicago: Aldine, 1968.

Glickman, A. S., Hahn, C. P., Fleishman, E. A., & Baxter, B. *Top management development and succession.* New York: Macmillan, 1968.

Goffman, E. *Asylums.* Garden City, N.Y.: Doubleday, 1961.

Goldsmith, D. B. The use of the personal history blank as a salesmanship test. *Journal of Applied Psychology,* 1922, **6,** 149–155.

Goldthorpe, J. H., Lockwood, D., Bechhofer, F., & Platt, J. *The affluent worker: Industrial attitudes and behavior.* Cambridge, London: Cambridge University Press, 1968.

Golembiewski, R. T. *The small group.* Chicago: University of Chicago Press, 1962.

Gomersall, E. R., & Myers, M. S. Breakthrough in on-the-job training. *Harvard Business Review,* 1966, **44** (4), 62–72.

Goodale, J. G. Effects of personal background and training on work values of the hard-core unemployed. *Journal of Applied Psychology,* 1973, **57,** 1–9.

Gouldner, A. Cosmopolitans and locals: Toward an analysis of latent social roles: I. *Administrative Science Quarterly,* 1958, **2,** 281–306. (a)

Gouldner, A. Cosmopolitans and locals: Toward an analysis of latent social roles: II. *Administrative Science Quarterly,* 1958, **2,** 444–480. (b)

Graen, G. Instrumentality theory of work motivation: Some experimental results and suggested modifications. *Journal of Applied Psychology Monograph,* 1969, **53,** 1–25.

Graen, G., Alvares, K., & Orris, J. Contingency model of leadership effectiveness: Antecedent and evidential results. *Psychological Bulletin,* 1970, **74,** 285–296.

Gross, B. M. *Organizations and their managing.* New York: Free Press, 1968.

Gross, N., Mason, W., & McEachern, A. *Explorations in role analysis.* New York: Wiley, 1958.

Guest, R. H. Men and machines: An assembly-line worker looks at his job. *Personnel,* May, 1955, 3–10.

Guion, R. M. *Personnel testing.* New York: McGraw-Hill, 1965.

Gulick, L. Notes on the theory of organization. In L. Gulick and L. Urwick (Eds.),

Papers on the science of administration. New York: The Institute of Public Administration, 1937.

Gustad, J. W. Psychological test reviews: Edwards Personal Preference Schedule. *Journal of Consulting Psychology,* 1956, **20,** 322–324.

Hackman, J. R. Group influences on individuals in organizations. In M. D. Dunnette (Ed.), *Handbook of industrial and organizational psychology.* Chicago: Rand-McNally, 1975.

Hackman, J. R., & Lawler, E. E. Employee reactions to job characteristics. *Journal of Applied Psychology,* 1971, **55,** 259–286.

Haire, M. Introduction—Recurrent themes and general issues in organization theory. In M. Haire (Ed.), *Modern organization theory.* New York: Wiley, 1959.

Haire, M., Ghiselli, E. E., & Gordon, M. E. A psychological study of pay. *Journal of Applied Psychology Monograph,* 1967, **51** (4, Whole No. 636).

Hakel, M. D., Dobmeyer, T. W., & Dunnette, M. D. Relative importance of three content dimensions in overall suitability ratings of job applicants' résumés. *Journal of Applied Psychology,* 1970, **54,** 65–71.

Hakel, M. D., Hollmann, T. D., & Dunnette, M. D. Accuracy of interviewers, certified public accountants, and students in identifying the interests of accountants. *Journal of Applied Psychology,* 1970, **54, 115–119.**

Hall, D. T., & Lawler, E. E. III Job design and job pressures as facilitators of professional-organization integration. *Administrative Science Quarterly,* 1970, **15,** 271–281.

Hall, D. T., and Lawler, E. E. Unused potential in R and D labs, *Research Management,* 1969, **12,** 339–354.

Hall, D. T., & Nougaim, K. E. An examination of Maslow's need hierarchy in an organizational setting. *Organizational Behavior and Human Performance,* 1968, **3,** 12–35.

Hall, D. T., & Schneider, B. *Organizational climates and careers.* New York: Seminar Press, 1973.

Hall, D. T., Schneider, B., & Nygren, H. T. Personal factors in organizational identification. *Administrative Science Quarterly,* 1970, **15,** 176–190.

Hall, R. H. The concept of bureaucracy: An empirical assessment. *American Journal of Sociology,* 1963, **69,** 32–40.

Hall, R. H., Haas, J. E., & Johnson, N. J. An examination of the Blau-Scott and Etzioni typologies. *Administrative Science Quarterly,* 1967, **12,** 118–139.

Halpin, A. W., & Croft, D. B. *The organizational climate of schools.* Washington, D. C.: U.S. Office of Education, Department of Health, Education, and Welfare, Contract No. SAE 543 (8639), 1962.

Harris, D. H. The assimilation of recent college graduates into engineering organizations: Final report. Technical Report T8-1276/501, Autonetics Division of North American Rockwell Corp., Anaheim, Calif., 1968.

Harrison, R. Choosing the depth of organizational intervention. *Journal of Applied Behavioral Science,* 1970, **6,** 181–202.

Harvey, E. Technology and the structure of organizations. *American Sociological Review,* 1968, **33,** 247–259.

Harvey, O. J., & Consalvi, C. Status and conformity to pressures in informal groups. *Journal of Abnormal and Social Psychology,* 1960, **60,** 182–187.

Heider, F. *The psychology of interpersonal relations.* New York: Wiley, 1958.

Hemphill, J. K. Relations between the size of the group and the behavior of superior leaders. *Journal of Social Psychology, 32,* 11–22.

Henchy, T., & Glass, D. C. Evaluation apprehension and the social facilitation of dominant and subordinate responses. *Journal of Personality and Social Psychology,* 1968, **10,** 446–454.

Herman, J. B., & Hulin, C. L. Studying organizational attitudes from individual and organizational frames of reference. *Organizational Behavior and Human Performance,* 1972, **8,** 84–108.

Herzberg, F. *Work and the nature of man.* Cleveland: World, 1966.

Herzberg, F., Mausner, B., Peterson, R. D., & Capwell, D. F. *Job attitudes: Review of research and opinion.* Pittsburgh: Psychological Service of Pittsburgh, 1957.

Herzberg, F., Mausner, B., & Snyderman, B. *The motivation to work.* New York: Wiley, 1959.

Hickson, D. J. Motives of work people who restrict their output. *Occupational Psychology,* 1961, **35,** 110–121.

Hickson, D. J. A convergence in organization theory. *Administrative Science Quarterly,* 1966, **11,** 229–237.

Hickson, D. J., Pugh, D. S., & Pheysey, D. Operations technology and organization structure: An empirical reappraisal. *Administrative Science Quarterly,* 1969, **14,** 378–397.

Hinrichs, J. R. The attitudes of research chemists. *Journal of Applied Psychology,* 1964, **48,** 21–32.

Hinton, B. L. An empirical investigation of the Herzberg methodology and two-factor theory. *Organizational Behavior and Human Performance,* 1968, **3,** 286–309.

Hitt, W. D. Two models of man. *American Psychologist,* 1969, **24,** 651–658.

Hodgson, R. C., Levinson, D. J., & Zaleznik, A. *The executive role constellation: An analysis of personality and role relations in management.* Boston: Harvard University Press, 1965.

Hofstede, G. H. *The game of budget control.* Assen, Netherlands: Van Gorcum, 1967.

Hollander, E. P. Conformity, status, and idiosyncrasy credit. *Psychological Review,* 1958, **65,** 117–127.

Hollander, E. P. Some effects of perceived status on responses to innovative behavior. *Journal of Abnormal and Social Psychology,* 1961, **63,** 247–250.

Hollander, E. P. *Leaders, groups and influence.* New York: Oxford University Press, 1964.

Homans, G. C. *The human group.* New York: Harcourt, Brace & World, 1950.

Homans, G. C. *Social behavior: Its elementary forms.* New York: Harcourt, Brace & World, 1961.

Hornstein, H. A., Benedict, B. A., Burke, W., Hornstein, M., & Lewicki, R. J. *Social intervention.* New York: Free Press, 1971.

House, R. J. A path-goal theory of leader effectiveness. *Administrative Science Quarterly,* 1971, **2,** 321–339.

House, R. J., Filley, A. C., & Kerr, S. Relation of leader consideration and initiating structure to R and D subordinates' satisfaction. *Administrative Science Quarterly,* 1971, **16,** 19–30.

House, R. J., & Miner, J. B. Merging management and behavioral theory: The interaction between span of control and group size. *Administrative Science Quarterly,* 1969, **14,** 451–464.

Hughes, E. C. The knitting of racial groups in industry. *American Sociological Review,* 1946, **11,** 512–519.

Hulin, C. L., & Blood, M. R. Job enlargement, individual differences, worker responses. *Psychological Bulletin,* 1968, **69,** 41–55.

Humphreys, L. G. Statistical definitions of test validity for minority groups. *Journal of Applied Psychology,* 1973, **58,** 1–4.

Hunt, J. McV. Motivation and social interaction. In O. J. Harvey (Ed.), *Motivation inherent in information processing and action.* New York: Ronald Press, 1963.

Indik, B. P. The scope of the problem and some suggestions toward a solution. In B. P. Indik and F. K. Berrien (Eds.), *People, groups and organizations.* New York: Teachers College Press, 1968.

Jackson, J. Structural characteristics of norms. In N. B. Henry (Ed.), *Dynamics of instructional groups* (The fifty-ninth yearbook of the National Society for the Study of Education). Chicago: University of Chicago Press, 1960.

Jackson, J. Structural characteristics of norms. In I. D. Steiner and M. Fishbein (Eds.), *Current studies in social psychology.* New York: Holt, Rinehart & Winston, 1965.

Jackson, J. A conceptual and measurement model for norms and roles. *Pacific Sociological Review,* 1966, **9,** 35–47.

Jackson, J. *Norms and roles: Studies in systematic social psychology.* New York: Holt, Rinehart & Winston, in press.

Janis, I. L. Group identification under conditions of external danger. *British Journal of Medical Psychology,* 1963, **36,** 227–238.

Janis, I. L. *Victims of groupthink: A psychological study of foreign-policy decisions and fiascos.* Boston: Houghton Mifflin, 1972.

Jaques, E. *Equitable payment.* New York: Wiley, 1961.

Jones, E. E., & Gerard, H. B. *Foundations of social psychology.* New York: Wiley, 1967.

Kahn, R. L. & Katz, D. Leadership practices in relation to productivity and morale. In D. Cartwright and A. Zander (Eds.), *Group dynamics: Research and theory.* (2nd ed.) Evanston, Ill.: Row, Peterson, 1960.

Kahn, R. L., Wolfe, D. M., Quinn, R. P., Snoek, J. D., & Rosenthal, R. A. *Organizational stress: Studies in role conflict and ambiguity.* New York: Wiley, 1964.

Kast, F. E., & Rosenzweig, J. E. *Organization and management: A systems approach.* New York: McGraw-Hill, 1970.

Katz, D., & Kahn, R. L. *The social psychology of organizations.* New York: Wiley, 1966.

Kaufman, H. *The Forest Ranger.* Baltimore: Johns Hopkins Press, 1960.

Kaufman, H., & Seidman, D. The morphology of organizations. *Administrative Science Quarterly,* 1970, **15** 439–452.

Kelley, H. H., & Lamb, T. W. Certainty of judgment and resistance to social influences. *Journal of Abnormal and Social Psychology,* 1957, **55,** 137–139.

Kelman, H. C. Effects of success and failure on "suggestibility" on the autokinetic situation. *Journal of Abnormal and Social Psychology,* 1950, **45,** 267–285.

Kelman, H. C. Processes of opinion change. *Public Opinion Quarterly,* 1961, **25,** 57–78.

Kemper, T. D. Reference groups, socialization and achievement. *American Sociological Review,* 1968, **33,** 31–45.

Kiesler, C. A. Group pressure and conformity. In J. Mills (Ed.), *Experimental social psychology.* New York: Macmillan, 1969.

Kilbridge, M. D. Reduced costs through job enlargement: A case. *The Journal of Business,* 1960, **33,** 357–362.

Kindall, A. F., & Gatza, J. Positive program for performance appraisal. *Harvard Business Review,* 1963, **41** (6), 153–157.

King, N. A clarification and evaluation of the two-factor theory of job satisfaction. *Psychological Bulletin,* 1970, **74,** 18–31.

Kirchner, W. K. "Real-life" faking on the Strong Vocational Interest Blank by sales applicants. *Journal of Applied Psychology,* 1961, **45, 273**–276.

Kirchner, W. K. "Real-life" faking on the Edwards Personal Preference Schedule by sales applicants. *Journal of Applied Psychology,* 1962, **46,** 128–130.

Klein, S. M. *Workers under stress: The impact of work pressure on group cohesion.* Lexington: University Press of Kentucky, 1971.

Korman, A. K. "Consideration," "Initiating structure," and organizational criteria: A review. *Personnel Psychology,* 1966, **19,** 349–361.

Kornhauser, A. *Mental health of the industrial worker.* New York: Wiley, 1965.

Lanzetta, J. T., & Hannah, T. E. Reinforcing behavior of "naive" trainers. *Journal of Personality and Social Psychology,* 1969, **11,** 245–252.

Latane, B. (Ed.). Studies in social comparison. *Journal of Experimental Social Psychology,* 1966, **2** (Supplement 1).

Lawler, E. E. Managers' job performance and their attitudes toward their pay. Unpublished doctoral dissertation, University of California, Berkeley, 1964.

Lawler, E. E. Ability as a moderator in the relationship between job attitudes and job performance. *Personnel Psychology,* 1966, **19,** 153–164. (a)

Lawler, E. E. Managers' attitudes toward how their pay is and should be determined. *Journal of Applied Psychology,* 1966, **50,** 273–279. (b)

Lawler, E. E. The multitrait-multirater approach to measuring managerial job performance. *Journal of Applied Psychology,* 1967, **51,** 369–381.

Lawler, E. E. Effects of hourly overpayment on productivity and work quality. *Journal of Personality and Social Psychology,* 1968, **10,** 306–314.

Lawler, E. E. Job attitudes and employee motivation: Theory, research, and practice. *Personnel Psychology,* 1970, **23,** 223–237.

Lawler, E. E. *Pay and organizational effectiveness: A psychological view.* New York: McGraw-Hill, 1971.

Lawler, E.E. Control systems in organizations. In M. D. Dunnette (Ed.), *Handbook of industrial and organizational psychology.* Chicago: Rand McNally, 1975.

Lawler, E. E., & Cammann, C. What makes a work group successful? In A. J. Marrow (Ed.), *The failure of success.* New York: Amacom, 1972.

Lawler, E. E., & Hackman, J. R. The impact of employee participation in the development of pay incentive plans: A field experiment. *Journal of Applied Psychology,* 1969, **53**, 467–471.

Lawler, E. E., Hackman, J. R., & Kaufman, S. Effects of job redesign: A field experiment. *Journal of Applied Social Psychology,* 1973, **3**, 49–62.

Lawler, E. E., & Porter, L. W. Perceptions regarding management compensation. *Industrial Relations,* 1963, **3**, 41–49.

Lawler, E. E., & Suttle, J. L. A causal correlational test of the need hierarchy concept. *Organizational Behavior and Human Performance,* 1972, **7**, 265–287.

Lawler, E. E., & Suttle, J. L. Expectancy theory and job behavior. *Organizational Behavior and Human Performance,* 1973, **9**, 482–503.

Lawrence, P. R., & Lorsch, J. W. *Organization and environment.* Boston: Harvard Business School, Division of Research, 1967.

Lawrence, P. R., & Lorsch, J. W. *Developing organizations: Diagnosis and action.* Reading, Mass.: Addison-Wesley, 1969.

League, B. J., & Jackson, D. N. Conformity, veridicality and self-esteem. *Journal of Abnormal and Social Psychology,* 1964, **68**, 113–115.

Leavitt, H. J. Management according to task: Organizational differentiation. *Management International,* 1962, **1**, 13–22.

Lefkowitz, J. Differential validity: Ethnic group as a moderator in predicting tenure. *Personnel Psychology,* 1972, **25**, 223–240.

Lesieur, F. G. *The Scanlon Plan: A frontier in labor-management cooperation.* Cambridge: M.I.T. Press, 1958.

Levinson, H. Management by whose objectives? *Harvard Business Review,* 1970, **48**, 125–134.

Levinson, H. *Organizational diagnosis.* Cambridge: Harvard University Press, 1972.

Levinson, H., Price, C. R., Munden, H. J., & Solley, C. M. *Men, management, and mental health.* Cambridge: Harvard University Press, 1962.

Lewin, K., Dembo, T., Festinger, L., & Sears, P. Level of aspiration. In J. McV. Hunt (Ed.), *Personality and the behavior disorders.* New York: Ronald Press, 1944.

Lieberman, S. The effects of changes in roles on the attitudes of role occupants. *Human Relations,* 1956, **9**, 385–402.

Liebow, E. *Tally's Corner: A study of Negro streetcorner men.* Boston: Little, Brown, 1967.

Likert, R. *New patterns of management.* New York: McGraw-Hill, 1961.

Likert, R. *The human organization: Its management and value.* New York: McGraw-Hill, 1967.

Likert, R., & Bowers, D. G. Organizational theory and human resources accounting. *American Psychologist,* 1969, **24**, 585–592.

Litterer, J. A. *The analysis of organizations.* New York: Wiley, 1965.

Litwin, G. H., & Stringer, R. A., Jr. *Motivation and organizational climate.* Boston: Graduate School of Business Administration, Harvard University, 1968.

Livingston, J. S. Pygmalion in management. *Harvard Business Review,* 1969, **47** (4), 81–89.

Locke, E. A. Motivational effects of knowledge of results: Knowledge or goal setting? *Journal of Applied Psychology,* 1967, **51**, 324–329.

Locke, E. A. Toward a theory of task motivation and incentives. *Organizational Behavior and Human Performance,* 1968, **3**, 157–189.

Locke, E. A. What is job satisfaction? *Organizational Behavior and Human Performance,* 1969, **4**, 309–336.

Locke, E. A., Cartledge, N., & Koeppel, J. Motivational effects of knowledge of results: A goal-setting phenomenon? *Psychological Bulletin,* 1968, **70**, 474–485.

Lopez, F. M., Jr. Current problems in test performance of job applicants: I. *Personnel Psychology,* 1966, **19**, 10–17.

Lott, A. J., & Lott, B. E. Group cohesiveness as interpersonal attraction: A review of relationships with antecedent and consequent variables. *Psychological Bulletin,* 1965, **64**, 259–309.

Lott, B. E. Attitude formation: The development of a color-preference response through mediated generalization. *Journal of Abnormal and Social Psychology,* 1955, **50**, 321–326.

Lowin, A. Participative decision making: A model, literature critique, and prescriptions for research. *Organizational Behavior and Human Performance,* 1968, **3**, 68–106.

Lowin, A., & Craig, J. R. The influence of level of performance on managerial style: An experimental object-lesson in the ambiguity of correlational data. *Organizational Behavior and Human Performance,* 1968, **3**, 440–458.

Macedonia, R. M. Expectation-press and survival. Unpublished doctoral dissertation, Graduate School of Public Administration, New York University, 1969.

Maier, N. R. F., & Solem, A. R. The contribution of a discussion leader to the quality of group thinking. *Human Relations,* 1952, **5**, 277–288.

March, J. G. Group norms and the active minority. *American Sociological Review,* 1954, **19**, 733–741.

March, J. G., & Simon, H. A. *Organizations,* New York: Wiley, 1958.

Margulies, N., & Wallace, J. *Organizational change: Techniques and applications.* Glenview, Ill.: Scott, Foresman, 1973.

Marrow, A. J., Bowers, D. G., & Seashore, S. E. *Management by participation.* New York: Harper & Row, 1967.

Martin, N. H., & Strauss, A. L. Patterns of mobility within industrial organizations. *Journal of Business,* 1956, **29**, 101–110.

Maslow, A. H. A theory of human motivation. *Psychological Review,* 1943, **50**, 370–396.

Maslow, A. H. *Motivation and personality.* New York: Harper, 1954.

Mayfield, E. C. The selection interview—a re-evaluation of published research. *Personnel Psychology,* 1964, **17**, 239–260.

McClelland, D. C. *Personality.* New York: Sloane, 1951.

McClelland, D. C. N achievement and entrepreneurship: A longitudinal study. *Journal of Personality and Social Psychology*, 1965, **1**, 389–392. (a)

McClelland, D. C. Toward a theory of motive acquisition. *American Psychologist*, 1965, **20**, 321–333. (b)

McClelland, D. C., Atkinson, J. W., Clark, R. A., & Lowell, E. L. *The achievement motive.* New York: Appleton Century Crofts, 1953.

McClelland, D. C., & Winter, D. G. *Motivating economic achievement.* New York: Free Press, 1969.

McGehee, W., & Thayer, P. W. *Training in business and industry.* New York: Wiley, 1961.

McGrath, J. E. Leadership behavior: Some requirements for leadership training. Office of Career Development, U.S. Civil Service Commission, 1962.

McGregor, D. An uneasy look at performance appraisal. *Harvard Business Review*, 1957, **35** (3), 89–94.

McGregor, D. *The human side of enterprise.* New York: McGraw-Hill, 1960.

McGregor, D. *The professional manager.* New York: McGraw-Hill, 1967.

McKelvey, W. Expectational noncomplementarity and style of interaction between profession and organization. *Administrative Science Quarterly*, 1969, **14**, 21–32.

Mellinger, G. C. Interpersonal trust as a factor in communications. *Journal of Abnormal and Social Psychology*, 1956, **52**, 304–309.

Meltzer, L., & Salter, J. Organizational structure and the performance and job satisfaction of physiologists. *American Sociological Review*, 1962, **27**, 351–362.

Merton, R. K. Bureaucratic structure and personality. *Social Forces*, 1940, **18**, 560–568.

Meyer, H. H., Kay, E., & French, J. P. Split roles in performance appraisal. *Harvard Business Review*, 1965, **43** (1), 123–129.

Miles, R. E. Human relations or human resources? *Harvard Business Review*, 1965, **43** (4), 148–163.

Miles, R. E., & Vergin, R. C. Behavioral properties of variance controls. *California Management Review*, 1966, **8** (3), 57–65.

Milkovich, G. T., & Anderson, P. H. Management compensation and secrecy policies. *Personnel Psychology*, 1972, **25**, 293–302.

Miller, E. J., & Rice, A. K. *Systems of organization.* London: Tavistock, 1967.

Miller, G. A., Galanter, E., & Pribram, K. H., *Plans and the structure of behavior.* New York: Holt, Rinehart & Winston, 1960.

Miller, N. E., & Dollard J. *Social learning and imitation.* New Haven: Yale University Press, 1941.

Mills, C. W. *White collar: The American middle classes.* New York: Oxford University Press, 1953.

Mills, T. M. *The sociology of small groups.* Englewood Cliffs, N.J.: Prentice-Hall, 1967.

Morse, J. J., & Lorsch, J. W. Beyond theory Y. *Harvard Business Review*, 1970, **48** (3), 61–68.

Morse, N. C., & Reimer, E. The experimental change of a major organizational variable. *Journal of Abnormal and Social Psychology*, 1956, **52**, 120–129.

Morse, N. C., & Weiss, R. The function and meaning of work and the job. *American Sociological Review*, 1955, **20**, 191–198.

Mudd, S. A. Group sanction severity as a function of degree of behavior deviation and relevance of norm. *Journal of Personality and Social Psychology,* 1968, **8,** 258–260.

Mumford, E., & Banks, O. *The computer and the clerk.* London: Routledge & Kegan Paul, 1967.

Murray, H. A. *Explorations in personality.* New York: Oxford University Press, 1938.

Newcomb, T. M. Attitude development as a function of reference groups: The Bennington study. In C. G. Swanson, T. M. Newcomb, & E. L. Hartley (Eds.), *Readings in social psychology* (Rev. ed.) New York: Holt, Rinehart & Winston, 1952.

Nolen, W. *The making of a surgeon.* New York: Random House, 1970.

Odiorne, G. S. A systems approach to training. *Training Directors Journal,* 1965, **19** (1), 3–11. (a)

Odiorne, G. S. *Management decision by objectives.* Englewood Cliffs, N.J.: Prentice-Hall, 1965. (b)

Opinion Research Corporation. *"Productivity" from the worker's standpoint.* Princeton: Author, 1965.

Organization for Economic Cooperation and Development. *Wages and labor mobility.* Paris, 1965.

Osgood, E. C., Suci, C. J., & Tannenbaum, P. H. *The measurement of meaning.* Urbana, Ill.: University of Illinois Press, 1957.

Oshry, B. I., & Harrison, R. Transfer from here-and-now to there-and-then: Changes in organizational problem diagnosis stemming from T-group training. *Journal of Applied Behavioral Science,* 1966, **2,** 185–198.

OSS Staff. *Assessment of men.* New York: Rinehart, 1948.

Parsons, T. Suggestions for a sociological approach to the theory of organizations I and II. *Administrative Science Quarterly,* 1956, **1,** 63–85, 225–239.

Parsons, T. *Structure and process in modern societies.* Glencoe, Ill.: Free Press, 1960.

Perrow, C. A framework for the comparative analysis of organizations. *American Sociological Review,* 1967, **32,** 194–208.

Peter, L. J., & Hull, R. *The Peter principle.* New York: Morrow, 1969.

Pettigrew, A. A behavioral analysis of an innovative decision. Unpublished doctoral dissertation, University of Manchester, England, 1970.

Pettigrew, T. F. Social evaluation theory: Convergences and applications. In J. D. Levine (Ed.), *Nebraska symposium on motivation.* Lincoln: University of Nebraska Press, 1967.

Pfiffner, J. M., & Sherwood, F. P. *Administrative organization.* Englewood Cliffs, N.J.: Prentice-Hall, 1960.

Porter, L. W. A study of perceived need satisfaction in bottom and middle management jobs. *Journal of Applied Psychology,* 1961, **45,** 1–10.

Porter, L. W. Job attitudes in management: I. Perceived deficiencies in need fulfillment as a function of job level. *Journal of Applied Psychology*, 1962, **46**, 375–384.

Porter, L. W. Job attitudes in management: IV. Perceived deficiencies in need fulfillment as a function of size of company. *Journal of Applied Psychology*, 1963, **47**, 386–397. (a)

Porter L. W. Where is the organization man? *Harvard Business Review*, 1963, **41** (6), 53–61. (b)

Porter, L. W. *Organizational patterns of managerial job attitudes.* New York: American Foundation for Management Research, 1964.

Porter, L. W. Turning work into nonwork: The rewarding environment. In M. D. Dunnette (Ed.), *Work and nonwork in the year 2001.* Monterey, Calif.: Brooks/Cole, 1973.

Porter, L. W., Crampon, W. J., & Smith, F. J. Organizational commitment and managerial turnover: A longitudinal study. Technical Report No.13, ONR Contract NR 151–315, University of California, Irvine, 1972.

Porter, L. W., & Ghiselli, E. E. The self perceptions of top and middle management personnel. *Personnel Psychology,* 1957, **10**, 397–406.

Porter, L. W., & Lawler, E. E. The effects of tall and flat organization structures on managerial job satisfaction. *Personnel Psychology,* 1964, **17**, 135–148.

Porter, L. W., & Lawler, E. E. Properties of organization structure in relation to job attitudes and job behavior. *Psychological Bulletin,* 1965, **64**, 23–51.

Porter, L. W., & Lawler, E. E. *Managerial attitudes and performance.* Homewood, Ill.: Irwin-Dorsey, 1968. (a)

Porter, L. W., & Lawler, E.E. What job attitudes tell about motivation. *Harvard Business Review,* 1968, **46** (1), 118–126. (b)

Porter, L. W., & Siegel, J. Relationships of tall and flat organization structures to the satisfaction of foreign managers. *Personnel Psychology,* 1965, **18**, 379–392.

Porter, L. W., & Steers, R. M. Organizational, work, and personal factors in employee turnover and absenteeism. *Psychological Bulletin,* 1973, **80**, 151–176.

Porter, L. W., & Stone, E. F. Job characteristics and job attitudes: A multivariate study. Technical Report No.23, ONR Contract NR 151–315, University of California, Irvine, 1973.

Porter, L. W., Van Maanen, J., Yeager, F., & Crampon, W. J. Continuous monitoring of employees' motivational attitudes during the initial employment period. Technical Report No.4, ONR Contract NR 151–315, University of California, Irvine, 1971.

Presthus, R. V. Toward a theory of organizational behavior. *Administrative Science Quarterly,* 1958, **3**, 48–72.

Pritchard, R. D., & Karasick, B. W. The effects of organizational climate on managerial job performance and job satisfaction. *Organizational Behavior and Human Performance,* 1973, **9**, 126–146.

Proshansky, H., & Seidenberg, B. *Basic studies in social psychology.* New York: Holt, Rinehart & Winston, 1965.

Psychology Today, New tool: Reinforcement for good work, 1972, **5** (11), 68–69.

Pugh, D. S. Modern organization theory. *Psychological Bulletin,* 1966, **66**, 235–251.

Pugh, D. S., Hickson, D. J., Hinings, C. R., & Turner, C. Dimensions of organization structure. *Administrative Science Quarterly,* 1968, **13**, 65–105.

Pugh, D. S., Hickson, D. J., & Hinings, C. R. An empirical taxonomy of structures of work organizations. *Administrative Science Quarterly,* 1969, **14,** 115–126. (a)

Pugh, D. S., Hickson, D. J., Hinings, C. R., & Turner, C. The context of organization structures. *Administrative Science Quarterly,* 1969, **14,** 91–114. (b)

Rackham, J., & Woodward, J. The measurement of technical variables. In J. Woodward (Ed.), *Industrial organization: Behavior and control.* London: Oxford, 1970.

Rhine, J. The effects of peer group influence upon concept-attitude development and change. *Journal of Social Psychology,* 1960, **51,** 173–179.

Rhode, J. G., & Lawler, E. E. Auditing charge: Human resource accounting. In M. D. Dunnette (Ed.), *Work and nonwork in the year 2001.* Monterey, Calif.: Brooks/ Cole, 1973.

Roethlisberger, F. J., & Dickson, W. J. *Management and the worker.* Cambridge: Harvard University Press, 1939.

Rosen, N. *Leadership change and work group dynamics—An experiment.* Ithaca, N.Y.: Cornell University Press, 1969.

Rosenberg, L. A. Group size, prior experience, and conformity. *Journal of Abnormal and Social Psychology,* 1961, **63,** 436–437.

Rosenberg, M. J. Cognitive structure and attitudinal affect. *Journal of Abnormal and Social Psychology,* 1956, **53,** 367–372.

Rosenberg, M. J. *Occupations and values.* Glencoe, Ill.: Free Press, 1957.

Rosenthal, R. The Pygmalion effect lives. *Psychology Today,* 1973, **7** (4), 56–63.

Rosenthal, R., & Jacobson, K. *Pygmalion in the classroom.* New York: Holt, Rinehart, & Winston, 1968.

Roy, E. Quota restriction and gold bricking in a machine shop. *American Journal of Sociology,* 1952, **57,** 427–444.

Sales, S. M. Supervisory style and productivity: Review and theory. *Personnel Psychology,* 1966, **19,** 275–286.

Sampson, E. E., & Brandon, A. C. The effects of role and opinion deviation on small group behavior. *Sociometry,* 1964, **27,** 261–281.

Sanford, N. Whatever happened to action research? *Journal of Social Issues,* 1970, **26,** 3–23.

Sarbin, T. R., & Allen, V. L. Increasing participation in a natural group setting: A preliminary report. *The Psychological Record,* 1968, **18,** 1–7. (a)

Sarbin, T. R., & Allen, V. L. Role theory. In G. Lindzey & E. Aronson (Eds.), *The handbook of social psychology* (2nd ed.) Reading, Mass.: Addison-Wesley, 1968. (b)

Schachter, S. Deviation, rejection and communication. *Journal of Abnormal and Social Psychology,* 1951, **46,** 190–207.

Schachter, S. *The psychology of affiliation.* Stanford, Calif.: Stanford University Press, 1959.

Scheflen, K. C., Lawler, E. E., & Hackman, J. R. Long-term impact of employee participation in the development of pay incentive plans: A field experiment revisited. *Journal of Applied Psychology,* 1971, **55,** 182–186.

Scheidlinger, S. *Psychoanalysis and group behavior: A study in Freudian group psychology.* New York: Norton, 1952.

Schein, E. H. The Chinese indoctrination program for prisoners of war. *Psychiatry,* 1956, **19,** 149–172.

Schein, E. H. How to break in the college graduate. *Harvard Business Review,* 1964, **42** (6), 68–76.

Schein, E. H. Organizational socialization and the profession of management. *Industrial Management Review,* 1968, **9,** 1–16.

Schein, E. H. *Process consultation: Its role in organizational development.* Reading, Mass.: Addison-Wesley, 1969.

Schein, E. H. *Organizational psychology* (2nd ed.) Englewood Cliffs, N.J.: Prentice-Hall, 1970.

Schein, E. H. The individual, the organization, and the career: A conceptual scheme. *Journal of Applied Behavioral Science,* 1971, **7,** 401–426.

Schlesinger, A. M. *A thousand days.* Boston: Houghton Mifflin, 1965.

Schneider, B. Organizational climate: Individual preferences and organizational realities. *Journal of Applied Psychology,* 1972, **56,** 211–217.

Schneider, B., & Bartlett, C. J. Individual differences and organizational climate: I. The research plan and questionnaire development. *Personnel Psychology,* 1968, **21,** 323–333.

Schultz, G. P. Variations in environment and the Scanlon Plan. In F. G. Lesieur (Ed.), *The Scanlon Plan.* Cambridge, Mass.: M.I.T. Press, 1958.

Scott, W. D. The scientific selection of salesmen. *Advertising and Selling,* 1915, **25,** 5–6, 95–96.

Scott, W. E. Activation theory and task design. *Organizational Behavior and Human Performance,* 1966, **1,** 3–30.

Scott, W. E. The behavioral consequences of repetitive task design: Research and theory. In L. L. Cummings & W. E. Scott (Eds.), *Readings in organizational behavior and human performance,* Homewood, Ill.: Irwin, 1969.

Scott, W. R. Theory of organizations. In R. E. L. Faris (Ed.), *Handbook of modern sociology.* Chicago: Rand McNally, 1964.

Seashore, S. *Group cohesiveness in the industrial work group.* Ann Arbor: Institute for Social Research, University of Michigan, 1954.

Selznick, P. *T.V.A. and the grass roots.* Berkeley, Calif.: University of California Press, 1949.

Selznick, P. *Leadership in administration,* Evanston, Ill.: Row, Peterson, 1957.

Shepard, H. A. Changing relationships in organizations. In J. G. March (Ed.), *Handbook of Organizations.* Chicago: Rand McNally, 1965.

Sheppard, H. L., & Herrick, N. Q. *Where have all the robots gone?* New York: Free Press, 1972.

Sherif, M. Formation of social norms: The experimental paradigm. In H. Proshansky and B. Seidenberg (Eds.), *Basic studies in social psychology.* New York: Holt, Rinehart & Winston, 1965.

Siegel, A. E., & Siegel, S. Reference groups, membership groups, and attitude change. *Journal of Abnormal and Social Psychology,* 1957, **55,** 360–364.

Sills, D. L. *The volunteers.* Glencoe, Ill.: Free Press, 1957.

Simon H. A. Comments on the theory of organization. *American Political Science Review,* 1952, **46,** 1130–1139.

Simon, H. A. *Administrative behavior* (2nd ed.) New York: Free Press, 1957.

Simon, H. A. On the concept of organizational goal. *Administrative Science Quarterly,* 1964, **9,** 1–22.

Skinner, B. F. *Walden two.* New York: Macmillan, 1948.

Slater, P. E. Role differentiation in small groups. *American Sociological Review,* 1955, **20,** 300–310.

Sloan, A. P., Jr. *My years with General Motors.* Garden City, N.Y.: Doubleday, 1964.

Sofer, C. *Men in mid-career: A study of British managers and technical specialities.* Cambridge, London: Cambridge University Press, 1970.

Sommer, R. Man's proximate environment. *Journal of Social Issues,* 1966, **22,** 59–70.

Sommer, R. Small group ecology. *Psychological Bulletin,* 1967, **67,** 145–152.

Sorenson, J. Professional and bureaucratic organization in large accounting firms. *The Accounting Review,* 1967, **42,** 553–565.

Sorenson, J. E., Rhode, J. G., & Lawler, E. E. The generation gap in public accounting. *Journal of Accounting,* 1973, **136,** 42–50.

Soujanen, W. W. The span of control—fact or fable? *Advanced Management,* 1955, **20** (November), 5–13.

Spriegel, W. R. Company practices in appraisal of managerial performance. *Personnel,* 1959, **38,** 9–12.

Staats, A. W., & Staats, C. K. Attitudes established by classical conditioning. *Journal of Abnormal and Social Psychology,* 1958, **57,** 37–40.

Stedry, A. *Budget control and cost behavior.* Englewood Cliffs, N.J.: Prentice-Hall, 1960.

Stedfry, A., & Kay, E. *The effects of goal difficulty on performance.* Publication BRS-19 by Behavioral Research Service, General Electric Co., Crotonville, N.Y., 1964.

Steele, F. I. The impact of the physical setting on the social climate at two comparable laboratory sessions. *Human Relations Training News,* 1968, **12,** No. 4.

Steele, F. I. Problem solving in the spatial environment. In *EDRA One* (Proceedings of the First Environmental Design Research Association Conference), Chapel Hill, 1969.

Steele, F. I. *Physical setting and organizational development.* Reading, Mass.: Addison-Wesley, 1973.

Steers, R. M. The concept of organizational goals: A research review. Unpublished manuscript, Graduate School of Administration, University of California, Irvine, 1971.

Steers, R. M. Task goals, individual need strengths and supervisory performance. Unpublished doctoral dissertation, University of California, Irvine, 1973.

Steers, R. M., & Porter, L. W. The role of task-goal attributes in employee performance. *Psychological Bulletin,* 1974, **81,** 434–452.

Stogdill, R. M. Personal factors associated with leadership. *Journal of Psychology,* 1948, **25,** 35–71.

Strauss, G. Some notes on power-equalization. In H. J. Leavitt (Ed.), *The social science of organization.* Englewood Cliffs, N.J.: Prentice-Hall, 1963.

Strauss, G. Organization development. In R. Dubin (Ed.), *Handbook of work, organization and society.* Chicago: Rand McNally, in press.

Strother, G. B. Problems in the development of a social science of organization. In H. J. Leavitt (Ed.), *The social science of organizations.* Englewood Cliffs, N.J.: Prentice-Hall, 1963.

Super, D. *The psychology of careers.* New York: Harper, 1957.

Svetlik, B., Prien, E., & Barrett, G. Relationships between job difficulty, employee's attitude toward his job, and supervisory ratings of the employee effectiveness. *Journal of Applied Psychology,* 1964, **48,** 320–324.

Taguiri, R., & Litwin, G. H. *Organizational climate: Explorations of a concept.* Boston: Graduate School of Business Administration, Harvard University, 1968.

Tajfel, H. Social and cultural factors in perception. In G. Lindzey and E. Aronson (Eds.), *The handbook of social psychology* (2nd ed.) Reading, Mass.: Addison-Wesley, 1969.

Tannenbaum, R., & Davis, S. A. Values, man, and organizations. *Industrial Management Review,* 1969, **10** (2), 67–86.

Tausky, C., & Dubin, R. Career anchorage: Managerial mobility motivations. *American Sociological Review,* 1965, **30,** 725–735.

Taylor, F. W. *Shop management.* New York: Harper, 1911. (a)

Taylor, F. W. *The principles of scientific management.* New York: Harper, 1911. (b)

Taylor, J. C. An empirical examination of a four-factor theory of leadership using smallest space analysis. *Organizational Behavior and Human Performance,* 1971, **6,** 249–266.

Thibaut, J. W., & Kelley, H. H. *The social psychology of groups.* New York: Wiley, 1959.

Thibaut, J. W., & Strickland, L. H. Psychological set and social conformity. *Journal of Personality,* 1956, **25,** 115–129.

Thompson, J. D. *Organizations in action.* New York: McGraw-Hill, 1967.

Thompson, J. D., & Bates, F. L. Technology, organization, and administration. *Administrative Science Quarterly,* 1957, **2,** 325–343.

Tosi, H. L. Rizzo, J. R., & Carroll, S. J. Setting goals in management by objectives. *California Management Review,* 1970, **12** (4), 70–78.

Trist, E. L., & Bamforth, K. W. Some social and psychological consequences of the longwall method of coal-getting. *Human Relations,* 1951, **4,** 1–38.

Turner, A. N., & Lawrence, P. R. *Industrial jobs and the worker.* Boston: Harvard University Graduate School of Business Administration, 1965.

Udy, S. H., Jr. *Organization of work.* New Haven: Human Relations Area Files Press, 1959.

Urwick, L. F. Executive decentralization with functional coordination. *Management Review,* 1935, **24,** 355–368.

Valenzi, E., & Andrews, I. R. Individual differences in the decision process of employment interviewers. *Journal of Applied Psychology,* 1973, **58,** 49–53.

Vernon, H. M. On the extent and effects of variety in repetitive work. Industrial Fatigue Research Board Report No. 26. London: H. M. Stationary Office, 1924.

Verplanck, W. S. The operant, from rat to man: An introduction to some recent experiments on human behavior. *Transactions of the New York Academy of Sciences,* 1955, **17,** 594–601.

Viteles, M. A. *Motivation and morale in industry.* New York: Norton, 1953.

Vroom, V. H. The effects of attitudes on perception of organizational goals. *Human Relations,* 1960, **13,** 229–240.

Vroom, V. H. *Work and motivation.* New York: Wiley, 1964.

Vroom, V. H. Organizational choice: A study of pre and post decision processes. *Organizational Behavior and Human Performance,* 1966, **1,** 212–225.

Vroom, V. H. Industrial social psychology. In G. Lindzey & E. Aronson (Eds.), *The handbook of social psychology* (2nd ed.) Reading, Mass.: Addison-Wesley, 1969.

Vroom, V. H. Leadership. In M. D. Dunnette (Ed.), *Handbook of industrial and organizational psychology.* Chicago: Rand-McNally, 1975.

Vroom, V. H., & Yetton, P. W. *Leadership and decision-making.* Pittsburgh: University of Pittsburgh Press, 1973.

Waldo, D. Organization theory: An elephantine problem. *Public Administration Review,* 1961, **21,** 210–225.

Walker, C. R. The problem of the repetitive job. *Harvard Business Review,* 1950, **28,** 54–58.

Walker, C. R., & Guest, R. H. *The man on the assembly line.* Cambridge: Harvard University Press, 1952.

Wallace, J. An abilities conception of personality: Some implications for personality measurement. *American Psychologist,* 1966, **21,** 132–138.

Walters, R. H., & Parke, R. D. Social motivation, dependency and susceptibility to social influence. In L. Berkowitz (Ed.), *Advances in experimental social psychology.* (Vol. I) New York: Academic Press, 1964.

Walters, R. W., & Associates *Job enrichment for results.* Reading, Mass.: Addison-Wesley, in press.

Walton, R. E. *Interpersonal peace making: Confrontations and third-party consultation.* Reading, Mass.: Addison-Wesley, 1969.

Walton, R. E. Frontiers beckoning the organizational psychologist. Invited address presented at the 79th Annual Meeting of the American Psychological Association, Washington, D.C., September, 1971.

Wanous, J. P. Occupational preferences: Perceptions of valence and instrumentality and objective data. *Journal of Applied Psychology,* 1972, **56,** 152–155.

Wanous, J. P. Effects of a realistic job preview on job acceptance, job attitudes, and job survival. *Journal of Applied Psychology,* 1973, **58,** 327–332.

Watson, J. B. *Behaviorism.* Chicago: University of Chicago Press, 1930.

Webster, E. C. *Decision making in the employment interview.* Montreal: Eagle Publishing, 1964.

Weiss, D. J., & Dawis, R. V. An objective validation of factual interview data. *Journal of Applied Psychology,* 1960, **44,** 381–385.

Weitz, J. Job expectancy and survival. *Journal of Applied Psychology,* 1956, **40,** 245–247.

Wexley, K. N., Singh, J. P., and Yukl, G. A., Subordinate personality as a moderator of the effects of participation in three types of appraisal interviews. *Journal of Applied Psychology*, 1973, **58**, 54–59.

Wexley, K. N., Yukl, G. A., Kovacs, S. Z., & Sanders, R. E. Importance of contrast effects in employment interviews. *Journal of Applied Psychology*, 1972, **56**, 45–48.

White, B. F., & Barnes, L. B. Power networks in the appraisal process. *Harvard Business Review*, 1971, **49** (3), 101–109.

Whitsett, D. A., & Winslow, E. K. An analysis of studies critical of the motivator-hygiene theory. *Personnel Psychology*, 1967, **20**, 391–415.

Whyte, W. F. *Street corner society.* Chicago: University of Chicago Press, 1943.

Whyte, W. F. *Human relations in the restaurant industry.* New York: McGraw-Hill, 1948.

Whyte, W. F. *Money and motivation.* New York: Harper, 1955.

Whyte, W. F. Pigeons, persons, and piece rates. *Psychology Today*, 1972, **5** (11), 66–68.

Wickstrom, W. S. *Developing managerial competence: Changing concepts—emerging practices.* New York: National Industrial Conference Board, Personnel Policy Study No. 189, 1964.

Wiener, M. Certainty of judgment as a variable in conformity behavior. *Journal of Social Psychology*, 1958, **48**, 257–263.

Woodward, J. *Management and technology.* London: H. M. Stationary Office, 1958.

Woodward, J. *Industrial organization: Theory and practice.* London: Oxford University Press, 1965.

Woodward, J. Technology, material control, and organizational behavior. In A. R. Negandhi & J. R. Schwitter (Eds.), *Organizational behavior models.* Kent, Ohio: Bureau of Economic and Business Research, Kent State University, 1970.

Work in America. Report of a special task force to the Secretary of Health, Education, and Welfare. Cambridge: M.I.T. Press, 1973.

Worthy, J. C. Organizational structure and employee morale. *American Sociological Review*, 1950, **15**, 169–179.

Yoder, D. Personnel management and industrial relations. Englewood Cliffs, N.J.: Prentice-Hall, 1956.

Yukl, G. Toward a behavioral theory of leadership. *Organizational Behavior and Human Performance*, 1971, **6**, 414–440.

Zajonc, R. B. Social facilitation. *Science*, 1965, **149**, 269–274.

Zajonc, R. B., & Sales, S. M. Social facilitation of dominant and subordinate responses. *Journal of Experimental Social Psychology*, 1966, **2**, 160–168.

Zald, M. N. Comparative analysis and measurement of organizational goals: The case of correctional institutions for delinquents. *Sociological Quarterly*, 1963, **4**, 206–230.

Zand, D. E. Trust and managerial problem solving. *Administrative Science Quarterly*, 1972, **17**, 229–239.

Ziller, R. C. Individuation and socialization: A theory of assimilation in large organizations. *Human Relations*, 1964, 17, 341–360.

NAME INDEX

SUBJECT INDEX